W9-DET-442

GLENCOE
LATIN 2

LATIN *and greek*

FOR AMERICANS

B.L. ULLMAN

CHARLES HENDERSON, JR.

New York, New York   Columbus, Ohio   Chicago, Illinois   Peoria, Illinois   Woodland Hills, California

About the Authors

B. L. Ullman (Ph.D., University of Chicago) enjoyed a distinguished career of teaching and scholarship at the Universities of Pittsburgh, Iowa, Chicago, and North Carolina. An internationally recognized authority on all aspects of the Roman world, ancient, medieval, and Renaissance, he was also a pioneer in modern methods of teaching Latin.

Charles Henderson, Jr. (Ph.D., University of North Carolina) collaborated with Professor Ullman on several revisions of this book. He has taught at New York University, the University of North Carolina, and Smith College, where he served as Chairman of the Classics Department and Assistant to the President.

Acknowledgments

The authors would like to thank the following individuals for their assistance in this revision of **Latin for Americans.**

Contributing Writers

David Driscoll (Ph.D., University of North Carolina) is Head of Latin and Classical Studies at The Masters School in Dobbs Ferry, NY. He has taught Latin and Greek at Gustavus Adolphus College, the University of Mississippi, and at schools in the Boston area.

Frances Knapp Clawson (A.B., Smith College; M.S., Nazareth College) has taught Latin in the Pittsford, NY, schools and lectured at Xiamen University, China.

Reviewer

Sue Wood, Indianapolis, Indiana

Front cover:

Ruins of the Temple of Vesta
Photo by Karen Tweedy-Holmes/CORBIS

The McGraw·Hill Companies

Send all inquiries to:
Glencoe/McGraw-Hill
8787 Orion Place
Columbus, OH 43240-4027

ISBN-13: 978-0-07-874253-8
ISBN-10: 0-07-874253-6

Printed in the United States of America.

2 3 4 5 6 7 8 9 027/055 12 11 10 09 08 07

CONTENTS

UNIT I

A ROMAN FAMILY

Araldo de Luca/CORBIS

UNIT II

TWO ROMAN STUDENTS IN ATHENS

The Bettmann Archive

UNIT III

LIVY

Bettmann/CORBIS

THE ARGONAUTS

Luca Tamagnini/Archivio e Studio Folco Quilici

SuperStock

UNIT V

DĒ BELLŌ GALLICŌ I

DĒ BELLŌ GALLICŌ II

Erich Lessing/Art Resource, NY

Robert Estall/Stone

UNIT
VII

DĒ BELLŌ GALLICŌ III–V

DĒ BELLŌ GALLICŌ VI–VII

Ronald Sheridan/Ancient Art & Architecture Collection

Jack Novak/SuperStock

UNIT
IX

PLINY'S LETTERS

LATIN LITERATURE

SEF/Art Resource, NY

OVID AND VERGIL

David Lees/CORBIS

INTRODUCTION

I n content, theme, and organization, this edition of **Latin for Americans, Level 2** retains the emphasis earlier editions have placed upon American ideals and their classical background. The textbook makes comparisons between ancient and modern ways of life, builds upon English vocabulary-building through the study of Latin roots, and provides thorough and yet simple explanations of the similarities and differences between English and Latin grammar. The reading selections are often accompanied by exercises intended to help the student analyze the real sense of what is being said, develop a feeling for the variety of meanings that depend on context in many Latin words, acquire the confidence to respond using the full resources of his or her own Latin vocabulary, and equally, to master English vocabulary. The teacher can use these exercises to foster both speaking and writing abilities and to encourage individual research, group discussion, and cross-disciplinary activities. In addition, the teacher can encourage students to practice speaking and writing using the idioms provided in the vocabulary lists.

It is not intended that all the Latin readings be completed by every class. The first three units present virtually all the essentials of second-year grammar, and the teacher should feel a certain freedom thereafter in matching the readings to the interests and abilities of the class. The wealth of material provides an ample choice for both regular classwork and for additional assignments. The reading in Caesar can well be postponed until the second semester, and there should be no need to feel that it must all be done. This edition contains the work of two female authors: Sulpicia and Hildegard von Bingen. Numerous full-color photos provide visual appeal and reinforcement to the reading topics.

The Workbook offers a wealth of supplemental practice, as does the accompanying Audio Program. The Transparencies can be used as enrichment to introduce students to various topics relating to the Roman world, such as politics, history, and culture. The Tests may be used to assess progress in the basic areas that are included in *Latin for Americans*: reading, comprehension, vocabulary, syntax, forms, word study and derivatives, and civilization.

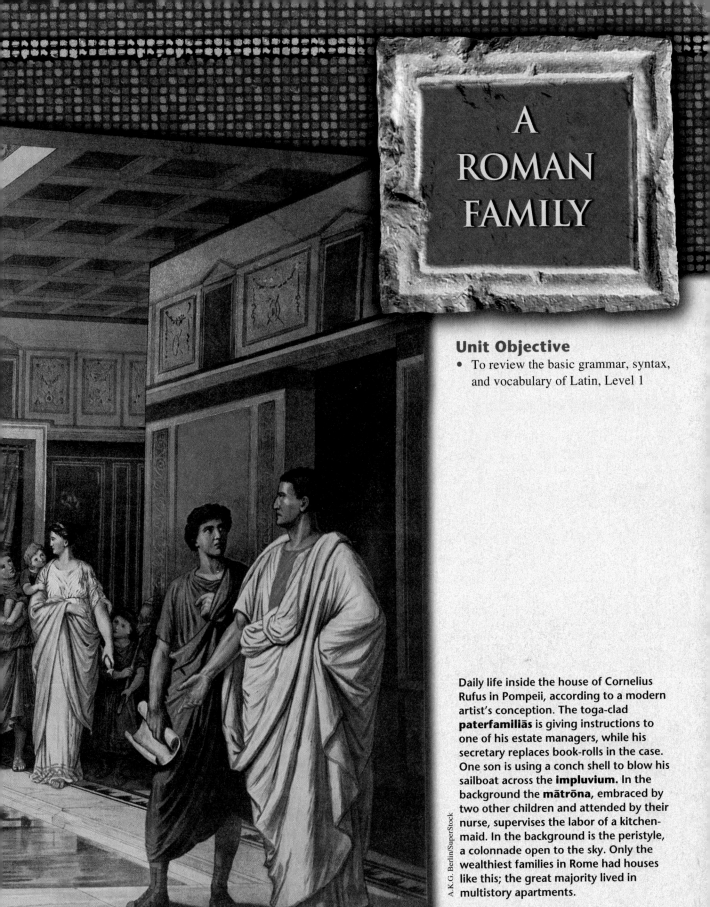

A ROMAN FAMILY

Unit Objective
- To review the basic grammar, syntax, and vocabulary of Latin, Level 1

Daily life inside the house of Cornelius Rufus in Pompeii, according to a modern artist's conception. The toga-clad **paterfamiliās** is giving instructions to one of his estate managers, while his secretary replaces book-rolls in the case. One son is using a conch shell to blow his sailboat across the **impluvium**. In the background the **mātrōna**, embraced by two other children and attended by their nurse, supervises the labor of a kitchen-maid. In the background is the peristyle, a colonnade open to the sky. Only the wealthiest families in Rome had houses like this; the great majority lived in multistory apartments.

A.K.G. Berlin/SuperStock

1

PUBLIUS AND SECUNDA

LESSON OBJECTIVES

Review:

- First and Second Declensions of Nouns and Adjectives
- Present Active Indicative System (Present, Imperfect, and Future Tenses) of the First and Second Conjugations and **Sum**
- Nominative (Subject and Predicate)
- Accusative (Direct Object)
- Ablative (Place Where, Time When)
- Agreement
- Apposition

Gilles Mermet/Art Resource, NY

In this late mosaic from Tunisia, a great Roman lady needs two slave-girls and a large array of cosmetic implements to ready herself for an appearance in public.

[1] So called after the emperor Augustus who, in the first century B.C., brought about a long period of peace after many years of civil war. The name "Augustus" (meaning something like *worthy of honor, revered, majestic*) was the honorary surname, or cognomen, conferred by the Roman Senate upon Julius Caesar's grandnephew (and adopted son) Octavian after Octavian obtained the supreme power. Following Augustus, Roman emperors regularly received the name, and a few female members of the imperial family enjoyed the title "Augusta."

[2] The second part of the word is an old genitive form; *paterfamilias* and *materfamilias* are used in English.

[3] adjective: *the father's (power)*

[4] respect

Secunda:	Ubi fuistī, Pūblī?
Pūblius:	In Forō Rōmānō fuī, Secunda.
Secunda:	Quem ibi vīdistī, Pūblī?
Pūblius:	Patrem nostrum et Augustum, prīncipem cīvitātis, vīdī, illum quī pācem cōnstituit. Nōnne dē hāc pāce audīvistī? "Pāx Augusta"[1] ā populō grātō appellātur.
Secunda:	Sī Augustus prīnceps cīvitātis est, estne pater noster, P. Caecilius Rūfus, prīnceps familiae?
Pūblius:	Ita est; nōn autem prīnceps sed paterfamiliās[2] appellātur. Māter nostra Fulvia māterfamiliās[2] est.
Secunda:	Quid facit paterfamiliās?
Pūblius:	Ille tōtam familiam regit—et līberōs et servōs. Etiam deōs familiae colit et sōlus omnia negōtia gerit. Auctōritās patris, quae ā nōbīs Rōmānīs "patria[3] potestās" appellātur, maxima est. Sī servum aut fīlium interficere cupit, potestātem habet. Sed nōn timēre dēbēs, nam hōc tempore nūllī patrēs Rōmānī id cupiunt. Pater noster bonus, nōn dūrus, est. Nōs eum amāmus. Omnēs servī eum colunt[4] quod sevērus sed aequus est.
Secunda:	Ubi nunc pater est?

Line numbers: 5, 10, 15, 20

Pūblius:	In Forō negōtia pūblica gerit; quondam mīles fuit. Nōbilis et īnsignis est. Sed quid tū hodiē fēcistī, Secunda?
Secunda:	Cum sorōre nostrā maiōre Caeciliā eram. Ea dē officiīs mātris nostrae verba fēcit. Māter domina servārum est et labōrem eārum regit. Ā patre nostrō semper cōnsulitur, 25 nam docta ācrisque est. Posteā māter mē docuit, nam puellae nōn saepe in lūdum mittuntur. Māter mē docuit dē factīs quae memoriā tenuit et dē hominibus clārīs quōs ipsa nōvit et dē eīs dē quibus in librīs lēgit.
Pūblius:	Bene. Quid aliud māter docuit? 30
Secunda:	Dē patre nostrō docuit. Pater "iūs trium līberōrum"[5] obtinuit, quod trēs līberōs habet, mē et tē et Caeciliam. Hoc iūs ab Augustō datum est quod in paucīs nōbilibus familiīs hōc tempore multī līberī sunt, et quod Augustus maiōrem esse numerum optimōrum cīvium Rōmānōrum cupit. Sed 35 tū, Pūblī, quī iam vir es, quid nunc faciēs?
Pūblius:	Studia in lūdō nostrō perfēcī; iam in Graeciam, ubi clārae scholae sunt, nāvigāre parō.
Secunda:	Ōh, fēlīx tū. Ego quoque in Graeciam nāvigāre cupiō.
Pūblius:	Sed hodiē aliud in mente volvō, nam crās optimus diēs aderit. 40
Secunda:	Quid est hoc?
Pūblius:	Sī bona puella eris, iam cognōscēs.

[5] Fathers having three children were exempted from certain taxes and were given preference in official positions. Compare modern income tax exemptions for married couples with children.

Questions

1. What legal right did a Roman father have over his family?
2. Whom did the Romans include under "family"?
3. For what great accomplishment was Augustus responsible?
4. What was the role of the **māterfamiliās,** according to Caecilia?
5. Why was the **iūs trium līberōrum** enacted, and what privileges did it confer?

The **ātrium** of the House of the Faun at Pompeii. Typically, the **ātrium** had a funnel-shaped roof designed so that rainwater would drain into the **impluvium** (*shallow pool*) in the foreground. The water would then be stored in a cistern for household purposes. In the distance, you can see the **peristȳlium,** or open area, at the rear of the house, where there was usually a garden and a fountain. The basic design of the Roman house can still be seen today in Italy and throughout Europe in former Roman provinces.

3

Form Review

First and Second Declension Nouns

Review the following models of the stems and endings of first and second declension nouns and adjectives. The stem (or base) of a noun is found by dropping the ending of the genitive singular. Remember that almost all nouns of the first declension (the **Ā/Ă**-declension) are feminine. (Exceptions are masculine agent nouns like **agricola, nauta, pīrāta, poēta.**) Almost all nouns of the second declension (the **O**-declension) are either masculine (nominatives in **-us, -er,** or **-r**) or neuter (nominatives in **-um**).

FIRST DECLENSION

	SINGULAR		PLURAL	
NOM.	**via**	*road*	**viae**	*roads*
GEN.	**viae**	*of the road*	**viārum**	*of the roads*
DAT.	**viae**	*to/for the road*	**viīs**	*to/for the roads*
ACC.	**viam**	*road* (obj.)	**viās**	*roads* (obj.)
ABL.	**viā**	*from/by/with the road*	**viīs**	*from/by/with the roads*

SECOND DECLENSION (M.) / SECOND DECLENSION (N.)

	SINGULAR	PLURAL	SINGULAR	PLURAL
NOM.	**servus** *slave,* etc.	**servī**	**signum** *sign,* etc.	**signa**
GEN.	**servī**	**servōrum**	**signī**	**signōrum**
DAT.	**servō**	**servīs**	**signō**	**signīs**
ACC.	**servum**	**servōs**	**signum**	**signa**
ABL.	**servō**	**servīs**	**signō**	**signīs**

Identify the base: **ager, agrī,** m., *field*
puer, puerī, m., *boy*
vir, virī, m., *man*
fīlius, fīlī, m., *son*
cōnsilium, cōnsilī, n., *plan*

Second declension nouns with nominatives ending in **-ius** or **-ium** have a single **-ī** in the genitive. In all declensions, the vocative, singular or plural, is like the nominative, except in the singular of second declension nouns ending in **-us,** where it becomes **-e,** or ending in **-ius,** where it

becomes **-ī: ser´ve!** *slave!* **fī´lī!** *son!* **fī´liī!** *sons!,* **Brū´te!** *Brutus!* **Caeci´lī!**
Caecilius! The accent does not change.

First and Second Declension Adjectives

Adjectives of the first and second declensions use the endings of first
and second declension nouns. To find the base (stem), drop the ending of
the nominative singular feminine or the genitive singular.

	FIRST AND SECOND DECLENSION ADJECTIVES					
	SINGULAR			PLURAL		
	M.	F.	N.	M.	F.	N.
NOM.	magnus *large*	magna	magnum	magnī	magnae	magna
GEN.	magnī	magnae	magnī	magnōrum	magnārum	magnōrum
DAT.	magnō	magnae	magnō	magnīs	magnīs	magnīs
ACC.	magnum	magnam	magnum	magnōs	magnās	magna
ABL.	magnō	magnā	magnō	magnīs	magnīs	magnīs

Identify the base: **miser, misera, miserum,** *unhappy*
                noster, nostra, nostrum, *our*
                līber, lībera, līberum, *free*
                vester, vestra, vestrum, *your*

First and Second Conjugation Verbs

The present, imperfect, and future tenses are formed from the present
stem of the verb. To find the present stem, drop the **-re** from the present
infinitive (second principal part), add the tense sign (if necessary) and the
personal ending.

PRESENT			
FIRST CONJUGATION (-Ā-)		SECOND CONJUGATION (-Ē-)	
SINGULAR	PLURAL	SINGULAR	PLURAL
portō *I carry,* etc.	portāmus	doceō *I teach,* etc.	docēmus
portās	portātis	docēs	docētis
portat	portant	docet	docent

IMPERFECT (TENSE SIGN -BĀ-)			
portābam *I was carrying, used to carry,* etc.	portābāmus	docēbam *I was teaching, used to teach,* etc.	docēbāmus
portābās	portābātis	docēbās	docēbātis
portābat	portābant	docēbat	docēbant

	FUTURE (TENSE SIGN **-BI-**)		
portābō *I will (shall) carry*, etc.	**portābimus**	**docēbō,** *I will (shall) teach*, etc.	**docēbimus**
portābis	**portābitis**	**docēbis**	**docēbitis**
portābit	**portābunt**	**docēbit**	**docēbunt**

The present, imperfect, and future of **sum** are irregular.

PRESENT		IMPERFECT		FUTURE	
sum *I am*, etc.	**sumus**	**eram** *I was*, etc.	**erāmus**	**erō** *I will (shall) be*, etc.	**erimus**
es	**estis**	**erās**	**erātis**	**eris**	**eritis**
est	**sunt**	**erat**	**erant**	**erit**	**erunt**

Practice

1. Decline **agricola līber, officium dūrum, poēta clārus.**
2. Tell the form(s) of **servō, optimōrum, paucīs, familiā, fīlī, fīliae, fīliī, virī, līberōs, negōtiīs.**
3. Give the second person singular of **obtineō** and the third person plural of **nāvigō** in the present, imperfect, and future active indicative.

In this modern painting of an ancient street scene, housewives and children gather at the public well to get water for their households. Water from mountain springs miles away was carried to the cities and piped to wells and fountains. Note the two-story houses and the ruts worn in the paving stones by the constant passage of carts.

SuperStock

Syntax Review

Nominative: Subject and Predicate Nominative

The *subject* of a finite verb is in the nominative case. A noun or an adjective used in the *predicate* with a linking verb (*is, are, seem, become, remain, be called,* etc.) is also in the nominative.

Pater noster bonus est.	*Our father is (a) good (man).*
Auctōritās patris "patria potestās" appellātur.	*A father's authority is called the "patria potestas."*

Accusative: Direct Object

The direct object of a transitive verb is in the accusative case.

Vīdī illum quī pācem cōnstituit.	*I saw that man who established peace.*
Māter mē docuit.	*Mother taught me.*

Ablative: Place Where

The ablative with **in** or **sub** expresses *place where.* The preposition may be omitted with certain words like **locō, locīs,** and **parte,** etc., and often in poetry.

In Forō Rōmānō negōtia gerit.	*He is transacting business in the Roman Forum.*
Studia in lūdō nostrō perfēcī.	*I have finished my studies in our school.*

Ablative of Time When or Within Which

Time when or *within which* is expressed by the ablative without a preposition.

Hōc tempore paucī līberī sunt.	*At this time there are few children.*
Illīs diēbus facilius erat fāmam merēre.	*In those days it was easier to gain fame.*
Quīnque mēnsibus eōs vīcerat.	*(With)in five months he had conquered them.*

Agreement of Adjectives

Adjectives agree in *gender, number,* and *case* (but not necessarily in ending) with the nouns they modify.

Pater tōtam familiam rēgit, et māter docta ācrisque est.	*Father runs the whole household, and Mother is well educated and quick-witted.*
Augustus maiōrem esse numerum optimōrum cīvium cupit.	*Augustus desires the number of the best citizens to be larger.*

Apposition

Appositives are nouns that further describe the noun that they are placed next to and with which they agree in *case*. It is often best to supply *as* in translating an appositive.

Augustum, principem cīvitātis	*. . . Augustus, chief of state . . .*
Caecilium, principem familiae, colunt.	*They respect Caecilius as head of the household.*

Translation

1. The slaves at that time often had harsh masters.
2. Do you not wish to hear about Publius, son of Rufus?
3. The mother taught the daughters, and the father the sons.
4. Rufus consulted Fulvia about the duties of the children and slaves.
5. There were few children in many Roman families in the time of Augustus.

VOCABULARY REVIEW

The following Vocabulary Review words should already be familiar to you. Remember that it is important to learn not only the basic meanings but also the essential facts about each word: for nouns, this means the genitive and gender; for adjectives, all three nominative forms; for verbs, the principal parts; and for each preposition, the case used with it. Try to think of an English derivative for each vocabulary word.

Nouns

fīlius	**negōtium**	**servus**
līberī	**officium**	**vir**
	populus	

Adjectives

dūrus	**paucī**

Verbs

appellō	**nāvigō**	**teneō**
doceō	**obtineō**	**timeō**
habeō		

WORD STUDY

Bases Many English words in the singular retain the exact form of the Latin original, even though the meaning may have changed: *arena, radius, victor, impetus, species*. Some of these even retain the Latin ending in the plural: e.g., *radii, data, indices*.

Other English words preserve only the Latin base: *duct, legion, long, tend, timid*. Others preserve the Latin base plus silent *-e: mode, grave, produce, dire*. Still others show a minor change of spelling in the base: *boon* (**bonus**), *example* (**exemplum**), *pair* (**pār**), *obtain* (**obtineō**).

Give two more examples of each of the four types of derivatives presented above. The next stage will be to review the prefixes and suffixes commonly attached to the bases of Latin words.

Derivatives Explain by derivation: *appellate, docile, nominal, officious, tenacity*.

READING IN THE LATIN WORD ORDER

When you read or listen to English you naturally take in the words as they come. So it is in Latin. When Romans were conversing, they understood each other as the words were spoken. They did not stop to look first for the subject, then for the verb, and finally for the object. That would have been unnatural. They read aloud, and, in reading as in speaking, they understood the meaning of the words in their Latin order. You should try to do the same. Let's consider the following sentence as an example.

Pūblius, hīs rēbus impulsus, litterās longās prīmā nocte ad patrem amīcī mittit.

Just take the words *as they come; at the same time, try to see what words belong together in phrases:*

Pūblius: The ending shows that it is nominative singular—for this reason it is probably the subject. In English, it will probably come first.

hīs rēbus: These words seem to go together (demonstrative and noun) and are either dative or ablative plural. You have to wait until you read more of the sentence before their meaning will be clear.

impulsus: This word, which is nominative singular masculine, looks like "impulse," which comes from the Latin verb meaning *impel*. It must agree with **Pūblius,** since it has the same gender, number, and case. The punctuation shows that **hīs rēbus** depends upon it; the latter is, therefore, the ablative of means. The sentence so far reads: "Publius, impelled by these things (facts) . . ."

litterās longās: These words clearly belong together because both have the same case, number, and gender. They are in the accusative plural and must be the direct object of some verb or else the subject of an infinitive— we cannot tell which until we go on.

prīmā nocte: the ā in **prīmā** shows that it is ablative singular in agreement with **nocte.** The latter suggests "nocturnal" but is a noun. The phrase, therefore, probably means *on the first night*—or could it possibly mean *in the first (part of the) night?*

ad patrem amīcī: The sense seems clear as it stands: "to the father of (his) friend," for **ad** always is followed by the accusative and **patrem** must be its object; **amīcī** is genitive singular and evidently depends upon **patrem.**

mittit: At last the sense of the whole passage is clear! **Mittit** is the verb and it agrees with the first word, **Pūblius,** for it is third person singular active. Now it is evident that **litterās longās** is the direct object of **mittit.** All the words seem to fall into line and make sense just as they stand.

We notice, as we go over the words again with the thought of the whole sentence more or less clearly in mind, that the first meaning of a word is not always the best and that the general sense of the passage (i.e., the "context") helps you decide the exact meaning to be given to each word. The complete sentence reads as follows:

> *Publius, influenced by these things, sends a long letter in the evening to his friend's father.*

Our experience with **litterās** shows that we must not forget a word that has not been fully explained; this is like "carrying" a number in adding up a column of figures or in multiplying.

If you adopt the plan just described, you will soon be able to grasp the thought naturally and more or less automatically, without so much conscious effort.

A NEW COUSIN

LESSON OBJECTIVES

Review:
- Third Declension of Nouns and Adjectives
- Ablative (Accompaniment, Manner)
- Dative (Indirect Object)

Lūx erat: Pūblius praeceps ad patrem P. Caecilium cucurrit et eī salūtem dīxit.

"Cūr properās?" pater rogāvit.

"Nōnne memoriā tenēs? Tempus adest quō Q. Fūrius erit noster."

Q. Fūrius amīcus firmus Pūblī erat. Familia Quīntī nōbilis sed pauper[1] 5
fuit. Pater eius sex līberōs sed pecūniam nōn magnam habuit. M. Caecilius, frāter P. Caecilī, magnam pecūniam sed nūllōs līberōs habuit.

"Nōnne cupis fīlium adoptāre?" Pūblius Mārcō dīxerat.

"Certē," respondit Mārcus. Omnēs Rōmānī fīliōs habēre cupiēbant quod fīliī nōmen familiae servābant, deōs familiae colēbant, "patriam 10
potestātem" cōnfirmābant. Multae erant adoptiōnēs inter Rōmānōs. Multī clārī Rōmānī adoptātī sunt. Fīlius minimus L. Aemilī Paulī ā P. Cornēliō Scīpiōne, fīliō ducis clārī, adoptātus est, et posteā P. Cornēlius Scīpiō Aemiliānus Āfricānus appellābātur. Augustus ipse ā C. Iūliō Caesare adoptātus erat, et nōmen tōtum quod tum sūmpsit erat C. Iūlius Caesar 15
Octāviānus. Posteā tertium cognōmen, "Augustus," dēcrētō senātūs[2] recēpit.

Pūblius Q. Fūrium ad M. Caecilium dūxerat.

"Quīntus puer magnī animī est. Eum adoptāre cupiō," dīxit Mārcus. "Cum meā familiā habitābit, sed saepe patrem, mātrem, frātrēs, sorōrēs vidēbit." 20

Id grātum patrī Quīntī fuerat, et nunc tempus aderat. Multī clientēs ad P. Caecilium iam veniēbant et salūtem dīcēbant. Cum clientibus et fīliō Caecilius in Forum prōcessit et ad aedificium praetōris[3] accessit. Q. Fūrius, pater suus, M. Caecilius, amīcī iam aderant. Q. Fūrius novam togam gerēbat. 25 30

Cum cūrā praetor condiciōnēs adoptiōnis prōposuit.

[1] *poor*

[2] *by decree of the senate*

[3] (gen. sing.) Praetors (*pree´tors*) were officials second in rank to the consuls with many civil or military duties. Here the praetor presides over the formal legal ceremony of adoption.

Ronald Sheridan/Ancient Art & Architecture Collection

A family scene, probably recording the day a boy received the toga virīlis as a sign of his entering manhood. The family unit was very important to Romans, and families without sons would often adopt a young man who would someday protect the family's estate and carry on the family name.

"Quīntum, fīlium meum, ā patriā potestāte meā līberō," pater Quīntī
35 ter dīxit.

Tum M. Caecilius dīxit, "Meus fīlius nunc est."

"Tuus fīlius nunc est," praetor dīxit. "In tuā potestāte nunc est. Nōmen
nōn iam Q. Fūrius est, sed M. Caecilius Fūriānus."

Omnēs magnō cum studiō Fūriānō novō et M. Caeciliō salūtem
40 dīxērunt; tum discessērunt.

"Nunc noster Fūriānus es," Pūblius Fūriānō dīxit.

"Tibi grātiās agō," Fūriānus respondit, et cum patre novō discessit.
Plūra dē Fūriānō et dē Pūbliō audiētis.

Questions

1. Who was Quintus Furius and how many siblings did he have?
2. Who adopted Quintus and why?
3. What was the name of Publius' uncle and how many children did he have?
4. Cite two famous adoptions from Roman history. Explain how the names of the adopted sons change. Then explain the change of Quintus' name.
5. What special provisions did Marcus make so that Q. Furius and his father would agree to the adoption?
6. How did the adoption change Quintus' legal status?

GRAMMAR

Form Review

Nouns of the Third Declension

Third declension nouns are either *consonant-stems* or *i-stems*. All of them, whether masculine, feminine, or neuter, have a genitive singular ending in **-is,** which you drop to find the stem. Unlike the consonant-stems, which have a genitive plural ending in **-um,** i-stem nouns have a genitive plural ending in **-ium.** To identify three major classes of i-stem nouns, see the details in the Grammar Appendix, pp. 512–513.

Nota Bene

Roman **praenōmina** (*first names*) were regularly abbreviated: **A. = Aulus, C. = Gaius, Cn. = Gnaeus, L. = Lūcius, M. = Mārcus, P. = Pūblius, Q. = Quīntus, T. = Titus, Ti. = Tiberius. Nōmina** were the family names, i.e., the names of the **gentēs. Cognōmina** were surnames designating a branch of the family and were often derived from some ancestor's physical or moral characteristics, or some heroic deed, e.g., Africanus from Scipio's victory in Africa. The reading in this lesson also exemplifies how, upon a person's adoption, his **nōmen** could be converted to a **cognōmen.**

CONSONANT-STEMS

	MASCULINE		FEMININE		NEUTER	
	SINGULAR	PLURAL	SINGULAR	PLURAL	SINGULAR	PLURAL
NOM.	mīles	mīlitēs	lēx	lēgēs	corpus	corpora
GEN.	mīlitis	mīlitum	lēgis	lēgum	corporis	corporum
DAT.	mīlitī	mīlitibus	lēgī	lēgibus	corporī	corporibus
ACC.	mīlitem	mīlitēs	lēgem	lēgēs	corpus	corpora
ABL.	mīlite	mīlitibus	lēge	lēgibus	corpore	corporibus

I-STEM NOUNS

	MASCULINE AND FEMININE		NEUTER	
	SINGULAR	PLURAL	SINGULAR	PLURAL
NOM.	cīvis	cīvēs	mare	maria
GEN.	cīvis	cīvium	maris	marium
DAT.	cīvī	cīvibus	marī	maribus
ACC.	cīvem	cīvēs (-īs)	mare	maria
ABL.	cīve (-ī)	cīvibus	marī	maribus

Adjectives of the Third Declension

Third declension adjectives fall into one of three categories, based on the number of endings they have in the nominative singular. They are declined like the preceding **i**-stem nouns, but regularly have **-ī** in the the ablative singular rather than **-e**. To find the base (stem), drop the ending of the nominative singular feminine or of the genitive singular.

THREE ENDINGS

	SINGULAR			PLURAL		
	M.	F.	N.	M.	F.	N.
Nominative	ācer	ācris	ācre	ācrēs	ācrēs	ācria
Genitive	ācris	ācris	ācris	ācrium	ācrium	ācrium
Dative	ācrī	ācrī	ācrī	ācribus	ācribus	ācribus
Accusative	ācrem	ācrem	ācre	ācrēs (-īs)	ācrēs (-īs)	ācria
Ablative	ācrī	ācrī	ācrī	ācribus	ācribus	ācribus

TWO ENDINGS

	SINGULAR		PLURAL	
	M., F.	N.	M., F.	N.
Nominative	fortis	forte	fortēs	fortia
Genitive	fortis	fortis	fortium	fortium
Dative	fortī	fortī	fortibus	fortibus
Accusative	fortem	forte	fortēs (-īs)	fortia
Ablative	fortī	fortī	fortibus	fortibus

ONE ENDING

	SINGULAR		PLURAL	
	M., F.	N.	M., F.	N.
Nominative	pār	pār	parēs	paria
Genitive	paris	paris	parium	parium
Dative	parī	parī	paribus	paribus
Accusative	parem	par	parēs (-īs)	paria
Ablative	parī	parī	paribus	paribus

Nota•Bene

Consonant-stems and **i**-stems frequently "borrow" each other's endings, especially in the ablative singular (**-ī** or **-e**), the accusative plural (**-ēs** or **-īs**), and even (rarely) in the genitive plural (**-um** or **-ium**). Some nouns like **turris,** *tower,* are "pure" **i**-stems and have **-im** in the accusative singular. Others, like **canis,** *dog,* and **iuvenis,** *young man,* which look as if they ought to be **i**-stems, always show **-e** in the ablative singular and **-um** in the genitive plural. Don't let these variations bother you! You are already accustomed to distinguishing the three possibilities for an **-ae** ending in the first declension or the four possibilities for an **-īs** ending in the first and second declensions, so this is nothing new.

Practice

1. Decline **frāter humilis, dux noster, pār nōmen.**
2. Tell the form of **condiciōnēs, patrī, sorōrum, omnium, fīlium, salūte, togīs, nōminibus, mātrum, lūcis, potestātēs.**

Syntax Review

Ablative of Accompaniment

The ablative with **cum** expresses accompaniment. When **cum** is used with a personal, reflexive, or relative pronoun, it is attached to the end of the pronoun, e.g., **mēcum, sēcum, quōcum.**

Cum clientibus Caecilius prōcessit.	*Caecilius proceeded with his clients.*
Fūriānus **cum patre novō** discessit.	*Furianus left with his new father.*
Possumne **tēcum** venīre?	*Can I come with you?*

Ablative of Manner

The ablative of manner with **cum** describes how something happens or is done. **Cum** can sometimes be omitted if an adjective modifies the noun.

Cum cūrā praetor condiciōnēs prōposuit.	*The praetor explained the conditions carefully.*
Omnēs **magnō cum studiō** Fūriānō salūtem dīxērunt.	*Everyone greeted Furianus with great enthusiasm.*
Pūblius et Fūriānus **magnō studiō** per viās cucurrērunt.	*Publius and Furianus ran through the streets with great enthusiasm.*

Notice that the ablative of manner is almost equivalent to an adverb: **cum cūrā** = *carefully;* **magnō studiō** = *with great enthusiasm* or *very enthusiastically.* Thus, ablatives of manner can be translated as adverbs.

Conversely, it is also possible to translate adverbs by treating them as ablatives of manner: **difficillimē** = *most difficultly* or *with very great difficulty.*

Dative of Indirect Object

The indirect object of a verb is in the dative. It is used with verbs of *giving, showing, telling, reporting,* etc., and in English is often preceded by *to* or *for.*

Omnēs **Fūriānō** salūtem dīxērunt.	*Everyone greeted (wished good health to) Furianus.*
"**Tibi** grātiās agō," Fūriānus respondit.	*"I give you thanks," answered Furianus.*
Magister **puellae** librum dedit.	*The teacher gave the book to the girl.*

Translation

1. Who came to the Forum with Publius?
2. A new name is given to the humble boy.
3. I shall tell everything *(neut. pl.)* to my father and mother.
4. Publius proceeds to the praetor with his father and Marcus.

VOCABULARY REVIEW

Nouns

condiciō	māter	salūs
dux	nōmen	soror
frāter	pater	toga
lūx	potestās	

Adjectives

ācer	omnis	plūs
humilis	pār	
nōbilis		

Verbs

respondeō	rogō	servō

WORD STUDY

Prefixes Review the prefixes **ab- (abs-)**, **dē-**, **ex- (ē-)**, and **sē-** in the Grammar Appendix, noting that each has a basic "from" meaning.

Select the proper form of each prefix and define its English derivative: **(ab)** *-rogate, -vert, -tain;* **(dē)** *-duct, -cease, -scribe;* **(ex)** *-lect, -tract, -vent;* **(sē)** *-parate, -cede.*

Derivatives Explain by derivation: *arrogance, humiliate, nomenclature, salutary, translucent.*

READING STRATEGY NEW WORDS

Reading Latin as Latin of course implies acquaintance with a certain number of Latin words. We shall take it for granted that at the beginning of the second year you know all the ordinary prepositions and conjunctions and several hundred of the most common nouns, adjectives, adverbs, and verbs that occurred almost every day in your first-year work.

In your reading you will probably discover many new words. Your first impulse may be to turn at once to the Dictionary at the end of the book for their meaning, but that always takes time and should be done only if other methods fail. There are three easier and better ways to determine the meaning of a new word. Sometimes just one of them, more often a combination of two or all three of them, makes it possible for you to find out the meaning of the word. Try all three before you turn to the Dictionary.

1. *Think of an English derivative from the Latin word* (about sixty percent of our English words come from Latin). The English derivative, if the same part of speech as the Latin original, will serve as a stopgap until you can find a synonym that may suit the sense better.
2. If you can think of no related English word, try to *recall a related Latin word;* for example, **amīcitia** suggests **amīcus,** which you already know.
3. If no related English or Latin word suggests itself, *guess the meaning from the context* and later check your guess by looking up the word in the Dictionary.

THE WOMEN HAVE THEIR SAY

LESSON OBJECTIVES
Review:
- Present Active Indicative System (Present, Imperfect, and Future Tenses) of the Third and Fourth Conjugations
- Ablative (Means)
- Infinitive as Subject and Object

Fulvia, māter Pūblī, cum sorōribus eius, Caeciliā et Secundā, Pūblium Rūfumque exspectābat.

"Dūrum est semper exspectāre," Secunda clāmāvit. "Virōs exspectāmus; nihil ipsae agimus. Vīta puerōrum et virōrum grātior est. In lūdum, in Forum, in loca pūblica prōcēdunt. Sed Rōma puellīs inimīca est." 5

"Quid? Nōnne Rōma clārās mulierēs Rōmānās semper memoriā tenet?" rogāvit Caecilia.

"Vērum est," erant verba Fulviae. "Quis Veturiam, quae Rōmam servāvit, memoriā nōn tenet? Coriolānus, fīlius Veturiae, lēgem prōposuerat, quae cīvitātī nōn grāta erat. Itaque inimīcī Coriolānum in 10
fugam dedērunt, et is ad Volscōs, hostēs Rōmānōrum, fūgit. Dux Volscōrum factus, ad portās Rōmae veniēbat et urbem occupāre parābat. Veturia cum aliīs ēgregiīs mulieribus Rōmānīs ad castra Coriolānī prōcessit pācemque petīvit. Coriolānus, verbīs mātris affectus, dīxit, 'Māter, Rōmam servāvistī.'" 15

A view of a part of the **Ātrium Vestae** in the Roman Forum. The area once contained the Temple of Vesta, the house in which the Vestals lived, a sacred grove, and the house of the Pontifex Maximus. The complex underwent many alterations and restorations often made necessary by fire. These statues of the Chief Vestals (some of their names can still be read) were set up in the last phase of its development, probably in the fourth century A.D.

Scala/Art Resource, NY

"Et quī Rōmānus factīs Cloeliae nōn permōtus est?" dīxit Caecilia. "Captīva, ē castrīs Etrūscōrum, hostium Rōmānōrum, fūgit et flūmen trānāvit."

"Eīs temporibus facilius erat fāmam merēre quod Rōmānī bellum
20 gerēbant," dīxit Secunda. "Sed nunc pāx est. Quid mulierēs in pāce efficere possunt?"

"Multa!" respondit Caecilia. "Nōnne Vestālēs officiīs sacrīs saepe Rōmam servāvērunt, deīs inimīcīs?[1] Et quis nōn Līviam[2] bonam memoriā tenēbit?"

25 "Sed in Forum nōn prōcēdunt."

"Nōnne Laelia ōrātiōnēs ēgregiās facere poterat?" Fulvia rogāvit. "Nōnne Hortēnsia causam Rōmānārum in Forō ēgit? In bellō cīvīlī triumvirī[3] mulierēs Rōmānās pecūniam dare iussērunt. Sed Hortēnsia in Forō dīxit: 'Cūr nōs pecūniam dare dēbēmus? Nūllam auctōritātem in
30 cīvitāte habēmus. Sī hostēs venient, pecūniam vōbīs dabimus, sed numquam prō cīvīlī bellō auxilium dabimus.' Hīs verbīs triumvirī concēdere coāctī sunt.

"Puerī Rōmānī dē hīs et dē Cornēliā, Claudiā, Lucrētiā, Tucciā, ipsā Caeciliā Metellā nostrā in lūdīs legunt audiuntque, et semper legent
35 audientque dum Rōma manēbit. Mulierēs Rōmānae bonae cīvitātem mūniunt. Ubi perīcula venient, parātae semper erunt."

[1] (ablative absolute) *when the gods were unfriendly*

[2] *Livia*, wife of Augustus

[3] *triumvirs*, a coalition of three (Octavian, Mark Antony, and a general named Lepidus) formed to prosecute the war against the murderers of Julius Caesar and to reform the Roman "Constitution."

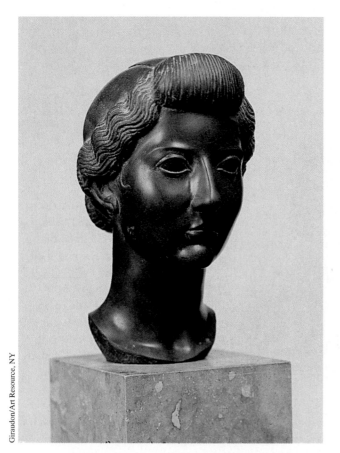

Questions

1. How did Caecilia and her mother answer Secunda's criticisms of her life as a girl in Rome?
2. Who was Veturia's son? How did she save Rome?
3. For what was Cloelia famous?
4. To what did Hortensia object? What did her speech accomplish?
5. What examples of the importance of Roman women in peacetime does Caecilia offer?
6. What light do these stories shed upon the status of women in ancient Rome?

Livia Drusilla (58 B.C.–A.D. 29) was the second wife of the emperor Augustus and a woman of keen political sensitivity. She was also the mother of Tiberius, Augustus' successor. During Augustus' reign, she became his valued counselor and ran his domestic life with integrity and grace.

GRAMMAR

Form Review

Third and Fourth Conjugation Verbs

Like the present system of first and second conjugation verbs, the present, imperfect, and future of third, third **-iō,** and fourth conjugation verbs are formed by taking the present stem and adding the tense sign (if any) and the personal endings.

PRESENT

pōnō *I put, am putting, do put,* etc.	**capiō** *I take, am taking, do take,* etc.	**mūniō** *I build, am building, do build,* etc.
pōnis	**capis**	**mūnis**
pōnit	**capit**	**mūnit**
pōnimus	**capimus**	**mūnīmus**
pōnitis	**capitis**	**mūnītis**
pōnunt	**capiunt**	**mūniunt**

IMPERFECT

ponēbam *I was putting, kept putting,* etc.	**capiēbam** *I was taking, kept taking,* etc.	**mūniēbam** *I was building, kept building,* etc.
ponēbās	**capiēbās**	**mūniēbās**
ponēbat	**capiēbat**	**mūniēbat**
ponēbāmus	**capiēbāmus**	**mūniēbāmus**
ponēbātis	**capiēbātis**	**mūniēbātis**
ponēbant	**capiēbant**	**mūniēbant**

FUTURE

pōnam *I shall put,* etc.	**capiam** *I shall take,* etc.	**mūniam** *I shall build,* etc.
pōnēs	**capiēs**	**mūniēs**
pōnet	**capiet**	**mūniet**
pōnēmus	**capiēmus**	**mūniēmus**
pōnētis	**capiētis**	**mūniētis**
pōnent	**capient**	**mūnient**

Marcus Agrippa, Augustus' great general, his head covered for the religious ceremony, is shown on the **Āra Pācis Augustae**, with a boy tugging at his toga. Behind him is his wife. This altar was probably the first Roman public monument to celebrate the family by including women and children.

Practice

1. Conjugate **fugiō** and **veniō** in the present, imperfect, and future active indicative.
2. Give the second singular of **gerō** and the first plural of **audiō** in the present, imperfect, and future active indicative.
3. Decline **magna cīvitās**.

Syntax Review

The Ablative of Means

The means or instrument by which a thing is done is expressed by the ablative without a preposition.

Coriolānus, verbīs mātris affectus, dīxit...	*Coriolanus, affected by (with) his mother's words, said . . .*
Nōnne Vestālēs officiīs sacrīs saepe Rōmam servāvērunt?	*Haven't the Vestals often saved Rome with (by means of) their sacred duties?*

Infinitive Used as Subject and Object

The infinitive is an indeclinable neuter noun derived from a verb. As a noun, it can be used as a subject (or predicate nominative).

Vidēre est crēdere.	*To see is to believe.*
Dūrum est expectāre.	*It is hard to wait.*
Tum facilius erat fāmam merēre.	*To earn fame then was easier.*

It can also be used as an object.

Dux Volscōrum urbem occupāre parābat.	*The leader of the Volsci was preparing to seize the city.*
Laelia ōrātiōnēs ēgregiās facere poterat.	*Laelia was able to make outstanding speeches.*

Note that the infinitive, since it has some of the characteristics of a verb, can itself take an object (see **fāmam, urbem, ōrātiōnēs** in the last three preceding examples).

When the infinitive, as object, describes another action of the same subject and completes the sense of verbs with meanings like *want, be able, begin, dare, be accustomed, hasten, ought, try,* etc., it is often called a *complementary infinitive.*

Translation

1. Can girls in these times win fame by good deeds?
2. Coriolanus did not occupy the city with his troops.
3. It was not easy for many Roman women at that time to earn money.
4. Will the men order the women to give money or will Hortensia's words compel the men to yield?

VOCABULARY REVIEW

Nouns

cīvitās	fuga	pāx

Adjectives

ēgregius	facilis

Verbs

afficiō	faciō	mūniō
agō	fugiō	occupō
cōgō	gerō	veniō
dō	iubeō	

Carmen Redondo/CORBIS

The round temple of Vesta in the Forum. It housed the sacred fire which the Vestals were to keep lit on pain of death, the **Palladium** (a small wooden image of Minerva which Aeneas was believed to have rescued from burning Troy), and other sacred objects in a room to which only the Chief Vestal had access.

WORD STUDY

Prefixes Review the prefixes **ad-, in-,** and **con-** in the Grammar Appendix, noting carefully that assimilation may take place, depending upon the initial sound of the base to which the prefix is attached.

Define **accēdō, adsum, inveniō, cōnfundō, commoveō;** *adverse, impel, inquire, comprehend.*

Apply the proper form of the prefix and define the resulting English compound: **(ad)** *-sim|ate, -gressive, -sent, -tribute;* **(in)** *-duce, -pede, -vert;* **(con)** *-fection, -lect, -mission, -rupt.*

Explain by derivation: *affectation, cogent, fugue, ingest.*

DAYS WITH BOOKS AND WRITERS

Araldo de Luca/CORBIS

This statue of Augustus Caesar in the uniform of a Roman general **(imperātor),** now in the Vatican Museum, was intended as a form of propaganda to display the emperor's military prowess. While Augustus was, according to his biographers, no mean soldier, this idealized statue also hints at the poise of an orator and the youthful confidence of a civil leader. The cuirass *(breastplate)* is covered not just with the symbols of military victories, but with signs of an empire in peace and prosperity under the blessing of the gods.

In pulchrō templō Apollinis, quod Augustus in bellō vōverat et posteā in Palātīnō cōnfēcerat, erat bibliothēca pūblica ubi multī librī, et Graecī et Latīnī, continēbantur. Ibi Pūblius et Fūriānus saepe diū manēbant. Saepe etiam per partem urbis in quā librāriōrum tabernae erant ambulābant. Prō
5 tabernīs pendēbant[1] librī ab auctōribus et novīs et nōtīs scrīptī. In tabernīs servī librāriōrum semper librōs dēscrībēbant. Magna taberna Sosiōrum grātissima Fūriānō Pūbliōque erat.

Quondam P. Ovidius Nāsō, poēta Rōmānīs eō tempore grātus, carmina legere parāvit. P. Caecilius Rūfus, pater Pūblī, amīcum poētae nōverat;
10 itaque Rūfus cum amīcō et cum fīliō Fūriānōque ad aedificium in quō Ovidius habitāvit prōcessit. Magnum erat studium Pūblī et Fūriānī; multa enim carmina Ovidī in tabernā Sosiōrum vīderant et explicāverant, et saepe Ovidium ipsum vidēre cupīverant. In viā Rūfus amīcusque multa dē poētīs dīcēbant.
15 "Ovidius poētārum Rōmānōrum optimus est," amīcus clāmāvit. "Ubi hominēs nōmina omnium aliōrum poētārum quī nunc sunt ex memoriā dēposuerint, nōmen Ovidī remanēbit."

---

[1] *hung*

"Bonus est, sed nōn est melior quam Vergilius et Horātius, quōs puerī audiēbāmus. Meliōrēs quam illī erant Rōma neque vīdit neque audīvit," dīxit Rūfus. 20

"Certē, certē, *Aeneidem,*[2] *Carmen Saeculāre*[3] nōn scrīpsit; *Amōrēs* et aliī librī eius grātī, sed nōn ēgregiī sunt. Sed multa dē novō librō eius, quī *Metamorphōsēs*[4] appellātur, audīvī."

"Augustusne eum librum vīdit?"

"Nesciō.[5] Ovidius autem Augustō nōn grātissimus esse vidētur. 25 Augustus Horātium et Vergilium memoriā tenet."

Ad aedificium in quō Ovidius habitābat vēnerant, et Ovidius iam librum novum recitābat. Carmen dē Orpheō et uxōre eius lēgit. Pūblius et Fūriānus magnō cum studiō audīvērunt. Carmine lēctō, ex aedificiō tardē excessērunt. 30

"Poēta certē est!" erant verba Pūblī.

[2] the *Aeneid,* an epic poem by Vergil

[3] *The Secular Hymn,* a poem by Horace written for the Secular (i.e., Century) Games, which were revived by Augustus in 17 B.C. to mark the end of an era.

[4] *Transformations,* a long poem dealing with supernatural changes, or miracles, from the creation of the world out of chaos to the fabled transformation of Julius Caesar into a star.

[5] = **nōn sciō**

Questions

1. What was the location of the public library in which Publius and Furianus often read? Who established it?
2. Where else did the boys see many books?
3. How did they learn about Ovid and his poetry?
4. Which poets did Augustus favor?
5. Which of his poems was Ovid reading? Where?

Giraudon/Art Resource, NY

Publius Vergilius Maro, or simply Vergil, was one of Rome's finest poets. His works include the *Eclogues,* ten poems praised for their beautiful recreations of pastoral life and song; the *Georgics,* a poem in four books dedicated to the art of farming; and the *Aeneid,* an epic poem that tells of the wanderings of Aeneas and the founding of Rome.

Nota•Bene

The personal endings in the **perfect active indicative** are different from all others, but they are the same for all conjugations, for all regular and irregular verbs, including **sum.**

⊞ GRAMMAR

Form Review

Perfect Active Indicative System

The perfect, past perfect, and future perfect tenses make up the perfect system. In the active voice, for all conjugations, these tenses are formed by dropping the **-ī** from the third principal part to get the perfect active stem, adding a tense sign when necessary, and then adding the personal endings.

PERFECT

portāvī	**docuī**	**posuī**	**cēpī**	**mūnīvī**
I carried, etc.	*I taught,* etc.	*I placed,* etc.	*I took,* etc.	*I fortified,* etc.
portāvistī	**docuistī**	**posuistī**	**cēpistī**	**mūnīvistī**
portāvit	**docuit**	**posuit**	**cēpit**	**mūnīvit**
portāvimus	**docuimus**	**posuimus**	**cēpimus**	**mūnīvimus**
portāvistis	**docuistis**	**posuistis**	**cēpistis**	**mūnīvistis**
portāvērunt	**docuērunt**	**posuērunt**	**cēpērunt**	**mūnīvērunt**

PAST PERFECT[6]

portāveram *I had*	**docueram** *I had*	**posueram** *I had*	**cēperam** *I had*	**mūnīveram** *I had*
carried, etc.	*taught,* etc.	*placed,* etc.	*taken,* etc.	*fortified,* etc.
portāverās	**docuerās**	**posuerās**	**cēperās**	**mūnīverās**
portāverat	**docuerat**	**posuerat**	**cēperat**	**mūnīverat**
portāverāmus	**docuerāmus**	**posuerāmus**	**cēperāmus**	**mūnīverāmus**
portāverātis	**docuerātis**	**posuerātis**	**cēperātis**	**mūnīverātis**
portāverant	**docuerant**	**posuerant**	**cēperant**	**mūnīverant**

FUTURE PERFECT

portāverō	**docuerō**	**posuerō**	**cēperō**	**mūnīverō**
I shall have	*I shall have*	*I shall have*	*I shall have*	*I shall have*
carried, etc.	*taught,* etc.	*placed,* etc.	*taken,* etc.	*fortified,* etc.
portāveris	**docueris**	**posueris**	**cēperis**	**mūnīveris**
portāverit	**docuerit**	**posuerit**	**cēperit**	**mūnīverit**
portāverimus	**docuerimus**	**posuerimus**	**cēperimus**	**mūnīverimus**
portāveritis	**docueritis**	**posueritis**	**cēperitis**	**mūnīveritis**
portāverint	**docuerint**	**posuerint**	**cēperint**	**mūnīverint**

[6] also called the *pluperfect*

PERFECT	PAST PERFECT	FUTURE PERFECT
fuī *I have been, was, etc.*	**fueram** *I had been, etc.*	**fuerō** *I shall have been, etc.*
fuistī	**fuerās**	**fueris**
fuit	**fuerat**	**fuerit**
fuimus	**fuerāmus**	**fuerimus**
fuistis	**fuerātis**	**fueritis**
fuērunt	**fuerant**	**fuerint**

Practice

1. Conjugate **videō** and **occupō** in the perfect active indicative.
2. Give the third person singular of **dīcō** and the third person plural of **veniō** in all tenses of the active indicative.

Syntax Review

Genitive

The genitive case is used to make one noun limit or define another. It can usually be translated by the preposition *of*.

Genitive of Possession

Possession is expressed by the genitive case.

taberna Sosiōrum	*the shop of the Sosii*
nōmina omnium aliōrum poētārum	*the names of all other poets*

Partitive Genitive (Genitive of the Whole)

The whole of which something is a part is expressed in the genitive case.

partem urbis	*part of the city*
Poētārum Rōmānōrum optimus est.	*Of Roman poets he is the best.*

Translation

1. Augustus had completed a new temple of Apollo on the Palatine.
2. Publius had read many books written by Greek and Latin authors.
3. Publius had read many poems of Ovid but had not seen the poet himself.
4. "Ovid has certainly been a good poet," said Publius to (his) father, "but Rome will always remember Vergil."

Nota•Bene

Videor, the passive of **videō,** *see,* very often means *seem* or *seem best* as well as *be seen.* **Ovidius Augustō nōn grātissimus poēta vidētur,** *To Augustus, Ovid does not seem to be a very pleasing poet.*

Nouns

amīcus	homō	pars
auctor		

Adjectives

grātus	novus

Verbs

clāmō	dīcō	nōscō
cōnficiō	legō	scrībō
contineō	maneō	videō, videor
cupiō		

Adverb

autem

WORD STUDY

Prefixes Review the prefixes **re-, prō-, sub-** in the Grammar Appendix. Only **sub-** is assimilated. **Re-** adds a *d* before vowels and before forms of **dō.**

Define according to the prefix: **recēdō, redigō, reddō, redūcō, prōmoveō, prōpellō, succēdō, sustineō;** *recession, proclaim, provide, subtract.*

Use the proper form of the prefix **sub-:** *-ficient, -ject, -cession, -gest, -port.*

Explain by derivation: *remain, refugee, repatriation, resumption, revoke, provocative, prescription, suspect, sustain.*

LESSON V

THE TWELVE TABLES OF THE LAW

LESSON OBJECTIVES
Review:
- Passive Indicative in all Tenses of all Four Conjugations
- Participles
- Uses of Participles
- Ablative (Absolute, Agent)

Quondam haec verba ā Pūbliō recitābantur, Secundā, sorōre parvā, audiente: "Adversus hostem aeterna auctōritās."[1]

Dē hīs verbīs Secunda Pūblium rogātūra erat, sed hic in Forum excesserat. Itaque Rūfus pater ā Secundā petītus est. Rūfō inventō, Secunda rogāvit:

"Quid est 'Adversus hostem aeterna auctōritās'? Pūblium haec dīcentem audīvī."

Pater explicāvit: "Haec sunt verba dē lēgibus Duodecim Tabulārum lēcta, quae ab omnibus puerīs Rōmānīs memoriae semper mandātae sunt, ab eō tempore quō scrīptae sunt."

"Quō tempore scrīptae sunt?"

"Prīmīs annīs cīvitātis, ubi Decemvirī potestātem habuērunt. Diū lēgēs Rōmānōrum, memoriā hominum retentae, nōn scrīptae erant. Sed ā populō Rōmānō scrīptae lēgēs petītae sunt, quod multae gravēs iniūriae ab hominibus verba lēgum nōn scientibus acceptae erant. Cōnsiliō clārissimōrum hominum cīvitātis petītō, hic modus optimus inventus est: trēs virī clārī in Graeciam missī sunt, ubi lēgēs Graecōrum cognōvērunt. Aliī ad Hermodōrum, Graecum in Italiā habitantem, missī sunt. Etiam nunc statua Hermodōrī, ā Rōmānīs posita, in Comitiō[2] stat. Tum summa potestās cīvitātis decem virīs data est, quī iussī sunt lēgēs Rōmānās dēscrībere. Ubi hī decem virī diū labōrāvērunt, magnum opus cōnfectum est. Lēgēs, in tabulīs duodecim scrīptae, in Forō positae sunt. Ibi ab omnibus per multōs annōs vīsae sunt, et ibi nunc videntur."

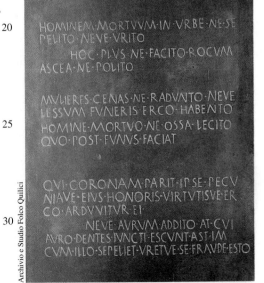

Archivio e Studio Folco Quilici

[1] *Against a foreigner the right (in property shall be) everlasting;* e.g., a Roman citizen could obtain legal possession of public land by settling on it; a foreigner could not.

[2] the *Comitium,* the area in the Forum where the people came together to vote

Plaster replica of a tablet from the Twelve Tables, now in a Roman museum. The originals were made of wood or bronze, but have all been lost, and the texts survive only in literary quotations. This copy contains several regulations about burial procedures, in a Latin so archaic that even Cicero and the scholars of his time had difficulty understanding it. But even now you should be able to recognize many of its words. The laws dealt with many matters: court procedures (lawsuits, witnesses, etc.), property rights, wills, crimes, rights and damages, the relationship between a **patrōnus** and his **clientēs**, as well as rules forbidding the bewitching of crops or making incantations.

"Eās saepe vīdī. Sed quae sunt illae lēgēs?"

35 "Multae sunt—dē poenīs, dē iniūriīs, dē familiīs, dē patriā potestāte, dē dēbitīs, dē viīs, dē sepulchrīs—dē iūre Rōmānō. Multae aliae lēgēs posteā dēcrētae sunt, sed lēgibus Duodecim Tabulārum potestās Rōmāna cōnfirmāta est. Ubi illae lēgēs āmissae erunt, tum potestās Rōmae āmittētur; illīs manentibus, Rōma aeterna erit."

Questions

1. Why couldn't Secunda ask Publius about the strange words he was reciting? Whom did she ask?
2. Why did the Roman people think that the laws should be written down?
3. Why were three men sent to Greece and others to Hermodorus?
4. The caption accompanying the illustration on page 27 tells you some of the subjects covered by the Twelve Tables. Name five others mentioned in the reading.
5. Can you think of some ways in which the origin and nature of the Twelve Tables and the U.S. Constitution are alike? In what ways are they not alike?

One of the laws of the Twelve Tables decreed that cemeteries had to be built outside the city limits. As a result, they were usually placed along the main highways near the city, as is this family tomb on the **Via Appia**.

Erich Lessing/Art Resource, NY

GRAMMAR

Form Review

Passive Voice

In the passive voice, the subject receives the action of the verb. To form the present passive system, Latin adds distinctive passive personal endings to the present stem for the present tense, or to that stem plus the tense signs for the imperfect or the future.

PRESENT PASSIVE

portor *I am (being) carried,* etc.	doceor *I am (being) taught,* etc.	pōnor *I am (being) placed,* etc.	capior *I am (being) taken,* etc.	mūnior *I am (being) fortified,* etc.
portāris	docēris	pōneris	caperis	mūnīris
portātur	docētur	pōnitur	capitur	mūnītur
portāmur	docēmur	pōnimur	capimur	mūnīmur
portāminī	docēminī	pōniminī	capiminī	mūnīminī
portantur	docentur	pōnuntur	capiuntur	mūniuntur

IMPERFECT PASSIVE

portābar *I was (being) carried*	docēbar *I was (being) taught*	pōnēbar *I was (being) placed*	capiēbar *I was (being) taken*	mūniēbar *I was (being) fortified*
portābāris	docēbāris	pōnēbāris	capiēbāris	mūniēbāris
portābātur	docēbātur	pōnēbātur	capiēbātur	mūniēbātur
portābāmur	docēbāmur	pōnēbāmur	capiēbāmur	mūniēbāmur
portābāminī	docēbāminī	pōnēbāminī	capiēbāminī	mūniēbāminī
portābantur	docēbantur	pōnēbantur	capiēbantur	mūniēbantur

FUTURE PASSIVE

portābor *I shall be carried*	docēbor *I shall be taught*	pōnar *I shall be put*	capiar *I shall be taken*	mūniar *I shall be fortified*
portāberis	docēberis	pōnēris	capiēris	mūniēris
portābitur	docēbitur	pōnētur	capiētur	mūniētur
portābimur	docēbimur	pōnēmur	capiēmur	mūniēmur
portābiminī	docēbiminī	pōnēminī	capiēminī	mūniēminī
portābuntur	docēbuntur	pōnentur	capientur	mūnientur

In the perfect passive system, the perfect passive participle (the fourth principal part) is combined with conjugated forms of the verb **sum.**

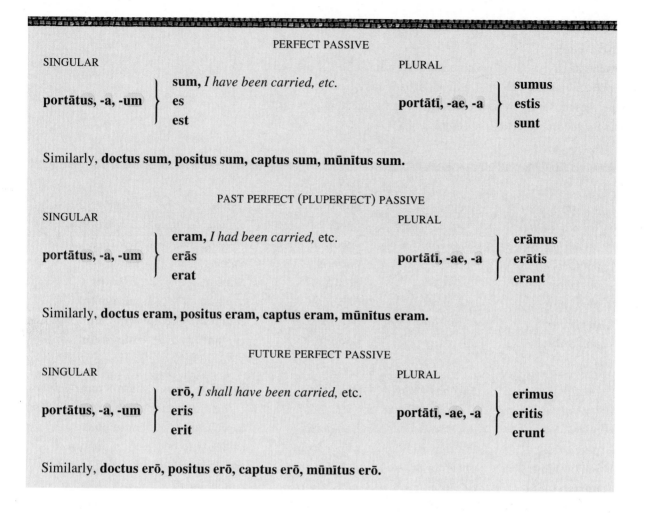

PERFECT PASSIVE

SINGULAR		PLURAL	
portātus, -a, -um	**sum,** *I have been carried, etc.* **es** **est**	**portātī, -ae, -a**	**sumus** **estis** **sunt**

Similarly, **doctus sum, positus sum, captus sum, mūnītus sum.**

PAST PERFECT (PLUPERFECT) PASSIVE

SINGULAR		PLURAL	
portātus, -a, -um	**eram,** *I had been carried, etc.* **erās** **erat**	**portātī, -ae, -a**	**erāmus** **erātis** **erant**

Similarly, **doctus eram, positus eram, captus eram, mūnītus eram.**

FUTURE PERFECT PASSIVE

SINGULAR		PLURAL	
portātus, -a, -um	**erō,** *I shall have been carried, etc.* **eris** **erit**	**portātī, -ae, -a**	**erimus** **eritis** **erunt**

Similarly, **doctus erō, positus erō, captus erō, mūnītus erō.**

Practice

1. Conjugate **āmittō** in the present passive, **inveniō** in the future passive, and **mandō** in the perfect passive indicative.
2. Give the third singular of **petō** and the third plural of **cōnficiō** in the six tenses of the passive indicative.

Participles

A *participle* is an adjective derived from a verb, and it retains the verb's characteristics of tense and voice. A Latin verb has four participles: present active, perfect passive, future active, and future passive. The future passive participle will be discussed in Lesson XXI.

The *present active participle* in Latin is formed by adding **-ns** in the nominative singular (**-ntis** in the genitive) to the present stem of any verb, e.g., **portāns, portantis,** *carrying.* Its stem ends in **-nt-** and it is declined like a third declension **i**-stem adjective of one ending (cf. **pār**).[3]

[3] The ablative singular regularly ends in **-e,** but in **-ī** when the participle is used as a simple adjective.

	SINGULAR		PLURAL	
M. F.	N.		M. F.	N.
portāns, *carrying*			**portantēs**	**portantia**
portantis			**portantium**	
portantī			**portantibus**	
portantem	**portāns**		**portantēs (īs)**	**portantia**
portante (ī)			**portantibus**	

Similarly, **docēns, -ntis; pōnēns, -ntis; capiēns, -ntis, mūniēns, -ntis.**

The *perfect passive participle* is the fourth principal part, declined like an adjective of the first and second declension, e.g., **portātus, -a, -um,** *having been carried, carried.*

Similarly, **doctus, -a, -um; positus, -a, -um; captus, -a, -um; mūnītus, -a, -um.**

The *future active participle* is formed by replacing the **-us** of the perfect passive participle with **-ūrus.** It too is declined like an adjective of the first and second declension, e.g., **portātūrus, -a, -um,** *about to carry, going to carry.*

Similarly, **doctūrus, -a, -um; positūrus, -a, -um; captūrus, -a, -um; mūnītūrus, -a, -um.**

Because participles are (verbal) adjectives, they must agree with the noun, stated or understood, that they modify in gender, number, and case.

Practice

1. Form and translate the participles of **dō, videō, mittō, sciō.**
2. Give in Latin: *having been said* (acc. sing. neut.); *learning* (dat. pl. masc.); *going to entrust* (gen. sing. fem.); *standing* (nom. pl. fem.); *sent* (abl. sing. neut.)

Syntax Review

Uses of Participles

Participles give Latin great flexibility of expression.

1. They can be used as simple adjectives modifying nouns and conveying the idea of action in a verb, e.g., **scrīptae lēgēs,** *written laws;* **Graecum in Italiā habitantem,** *a Greek living in Italy.*

2. They can be used as nouns alone (substantives) or as modifiers of a noun that is not expressed but is to be understood, e.g.,

> **spectantēs** (nom. pl. masc./fem.) *the ones watching,* i.e., *spectators*
>
> **facta** (nom. pl. neut.) *the things (having been) done,*
> i.e., *deeds*

dē dēbitīs (abl. pl. neut.)	*about the things having been owed,* i.e., *about debts*
captae (gen. sing. fem.)	*of the captive woman*
futūra (acc. pl. neut.)	*those things about to be,* i.e., *the future*

3. They can be used as part of a whole clause introduced by words like *who, which, while, when, after, since, because, although, if,* e.g.,

ab hominibus verba lēgum nōn scientibus	*by men who did not know the words of the laws*
Lēgēs, in tabulīs duodecim scrīptae, in Forō positae sunt,	*The laws, after they had been written on twelve tablets, were set up in the Forum.*

When used this way, the Latin participle can have a great variety of translations in English, depending upon your interpretation of the context. Use your imagination to figure out which meaning is best.

It is also important to understand that in Latin the participle indicates a time relative to that of the main verb. The present participle describes an action going on *at the same time as* the time of the main verb, the perfect participle a time *before* that of the main verb, and the future participle a time *after* that of the main verb.

Pūblium haec dīcentem audīvī.	*I heard Publius saying these things* i.e., ***at the same time as** he said them.*
Illīs lēgibus manentibus, Rōma aeterna erit.	*As long as (**at the same time**) those laws (will) remain, Rome will be eternal.*
Lēgēs scrīptae in Forō positae sunt.	*The laws were set up in the Forum after they had been written down, i.e., they were written down **before** they were set up.*
Aliī ad Hermodōrum missī sunt eius cōnsilium rogātūrī.	*Others were sent to Hermodorus who were going to ask his advice, i.e., **after** they were sent.*

4. By far the most common use of the perfect passive and future active participles is to form compound tenses of the verb. You already know how the perfect passive participle is combined with conjugated forms of **sum** to create the entire perfect passive system, and how the future active participle with **sum** can produce an alternate form of the future tense (usually called the *periphrastic*), e.g., **rogātūrī sumus,** *we are about to ask;* **rogātūra erat,** *she was going to ask.*

But here the present active participle is different. The present active participle ending in *-ing,* e.g., *carrying, doing,* etc., can be used in English to form the progressive tenses, *but **not** in Latin.* You do *not* say **portāns sum** for *I am carrying;* **portō** by itself is enough.

Ablative Absolute

To describe the circumstances under which the rest of the action in a sentence occurs, Latin will often use the ablative case of a noun accompanied by a modifying participle. This construction is called the *ablative absolute.* Less often it will be composed of two nouns in the ablative or a noun and an adjective in the ablative. This phrase in the ablative can usually be translated as a whole clause, which you may introduce with a word like *when, while, because, since, although, if,* etc., when the context seems to require it.

Secundā audiente,...	*while Secunda was listening, . . .*
Rūfō inventō,...	*Rufus having been found, . . .*
Numā rēge,...	*when Numa was king, . . .*

Ablative of Agent

The ablative with **ā** or **ab** is used with a passive verb to indicate the person (or sometimes an animal or a personalized abstraction, like *Luck*) by whom something is done.

Verba ā Pūbliō recitābantur.	*Words were being recited by Publius.*
lēgēs āb omnibus puerīs Rōmānīs memoriae mandātae	*laws committed to memory by all Roman boys*
statua in Forō ā Rōmānīs posita	*a statue placed in the Forum by the Romans*

Richard T. Nowitz/CORBIS

A coin from Jerusalem showing Augustus wearing a victor's wreath. Coins make excellent propaganda, because they are good for name and face recognition, and are widespread. Are you looking at the *obverse* or the *reverse* of this coin?

Translation⁴

1. (As) Publius (was) reciting these strange words, Secunda could not understand his eagerness.
2. Having found her father, Secunda asked about the words (which she had) heard.
3. Her father said, "The words (which you have) heard were selected from the laws."
4. "These laws, placed in the Forum, can be seen by all Romans. While they remain, we shall be free."
5. These temples were repaired when Augustus was leader.

VOCABULARY REVIEW

Nouns

annus	iūs	opus
auctōritās	lēx	prīnceps
hostis	modus	

Adjectives

clārus	gravis

Verbs

āmittō	mandō	pōnō
audiō	mittō	sciō
cognōscō	petō	stō
inveniō		

Adverb

ubi

Translation Strategy: Participial Phrases

A neat way Latin often uses to break a sentence into manageable elements is to "trap" between a noun and the participle that modifies it a phrase which fills out the meaning of the whole participial phrase.

verba dē lēgibus lēcta	*words chosen from the laws*
ab hominibus verba lēgum	*by men who did not know (not*
nōn scientibus	*knowing) the words of the laws*
Graecum in Italiā habitantem	*a Greek living in Italy*

So, as your eyes pass over the words of a Latin sentence, be alert to the possibility that, following some noun or pronoun and after an adverb, or a prepositional phrase, or even a direct object, a participle may be lying in wait to modify it.

WORD STUDY

Prefixes Review the prefixes **in-** *(negative)*, **dis-**, **per-** in the Grammar Appendix. All three may be assimilated. **Per-**, like **con-**, may have the intensive meaning *very,* or *thoroughly.* Define according to the prefix: **incertus, inimīcus, dīmittō, dispōnō, perficiō, perlegō;** *inaudible, ingrate, dissimilar, permission.*

Select the proper form of each prefix: **(in)** *-dispensable, -legal, -proper, -responsible;* **(dis)** *-gest, -vert, -claim;* **(per)** *-manent, -turb.*

Explain by derivation: *imperfect, incognito, command, dissent, invisible, ignoble.*

THE SENATE IN SESSION

Pūblius per iānuam vēnit, ad quam Fulvia māter diū exspectāverat. "Ubi fuistī?" Fulvia rogāvit. "Tardus es."

"Ad Cūriam Iūliam cum patre prōcessī," Pūblius respondit. "Putō patrem mox ventūrum esse. In Comitiō, ad Cūriam, stābam. Iānuā nōn
5 clausā, multa audīvī et vīdī. Multī patrēs,[1] inter quōs clārissimōs cīvitātis vīdī, per viās in Cūriam convēnērunt. Quibus[2] iam sedentibus, cōnsulēs accessērunt, tum Augustus ipse. Post sacrificium nūntiātum est ōmina[3] bona esse. Tum Augustus litterās multās et longās lēgit."

"Dē quō?"

10 "Audīre nōn poteram quod multī puerī ad iānuam stābant, virōs prementēs et clāmantēs. Quem putās eōs dīmīsisse? Fūriānus hoc fēcit! Puerīs dīxit Augustum, prīncipem cīvitātis, patrēs dē gravibus rēbus cōnsulere; deōs vocātōs esse et adesse; eōs puerōs clāmantēs deīs iniūriam facere; eōs poenam datūrōs esse—haec et multa alia. Quō modō, nōn vīdī;

[1] *senators.* Originally the Senate was composed of the heads *(fathers)* of the prominent families.

[2] = **His**

[3] *omens*

The Senate's usual functions were to advise the magistrates, to discuss and approve laws before they were ratified by the voters (the Comitia), to decide and confirm appointments and budgetary matters, to conduct foreign and domestic relations, and to deal with matters of religion.

Robert E. Bright/Photo Researchers

A view across the Forum from the Palatine Hill. In the right background is the ancient Senate house (the **Cūria**). The open area in front of it was the **Comitium**, where the people came together to vote. The Arch of Septimius Severus was a much later addition. Three columns of the Temple of Castor and Pollux are in the left center.

sed Fūriānus coēgit puerōs discēdere. Magnam vōcem habet; puerōs eum   15
timuisse putō.

"In Cūriā Augustus iam rogābat, 'Quās litterās habētis?' et patrēs
litterās legere iussit. Litterīs omnibus lēctīs, cōnsul verba fēcit: multōs
Rōmānōs dominōs, virōs clārissimōs, ā servīs oppressōs et interfectōs
esse; hoc malum esse; servōs cīvium Rōmānōrum interfectōrum prehendī   20
et torquērī et tum interficī dēbēre."

"Cuius modī erant sententiae?"

"Paene omnēs patrēs sēnsērunt cōnsilium cōnsulis bonum futūrum esse;
paucī putāvērunt hanc poenam ācriōrem futūram esse. Augustus nūntiāvit
maiōrem partem patrum cōnsilium cōnsulis probāre."   25

"Quae erat sententia patris tuī?"

"Verba multa nōn fēcit, et ea audīre nōn poteram; sed putō eum in parte
cōnsulis sēnsisse. Sententiīs datīs, Augustus dīxit: 'Nihil[4] vōs teneō,' et   [4] *not*
omnēs patrēs ē Cūriā discessērunt."

Questions

1. Where had Publius been and what events had he witnessed there?
2. How did Furianus distinguish himself?
3. In what way was the meeting of the Senate opened?
4. What was the consul's proposal? Was it universally accepted?
5. On what reasoning were, and still are, senators chosen or elected from the older citizens?

GRAMMAR

Form Review

Infinitives

Infinitives are verbal nouns and may be used as the subjects or objects of verbs. They have three tenses—present, perfect, and future—and two voices—active and passive. The future passive infinitive is rare and is not used in this book.

PRESENT ACTIVE

The present active infinitive is the second principal part, formed by adding **-re** to the present stem.

portāre, *to carry*   **docēre   pōnere   capere   mūnīre**

PRESENT PASSIVE

In the first, second, and fourth conjugations, form the present passive infinitive by changing the final **-e** of the present active infinitive to **-ī**. In the third conjugation change the final **-ere** to **-ī.**

portārī, *to be carried*   **docērī   pōnī   capī   mūnīrī**

PERFECT ACTIVE

Form the perfect active infinitive by dropping the final **-ī** of the third principal part and adding **-isse.**

portāvisse, *to have carried*   **docuisse   posuisse   cēpisse   mūnīvisse**

PERFECT PASSIVE

Form the perfect passive infinitive by using the perfect passive participle (the fourth principal part) plus **esse.**

portātus, -a, -um esse, *to have been carried*
doctus, -a, -um esse
positus, -a, -um esse
captus, -a, -um esse
mūnītus, -a, -um esse

FUTURE ACTIVE

Form the future active infinitive by dropping the **-us, -a, -um** of the perfect passive participle, and adding **-ūrus, -a, -um** plus **esse.**
portātūrus, -a, -um esse, *to be about to carry*
doctūrus, -a, -um esse
positūrus, -a, -um esse
captūrus, -a, -um esse
mūnītūrus, -a, -um esse

The infinitives of **sum** have active forms.

PRESENT	**esse,**	*to be*
PERFECT	**fuisse,**	*to have been*
FUTURE	**futūrus, -a, -um esse,**	*to be about to be*

Forms and Use of the Relative Pronoun

The relative pronoun, *who, which, that,* refers back to an antecedent with which it agrees in gender and number. It takes its case, however, from its use in the clause it introduces.

SINGULAR			PLURAL		
M.	F.	N.	M.	F.	N.
quī	quae	quod	quī	quae	quae
cuius	cuius	cuius	quōrum	quārum	quōrum
cui	cui	cui	quibus	quibus	quibus
quem	quam	quod	quōs	quās	quae
quō	quā	quō	quibus	quibus	quibus

Virī ad Hermodōrum quī in Italiā habitābat missī sunt.	*Men were sent to Hermodorus* (acc. sing. masc., object of the preposition **ad**) *who* (nom. sing. masc., subject of **habitābat**) *was living in Italy.*
Patrēs, inter quōs clārissimōs cīvitātis vīdī, convēnērunt.	*Senators,* (nom. pl. masc., subject of **convēnērunt**) *among whom* (acc. pl. masc., object of **inter**) *I saw the most distinguished men of the state, came together.*
Patrēs in Cūriam convēnērunt. Quibus iam sedentibus, cōnsulēs accessērunt.	*The senators* (nom. pl. masc., subject of **convēnērunt**) *came together into the Senate House. While they* (abl. pl. masc. in an ablative absolute) *were just taking their seats, the consuls approached.*

All three of the preceding examples demonstrate that while the relative pronoun agrees with its antecedent in gender and number, *its **case** is determined by its use **in its own clause***. The last example shows how Latin will often begin a new sentence with a relative pronoun whose antecedent is in the preceding sentence. Here English uses a demonstrative pronoun instead of the relative. Often an entire preceding sentence or even a whole paragraph is the antecedent, as when, after successfully proving a theorem in geometry, you proudly write **Q.E.D. (Quod erat demōnstrandum),** *Which* (or *This*) *(is) what was to be proved.*

Forms and Use of the Interrogative Pronoun

The interrogative pronoun **quis? quid?** asks the question *who? what?*

	SINGULAR		PLURAL		
	M. F.	N.	M.	F.	N.
NOM.	**quis?** *who?*	**quid?** *what?*	**quī?**	**quae?**	**quae?**
GEN.	**cuius?** *whose?*	**cuius?** *of what?*	**quōrum?**	**quārum?**	**quōrum?**
DAT.	**cui?** *to/for whom?*	**cui?** *to/for what?*	**quibus?**	**quibus?**	**quibus?**
ACC.	**quem?** *whom?*	**quid?** *what?*	**quōs?**	**quās?**	**quae?**
ABL.	**quō?** *by whom?*	**quō?** *by what?*	**quibus?**	**quibus?**	**quibus?**

Quis multās et longās litterās lēgit?	*Who read many long letters?*
Quem putās eōs dīmīsisse?	*Who do you think sent them away?*[5]

Forms and Use of the Interrogative Adjective

The forms of the interrogative adjective *which? what?* are the same as the relative pronoun. The interrogative adjective modifies a noun (or other substantive) and will agree with it in gender, number, and case.

Quās litterās habētis?	*What letters do you have?*
Cuius modī erant sententiae?	*Of what sort were the opinions?*

Practice

1. Give the present infinitive, active and passive, of **appellō, cōgō,** and **sentiō;** the perfect infinitive, active and passive, of **nūntiō, probō,** and **afficiō;** the future active infinitive of **exspectō, respondeō,** and **accēdō.**

2. Give the Latin for *whose* (pl.); *whom?* (fem. sing.); *to whom?* (masc. sing.); *what boy?* (nom. sing.); *who?* (fem. sing.); *by whom?* (pl.); *whose?* (masc. sing.); *to whom?* (pl.); *by whom?* (fem. sing.); *what?* (acc. sing.)

---

[5] Good English uses *Who* here because it is separated from the verb by the phrase *"do you think,"* which is regarded as parenthetical.

Syntax Review

Infinitive with Subject Accusative

The subject of an infinitive is in the accusative case.

Tē (subj.) **intellegere hoc** (obj.) **grātissimum est.**	*That you understand this (For you to understand this) is very gratifying.*
Fūriānus dīxit deōs adesse.	*Furianus said that the gods were present.*

Infinitive in Indirect Statement

Statements that report *indirectly* the thoughts or words of another, used as objects of verbs of *saying, declaring, knowing, thinking, hearing, perceiving,* etc., have verbs in the infinitive with their subjects in the accusative. (In *direct* statements, the verb has a finite form and its subject is in the nominative.) Since in most cases of indirect statement both the subject and the object of the infinitive are in the accusative, you must depend upon the context to tell you which is subject and which is object.

Fūriānus dīxit Augustum cōnsulere patrēs.	*Furianus said that Augustus was consulting the senators.*
Puerōs Fūriānum timuisse putō.	*I think that the boys were afraid of Furianus.*
Paucī putāvērunt hanc poenam ācriōrem futūram esse.	*A few thought that this punishment would be too harsh.*

Tenses of the Infinitive

Like the participles, the three tenses of the infinitive, whether they are in the active or passive voice, represent the action as taking place *relative* to the time of the main verb, and their translations will therefore vary accordingly.

The present infinitive represents an action as going on *at the same time as* that of the main verb.

Hodiē putō deōs adesse.	*Today I think the gods are present.*
Herī putāvī deōs adesse.	*Yesterday I thought the gods were present.*
Crās putābō deōs adesse.	*Tomorrow I shall think that the gods are present.*

The perfect infinitive represents an action as having gone on *before* the time of the main verb.

Hodiē putō deōs adfuisse.	*Today I think the gods were present (yesterday).*
Herī putāvī deōs adfuisse.	*Yesterday I thought the gods had been present (day before yesterday).*
Crās putābō deōs adfuisse.	*Tomorrow I shall think that the gods were present (today or yesterday).*

The future infinitive represents an action as taking place *after* the time of the main verb.

Hodiē putō deōs adfutūrōs esse.	*Today I think that the gods will be present (tomorrow).*
Herī putāvī deōs adfutūrōs esse.	*Yesterday I thought that the gods would be present (today).*
Crās putābō deōs adfutūrōs esse.	*Tomorrow I shall think that the gods will be present (day after tomorrow).*

Translation

1. Publius had heard that the consuls would come into the Forum.
2. The consul reported that many Romans were being killed by slaves.
3. Fulvia asked, "Did your father feel that the consul's opinion was good?"
4. Fulvia did not know that Publius had been with his father in the Forum.

▦ VOCABULARY REVIEW

Nouns

auxilium	poena	vōx
cōnsilium	sententia	

Adjective

tardus

Verbs

accēdō	exspectō	probō
adsum	interficiō	putō
claudō	nūntiō	sentiō
dēbeō	opprimō	vocō
dīmittō	premō	

Adverbs

crās	herī	hodiē [hōc + diē]

WORD STUDY

Suffixes The suffix **-ia** and its various combinations (**-cia, -tia, -antia, -entia**) form many nouns in Latin. Note the way they change in English.

LATIN	ENGLISH
-ia	*-y* (usually)
-tia (or **-cia**)	*-ce*
-antia	*-ance, -ancy*
-entia	*-ence, -ency*

Give the English forms of **glōria, prōvincia, iniūria, clēmentia, cōnstantia, Germānia, iūstitia.**

What must be the Latin words from which come *memory, providence, science, Thessaly, audience, instance?*

LESSON OBJECTIVES

Review:
- Numerals and Pronominal Adjectives
- Demonstratives: **Hic** and **Ille**
- Conjugation of **Possum**
- Ablative of Respect

HOLIDAYS

Mēnsis Mārtius iam aderat—ōlim prīmus novī annī inter Rōmānōs. Omnēs Caeciliī servīque suī vestibus nōvīs īnsignēs erant. Negōtium nūllī hominī mandābātur quod mūnera tōtīus cīvitātis ob fēriās dēposita erant. Pūblius Fūriānusque per Forum prōcēdēbant inter multōs hominēs, aliōs ad
5 templum properantēs, aliōs stantēs, omnēs novās vestēs gerentēs. Pūbliō et Fūriānō aedificia adōrnāta spectantibus,[1] per Forum nūntiātum est Vestālēs ignem Vestae magnā cum cūrā exstīnxisse māteriamque ad novum ignem dīligenter iam collēgisse. Duo virī ad Pūblium stābant; alter alterī dīxit: "Bene est. Illō igne semper manente, Rōma superārī nōn potest."
10 Nunc vōcēs audīrī poterant: "Saliī![2] Saliī veniunt!"
Illī salientēs per viās veniēbant, armātī et ancīlia ferentēs. (Dictum est temporibus antīquīs ūnum ex ancīlibus dē caelō cecidisse. Rōmānī, nōn cupientēs hoc sacrum rapī, iusserant virum fabricā callidum[3] XI alia huic simillima facere. Itaque nēmō nunc, XII ancīlia spectāns, illud ūnum
15 sacrum et vērē antīquum cognōscere potest.) Saliī currēbant, ancīlia quae ferēbant ostendentēs. Officium hōrum sacerdōtum erat mala ē portīs Rōmānīs expellere.

[1] ablative absolute

[2] *the Sā´liī,* Jumpers (priests of Mars who leapt about, brandishing their shields, **ancilia**)

[3] *skilled in metalworking*

This wall painting from Ostia appears to be a celebration carried out by girls bearing torches in honor of Artemis, who, besides being the virgin huntress, presided over the transition from girlhood to womanhood and over other stages in a woman's growth. Her image can be seen on a pedestal at the left.

C. M. Dixon/Photo Resources

Aliae antīquissimae fēriae erant multae numerō, variae natūrā et
auctōritāte: Cereālia et Parīlia (vel Palīlia), hae fēriae pāstōrum, quōrum
dea Palēs erat, illae agricolārum, quī Cererem colēbant; fēriae Latīnae, ubi 20
omnēs Latīnī Iovem in monte Albānō colēbant; Cōnsuālia, ubi equī pede
celerēs in Circō currēbant; Lupercālia, ubi duo virī per viās percurrēbant,
rīdentēs et omnēs fēminās quās vidēbant verberantēs; Parentālia, ubi
sepulchra tōtīus Rōmae adōrnābantur; et aliae. Pontificēs sōlī illās omnēs
memoriā tenuērunt, sed Pūblius aliīque līberī Rōmānī multās memoriā 25
tenuērunt quod, studiīs intermissīs, lūdere potuērunt.

Questions

1. Give several reasons why the month of March was special for the
   Romans.
2. Explain the symbolism in what the Vestals did at this time.
3. What method was adopted of preventing the theft of the one sacred
   shield?
4. Which festival was important for the farmers? the shepherds? the Latins?
5. What ceremonies took place during the Parentalia?

▦ GRAMMAR

Form Review

Numerals and Pronominal Adjectives

Cardinal numbers, the major ones with which we count 1, 2, 3, etc.,
are adjectives. Only four have some slight irregularity in declension; the
rest of the cardinals through one hundred are indeclinable. **Ambō,** *both,* is
declined like **duo.**

	M.	F.	N.	M.	F.	N.
Nominative	**ūnus,** *one*	**ūna**	**ūnum**	**duo,** *two*	**duae**	**duo**
Genitive	**ūnīus**	**ūnīus**	**ūnīus**	**duōrum**	**duārum**	**duōrum**
Dative	**ūnī**	**ūnī**	**ūnī**	**duōbus**	**duābus**	**duōbus**
Accusative	**ūnum**	**ūnam**	**ūnum**	**duōs**	**duās**	**duo**
Ablative	**ūnō**	**ūnā**	**ūnō**	**duōbus**	**duābus**	**duōbus**

	M. F.	N.	M. F. N. *(adj)*	N. *(noun)*
Nominative	**trēs,** *three*	**tria**	**mīlle,** *thousand*	**mīlia,** *thousands*
Genitive	**trium**		**mīlle**	**mīlium**
Dative	**tribus**		**mīlle**	**mīlibus**
Accusative	**trēs**	**tria**	**mīlle**	**mīlia**
Ablative	**tribus**		**mīlle**	**mīlibus**

Pronominal adjectives, so called because they are often used as pronouns, show many of the same minor irregularities in declension as **ūnus** above, namely **-īus** or **-ĭus** throughout the genitive singular and **-ī** throughout the dative singular. In the plural they are regular first and second declension adjectives. Learn these pronominal adjectives as well as the other words in the Vocabulary Review.

Don't condemn these adjectives as "irregular" just because they show an **-īus** or **-ĭus** in the genitive and **-ī** in the dative singular. The relative, interrogative, indefinite pronouns, and other demonstratives do exactly the same thing.

alius, alia, aliud,[4] *other*

ūllus, -a, -um, *any*

sōlus, -a, -um, *alone, only*

uter, utra, utrum,
   which (of two)

uterque, utraque, utrumque,
   each (of two)

alter, altera, alterum, *the other*
   (of two)

nūllus, -a, -um, *no, none*

tōtus, -a, -um, *whole, entire*

neuter, neutra, neutrum,
   neither (of two)

Demonstratives

The *demonstratives* **hic,** *this,* and **ille,** *that,* can likewise be used as adjectives or pronouns to point out something near (**hic**) or far (**ille**). **Hic** shows the characteristic **-īus** in the genitive singular and **-ī** in the dative singular, and in some cases a final **-c** (the remnant of an archaic **-ce,** an emphatic *here!*). **Ille** shows the characteristic **-īus** (gen. sing.), **-ī** (dat. sing.), and **-ud** in the neuter nominative and accusative singular, but is entirely regular in the plural.

	SINGULAR			PLURAL		
	M.	F.	N.	M.	F.	N.
Nominative	hic	haec	hoc	hī	hae	haec
Genitive	huius	huius	huius	hōrum	hārum	hōrum
Dative	huic	huic	huic	hīs	hīs	hīs
Accusative	hunc	hanc	hoc	hōs	hās	haec
Ablative	hōc	hāc	hōc	hīs	hīs	hīs

	SINGULAR			PLURAL		
	M.	F.	N.	M.	F.	N.
Nominative	ille	illa	illud	illī	illae	illa
Genitive	illīus	illīus	illīus	illōrum	illārum	illōrum
Dative	illī	illī	illī	illīs	illīs	illīs
Accusative	illum	illam	illud	illōs	illās	illa
Ablative	illō	illā	illō	illīs	illīs	illīs

[4] Regularly uses **alterĭus** instead of **alĭus** in the genitive singular.

Forms of *Possum*

The verb **possum, posse, potuī** is a combination of **pot(is)**, *able,* and forms of **sum.** In the present tense, the **-t-** in the stem is assimilated to a following **-s.** In the imperfect and future, the **-t-** remains because it is not followed by an **-s.** In the perfect system, **possum** is perfectly regular.

PRESENT	IMPERFECT	FUTURE
possum *I am able, I can,* etc.	**poteram** *I was able, I could,* etc.	**poterō** *I shall be able,* etc.
potes	**poterās**	**poteris**
potest	**poterat**	**poterit**
possumus	**poterāmus**	**poterimus**
potestis	**poterātis**	**poteritis**
possunt	**poterant**	**poterunt**

PERFECT	PAST PERFECT (PLUPERFECT)	FUTURE PERFECT
potuī *I have been able, could,* etc.	**potueram** *I had been able,* etc.	**potuerō** *I shall have been able,* etc.
potuistī	**potuerās**	**potueris**
potuit	**potuerat**	**potuerit**
potuimus	**potuerāmus**	**potuerimus**
potuistis	**potuerātis**	**potueritis**
potuērunt	**potuerant**	**potuerint**

Syntax Review

Ablative of Respect

The ablative of *respect* tells in what specific and limited respect a certain statement is true. No preposition is used in Latin.

virum fabricā callidum	*a man skilled in metalworking*
fēriae multae numerō, variae natūrā	*festivals many in number, various in nature*

Practice

1. Decline **hoc mūnus, alius nūntius, illa lēx.**
2. Give the third person singular of **possum** in all tenses of the indicative.
3. Give all the participles and infinitives of **exspectō** and **ostendō.**
4. Give the third person plural of **lūdō** in all tenses, active and passive, of the indicative.

Translation

1. Roman festivals were strange in nature and many in number.
2. At these times all the business of the entire people was always laid aside.
3. Some hastened to the Forum, others quickly proceeded to the temples.
4. The former *(those)* looked at the decorated buildings; the latter *(these)* worshiped the gods.

VOCABULARY REVIEW

Nouns

māteria	nēmō	tempus
mēnsis	numerus	vestis
mūnus	pēs	

Adjectives

celer	similis	vērus

Verbs

cadō	lūdō	properō
currō	ostendō	rapiō
expellō	possum	spectō

Adverb

semper

WORD STUDY

Suffixes   Review the suffixes **-tās** *(-ty)*, **-or** *(-or)*, and **-iō** *(-ion).* (See the Grammar Appendix.)

Give the English forms of **nōbilitās, gravitās, condiciō, vocātiō.**

What are the Latin words from which are derived *utility, facility, paucity, production, retention?*

Give and define, according to their etymology, four English words formed by adding the suffix *-or* to the present stem (base) of Latin verbs you have already studied, and four more formed by adding *-or* to the stem of the perfect participle.

Give five English words formed by adding the suffix *-ion* to Latin verbs and five formed by adding the suffix *-ty* to Latin adjectives.

READING STRATEGY — CORRELATIVES

Another help in making your way through a complex Latin sentence is to recognize *correlatives,* mutually related words. They regularly will reveal a parallel grammatical construction that makes understanding easier. Reading a sentence aloud before attacking the translation will often make them pop up like signposts. Since there are a great many of these correlatives in Latin (and in English), let's review some of the ones you have already come across.

et... et...,	*both . . . and . . .*
aut (vel)... aut (vel)...,	*either . . . or . . .*
neque... neque...,	*neither . . . nor . . .*
alius (aliī)... alius (aliī)...,	*one (some) . . . another (others)*
alter (alterī)... alter (alterī)	*the one (some,* literally, *the ones) . . . the other (the others) . . .*
hic... ille...,	*this man . . . that man . . . ,* or, *the latter* (nearer) *. . . the former* (farther)
nōn sōlum... sed etiam...	*not only . . . but also . . .*

SUPERSTITIONS

Quondam Rūfus, in Forum ad negōtium prōcēdēns, caelum spectāvit avēsque trēs in dextrā parte vīdit.

"Signum est!" dīxit. "Fortūna negōtiō meō amīca erit!"

Ita accidit: negōtium bene ēvēnit; itaque Rūfus semper putāvit avēs
5   fortūnam bonam eī negōtiō dedisse.

Plūrimī Rōmānī signa et ōmina semper exspectābant—in caelō, in terrā, in flūminibus. Putābant deōs ipsōs ad hominēs somnō oppressōs saepe accēdere et eōs monēre. Multī Rōmānī in templīs cōnsilium ā deīs petēbant; etiam ibi somnum capiēbant. Eī quī nōn valēbant Aesculāpium
10 hōc modō cōnsulēbant; sed omnēs Apollinem hominibus ūtilissimum deōrum esse ob respōnsa eius putābant. Haec respōnsa plūrima, sed nōn saepe clārissima,[1] per sacerdōtēs eius dabantur.

Rūfus, deōs familiae colēns, eadem verba semper dīcēbat, eadem mūnera sacra eōdem modō semper efficiēbat, familiā spectante. Putābātur,
15 deīs nōn ita vocātīs, familiam gravissimam poenam datūram esse.

Etiam mortuōs Rōmānī cum cūrā colēbant quod putābant hōs facillimē et celerrimē ad amīcōs in terrā manentēs venīre posse et eōs terrēre; et

[1] The responses of oracles were often so worded that they could be interpreted in two opposite ways. So they were always right!

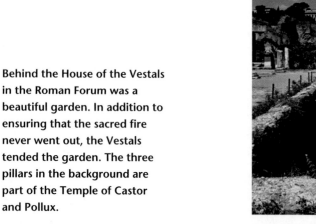

Behind the House of the Vestals in the Roman Forum was a beautiful garden. In addition to ensuring that the sacred fire never went out, the Vestals tended the garden. The three pillars in the background are part of the Temple of Castor and Pollux.

Hugh Rooney; Eye Ubiquitous/CORBIS

mortuōs, sepultūrā nōn datā, per omnēs terrās iter dūrum facientēs, multōs
annōs in labōre gravī agere cōgī.

Tempore magnī perīculī deī et virī mortuī in viīs ipsīs appāruisse dictī   20
sunt. Post pugnam Rēgillēnsem[2] Castor Polluxque in Forum vēnisse
nūntiābantur. Caesare interfectō, virī mortuī et novissima animālia in
Italiā vidēbantur—ōmina gravissima, quae mōnstrāre putābantur fortūnam
inimīcīs Caesaris dūram futūram esse.

Eō tempore fortūnam graviōrem et sacriōrem esse crēdēbant quam   25
nunc. Virī quibus haec dea amīca fuerat deīs grātiōrēs erant (ita putābant)
quam aliī quibus inimīca fuerat. Omnēs mīlitēs fortius et ācrius sub duce
quī fortūnae grātus erat pugnābant—et ob eam causam saepius vincēbant.

Rōmānī, mala timentēs, fortasse stultī nōbīs videntur; sed nōnne ipsī
multa eiusdem generis nunc facimus vel audīmus?   30

[2] The battle against the Latins at Lake Regillus in 498 B.C. when these twin gods brought news of the victory to Rome.

Questions

1. In what places did Romans look for signs from the gods?
2. What strange way of seeking a god's advice did many Romans use when inside his temple?
3. Why was Apollo considered to be the most useful of the gods?
4. Why were the Romans so careful and cautious in carrying out their domestic religious practices?
5. According to the passage, how were war, politics, and superstitious religious beliefs interrelated?

▦ GRAMMAR

Form Review

Demonstratives *Is, Īdem* and Intensive *Ipse*

The *demonstratives* **is** *(he, she, it; this, that),* **īdem** *(the same)* and the *intensive* **ipse** *(-self, the very)* are declined as follows. Remember that these same forms can stand alone as pronouns or be used as adjectives to modify nouns.

| | SINGULAR | | | PLURAL | | |
	M.	F.	N.	M.	F.	N.
NOM.	**is,** *he, it*	**ea,** *she, it*	**id,** *it*	**eī (iī),** *they*	**eae,** *they*	**ea,** *they*
GEN.	**eius,** *his, its (of him, of it)*	**eius,** *hers, its (of her, of it)*	**eius,** *its (of it),* etc.	**eōrum,** *theirs, (of them),* etc.	**eārum,** *theirs*	**eōrum,** *theirs*
DAT.	**eī**	**eī**	**eī**	**eīs (iīs)**	**eīs (iīs)**	**eīs (iīs)**
ACC.	**eum**	**eam**	**id**	**eōs**	**eās**	**ea**
ABL.	**eō**	**eā**	**eō**	**eīs (iīs)**	**eīs (iīs)**	**eīs (iīs)**

	SINGULAR			PLURAL		
	M.	F.	N.	M.	F.	N.
NOM.	**īdem,**	**eadem,**	**idem,**	**eīdem (īdem)**	**eaedem**	**eadem**
	the same (man)	*the same (woman)*	*the same (thing)*, etc.			
GEN.	**eiusdem**	**eiusdem**	**eiusdem**	**eōrundem**	**eārundem**	**eōrundem**
DAT.	**eīdem**	**eīdem**	**eīdem**	**eīsdem**	**eīsdem**	**eīsdem**
ACC.	**eundem**	**eandem**	**idem**	**eōsdem**	**eāsdem**	**eadem**
ABL.	**eōdem**	**eādem**	**eōdem**	**eīsdem**	**eīsdem**	**eīsdem**

	SINGULAR			PLURAL		
	M.	F.	N.	M.	F.	N.
NOM.	**ipse,**	**ipsa,**	**ipsum,**	**ipsī,**	**ipsae,**	**ipsa,**
	-self	*-self*	*-self*, etc.	*-selves*	*-selves*	*-selves*
GEN.	**ipsīus**	**ipsīus**	**ipsīus**	**ipsōrum**	**ipsārum**	**ipsōrum**
DAT.	**ipsī**	**ipsī**	**ipsī**	**ipsīs**	**ipsīs**	**ipsīs**
ACC.	**ipsum**	**ipsam**	**ipsum**	**ipsōs**	**ipsās**	**ipsa**
ABL.	**ipsō**	**ipsā**	**ipsō**	**ipsīs**	**ipsīs**	**ipsīs**

Remember that comparative adjectives are third declension adjectives but are *not* **i**-stems. They have **-e** in the ablative singular, **-um** in the genitive plural, and **-a** in the neuter nominative and accusative plural.

Comparison of Regular Adjectives and Adverbs

Adjectives in Latin form their *comparative* degree (*-er, more _____, rather _____, too _____* in English) by adding **-ior** (M. and F.), **-ius** (N.) to the base of the positive. These comparative adjectives in **-ior, -ius** belong to the third declension but are not **i**-stems. Their base, except in the neuter nominative and accusative singular, is **-iōr-**. The great majority of adjectives form their *superlative* degree (*-est, most _____, very _____* in English) by adding **-issimus, -a, -um** to the base of the positive. If their nominative singular masculine ends in **-r** or **-er,** then the superlative will end in **-errimus, -a, -um.** Six adjectives (only) whose base ends in **-l-** have a superlative ending in **-illimus, -a, -um: facilis, difficilis, similis, dissimilis, gracilis,** and **humilis.** Study the following examples.

ADJECTIVES

POSITIVE	COMPARATIVE	SUPERLATIVE
altus, -a, -um, *high*	**altior, -ius,** *higher*	**altissimus, -a, -um,** *highest*
fortis, -e, *strong*	**fortior, -ius,** *stronger*	**fortissimus, -a, -um,** *strongest*
līber, -a, -um, *free*	**līberior, -ius,** *freer*	**līberrimus, -a, -um,** *freest*
ācer, ācris, ācre, *sharp*	**ācrior, -ius,** *sharper*	**ācerrimus, -a, -um,** *sharpest*
facilis, -e, *easy*	**facilior, -ius,** *easier*	**facillimus, -a, -um,** *easiest*
ūtilis, -e, *useful*	**ūtilior, -ius,** *more useful*	**ūtilissimus, -a, -um,** *most useful*

ADVERBS		
POSITIVE	COMPARATIVE	SUPERLATIVE
altē, *highly*	**altius,** *more highly*	**altissimē,** *most highly*
fortiter, *strongly*	**fortius,** *more strongly*	**fortissimē,** *most strongly*
līberē, *freely*	**līberius,** *more freely*	**līberrimē,** *most freely*
ācriter, *sharply*	**ācrius,** *more sharply*	**ācerrimē,** *most sharply*
facile,[3] *easily*	**facilius,** *more easily*	**facillimē,** *most easily*
ūtiliter, *usefully*	**ūtilius,** *more usefully*	**ūtilissimē,** *most usefully*

There are other ways of comparing adjectives and adverbs in Latin, and some forms of comparison are irregular. You will learn about them later.

Practice

1. Decline **idem iter** and **ipsa lēx.**
2. Identify the forms of **ipsī, eius, illud, eundem, ipsō, eī, haec, id, hoc, hōc, ipsīus.**
3. Compare **tardus, celer, humilis, gravis, clārus; grātē, graviter, amīcē, nōbiliter.**

Superstition

Syntax Review

Dative with Adjectives

Certain adjectives like **amīcus** *(friendly),* **aptus** *(suited),* **idōneus** *(suitable),* **pār** *(equal),* **proximus** *(next),* **similis** *(like),* **ūtilis** *(useful),* and their opposites, are often followed by the dative. In many cases the English idiom is the same.

Fortūna amīca meō negōtiō erit.	*Fortune will be friendly to my business.*
Apollō, hominibus ūtilissimus deōrum	*Apollo, for mankind the most useful of the gods*

[3] irregular

In the *positive* degree, adverbs are formed from first and second declension adjectives by adding **-ē** to the stem. Third declension adjectives form the corresponding adverbs by adding **-iter.** In the *comparative* degree, the adverb is the same as the neuter accusative singular of the comparative adjective, i.e., with an ending in **-ius.** Adverbs in the *superlative* degree are formed like those from first and second declension adjectives, i.e., by adding a final **-ē** to the stem.

Translation

1. The Romans consulted the gods themselves about signs.
2. They thought that Fortune was a goddess friendly to some, unfriendly to others.
3. Soldiers fought more bravely under a leader to whom Fortune was more kind.
4. When Caesar was killed,[4] very strange (things) of the same kind were seen.

VOCABULARY REVIEW

Nouns

animal	genus	mīles
avis	iter	signum
flūmen		

Adjectives

īdem	ipse	ūtilis
inimīcus	is	

Verbs

accidō	efficiō	valeō
capiō	moneō	vincō
cōnsulō	terreō	

The goddess **Fortūna** was the "bearer" of luck—either good or bad. (Her name is related to the verb **ferō**, *bear*, and originally she was associated with fertility). She is often portrayed holding a wheel of fortune, a ship's rudder, or, as here, a cornucopia. She was highly important in Roman cult worship, and even the emperor, it is said, kept a golden statuette of her in his bedroom.

Ronald Sheridan/Ancient Art & Architecture Collection

[4] Use ablative absolute.

WORD STUDY

Prefixes Review the prefixes **inter-, ob-, ante-, trāns-** in the Grammar Appendix.

Define according to the prefix: **antecēdō, intercipiō, occurrō, oppugnō, trānsmittō, trādūcō;** *intercede, interscholastic, opposition, antedate, transcription, transportation.*

Add the proper form of **ob-:** *-casion, -fice, -ject, -lige, -press.*

Explain by derivation *admonition, deterrent, invalid, public utility.*

THE BIG SHOW

On the base of an Egyptian obelisk brought to Constantinople (now Istanbul, Turkey) is a frieze showing the Emperor Theodosius I (A.D. 346–395) presiding at the races in the hippodrome and holding the wreath with which to crown the winner. He is flanked by his two sons and other members of his court. The spectators sit below in rows. Theodosius, a Christian, is blamed for banning the "pagan" Olympic Games in Greece in A.D. 393, but clearly athletic contests continued throughout the Roman Empire for many years.

Ronald Sheridan/Ancient Art & Architecture Collection

[1] *unlimited.* The lavish banquet on the night before the **mūnera** was not just free to the combatants, but it and the training schools (**lūdī**) were opened to the public, who thus got a chance to see their favorite gladiators close up.

E x extrēmīs viīs, ē Forō, dē summō monte Aventīnō et dē Caeliō, ex omnibus partibus Rōmae hominēs ad lūdōs gladiātōriōs prōcēdēbant. Proximō diē Augustus maxima mūnera gladiātōria datūrus erat; nunc gladiātōribus cēna lībera[1] in lūdīs dabātur, et multī Rōmānī, ad hōs
5 properantēs, gladiātōrēs spectātūrī erant. Pūblius et Fūriānus magnō studiō per viās cucurrērunt. Gladiātōribus prīmīs spectātīs, Pūblius clāmāvit, "Haec mūnera meliōra quam omnia alia erunt; hī sunt optimī gladiātōrēs quōs vīdī."

Nunc diēs mūnerum aderat. Amphitheātrum hominibus complētum est.
10 In īnferiōre parte Pūblius cum Fūriānō sedēbat. Vir Pūbliō proximus dīxit Augustum duo mīlia gladiātōrum ad haec mūnera parāvisse. Pūblius, coniūrātiōnem Spartacī memoriā tenēns, spērāvit nūllum perīculum Rōmae futūrum esse; sed Augustus ipse aderat, et Pūblius scīvit illīus potestātem maximam esse.

In arēnam prōcēdēbant plūrimī gladiātōrēs, armīs variīs īnsignēs. Firmō 15
pede inter clāmōrēs spectantium ad Augustum accessērunt et eī salūtem
dīxērunt.

"Vidēsne illōs decem quī arma eiusdem generis gerunt?" rogāvit
Fūriānus.

"Videō. Putō eōs esse captīvōs, ex ulteriōre Galliā missōs. Ācrēs 20
videntur, sed nōnne putās illōs septem Aethiopēs melius pugnātūrōs esse?
Sed quis est ille? Veturiumne, cīvem Rōmānum, in arēnā videō?"

"Ipse est. Pessimus ille homō damnātus est quod patrem et amīcum
interfēcerat."

Prīmum octō paria² servōrum eiusdem gentis, ab ultimā Sarmatiā,³ 25
prōcessērunt; sed minus ācriter pugnāvērunt quam populus exspectābat et,
omnibus irrīdentibus, ex arēnā discessērunt. Posteā decem Thrācēs cum
decem Britannīs melius pugnāvērunt. Ūnus ē Britannīs,⁴ quī valēbat et
optimē pugnābat, spectantibus grātus erat. Hic, ā Thrāce difficillimē
superātus, nōn interfectus est et clāmōribus populī līberātus est. Tum 30
hominēs cum animālibus, animālia cum animālibus pugnāvērunt. Tandem
Veturiō sōlō adductō, leō ācer in arēnam missus est. Leō ā Veturiō
vulnerātus est, sed hunc interfēcit.

Mūnera huius modī nunc crūdēlissima videntur; sed auctōritātem
Augustī plūrimum cōnfirmāvērunt quod populō Rōmānō maximē 35
grāta erant.

² *pairs,* from **pār**
³ See map pp. 158–159
⁴ With cardinal numerals (except **milia**) **ex (ē)** or **dē** is usually used instead of the partitive genitive.

Questions

1. On the one hand, Publius was optimistic about what? On the other, what earlier historical event gave him concern?
2. Describe the gladiators' entrance into the arena.
3. Why was Veturius forced to fight?
4. Name five of the nationalities represented among the gladiators, and three types of combat which were presented.
5. What political value did these gladiatorial **mūnera** have?

This violent mosaic in Rome honors by name a number of popular gladiators. Not all, however, were still active. Astivus and Rodan have met their fate. (The letter Θ, **theta**, is the first letter of the Greek word for *dead*.)

SEF/Art Resource, NY

GRAMMAR

Form Review

Irregular Comparison of Adjectives

In Latin as in English, some very common adjectives are compared irregularly. Linking these words to their English derivatives will be a great help in learning them. All except **plūs** are declined regularly.

POSITIVE	COMPARATIVE	SUPERLATIVE
bonus, -a, -um, *good*	**melior, melius,** *better*	**optimus, -a, -um,** *best*
malus, -a, -um, *bad*	**peior, peius,** *worse*	**pessimus, -a, -um,** *worst*
magnus, -a, -um, *great*	**maior, maius,** *greater*	**maximus, -a, -um,** *greatest*
parvus, -a, -um, *small*	**minor, minus,** *smaller*	**minimus, -a, -um,** *smallest*
multus, -a, -um, *much*	**—, plūs,** *more* (quantity)	**plūrimus, -a, -um,** *most*
multī, -ae, -a, *many*	**plūrēs, plūra,** *more* (number)	**plūrimī, -ae, -a,** *most, very many*

Here are some additional words whose comparisons will prove useful. Some of them are rarely used in the positive except with special meanings, but have an obvious relation in meaning to the preposition given with them here in parentheses.

POSITIVE	COMPARATIVE	SUPERLATIVE
exterus, -a, -um, *outside* (**extrā,** *outside of*)[5]	**exterior, -ius,** *outer*	**extrēmus, -a, -um,** *outermost*
īnferus, -a, -um, *low* (**īnfrā,** *beneath*)[5]	**īnferior, -ius,** *lower*	**īnfimus, -a, -um (īmus),** *lowest*
——— (**intrā,** *within*)[5]	**interior, -ius,** *inner*	**intimus, -a, -um,** *innermost*
posterus, -a, -um, *following* (**post,** *after*)[5]	**posterior, -ius,** *later*	**postrēmus, -a, -um,** *last*
superus, -a, -um *above* (**super,** *above*)[5]	**superior, -ius,** *higher*	**suprēmus, -a, -um (summus),** *highest*
(**ante,** *before*)[3]	**anterior, -ius,** *earlier*	———
(**prae,** *in front of*)[3]	**prior, -ius,** *earlier*	**prīmus, -a, -um,** *first*
(**prope,** *near*)[3]	**propior, -ius,** *nearer*	**proximus, -a, -um,** *nearest, next*
(**ultrā,** *beyond*)[3]	**ulterior, -ius,** *farther*	**ultimus, -a, -um,** *farthest*

[5]All these prepositions govern the accusative case except **prae,** which takes the ablative.

Irregular Comparison of Adverbs

The most important adverbs with irregular comparisons are listed here. Notice that even some of those that do not follow the rules for regular comparison (Positive: **-ē** or **-iter,** Comparative: **-ius,** Superlative: **-ē**) still look like the neuter accusative singular of the adjectival form, e.g., **facile** (which you have learned earlier), **multum, plūrimum,** and **prīmum.**

bene, *well*	**melius,** *better*	**optimē,** *best*
male, *badly*	**peius,** *worse*	**pessimē,** *worst*
magnopere, *greatly*	**magis,** *more*	**maximē,** *most*
parum, *a little*	**minus,** *less*	**minimē,** *least*
multum, *much, a lot*	**plūs,** *more*	**plūrimum,** *very much, most*
diū, *(for a) long (time)*	**diūtius,** *(for a) longer (time)*	**diūtissimē,** *(for a) very long (time)*
prope, *near*	**propius,** *nearer*	**proximē,** *nearest*
saepe, *often*	**saepius,** *more often*	**saepissimē,** *most often*
——	**prius,** *before*	**prīmum,** *first*

Practice

1. Compare **multus, malus, dūrus, parvus, ācer.**
2. Compare **bene, diū, līberē, multum, celeriter.**
3. Give the positive of **optimus, minimus, peius, magis, humillimus;** the comparative of **minimē, bonus, prīmum, ācerrimus, altē;** the superlative of **magnus, facilius, graviter, propius.**

Syntax Review

Uses of the Ablative

The ablative case is really three concepts combined into one set of endings. With that in mind, let's inspect the nine ablatives you have studied so far.

The first concept is *separation,* where the ablative's basic and original meaning (**ab,** *away from;* **lātus,** *carried*) is *from.* Under *separation* we can group:

1. the ablatives that follow the prepositions that mean *from,* **ab, dē, ex,** and others.
2. the ablative of *(personal) agent,* in which the person *by whom* something is done is considered the source from which the result comes.

The second idea is that of *means,* or *instrument,* or *association,* i.e., how, or with what or whom something is done or true. Under this heading we can group:

3. the ablative of *means;*
4. the ablative of *accompaniment,* with **cum;**
5. the ablative of *manner,* with or without **cum;**
6. the *ablative absolute,* which tells you under what circumstances another action took/takes/will take place.

The third idea behind the ablative is *locative,* i.e., position in time or space. Here we can put:

7. the ablative of *place where,* with or without prepositions like **in** or **sub** when motion is not involved;
8. the ablative of *time when* or *within which.*
9. the ablative of *respect* (or *specification*).[6]

The boundaries between these three concepts are not always clear, so that some overlapping of uses does occasionally occur. The purpose of learning the names for these various uses is not just an end in itself, but to clarify your understanding of the meaning the author intended.

---

[6] Can also be considered as instrumental

Practice

Divide the class into as many gladiatorial **lūdī** (Britons, Galatians, Gauls, Germans, Thracians, Spaniards, Syrians, Scythians, etc.) as it takes to get about four combatants per school. Here are the types of combat: 1) identify by name every ablative in the reading for this lesson; then 2) in the English paragraph that follows, identify by its ablative name every word or phrase that would be ablative in Latin; and finally 3) for double credit, see how many of these words or phrases your team can turn into Latin. (Your teacher can help with unfamiliar vocabulary.)

Dogs and cats by nature being enemies, there was little we could now do without the aid of the fire department. Within a very brief time, they were in the woods with us, happy to be liberated from a day of pinochle and banjo-picking in the fire station. Led by a captain, Leo by name, they took their ladders from the fire truck with supreme confidence, put them against the tree, and with great celerity got themselves only a foot away from the cat, the dog barking all the while. But no cat was quicker than this one nor more independent in spirit. Its ultimate safety now being certain, it undertook a program of feline aerial acrobatics for the benefit of the spectators, calmly walking in and out among the branches, or under them, or leaping from one to another, always just out of reach. Leo again and again tried to dislodge Kitty, using a long pole, but failed miserably. Much later, after a very long time, he climbed down from the tree and sat with his allies on the ground, frustrated, covered with sweat, and complaining from the bottom of his heart that "no cat-rescue duty had ever been worse than this." While the firefighters were putting their gear back onto the truck and we were being impressed by the spotless condition in which they kept it, the cat quietly descended down the tree and perched on the driver's seat, without doubt looking for more of the attention which it had recently enjoyed and of which it was now about to be deprived by the firefighters' departure.

Translation

1. Do you not think that these shows were very cruel?
2. Many prisoners and slaves were killed in the arena (while) Romans looked on.
3. In the gladiatorial schools were very many men sent from the farthest parts of Gaul.
4. To these shows many thousands of the best citizens hurried with the greatest eagerness.
5. In those times, condemned men (**damnātī**) often fought with the gladiators and were killed by them.

▤ VOCABULARY REVIEW

In addition to learning the forms and meanings of the adjectives and adverbs compared in the previous sections, review the following words.

Nouns

arma	**gēns**	**perīculum**
cīvis	**mōns**	**studium**

Verbs

addūcō	**prōcēdō**	**spērō**
cōnfirmō		

Sports and spectacles were important not only in Rome but also in the provinces. The remains of this Roman amphitheater in El Djem, Tunisia, indicate that it was of substantial size. Built in A.D. 238 by the emperor Gordianus, it had thirty-five thousand seats. It has been partially dismantled over the centuries to build the Arab city around it.

Gianni Tortoli/Photo Researchers

WORD STUDY

Spelling The spelling of words in English, one of the most difficult things for non-native speakers of the language to master, is often made easier by considering the Latin words from which they come.

The Latin double consonant is usually kept in English, except at the end of a word: *expelled,* but *expel* (from **pellō**). Give five additional examples.

Since assimilation of prefixes often caused a doubling of consonants, it is frequently possible to obtain help in spelling by analyzing the word. Compare *dis-miss* and *dis-similar, ad-monition* and *af-fection, dis-tention* and *dis-sension, im-modest* and *il-legible.*

VOCABULARY

Circle the word that best completes each sentence.

1. Verbīs Fūriānī _____, puerī clāmantēs
   discessērunt.
   a. affectī
   b. cōnfectī
   c. effectī
   d. interfectī

2. In familiā Rōmānā regere labōrem servārum
   _____ mātris erat.
   a. auxilium
   b. cōnsilium
   c. perīculum
   d. officium

3. _____ Q. Fūrius, pater suus, et Caeciliī in
   Forum ob adoptiōnem prōcēdunt.
   a. Crās
   b. Herī
   c. Hodiē
   d. Ante

4. Iuvenēs dīxit sē in Graeciā _____ antīquum
   templum vīsūrōs esse.
   a. graviter
   b. vērē
   c. nōbiliter
   d. tardē

5. _____ tōtīus cīvitātis illō diē dēposita erant.
   a. iūra
   b. itinera
   c. mūnera
   d. perīcula

GRAMMAR

Complete each sentence with the correct case endings.

6. Secunda putāvit vir___ Rōmānōs ill___
   tempore vītam grātiōr___ quam fēmin___
   ag___.

7. Dux hōrum mīlit___ simil___ princip___ suā
   auctōritāt___ erat.

8. Condiciōn___ pācis cōnfirmātīs, familiae
   meliōr___ cum salūt___ iter fac___ poterunt.

9. Crās Cornēlia et Pūbliō et Fūriān___, nov___
   frātr___, grāti___ ob e___ auxilium ag___.

10. Poēta qu___ audīverant oper___ clārius
    legent_____ optim_____ vīs___ est.

TRANSLATION

Translate the following sentences.

11. Patrēs Rōmānī līberīs saepissimē dīcēbant
    lēgēs Duodecim Tabulārum, scrīptās auxiliō
    cōnsiliōque Graecōrum, potestātem cīvitātis
    semper cōnservātūrās esse.

12. Hoc est aedificium in quō, condiciōnibus
    adoptiōnis prōpositīs et acceptīs, clientibus et
    amīcīs patrum exspectantibus, Q. Fūrius,
    īnsignis veste novā, frāter Pūblī appellātus est.

13. Duae sorōrēs ā suā mātre docēbantur dē
    mulierum antīquārum Rōmānārum sententiīs et
    factīs quae memoriā tenēre dēbēbant, nam
    puellae in scholam nōn saepe mittī poterant.

14. Multōs mēnsēs quattuor amīcī, pictūrās avium
    pulcherrimārum petentēs, per omnēs urbēs
    illīus prōvinciae prōcesserant; nunc quam
    celerrimē et magnō cum studiō eās inventās in
    Italiam importābant.

15. Dux, cum paucīs mīlitibus in castrīs sub monte manēns, hostibus nōn scientibus, māteriam ē silvā movērī iussit prīmā lūce.

INVESTIGATION

Find the answers to these questions from any lesson in Unit I.

16. The second wife of Augustus, named _____, also became his trusted political advisor.
17. The Latin title of the poet Ovid's great work on "Transformations" and mythology is _____.
18. **Cereālia, Parīlia,** and **Lupercālia** were the names of Roman _____.
19. The letters **Q.E.D.,** which are an abbreviation for the Latin phrase _____, are written after successful proof of a theorem in geometry.
20. The name of the Roman woman credited with making a speech in the Forum to protest the demand for women's monetary aid in the civil war was _____.

CULTURE

Vērum aut Falsum? Indicate whether each statement is true or false.

21. In the Augustan Age, Roman tax laws discouraged upper-class families from having more than one child.
22. A Roman's **cognōmen** might have been derived from an ancestor's physical characteristic.
23. Gladiators and their fans were usually treated to a great banquet on the day of the big games in the arena.

24. Few Romans ever saw the laws of the Twelve Tables because they were kept locked in a temple.
25. The poet Vergil's work in four books dedicated to the art of farming is called the *Georgics*.

FROM LATIN TO ENGLISH

Apply your knowledge of Latin roots to determine the best meaning of the italicized words.

26. They maintained an impressive *aviary* on their estate.
    a. place for bees
    b. place for fish
    c. place for birds
    d. place for trees
27. The tale was about an *ingrate* who became king.
    a. rich man
    b. cruel man
    c. foreigner
    d. thankless man
28. The entrance fee seemed *nominal* to me.
    a. exorbitant
    b. fair
    c. insignificant
    d. unusual
29. That member will *facilitate* the work of the committee.
    a. destroy
    b. aid
    c. hinder
    d. question
30. The school wishes to *mandate* a dress code.
    a. abolish
    b. revise
    c. require

UNIT
II

TWO ROMAN STUDENTS IN ATHENS

Unit Objectives

Read:

- Two Roman Students Visit Greece

Learn:

- Subjunctive of All Four Conjugations, **Sum** and **Possum**; Conjugation of **Ferō, Eō, Fīō, Volō, Nōlō**; Deponent Verbs; Indefinite Pronouns and Adjectives; Future Passive Participle, the Gerund, and their Uses; Uses of the Subjunctive: Volitive Subjunctive, Purpose Clauses, Result Clauses, Indirect Questions; Sequence of Tenses in Subjunctive Clauses; Temporal Clauses with **Ubi, Postquam,** and **Cum**; Dative (Agent, Special Verbs, Purpose, Reference); Ablative (Measure of Difference)

Review:

- Fourth and Fifth Declensions of Nouns; Personal and Reflexive Pronouns; Accusative of Extent

Many Greek cities and towns had for their defense an acropolis, a "high city," on which they built a temple or temples to the deities protecting the city. The most famous of these, and Greece's most widely recognized monument, is the Parthenon in Athens, dedicated to Athena.

George Grigoriou/Getty Images

LESSON OBJECTIVES

- Review Fourth Declension Nouns
- The Present Subjunctive, Active and Passive, of the Second, Third, and Fourth Conjugations
- Volitive Subjunctive

LESSON X

THE FAREWELL DINNER

Quondam domus nōbilis familiae Rōmānae, Caeciliae, maximē perturbābātur. Pūblius, fīlius P. Caecilī Rūfī, et Fūriānus, fīlius adoptātus M. Caecilī, diū in animō habuerant ad Graeciam nāvigāre et clārōs philosophōs Graecōs audīre; et nunc proximum diem exituī cōnstituerant.

5 Nōna hōra fuit—hōra cēnae. Cēna in ātriō domūs, nōn in trīclīniō,[1] parāta erat quod adfutūrī erant paucī. In ātrium, in quō mulierēs exspectābant, ē balneīs vēnērunt virī.

Rūfus manibus signum dedit et clāmāvit: "Cēna pōnātur."

Virīs accumbentibus[2] et mulieribus sedentibus, soleae sunt dēpositae,
10 et mēnsa ā servīs in ātrium portāta est. Mēnsā positā, aqua et mappae[3] omnibus datae sunt.

[1] dining room
[2] The men *reclined* on couches, resting on their left elbows.
[3] napkins

Virīs accumbentibus et mulieribus sedentibus, mēnsa ā servis in ātrium portāta est. This relief of men and women at dinner has the quality of a family portrait. The small figure in the center is probably a son; to the left, a slave reads from a scroll. When this course is over, slaves will remove the platter from the three-legged table and replace it with the next course.

Prīma pars cēnae, prōmulsis,[4] in ātrium importāta est—ōva et lactūca,[5] tum mulsum.[6] Aquā et mappīs iterum datīs, cēna ipsa portāta est. Cibus bonus erat, nostrō similis. Per cēnam multa dē Graeciā et Graecīs dicta sunt.

Magnum erat studium Pūblī et Fūriānī quod in Graeciam prōcessūrī erant et tempus exitūs aderat. Sed Rūfus verba gravia Mārcō dīxit: "In terram illīs novam prōcēdere cōnstituērunt. Cupiāmus eōs vītam dignam āctūrōs esse." "Semper memoriā teneant sē Rōmānōs esse," respondit Mārcus. "Nē iniūstē faciant—tum vītam dignam agent."

Sed nōn omnia gravia sēriaque erant. "Noster Musaeus Caecilius[7] prōdūcātur!" clāmāvit Pūblius.

"Et carmen Graecum canat!" addidit Fūriānus.

Postquam Musaeus carmen Hōmērī recitāvit, Rūfus dīxit: "Nunc linguīs faveāmus[8] et deōs colāmus." Ubi Larēs in mēnsā positī sunt, Rūfus cibum et vīnum ad eōs posuit. Omnibus stantibus, silentium factum est. Tum, Laribus magnā cum cūrā remōtīs, secunda mēnsa[9] in ātrium portāta est— dulcia et frūctūs. Cēnā perfectā "ab ōvō usque ad māla,"[10] Rūfus dīxit, "Dāvus veniat et saliat." Davus, servus ingeniōsissimus, prīmō tardē saltāvit, tum violenter, tum in manibus, tum in capite stetit, et multa alia rīdicula fēcit. Tōta familia saepissimē rīdēbat et applaudēbat.

Sed nunc erat tempus discēdere. Servī soleās parāre iussī sunt, et omnēs magnō silentiō discessērunt.

15

20

25

30

[4] (nom.) *first course*
[5] *eggs and lettuce*
[6] *wine mixed with honey*
[7] *our friend Musaeus.* From his Greek name, we may suppose that Musaeus was an ex-slave, a freedman (**libertus**), to whom the paterfamilias Rufus had granted freedom. Perhaps he had been Publius' and Furianus' pedagogue and tutor and had filled them with stories from Homer and Greek literature. In any case, Musaeus was now a genuine member of the Caecilian household, but probably not yet close enough to be invited to this intimate family dinner.
[8] literally, *let us favor with our tongues,* i.e., by refraining from evil words; therefore, *let us keep silent*
[9] Since dessert was brought in on a separate table, **secunda mēnsa** came to mean *dessert.*
[10] *from eggs to apples* (like our "from soup to nuts"), a proverbial expression from the Roman practice of beginning a dinner with *eggs* and ending with *apples,* which came to mean *from beginning to end*

Questions

1. Where were Publius and Furianus planning to go? Why? IOK
2. Where was the dinner, and at what time was it served?
3. Where had the men been before dinner?
4. Describe the preliminaries to the meal, before the first of the food and drink was served.
5. What was the first course, and what were the subjects of conversation?
6. What were Rufus' concerns as expressed to his brother Marcus?
7. What types of entertainment were there?
8. What religious ritual was performed before dessert?
9. What was served for the final course?
10. In what ways do Roman dining customs seem unusual to you?

What are **mala?** What are **māla?** What are **mala māla?** The fourth declension is another place where the difference between long and short vowels in the endings becomes important. **Cornū** is easy, but in the declension of **cāsus,** the long **-ūs** could be any one of three things.

Review of Fourth Declension Nouns

Most of the nouns of the fourth declension that end in **-us** are masculine. There are only two important exceptions, **manus** and **domus,**[11] which are feminine. There are also very few neuter nouns ending in **-ū.** The only one used in this book is **cornū.**

	SINGULAR	PLURAL	SINGULAR	PLURAL
NOM.	cāsus	cāsūs	cornū	cornua
	chance, etc.		*horn,* etc.	
GEN.	cāsūs	cāsuum	cornūs	cornuum
DAT.	cāsuī	cāsibus	cornū	cornibus
ACC.	cāsum	cāsūs	cornū	cornua
ABL.	cāsū	cāsibus	cornū	cornibus

Practice

Decline **exitus ipse, illa manus.**

Subjunctive Mood

You have previously studied the forms of the *indicative mood,* which presents actions and states of being as facts, and is also used to ask questions. You have also learned separate forms for the *imperative mood,* which issues orders or commands. We now take up the forms of the

Reclining at the dinner table was a city custom not always followed in the countryside or in the provinces, as shown in this relief from Germany.

C.M. Dixon/Photo Resources

[11] **Domus,** in addition to its regular fourth declension forms, has some alternate forms from the second declension. It also has one important locative form: **domī,** *at home.*

subjunctive mood, which, in both Latin and English, gives more of the speaker's or writer's opinion or attitude toward the truth of a statement.

The subjunctive in Latin has only four tenses, active and passive: present, imperfect, perfect, and past perfect. The personal endings are the same as for the indicative, so you need concentrate mostly on the tense signs and the mood signs.

PRESENT ACTIVE

doceam,	**pōnam,**	**capiam,**	**mūniam,**
I may teach, etc.	*I may put,* etc.	*I may take,* etc.	*I may fortify,* etc.
doceās	**pōnās**	**capiās**	**mūniās**
doceat	**pōnat**	**capiat**	**mūniat**
doceāmus	**pōnāmus**	**capiāmus**	**mūniāmus**
doceātis	**pōnātis**	**capiātis**	**mūniātis**
doceant	**pōnant**	**capiant**	**mūniant**

PRESENT PASSIVE

docear, *I may*	**pōnar,** *I may*	**capiar,** *I may*	**mūniar,** *I may be*
be taught, etc.	*be put,* etc.	*be taken,* etc.	*fortified,* etc.
doceāris	**pōnāris**	**capiāris**	**mūniāris**
doceātur	**pōnātur**	**capiātur**	**mūniātur**
doceāmur	**pōnāmur**	**capiāmur**	**mūniāmur**
doceāminī	**pōnāminī**	**capiāminī**	**mūniāminī**
doceantur	**pōnantur**	**capiantur**	**mūniantur**

Note the similarities and differences between the future indicative and the present subjunctive in the third and fourth conjugations.

As you can see, the mood sign of the *present subjunctive* in the second, third, and fourth conjugations is **-ā.** Added directly to the present stem, it causes the loss of the short stem vowel (**-ĕ**) of the third conjugation (**pōnam**) and the shortening of the long stem vowels of the second (**-ē**) and the fourth (**-ī**) conjugations (**doceam, mūniam**). The forms of the present subjunctive in the first conjugation will be given later.

Practice

Give the present subjunctive, active and passive, of **perficiō** in the first plural; of **colō** in the second singular; of **cōnstituō** in the second plural; of **teneō** in the third singular; and of **audiō** in the third plural.

Meanings of the Subjunctive

In English, various *auxiliary verbs,* such as *let, may, might, should,* and *would,* are used to express ideas that are not presented as simple facts, e.g., *She **may be** a queen,* or *I **might** agree,* or *We **would** hope that this is so.* In addition, English preserves some separate verb forms, the true subjunctives, which we may also use, e.g., *If this **be** true* (subjunctive), or *If this **should be** true* (auxiliary); *We **would** hope* (auxiliary) *that this **be** so* (subjunctive).

In Latin, the subjunctive mood is often used to express such ideas and even to state facts. *There are many possibilities for translating the subjunctive, depending upon the context, and only one is given above as a sample.*

Volitive Subjunctive

The *volitive subjunctive* (from Latin **volō,** *wish*) is used to express the speaker's *will* that something be done.

Cēna pōnātur.	*Let dinner be served.*
Semper memoriā teneant...	*Let them always remember . . .* or *They should always remember . . .*
Nē iniūstē faciant.	*Let them not act unjustly.*

This is also called the *jussive subjunctive* (from Latin **iubeō,** *order*), because it gives a type of command somewhat softer than the imperative. In the first person, it can also be called the *hortatory subjunctive* because it encourages or exhorts an action.

Linguīs faveāmus et deōs colāmus.	*Let us be silent and worship the gods.*

Note that in these examples:
1) the subjunctives can be translated by *let* or, with a little shifting about, by *should;*
2) the negative is **nē;**
3) the subjunctive can serve independently as the main verb.[12]

---

[12] The subjunctive (from Latin **sub + iungō,** *join under*) gets its name from being used in many types of dependent (subordinate) clauses. But it can also be used independently, as the main verb in a sentence as in the examples given here.

Practice

Translate the following phrases into Latin: *let us yield, let him not fear, let her be banished, let them read, let us be found, let them not worship money.*

Translation

1. Let us hear about the departure of Publius and Furianus.
2. A great dinner was prepared, during which Publius' father spoke.
3. Then the father said, "Let my boy always remember that Romans are brave."
4. "Let him live a worthy life in Greece; let him remain dutiful and remember home and the gods."

▦ VOCABULARY

Nouns

ātrium, -ī n. *atrium, hall*   (atrium)
balneum, -ī n. *bath*
exitus, -ūs m. *outcome, departure*   (exit)
mulier, mulieris f. *woman, wife*
silentium, -ī n. *silence*   (silence)

Adjectives

dignus, -a, -um *worthy*   (dignify, dignitary)
nōnus, -a, -um *ninth*   (nonagenerian)

Verbs

canō, -ere, cecinī, cantus *sing (about), tell*   (chant, cantata)
cōnstituō, -ere, -stituī, -stitūtus   [stō]
  determine, decide
perturbō, 1[13] *disturb, throw into confusion*   (perturb)

Adverb

iterum *again*   (iterate, reiterate)

---

[13] From now on, if first conjugation verbs (both active and deponent) have regular principal parts (i.e., **portō**), they will simply be indicated by a **1**.

WORD STUDY

Vowel Changes In Latin, when a prefix is added to a word, as **in-** to **capiō,** or **con-** to **teneō,** the root vowel is often changed. This change is carried over into English.

Short **-a-** and short **-e-** before any single consonant except **-r-** usually become short **-i-.**

Short **-a-** before two consonants usually becomes short **-e-.**

The diphthong **-ae-** usually becomes long **-ī-,** and **-au-** becomes long **-ū-.**

PREFIX	+	WORD	=	NEW WORD	(ENGLISH)
in	+	**capiō**	=	**incipiō**	(incipient)
ex	+	**faciō**	=	**efficiō**	(efficient)
in	+	**factus**	=	**infectus**	(infection)
con	+	**teneō**	=	**contineō**	(continent)
in	+	**aequus**	=	**inīquus**	(iniquity)
ex	+	**claudō**	=	**exclūdō**	(exclude)

Give some additional examples of these rules by using different prefixes with the Latin words above; give also the English derivatives. Apply these rules to **agō, cadō, caedō, damnō, habeō,** and **statuō,** and give English derivatives. Not all the prefixes can be attached to each of these words.

Did You Know?

Tourism is nothing new. Greeks and Romans went as far as Egypt to see the sights, and Roman generals, even on campaign in the East, would divert to a famous temple or site. Among wealthy Romans the favorite destination was mainland Greece, where Roman relations had once been hostile but later became admiring. Athens itself was the prime attraction, but nearby Eleusis was famous for its religious festivals, especially those of the Mystery rites, whose exact nature is still a matter of continuing debate. Thebes was noted for its position in legend as the home of Oedipus, and in history as both foe and ally of Athens; in the fourth century B.C. it became the most powerful Greek city. Lying under Mount Parnassus, Delphi, with its natural beauty and areas dedicated to Apollo, the Muses, and Athena, not to mention its famous oracle, brought many curious visitors.

LESSON XI

ON THE WAY

LESSON OBJECTIVE
- Purpose Clauses with **Ut** and **Nē** and the Subjunctive

Nunc diēs aderat. Impedīmentīs et servīs parātīs, familia tōta domum relīquit et ex urbe ad portam Capēnam pedibus prōcessit, quod ob viās angustās nūllae raedae[1] in urbe erant. Ad portam Pūblius et Fūriānus et servī in raedam, quattuor equīs trāctam, ascendērunt, mātre et sorōribus flentibus et omnibus "Valēte!" clāmantibus. 5

Portā relīctā, in Appiā Viā prōcessērunt, quae iam ad flūmen parvum dēscendēbat. Tum via plāna multa mīlia passuum per agrōs tetendit. Pūblius Fūriānō dīxit, "Cōnsistāmus ut sepulchrum clārae nostrae cognātae,[2] Caeciliae Metellae, videāmus." Multa alia sepulchra vīdērunt, inter quae īnsigne erat id Messālae Corvīnī.[3] Vīdērunt Campum Sacrum 10 Horātiōrum, ubi Horātiī cum Cūriātiīs temporibus antīquīs pugnāverant.

Posteā ad palūdēs Pomptīnās vēnērunt, trāns quās nautae nāvigiō parvō prīmīs hōrīs noctis multōs hominēs trānsportāre parābant. "Properāre dēbēmus," Fūriānus dīxit, "ut in nāvigium ascendāmus, nam multī aliī ascendere cupiunt." Ob numerum ascendentium magnum perīculum erat. 15

[1] *carriages*
[2] *relative*
[3] *Messā´la Corvī´nus*

The tomb of Caecilia Metella along the Appian Way near Rome. The patrician Caecilii Metelli were so important in republican Rome and produced so long a line of distinguished generals and politicians that they claimed that they "owned the consulship." Caecilia was the daughter of Quintus Caecilius Metellus Creticus who subdued Crete in 68–66 B.C. She married into the family of the triumvir Crassus.

E. Streichan/SuperStock

"Iam satis est!" eī clāmāvērunt quī in nāvigiō locum invēnerant; "prōcēdāmus nē omnēs submergāmur." Tandem nautae nāvigium solvunt et omnēs gaudent. Sed ob culicēs et rānās[4] nēmō dormīre poterat. Praetereā nauta dē amīcā suā absentī cantābat. Duōs hominēs īrātōs nautam in aquam

20 ēicere cupientēs aliī nautae retinuērunt. Tandem septimā hōrā noctis ad terram accessērunt sed plūrimī in nāvigiō ad hōram octāvam vel decimam mānsērunt.

Tum Pūblius dīxit, "Celerius prōcēdāmus nē in hīs palūdibus pessimīs vītam āmittāmus et ut noctem quārtam in vīllā hospitis[5] patris meī

25 agāmus." Hōc factō, sextō diē in forum Capuae, ultimae urbis Appiae Viae, pervēnērunt.

Quid in hāc urbe accidit? Aliō diē dē hōc legētis.

4 *mosquitoes and frogs*

5 *host.* Wealthy Roman travelers could stay at their own villas or at those of their guest-friends, who enjoyed the same reciprocal hospitality when they themselves were on a journey.

Questions

1. Where did the entire family go to see Publius and Furianus leave? How?
2. Why did the boys leave from that spot and not from home?
3. What monuments did Publius and Furianus see along the way?
4. What was the countryside like in the first stage of the journey?
5. When did they arrive at the Pomptine marshes, and what was Furianus' concern there?
6. What were the hardships and disturbances they faced in crossing them?
7. Why did two men want to throw the sailor into the water?
8. What did most people do when the ferry was taking on passengers, and why?
9. How many days did the journey from Rome to Capua require?
10. What importance did Capua have at that time?
11. What concerns did Publius have?

Remains of the amphitheater at Capua. Founded by Etruscans sometime before 600 B.C., later captured by Oscan-speaking invaders in the fifth and fourth centuries B.C., Capua became linked to Rome by the Appian Way in 318 B.C., surviving numerous reversals of fortune down to the eighth century A.D. In 211 B.C. it revolted from Roman hegemonic control to side with Hannibal and was severely punished.

John Heseltine/CORBIS

GRAMMAR

Purpose Clauses with *Ut* and *Nē* and the Subjunctive

Properāre dēbēmus ut nāvigium ascendāmus.	*We ought to hurry so that we may get on the boat,* or . . . *in order to get on the boat,* or . . . *to get on the boat.*
Prōcēdāmus nē omnēs submergāmur.	*Let us go on so that we may not all be drowned,* or . . . *so we won't all be drowned,* or . . . *so that we aren't all drowned,* or . . . *so as not to be drowned, all of us.*
Celerius prōcēdāmus nē in hīs palūdibus vītam āmittāmus.	*Let's go faster so that we may not lose our lives in these swamps,* or . . . *lest we lose our lives in these swamps,* or . . . *so as not to lose our lives in these swamps,* or . . . *so we don't lose our lives in these swamps.*

In the examples above, observe:

1. In the subordinate clauses, the verbs **ascendāmus, submergāmur,** and **āmittāmus** express the *purpose* of the acts indicated by the main verbs.
2. The conjunction **ut** introduces the positive clause and **nē** the negative.
3. English has a number of ways, some formal, some informal, of expressing purpose, often with the infinitive (see *to get, to be drowned,* and *to lose* in the examples). Latin prose authors never use the infinitive this way and, to express purpose with **ut** or **nē** and the subjunctive, *Latin must always use a finite form of the verb.*

Practice

Find all examples of purpose clauses in the lesson's reading. Translate them in a variety of ways.

Translation

1. Is the sailor singing to scare the frogs?
2. Hurry, Furianus, in order not to be left behind.
3. Publius will hurry in order to proceed to Greece.
4. So as not to see Mother weeping, we will not wait.
5. Let us often stop to see famous places near the road.

Nota·Bene

Note that the subjunctive can be used as the main verb in a sentence. In the reading, **cōnsistāmus, prōcēdāmus** (twice) are volitive subjunctives *and* main verbs. They are examples of *independent* uses of the subjunctive.

VOCABULARY

Nouns

hospes, hospitis m.   (hospice, hospitality)
   host, guest, guest-friend
palūs, palūdis f. *swamp*   (paludal)

Adjectives

decimus, -a, -um *tenth*   [decem]
octāvus, -a, -um *eighth*   [octō]
quārtus, -a, -um *fourth*   [quattuor]
septimus, -a, -um *seventh*   [septem]
sextus, -a, -um *sixth*   [sex]

Verbs

dēscendō, -ere, dēscendī, dēscēnsus   (descendant, descent)
  descend
fleō, flēre, flēvī, flētus *weep (for)*

Conjunctions

nē *(so) that . . . not, lest*
ut *(in order) that, so that*

WORD STUDY

Derivatives *Cardinal* numbers are the basic numbers, e.g., *one, two, three*, etc. *Ordinal* numbers indicate the numerical order, e.g., *first, second, third*, etc. Both types are adjectives.

Derive the Latin ordinal numerals (i.e., **prīmus,** etc.) from the following English words and arrange them in the proper order: *tertiary, quintuplet, noon, quartet, secondary, octave, primary, decimal.*

Give the Latin cardinal numerals (**ūnus,** etc.) for the following Spanish cardinal numerals: *tres, cinco, siete, dos, ciento, nueve, cuatro, ocho, seis, diez.*

Translate the following Spanish sentence: *En las* (the) *primeras horas de la* (of the) *noche muchos hombres fueron transportados por navío.*

THE HAZARDS OF TRAVEL

Capua hōc tempore urbs amplissima atque pulcherrima erat, maxima omnium in hāc parte Italiae. In plānissimō locō posita, viās lātās optimāsque habuit. Ut urbem vidērent, Fūriānus Pūbliusque ūnum diem manēre cōnstituērunt. Homō quīdam[1] eōs vidēns dīxit: "Ut omnia bene hodiē videātis ducem habēre dēbētis. Ego vōbīs omnia mōnstrābō; 5 deinde vōbīs optimam cēnam dabō; meliōrem enim cibum in nūllā urbe inveniētis." Puerī auxilium ducis accēpērunt. Sed paucīs aedificiīs mōnstrātīs, homō in viā angustā pecūniam ex manū Pūblī rapuit et fūgit. Sed clāmōre iuvenum audītō, duo mīlitēs hominem pessimum comprehendērunt. 10

Itaque iuvenēs grātō animō Capuam relīquērunt. Iter nunc per montēs et silvās faciēbant, et via mala erat. Fūriānus Pūbliō dīxit, "Raedae adhaereāmus, nē ēiciāmur." In hīs regiōnibus nūllī hospitēs Rūfī habitāvērunt; itaque in caupōnam,[2] appellātam "Ad[3] Elephantum,"

[1] *a certain* (nom.)
[2] *inn*
[3] *at (the Sign of)*

Archivo Iconografico, S.A./CORBIS

This well-preserved section of the Appian Way outside Rome testifies to the durability of Roman roads even as it suggests some of the hardships of travel. Robbery, pickpocketing, unsanitary inns, drought, dust, and mosquitoes plagued the unwary traveler at various times in history, particularly in the later Empire and after its fall.

15 accēdere coāctī sunt, ut noctem ūnam agerent. Sed caupōna sordida erat,
neque dormīre facile erat. Proximō diē hominēs armātōs in viā vīdērunt;
sed servī arma cēpērunt, et hominēs fūgērunt. Deinde maxima tempestās
commōta est, et ad vīllam dēsertam properāvērunt nē tempestāte
opprimerentur. Tandem, quārtō decimō diē, ad portās Brundisī pervēnērunt.
20 In hōc locō raedam relīquērunt nāvemque celeriter petīvērunt, nē morā
impedīrentur et ut quam mātūrissimē ad Graeciam veherentur. Sed
gubernātor dīxit, "Magna nunc tempestās in marī est. In hōc locō hodiē
maneāmus, nē perīculum suscipiāmus." Itaque, litterīs ad familiam missīs,
Pūblius et Fūriānus apud[4] hospitem mānsērunt.

[4] *at (the house of)*

Questions

1. What distinguished Capua as a city?
2. How long did the young men stay there?
3. Who encountered them there, and what did he offer them?
4. What happened after they had seen some of Capua's sights?
5. How did the soldiers there help?
6. What was the road like leading out of Capua?
7. Why were they forced to stay at the Elephant Inn?
8. What two hazards did they face after leaving the inn? How did they deal with them?
9. How long did it take for them to travel from Rome to the port of Brundisium?
10. Why did they hurry to board the ship? Did they succeed in leaving port quickly? Why or why not?

While the diners sit or recline at leisure, slaves and cooks around them tend to their every wish: wine from the storeroom, meat, bread, and other delicacies. Notice the three ovens and the large platters on which the food was prepared and brought to the **triclinium.**

Alinari/Art Resource, NY

GRAMMAR

Imperfect Subjunctive

The imperfect subjunctive of all verbs, regular and irregular, looks like the present active infinitive with the personal endings, active or passive, added to it, e.g., **portāre-m** (active), **portāre-r** (passive), etc.[5] Only one translation is given below because, like all subjunctives, its translation will vary and be determined by the type of clause in which it is found.

IMPERFECT SUBJUNCTIVE

ACTIVE

portārem *I might carry*, etc.	**docērem** *I might teach*, etc.	**pōnerem** *I might put*, etc.	**caperem** *I might take*, etc.	**mūnīrem** *I might fortify*, etc.
portārēs	**docērēs**	**pōnerēs**	**caperēs**	**mūnīrēs**
portāret	**docēret**	**pōneret**	**caperet**	**mūnīret**
portārēmus	**docērēmus**	**pōnerēmus**	**caperēmus**	**mūnīrēmus**
portārētis	**docērētis**	**pōnerētis**	**caperētis**	**mūnīrētis**
portārent	**docērent**	**pōnerent**	**caperent**	**mūnīrent**

PASSIVE

portārer *I might be carried*, etc.	**docērer** *I might be taught*, etc.	**pōnerer** *I might be put*, etc.	**caperer** *I might be taken*, etc.	**mūnīrer** *I might be fortified*, etc.
portārēris	**docērēris**	**pōnerēris**	**caperēris**	**mūnīrēris**
portārētur	**docērētur**	**pōnerētur**	**caperētur**	**mūnīrētur**
portārēmur	**docērēmur**	**pōnerēmur**	**caperēmur**	**mūnīrēmur**
portārēminī	**docērēminī**	**pōnerēminī**	**caperēminī**	**mūnīrēminī**
portārentur	**docērentur**	**pōnerentur**	**caperentur**	**mūnīrentur**

Imperfect Subjunctive of *Sum* and *Possum*

The imperfect subjunctives of **sum** and **possum** are formed regularly.

essem, *I might be,* etc.	**essēmus**	**possem,** *I might be able,* etc.	**possēmus**
essēs	**essētis**	**possēs**	**possētis**
esset	**essent**	**posset**	**possent**

---

[5] The **-ē-** before the ending is long except before final **-m, -r, -t, -nt,** and **-ntur.**

Practice

1. Conjugate **vehō** in the present and imperfect subjunctive active; **terreō** in the present and imperfect subjunctive passive.
2. Tell the forms of **flēmus, cōnstituātur, dēscenderētis, perficiēmus, sentīrētur, possētis, cōnfīrmārēmur, accident, valētis, opprimātur.**

Sequence of Tenses

In English and Latin, a subordinate verb that is in the indicative or subjunctive shifts its tense in relation to that of the main verb. Study the following examples.

(indirect statement)	*They say that he is at home.*
	They said that he was at home.
(subjunctive in purpose clause)	*He studies/will study (so) that he may learn.*
	He studied (so) that he might learn.

Sequence of Tenses in Purpose Clauses

The subjunctive has no future tense in Latin. In dependent purpose clauses, the only tenses that can be used are the present and imperfect, as follows.

The *present* subjunctive is used when the main verb is *present* or *future.*

Venīmus ut videāmus.   *We come (so) that we may see.*

The *imperfect* subjunctive is used when the main verb is past (i.e., imperfect, perfect, or past perfect).

Vēnimus ut vidērēmus.   *We came (so) that we might see.*

Translation

1. They remained one day to see Capua.
2. So as not to lose their money, they left Capua.
3. They sought fresh horses so as not to be hindered by the bad roads.
4. They hurried (on) to spend the night in the villa of a guest-friend.
5. They hurried to the ship in order to sail to Greece and not spend another night in Italy.

⊞ VOCABULARY

Nouns

aedificium, -ī n. *building*   (edify)

gubernātor, -ōris m. *pilot, helmsman*   (governor, gubernatorial)

iuvenis, -is m. *young man*   (juvenile)

mora, -ae f. *delay*   (moratorium)

tempestās, -tātis f. *storm*   [tempus]

Adjectives

amplus, -a, -um *great, magnificent*   (ample, amplify)

angustus, -a, -um *narrow*   (anguish)

matūrus, -a, -um *early, quick, ripe*   [matūrō]

sordidus, -a, -um *dirty, disreputable*   (sordid)

Verbs

adhaereō, -ēre, -haesī, -haesus   [haereō]
     stick (to), cling (to)

ēiciō, -ere, ēiēcī, ēiectus *throw out*   [iaciō]

vehō, -ere, vēxī, vectus *carry*   (vehicle, vector)

Adverb

deinde *then, thereafter*

Conjunction

enim (never the first word in a sentence) *for*

An elaborate traveling carriage, with curtains that could be let down for privacy to make the ordinary carriage (**raeda**) into a **carrūca dormitōria**. Still, as it rocketed down the road behind four horses, Publius and Furianus probably were glad they knew of the villa of a guest-friend at which they could get a good night's sleep. Carriages of this type seem to have been an idea borrowed from the Gauls by the Romans.

North Wind Picture Archives

WORD STUDY

Suffixes The following suffixes have no sharply defined meanings, but if you know them you can recognize many English derivatives: **-ium** (English *-e* or *-y*), **-tium** (English *-ce*), **-men** (English *-men, -min, -me*), **-tūs** (English *-tue*).

Give the English form of **studium, officium, aedificium, sacrificium, spatium, volūmen, crīmen, virtūs.**

What must be the Latin words from which are derived *silence, commerce, remedy, prodigy, culmin(ate), lumin(ous), crimin(al)?*

Explain by derivation *amplifier, descendant, immature, manual, moratorium, vehicle.*

Did You Know?

Travel and *travail* ("hard labor") come from the same Latin word, **trēpālium** (**trēs + pālus,** *three stakes*), a *three-pronged device* used in medieval times as an instrument of torture. Think of that the next time the pilot turns on the seat-belt light for a horrendous landing, you have gone six hours without food, and your luggage turns up missing!

LESSON XIII

SIGHT-SEEING AT BRUNDISIUM

LESSON OBJECTIVES
- Conjugation of **Ferō**
- Present Subjunctive of the First Conjugation

Pūblius et Fūriānus Brundisī[1] diū mānsērunt ut sine perīculō trāns mare
nāvigārent. Hōc tempore urbem explōrāvērunt. Namque in hāc urbe multa
loca clāra erant. Multī ad hunc portum vēnērunt ut ad Graeciam Asiamque
nāvigārent—mercātōrēs, imperātōrēs, exercitūs, nūntiī litterās ferentēs.

Fūriānus Pūbliō dīxit: "Haec urbs clāra est. Nōnne memoriā tenēs   5
Cicerōnem in exsilium ēiectum ad hunc locum vēnisse ut nāvis eum ad
Graeciam ferret? Ūnus amīcus eum dolentem excēpit, cui numquam
satis grātiās agere poterat. Sed posteāquam Cicerō ex exsiliō revocātus
Brundisium[2] diē nātālī colōniae ipsīus vēnit, omnēs cīvēs cum maximō
gaudiō eum excēpērunt."   10

Tum Pūblius dīxit: "Rēctē dīcis. Posteā in hōc oppidō Pompeius[3] cōpiās
collēgit ut trāns mare fugeret. Caesar ad oppidum properāvit ut eum
interclūderet. Sed sine nāvibus eum retinēre nōn poterat. Prōcēdāmus ad
portum et propriīs oculīs spectēmus locum in quō Caesar exitūs portūs
impedīre temptāvit." "Bene," respondit Fūriānus. Itaque duo amīcī   15
prīmum ad locum ēditum prōcessērunt ut tōtam regiōnem vidērent.

[1] *at Brundisium*
[2] *to Brundisium*
[3] Pompey, Caesar's great rival for power during the Civil War

G. Tortoli/Ancient Art & Architecture Collection

**The Appian Way began in Rome
and originally ended in Capua.
It was eventually extended to
Brundisium, on the southeast
coast of Italy. This original
Roman column marks the end of
the Appian Way at Brundisium,
now the city Brindisi, and still a
major point of departure for
Greece.**

Asclepius (the son of Apollo and Coronis, a young woman from Thessaly) was the Greek god of medicine. He was taught the art of healing by the wise centaur Chiron. The Romans called him Aesculapius and in 291 B.C. dedicated a temple to him on the island in the Tiber River, where still today a hospital stands. In this Greek relief from the fourth century B.C., he is shown treating a patient.

Y ou have now had the four "irregular" second singular present imperatives of the third declension: **dīc, dūc, fac,** and **fer.** Constantly in use, they lost the regular **-e** ending.

Deinde dē locō ēditō dēscendērunt et portum ipsum spectāvērunt. Quā parte⁴ portus angustissimus erat Caesar opera et ratēs⁵ collocāverat, sed Pompeius, nē interclūderētur, nāvibus opera rūperat et fūgerat.

20   "Certē haec urbs multa clāra facta vīdit et multōs et gravēs cāsūs tulit," inquit Pūblius.

Questions

1. What did the boys do while they waited for good weather?
2. Who else was waiting to board ship?
3. Why was Brundisium famous?
4. When did Cicero stop there?
5. What kind of reception did he get?
6. What did Caesar try to accomplish there?
7. Why did they go to an elevated location?
8. How did Pompey escape?

GRAMMAR

Conjugation of *Ferō*

The conjugation of **ferō** is irregular in the present tense only; in all other tenses it is conjugated like a verb of the third conjugation. Its last two principal parts are "borrowed" from a different verb.

ACTIVE		PASSIVE	
ferō, *I carry,* etc.	**ferimus**	**feror,** *I am carried,* etc.	**ferimur**
fers	**fertis**	**ferris**	**feriminī**
fert	**ferunt**	**fertur**	**feruntur**

The present active infinitive **ferre** is contracted from **ferĕre,** while the present passive infinitive **(ferrī)** is formed by changing the final **-e** to **-ī,** as in other verbs. The imperatives are **fer** (sing.) and **ferte** (pl.). The subjunctive is regular throughout.

	INDICATIVE	
	ACTIVE	PASSIVE
IMPERFECT	**ferēbam,** etc.	**ferēbar,** etc.
FUTURE	**feram, ferēs, feret,** etc.	**ferar, ferēris, ferētur,** etc.
PERFECT	**tulī,** etc.	**lātus sum,** etc.
PAST PERFECT	**tuleram,** etc.	**lātus eram,** etc.
FUTURE PERFECT	**tulerō,** etc.	**lātus erō,** etc.

	SUBJUNCTIVE[6]	
	ACTIVE	PASSIVE
PRESENT	**feram, ferās, ferat,** etc.	**ferar, ferāris, ferātur,** etc.
IMPERFECT	**ferrem,** etc.	**ferrer,** etc.

Present Subjunctive of the First Conjugation

The mood sign of the present subjunctive in the first conjugation is **-ē-**, not **-ā-** as in the other conjugations. Only two of several possible translations are suggested below.

ACTIVE		PASSIVE	
portem *I should carry,* etc.	**portēmus** *we should carry, let us carry,* etc.	**porter** *I should be carried,* etc.	**portēmur** *we should be carried, let us be carried,* etc.
portēs	**portētis**	**portēris**	**portēminī**
portet	**portent**	**portētur**	**portentur**

Practice

1. Give the third person singular of **ferō** in all tenses of the indicative, active and passive, and in the present and imperfect subjunctive, active and passive.
2. Give all the infinitives and participles of **ferō**.
3. Conjugate in the present and imperfect subjunctive, active and passive: **colligō, cōnfirmō, dēbeō.**
4. Tell the form of **dolent, excipiāmur, nūntiētur, ferrētis, properent, rumperet, cōnstituantur, perficient, moneāminī, occupās.**

---

[6] The perfect and past perfect forms are regular and will be presented later.

Isola Tiberina, the ancient crossing place of the Tiber nearest Rome and associated with Aesculapius the god of healing. The island's hospital continues (since 1548) the island's commitment to spiritual and physical healing.

Vittoriano Rastelli/CORBIS

Translation

1. Publius and his friend proceeded toward the harbor to sail to Greece.
2. "Let us hurry (on) so that we shall not be left behind," said Publius.
3. His friend replied, "Let us proceed to an elevated place to see the whole region."
4. Caesar obstructed this harbor in order that Pompey's ships might not escape.

VOCABULARY

Nouns

mercātor, -ōris m. *merchant*   (mercantile)
oculus, -ī m. *eye*   (binocular, monocle)
portus, -ūs m. *harbor, port*   **[portō]**

Adjective

ēditus, -a, -um *elevated*   **[dō]**

Verbs

colligō, -ere, -lēgī, -lēctus *collect*   **[legō]**
doleō, -ēre, doluī, dolitūrus *grieve*   (dolor)
excipiō, -ere, -cēpī, -ceptus *receive*   **[capiō]**
ferō, ferre, tulī, lātus *carry, bear, bring*   (fertile, refer, relate)
rumpō, -ere, rūpī, ruptus *break*   (interrupt, rupture)

Adverb

rēctē *rightly*   **[regō]**

Conjunctions

namque *for*
posteāquam *after*

C.M. Dixon/Photo Resources

A touching funerary frieze of a man and his family, including a family pet horse. The instruments pictured overhead make it probable that the deceased was a surgeon. The snake in the tree is—strange for us—a symbol of immortality and of the god-healer Aesculapius, in whom physicians placed their trust.

WORD STUDY

Latin in Medicine Ask your family doctor or pharmacist about the use physicians make of Latin words and phrases every day. The science of anatomy, with which all physicians must be familiar, uses a large number of Latin terms. In writing prescriptions, physicians use Latin constantly, and pharmacists must be able to understand it. The symbol ℞ at the top of a prescription stands for **recipe,** *take.*[7] Other examples are: **aq(ua) pur(a),** *pure water;* **aq(ua) dest(illata),** *distilled water;* **t(er) i(n) d(ie),** *three times a day;* **cap(iat),** *let him/her take;* **gtt. (abbreviation for guttae),** *drops;* **sig(na),** *write;* **stat(im),** *at once;* **a(nte) c(ibum),** *before meals;* **p(ost) c(ibum),** *after meals;* **det(ur),** *let it be given.*

Explain *condolence, corruption, dilated, inoculate, oculist, rupture.*

---

[7] The stroke through the R is a sign of abbreviation, like our period.

LESSON OBJECTIVES

- Result Clauses with **Ut** and **Ut Nōn**
- Review Purpose and Result Clauses

A LETTER FROM ATHENS

Bettmann/CORBIS

Of the painted Stoa we have only ruins, but there is a lot of literary testimony to it and the activities that went on there. It got its name because it housed paintings of Athenian military victories (real or legendary) by Greece's most famous artists. As a general meeting place and site for lectures, it provided a kind of classroom for the professors who taught there. It was here that Zeno is said to have later founded the philosophy that came to be known as Stoicism.

¹ **salūtem plūrimam dicit,** *sends heartiest greetings.* These words are regularly abbreviated.

² i.e., in the Roman civil wars before Octavian (Augustus) overcame his rivals

Pūblius patrī et mātrī et sorōribus suīs s. p. d.¹ Sī valētis, bene est; valeō. Nunc valeō; sed nōn semper valuī. Namque Brundisiō post longam moram relīctō, posteāquam nāvis parva in mare lātum prōcessit, tanta tempestās commōta est ut putārem undās altās nāvem frāctūrās esse.

5 Fūriānus autem dīxit, "Nautae ita perītī sunt ut nāvem facile servent." Sed ego respondī: "Hoc nōn iam ferre possum. In īnferiōrem partem properēmus ut ibi somnum capiāmus et clārum caelum spērēmus."

Dēscendimus. Nāvis ita volvēbātur ut mors ab omnibus spērārētur; sed post diem longum et noctem longiōrem ad urbem Graecam Dyrrachium

10 pervēnimus. Viīs tam malīs iter per Graeciam fēcimus ut paene cōnficerēmur. Per oppida dēserta, per agrōs nōn cultōs, per urbēs bellīs cīvīlibus² oppressās prōcessimus. Tandem ad clāram urbem Athēnās pervēnimus, quae urbs ita pulchra est ut omnia dē eā scrīpta nōn satis dīcant. Agora, quae est forum Athēnārum, et Acropolis, Capitōliō Rōmānō

similis, ita ēgregiae sunt ut nōn satis laudentur. Sed in proximīs litterīs 15
plūs dē urbe scrībam. Nunc dē studiīs audīre cupitis.

Ubi ad portam Athēnārum accessimus, vīdimus multōs vestem
scholasticam gerentēs et tantīs clāmōribus vocantēs ut cōnsisterēmus et
cum silentiō eōs spectārēmus.[3] "Nōnne petitis scholam Philippī?" "Nōnne
petitis scholam Lycurgī?" et alia clāmābant. "Ad scholam Enchōriōnis 20
rhētoris[4] prōcēdimus," dīximus. Deinde ab aliīs relīctī sumus, ab aliīs
prehēnsī. In aedificium parvum ductī sumus, et iānua clausa est. Tam diū
ibi mānsimus ut putārēmus illōs numquam reversūrōs esse. Tandem nē
perterrērēmur līberātī sumus et ab illīs rīdentibus ad cēnam ductī sumus,
post quam omnibus modīs lūdificātī[5] sumus. Tum ad balnea ductī vestem 25
scholasticam accēpimus. Posterō diē ad numerum scholasticōrum
Enchōriōnis, quī grātus vidētur, ascrīptī sumus. Crās studia incipiēmus.
Cum Graecā familiā ad Agoram habitāmus.

Vidētis omnia bona esse. Saepe scrībēmus et saepe litterās
exspectābimus. Valēte. 30

[3] The following description of student life in Athens is based on that given by Libanius in the fourth century A.D., but it is probably substantially correct for the age of Augustus.

[4] professor of rhetoric

[5] made fun of

Questions

1. Why hadn't Publius been well?
2. What did Publius think would happen to the ship?
3. Why didn't Furianus worry?
4. What did they do to cope with the problem?
5. How long did it take them to reach land?
6. What were their impressions as they traveled through northwest Greece?
7. What was their impression of Athens?
8. Whom did they see first on their arrival there?
9. What joke was played on them?
10. Where did they find a place to stay?

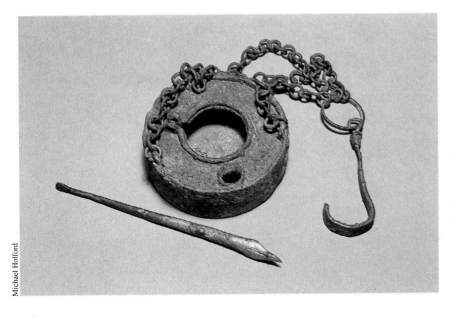

Michael Holford

Roman inkpot and pen dating from the first century A.D. Originally, the inkpot had a hinged lid. With the attached chain, travelers could easily take their writing implements with them to correspond with those at home. In Roman times, ink was made from **sepia**, a pigment in the body of the cuttlefish.

GRAMMAR

Result Clauses with *Ut* and *Ut Nōn*

A result clause is a subordinate clause used to express an action that results from the action or state of the main verb. In Latin, the result clause is introduced by the conjunction **ut**; for a negative, use **ut... nōn.** The verb is in the subjunctive, following the rules for the sequence of tenses.

Usually, one of the following words appears in the main clause to signal that a result clause will follow.

ita *(so)*
sīc *(so)*
tālis *(such)*
tam *(so, such)*
tantus, -a, -um *(so great)*
tot *(so many)*

Tanta tempestās commōta est ut putārem...	*So great a storm was stirred up that I thought* . . .
Viīs tam malīs iter per Graeciam fēcimus ut paene conficerēmur.	*We made our way through Greece by roads so bad that we were almost exhausted.*
(Haec aedificia) ita ēgregia sunt ut nōn satis laudentur.	*(These buildings) are so remarkable that they are not praised enough.*

Observe:

1. The verbs of the subordinate clause are in the subjunctive and express the *result* of the state or act described in the main clause.

2. The negative is **nōn.**

3. The tense sequence is the same as in purpose clauses.

Such words as **ita** and **tantus,** used in main clauses to point to subordinate clauses of result, are like signboards which seem to say, "Stop, Look, Think! A Result Clause Is Coming!"

Summary of Purpose and Result Clauses

IN LATIN

Purpose Clauses

1. Subjunctive

2. Introduced by **ut**, negative **nē**

Result Clauses

1. Subjunctive
2. Usually prepared for by **ita, tam,** etc.
3. Introduced by **ut**, negative **ut... nōn**

IN ENGLISH

1. a. Infinitive
   b. Indicative with auxiliaries *may* and *might*

2. a. No introductory word or introduced by *(in order) that, so that,* etc.

1. Indicative
2. Usually prepared for by *so,* etc.

3. Introduced by *that*

Translation

1. We hurried into a building in order not to see the storm.
2. The storm on the sea was so great that all were frightened.
3. The waves were so high that the ship did not easily proceed.
4. Leaving the ship behind, we hurried toward the city (of) Athens.
5. This city is so adorned with such beautiful buildings that it is praised by all.

Vanni/Art Resource, NY

Caryatid is a term for an architectural support that is wholly or partially in female human form, named for the priestess of Artemis in the Greek city Caryae. Here is the Porch of the Maidens, on the south face of the Erechtheum on the Acropolis, fifth century B.C. The porch was a source of inspiration to Roman architects, who made good use of the type at Hadrian's Villa at Tivoli.

VOCABULARY

Noun

somnus, -ī m. *sleep*   (somnolent)

Adjectives

perītus, -a, -um *skilled*
posterus, -a, -um *following*   [post]
tantus, -a, -um *so great*   (tantamount)

Verbs

perterreō, -ēre, -terruī, -territus   [terreō]
  scare thoroughly, alarm
prehendō, -ere, -hendī, -hēnsus   (apprehend, prehensile)
  grasp, seize
rideō, ridēre, rīsī, rīsus *laugh (at)*   (risible, ridicule)
volvō, -ere, volvī, volūtus   (revolve, revolution)
  roll, turn over

Adverbs

ita *so, in such a way, thus*
saepe *often*
satis *enough*   (sate, satisfactory)
tam *so, such* (with adjectives
  and adverbs)

WORD STUDY

Spelling Difficulties of English spelling due to silent or weakly sounded letters or to other causes are often cleared up by examination of the Latin. Give the Latin originals of the following words: *ascension, assign, comparative, conscience, consensus, debt, deficit, desperation, doubt, laboratory, receipt, reign, repetition, separate.*

Derivatives of compounds of **capiō** have **ei:** *receive, deceive, conceive, perceive.*

Explain by derivation *apprehension, penultimate, posterity, vestments, somniferous.*

Fifteen states in the United States have towns named Athens.

A GOSSIPY LETTER FROM ROME

M. ■ Caecilius Fūriānō suō. Rogāvistī, "Quid agit rēs pūblica?" Cōnsulēs proximī annī creātī sunt—Lepidus et Taurus. Ille Augustō cārus est. Maiōrēs eius erant Sulla et Pompeius, Caesaris inimīcus, sed Augustus tam concordiam cupit ut memoriam rērum eius modī dēpōnere possit.

Hic nūntius[1] multō gravior erit: Corellius, tribūnus, iam[2] decem diēs 5 mortuus est. Omnēs amīcī eius spem habuerant eum aegrum paucīs diēbus diūtius vīctūrum[3] esse, ut frātrem, ex Galliā properantem, vidēre posset; sed hoc nōn permissum est. Fūnus īnsigne erat—ōrātiō ante domum habita, pompa longa, cornicinēs,[4] plūrimae imāginēs,[5] rogus[6] multōs pedēs altus (sed tot hominēs aderant ut difficile esset rogum vidēre), sepulchrum 10 ēgregium.

Ovidius poēta, ex urbe ad oppidum barbarum expulsus, iam paene duōs annōs litterās supplicēs ad Augustum scrībit, sed hic nōn commovētur. Augustī autem silentium tantum est ut nēmō causam poenae Ovidī cognōscere possit. Ovidius librum novum ēdidit, quem emam et mittam ut 15 legere possīs.

[1] *news*

[2] The present tense is used with **iam** where the English idiom calls for the present perfect: *has now been dead.*

[3] from **vivō**

[4] *buglers*

[5] *wax masks* of ancestors who had held high public office. These were kept in a shrine in the house and served as a portrait gallery. At funerals they were worn by hired mourners so that it seemed as if all of a person's great ancestors were at the funeral.

[6] *funeral pyre*

Baths of Hadrian at Leptis Magna, Libya, North Africa. Roman baths, found in nearly every city or town in the Empire, provided a welcome respite from the hard work of the advancing day. Statues of the donors' friends and family often decorated the wall niches in the manner of some modern libraries and museums.

7 not from **exercitus**, *army!*
8 dative with **adsum**
9 *lunch*
10 *train myself, exercise*

Nōvistīne Calpurnium, quī tantam pecūniam habet ut domus ūna eam capere nōn possit—illum quī aedificia incēnsa celeriter emit, tum, igne operā servōrum exercitōrum[7] exstīnctō, reficit? Agrum magnum ēmit.
20 Multōs diēs iam cupiō agrum parvum emere, ut agricola in ōtiō sim. In Sabīnīs pulchrum agrum quī nōn multīs mīlibus passuum ab eō Horātī poētae abest, invēnī. Quid dē hōc putās?

Diēs omnēs paene similēs sunt. Surgō; clientibus audītīs, in Forum prōcēdō, ut aut iūdicia audīre possim aut senātuī[8] adsim; prandium[9] capiō;
25 dormiō; exerceor;[10] in thermās Agrippae prōcēdō, et ibi amīcōs videō. Tum est cēna, tum quiēs. Haec cotīdiē agimus. Quid agit Fūriānus meus?

Questions

1. With which consul was Augustus on particularly good terms?
2. Why was this surprising?
3. What was Augustus' policy according to Publius' uncle?
4. What was the important news story that he had to report?
5. What elements made up the **fūnus?**
6. Where was Ovid exiled?
7. What had he been doing while in exile?
8. What was the reason for his punishment?
9. How much money did Marcus claim Calpurnius had?
10. How did he make that much money?
11. What was Marcus about to purchase?
12. What was a typical day for Furianus' father?

Mille in the singular is an indeclinable adjective, a neuter **i**-stem noun in the plural. **Mīlle passūs** = *a mile;* **mīlia passuum** (gen.) = *miles.*

GRAMMAR

Review of Fifth Declension Nouns

The fifth declension includes comparatively few words. All are feminine except **diēs,** which is usually masculine. **Rēs** and **diēs** occur constantly and should be memorized. Other nouns of this declension usually have no plural.

	SINGULAR	PLURAL	SINGULAR	PLURAL
NOM.	**diēs** *day*	**diēs** *days*	**rēs** *thing*	**rēs** *things*
GEN.	**diēī**	**diērum**	**reī**	**rērum**
DAT.	**diēī**	**diēbus**	**reī**	**rēbus**
ACC.	**diem**	**diēs**	**rem**	**rēs**
ABL.	**diē**	**diēbus**	**rē**	**rēbus**

Subjunctive of *Sum* and *Possum*

The present subjunctive of **sum** and **possum** has **-ī-** as its mood sign.

sim *I may be,* etc.   **sīmus**   **possim** *I may be able,* etc.   **possīmus**

sīs   **sītis**   **possīs**   **possītis**

sit   **sint**   **possit**   **possint**

Practice

1. Decline **ipsa rēs pūblica, multī diēs.**
2. Give the second person singular of **sum** and the second person plural of **possum** in all tenses of the indicative and in the present and imperfect subjunctive.
3. Tell the forms of **sumus, erunt, potuistī, posset, fuērunt, possint, esset, poterō, posse, fuerāmus.**

Ablative of Measure of Difference

Hic nūntius multō gravior erit.   *This news will be much more serious* (literally, *more serious by much*).

(Ager)... nōn multīs mīlibus passuum... abest.   *(The farm) is not many miles distant* (literally, *not distant by many miles*).

Observe:

The ablative is used without a preposition to express the measure of difference. Find all the examples of this construction in the reading on pages 95 and 96.

Review of Accusative of Extent

The extent of time or space is put in the accusative case.

Corellius... iam decem diēs mortuus est.   *Corellius has now been dead for ten days.*

rogus multōs pedēs altus   *a funeral pyre many feet high*

Find two other examples of this construction in the preceding reading.

Translation

1. Consuls were elected a few days before.
2. Ovid was banished to a town which was many miles away.
3. For two years Marcus had desired to buy a small farm so that he might be a farmer.
4. For many months Calpurnius had been setting buildings on fire so that he could buy them.

▦ VOCABULARY

Nouns

cliēns, -entis m. *client* (clientele)
maiōrēs, -um m. pl. *ancestors* [magnus]
opera, -ae f. *work, effort* [opus]
quiēs, -ētis f. *rest* (quiescence, quiescent)

Adjectives

aeger, -ra, -rum *sick*
tot, *so many* (indeclinable)

Verbs

ēdō, -ere, ēdidī, ēditus *give out, publish,* [dō]
   utter, inflict
incendō, -ere, incendī, incēnsus (incendiary, incense)
   set on fire, burn
reficiō, -ere, refēcī, refectus *repair* [faciō]
surgō, -ere, surrēxī, surrēctūrus *rise* [regō]

Adverb

cotīdiē *daily* [diēs]

Scala/Art Resource, NY

This fresco of a Roman poet (note the laurel wreath and the book, symbols of intellectual activity) is thought by some to be a portrait of Ovid. It is found among paintings from mythology and legend in the Duomo (cathedral) at Orvieto, Italy. Ovid was born in 43 B.C., the year after the assassination of Julius Caesar. Although his father had wanted him to follow the usual political career, Ovid was drawn more to the literary life of Rome and by the time he was thirty had established himself as a major poet. Ovid's *Metamorphōsēs* (Transformations) is one of our principal sources for Greek and Roman mythology, and you will read selections from them later in this book.

WORD STUDY

Prefixes For meaning and use of **prae-** *(pre-)*, **contrā-** *(contra-, counter-)*, **bene-** *(bene-)*, **male-** *(male)*, see the Grammar Appendix, p. 510. Define according to the prefix: *prevent, premonition, predict, preclude, prerequisite, counterirritant, contradict, counterrevolutionary, benefactor, benediction, malefactor, malediction.*

What is the difference between a modern consul and an ancient Roman consul?

Explain *ignition, incendiary, refectory, resurrection, vivid.*

LESSON XVI

ALMA MATER

LESSON OBJECTIVES

- Past Perfect (Pluperfect) Active Subjunctive of All Four Conjugations, **Sum** and **Possum**
- Time Clauses with **Ubi, Postquam, Cum**
- Sequence of Tenses

Cum[1] Pūblius Fūriānusque Athēnās[2] iter facerent, multōs Rōmānōs in viā vīdērunt. Paucīs diēbus postquam Athēnās pervēnērunt, multō plūrēs Rōmānōs vīdērunt. Namque plūrimī aliī Rōmānī eiusdem aetātis ad hanc urbem īnsignem vēnerant ut philosophōs rhētorēsque Graecōs audīrent. Tam clārī erant illī quī multōs annōs in hāc urbe docuerant ut multī discipulī ad eōs ex omnibus terrīs venīrent.

Cum amīcī duo paucōs diēs in urbe fuissent et multōs magistrōs audīvissent, Fūriānus Pūbliō dīxit: "Nōnne exīstimās magistrum nostrum Enchōriōnem acūtum et optimum omnium esse?" "Rēctē dīcis," respondit amīcus. "Gaudeō[3] quod patrēs nostrī eum ēlēgērunt. Cēterōs quidem nōn contemnō, sed ille certē optimus est. Eō ōrātiōnem habente,[4] mīrō modō affectus sum. Praetereā ea quae ille docet Rōmānīs ūtilissima sunt. Nam Rōmānī in forō senātūque ōrātiōnēs habent." Tum Fūriānus dīxit: "Etiam ea quae philosophī docent ūtilia sunt ut vītam bonam agāmus. Rōmānī quidem sumus, et Rōmānīs ūtilissimum est ōrātiōnēs habēre posse. Sed etiam hominēs sumus, et vīta bona ūtilior est quam ōrātiō bona."

[1] *when.* This is not the preposition *with,* but rather the conjunction **cum,** introducing a time clause with the subjunctive, about which you will learn in this lesson.
[2] *to Athens*
5 [3] *rejoice*
[4] *delivering*

10

15

The Acropolis of Athens, as seen from the meeting place of the Athenian assembly. Remarkably pleasing for the symmetry of geometric form and design, this ancient fortress served both for religious sanctuary and defensive protection—functions symbolized in the goddess Athena. A pedestal seen just left of the entranceway once had statues of Antony and Cleopatra superimposed.

CORBIS

Cum haec aliaque ab amīcīs duōbus nostrīs dē philosophīs rhētoribusque dicta essent, tandem Fūriānus dīxit: "Cōnsentīmus Enchōriōnem optimum esse. Gaudeāmus igitur quod in eius scholā 20 sumus. Vīvat[5] schola Enchōriōnis!"

[5] (long) live!

Questions

1. Whom did Publius and Furianus see on their way to Athens?
2. What explains the fact that many Romans of Publius' age were in Athens with them?
3. What was Furianus' opinion of his teacher?
4. How did their teacher Enchorio affect Publius when he spoke?
5. Why did Publius especially value his teaching?
6. What was most valuable for Furianus?
7. What is more useful than a good speech?

Young women were taught the fine arts of needlework and music. This wall painting from Pompeii shows a young lady playing the cithara, an ancient stringed instrument resembling a lyre.

The Metropolitan Museum of Art, Rogers Fund, 1903. (03.14.5) Copyright © 1986 By The Metropolitan Museum of Art.

GRAMMAR

Past Perfect (Pluperfect) Active Subjunctive

The *past perfect subjunctive active* for all verbs looks like the perfect active infinitive plus the active personal endings, as **portāvisse-m,** etc. The English translation will vary with the context in which the subjunctive is found, but is usually like the indicative ("had" + perfect participle).

PAST PERFECT ACTIVE

portāvissem	docuissem	posuissem	cēpissem	mūnīvissem
portāvissēs	docuissēs	posuissēs	cēpissēs	mūnīvissēs
portāvisset	docuisset	posuisset	cēpisset	mūnīvisset
portāvissēmus	docuissēmus	posuissēmus	cēpissēmus	mūnīvissēmus
portāvissētis	docuissētis	posuissētis	cēpissētis	mūnīvissētis
portāvissent	docuissent	posuissent	cēpissent	mūnīvissent

Similarly, **fuissem,** etc., **potuissem,** etc.

Practice

Conjugate the following verbs in the past perfect active subjunctive:
incendō, cōnsentiō, possum.

Time Clauses with *Ubi, Postquam, Cum*

When the Romans wanted to indicate the *time* at which an act occurred in the past, they used **ubi** *(when),* **postquam** *(after),* or the conjunction **cum** *(when)* and the imperfect, perfect, or past perfect indicative in the subordinate time clause.

Ubi	vidēbās,		*When*	*you were seeing this,*	
Postquam id	vīdistī,	excessistī.	*After*	*you saw (or had seen) this,*	*you left.*
Cum	vīderās,		*When*	*you had seen this,*	

On the other hand, when they merely wanted to *describe the circumstances* under which the past act took place, they used **cum** with the imperfect or past perfect subjunctive in the subordinate clause and the indicative in the main clause. This use of **cum** with the subjunctive is extremely common.[5]

---

[5] These **cum** clauses with the subjunctive are sometimes called *descriptive* (or *circumstantial*) **cum** clauses.

Cum iuvenēs Athēnās iter facerent, multōs Rōmānōs vidērunt.	*When the young men were on the way to Athens, they saw many Romans.*
Cum duo amīcī multōs magistrōs audīvissent, Enchōriōnem ēlēgērunt.	*When the two friends had listened to many teachers, they chose Enchorio.*

Find the other **cum** clauses in the reading on pages 99 and 100. Are there any instances of the preposition **cum** (+ ablative)?

Sequence of Tenses

The way in which the tenses of the subjunctive are paired with the tenses of the indicative is called the *sequence of tenses.* You have already seen the sequence of tenses when you studied purpose clauses and result clauses.

PRIMARY TENSES (those referring to the present or future)
> *Indicative:* present, future, future perfect
> *Subjunctive:* present, perfect

SECONDARY TENSES (those referring to the past)
> *Indicative:* imperfect, perfect, past perfect
> *Subjunctive:* imperfect, pluperfect

Primary indicative tenses are followed by *primary subjunctive tenses, secondary* by *secondary.*

Translation

1. When Publius was traveling with his friend, he saw many noted men.
2. A few days later the two friends arrived at **(ad)** the most beautiful city of Greece.
3. When they had seen and heard all the teachers, they said that their own teacher was the best.
4. After they had been[6] in the city for a long time, they agreed that their fathers had chosen wisely.

---

[6] Use perfect indicative.

VOCABULARY

Adjectives

acūtus, -a, -um *sharp* (acute, acuteness)

cēterī, -ae, -a *the other(s)* (et cetera)

īnsignis, -e *noted* **[signum]**

mīrus, -a, -um *wonderful* (admire, mirage)

Verbs

cōnsentiō, -īre, -sēnsī, -sēnsus *agree* **[sentiō]**

contemnō, -ere, -tempsī, -temptus *despise* (contempt, contemptuous)

existimō, 1 *think* (estimate)

Adverbs

praetereā *besides*

quidem *at least, to be sure*
  (follows the word it emphasizes)

nē... quidem *not even*

Conjunction

cum *when*

WORD STUDY

Musical Terms Most of our musical terms come from Italian and thus ultimately from Latin. Explain the following, all derived from Latin words used in this book: *accelerando* (**celer**), *allegro* (**alacer**), *alto, cantabile, cantata, con amore, contralto, crescendo, da capo* (**dē capite**), *diminuendo* (**minuō**), *duet, finale, forte, fortissimo, libretto, mezzoforte* (**medius**), *octave, opus, piano, quintet, ritardando* (**tardus**), *sextet, solo, sonata, soprano* (**super**), *tempo, trio, vivace.*

LESSON OBJECTIVES
- Perfect System of the Subjunctive, Active and Passive
- Summary of Sequence of Tenses

ATHENS THE BEAUTIFUL

¹ *a little later* (lit., *later by a little*)

² *ivory*

³ *colonnade*

⁴ vocative of **meus**

⁵ This could be future indicative, *will I?* or present subjunctive, *may I?* We will never know precisely what was in Secunda's mind.

Vanni/Art Resource, NY

Through the columns of a portico you can see in the foreground the Propylaea, with its steps that give entrance to the Acropolis. In the background is the Temple of Athena Nike, with Ionic columns, on a site dedicated to Athena in the fifth century B.C. after the Greeks' victory over the Persians. Twice it has had to be largely reconstructed, once in the nineteenth century (because of damage in wartime) and once in the twentieth (to strengthen its foundation).

Paulō post¹ Pūblius litterās ad patrem mātremque mīsit, in quibus multa mīra dē urbe Athēnīs nārrāta sunt.

"Cum ad hanc urbem accessissēmus," scrīpsit, "cupīvimus quam prīmum Parthenōnem, templum Minervae, vidēre. In monte stat quī
5 Acropolis appellātur. Huius montis portae, quārum nōmen est Propylaea, tam pulchrae sunt ut eō tempore diū spectantēs steterīmus. Ad Propylaea est templum parvum in quō est statua Victōriae sine ālīs facta. Cum dē hāc rogāvissēmus, respōnsum est: 'Dea Victōria ita facta est nē ab urbe discēderet.' Saepe dictum est Parthenōnem pulcherrimum esse omnium
10 aedificiōrum; cum per Propylaea prōcessissēmus et ad Parthenōnem ipsum vēnissēmus, hoc intellegere poterāmus. In eō est statua Athēnae, altior quam sex virī. Dea ipsa ex ebore² facta est, vestis et arma ex aurō. Ita īnsignis est ut nēmō eam nōn permōtus spectāre possit, nēmō memoriam eius dēpōnere possit. Cum Parthenōnem vīdissēmus, ad aliud
15 templum Athēnae prōcessimus, cuius in porticū³ sunt columnae in fōrmā fēminārum. Cum Acropolis relīcta esset, in Agoram dēscendimus. Ibi, inter alia, aedificium ā Caesare Augustōque factum vīdimus.

"Cum in urbe multōs diēs fuissēmus, et cotīdiē multa alia clāra loca invenīre potuissēmus, haec optima vīsa sunt: Stadium; Olympiēum,
20 maximum templum Graeciae; Acadēmia, quae mīlle passibus ab urbe abest et in quā clārī philosophī docent. Tempus tam breve est et nōs tam dēfessī sumus ut lūdīs in theātrō habitīs nōndum adfuerīmus; theātrum autem vīdimus, et exīstimāmus id pulcherrimum esse.

"Sed urbs tanta est ut nōndum omnia loca aedificiaque amplissima ā
25 nōbīs inventa sint. Sed quam prīmum ea petēmus et dē eīs scrībēmus."

Cum litterae lēctae essent, Rūfus multa alia dē Athēnīs tam grāta nārrāvit ut tandem Secunda dīceret, "Ōh! Quō tempore ego, mī⁴ pater, discēdam⁵ ad illam scholam? Ad eam urbem tam pulchram statim prōcēdere cupiō!"

Questions

1. What had the boys wanted to see first in Athens?
2. Where was it located, and what building stood in front of it?
3. What is distinctive about the temple situated near the Propylaea?
4. Why was the statue of Victory made without wings?
5. How high was the statue of Athena, and what was it made of?
6. What was distinctive about the "other" temple to Athena?
7. What buildings seemed most impressive to them?
8. How many plays did they see?
9. What was Secunda's reaction after reading the letter?

GRAMMAR

Perfect System of the Subjunctive, Active and Passive

The *perfect active subjunctive* looks very much like the future perfect active indicative, with one exception. The first person singular, **portāverim**, ends in **-rim** instead of **-rō**. Unlike the future perfect indicative, the perfect subjunctive has long **-ī-** before the personal endings in the tense sign **-erī-**, except, of course, before the final **-m, -t,** and **-nt.** See the Grammar Appendix, pp. 520–530 for a review of the *past perfect active subjunctive.*

To form the *perfect passive* and *past perfect passive subjunctive,* use the present and imperfect subjunctive of **sum** with the perfect passive participle.

> The perfect subjunctive, like the perfect indicative, states an act as finished from the present point of view; while the past perfect subjunctive, like the past perfect indicative, represents an act as finished from the past point of view.

PERFECT ACTIVE			PERFECT PASSIVE		
	Similarly,				Similarly,
portāverim	docuerim, etc.			sim	doctus, -a, -um sim, etc.
portāverīs	posuerim, etc.	portātus, -a, um	{	sīs	positus, -a, -um sim, etc.
portāverit	cēperim, etc.			sit	captus, -a, -um sim, etc.
portāverīmus	mūnīverim, etc.			sīmus	mūnītus, -a, -um sim, etc.
portāverītis		portātī, -ae, a	{	sītis	
portāverint				sint	

PAST PERFECT ACTIVE (Lesson XVI)			PAST PERFECT PASSIVE		
	Similarly,				Similarly,
portāvissem	docuissem, etc.			essem	doctus, -a, -um essem, etc.
portāvissēs	cēpissem, etc.	portātus, -a, -um	{	essēs	positus, -a, -um essem, etc.
portāvisset	posuissem, etc.			esset	captus, -a, -um essem, etc.
portāvissēmus	mūnīvissem, etc.			essēmus	mūnītus, -a, -um essem, etc.
portāvissētis		portātī, -ae, a	{	essētis	
portāvissent				essent	

Practice

1. Give the first person singular of **intellegō,** the second person singular of **ferō,** the third person singular of **līberō,** and the third person plural of **reficiō** in all tenses of the subjunctive, active and passive.

2. Tell the form of **prehendātur, cōnsēnsisset, contemnī, contempsī, potuerīs, incēnsus sit, dolērent, ruptī essent, vexissēmus, exīstimārem, sītis.**

Summary of Sequence of Tenses

In Lesson XII, page 82, and in Lesson XVI, page 102, you were given an introduction to the *sequence of tenses*. The principles summarized here are easy enough to see in operation when you are translating from Latin to English, and important to use when you are translating from English to Latin.

PRIMARY TENSES (referring to the present or future)
    Indicative: Present, future, future perfect
    Subjunctive: Present or perfect

SECONDARY TENSES (referring to the past)
    Indicative: Imperfect, perfect,[6] past perfect
    Subjunctive: Imperfect or past perfect

Primary tenses are followed by primary tenses, secondary by secondary.

    Cum Rūfus litterās lēgisset...   *When (once, after) Rufus had read the letter . . .*

Notice how **cum** with the past perfect subjunctive can also be translated by *once* or *after.*

[6] The perfect, even when translated with *has* or *have,* is generally regarded as secondary.

This statue of Victory (Nike) was found in the Aegean on the island of Samothrace where it had been placed to commemorate a Greek naval victory in the second century B.C. She appears to be alighting on the prow of the winning admiral's ship, with the wind sweeping back her garments. The rigid marble from which she and her clothing have been carved has been miraculously transformed into something fluid and almost transparent. This masterpiece of Hellenistic art is now one of the chief attractions at the Louvre in Paris.

Erich Lessing/Art Resource, NY

The Olympieum, in Athens, is one of the largest Greek temples known. It was begun by the Athenians in the sixth century B.C. and finally finished by the Roman emperor Hadrian, a great admirer of Greek culture, in the second century A.D. Note the height of the majestic Corinthian columns.

Bettmann/CORBIS

Translation

1. When Publius had been in the city a few days, he sent a letter to his father.
2. When Publius' sister had read his long letter, she asked many things about Athens.
3. The city was so large that he had not been able to see all the famous places.
4. A little later, when he stood before the Parthenon, he exclaimed, "This is the most beautiful of all temples!"

Three orders of classical architecture illustrated here, Doric *(top left),* Corinthian *(right),* and Ionic *(bottom),* are notably different in the capitals of their columns. The Doric is the simplest, the Corinthian the most ornate. The Ionic capital is distinguished by its rolled shape.

VOCABULARY

Nouns

āla, -ae f. *wing*   (alate)
passus, -ūs m. *step, pace;* **mīlle passūs** *mile*   (pass, pace)
   (pl. **mīlia passum**)

Adjective

dēfessus, -a, -um *tired*

Verb

dēpōnō, -ere, -posuī, -positus   **[pōnō]**
   put aside, put down

Adverbs

nōndum *not yet*
quam prīmum *as soon as possible*
statim *at once, immediately*
tandem *finally, at last*   (tandem)

WORD STUDY

Suffixes For the meaning and use of **-ilis,** *(-ile, -il),* **-bilis** *(-ble, -able, -ible),* **-āris** *(-ar),* **-ārius** *(-ary),* consult the Grammar Appendix, p. 510. Give the English forms of **agilis, fertilis, memorābilis, possibilis, volūbilis, particulāris, necessārius.**

What are the Latin words from which are derived *facile, docile, delectable, defensible, fragile, noble, popular, primary?* Find five other examples of each of the suffixes *-ble (-able, -ible), -ar,* and *-ary* in English words derived from Latin words already studied.

Did You Know?

The Roman mile was one thousand paces **(mīlle passūs),** close to 1620 yards (1480 meters or 4860 feet). The mile as measured in the United States and Great Britain is 1760 yards (1610 meters or 5280 feet). Try this out: pace off a thousand paces on a running track whose length you know accurately. Measure the distance you have covered. Which are you more nearly like, the Roman soldiers and engineers who established the Roman mile, or the Englishmen who, prior to the nineteenth century, gave us a mile close in length to the one we use today?

LESSON XVIII

LESSON OBJECTIVE
• Deponent Verbs

A REQUEST FOR FUNDS

Pūblius patrī et mātrī et sorōribus suīs s. p. d.[1] Sī valētis, bene est; valeō. Cum magnō gaudiō litterās vestrās hodiē accēpī, quās ante vīgintī quīnque diēs[2] scrīpsistis. Cum litterās lēgissem, Fūriānō eās dedī ut legeret. Cum dē Rōmā et amīcīs nostrīs locūtī essēmus, Fūriānus dīxit Rōmam longē abesse. Sed fēlīcēs sumus, nam amīcōs hīc habēmus, et urbs 5 pulcherrima est.

   Vīta nostra tam quiēta est ut paene nihil scrībere possim. Sed tamen ūna rēs est dē quā scrībere necesse est. Potesne, pater, sine morā pecūniam mittere? Doleō quod haec scrībere necesse est, sed nōn est mea culpa. Omnia enim in hāc urbe tam cāra sunt ut paene tōta pecūnia mea 10 cōnsūmpta sit. Enchōriō magister tam amīcus est ut multī mē fīlium, nōn discipulum eius, esse arbitrentur. Sum tōtōs diēs cum eō et saepe noctis partem, nam mēcum saepe cēnat. Hīs temporibus dē multīs rēbus ita bene loquitur ut multa ūtilia audiam. Ob hanc causam eum saepe ad cēnam vocō. Hōc modō pecūnia celeriter cōnsūmitur. 15

   Etiam ob aliam causam pecūniam habēre necesse est. Cum ab Enchōriōne multa dē partibus Graeciae dicta essent, dē Delphīs eum

[1] See Lesson XIV, note 1, page 90.
[2] *twenty-five days ago* (literally, *before twenty-five days*)

Michael Nicholson/CORBIS

Praetereā locus ipse pulcherrimus erat—et est. The great natural beauty of Delphi, in the mountains about 75 miles west of Athens, never fails to fill the visitor with a sense of wonder. In the foreground is a Greek theater which was restored by the Romans.

rogāvī. Ille respondit omnēs Delphōs propriīs oculīs vidēre dēbēre. Itaque
quam celerrimē proficīscī cupimus ut illum locum videāmus. Enchōriō
20 pollicitus est nōbīscum proficīscī et omnia mōnstrāre atque explicāre.
Arbitror eum omnia scīre. Ita bene verba facit ut omnēs discipulōs mīrō
modō affēcerit. Valēte.

Questions

1. How long did the letter from Publius' parents take to arrive in Athens?
2. Why was Publius happy?
3. What was Publius' chief reason for writing a reply?
4. Why was it necessary for him to write?
5. Where has a lot of Publius' money gone?
6. What justification does Publius give for having his teacher over
   to dinner?
7. What is the other reason he needs money?
8. In what way will Enchorio take part in the trip?

GRAMMAR

Deponent Verbs

Some Latin verbs are *active* in meaning but *passive* in form. They are
called *deponents,* because they have *put away* (**dēpōnō**) their active forms:
arbitror, *I think,* (not *I am thought*). Deponent verbs are found in all four
conjugations and are conjugated throughout the indicative and subjunctive
like the passive of regular verbs of their respective conjugations.

Participles and Infinitives of Deponent Verbs

Note that some of the participles and infinitives of deponent verbs do
not follow this rule. The present and future participles and the future
infinitive (formed from the future participle) are active in both form and
meaning. The perfect participle and perfect infinitive, while passive in
form, are active in meaning.

	PARTICIPLES	FORM	MEANING
PRESENT	**arbitrāns** *thinking*	active	active
PERFECT	**arbitrātus** *having thought*	passive	active
FUTURE	**arbitrātūrus** *going to think*	active	active
	INFINITIVES	FORM	MEANING
PRESENT	**arbitrārī** *to think*	passive	active
PERFECT	**arbitrātus esse** *to have thought*	passive	active
FUTURE	**arbitrātūrus esse** *to be going to think*	active	active

Remains near Delphi of the Rotunda Temple at the Sanctuary of Athena. Originally on this extremely ancient site (perhaps occupied since 5000 B.C.), a shrine was dedicated to the worship of an Earth Goddess. Later the area was dedicated to the gods of Olympus, especially Athena, the goddess of wisdom, who preserved reverence for the female aspects of civilization as a legacy of the Earth Mother. The temple itself, built in the fourth century B.C., has a circular shape unusual in Greece.

Practice

1. Give and translate the third person singular of **proficīscor** and the third person plural of **polliceor** in all tenses of the indicative.
2. Give the second person singular of **arbitror** and the second person plural of **loquor** in all tenses of the subjunctive.
3. Give all the participles of **proficīscor** and the infinitives of **loquor.**

Translation

1. When Publius had spent all his money, he sent a letter to his father.
2. He said that his teacher spoke so well that he often invited him to dinner.
3. He wrote that his teacher had promised to set out with him (**sēcum**) to see Delphi.
4. Publius was with him so often (**totiēns**) that many thought that he was the teacher's son.

VOCABULARY

Nouns

culpa, -ae f. *blame, fault*   (culpable, exculpate)
gaudium, -i n. *joy*

Adjectives

cārus, -a, -um *dear, expensive, esteemed*   (cherish)
fēlīx, -īcis (gen.) *happy, fortunate, successful* (felicitation)
necesse *necessary* (indeclinable)
quiētus, -a, -um *quiet*   **[quiēs]**
vīgintī *twenty* (indeclinable)

Verbs

arbitror, arbitrārī, arbitrātus *think*   (arbitrate, arbitration)
cōnsūmō, -ere, -sūmpsī, -sūmptus   **[sūmō]**
  use up, spend
loquor, loquī, locūtus *talk*   (loquacious, circumlocution)
polliceor, pollicērī, pollicitus *promise*
proficīscor, proficīscī, profectus *set out, start*

Adverb

hīc *here, in this place*   **[hic]**

WORD STUDY

Science Derivatives Thousands of words used in all branches of science and technology come from Greek and Latin roots. Here are a few examples: *antenna* in Latin means *sail yard; carbon* is from **carbō**, *coal; detector* (**dē, tegō**); *deterrent* (**dē, terreō**); *element* (**elementum,** *first principle*); *exhaust* (**ex, hauriō**); *flux* (**fluō**); *neutron* (**neuter**); *nucleus, nuclear, thermonuclear* (**nucleus,** *little nut,* from **nux,** *nut; thermo-* is from a Greek word meaning *heat*) *operational* (**opus**); *radar, radiation, ray* (**radius,** *ray*); *rotate* (**rota,** *wheel*); *sensor* (**sentiō**); *vehicle* (**vehō**).

Look up the meanings of the Latin words you do not understand in the dictionary at the back of this book.

LESSON XIX

A WEDDING

Pūbliō in Graeciā studente, rēs grātissima Rōmae[1] agēbātur—nūptiae
Caeciliae, sorōris Pūblī, et M. Iūnī Vorēnī. Paucīs mēnsibus ante Caeciliīs
Iūniīsque in ātrium Rūfī cum amīcīs ingressīs, pater Vorēnī cum fīliō ante
Rūfum et Caeciliam cōnstiterat Rūfumque rogāverat: "Spondēsne fīliam
tuam fīliō meō uxōrem?"[2] Rūfus responderat: "Spondeō." Tum Vorēnus   5
Caeciliae ānulum,[3] Caecilia Vorēnō pulchrum servum dederat, et patrēs
inter sē dē dōte[4] ēgerant—quantum Rūfus in animō habēret dare, quō
modō pecūnia parārī posset.

    Tandem diēs nūptiārum aderat. Prīdiē Caecilia mūnera Laribus dederat;[5]
nunc, sōle oriente, ōminibus optimīs nūntiātīs, ā mātre ad nūptiās   10
parābātur, et cum eā amīcae loquēbantur. Māter flammeum[6] et deinde
corōnam in caput Caeciliae posuit.

    "Mīror quid frāter meus agat," dīxit Caecilia, "et quid arbitrātūrus sit,
nūntiō dē mē allātō."[7]

    Nunc Caecilia cum mātre amīcīsque in ātrium adōrnātum dēscendit, ubi   15
Rūfus et pontifex exspectābant. Cum Vorēnus et amīcī in ātrium ingressī
essent, prōnuba[8] manūs Caeciliae et
Vorēnī iūnxit, et Caecilia dīxit, "Ubi tū
Gāius, ego Gāia."[9] Eīs nunc sedentibus,
pontifex deōs (maximē Iūnōnem)   20
vocāvit. Deinde omnēs "Fēlīciter!"
clāmāvērunt. "Spērō vōbīs omnia bona
futūra esse, vītam vestram longam!"

    "Nōn iam nostra est," Rūfus Vorēnō
dīxit, "sed tua."   25

    Nōnā hōrā cēna maxima allāta est, et
Rūfus nūntiāvit, "Nōs cibō reficiāmus."
Omnēs uxōrem pulchram mīrātī sunt.

[1] *at Rome*
[2] *(as) wife*
[3] *ring*
[4] *dowry*
[5] On the eve of her marriage, the Roman girl dedicated her toys and childhood clothes to the household gods.
[6] *bridal veil* (flame-colored)
[7] from **afferō**
[8] the *matron* who attended the bride
[9] an old formula, equivalent to *Where you are John Doe, I am Mary Doe*, i.e., using generic rather than real names

Nimatallah/Art Resource, NY

The bride and groom ate a special cake. Then there was a procession to the bride's new home, where her husband was waiting for her. After a ceremony, the groom carried his bride over the threshold. This husband and wife are depicted on a sarcophagus in Rome.

14 With these gifts, symbols of the
essentials of domestic life, the
bride becomes the mistress of the
house.

Vesperī omnēs in viam sē recēpērunt. Ibi, mātre flente et Caeciliam
30 retinente, aliī pompam parāvērunt. Subitō Vorēnus Caeciliam rapuit ex
amplexū[10] mātris et pompa profecta est, amīcīs canentibus, rīdentibus,
"Talassiō!"[11] clāmantibus. Cum ad iānuam domūs Vorēnī accessissent,
Caecilia eam vittīs[12] adōrnāvit. Postquam Vorēnus uxōrem per iānuam
portāvit,[13] Caecilia iterum dīxit, "Ubi tu Gāius, ego Gāia." In ātriō Vorēnus
35 mātrōnae novae ignem aquamque dedit.[14] Posterō diē cēna altera data est,
ubi Caecilia deīs sacrificāvit. Familia eius nōn iam Caecilia, sed Iūnia erat.

Questions

1. Who was engaged to marry?
2. Where did the formal ceremony for engagement take place, and who
   was involved?
3. What exchange took place at that time?
4. What preparations were made the day before the wedding, and how was
   the bride dressed?
5. What did the matron do at the wedding?
6. What did the priest do?
7. What did everybody say to wish them well?
8. What events or actions signify that Caecilia now belongs to Vorenus'
   family?
9. Was the significance of Vorenus' gift to his bride real or symbolic?
10. What Roman customs persist in marriage ceremonies today?

In this second century A.D.
relief, the matron, in the rear,
embraces the bridal couple as
they join hands. One of the
witnesses stands to the right.
The groom holds what may be
the marriage contract. In earlier
days, beards were rare among
Roman men.

Ronald Sheridan/Ancient Art & Architecture Collection

GRAMMAR

Review of Personal Pronouns

The personal pronouns for the first and second persons are as follows. The third person personal pronoun is **is, ea, id,** *(he, she, it)* which was reviewed earlier in Lesson VIII.

	SINGULAR	PLURAL		SINGULAR	PLURAL
NOM.	**ego** *I*	**nōs** *we*		**tū** *you* (sing.)	**vōs** *you* (pl.)
GEN.	**meī** *of me*, etc.	**nostrum (nostrī)** *of us*, etc.		**tuī** *of you*, etc.	**vestrum (vestrī)** *of you*, etc.
DAT.	**mihi**	**nōbīs**		**tibi**	**vōbīs**
ACC.	**mē**	**nōs**		**tē**	**vōs**
ABL.	**mē**	**nōbīs**		**tē**	**vōbīs**

Review of Reflexive Pronouns

The reflexive pronouns for the first and second persons are the same as the preceding personal pronouns in form, except that there is no nominative. Since a reflexive refers *back* to the nominative, it does not have a nominative form.

In the third person singular and plural, Latin has separate reflexive pronoun forms used in place of **is, ea, id.** The forms and meanings are as follows.

	SINGULAR AND PLURAL
NOM.	—
GEN.	**suī** *of himself/herself/itself/oneself/themselves*
DAT.	**sibi**, etc.
ACC.	**sē (sēsē)**
ABL.	**sē (sēsē)**

laus suī	*praise of oneself*
Ānulōs sibi ēmērunt.	*They bought rings for themselves.*
Nōs cibō reficiāmus.	*Let's refresh ourselves with food.*
Caecilia sē laudāvit.	*Caecilia praised herself.*
Corōnam ā sē remōvit.	*He/she took off the wreath (i.e., removed the wreath from himself/herself.)*

Nota•Bene

If a direct question requires a *yes/no* answer, it is introduced by **num** in the indirect question.

DIRECT: **Pecūniamne invēnistī?** *Did you find the money?*

INDIRECT: **Rogāvit num pecūniam invēnissem.** *He asked whether I had found the money.*

Practice

1. Conjugate reflexively and translate the present and perfect tenses of **ego mē moneō, tū tē monēs,** etc.; **ego mihi crēdō,** etc.
2. Give the third person singular active of **sē contemnere** in all tenses of the indicative and subjunctive.
3. Translate **ab eīs, nōbīscum, dē tē, sēcum.**

Indirect Questions

An *indirect question* in Latin is introduced by a verb of *asking, knowing, saying, perceiving,* etc. and an *interrogative* word. In the indirect question, the verb of the original direct question is in the subjunctive and follows the rule for sequence of tenses. Compare the following direct and indirect questions.

Quid frāter meus agit?	*What is my brother doing?*
Mīror quid frāter meus agat.	*I wonder what my brother is doing.*
Patrēs inter sē dē dōte ēgerant—quantum Rūfus in animō habēret dare.	*The fathers had discussed the dowry between themselves— how much Rufus intended to give.*

Observe:

The first sentence is a simple, *direct* question, and the Latin verb is in the *indicative*.

The second sentence is complex, containing the same question but in *indirect* form, reduced to a subordinate clause, and its verb in Latin is in the *subjunctive*.

In the last two sentences, the whole subordinate clause is the direct object of the main verb. Indirect questions depend on verbs of *asking, learning, knowing, telling, wondering,* etc. (**rogō, cognōscō, sciō, dīcō, mīror,** etc.) The regular rules of sequence apply.

To review the sequence of tenses, study the following sentences, paying attention to the clocks.

I   Time: 3 P.M.   Place: Schoolroom   *you*

  Rogō quid faciās.
I ask (now) what you are doing (now).
Primary Tense ------ Present Subjunctive

  Rogō quid fēcerīs.
I ask (now) what you did (earlier).
Primary Tense ------ Perfect Subjunctive

  Rogāvī quid facerēs.
I asked (then) what you were doing (then).
Secondary Tense ------ Imperfect Subjunctive

  Rogāvī quid fēcissēs.
I asked (then) what you had done (earlier).
Secondary Tense ------ Past Perfect Subjunctive

Summary of Indirect Statements and Indirect Questions

IN LATIN

Indirect Statements
1. Infinitive
2. No introductory word

Indirect Questions
1. Subjunctive
2. Introduced by an
   interrogative word

IN ENGLISH

1. Indicative
2. Introduced by *that*

1. Indicative
2. Introduced by an
   interrogative word

Translation

1. Caecilia wondered what Publius thought about the wedding.
2. Her (girl) friends asked her how much money was being given.
3. She kept asking herself where Publius then was and what he was doing.
4. When the procession had started, the friends asked themselves how Vorenus and Caecilia would enter.

▦ VOCABULARY

Nouns

ōmen, ōminis n. *omen, sign*   (ominous)

pontifex, pontificis m. *priest*   [pōns + faciō]

vesper, vesperī m. *evening;*   (vespers, vespertine)
  vesperī *in the evening* (loc.)

Adjective

quantus, -a, -um *how great, how much*   (quantum, quantify)

Verbs

ingredior, ingredī, ingressus   (ingredient)
  step into, enter

mīror, 1 *wonder, admire*   [mīrus]

orior, orīrī, ortus *rise*   (orient, oriental)

spondeō, -ēre, spopondī, spōnsus   (respond, spouse)
  promise, pledge, engage

studeō, -ēre, studuī,— *be eager (for), study*   (student, studious)

Adverbs

prīdiē *on the day before*   [diēs]

subitō *suddenly*

WORD STUDY

Spelling The base ending of the Latin present participle (**-ant, -ent, -ient,** according to conjugation) is used as a suffix in English. All English words derived from the first conjugation have *-ant;* most of those derived from the other conjugations have *-ent;* but some derived through the French have *-ant.* Give examples.

The addition of **-ia** to the base ending of the present participle gives a suffix **-antia, -entia** (*-ance, -ence, -ancy, -ency* in English). The same rule for spelling which was given above holds true. Give examples.

Explain *ingredient, loquacity, miracle, orient, quantity, soliloquy, sponsor, vespers.*

THE TRIP TO DELPHI

**LESSON
OBJECTIVES**
• Indefinite Pronouns
  and Adjectives
• Conjugation of **Eō**

Pater Pūbliō pecūniam praebuerat ut is et Fūriānus Delphōs[1] īrent.
Cum diēs cōnstitūtus adesset, ad Enchōriōnem iērunt, quī pollicitus erat
cum eīs īre. Itaque hī trēs cum servīs aliquibus ex urbe Athēnīs exiērunt.

Cūr cupīvērunt Delphōs vidēre? Quod hic locus erat, ut ita dīcam,[2]
templum tōtīus Graeciae. In hōc locō erat īnsigne ōrāculum Apollinis.
Multī ex omnibus partibus terrae vēnērunt ut ōrāculum cōnsulerent.
Praetereā locus ipse pulcherrimus erat—et est.

Itaque amīcī nostrī duo per sacram viam eunt quae ad urbem clāram
Eleusim[3] dūcit et ex illā urbe ad aliam urbem clāram, Thēbās,[3] prōcēdunt.
Cum post paucōs diēs ad fīnem itineris vēnissent, gaudiō et admīrātiōne   10
complētī sunt. Namque urbs sub monte Parnassō[3] posita pulcherrima erat.
Fōrmam maximī theātrī habēbat. Ab[4] ūnā parte erant saxa alta; ab alterā,
arborēs et flūmen et alter mōns.

Haec omnia diū mīrātī ad fontem īnsignem Castalium vēnērunt. Omnēs
quī ōrāculum cōnsulēbant aquā huius fontis sē lavābant. Hic fōns Apollinī   15
Mūsīsque sacer erat.

[1] Like **Delphi,** the names of many
cities are plural, e.g., **Athēnae,
Syracūsae,** etc.
[2] so to speak [literally, *that I may say
(it) so*]
5   [3] Apposition
[4] on (literally, *from*)

Vanni/Art Resource, NY

From the sixth century B.C. on,
many cities of Greece used
Delphi to demonstrate their
reverence for Apollo and their
own prominence by dedicating
buildings called "treasuries" in
which they displayed trophies
from successful battles,
deposited valuable offerings,
and carried out the worship of a
particular cult. Pictured here is
the Treasury of the Athenians
(ca. 490 B.C.), stationed along
the Sacred Way that led upward
to the great Temple of Apollo. In
the first century B.C. Roman
armies raided the site, but later
Roman emperors protected the
sanctuary. Today Delphi rivals
Athens as the principal tourist
attraction in Greece.

[5] *treasuries* (nom. pl. m.); **appellāta** agrees with **aedificia... quae.**

[6] *mottoes*

[7] For the "Seven Wise Men of Greece," see p.125.

[8] *nothing in excess. [literally, lest (you do) anything too much]*

Tum viātōrēs nostrī aedificia aliqua cōnspexērunt quae thēsaurī[5] appellāta sunt. Haec cīvitātēs quaedam Graecae propter victōriam aliquam aedificāvērunt. Auctor quīdam Graecus dīxit Cnidiōs nōn ob rēs in proeliō
20 bene gestās thēsaurum aedificāvisse sed ut opēs suās ostenderent. In hīs aedificiīs et in aliīs partibus urbis erant tria mīlia statuārum.

Hīs aedificiīs vīsīs, templum Apollinis ingressī statim sententiās[6] septem sapientium Graecōrum[7] litterīs magnīs īnscrīptās cōnspexērunt: "Cognōsce tē ipsum," "nē quid nimis,"[8] et cētera. Sed in ōrāculum ipsum
25 ingredī nōn potuērunt quod ōrāculum tam sacrum erat ut paucī ingrederentur.

Itaque ad fontem rediērunt et eum et saxa et arborēs et caelum iterum mīrātī ad cēnam vesperī discessērunt.

Questions

1. Who went on the trip to Delphi, and who provided the funds?

2. What was the chief reason why many people went to Delphi?

3. What two famous cities did they stop at en route to Delphi?

4. Describe the topography (natural setting) of Delphi.

5. What spring did they visit, and why was it important?

6. Why did some Greek city-states erect buildings at Delphi?

7. What was the real reason, according to one Greek author, why the Cnidian Greeks had built their treasury?

8. What proverbs did they see in the temple of Apollo?

9. Why were they prevented from going into the oracle itself?

Did You Know?

Did you know that a *museum* is the "place of the Muses," the home of the goddesses that preside over the arts and sciences? They were the daughters of Zeus and Mnemosyne, goddess of memory, and their principal cults were located on Mt. Olympus and Mt. Helicon. They were naturally associated with the legendary singers, Orpheus and Musaeus, and with Apollo, the god of music and poetry. Their number and functions differed from time to time, but when they were finally assembled into a standard list, they were nine: Calliope (epic poetry), Clio (history), Euterpe (flute-playing), Erato (lyric poetry), Melpomene (tragedy), Thalia (comedy), Polyhymnia (hymns), Urania (astronomy), and Terpsichore (dancing).

Not just poets sought the Muses' blessing; philosophers like Plato and Aristotle incorporated museums in their schools.

Boltin Picture Library

The Temple of Apollo was the goal of those who wished to consult the Delphic Oracle about personal matters or questions of political policy or to secure the god's blessing upon a course of action already decided upon. In its innermost recess, where lay a stone marking the "center of the earth," the Pythian priestess, in a frenzy and waving a laurel branch, gave forth strange utterances which her attendants and the priests of Apollo transformed into an often-ambiguous answer. The oracle at Delphi was the most important of about twenty in the Greek world and played a major role in the early political history of Greece.

GRAMMAR

Indefinite Pronouns and Adjectives

Indefinite pronouns refer to persons and things that are not specifically identified.

After four special words **(si, nisi, nē, and num),** the pronoun **quis** (declined like the interrogative) and the adjective **quī** (defined like the relative)[9] are indefinite and mean *any.* For the declensions, review Lesson VI and the Grammar Appendix, p. 518.

Sī quis mē tanget, dolēbit.	*If anyone touches (will touch) me, he will be sorry.*
Nisi qua puella studēbit, poenam dabit.	*If any girl doesn't study (unless any girl will study), she will pay the penalty.*
Fugiō nē quis mē capiat.	*I am fleeing lest anyone (so that no one may) capture me.*
Nē quid nimis.	*Not anything in excess.*

The indefinite pronoun **aliquis,** a compound of **quis,** often means *someone*—"I don't know who." It is declined like **quis,** except that it has **aliqua** in the nominative and accusative plural neuter.

The indefinite adjective **aliquī, aliqua, aliquod** is declined like the relative pronoun **quī, quae, quod.**[9]

---

[9] But anywhere in the declension of the relative adjective **quae** appears, it *may* be replaced in the indefinite by **qua.** Similarly, in the indefinite adjective, **aliquae** is generally replaced by **aliqua.**

SINGULAR

	MASCULINE + FEMININE	NEUTER
NOM.	**aliquis** *someone*, etc.	**aliquid** *something*, etc.
GEN.	**alicuius**	**alicuius**
DAT.	**alicui**	**alicui**
ACC.	**aliquem**	**aliquid**
ABL.	**aliquō**	**aliquō**

PLURAL

	MASCULINE	FEMININE	NEUTER
NOM.	**aliquī** *some men*, etc.	**aliquae** *some women*, etc.	**aliqua** *some things*, etc.
GEN.	**aliquōrum**	**aliquārum**	**aliquōrum**
DAT.	**aliquibus**	**aliquibus**	**aliquibus**
ACC.	**aliquōs**	**aliquās**	**aliqua**
ABL.	**aliquibus**	**aliquibus**	**aliquibus**

Aliquis dīcat...	*Someone may say . . .*
Propter victōriam aliquam...	*On account of some victory . . .*

Quīdam, *a certain one,* is less indefinite than **quis** and **aliquis.** It often means "someone whose name I could mention but won't"; sometimes it is almost like our indefinite article *a.* It is declined almost like the relative pronoun **quī, quae, quod,**[10] the suffix **-dam** being indeclinable.

The indefinite adjective **quīdam, quaedam, quoddam** is declined like **quīdam** except that it has **quoddam** instead of **quiddam.**

SINGULAR

	MASCULINE	FEMININE	NEUTER
NOM.	**quīdam** *a certain man*, etc.	**quaedam** *a certain woman*, etc.	**quiddam** *a certain thing*, etc.
GEN.	**cuiusdam**	**cuiusdam**	**cuiusdam**
DAT.	**cuidam**	**cuidam**	**cuidam**
ACC.	**quendam**	**quandam**	**quiddam**
ABL.	**quōdam**	**quādam**	**quōdam**

PLURAL

	MASCULINE	FEMININE	NEUTER
NOM.	**quīdam** *certain men*, etc.	**quaedam** *certain women*, etc.	**quaedam** *certain things*, etc.
GEN.	**quōrundam**	**quārundam**	**quōrundam**
DAT.	**quibusdam**	**quibusdam**	**quibusdam**
ACC.	**quōsdam**	**quāsdam**	**quaedam**
ABL.	**quibusdam**	**quibusdam**	**quibusdam**

[10] Except in the neuter nominative singular **quiddam,** the accusative singular **quendam, quandam, quiddam,** and in the genitive plural **quōrundam, quārundam, quōrundam.**

Quendam (quandam) vīdī quī (quae) tē amat.	*I saw a certain fellow (lady) who loves you.*
Quaedam cīvitātēs Graecae thesaurōs aedificāvērunt.	*Certain Greek cities built treasuries.*
Quaedam mātrēs suōs fīliōs nimis amant.	*Certain mothers love their sons too much.*
Quīdam fīliī suās mātrēs nimis amant.	*Certain sons love their mothers too much.*

Conjugation of *Eō*

Eō, īre, iī (īvī), itūrus, which can mean either *go* or *come,* is irregular in the present, future, and perfect. Note that the stem vowel **ī-** is changed to **e-** before **a, o, u.** In the perfect system, **-v-** is often inserted between stem and ending, e.g., **īvī, īvistī,** etc. Since **eō** is intransitive, passive forms are rare.

INDICATIVE			SUBJUNCTIVE
	PRESENT		
eō	īmus	eam	eāmus
īs	ītis	eās	eātis
it	eunt	eat	eant
IMPERFECT	**ībam,** etc.	**īrem,** etc.	
FUTURE	**ībō, ībis,** etc.		
	PERFECT		
iī (īvī)	iimus	**ierim,** etc.	
īstī	īstis		
iit	iērunt		
PAST PERFECT	**ieram,** etc.	**īssem,** etc.	
FUTURE PERFECT	**ierō,** etc.		
INFINITIVES	**īre** (pres. act.)	**īsse** (perf. act.)	**itūrus esse** (fut. act.)
PARTICIPLES	**iēns, euntis** (gen.) (pres. act.)		**itūrus, -a, -um** (fut. act.)
IMPERATIVES	**ī** (sing.) **īte** (pl.)		

For the full conjugation see the Grammar Appendix, p. 529.

Practice

1. Decline in the singular: *if anything; some building; a certain animal.*
2. Give the third person singular of **eō**, the first person plural of **exeō**, and the third person plural of **redeō** in all tenses of the active indicative and subjunctive.

Translation

1. Some often returned to see the place and to consult the oracle.
2. Delphi was so famous that many thousands of people went to see it.
3. This beautiful place was called by some the temple of entire (all of) Greece.
4. Publius got money from his father in order to go to the city (of) Delphi.
5. If anyone desired to consult the oracle about a certain matter, do you know what he did first?

VOCABULARY

Nouns

arbor, -oris f. *tree* (arboreal, arboretum)
fōns, fontis m. *spring, source* (fountain, font)
ops, opis f. *aid;* (pl.) *wealth* (opulent)
saxum, -ī n. *rock*

Pronouns

aliquis, aliquid *someone, something,* [alius + quis]
   anyone, anything
quīdam, quaedam, quiddam *a certain one*
   or *thing*

Adjectives

aliquī, aliqua, aliquod *some, any* [alius + quī]
quīdam, quaedam, quoddam *certain, some*
sapiēns, -ntis (gen.) m. *wise* (sapient, insipid)

Verbs

compleō, -ēre, -ēvī, -ētus *fill* (completion)
eō, īre, iī (īvī), itūrus *go, come*
exeō, exīre, exiī, exitūrus *go out (from)* [eō]
praebeō, -ēre, -uī, -itus *furnish* [prae + habeō]
redeō, -īre, rediī, reditūrus *go back, return* [eō]

Preposition

propter (with acc.) *on account of*

WORD STUDY

Study the following Latin legal phrases used in English.

Supersedeas. *(I command that) you suspend (proceedings).*
Ne exeat. *Let him not go out (of the jurisdiction of the court).*
Caveat emptor. *Let the buyer beware (for he buys at his own risk).*
Scire facias. *(I demand that) you cause to know (why a certain court action should not be carried out).*
Habeas corpus. *(I command that) you have the body (of a certain person brought into court),* a writ issued by a judge to see whether a person is justly imprisoned.

Look up the meanings of **mandamus, nunc pro tunc, post mortem, prima facie, pro bono publico.**

Place names

There are towns named *Delphi* in Indiana and Pennsylvania, and one named *Delphi Falls* in New York. Iowa, North Carolina, and Ohio have towns named *Castalia* and Tennessee has *Castalian Springs. Parnassus* is a town in Virginia and also in Pennsylvania.

The Seven Wise Men of Greece

A common practice of the scholars of antiquity was the drawing up of lists (called *canons*) of persons considered outstanding in their fields. Thus there have been preserved for us canons of The Ten Attic Orators, The Nine Lyric Poets, and The Seven Wise Men. Here is one version of the names of the Seven Wise Men, with one of the sayings each is supposed to have made famous. Many of these men were politicians or poets, as well as philosophers. All of them lived between 620 and 550 B.C.

Cleobulus of Rhodes	*Moderation is the chief good.*
Periander of Corinth	*Forethought in all things.*
Pittacus of Mytilene	*Know your opportunity.*
Bias of Priene	*Too many workers spoil the work.*
Thales of Miletus	*To go into debt brings ruin.*
Chilon of Sparta	*Know thyself.*
Solon of Athens	*Nothing in excess.*

The last three mottoes are said to have been inscribed on the temple of Apollo at Delphi. Give some modern counterparts of these sayings.

Duo ex Septem Sapientium Graecōrum. Solon the Athenian, poet and lawgiver *(left)*, brilliantly resolved disputes over land, debts, and the enslavement of citizens, so averting a catastrophic civil war. Thales the Milesian *(right)*, a philosopher best known for his dictum that moisture was the basis of all life, stunned all Greece with his prediction of a solar eclipse in 585 B.C. What task was most difficult for anyone? To "know thyself," he replied.

LESSON XXI

TOTALITARIANISM AND DEMOCRACY

LESSON OBJECTIVES
- Formation and Use of the Future Passive Participle
- Dative of Agent

Quōdam diē Pūblius Fūriānusque cum aliīs adulēscentibus dē Spartā Athēnīsque loquēbantur. "Certē omnibus concēdendum est Spartānōs antīquōs omnium fortissimōs fuisse," ūnus ē Graecīs dīxit; "nōnne Leōnidam memoriā tenēs, quī cum CCC cīvibus apud Thermopylās[1] tam fortiter pugnāvit? Alacrī animō suōs ad id proelium hortātus est quō peritūrī erant."

"Ea quae dīcis nōn negō," alter dīxit, "sed Athēniēnsēs quoque fortēs fuērunt. Fortēs quidem Spartānī fuērunt sed aliās virtūtēs nōn habuērunt. Lycurgus,[2] dux ille antīquus, ob sevēritātem lēgum accūsandus est."

Deinde Fūriānus rogāvit quid Pūblius arbitrārētur. "Concēdō Athēniēnsēs meliōrēs esse," hic respondit. "Vīta dūra puerīs Spartānīs agenda erat. Septem annōs nātī[3] mātrēs relinquēbant ut ad bellum instituerentur. Cēnās ipsī parābant ex pessimīs cibīs, nam Spartānī crēdēbant famem optimum condīmentum cibī esse. Puerī flagellīs[4] caesī sunt, patribus ad patientiam hortantibus, ut dolōrem ferre discerent."

"Etiam peior," quīdam adulēscēns Athēniēnsis dīxit, "erat vīta eōrum quōs Spartānī vīcērunt. Nōn sōlum servī factī sunt sed etiam multae iniūriae eīs ferendae erant. Ā quibusdam sēcrētō[5] observābantur. Ille servus quī faciem hominis līberī habuit caesus est. Vestis servīlis omnibus servīs gerenda erat. Cotīdiē caesī sunt ut memoriā tenērent sē servōs esse."

"Nōn negō vītam servōrum miserrimam esse," Fūriānus dīxit, "sed pessima erat vīta Spartānōrum ipsōrum. Etiam in pāce semper in castrīs habitābant. Lībertās eīs nōn nōta fuit. Omnia prō patriā facienda erant; nihil tamen patria prō populō fēcit. 'Prō bonō pūblicō' significāvit 'prō bonō reī pūblicae,' nōn 'prō bonō cīvium.'"

"Vērum dīcis," Athēniēnsis dīxit. "Memoriā teneāmus verba nōbilis Periclis, quī dīxit rem pūblicam Athēniēnsium in manibus plūrimōrum, nōn paucōrum, esse; cīvibus ēgregiīs omnium generum mūnera pūblica praemia esse; iūra paria omnibus esse. Athēniēnsibus lībertās cārissima fuit; itaque illī nōn īrātī fuērunt sī aliī fēcērunt id quod cupīvērunt. Puerī eōrum in pāce vīxērunt nec ad bellum semper īnstitūtī sunt. Alacrī tamen animō in bellō pugnāvērunt et periērunt. Artēs līberālēs coluērunt; itaque eōrum urbs schola Graeciae fuit."

[1] *at Thermop´ylae,* a mountain pass in Greece
[2] *Lycur´gus,* the Spartan king who was supposed to have originated their way of life
[3] *at the age of seven* (literally, *born seven years*)
[4] *whips*
[5] *secretly.* Often an ablative is used as an adverb.

Pericles, 495–429 B.C., was a major political leader in Athens during a time when Athenian culture and military power were at their height. Among other things, he initiated a great public building program that included the Parthenon.

"Vērum est," Pūblius dīxit; "etiam nunc haec urbs schola est, nōn sōlum
35 Graeciae sed etiam orbis terrārum. Athēnae statuās pulcherrimās, aedificia
ēgregia, librōs optimōs nōbīs dedērunt. Spērō omnēs gentēs semper
Athēnīs, nōn Spartae, similēs futūrās esse."

Questions

1. What claim did one of the Greek youths make about the Spartans?
2. Why was Leonidas famous?
3. For what reason did the second Athenian think Lycurgus should be criticized?
4. How does Publius answer the question, "Which Greek city produced the better citizens?"
5. What do we learn about the life of Spartan boys from Publius?
6. What do we learn about the life of the people the Spartans held as subjects?
7. What three political principles did the Athenian Pericles lay down?
8. What was dearest to the Athenians?
9. What proud title is claimed for Athens in Publius' last remarks? How is the claim supported?
10. What are some factors that might make this picture of Sparta less than fully objective?

GRAMMAR

Future Passive Participle

The *future passive participle* (often called the *gerundive*) is a verbal adjective formed by adding **-ndus, -a, -um** to the present stem of any verb: **porta-ndus, -a, -um** *(about) to be carried*. In the case of **-iō** verbs add **-endus: mūni-endus, capi-endus.** The stem vowel is shortened before **-nd-.**

portandus, -a, -um	*(about) to be carried*
docendus, -a, -um	*(about) to be taught*
ponendus, -a, -um	*(about) to be put*
capiendus, -a, -um	*(about) to be taken*
mūniendus, -a, -um	*(about) to be built*

Practice

Give the future passive participle of **caedō, negō, compleō, excipiō.**

Use of the Future Passive Participle with the Dative of Agent

Omnibus concēdendum est Spartānōs... fortissimōs fuisse.	*It is to be granted by all that the Spartans were the bravest,* i.e., *it must* (or *ought* or *has to) be granted.*

Vīta dūra puerīs Spartānīs agenda erat.	*A hard life had to be lived by Spartan boys.*
Omnia prō patriā eīs facienda erant.	*Everything (all things) had to be done by them for the fatherland.*

Observe:

When used with a form of **sum** as a predicate adjective, the future passive participle naturally expresses *obligation* or *necessity*.

The person upon whom the obligation rests is expressed by the dative; this is called the *dative of agent*.[6] To help you understand how the dative may be used to express agency, consider the following example.

Eīs omnia neganda erant.	*For them everything had to be denied,* i.e., to them fell the need of denying everything, or *They had to deny everything.*

Translation[7]

1. Spartan boys had to be trained for war.
2. What ought to be done by us for our country?
3. Publius asked why Lycurgus had to be blamed by us.
4. Did dinner have to be prepared by the boys themselves?
5. No one need (ought to) embellish (adorn) a beautiful face.

Bettmann/CORBIS

This Roman mosaic shows a skeleton pointing to the Greek motto ΓΝΩΘΙ CAYTON, **gnōthi sauton**, which in Latin is **cognōsce tē ipsum.** The point here is to realize that you are mortal and that life is brief.

---

[6] Distinguish the dative of agent, regularly used with the future passive participle, from the ablative of personal agent with **ā** or **ab,** regularly used with the passive voice of verbs.

[7] Use the future passive participle in each of these sentences.

VOCABULARY

Nouns

adulēscēns, -entis m. *young man*   (adolescent, adolescence)
faciēs, faciēī f. *face, appearance*   (facet, deface)
famēs, -is (abl. **famē**) f. *hunger*   (famine, famish)

Adjective

alacer, -cris, -cre *eager*   (alacrity)

Verbs

accūsō, 1 *blame, criticize*   [causa]
caedō, -ere, cecīdī, caesus *cut, beat, kill*   (fratricide, incision)
concēdō, -ere, -cessī, -cessūrus   [cēdō]
     withdraw, grant
hortor, 1 *urge*   (hortatory, exhortation)
īnstituō, -ere, īnstituī, īnstitūtus   [stō]
     establish, train
negō, 1 *deny, say . . . not*   (negate, negation)
pereō, -īre, -iī, -itūrus *perish*   [eō]
significō, 1 *mean*   [signum + faciō]

Adverb

quoque *too* (follows the word it emphasizes)

Ancient Art and Architecture Collection

"Go, stranger, and tell the Lacedaemonians that we lie here obedient to their laws." So reads the epitaph over Leonidas and his three hundred Spartan companions, who fought and fell at Thermopylae (*Warm Gates*) before the advancing hordes of Xerxes' army. Spartan heroism in that battle, even if futile in its result, established the noble ideal of sacrifice in war for posterity to admire.

The Athenian Ephebic Oath

Athenian boys who were sons of citizens were drafted into the army at thirteen. Known as *ephebi,* they were given military training for two years. The following oath of allegiance that they took is a model for the citizens of any democracy.

> I will not disgrace my sacred arms nor desert my comrade, wherever
>   I am stationed.
> I will fight for things sacred and things profane.
> And both alone and with all to help me I will transmit my fatherland
>   not diminished but greater and better than before.
> I will obey the ruling magistrates who rule reasonably and I will
>   observe established laws and whatever laws in the future may be
>   reasonably established.
> If any person seek to overturn the laws, both alone and with all to
>   help me, I will oppose him.
> I will honor the religion of my fathers.
> I call to witness the Gods . . . the borders of my fatherland, the
>   wheat, the barley, the vines, and the trees of the olive and the fig.[8]

This oath has served as a model for many others, such as the Girl Scout Promise and Law, the Boy Scout oath, the oath of allegiance of naturalized citizens, and the oath taken by those enlisting in the armed forces of the United States.

Athenian Democracy

The famous speech praising Athens, which the Greek historian Thucydides ascribed to the great Athenian leader Pericles, contains many passages which, although they are nearly two thousand five hundred years old, still represent the ideals and hopes of all democratic people today.

> Since our state exists for the many, and not for the few, it is
> called a democracy. Before the law all share equal justice in their
> private disputes, and as for the status of the individual, if a man
> distinguishes himself in any way, he is advanced, not on the basis
> of his class, but of his merit; and not even a poor man, if he is able
> to serve the state, is hindered by the obscurity of his condition. We
> live in freedom, not only in our public affairs, but in our private
> lives as well, not putting on . . . sour . . . looks if our neighbor
> does as he pleases. Yet while we live without constraint as private
> citizens, a sense of reverence prevents us from breaking the
> public laws.

---

[8] Fletcher Harper Swift, "The Athenian Ephebic Oath in American Schools and Colleges," trans. Clarence A. Forbes, *University of California Publications in Education* 11 (1947): p. 4.

We are lovers of beauty, yet simple in our tastes, and we cultivate the mind without loss of manliness. We use our money not for talk or show, but when there is a real need for it . . . It is a disgrace, not for a man to admit poverty, but to do nothing to avoid it.

We regard a person who takes no part in public affairs not just as an unambitious but rather as a useless person, and we are all, if not originators of state policy, as least sound judges of it.

To sum up: I say that Athens is the school of Greece, and that our individual citizen seems to adapt himself independently, and with the utmost versatility and grace, to the greatest variety of activities.[9]

---

[9] Thucydides, *History of the Peloponnesian War* II, 35–46.

ATHLETICS, PATRIOTISM, AND FREEDOM

Quōdam diē Pūblius et Fūriānus ē scholā cum duōbus adulēscentibus
Graecīs exiērunt. Accidit ut per viās gradientēs statuam virī currentis, ā
clārō Myrōne[1] factam, cōnspicerent. Itaque cōnstitērunt ut eam spectārent.

"Nōnne Graecī semper virōs currentēs amant?" Pūblius quaesīvit.

"Sī quis celerrimē currit," respondit ūnus ē Graecīs, "cārissimus urbis
suae est; et sī quis in lūdīs Olympicīs vincit, cārissimus est tōtīus Graeciae.
Illī lūdī, īnsignēs et antīquissimī, in urbe Olympiā Iovī celebrantur. Hōc
ipsō annō habentur et post quattuor annōs iterum habēbuntur. Indutiīs[2] per
tōtam Graeciam factīs, ad hanc urbem virī ex omnibus urbibus Graeciae
eunt ut ibi contendant. Virō sē nōn dignō modō gerentī, virō quī fraudem
fēcit, nōn permittitur ut contendat. Victōrēs corōnās, statuās, carmina
accipiunt."

"Nōnne audīvī dē quōdam virō quī tempore magnī perīculī longē
cucurrit?" Fūriānus quaesīvit.

5

10

[1] *Myron,* a Greek sculptor

[2] *truce* (pl., translate as sing.). To allow travel to the Olympic Games to take place, hostilities between the Greek city-states were suspended.

Scala/Art Resource, NY

The ancient Greeks embraced the ideal of a sound body and a sound mind, and regular physical workouts were a part of their daily routine and education. Wrestling and boxing were among the original Olympic events, along with many of the field events you can see at a track meet today. This portrait of an exhausted boxer, now in a Roman museum, is a masterpiece of realistic Hellenistic art. This man was probably a professional—notice his battered face and the gloves made of leather straps with metal studs, designed to inflict as much damage as possible. He seems to be looking up at his trainer, wondering if he should stand up for the next round.

name as Philippides; perhaps they have confused two different men. That one man could run the 149 miles from Marathon to Sparta at such speed is not impossible (in 1983 a runner covered the distance in 22 hours), but that he could then turn around, run back to Marathon, fight in the battle, and then run back 26 miles to Athens, seems quite impossible. Nevertheless, it is a wonderful story of endurance, even with its tragic ending, and the battlefield has given its name to the long-distance run (26.22 miles or 42.195 kilometers) that now climaxes the Olympic Games.

15 "Pheidippidēs[3] erat," respondit alter ē Graecīs. "Nūntius eī portandus erat. Ducēs Persārum, cum multīs mīlibus mīlitum in Graeciam prōgressī, ad campum quī Marathōn appellātur dēscendērunt. Athēniēnsēs cōnstituērunt ut Pheidippidēs quīdam ad urbem Spartānōrum īret ut auxilium peteret. Etsī haec urbs circiter centum quīnquāgintā mīlia 20 passuum aberat, ille secundō diē ad eam pervēnit et eōs hortātus est ut auxilium mitterent. Spartānī autem ob fēriās cōnstituērunt nē īrent. Itaque Athēniēnsibus sōlīs Persae dūrī expellendī erant, et Graecia servāta est. Post hoc proelium ad urbem Athēnās celeriter cucurrit sed posteāquam in urbem pervēnit 'Victōria!' clāmāns subitō mortuus est."

25 "Graecī fortēs sunt," dīxit Pūblius, amīcīs suīs Graecīs relīctīs. "Nōnne mīrāris quō modō accidat ut Rōmānōs nōn vīcerint?"

Questions

1. What did Publius and Furianus see one day while walking through the streets?
2. What observation does Publius make about fast runners?
3. How often were the ancient Olympics held, and in whose honor were they held?
4. What prizes were the victors given?
5. What was Pheidippides' mission?
6. What was the need for speed?
7. What was the result of his mission? Why?
8. When did he die?
9. What are some answers to the indirect question posed by Publius at the end of the passage?

After the re-institution of the Olympic Games in 1896 in Athens, participation has gradually become global and the variety of competitions greatly increased. Women, who had their own games in ancient Olympia but were not allowed to compete at the men's Olympics, were admitted to the modern games in 1900, and some of their contests have become even more popular and exciting than the men's. Although the games are meant to honor individual prowess, the tendency to make them showplaces of national pride has seemed irresistible, both then and now. Can you translate **citius, altius, fortius,** the motto of the Olympic Games?

Duomo/CORBIS

GRAMMAR

Noun Clauses [4]

You have already studied *indirect questions* (Lesson XIX) in which the whole clause containing the indirect question can be considered an object of the main verb and therefore the equivalent of a noun. Here are two more types of *noun clauses,* in which the whole object clause can be thought of as a noun and in which the verb is in the subjunctive.

Volitive Noun Clauses (Indirect Commands)

Verbs expressing the subject's *will, command, request, advice, decision,* etc.,[5] generally have as objects clauses introduced by **ut** or **nē** with the verb in the subjunctive and following the sequence of tenses.

Cōnstituērunt ut statuam spectārent.	*They decided that they would look at the statue,* or *They decided to look at the statue.*
Petīvit ā Spartānīs ut auxilium ferrent.	*He sought from the Spartans that they bring aid,* or *He asked the Spartans to bring aid.*
Persuāsit (imperāvit) mihi ut librum legerem.	*She persuaded (ordered) me that I should read the book,* or *She persuaded (ordered) me to read the book.*

Noun Clauses of Result

Some clauses of result are also the equivalent of nouns. Verbs meaning *happen* (such as **accidō**), *cause, bring about, effect* (such as **efficiō**), or *permit* (such as **permittō**) are generally followed by a result clause introduced by **ut,** with the verb in the subjunctive, following the sequence of tenses. The negative in these clauses is **nōn.**

Accidit ut... statuam... cōnspicerent.	*It happened that they caught sight of the statue,* or, freely, *They happened to catch sight of the statue.*
Effēcērunt ut Persae Graeciam nōn occupārent.	*They brought it about that the Persians did not occupy Greece.*

---

[4] also called *substantive clauses*

[5] Such verbs take different constructions: **imperō, mandō, persuadeō** take the dative of the person ordered, persuaded, etc.; **moneō, ōrō, rogō** take the accusative of the person warned, begged, asked, etc.; **petō, quaerō, postulō** take the ablative with **ab (ā)** of the person asked.

Practice

In the reading, identify the type of every clause in which the verb is subjunctive.

Translation

1. Did the messenger ask the Spartans[6] not to send aid?
2. By his speed he caused the Persians[6] to be defeated.
3. A messenger had to be sent to the city by the Greeks.
4. The Greeks determine that the defeated general should pay the penalty.

VOCABULARY

Nouns

campus, -ī m. *plain*   (campus, champagne)
fēriae, -ārum f. *festival, holidays*

Verbs

gradior, gradī, gressus *step, walk*   (grade, gradient)
morior, morī, mortuus *die*   [mors]
prōgredior, prōgredī, prōgressus   [gradior]
   step forward, advance
quaerō, -ere, quaesīvī, quaesītus   (query, quest)
   seek (from), inquire (of)

Adverb

circiter *about*   [circum]

Conjunction

etsī *although*

---

[6] Make this the subject of the verb in the subordinate clause.

WORD STUDY

Suffixes For the meaning and use of the suffixes **-ānus** *(-an, -ane, -ain)*, **-ālis** *(-al)*, **-icus** *(-ic)*, **-īlis** *(-ile, -il)*, **-īvus** *(-ive)*, **-ōsus** *(-ous, -ose)*, see the Grammar Appendix, p. 510. Give the English forms of **hūmānus, urbānus, mortālis, cīvicus, virīlis, āctīvus, cūriōsus, bellicōsus.**

What must be the Latin words from which the English words *meridian, certain, liberal, classic, passive,* and *morose* are derived? Give three other examples of each of the above suffixes in English words.

Frequently several suffixes are used together in the same word. Sometimes these are joined together so closely that we think of them as one suffix. Particularly common is the attachment of noun suffixes to adjectives to form nouns, and vice versa: *simil-ar-ity, hum-an-ity, fert-il-ity, act-iv-ity.* Sometimes several adjective suffixes are used together: *republ-ic-an.*

Out of the Latin participle **nātus** we make the noun *nat-ion,* then the adjective *nat-ion-al,* then the verb *nat-ion-al-ize,* then the noun *nat-ion-al-iza-tion.* Sometimes even more suffixes are used.

Do you know any towns named *Olympia, Marathon,* or *Sparta?*

Archivo e Studio Folco Quilici

A copy of the *Discus Thrower,* or *Discobolus,* by the Greek sculptor Myron (fifth century B.C.), noted for his ability to portray figures in action. Unfortunately, the original bronze statue, much more carefully crafted, has been lost.

Did You Know?

The Battle of Marathon, 490 B.C., was a major turning point in history. It represents the first time that a group of free citizens, the Athenians, having settled their differences (there had been many) and having established a government in which each citizen had a vote (although slaves did not), were able to band together with other allies to protect their own liberty and defeat the much larger forces of an absolute ruler, Darius, King of Persia. Ten years later, after Thermopylae, at the naval battle of Salamis (479 B.C.), they were again the saviors of Greek freedom against an even more formidable Persian monarch, Xerxes, Darius' son. Thereupon the Athenians used their naval power to establish their own empire over their one-time allies, using the tribute exacted from them to beautify Athens rather than defend them against the waning threat from Persia. In the last quarter of that century, Sparta, fearing Athens' growing domination, attacked and brought Athens to its knees. This left a power vacuum which Thebes filled until the Macedonians, at the end of the fourth century B.C., under Philip and his son Alexander the Great, conquered all of Greece, the Middle East, and even Egypt. Thereafter, Macedonians controlled the eastern end of the Mediterranean; Greek colonies in Italy and the Carthaginian and Etruscan commercial empires controlled its western end until the rise of Rome. After the expulsion of the kings (509 B.C.), Rome's experience with representative government and elected officials, although the patrician senators only gradually and grudgingly granted political rights to the plebeians, lasted for nearly five centuries, until Rome, after a century of civil war, turned from a republic into an empire under a single man, Augustus Caesar. So ancient history teaches us that power is regularly abused and results in despotism, that peoples have often had to fight to win the right to govern themselves, and that freedom, once it has been won, is fragile and must be vigilantly guarded.

NATIONAL HEROES

LESSON OBJECTIVES
- Formation and Use of the Gerund
- Expressions of Purpose with the Gerund and Future Passive Participle

Dē virīs clārīs Pūblius et Fūriānus saepe cum adulēscentibus duōbus Graecīs loquēbantur. Pūbliō maximē grātum erat dē Graecō Dēmosthene audīre—quī puer vōcem pessimam habuerat, sed quī eam exercuerat loquendō ad lītus maris, clāmandō dum currit,[1] prōnūntiandō dum aliquid in ōre habet;[1] et quī tandem prīmum locum inter omnēs ōrātōrēs attigerat. "Ille sōlus melior quam Cicerō erat et etiam Rōmānīs laudandus et in honōre habendus est," quondam dīxit Pūblius.

Fūriānus dē rēbus mīlitāribus locūtus est factaque Caesaris, Scīpiōnis, Pompeī, Marī nārrāvit. Sed ūnus ē Graecīs dīxit: "Mihi grātissimus imperātōrum Graecōrum est Themistoclēs. Tempore maximī perīculī, potestātem Athēnārum nāvibus summam fēcit, Athēnās optimē mūnīvit, Persārum exercitum tandem ē Graeciā expulit."[2]

"Multī Rōmānī Graecīs similēs sunt," quōdam diē Pūblius dīxit. "Vergilius, clārissimus poēta Rōmānus, quī carmen dē Trōiānīs et dē Rōmā cōnstituendā scrīpsit, similis Homērō est, quī dē bellō Trōiānō scrīpsit. Numa autem, quī temporibus antīquīs lēgēs quās ā deīs accēperat Rōmānīs dedit, similis Solōnī est, quī lēgēs īnstituit ad Athēnās reficiendās."

"At quī Rōmānus philosophīs Graecīs pār est?" alter ē Graecīs quaesīvit. "Cicerō, Lucrētius, quī dē atomīs et dē orīgine hominum rērumque scrīpsit, aliī philosophī Rōmānī—hī ad Graeciam audiendī et discendī causā vēnērunt. Quis Sōcratem memoriā nōn tenet, quī puerōs interrogandō docēbat et eōs ad bene vīvendum īnstituēbat; quī malī[3] expellendī et bonī[3] mōnstrandī grātiā semper labōrābat; quī ob sententiās suās occīsus est?"

"At quī Graecus Augustō nostrō pār est?" respondit Fūriānus. "Periclēs quidem īnsignis erat—Athēnās adōrnāvit, auctōritātem urbis auxit, pāce regēbat. Augustus autem nōn sōlum Rōmam adōrnāvit auxitque—urbem quam ex latere[4] factam accēpit nunc marmoream relinquit—sed etiam nunc omnēs terrās pāce, sapientiā, iūstitiā regit."

Et duo Graecī concessērunt Augustum īnsignem esse.

[1] In translating use the English past tense.

[2] As the Athenians prepared for war, the oracle at Delphi ominously predicted that the Persians would devastate Greece and that "many of the offspring of women" would die, but that her "wooden walls" would save Athens. It was Themistocles, unlike his fellow-generals, who saw that by "wooden walls" was really meant ships of wood, not actual walls. And, after the Persians had overrun much of Greece, at the battle of Salamis (479 B.C.), the Greek fleet, enlarged and made ready by Themistocles' policies, decisively defeated the Persians, who suffered great losses of men. So the Delphic oracle was right on all counts.

[3] Neuter of the adjective, used as a noun: *evil, good*

[4] From **later, lateris**, m., *brick*. Augustus and his subjects were proud of his program of rebuilding and beautifying Rome after the damage done by age and the Civil Wars.

5

10

15

20

25

30

Ronald Sheridan/Ancient Art & Architecture Collection

Ronald Sheridan/Ancient Art & Architecture Collection

Demosthenes (384–322 B.C.) was the greatest orator of the ancient world and a great champion of Athenian freedom. Tradition has it that he perfected his delivery by practicing near the seashore, with pebbles in his mouth, to overcome the sound of the waves. His style was varied, by turns plain and smooth, or fiery, explosive, and grand. A series of his speeches called *Philippics* was an attempt to unite the Athenians against the threat posed by Philip of Macedon, a cause which eventually cost him his life.

The blind poet Homer (eighth century B.C.) is credited with being the author of the two earliest and finest examples of Greek epic poetry, the *Iliad* and the *Odyssey*. Nothing about his life is certain, but it is generally agreed that he was the greatest poet who ever lived.

Questions

1. By what three means did Demosthenes correct his handicaps in speaking?
2. What opinion did Publius have of Demosthenes as an orator?
3. Why did one of the Greeks praise Themistocles?
4. To what Greek was Vergil compared, and what is the basis of the similarity?
5. What is the difference between the ways in which Numa and Solon produced their laws?
6. What did the Roman poet/philosopher Lucretius write about?
7. What four things made Socrates famous?
8. Which of the achievements attributed here to Augustus do you regard as most important?

▦ GRAMMAR

Gerund

The *gerund* corresponds to the English verbal noun ending in *-ing,* as in *We learn by doing.* In Latin it is declined only in the singular; it has no nominative and only four cases, formed by adding **-ndī, -ndō, -ndum, -ndō** to the present stem in the first three conjugations: **portandī, monendī, ponendī,** but with an **-e-** inserted in the **-iō** verbs: **capiendī, mūniendī.** Where the nominative of this verbal noun is needed, Latin uses the present active infinitive.

Vidēre est crēdere.   *See**ing** is believ**ing**.* (English, but in Latin, literally, *To see is to believe*.)

Note these differences between the gerund and the future passive participle (often called the *gerundive*).

GERUND	FUTURE PASSIVE PARTICIPLE
1. Is a *verbal noun*	**1.** Is a *verbal adjective*
2. Has only four singular endings (**-ī, -ō, -um, -ō**) and is neuter	**2.** Has thirty forms (**-us, -a, -um,** etc.)
3. Is always *active* (translate "-ing")	**3.** Is *passive* ("to be," "must be"), but see page 142 below.
4. Never agrees with anything	**4.** Always agrees with a noun or pronoun

Practice

1. Give the gerunds of **laudō, moneō, regō, fugiō, audiō.**
2. Decline the gerunds of **nārrō** and **pōnō,** as well as the future passive participles of **capiō** and **tangō.**

Uses of the Gerund and the Future Passive Participle

The gerund, being a *noun,* may have noun constructions, e.g., as object of a preposition, ablative of means, etc., but, since it has no nominative, it cannot be the subject. Being a *verbal* noun, it can also be modified by an adverb, but using the gerund to govern a direct object is generally avoided.

Vōcem exercuit saepe loquendō ad lītus maris.   *He trained his voice by constantly speaking at the seashore.*

Sōcratēs, quī puerōs interrogandō docēbat... (**puerōs** here is the object of **docēbat,** not of **interrogandō**)   *Socrates, who taught boys by asking questions* . . .

The gerund does not usually have an object. To avoid using the gerund with an object, the future passive participle is used instead, modifying the noun, and conveniently translated as if *active* ("-ing").

Sōcratēs interrogandīs puerīs sententiās falsās **exposuit.**	*Socrates, by asking boys questions, exposed their false opinions* (literally, *by boys to be questioned*).
Carmen... dē cōnstituendā Rōmā scrīpsit, with the gerundive and not **dē Rōmam cōnstituendō** (gerund).	*He wrote a poem about founding Rome* (literally, *about Rome to be founded*).

When the preposition **ad** is used, the phrase with the gerund or the future passive participle regularly expresses *purpose*.

Sōcratēs puerōs ad bene vīvendum īnstituēbat.	*Socrates trained boys to live well* (literally, *toward living well*).
Solōn lēgēs īnstituit ad Athēnās reficiendās.	*Solon established laws for rebuilding Athens* (literally, *for Athens to be rebuilt*).

Purpose is also expressed by **causā** or **grātiā,** *for the sake of,* used as prepositions, but following the gerund or future passive participle (in the genitive).

Malī expellendī... grātiā semper labōrābat.	*He always worked for the sake of expelling evil.*

Question: Is **expellendī** here a gerund or a future passive participle?

Translation

Translate the words in italics, using the gerund or the future passive participle (gerundive), as the case may be. By now you know other ways to express purpose, but do not use them here.

1. He sat down *to read*.
2. We felt the joy *of giving*.
3. I have come *to seek aid*.
4. This is no time *for talking*.
5. She gained fame *by writing*.
6. He sat down *to read a book*.
7. We felt the joy *of giving money*.
8. He gained fame *by writing books*.
9. He leaned forward *for-the-sake-of seeing*.
10. She leaned forward *for-the-sake-of seeing the man*.

Art Resource, NY

This section of a painting by Raphael (1483–1520), called *School of Athens,* shows Plato (left) and Aristotle in a discussion surrounded by their followers, who listen intently to every word. The painting is on display in the Vatican Museum.

⊞ VOCABULARY

Nouns

honor, -ōris m. *honor*   (honorable, honorary)

imperātor, -ōris m. *commander, general*   **[imperō]**

lītus, lītoris n. *shore*   (littoral)

ōs, ōris n. *mouth*   (oral)

Verbs

attingō, -ere, attigī, attāctus *touch, reach*   **[tangō]**

discō, -ere, didicī, —*learn*

interrogō, 1 *ask, question*   **[rogō]**

occīdo, -ere, occīdī, occīsus *kill, cut down*   **[caedō]**

prōnūntiō, 1 *recite*   **[nūntiō]**

Adverb

nōn sōlum... sed etiam *not only . . . but also*

Conjunction

at *but*

Scala/Art Resource, NY

Sōcratem... quī puerōs interrogandō docēbat et eōs ad bene vīvendum instituēbat. This "Socratic method" of calmly eliciting answers rather than arguing points in debate is still viewed by many teachers as an ideal way to teach. For the stubborn Romans, ever doubtful of the value of speculative philosophy, Socrates' emphasis on ethics and unflinching obedience to the laws in the face of death probably were considered his most noble characteristics.

WORD STUDY

Spanish Derivatives Spanish is so much like Latin that it is easy for those knowing Latin to recognize hundreds of Spanish words, especially if a few simple principles concerned with the loss or change of letters are known. Spanish nouns are usually not derived from the Latin nominative but from a common form made from the other cases.

Remembering that final letters and syllables often are lost in Spanish, give the Latin for *alto, ánimo, ceder, constituir, dar, fácil, gente, libro, orden, responder.*

Remembering that double consonants become single, give the Latin from which are derived *aceptar, común, difícil, efecto.*

Remembering that *e* often becomes *ie*, and *o* becomes *ue*, give the Latin for *bien, ciento, cierto, tierra; bueno, cuerpo, fuerte, muerte, nuestro, puerto.*

Since *c* and *q* sometimes become *g*, and *t* becomes *d*, what must be the Latin words from which are derived *agua, amigo, edad, libertad, madera, madre, padre, todo?*

Since *li* becomes *j*, and *ct* becomes *ch*, from what Latin words are the following derived: *ajeno, consejo, mejor; dicho, noche, ocho?*

A VISIT TO THE ACADEMY

LESSON
OBJECTIVES
• Conjugation of **Fīō**
• Predicate Nouns and
  Adjectives with
  Certain Verbs

Saepe Pūbliō et Fūriānō grātum erat per urbem Athēnās ambulāre et
virōs maximae auctōritātis causās ōrantēs audīre. Saepe autem grātius
vidēbātur urbem relinquere sēque ad locum pulchrum et quiētum,
Acadēmiam, legendī grātiā recipere.

Quōdam diē eō tardē prōcēdēbant, librōs carminum ferentēs.

"Quot Rōmānī dignī per hanc ipsam viam ambulāvērunt!—Rōmānī
quī posteā clārissimī factī sunt," dīxit Pūblius. "Nōs quoque in studiīs
dīligentēs sīmus ut clārī fīāmus—tū ut dux īnsignis fīās, ego ōrātor."

Nunc inter arborēs Acadēmiae stābant. Hae erant novae sed iam altae.

"Quā magnitūdine arborēs fīunt!" Pūblius dīxit. "Audīvī quōsdam
Athēniēnsēs dīcere hās paucīs annīs tam altās quam[1] illās antīquās futūrās
esse. Nam Sulla, quī illās cecīdit ut ē
māteriā īnstrūmenta bellī fierent, rēs
pulchrās contempsit. Statuās quidem ē
Graeciā tulit; hoc autem fēcit ut magnam
praedam in urbem Rōmam referret."

Nunc sub arbore altā librōs quōs sēcum
tulerant legunt. Tum Fūriānus dīxit, "Mihi
grātissimum est ad hunc locum venīre
carminum Horātī legendōrum causā, quod
hīc Horātius ipse carmina legēbat et
scrībēbat. Horātius, quī vir corpore parvō
et rotundō erat, bellō erat inimīcus—Sullae
dissimillimus. Nūntiō bellī allātō, nōn
perturbātus est. Brūtus sōlus eum
permovēre potuit (saepe mīror quō modō)
ut tribūnus mīlitāris fieret et ad bellum
proficīscerētur. Brūtō et Cassiō ad urbem
Philippōs[2] victīs, Horātiō scūtum
relinquendum fuit (memoriāne tenēs?)
ipseque fūgit. Posteā ab Augustō, contrā
quem arma tulerat, amīcus dēlēctus est, et
nōtissimus poēta factus est."

Giraudon/Art Resource, NY

[1] **tam... quam,** (so) as . . . (just) as

[2] Brutus ("the noblest of them all")
and Cassius (he of "the lean and
hungry look,") as Shakespeare
called them, along with the other
conspirators, had killed Caesar and
fled with their forces to Greece.
They were pursued there by Mark
Antony and the young Octavian.
In 42 B.C. at Philippi, in
northeastern Greece, first Cassius
and then Brutus were decisively
defeated and took their own lives.
However, among those senators
who had resisted Julius Caesar and
longed for the power they had
had in the old republic, they
remained heroes well into the first
century A.D.

L. Cornelius Sulla (138–79 B.C.)
was a patrician of extraordinary
talents but arrogant, ruthless,
and supremely self-confident.
In his rise to power he was sup-
ported by the senatorial party
and eventually came to open
warfare against his former com-
mander Marius. On the defeat of
Marius' party, Sulla did all in his
power to enhance the power of
the Senate, even resorting to
large-scale massacres of his
opponents and confiscations of
their property (called proscrip-
tions). From his death on, Rome
was subjected to almost con-
tinuous civil strife, caused by the
ambitions of powerful men like
Julius Caesar and Pompey, until
Octavian succeeded in subduing
all his rivals and became
Augustus Caesar.

"Hīc saepe dē philosophīs admoneor,"[3] dīxit Pūblius; "de Platōne, 35 quī prīmus hīc docuit; dē Aristotele, quī rēgem Alexandrum īnstituit; dē Carneade, quī nunc prō iūstitiā, nunc contrā eam, verba īnsignia facere potuit."

Subitō accessērunt duo Graecī. Ab hīs certiōrēs factī rhētorem[4] clārum causam in Agorā ōrātūrum esse et tempus adesse, Pūblius et Fūriānus 40 librōs celeriter volvērunt et nōn iam morātī ex Acadēmiā exiērunt.

Questions

1. What attracted Publius and Furianus to the Academy?
2. What did each hope to become by studying so diligently?
3. What had Sulla done to the Academy?
4. What had Sulla taken back to Rome?
5. Which author's poems were most pleasing to Furianus?
6. What was the poet like? What had he (jokingly) admitted to doing at Philippi?
7. What policy of Augustus is hinted at by his treatment of that poet?
8. How are academies today like or unlike the original Academy in Athens?

GRAMMAR

Conjugation of *Fīō*

Faciō has no passive in the present, imperfect, or future tenses. To express *be made, be done, become* in these tenses, the Romans used the irregular verb **fīō**, which, although it is for the most part active in form, has passive meanings.

INDICATIVE			SUBJUNCTIVE	
PRESENT	IMPERFECT	FUTURE	PRESENT	IMPERFECT
fīō *I become,* etc.	**fīēbam** *I became,* etc.	**fīam** *I shall become,* etc.	**fīam**	**fierem**
fīs	**fīēbās**	**fīēs**	**fīās**	**fierēs**
fit	**fīēbat**	**fīet**	**fīat**	**fieret**
----[5]	**fīēbāmus**	**fīēmus**	**fīāmus**	**fierēmus**
----	**fīēbātis**	**fīētis**	**fīātis**	**fierētis**
fīunt	**fīēbant**	**fient**	**fiant**	**fierent**

IMPERATIVE		INFINITIVE
SINGULAR	PLURAL	PRESENT
fī *become*	**fīte** *become*	**fierī** *(to) become*

5 This mark indicates that the form does not occur.

Remember:

The stem vowel is long throughout, except before **-er** and final **-t.**

The perfect tenses of **faciō** are regular in the passive: **factus sum** (*I became, was made*); **factus eram** (*I had become, been made*), etc.

The future passive participle and the gerund are also formed from **faciō**: **faciendus, -a, -um** (*going to be made*); **faciendī** (active; *making, doing*).

Compounds of **faciō,** such as **cōnficiō** and **efficiō,** form the passive regularly: **cōnficior, efficior,** etc.

Predicate Nouns and Adjectives

Like **sum** and **maneō,** etc., **fīō** and such passive forms as **appellor** (*be called*), **dēligor** (*be selected*), and **videor** (*seem*), etc., may be used with predicate nouns or adjectives.

Dīligentēs sīmus ut clārī fīāmus.	*Let us be diligent so that we may become famous.*
Inter ruīnās urbis mātrēs aequae mānsērunt.	*Amid the ruins of the city the mothers remained calm.*
Mihi Clāra tam pulchra quam Diāna vidētur.	*To me Clara seems as beautiful as Diana.*
Carolus appellor.	*I am called Charles.*

Find all examples of this construction in the reading on pages 145 and 146.

Translation

1. Horace, who had borne arms against Augustus, became a noted poet.
2. "Let us strive to become men of the greatest influence," said Publius to Furianus.
3. Leaving the city behind, let us retire[6] to the Academy, carrying our books with us.
4. Sulla, who had come to Greece for the sake of waging war, carried back many beautiful things.

VOCABULARY

Nouns

scūtum, -ī n. *shield*	(escudo, escutcheon)[7]
tribūnus, -ī m. *tribune*	(tribunal, tribunate)

Adjectives

dīligēns, -entis (gen.) *careful*	[legō]
quot *how many; as (many as)* (indeclinable)	(quote, quotient)

---

[6] Consult the Dictionary.
[7] For the initial **e-** see page 211.

Verbs

dēligō, -ere, dēlēgī, dēlēctus *select*   **[legō]**

fīō, fierī, —, (factus) *be made, become;*   (fiat, justify)
  certior fīō *be informed* (literally, *be*
  made more certain)

moror, 1 *delay*   (moratorium)

ōrō, 1 *beg, plead*   (orator)

referō, referre, rettulī, relātus *bring back*   **[ferō]**

Adverb

eō *there, to that place*

WORD STUDY

Prefixes For the meaning and use of **circum-** *(circum-)* and **super-** *(super-, sur-),* see the Grammar Appendix. Define according to the prefix: *circumscribe, circumference, circuit, supervise, survive.*

Prefixes often have intensive force; this is especially true of **con-, ex-, ob-, per-: cōnficiō,** *do up, do thoroughly;* **efficiō,** *complete;* **occīdō,** *cut up, kill;* **perficiō,** *do through and through, finish.* Define according to the intensive use of the prefix: *complement, commotion, conserve, emotion, extensive, obtain, persist, permanent.*

Believe it or not, *squire* comes from **scūtiger,** *shield-bearer* of the medieval knight. A "blot on the escutcheon," (meaning a "disgrace") is a blot on the *shield,* with its coat of arms.

Explain *fiat, gradual, inquisitive, interrogation, littoral, perturbation, progressive.*

ATHENS AND ROME

Fūriānus patrī s. p. d. Quaeris quibus modīs Rōma et Athēnae inter sē[1] differant et utram urbem magis amem. Mihi quidem respondēre difficile est. Rōma patria mea est et ob eam rem mihi cārissima est. Num vīs mē Rōmam et Rōmānōs accūsāre? Iam dē aedificiīs amplissimīs quae hīc vīdimus scrīpsī. Sed Rōma quoque aedificia pulchra habet. Viae Rōmānae 5 certē meliōrēs sunt. Omnia sordidiōra hīc sunt—viae, aedificia prīvāta, hominēs. Nūllae cloācae[2] sunt. Aliquis Rōmānus hūc mittendus est ad cloācās faciendās. Aqua ita mala est ut multī pereant. Nōnne vult aliquis Rōmānus aquaeductum hīc facere?[3] Cum autem Acropolim cōnspiciō, tum haec urbs pulcherrima omnium esse vidētur, neque iam[4] peiōra[5] 10 memoriā teneō.

Haec dē urbe ipsā; nunc dē populō quaedam dīcere volō. Concēdō Graecōs multās virtūtēs habēre, sed hae nōn sunt virtūtēs Rōmānae. Nostrī sunt fortēs atque prūdentēs, maximē labōrant et optimē regunt. Graecī autem optimī philosophī, rhētorēs, poētae, medicī sunt et optima templa 15 pulcherrimāsque statuās faciunt.

[1] *from each other* (literally, *among themselves*)
[2] *sewers*
[3] This was actually done later at the Emperor Hadrian's expense.
[4] *longer*
[5] *the more disagreeable things*

Ronald Sheridan/Ancient Art & Architecture Collection

Roman matrons enjoyed more freedom than did their Greek counterparts. When they came to their marriages from prominent families and with substantial dowries, it was prudent of their husbands to treat them well and listen to their advice, even if legally they were, in theory, totally under their husbands' control. Another important basis for their influence was they were in charge of the early nurturing of the children who someday, it was hoped, would uphold the honor of the families, both hers and her husband's.

[6] *it makes a difference (literally, there is between)*

[7] *whether*

Multōs amīcōs Graecōs habeō; itaque nōlō omnēs Graecōs accūsāre. Sed Rōmānī mihi cāriōrēs sunt. Quīdam dīcunt perfidiam Graecōrum nōtam esse; quamquam nōn negō Graecōs loquī dē perfidiā Rōmānā.

20 Interest[6] utrum[7] Rōmānus an Graecus sīs. Ita omnēs populī aliōs contemnunt. Nōnne nōs loquimur etiam dē Pūnicā perfidiā? Sed, sī mē rogās, dīcō in tabernīs Graecīs fraudēs frequentiōrēs esse quam in Rōmānīs.

Etsī multī servī in Ītaliā sunt, numquam tot servōs vīdī quot in hāc urbe. Omnia ā servīs fīunt; cīvēs enim ipsī nōn labōrant.

25 Maximē autem condiciō mulierum differt. Mulierēs Graecae nōn habent eandem lībertātem quam Rōmānae. Apud nōs mātrōnae in honōre sunt, sed nōn hīc. Virī volunt uxōrēs nihil vidēre, nihil audīre, nihil quaerere. Sed tamen puellae quās vīdī tam pulchrae quam statuae deārum fuērunt.

Questions

1. What were Furianus' parents asking him?
2. What did he previously write them a letter about?
3. What is Furianus' main criticism of Athens?
4. If Furianus were in charge of public works, whom would he appoint to do what?
5. What, in his view, do Greeks do best? What do Romans do best?
6. Does he concede that his judgement about Greeks might be biased? How?
7. Who, according to Furianus, has more slaves?
8. What is his assessment of the status of women in Greek and Roman society?

▦GRAMMAR

Conjugation of *Volō* and *Nōlō*

The present indicative and subjunctive of both **volō** and **nōlō** are irregular. The present subjunctive has the tense sign **-ī-**, as in **sim.** The other tenses are regularly formed. There is no passive.

PRESENT INDICATIVE		PRESENT SUBJUNCTIVE	
volō *I want,* etc.	**nōlō** *I do not want,* etc.	**velim** *I should want,* etc.	**nōlim** *I should not want,* etc.
vīs	**nōn vīs**	**velīs**	**nōlīs**
vult	**nōn vult**	**velit**	**nōlit**
volumus	**nōlumus**	**velīmus**	**nōlīmus**
vultis	**nōn vultis**	**velītis**	**nōlītis**
volunt	**nōlunt**	**velint**	**nōlint**
IMPERATIVE	INFINITIVE	IMPERATIVE	INFINITIVE
---- ----	**velle**	**nōlī nōlite**	**nōlle**

Observe:

The present stem of **volō** is **vol-** in the indicative, **vel-** in the subjunctive.

Nōlō is a combination of **nōn + volō.**

The imperfect subjunctive of both **volō** and **nōlō** looks like the infinitive plus the personal endings.

A very common way of expressing a negative command in Latin is to use the imperative of **nōlō** plus the infinitive of another verb.

Nōlī mē tangere!	*Don't touch me!* (literally, *Be unwilling to touch me!*)
Nōlīte timēre!	*Don't be afraid!*

Practice

1. Give the second person singular of **volō** and the third person plural of **nōlō** in all tenses of the indicative and subjunctive.
2. Conjugate the following verbs in all tenses of the indicative and subjunctive, giving the first person singular of the first verb, the second person singular of the second verb, etc.: **prōgredior, sum, ferō, fīō, possum, eō.**

Translation

1. Do you wish to know which city (of the two) I like more?
2. It is very difficult for me to say because they are so unlike.
3. I don't wish to criticize the Greeks, but they seem to be willing to talk rather **(potius)** than (to) work.
4. I have always been willing, however, to say that the Greeks surpass us in all the arts.

-**ne** added to the first word in a sentence asks a question that expects a *Yes/No* answer.

Nōnne expects a *Yes* answer.
Num expects a *No* answer.

Interrogative pronouns, adjectives, and adverbs ask questions which expect a specific factual answer.

Scala/Art Resource, NY

The Cloaca Maxima was the greatest of the sewers and drains built by the Tarquins in the sixth century B.C. to drain Rome's marshlands. One of its effects was to create firm ground on which to build the Forum. Though rebuilt many times, it remains in use to this day.

VOCABULARY

Noun

perfidia, -ae f. *treachery*   (perfidious, perfidy)

Adjective

prūdēns, prūdentis (gen.) *sensible*   **[videō]**

Verbs

differō, differre, distulī, dīlātus *differ*   **[ferō]**

nōlō, nōlle, nōluī, — *not want, not wish,*
    be unwilling   **[volō]**

volō, velle, voluī, — *want, wish, be willing*   (volition, volitive)

Adverbs

hūc *here, to this place*   **[hic]**

num (introduces question expecting
    negative answer), *whether*

Conjunctions

an *or* (in double questions)

quamquam *although*

WORD STUDY

Latin Phrases Study the following English phrases borrowed from Latin.

per se	*by itself*
hic iacet	*here lies*
in re	*in the matter (of)*
nolens volens	*willy-nilly*
Deo volente	*God willing*
Fiat panis	*Let there be bread* (motto of the Food and Agriculture Organization of the United Nations)

A *prudent* person is *forward-looking* (**prō-vidēns**). A *perfidious* person (breaks) *through* (the bond of) *trust* (**fidēs**). Another case of this pejorative meaning for the prefix **per** is *perjure*. The *interest* on a loan *is* (the difference) *between* what you borrowed and what you have to pay back.

THE HOMECOMING

LESSON OBJECTIVES
Forms:
- Dative with Special Verbs
- Dative of Purpose
- Dative of Reference

Tandem diēs aderat quō, studiīs perfectīs, Athēnae Pūbliō Fūriānōque relinquendae erant.

"Illīs invideō quī nunc in Graeciā, nunc in Italiā habitant," dīxit Fūriānus, volēns Rōmam vidēre, nōlēns tamen Athēnās dēserere.

Certiōrēs autem ā mercātōre factī viās bonās esse, sibi persuāsērunt ut 5
sine morā proficīscerentur. Nūntiō allātō latrōnēs[1] viātōribus nocēre, servīs armātīs ut praesidiō impedīmentīs essent, per Graeciam iter fēcērunt.[2]
Marī quiētō, in portum Brundisī sine cāsū nāvigāvērunt, et ibi duōs diēs mānsērunt quod quaedam vidēre volēbant: locum ubi Augustus nōmen Caesaris accēperat, et aedificium in quō Vergilius mortuus erat postquam ē10 Graeciā rediit. Hoc tam grātum Pūbliō erat ut discēdere nōllet. Fūriānus autem dīxit, "Nōnne dēsīderās quam prīmum domum tuam vidēre?"

"Dēsīderō!"[3] respondit Pūblius. Itaque quam celerrimē profectī sunt.

Magnum erat gaudium familiae Caeciliae, adulēscentibus duōbus dēfessīs vesperī reversīs. Sōle oriente, clientēs vēnērunt, et paene tōtum 15

[1] *bandits*

[2] Notice that in this sentence the idea of "saying" **nūntiō allātō** introduces indirect statement, and the idea of action in **servis armātīs** introduces a purpose clause.

[3] *Yes* was often expressed in conversation by repeating the verb.

The origins of Greek drama, both tragedy and comedy, go back to the satyr play, which celebrated the life and great deeds of the god Dionysus. Pictured in the mosaic here *(left to right)* are two young actors next to a musician who plays the **diaulos** or *double pipe,* an old man (perhaps the playwright Aeschylus), and various stagehands. Note the masks.

Alinari/Bridgeman Art Library

[4] **Iste** often has a derogatory sense.

[5] *ghosts*

[6] *pantomime, ballet dancer.* Accompanied by musicians and a chorus, a masked pantomime would silently act out in his dance scenes from tragedy or mythology.

[7] See page 264.

[8] *both*

diem ātrium clientibus et amīcīs salūtem dīcentibus complētum est. Posteā Caeciliī ad Campum Mārtium in pulchrās thermās Agrippae iērunt. Ibi cum aliīs amīcīs locūtī, sē exercuērunt et lāvērunt.

Proximō diē, rogātus quid facere vellet, Pūblius dīxit sē velle in Circum
20 īre. Pater respondit nōn circēnsēs lūdōs, sed scaenicōs eō diē darī; quendam poētam quoque carmina sua lēctūrum esse. Pūblius dīxit sē nōlle istum[4] poētam ignōtum audīre; lūdōs autem scaenicōs sibi placēre et eōs vidēre velle.

Fābula, ā Plautō dē lārvīs[5] scrīpta, grāta erat. Tum pantomīmus[6] labōrēs
25 Herculis exprimēns tam bene saltāvit ut populus alacer clāmāret, ad pantomīmum curreret, pecūniam iaceret. Etiam Augustus eī corōnam dedit, quam accipere maximō honōrī pantomīmō erat. Lūdīs perfectīs, omnēs per Forum reversī sunt.

Pūblius et Fūriānus nunc vītam cīvium Rōmānōrum iniērunt. Post
30 aliquod tempus Pūblius quaestor[7] creātus est, perque tōtum cursum honōrum īre parāvit. Fūriānus, tribūnus mīlitum[7] factus, auxiliō ducī ab hostibus circumventō missus est, sēque tam fortiter gessit ut lēgātus[7] fieret. Itaque et Pūblius et Fūriānus vītā suā magnam auctōritātem familiae Caeciliae et servāvērunt et auxērunt.

35 Ut fīnem faciāmus: posteā Caecilia Vorēnusque parentēs factī sunt īnfantis quī tam ēgregiae mīraeque pulchritūdinis erat et quī omnibus sīc placēbat ut ambae[8] familiae numquam eius aequālem vīdissent—ita dīxērunt!

Questions

1. Whom did Furianus envy?
2. What were the conditions, by land and sea, of the trip home?
3. How long did they stay in Brundisium and what did they see there?
4. How did the Caecilii spend the first day after the boys' return? The second day?
5. What sort of entertainment did Publius prefer?
6. On what grounds did he refuse his father's suggestion?
7. What story did the pantomime act out in his dance?
8. Describe the entrance of Publius and Furianus into their public careers.
9. What noteworthy thing has happened to Caecilia?

GRAMMAR

Dative with Special Verbs

With some verbs, such as **imperō, permittō,** and **persuādeō,** an indirect personal object is used in addition to a subordinate **ut** clause as direct object.

Servīs imperāvit ut impedīmenta parārent.	*He ordered the slaves to get the baggage ready.*
Sibi persuāsērunt ut sine morā proficīscerentur.	*They persuaded themselves to set out* (literally, *that they should set out*) *without delay.*

A number of other special intransitive verbs, such as **invideō** *(look with a sidewise disapproving glance toward, envy),* **noceō** *(be harmful to, injure),* **placeō** *(be pleasing to, please),* etc., take an (indirect) object in the dative case. Almost always, by looking closely at their real meaning in Latin, you can see why they take an indirect object rather than a direct object.[9] It is best to learn these verbs as they occur. See the Grammar Appendix, p. 496.6.

Illīs invideō quī in Italiā habitant.	*I envy those who live in Italy.*
Voluērunt nōbīs placēre.	*They wanted to please us.*
Latrōnēs viatōribus nocēbant.	*Bandits were harming travelers.*

Datives of Purpose and Reference

The dative alone may be used to express *purpose.*

Locum castrīs dēlēgit.	*He chose a place for the camp.*

The dative alone may also be used to indicate the interested party, i.e., the person concerned or *referred to.* It is often literally translated by *for.*

Mihi bellum magnum malum est.	*As far as I am concerned* (literally, *for me*) *war is a great evil.*
Secunda pulchrior multīs erat.	*In the eyes of many* (literally, *for many*) *Secunda was more beautiful.*

---

[9] Would you believe that **persuādeō** really means *make very sweet for?* It comes from **suāvis, -e,** *sweet.*

These two datives, *purpose* and *reference,* are often used together, usually after a form of **sum.** The combination can be called the *double dative* construction.

Armātī sunt ut praesidiō impedīmentīs essent.

They were armed so as to be (for) a guard (with reference) to the baggage.

Fūriānus... auxiliō ducī missus est.

Furianus was sent to aid (literally, for an aid with reference to) a general.

Practice

1. Find and explain the use of every noun/pronoun in the dative in the reading.
2. Find and explain the use of every reflexive pronoun in the reading.

Translation

1. They were informed that bandits were harming travelers.
2. Furianus, however, persuaded Publius to start as soon as possible.
3. They armed the slaves as a protection for themselves and the baggage.
4. It was pleasing to them to see home again, and they said that they wanted to make the journey as swiftly as possible.

VOCABULARY

Noun

quaestor, -ōris m. *quaestor (an officer who might be a quartermaster in the army, a trial judge, or treasury official)* **[quaerō]**

Adjectives

aequālis, -e *equal* **[aequus]**

ignōtus, -a, -um *unknown* **[nōscō]**

Verbs

circumveniō, -īre, -vēnī, -ventus *surround* **[veniō]**

dēsīderō, 1 *long for, strongly desire* (desire, desideratum)

exprimō, -ere, -pressī, expressus *press out, express, portray* **[premō]**

ineō, -īre, iniī, initūrus *enter in or upon* **[eō]**

persuādeō, -ēre, -suāsī, -suāsūrus   (persuasive, persuasion)
  persuade
placeō, -ēre, placuī, placitūrus *please*   (placate, placid)
revertō, -ere, revertī, reversus (sometimes   **[vertō]**
  deponent) *turn back, return*

WORD STUDY

Suffixes For the meaning and use of **-tūdō** (*-tude*), **-mentum**
(*-ment*), **-ūra** (*-ure*), **-faciō, -ficō** (*-fy*), see the Grammar
Appendix, p. 510. Give the English forms of **multitūdō,
servitūdō, argūmentum, agricultūra, pictūra.**

What must be the Latin words from which are derived *altitude,
solitude, instrument, moment,* and *conjecture, stultify?*

Give three other examples of each of the preceding suffixes in
English words.

Explain *casualty, circumvent, imprudence, initiative, innocent,
legation.*

READING STRATEGY   NOUNS DERIVED FROM PERFECT PASSIVE PARTICIPLES

You will remember that many fourth declension nouns are related to
verbs, for example, **exercitus (exerceō)** and **exitus (exeō).** The nominative
singular of the noun regularly looks like the nominative singular masculine
of the verb's perfect passive participle. Generally they describe an action
and can often be translated by the English verbal noun (the *gerund*) ending
in *-ing:* **vīsus (videō),** *seeing,* i.e., *sight* or *vision.*

Translate these sayings and identify the verbs related to the fourth
declension nouns.

   Labor sine lūsū Jōhannem (*Jack*) **brūtum** (*dull*) **facit.**
   Fiat nōn mandātū tuō, sed rogātū (a rule of good manners).
   Facile dictū, difficile factū (Tell this to a boaster!).
   Plūrimum sūmptūs, minimum quaestūs (=**quaesītūs,** *of profit;* a
     shopkeeper's motto).
   Facilis dēscēnsus Avernō (from Vergil).

From your knowledge of the basic verbs, assign a meaning to these
Latin nouns: **arbitrātus, cāsus, cōnsēnsus, cursus, flētus, gressus,
habitus, impulsus, ingressus, intellectus, monitus, reditus, status.**

50°

20°   10°   0°   10°

OCEANUS ATLANTICUS

MARE GERMANICUM

HIBERNIA

Eboracum

BRITANNIA
Londinium

Saxones
Albis

MARE SUE

GERMANIA

Belgae
Rhenus
GERMANIA

Sequana
Remi
Lutetia
Matrona

Liger

GALLIA
Celtae
Genua

RAETIA

NORICUM
PANNONIA

Lugdunum
Helvetii
ALPES
Mediolanum
Padus

40°

Garunna
AQUITANIA
Narbo
Rhodanus
Genua
Rubico
ILLYRICUM

PYRENAEI

Numantia
Hiberus
Massilia

HISPANIA

Tagus
LUSITANIA

Tarraco

Saguntum

CORSICA

Roma
Ostia
ITALIA
Cannae
Neapolis
Dyrrachiu
Pompeii
Tarem

Atlas
Corduba

Gades
Nova Carthago

BALEARES

SARDINIA

MARE
MARE

MAURETANIA

NUMIDIA

AFRICA

Utica
SICILIA
Aetna
Carthago
Syracusae

Zama

MELITA

ATLAS

Thapsus

M E D I

30°

Leptis Magna

〰〰〰〰 Roman Walls

Roman Territory 264 B.C. *Before Punic Wars*

Added Territory 238-201 B.C. *After First and Second Punic Wars*

Added Territory 133 B.C.

Added Territory 44 B.C. *Death of Caesar*

Added Territory 14 A.D. *Death of Augustus*

Added Territory Second Century A.D.

158

0°   10°

IMPERIUM ROMANUM

SARMATIA

Tanais

SCYTHIA

DACIA

Danuvius

MOESIA

THRACIA

DONIA

Phillipi

Thessalonica

Pharsalus

Troia

ASIA

Mare

Corinthus

Athenae

Aegaeum

ECIA

Sparta

CRETA

RRANEUM

Cyrene

Byzantium

Bosporus

BITHYNIA

GALATIA

PAMPHYLIA

CILICIA

LYCIA

RHODUS

CYPRUS

PONTUS EUXINUS

PONTUS

CAPPADOCIA

Antiochia

PHOENICIA

Palmyra

SYRIA

Damascus

Tyrus

PALAESTINA

Hierosolyma

CAUCASUS

MARE CASPIUM

ARMENIA

ASSYRIA

Euphrates

MESOPOTAMIA

Tigris

Babylon

PARTHIA

Alexandria

ARABIA

AEGYPTUS

Nilus

Scale of Miles

0   100   200   300   400   500

30°   40°   50°   60°   50°   40°   30°

OUR HERITAGE

GREEKS AND ROMANS

The civilizations of the Greeks and Romans, although they eventually became closely intertwined, differed from each other in many respects and were never identical. The peoples were members of different ethnic groups, nomadic tribes who began their migration from somewhere in western Asia around 2000 B.C. They spoke different versions of the same original tongue, but those languages were about as different as French and German are today. Their original religious beliefs and practices were different. The Greeks became a nation of farmers, seafarers, and colonizers with far-flung commercial interests. Those who became the Romans were originally an agricultural people until, by wars of defense or encroachment, they spread their dominion over all of Italy and the Mediterranean. Their social values were different: the Romans looked to power, status, and prestige, the Greeks to intellect, individualism, and privacy. The political developments in each country were different: the Greeks grouped themselves into a large number of fiercely independent and often rival city-states; the Romans transformed the hostility of their adversaries into loyalty and dependency upon one capital city, Rome. For a brief period after the Persian Wars, the Greeks enjoyed a nearly pure democracy; the Romans evolved a representative system which eventually collapsed into one-person rule.

Underground tomb paintings, like this one from Tarquinia of a lyre-player, give us precious insights into the life of the Etruscans, who developed a highly refined and luxurious culture and greatly influenced early Rome, but left us almost nothing in the way of literature. Notice the birds, picking away at the olives, and to the right, cement patches where the stucco, damaged by light, changes of temperature in the tombs, and moisture (even that from the breath of tourists), has fallen away and left mutilated the original work of art.

Nimatallah/Art Resource, NY

The earliest important contact of the Romans with Greek culture was an indirect one, through the Etruscans. This people who lived north of Rome borrowed a number of things from the Greeks, such as the alphabet, forms of architecture, and some religious practices, and transmitted them to the Romans. Later the Romans met Greek culture directly as they moved south to the Greek colonies in Italy and Sicily. In the second century B.C., Greece itself came under Roman rule, which directly inspired the importation of Greek culture and customs. The poet Horace noted:

Graecia capta ferum
   victōrem cēpit et artēs
Intulit agrestī Latiō...

Captured Greece took captive its
   fierce conqueror and
brought the arts to rustic Latium . . .
    (*Epist.* II, 1, 156–157)

Though Greece was defeated by Roman arms, uncivilized Rome was conquered by Greek culture. The Romans began to develop their own art and literature, which imitated Greek art and literature, but added the stamp of their own individuality. So Vergil, inspired by Homer, produced a masterpiece quite unlike Homer's. Greek architecture was imitated, but one can always tell a Roman building from a Greek building. The Romans generally preferred the Corinthian style and, unlike the Greeks, often placed their temples and other buildings on a high base. The round temple with a dome is distinctly Roman. Greek sculpture attained a beauty never since equaled, but the Romans excelled in making realistic portrait statues. The Greeks were superior in mathematics, especially geometry (the name of their greatest geometrician, Euclid, still is a synonym for geometry); the Romans developed applied mathematics, such as surveying and engineering.

Vanni Archive/CORBIS

This Greek temple to Hera (earlier believed to be a temple to Poseidon, and still so called) is celebrated as the most beautiful of all Doric temples in Italy. Two other great temples stand near it in Paestum. Originally called Poseidonia, Paestum was founded in the seventh century B.C. by Greeks who had been exiled from Sybaris, a Greek colony in southern Italy. Having been overrun at times by the native Lucanians, it eventually came under Roman control in 273 B.C.

One frame of a frieze from the Villa of the Mysteries at Pompeii. It shows a matron attended by her helpers preparing the preliminary rites of purification for an initiation into the rites of Dionysus (Bacchus). This cult, adopted from the Greeks living in southern Italy, became so extensive that it alarmed the Roman Senate, fearful of any secret society that seemed to embrace orgiastic rituals and threatened to break down conventional morality.

Scala/Art Resource, NY

For a thousand years after the fall of the Roman Empire, Greek thought and art were preserved in western Europe only through Latin literature and tradition. The civilization of western Europe, and therefore of the United States, developed from this Roman tradition with its Greek borrowings. Just as the Romans had been inspired by Greek culture, so now the world was imbued with the Greco-Roman style. Then, through the interest created by the praise of Greek literature found in the works of Roman writers, Greek once again became a language of interest during the Renaissance, and the world supplemented its huge Roman inheritance by borrowing directly from the Greeks. Therefore the Roman hospitality to Greek ideas has enabled the transmission of two very different cultures. Without Rome, Greek culture might not have been preserved at all, or at least the modern world would not have been prepared to appreciate and welcome it.

Vergil, the great poet who described Rome's ideals, stated that others (meaning the Greeks) were better sculptors, orators, astronomers, but:

Tū regere imperiō populōs, Rōmāne, mementō. Hae tibi erunt artēs pācīque impōnere mōrem, parcere subiectīs et dēbellāre superbōs.	*Roman, remember (your mission) to rule the nations with your power. These will be your arts: to impose civilization on peace, to spare the conquered, and subdue the proud.* (*Aeneid* VI, 851–853)

To help you understand the nature of these two cultures and the way in which both have evolved to form one basis of what we call "Western civilization," consider the following questions. Many of them deal in different and modern forms with issues that still, after two and a half millennia, are worthy of our attention. They are posed to stimulate discussion and there are no easy, complete, and absolute answers.

What do you believe would have been the attitude of these two peoples, Greeks and Romans, toward the idea of: a United Nations? of NATO? of abolishing slavery? of a government based on the checks and balances among its separate powers? of one person, one vote? of capital punishment? of ending racial discrimination? of the public welfare as a duty of government? of capitalism? of freedom of speech? of subsidizing the arts? of exploring unknown lands? of the death penalty? of defining and living the "good life"?

Uses of the Subjunctive

INDEPENDENT: VOLITIVE

IN LATIN	IN ENGLISH
Present subjunctive	*Let . . .*
EXAMPLE: **Lūx fīat.**	*Let there be light.*

DEPENDENT

Purpose Clauses

1. Present or imperfect subjunctive	1. Infinitive	1. Indicative with auxiliaries *may* or *might*
2. Introduced by **ut**, negative **nē**	2. No introductory word	2. Introduced by *(in order) that*, etc.
EXAMPLE: **Edimus ut vīvāmus.**	*We eat to live.*	*We eat that we may live.*

Result Clauses

1. Subjunctive	1. Indicative
2. Usually prepared for by **ita, tam,** etc.	2. Usually prepared for by *so,* etc.
3. Introduced by **ut**, negative **ut... nōn**	3. Introduced by *that*
EXAMPLE: **Ita vīvāmus ut nōs laudent.**	*Let us live in such a way that they will praise us.*

Noun Clauses: Volitive

1. Subjunctive; clause is object of such verbs as **cōgō, cōnstituō, imperō, petō,** etc.	1. Indicative	1. Infinitive
2. Introduced by **ut**, negative **nē**	2. Introduced by *that*	2. No introductory word
EXAMPLE: **Cōnstituimus nē ad lūdōs īrēmus.**	*We decided not to go to the games.*	

Noun Clauses: Result

1. Subjunctive; clause is object of such verbs as **accidō, efficiō,** etc.	1. Indicative
2. Introduced by **ut**, negative **ut... nōn**	2. Introduced by *that*
EXAMPLE: **Accidit ut caderem.**	*It happened that I fell.*

UNIT II REVIEW

Noun Clauses: Indirect Questions

1. Subjunctive; clause is object of verbs of *asking,* etc.: **rogō, cognōscō,** etc.
2. Introduced by an interrogative word: **quis, quid, cūr, ubi,** etc.

EXAMPLE: **Dīc mihi cūr vēnerīs.**

1. Indicative

2. Introduced by an interrogative word: *who, what, why, where,* etc.

Tell me why you have come.

Time Clauses

1. With **ubi** or **postquam,** always indicative
2. With **cum** in secondary sequence, subjunctive

1. With *when,* indicative

2. With *when,* indicative

Sequence of Tenses

1. Primary tenses (referring to the present or future)

   INDICATIVE: Present, future, future perfect

   SUBJUNCTIVE: Present or perfect

2. Secondary tenses (referring to the past)

   INDICATIVE: Imperfect, perfect, past perfect

   SUBJUNCTIVE: Imperfect or past perfect

Primary tenses are followed by primary tenses, secondary by secondary.

Summary of Purpose Constructions

1. **Ut** clause with subjunctive

   Venīmus ut Claudiam laudēmus.
   We come to praise Claudia.

2. Dative

   Cui bonō est?
   Whom does it benefit (literally, *To whom is it for a good*)?

3. **Ad** with gerund

   Ad laudandum venīmus.
   We come to praise.

4. **Ad** with future passive participle

   Ad Claudiam laudandam venīmus.
   We come to praise Claudia.

5. **Causā** or **grātiā** following the gerund

   Laudandī grātiā venīmus.
   We come for the sake of praising.

6. **Causā** or **grātiā** following the future passive participle modifying a noun

   Claudiae laudandae grātiā venīmus.
   We come for the sake of praising Claudia.

UNIT II ASSESSMENT
LESSONS X–XXVI

VOCABULARY

Circle the word that best completes each sentence.

1. Amīca mihi auxilium _____ ut ego opus perficerem.
   a. contempserat
   b. negāverat
   c. praebuerat
   d. rūperat

2. Cum pontifex ōmen fēlix prōnūntiāvisset, populus magnō cum gaudiō _____.
   a. vēxit
   b. flēvit
   c. dēposuit
   d. adhaesit

3. Nōs _____ ad mare cum nostrīs amīcīs cārissimīs reficiāmus!
   a. pollicendō
   b. gradiendō
   c. hortandō
   d. moriendō

4. Iuvenēs in saxō _____ stetērunt, dē quō trāns mare spectāre potuērunt.
   a. aegrō
   b. dēfessō
   c. ēditō
   d. perītō

5. Pūblius dīxit: "Quī in marī vītam ēgit optimus _____ ad nōs trānsportandōs in Graeciam erit."
   a. gubernātor
   b. imperātor
   c. mercātor
   d. pontifex

GRAMMAR

Complete each sentence with the correct case endings.

6. Tribūnus mīrābā___ qu___ mīlitēs in angustō itiner___ sine armīs esse___ et ubi scūta relīq___.

7. Crās Rūfus virōs īnsign___ in ātri___ fer___, et posteā omnēs ad forum et balne___ novius quīntā hōr___ ībunt.

8. Cornēlia exīstimāvit sē septem di___ omn___ amīc___ vidend___ gratiā ibi morātūr___ ___.

9. Pontifex tam quiēt___ locūt___ ___ ut eius verba ab aegr___ cīvibus nōn audīr___.

10. Vesperī nōs ad illum port___ ībimus ut dēscend___ ad lītus et cum quōdam mercātōr___ dē emend___ māteriā loquāmur.

TRANSLATION

Translate the following sentences.

11. Aliquis dīcat sē nōn sōlum fontem sacrum attingere sed etiam ad ōrāculum ipsum prōgredī velle.

12. Sapiēns iuvenibus persuāsit ut saepe interrogārent, dīligenter discerent, iūstē vīverent, et hōc modō dignī cīvēs fierent.

13. Ager parvus, quem P. Caecilius Rūfus emere voluit ut locus familiae ōtiō esset, paucīs mīlibus passuum ab urbe aberat.

14. Tempestās tanta est ut magnae undae in lītus sē frangerent, saxa dē montibus caderent, populus etiam quaerēret num deī urbem servārent.

15. Pūbliō Fūriānōque dē itineribus tam diū loquentibus, omnēs Caeciliī alacriter cōnstituērunt ut in Graeciam quōrundam aedificiōrum videndōrum causā quam prīmum proficīscerentur.

INVESTIGATION

Find the answers to these questions from any lesson in Unit II.

16. The great Athenian lawmaker named _____ is credited with having said *"Nothing in excess."*

17. All modern day marathons cover a distance of _____ and are named for the Greek town from which the legendary runner named _____ ran to Athens to announce the Greek victory.

18. The port city from which most ancient Romans would depart for Greece and other destinations in the East was named _____.

19. Many Greek city-states were defended by an **acropolis,** a word that means _____.

20. A Roman warship with high sides to protect the two tiers of rowers was called a _____.

CULTURE

Vērum aut Falsum? Indicate whether each statement is true or false.

21. Most of our musical terms are derived from French words which in turn came from Latin.

22. A Roman bride traditionally wore a blue veil at her wedding ceremony.

23. The oracle at Delphi was chiefly dedicated to Aesculapius, the Roman god of medicine.

24. The Battle of Marathon was an important turning point in the wars between Greece and Persia.

25. Sulla was a powerful patrician who worked relentlessly to enhance the power of the Senate.

FROM LATIN TO ENGLISH

Apply your knowledge of Latin roots to determine the best meaning of the italicized words.

26. Her speech was filled with words of *exhortation.*
    a. criticism
    b. anger
    c. devotion
    d. encouragement

27. The witness insisted on telling the *sordid* details.
    a. erroneous
    b. disgraceful
    c. exciting
    d. important

28. The committee had proposed and passed a *moratorium.*
    a. new policy
    b. death sentence
    c. delay in proceedings
    d. code of conduct

29. His idea was accepted with *alacrity.*
    a. promptness
    b. hesitancy
    c. anger
    d. silence

30. The general *conceded* that the battle would be difficult.
    a. denied
    b. feared
    c. granted
    d. hoped

LIVY

Unit Objectives

Read:

- Stories of Roman History from Livy, Aulus Gellius, and Eutropius

Learn:

- Dative with Compound Verbs
- Conjugation of **Mālō**
- Locative Case
- More about **Cum** Clauses
- Impersonal Verbs
- Omission of **Sum**
- Relative Pronoun as a Connector
- Place to Which without a Preposition
- **Quisque** and **Quisquam**
- Passive Imperative
- Relative Purpose Clauses

Review:

- Future Passive Participle and Gerund; Datives of Purpose, Reference, and Agent; Volitive Clauses; Indefinite Pronouns; Result Clauses; Ablative (Separation, Measure of Difference, Description); Genitive (Description of the Whole)

The Oath of the Horatians. In this great example of classicist painting by Jacques-Louis David (1748–1825), the father of the triplet Horatian brothers presents them with their swords before they go to battle the triplet Curiatians to decide which city shall rule Latium—Rome or Alba. To the right huddle their mother and the sister (who was betrothed to one of the Curiatians), each fearful for her own reasons of the outcome. The reading in Lesson XXVII will tell you who won.

Erich Lessing/Art Resource, NY

169

A GREAT HISTORIAN

Livy was one of Rome's most famous historians. Living nearly two thousand years ago in the time of Augustus, he was eyewitness to civil wars, the fall of the Republic, and the establishment of the Principate. In 142 books, his history began with the origins of Rome and went down to 9 B.C. Only thirty-five of the original books survive, but there are very brief summaries of most of the others. Livy's work is of crucial importance for the history of Rome, and it has always been the dream of scholars to find the lost books.

Livy truly believed that ancient history had lessons to teach the reader. He calls the episodes in his history **documenta** *(means of teaching)* placed as if on a **monumentum** *(a means of advising),* so that the viewer (or reader) could learn what courses of action would produce good or bad results.

Livy was not what we could call a "scientific" historian. He did almost no independent research and relied upon earlier accounts by often

In the nineteenth century it became fashionable to create images of famous persons, especially ancient writers, for whom no bust or sculpture could be found. This etching of Livy is totally imaginary and it is very unlikely that he looked so much like a movie star. But he was unquestionably a star: Pliny the Younger *(Epist. 2.3)* writes that Livy's *History* had made Livy so famous that a man from Cadiz, near Gibraltar, traveled all the way to Rome to get a glimpse of him and, having achieved his goal, turned around immediately and went back home!

Bettmann/CORBIS

untrustworthy sources. But, while the old Roman tales that Livy weaves into his early history of Rome may be mere legends, they are, nevertheless, like the story of George Washington and the cherry tree, of great importance, interest, and drama, and give us good insight into Roman character and ideals. One historian says of these stories:

> If now we take a general view of this wonderful collection of legends, caring little whether the details be wholly or in part imaginary, but regarding the heroes and heroines as at least a gallery of moral types, we may gain a fair notion of the kind of greatness that carried Rome, the city of the Tiber, to the headship of the ancient world. It is simple enough. There is a plain devotion to duty, a disregard of personal inclinations, a pride that disdains submission, a constancy of the finest temper. There is a clear grasp of the object of the hour and a willingness to take the necessary steps . . . We are not dealing with a clever people, like the Greeks. Here there is no constellation of brilliant stars, but a succession of good citizens, able to cooperate and to obey, and preeminent among peoples ancient or modern in steadiness of nerve.

The stories in the following thirteen lessons are adapted chiefly from Livy. However, some parts are based on Eutropius, a writer in the fourth century A.D., who wrote a very brief history of Rome, in the early portion of which he used an abridged edition of Livy.

Questions
1. Can you name any prominent citizens of the world today who have shown qualities similar to those mentioned in the quotation?
2. What are some of the legends in our history that have become part of our historical tradition?

EARLY KINGS OF ROME

[1] *having been founded.* The title of Livy's history was **Ab urbe conditā**, *From the Founding of the City* (literally, *from the city having been founded*).

[2] *because of their habit of (fighting) battles*

[3] *at Rome*

[4] *triplet*

[5] historical present; Grammar Appendix, p. 501

Rōmānum imperium ā Rōmulō initium habet, quī urbem parvam in Palātīnō cōnstituit. Urbe conditā,[1] quam ex nōmine suō Rōmam vocāvit, haec ēgit: multitūdinem fīnitimōrum in cīvitātem recēpit et centum ex seniōribus dēlēgit, quōs senātōrēs nōmināvit quod senēs erant. Hōrum
5 cōnsiliō omnia ēgit.

Post mortem Rōmulī Numa Pompilius rēx creātus est, quī nūllam partem quidem Rōmae adiēcit, sed nōn minus cīvitātem quam Rōmulus iūvit; nam lēgēs mōrēsque Rōmānīs cōnstituit, quī cōnsuētūdine[2] proeliōrum ā fīnitimīs sēmibarbarī putābantur. Annum dīvīsit in decem
10 mēnsēs et multa sacra ac templa Rōmae[3] cōnstituit.

Huic successit Tullus Hostīlius. Hōc rēge, Rōmānī cum Albānīs bellum gerēbant. Forte in duōbus exercitibus erant trigeminī[4] frātrēs et aetāte et vīribus parēs. Horātiī erant Rōmānī; Cūriātiī, Albānī. Cum hīs agunt[5] rēgēs, ut hī sōlī prō suā patriā exercitūque pugnent.

The story of the founding of Rome by Romulus was spread throughout the Roman empire. This reproduction of the famous Etruscan statue of the she-wolf is in Spain. Romulus was the first of the seven kings of Rome.

Archive Iconografico, S.A./CORBIS

Tempore cōnstitūtō, arma capiunt.[5] Duo Rōmānī, vulnerātīs tribus
Albānīs, interfectī sunt. Forte tertius Rōmānus integer fuit; tribus Cūriātiīs 15
sōlus nōn pār erat, sed contrā singulōs ferōx. Itaque, ut cum singulīs
pugnāret, fūgit. Tum respiciēns videt[5] eōs magnīs intervāllīs sequentēs;
ūnus nōn multō[6] abest. In eum magnō impetū rediit; et dum Albānus
exercitus clāmat[5] Cūriātiīs ut opem ferant frātrī, iam Horātius, caesō hoste, 20
secundam pugnam petēbat et alterum Cūriātium interfēcit. Iamque singulī
supererant,[7] sed nec spē nec vīribus parēs. Tertiō Cūriātiō quoque
interfectō, Rōmānī cum gaudiō Horātium accipiunt.[5]

Horātī soror spōnsa ūnī ex Cūriātiīs erat. Cum Horātius ad urbem
accēderet, soror eum vīdit gerentem palūdāmentum[8] Cūriātī quod ipsa 25
cōnfēcerat. Eam flentem[9] frāter interfēcit. "Abī[10] ad spōnsum," inquit,
"oblīta[11] frātrum mortuōrum vīvīque,[12] oblīta patriae. Sīc eat[13] quaecumque
Rōmāna[14] lūgēbit hostem."

[6] *far*
[7] from **supersum**
[8] *cloak*
[9] *as she wept*
[10] *Go*
[11] *since you have forgotten,* with genitive (= *are forgetful of*)
[12] refers to himself: *and (your one) living (brother)*
[13] = **pereat**
[14] *any and every Roman woman who*

Questions

1. What institution did Romulus establish as a restraint on the power of his monarchy?
2. How did this institution get its name?
3. How is Numa said to have changed the Romans?
4. What two areas beside government did Numa affect?
5. How does Tullus Hostilius' name suggest the character of his rule?
6. What coincidence produced a very unusual battle between the Romans and the Albans?
7. The opening rounds of the battle had what result on each side?
8. What clever tactic did the one remaining Horatius use against his adversaries?
9. Can you apply the Latin motto **dīvide et imperā** to this story?
10. Is Horatius' stern lesson to his sister justifiable?

GRAMMAR

Dative with Compound Verbs

You have seen that many verbs are compounded by adding a prefix.
Very often this compounding changes the meaning of the verb and causes
it to be followed by the dative. The English equivalent often calls for *to* or
for. The most common prefixes are:

ad	circum	in	ob	prae	sub
ante	cum	inter	post	prō	super

If the simple form of the verb is transitive, the compounded form can take both the dative and a direct object in the accusative.

Huic successit Tullus Hostīlius.	*Tullus Hostilius succeeded (to) him.*
Nūllam partem Rōmae adiēcit.	*He added no part to Rome.*
pācī impōnere mōrem	*to impose custom on peace*

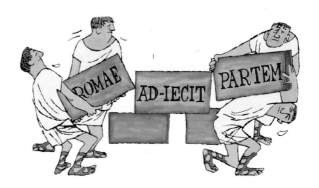

Translation

1. Whom did Tullus Hostilius succeed?
2. After killing two Albans, Horatius approached the third.
3. Numa added no hill to Rome, but he gave the Romans laws.
4. Numa divided the year into months and established many customs.

VOCABULARY

Nouns

cōnsuētūdō, -dinis f. *custom*	(customary, customize)
fors, fortis f. *chance*	(fortuity, fortune)
initium, -tī n. *beginning*	[eō]
mōs, mōris m. *custom;* pl. *character*	(moral, moralize)
senex, senis m. *old man;* adj. *old; senior*	(senility)

Adjective

vīvus, -a, -um *living*	(vivid, vivarium)

Verbs

iuvō, iuvāre, iūvī, iūtus *aid*	(adjutant)
sequor, sequī, secūtus *follow*	(prosecute, sequence)
succēdō, -ere, -cessī, -cessūrus *succeed*	[cedo]

WORD STUDY

Derivatives There are many interesting derivatives of **sequor.**
From it was derived **secundus,** English *second,* whose chief
meaning therefore is *following.* Its use as a measure of time arose
thus: **hōra** means *hour;* **hōra minūta** means a *diminished hour,* or
minute (from **minuō,** *make less,* which comes in turn from
minus); **hōra minūta secunda** means a *second-degree minute,* or
smaller division of a minute. The *sequence* of tenses refers to the
way one verb *follows* another in the use of a tense. A *suit* of
clothes is one which the various pieces *follow* or match one
another. A *suite* of rooms consists of several rooms *following* one
another, i.e., one after the other. What is a *suitor?* An *executive?*
A *prosecutor?*

Suitor

OUT GO THE KINGS

[1] noun

[2] The Sabines, neighbors of Rome to the northeast, were so stern and moralistic a people and such stubborn warriors that the later Romans greatly admired their tough and simple ways. It seems clear that these legends reflect the fact that early Rome was a mingling of three peoples: the basic stock were Latins, but Kings Numa and Ancus had Sabine connections, and the Tarquins originally were Etruscans.

[3] *sewers*

[4] *glory* (literally, *light*)

[5] *dative*

[6] *let us train (him) in good arts*

[7] *he was the first of all to*

Post Hostīlium Ancus Mārcius suscēpit imperium, tum Prīscus Tarquinius. Circum[1] Rōmae aedificāvit. Lūdōs Rōmānōs īnstituit. Vīcit īdem Sabīnōs.[2] Mūrōs fēcit et cloācās.[3] Capitōlium aedificāvit.

Eō tempore rēs mīra accidit. Servius Tullius puer erat rēgis servus. In
5 capite huius puerī dormientis flamma appāruit multōrum in cōnspectū.
Cum quīdam aquam ad exstinguendum ferret, ab rēgīnā retentus est, quae
movērī vetuit puerum. Tum cum somnō etiam flamma abiit. Tum rēgīna
rēgī sēcrētō "Vidēsne, Tarquinī," inquit, "hunc puerum tam humilem? Hic
lūmen[4] rēgnō nostrō erit praesidiumque nōbīs; eī[5] amīcī sīmus et bonīs
10 artibus īnstituāmus."[6] Hōc factō, puer fit vir īnsignis. Cum marītus
quaererētur fīliae[5] Tarquinī, nēmō Rōmānus cum Tulliō cōnferrī potuit,
rēxque sē fīliam suam eī spondēre mālle dīxit. Post mortem Tarquinī
Servius, quī servus fuerat, rēx factus est.

Servius Tullius montēs trēs, Quirīnālem, Vīminālem, Ēsquilīnum, urbī
15 adiūnxit; fossās circum mūrum dūxit. Prīmus[7] omnium cēnsum habuit, quī
adhūc per orbem terrārum nōn cognitus erat. Sub eō Rōma, omnibus in
cēnsum dēlātīs, habuit LXXXIIII mīlia cīvium.

This painting by Titian (1477–1576) shows the noble Roman matron Lucretia. Tarquinius Superbus was the last of the seven kings to rule Rome. He was expelled by the Senate after his son Sextus assaulted the beautiful and virtuous Lucretia, and his banishment meant the end of monarchy and the beginning of republican government in Rome.

Erich Lessing/Art Resource, NY

Walls and trenches were typically built to help defend a settlement from outsiders. This picture shows part of the reconstructed wall around the Aventine, one of the seven hills of Rome. Some writers, including Livy, attribute this wall to King Servius Tullius.

L. Tarquinius Superbus, fīlius Prīscī Tarquinī, Tullium occīdit et Rōmae rēgnāvit. Cum fīlius eius nōbilissimam mātrōnam Lucrētiam iniūriā affēcisset, eaque dē iniūriā marītō et patrī et amīcīs dīxisset, in omnium cōnspectū Lucrētia sē occīdit. Propter quam causam L. Iūnius Brūtus populum contrā Tarquinium incitāvit. Posteā exercitus quoque istum[8] crūdēlem rēgem relīquit. Cum imperāvisset annōs XXV, cum uxōre et līberīs suīs fūgit. Septem rēgēs CCXXXXIIII annōs rēgnāverant. Mors fortis mulieris cīvitātem līberāvit, nam post hoc duo cōnsulēs, quī singulōs annōs imperium habuērunt, ā populō creātī sunt.

[8] that; acc. sing. masc. of **iste**

Questions
1. How many kings had Rome before Ancus Marcius?
2. What building projects did Priscus Tarquinius accomplish?
3. What was the original status of Servius Tullius at the palace?
4. What miracle occurred during Tarquin's reign, and how did the queen interpret it?
5. Why was Servius considered a suitable candidate for the hand of the king's daughter?
6. What alterations to Rome did Servius Tullius accomplish?
7. How did Tarquinius Superbus manage to become king?
8. How did Lucretia react to the crime committed against her?
9. What happened to the royal family?
10. What effect did Lucretia's death have upon the government at Rome?
11. How long was there a monarchy at Rome? How many kings?

GRAMMAR

Conjugation of *Mālō*

Mālō (= **magis volō,** *want more, prefer*) has the same irregularities as **volō.**

PRESENT INDICATIVE		PRESENT SUBJUNCTIVE	
mālō	*I prefer,* etc.	**mālim**	*I should prefer,* etc.
māvīs		**mālīs**	
māvult		**mālit**	
mālumus		**mālīmus**	
māvultis		**mālītis**	
mālunt		**mālint**	

The infinitive is **mālle.** For full conjugation, see the Grammar Appendix, pp. 529–530.

The Locative Case

As you know, the ablative with **in** is used to express "place where": **in Italiā,** *in Italy.* But names of towns, as well as **domus** and a few other words, have a special case form, the *locative,* to express this idea. The ending of this case is the same as the genitive in the singular nouns of the first and second declensions, and the same as the ablative elsewhere. No preposition is used: **Rōmae,** *at Rome;* **domī,** *at home;* **Athēnīs,** *at Athens;* **Carthāgine (-ī),** *at Carthage.*

Review of *Cum* Clauses

Review **cum** clauses in Lesson XVI and identify the type of those used in the reading on pages 176 and 177.

Translation

1. "Dear Servius," the queen said, "we prefer to be your friends."
2. The power of the state was given to the boy when the king had died.
3. When the flame appeared on the boy's head, the king adopted him.
4. When he had ruled many years, he lost his power on account of his own son.

▦ VOCABULARY

Nouns

cōnspectus, -ūs m. *sight*   **[spectō]**
fossa, -ae f. *trench*   (fossil)
mūrus, -ī m. *wall*   (mural, intramural)

Verbs

adiungō, -ere, adiūnxī, adiūnctus *join to*   **[iungō]**
dēferō, dēferre, dētulī, dēlātus *offer, enroll*   **[ferō]**
inquit *he/she said* (never first word)
mālō, mālle, māluī, — *prefer*
vetō, vetāre, vetuī, vetitus *forbid*   (veto)

Adverb

adhūc *up to this time, still*

A very few first conjugation verbs do not have the familiar **-āre, -āvī, -ātus** principal parts you know so well and which are now marked in the Vocabulary sections with a **1.** By now you should have also mastered the principal parts of four of these exceptions: **dō, stō, iuvō,** and **vetō.** There is only one more used in this book: **lavō, lavāre, lāvī, lautus,** *wash, bathe.*

WORD STUDY

Prefixes The prefix **sēmi-** means *half* or *partly:* **sēmibarbarus,** *semibarbarous. Semiannual* means *occurring every half year.*

The prefix **bi-** or **bis-** means *twice* or *two:* **biennium,** *a period of two years* (from **annus**). Distinguish carefully *semiannual* and *biennial, semimonthly* and *bimonthly.* **Bi-** is often found in chemical terms: *bicarbonate, bichloride.*

The prefix **ūn-, ūni-** (from **ūnus**) means *one: uniform.*

The prefix **multi-** (from **multus**) means *much, many: multiform, multicellular, multimillionaire.*

Give three other examples of each of these prefixes.

Explain *adjunct, fortuitous, revive, successor, defer, consequence.*

LESSON OBJECTIVES
- Review the Future Passive Participle
- Review the Gerund
- Review Dative of Agent

HOW BRUTUS GOT HIS NAME

[1] *snake*
[2] *slipping*
[3] *to Delphi*
[4] with **ex**: *on purpose*
[5] **brūtus, -a, -um** means *stupid.*
[6] *escaping notice*
[7] *wait for, bide*
[8] *laughingstock*
[9] *to chance*
[10] *had another meaning (literally, looked in another direction)*

Altera fābula dē Brūtō nunc nārranda est. Dum Tarquinius, ultimus rēgum Rōmānōrum, Iovis templum Rōmae aedificat, ōmen terribile vīsum est: anguis[1] ex columnā ēlāpsus,[2] rēgis pectus anxiīs cūrīs implēvit. Itaque duōs fīliōs Delphōs[3] ad ōrāculum cōnsulendum mīsit. Comes eīs additus
5 est L. Iūnius. Hic ex industriā[4] imitātus stultitiam, cum sē suaque praedae esse rēgī sineret, Brūtī[5] quoque nōn recūsāvit cognōmen, ab Tarquiniō datum, ut, sub eō cognōmine latēns,[6] līberātor ille populī Rōmānī opperīrētur[7] tempora sua. Is tum ab Tarquiniīs, fīliīs rēgis, ductus est Delphōs, lūdibrium[8] vērius quam comes. Quō postquam vēnērunt, perfectīs
10 patris mandātīs, cupīdō incessit animōs iuvenum rogandī ad quem eōrum rēgnum Rōmānum esset ventūrum. Ex īnfimō vōcem redditam audiunt: "Imperium summum Rōmae habēbit quī vestrum prīmus, ō iuvenēs, ōsculum mātrī dederit." Tarquiniī sortī[9] permittunt uter prior, cum ad patriam rediissent, mātri ōsculum daret. Brūtus aliō putāns spectāre[10]
15 vōcem ōrāculī, velut si prōlāpsus cecidisset, terram ōsculō contigit, quod ea commūnis māter omnium mortālium erat. Et sīc ēvēnit: post fugam Tarquinī et fīliōrum suōrum, Brūtus et L. Collatīnus, duo cōnsulēs, imperium Rōmae obtinuērunt.

This photo is of the area of the sacred spring at Delphi. The sons of Tarquin went to consult the oracle at Delphi to learn the significance of the snake omen. The oracle often gave answers that were ambiguous so that no matter what the outcome, the prophesy was accurate. What happened when the Tarquins posed their question?

Boltin Picture Library

Questions

1. What omen did King Tarquinius see, and how did it affect him?
2. Who was sent to Delphi? Why?
3. Why did Lucius Junius go along?
4. How did Brutus pretend to be stupid?
5. Why did he pretend to be stupid?
6. After the two sons had done what their father asked, what additional question did they ask the oracle?
7. What was the oracle's answer?
8. How did the sons intend to decide who would be first?
9. How did the sons interpret this response? What different meaning did Brutus see in it? Who was right?
10. Now that you know the story of Brutus, how would you interpret the omen of the snake?

The Metropolitan Museum of Art, Rogers Fund, 1947. (47.11.3) Copyright © 1991 By the Metropolitan Museum of Art.

Statue of an Etruscan soldier helping a wounded comrade. The Etruscans flourished in central Italy from the eighth to the first centuries B.C. They were well regarded for their seamanship and established a relationship with the Phoenicians in Carthage. Eventually, they were assimilated into the Roman population.

▦ GRAMMAR

Review of the Future Passive Participle and the Gerund

Review the future passive participle and the gerund in Lessons XXI and XXIII. Also see the Grammar Appendix, pp. 520–530.

Find all the examples of these in the reading on page 180.

Translation

1. Who did Brutus think was the mother of all people?
2. A temple had-to-be-built at Rome by the citizens.[10]
3. Brutus did not think that he had-to-fear[10] the king.
4. The two young men went to the oracle for the purpose of asking[11] which would be king.

▦ VOCABULARY

Nouns

comes, -itis m., f. *companion*   [eō]
pectus, pectoris n. *breast, heart*   (pectoral)
stultitia, -ae f. *stupidity*   (stultification, stultify)

Verbs

contingō, -ere, -tigī, -tāctus *touch*   [tangō]
impleō, -ēre, implēvī, implētus *fill*   (implement)
sinō, -ere, sīvī, situs *allow*

Adverb

velut *as if*

▦ WORD STUDY

Derivatives Comes (**cum + eō**) is one who "goes with" you; a *companion* (**cum + pānis**) is one who shares "bread with" you.

Explain *additive, comity, contingency, elapse, juvenile, latent, narrative, osculatory, pectoral, ultimatum.*

Explain how *habit* can equal *custom* and *costume.*

---

[10] Use the dative of agent.
[11] Use the gerund with **ad** or **causā.**

HOW "LEFTY" (SCAEVOLA) GOT HIS NAME

LESSON OBJECTIVE
- More about Latin Sentence Structure

Tarquinius, ut reciperet rēgnum, bellum Rōmānīs intulit, Porsenā, rēge Etrūscōrum, auxilium ferente. Illō tempore Horātius Coclēs pontem dēfendit et Rōmam servāvit. Urbs tum obsidēbātur ā Porsenā, et frūmentī erat inopia. Sedendō[1] expugnātūrum sē urbem Porsena spērābat. Tum C. Mūcius in hostium castra īre cōnstituit. Nē forte[2] ā mīlitibus Rōmānīs retraherētur, senātum adiit. "Trānsīre Tiberim," inquit, "patrēs, et in castra hostium īre volō. Deīs iuvantibus, magnum in animō factum fīxum habeō." Probant patrēs. Abditō intrā vestem gladiō, proficīscitur. Ubi eō vēnit, in multitūdine hostium ad rēgis tribūnal[3] cōnstitit. Ibi stīpendium mīlitibus forte dabātur, et rēgis scrība,[4] quī rēgī simillimus ōrnātū[5] erat, multa   10 agēbat. Mūcius Porsenam nōn cognōverat, neque rogāre volēbat, nē ipse aperīret quis esset; itaque scrībam, quem rēgem esse crēdidit, prō rēge occidit. Deinde postquam per hostēs territōs gladiō viam sibi ipse fēcit, rēgis mīlitēs eum prehēnsum retrāxērunt. Ante tribūnal rēgis stāns, tum

[1] *by remaining encamped.* What literally?
[2] *not from* **fortis, -e**
[3] *tribunal, platform*
[4] *secretary*
[5] *dress*

Museum of Fine Arts, Budapest Hungary/Bridgeman Art Library

"Cīvis sum Rōmānus." With three simple words Mucius Scaevola confronts the Etruscan king Porsena and sets the stage for a showdown. Livy writes that the king is so astonished and impressed by Mucius' stoic fortitude that he sets the Roman spy free. In later history, Roman citizenship conferred enormous legal and economic benefits on its holder, including immunity from any torture or violence.

6 to be feared

7 toward you

8 the issue will be between you and individual (enemies)

9 at the same time

10 look you

11 how

12 Why dative?

13 Left-handed ("Lefty"); pronounced Seev'ola

15 quoque in tantō perīculō timendus[6] magis quam timēns, "Rōmānus sum," inquit, "cīvis; C. Mūcium mē vocant. Hostem occīdere voluī, sed morī sciō. Nec ego sōlus in tē[7] hōs animōs habeō. Nūllus exercitus timendus tibi, nūllum proelium timendum est; ūnī tibi cum singulīs rēs erit."[8] Tum rēx simul[9] īrā commōtus perīculōque perterritus, ignem circumdarī 20 iussit ut Mūcius īnsidiās statim explicāre cōgerētur. Mūcius autem, "Ēn tibi,"[10] inquit, "ut sentiās quam[11] vīle corpus sit eīs quī magnam glōriam vident," dextramque manum ignī[12] ad sacrificium factō iniēcit. Rēx, tantam virtūtem mīrātus, Mūcium līberum dīmīsit. Huic Mūciō posteā, quod dextram manum āmīserat, nōmen Scaevolae[13] datum est.

Questions

1. Why did Tarquin bring war on the Roman? Who was his ally?
2. By what means were they trying to subdue Rome?
3. From whom did Mucius get approval for his plan and why?
4. What was his plan?
5. What did Mucius take with him to execute his plan?
6. Why was there a crowd at the king's tribunal?
7. What mistake did he make in carrying it out?
8. What effect did Mucius have upon his captors, even when captured?
9. What did Mucius have to say to the king, and what was the point of his remarks?
10. What effect did Mucius' courage have on the king and on himself?
11. What Roman character trait is Livy illustrating in this story?

GRAMMAR

Latin Sentence Structure

| **Mīlitēs eum prehēnsum retrāxērunt.** | *The soldiers seized him and pulled him back.* |

Note the striking difference between Latin and English sentence structure. Latin prefers to vary the construction by use of participles (including the ablative absolute) and subordinate clauses of various sorts. English prefers coordinate constructions connected by *and*.

Translation

1. Mucius said that Rome was to be saved by him.
2. When Rome was being besieged, Mucius approached the senate.
3. He was to be feared by the enemy, for he had come to free Rome by fighting.
4. He set out for the enemy's camp for the purpose of killing the king.

⊞ VOCABULARY

Nouns

inopia, -ae f. *lack*	[ops]
īnsidiae, -ārum f. pl. *plot, ambush*	[sedeō]
stīpendium, -dī n. *pay*	(stipend, stipendiary)

Verbs

abdō, -ere, abdidī, abditus *put away, hide*	[dō]
aperiō, -īre, aperuī, apertus *open, reveal*	(aperture)
circumdō, -dare, -dedī, -datus *put around*	[dō]
fīgō, -ere, fīxī, fixus *fix*	(fixate, fixture)
obsideō, -ēre, obsēdī, obsessus, *beseige*	[sedeō]

Preposition

intrā (with acc.) *within*	(intragalactic, intramural)

WORD STUDY

Spelling We have many silent consonants in English words. They cause trouble in spelling. In some cases the difficulty is cleared up by thinking of the Latin original, for Latin has no silent letters. Compare the following, often misspelled: *debt* (**dēbitus**), *honor* (**honor**), *assign* (**signum**), *mortgage* (**mortem**), *receipt* (**receptus**). Can you think of other instances?

LESSON OBJECTIVE
- Impersonal Verbs

THE PLEBEIANS GO ON STRIKE[1]

[1] In this reading, adapted from Livy II, 23, 1–15; 31, 7–33, 11, the plebeians, long oppressed by forced military service, food shortages, and debt, at last in 494 B.C. moved out of Rome in protest. The "strike" was settled by a compromise: in return for their renewed allegiance, the plebeians were allowed to create tribunes who had the power to veto legislation and to protect them against harm from the Senate and the consuls. No patrician could be a **tribūnus plēbis**.

[2] *after the expulsion of the kings.* What literally?

[3] *another's money,* i.e., *debt.* It is prudent for a debtor to think of debt as someone else's money.

[4] i.e., *the plebeians*

[5] *go into debt*

[6] *chains*

[7] They called the roll in the draft.

[8] *before arms are (to be) given (to them)*

Paulō post rēgēs exāctōs[2] bellum cīvīle propter aes aliēnum[3] inter senātōrēs et plēbem oritur. Hōrum[4] multī dīxērunt sē in fīnibus hostium prō lībertāte et imperiō pugnantēs ā cīvibus domī oppressōs esse, tūtiōremque in bellō inter hostēs lībertātem plēbis esse quam in pāce inter
5 cīvēs. Quīdam, quī Sabīnō bellō fortis mīles fuerat, "Mē absente," inquit, "ager vāstātus est, vīlla incēnsa, tribūtum imperātum. Aes aliēnum facere[5] mē oportēbat. Posteā agrum āmīsī et ā crēditōribus in vincula[6] coniectus sum." Hōc audītō, multitūdō postulāvit ut senātus vocārētur. Senātū convocātō, nūntiātur Volscōs ad urbem oppugnandam venīre. Omnēs,
10 inimīcitiā dēpositā, pugnant, hostēsque vincuntur. Sed post bellum senātus nihil dē plēbe ēgit. Tum aliud bellum oritur. Cōnsulēs nōmina cīvium legunt.[7] Cum ad suum nōmen nēmō respondēret, omnēs dīcunt lībertātem reddendam esse priusquam arma danda,[8] ut prō patriā cīvibusque, nōn prō dominīs pugnent. Dictātor plēbī meliōrem condiciōnem post bellum
15 pollicitus est. Sed, bellō cōnfectō, nihil āctum est.

The Sabines were an ancient people who lived in the hills northeast of Rome. Tradition says that the abduction of the Sabine women, supposedly to provide wives for the followers of Romulus, may have explained the Sabine population in Rome.

Bettmann/CORBIS

The Roman Senate was the dominant branch of the government during the Republic. It began with a membership of three hundred, then grew to six hundred under Sulla, increased to nine hundred under Julius Caesar, and was brought back to six hundred by Augustus. Senators were primarily wealthy aristocrats or large landowners; others obtained senatorial rank by virtue of holding a magistracy. Senators were forbidden to engage in large-scale business.

Tum plēbs in Sacrum montem sēcessērunt.[9] Hic mōns trāns Aniēnem flūmen est tria ab urbe mīlia passuum. Patribus[10] placuit ad plēbem mittī Menēnium Agrippam. Is hanc fābulam nārrāvit:

"Ōlim reliquae partēs corporis hūmānī īrātae erant quod suā cūrā, suō labōre ventrī[11] omnia quaerēbantur, quī ipse nihil agēbat. Coniūrāvērunt nē manūs[12] ad ōs cibum ferrent, nec ōs acciperet, nec dentēs cōnficerent.[13] Dum ventrem hōc modō vincere volunt, ipsa membra paene moriuntur. Inde appāret ventrem nōn magis alī quam alere." Cum Menēnius ostendisset quam[14] corporis discordia similis esset īrae plēbis, pāx facta est hāc condiciōne, ut tribūnī plēbis creārentur neque ūllī patrī[15] licēret eum magistrātum capere. Tribūnī accēpērunt potestātem auxilī dandī[16] contrā cōnsulēs.

20

25

[9] 494 B.C.; as **plēbs** is plural in thought, the plural verb is used; so in English, we may say "The committee *is* meeting," when the committee is thought of as a whole, or "The committee *are* not agreed," when we think of individual members.

[10] *senators*

[11] *for the stomach*

[12] subject of **ferrent**. The parts of the body went on strike against the stomach.

[13] *"do up,"* i.e., *chew up*

[14] *how,* introducing an indirect question

[15] *patrician*

[16] i.e., to a citizen who appealed to them

Questions

1. What causes of the civil strife between the patricians and the plebeians are mentioned here?
2. What grievances did the soldier who fought in the Sabine War express?
3. What was expected of the plebeians in time of war?
4. What happened the next time the senate called out the plebeians and enlisted them for military service?
5. What did the dictator promise? Was the promise kept?
6. To what place did the *plebs* secede, and where was this located?
7. What was the tale of "conspiracy" the Menenius Agrippa told? What was its moral?
8. On what conditions did the *plebs* come to terms with the *patres?*

GRAMMAR

Impersonal Verbs

Some verbs are at times used impersonally, either without an expressed subject or with a clause as subject. Compare **nūntiātur** in line 9 of the reading and **appāret** in line 23.

Other verbs are used only impersonally and therefore have no forms in the first and second persons. Note the differences in construction.

1. With **licet** the dative of the person is used.

> **Mihi hoc facere licet.**   *It is permitted to me to do this; I may do this.*

2. With **oportet** the accusative is used as subject of the infinitive.

> **Mē hoc facere oportet.**   *It is necessary that I do this; I must (ought to) do this.*

3. With the impersonal form **placet** the dative is used and it generally has the idiomatic sense *it is decided by* (literally, *it is pleasing to*).

> **Mihi placet.**   *It is decided by me; I have decided.*

Translation (Use the proper impersonal construction in each sentence.)

1. No senator will be allowed (permitted) to oppress the common people.
2. It will not be necessary (for) them to demand better conditions.[17]
3. The citizens ought not to be seized and thrown into chains by creditors.[17]
4. It has been agreed (decided) by the senate to make peace by promising certain conditions.

Nota•Bene

Remember that necessity may also be expressed in two other ways.

Hoc facere dēbeō. or
Hoc mihi faciendum est.

VOCABULARY

Nouns

aes, aeris n. *bronze, money*
magistrātus, -ūs m. *magistracy, office*   [magister]
plēbs, plēbis f. *common people*   (plebeian, plebiscite)

Adjective

tūtus, -a, -um *safe, guarded*   (tutelage, tutor)

---

[17] Translate in two ways.

Verbs

alō, -ere, aluī, alitus *feed, nourish*   (alimony, coalition)

coniūrō, 1 *conspire*   (conjure)

licet, -ēre, licuit or **licitum est** *it is permitted*   (illicit, licit)

oportet, -ēre, oportuit *it is necessary*

oppugnō, 1 *attack*   **[pugnō]**

postulō, 1 *demand*   (postulant, postulate)

Conjunction

priusquam *before*

WORD STUDY

Terms Used in Geometry The following words are commonly used in geometry. Define them and find other geometrical or mathematical terms derived from Latin.

acute (**acūtus**)	locus (**locus**)
adjacent (**ad-, iaceō**)	median (**medius**)
circumscribe (**circum-, scrībō**)	plane (**plānus**)
coincide (**co-, incidō**)	quadrilateral (**quattuor, latus**)
complementary (**compleō**)	Q.E.D. (**quod erat dēmōnstrandum**)
concurrent (**con-, currō**)	Q.E.F. (**quod erat faciendum**)
equidistant (**aequus, dis-, stō**)	subtend (**sub-, tendō**)
equilateral (**aequus, latus**)	tangent (**tangō**)
inscribe (**in-, scrībō**)	transversal (**trāns-, vertō**)

Can you think of others? Make a poster to organize and illustrate the different terms you know.

Civil Liberty and Democracy

As stated in the American Declaration of Independence, we believe that people have "certain unalienable rights," and "that to secure these rights Governments are instituted among Men, deriving their just powers from the consent of the governed."

But in ancient Rome, even after the expulsion of the kings, the common people had very little voice in the way in which they were governed by the senatorial and patrician oligarchy *(rule by the few)*. They struggled for several hundred years for the right to hold certain political and military offices, for intermarriage among the classes, for fair taxes, and for adequate protection in the courts. Our word *plebiscite,* a vote of the people, is an inheritance from that struggle. The history of Rome shows that the fight for liberty and democracy is never completely won, that we must always be on the alert to defend both, that we must never take them for granted.

The new office of tribune, open only to plebeians, had the power of veto over the actions of the patrician consuls and senate. This led to a system of checks and balances that was adopted in the Constitution of the United States. We use the Roman tribune's word **vetō,** *I forbid,* of the President's power to reject the acts passed by Congress. Compare too the veto power in the Security Council of the United Nations.

The settlement of the strike has a lesson for us. It was ended by mediation and through concessions by both sides. The plebeians did not strike in order to destroy their country but because they had just grievances, which they wanted to settle by peaceful means.

Latīnum Hodiernum
Pictūrae Mōbilēs

Amāsne tēlevīsiōnem? Habēsne domī māchinam ad tēlevīsiōnem accommodātam? An pictūrae mōbilēs quae in theātrīs videntur magis tibi placent? Vīdistīne tālēs pictūrās quae dē vītā antīquā agunt? Inter eās est *Iūlius Caesar,* illa fābula quam Pīlīvibrātor (Anglicē Shakespeare) scrīpsit, et *Antōnius et Cleopātra.* Deinde sunt eae quae dē Rōmānīs et Christiānīs agunt, ut *Quō Vādis, Chlamys,*[18] *Dēmētrius et Gladiātōrēs, Ben Hur, Gladiātor.* Hae omnēs nimis crūdēlitātem īnsāniamque imperātōrum, gladiātōrēs in arēnā pugnantēs, Christiānōs leōnibus aliīsque ferīs animālibus obiectōs dēscrībunt sed tamen spectācula iūcunda praebent, quae mīlitēs, senātōrēs, Vestālēs, gladiātōrēs mōnstrant, nec nōn[19] amphitheātra, templa, aedificia antīqua. Similis est pictūra *Spartacus* appellāta, quae dē servīs ā Rōmānīs crūdēlibus oppressīs agit. Sed mihi maximē placent pictūrae mōbilēs quae quidem dē vītā hodiernā agunt, Rōmae tamen factae, pulcherrimōs prōspectūs praebent, et ruīnās Rōmānās et aedificia moderna, nam antīqua et hodierna Rōmae nunc ita cōnfūsa sunt ut ōva mixta vel carō modō Hamburgiēnsī cocta. Plūrēs pictūrās huius generis vīdimis, e.g., *Fēriae Rōmānae* et *Trēs Nummī in Fonte;* aliae certē prōdūcentur.

Quod tot pictūrae huius generis nunc in theātrīs nostrīs mōnstrantur nōn sine ratiōne est: conicere possumus haec spectācula Americānīs grātissima esse, rēs Rōmānās nōbīs iūcundissimās, vītam antīquam et imperium Rōmānum populō nostrō magnae cūrae esse.

---

[18] *the Robe*
[19] *and also*

EXTRA! ROME CAPTURED BY THE GAULS[1]

LESSON OBJECTIVES
- Review Genitive of the Whole
- More about **Cum** Clauses

Gallī, Italiae dulcibus frūctibus maximēque vīnō captī, Alpēs trānsiērunt et contrā Rōmānōs prōcessērunt. Sed cum Rōmānī pugnantēs cum fīnitimīs populīs saepe dictātōrem creāvissent, eō tempore nihil extraōrdināriī[2] imperī aut auxilī quaesīvērunt. Plūrimum terrōris ad Rōmānōs celeritās hostium tulit. Ad flūmen Alliam Rōmānī superātī sunt. Maxima pars eōrum ad urbem Veiōs fūgit; nihil praesidī Rōmam[3] mīsērunt. Aliī Rōmam petīvērunt et, nē clausīs quidem portīs urbis, in arcem fūgērunt. Tam facile Rōmānī victī erant ut Gallī mīrantēs prīmum stārent, īnsidiās verentēs. Deinde ad urbem prōgressī sunt. Cum equitēs rettulissent nōn portās urbis clausās, nōn mīlitēs in mūrīs esse, veritī tamen īnsidiās et noctem, inter Rōmam atque flūmen Aniēnem castra posuērunt.

Cum spēs nūlla urbis dēfendendae esset, Rōmānī cōnstituērunt ut iuventūs mīlitāris[4] cum mulieribus ac līberīs in arcem Capitōliumque concēderet. Ibi, frūmentō collātō, deōs hominēsque et Rōmānum nōmen dēfendere parant.

5

10

15

[1] This was in 390 B.C. Many believe that because the buildings which held the records of early Rome were burned in this sack by the Gauls, the history of Rome before 390 B.C. is seriously flawed. Rome was not again captured by a foreign enemy for eight hundred years.

[2] The genitive of second declension adjectives is not contracted like that of nouns.

[3] *to Rome*

[4] *capable of bearing arms*

Bettmann/CORBIS

Livy's narrative of the Gallic sack of Rome tells how the Gauls entered the city, motivated chiefly by love of Italian food and drink. Roman vigilance on this occasion had failed, but resolute adherence to ancestral customs—the **mōs maiōrum**—made possible a determined resistance. Here the Gauls indulge their appetites in food, drink, and sport, without any apprehension for the future.

5 *houses*

6 *resolved*

7 *ivory chairs*

8 *full of reverence*

9 *stroking his (i.e., the old man's) beard*

10 *ivory staff—part of the insignia of a triumphing general. He was seated, as we might say, in full uniform, wearing all his medals, awaiting his doom.*

11 *struck. What are* percussion *instruments?*

12 *No one is spared.*

13 *try*

Senēs autem in aedibus[5] suīs adventum hostium obstinātō[6] ad mortem animō exspectāre māluērunt. Eī quī magistrātūs gesserant, augustissimā veste vestītī in mediō aedium in eburneīs sellīs[7] sēdērunt. Posterō diē Gallī
20 urbem ingressī ad praedam properant. Venerābundī[8] spectābant sedentēs virōs, quī ob vestem et maiestātem gravitātemque deīs simillimī vidēbantur. Cum Gallī, ad eōs sedentēs velut ad imāginēs versī, stārent, ūnus ē senibus Gallum barbam suam permulcentem[9] scīpiōne eburneō[10] percussit.[11] Hoc initium caedis fuit. Cēterī in aedibus suīs interfectī sunt.
Post prīncipum caedem nēminī parcitur,[12] dīripiuntur aedificia, iniciuntur
25 ignēs. Sed arcem capere Gallī nōndum cōnantur.[13]

Questions

1. What were the attractions that led the Gauls into Italy?
2. What usual step, when attacked by their neighbors, did the Romans this time fail to take?
3. Where were the Roman troops defeated, and where did they go?
4. Why did the Gauls hesitate to follow up on their victory?
5. In what way did the Romans prepare for their defense?
6. What is the difference between an **urbs** and an **arx?**
7. How did the seniors and the ex-magistrates prepare for the Gauls' arrival?
8. How did their appearance impress the Gauls?
9. What action triggered the slaughter?
10. What happened to the city?
11. In what way was the Romans' plan of defense successful?

GRAMMAR

Review of Genitive of the Whole[14] (Lesson IV)

nihil imperī	*no power*
plūrimum terrōris	*a great deal of terror*

The genitive of the whole *represents the whole to which a part belongs.* It may depend on any noun, pronoun, adjective, or adverb that implies part of the whole. Ordinarily the construction is the same as English and causes no trouble (second example). At times, where the genitive is used in Latin with such words as **nihil, satis, quid** (first example), we prefer in English to use an adjective modifier. Still, we sometimes use such expressions as *nothing of good.*

[14] also called the Partitive Genitive

With cardinal numerals and **quīdam** the ablative with **dē** or **ex** is preferred to the genitive of the whole.

ūnus ē senibus   *one of the old men*

More about *Cum* Clauses

Review **cum** clauses in Lesson XXVIII. In some clauses **cum** *(when)* is best translated as *since,* in others by *although.* In such clauses the subjunctive is always used.

Cum spēs nūlla urbis dēfendendae esset...	*Since* (literally, *when*) *there was no hope of defending the city . . .*
Sed cum Rōmānī... saepe dictātōrem creāvissent...	*But although the Romans had often appointed a dictator . . .*

Find at least one example of each of these uses in the reading on pages 191 and 192.

Translation

1. Nothing (of) good is inspired by a great deal of terror.
2. Of all the Romans, the old men alone determined to die in the city.
3. Although the gates had not been closed, the rest withdrew to the citadel.
4. Since the Romans feared the approach of the enemy's horsemen, they fled and left no (nothing of a) guard.

▦ VOCABULARY

Nouns

adventus, -ūs m. *arrival*	[veniō]
arx, arcis, f. *citadel*	
caedēs, -is f. *slaughter*	[caedō]

Adjective

mīlitāris, -e *military*	[mīles]

Verbs

dīripiō, -ere, dīripuī, dīreptus *plunder*	[rapiō]
parcō, -ere, pepercī, parsūrus (w. dat.) *spare*	(parsimonious)
vereor, verērī, veritus *fear*	(revere)

WORD STUDY

Prefixes Review the prefix **inter-** in the Grammar Appendix. The preposition **intrā** *(within, inside)* is also used as a prefix in English. The two must be carefully distinguished: an *intercollegiate* contest is one *between* two (or more) colleges; an *intracollegiate* contest is one *within* a single college, as when the freshmen and sophomores play a game. What is the difference between *interscholastic* and *intrascholastic, interstate* and *intrastate?*

Intrō- *(within)* is also used as a prefix: **intrōdūcō,** *introduce, introspection, introvert*

Extrā- *(outside)* is found in *extraordinary* (from **ōrdō**).
Define *extralegal, extramural, intracellular, intravenous.*

A WAKE-UP CALL SAVES ROME SWEET HOME

LESSON OBJECTIVES
- Review Uses of the Dative
- Omission of Forms of **Sum**

Arx Capitōliumque in magnō perīculō fuērunt. Nam Gallī nocte tantō silentiō in summum ēvāsērunt ut nōn custōdēs sōlum fallerent sed nē canēs quidem excitārent. Ānserēs[1] nōn fefellērunt, quōs sacrōs[2] Iūnōnī in summā inopiā cibī[3] Rōmānī tamen nōn occīderant. Quae rēs Rōmānīs salūtī fuit; nam clangōre[4] eōrum excitātus est M. Mānlius, quī, armīs raptīs, ad arma   5 cēterōs vocāvit. Eī Gallōs facile dēiēcērunt.

Sed posteā nōn sōlum cibus sed etiam spēs dēfēcit. Tum tribūnīs mīlitum negōtium datum ut pācem facerent. Ācta rēs est, et mīlle pondō[5] aurī pretium factum est. Pondera[6] ab Gallīs allāta inīqua et, tribūnō Rōmānō recūsante,[7] additus est ā Gallō ponderī gladius, audītaque vōx   10 Rōmānīs nōn ferenda,[8] "Vae[9] victīs!"

Sed dī[10] et hominēs prohibuērunt esse redēmptōs Rōmānōs. Nam nōndum omnī aurō pēnsō, Camillus, quī absēns iterum dictātor creātus erat, vēnit. Gallōs discēdere iubet et eīs imperat ut sē ad proelium expediant. Suōs ferrō,[11] nōn aurō, recipere patriam iubet. Gallī in Rōmānōs 15 currunt sed vincuntur; castra capiuntur; nē nūntius quidem proelī relīctus.

Sed nunc plēbs voluit ruīnās Rōmae relinquere et in urbem Veiōs migrāre. Camillus ōrātiōnem vehementem habuit et eōs mōvit:

"Nōnne tenet vōs haec terra quam mātrem appellāmus? Mihi quidem, cum patria in mentem venit, haec omnia occurrunt: collēs campīque et   20

---

[1] *geese*

[2] *(being) sacred*

[3] *(although) in the greatest need of food*

[4] *honking*

[5] used as an indeclinable noun: *pounds*

[6] *weights,* for weighing the gold. When the Romans complained that the weights were heavier than the bargain specified, the Gaul insolently threw in a sword as an additional weight.

[7] i.e., the weights

[8] *intolerable to Romans.* What literally?

[9] *woe*

[10] for **dei**

[11] English would say *steel.*

North Wind Picture Archives

The Capitoline, the least inhabited of Rome's seven hills, was the site of a fortified citadel and the center of the state religion. At its summit was the Capitolium, the magnificent temple dedicated to Jupiter, Juno, and Minerva. According to legend, in 390 B.C. the geese caged nearby and sacred to Juno awakened M. Manlius Capitolinus at a moment of great crisis.

Tiberis et hoc caelum sub quō nātus ēducātusque sum. Nōn sine causā dī hominēsque hunc urbī cōnstituendae locum ēlēgērunt, marī propinquum, regiōnum Italiae medium. Argūmentō[12] est ipsa magnitūdō tam novae urbis. Nōn singulae urbēs, nōn coniūnctī cum Aequīs Volscī, nōn tōta

25 Etrūria bellō vōbīs pār est. Hīc Capitōlium est ubi, quondam capite hūmānō inventō, ā deō respōnsum est[13] in eō locō caput imperī futūrum esse. Hīc Vestae ignēs, hīc ancīlia dē caelō dēmissa, hīc omnēs dī propitiī[14] manentibus vōbīs."

Questions

1. Why was the danger to Rome so great?
2. Why had the geese not been killed although the Romans were faced with famine?
3. What actions did Manlius take?
4. What task was given to the military tribunes?
5. What was the price of peace? Was the bargain faithfully kept?
6. Why and how did one Gaul "add insult to injury?"
7. What orders did Camillus give to the Gauls? To the Romans?
8. How badly were the Gauls beaten in the ensuing battle?
9. What did the plebeians want to do?
10. What arguments did Camillus use to dissuade the people from their plan?
11. To what elements in Roman character does each argument appeal?

The top of the Capitoline Hill is now occupied by a square called the Piazza del Campidoglio. Palaces (two of them now museums) surround the piazza on three sides and on the fourth is an impressive staircase flanked by giant ancient marble horses, which were relocated to this site by Michelangelo in the sixteenth century. In the center of the square stands a copy of an equestrian statue of the emperor Marcus Aurelius. The original, perhaps saved from destruction during the Middle Ages because it was thought to portray the Christian emperor Constantine, has been restored and can now be seen in the Palazzo Nuovo.

C.M. Dixon/Photo Resources

Roman armor pieces included body armor (**arma, lōrīca**), shield (**scūtum**), helmet (**galea**), a short stabbing dagger (**sīca, pūgiō**), a sword (**gladius**), and a heavy and a light javelin (**pīlum**).

Archivio e Studio Folco Quilici

GRAMMAR

Review of Uses of the Dative

Review the datives of purpose and reference in Lesson XXVI. Find all the examples of these and the other dative constructions in the reading on pages 195 and 196.

Omission of Forms of *Sum*

English will occasionally omit some form of the verb *to be,* as in a sentence like *They were known (to have been) lost at sea.* In informal English, contraction of very common forms of *to be* (and of a few other words) reduces their impact upon the ear without destroying the sense intended: *She's a great rider; he's less proficient.* In English, too, you will sometimes find complete omission of forms of the verb *to be: Glad to see you!* or *He's a poet, his sister an artist.*

In Latin, to the contrary, a form of **sum** is very often omitted when it might be used 1) as a simple linking verb (or *copula*), or 2) in compound tenses of the indicative or infinitive.

There are at least five examples of this common Latin usage in the reading. Can you find them?

Translation

1. What circumstance was a (source of) safety to the Romans?
2. "The gods," said he, "have chosen Rome as a home for themselves."
3. The Romans had made peace with the Gauls by paying (*fut. pass. part.*) money.
4. When the Gauls were already near the top (of the) hill, the Romans threw them down.

▓ VOCABULARY

Nouns

collis, -is m. *hill*
custōs, -ōdis m. *guard* (custodian, custody)
mēns, mentis f. *mind* (mental, dementia)

Adjectives

inīquus, -a, -um *uneven, unjust* [aequus]
propinquus, -a, -um *near*
vehemēns, vehementis (gen.) *vigorous* [vehō]

Verbs

dēficiō, -ere, dēfēcī, dēfectus *fail* [faciō]
dēiciō, -ere, dēiēcī, dēiectus [iaciō]
  throw down, dislodge
ēvādō, -ere, ēvāsī, ēvāsūrus (evade, evasive)
  go out, climb, escape
nāscor, nāscī, nātus *be born* (Renaissance, nascent)
occurrō, -ere, occurrī, occursūrus [currō]
  meet, occur
pendō, -ere, pependī, pēnsus (pendant, compensate)
  hang, weigh, pay

WORD STUDY

Spelling Many English words containing *c, g,* or *s* sounds are often misspelled. When these are derived from Latin, it will be helpful to think of the Latin original: *circumstance, voice, concern, suggest, legislation, origin, cordial, graduate, presume, vision, decision.*

Explain *alimentary, custodian, deficient, dementia, expenditure, illicit, impend, iniquitous, nascent, nativity, occurrence, propinquity.*

Explain the difference between *liberty* and *license.*
Illinois and New York have towns named *Manlius.*

LESSON XXXIV

THE TWO MANLII TORQUATI, OR COURAGE AND DISCIPLINE[1]

LESSON OBJECTIVES
- Review Volitive Clauses
- Review the Indefinite Pronouns **Quis, Aliquis,** and **Quīdam**

Gallī contrā Rōmānōs pugnābant. Quīdam ē Gallīs quī et vīribus et magnitūdine et virtūte cēterīs praestābat prōcessit et vōce maximā clāmat: "Sī quis mēcum pugnāre vult, prōcēdat." Omnēs recūsant propter magnitūdinem eius atque immānem[2] faciem. Deinde Gallus rīdēre incipit atque linguam ēicere. Tum T. Mānlius, mīles Rōmānus, prōcessit et contrā 5 Gallum cōnstitit. Gallus, quī longiōrem gladium habuit, scūtō prōiectō, exspectābat; Mānlius scūtō scūtum percussit[3] atque Gallum dē locō dēiēcit. Eō modō sub Gallī gladium successit atque breviōre suō gladiō eum interfēcit. Torquem auream[4] eius dētrāxit eamque sibi in collum impōnit. Quō ex factō ipse posterīque eius Torquātī sunt nōminātī. 10

Postquam Torquātus cōnsul factus est, bellum contrā Latīnōs susceptum est. Latīnī Rōmānīs similēs erant linguā, mōribus, armōrum genere, īnstitūtīs mīlitāribus. Itaque Torquātus et alter cōnsul cōnstituērunt maximā cum cūrā pugnāre et imperāvērunt nē quis extrā ōrdinem in hostēs pugnāret. 15

Forte inter cēterōs quī ad explōrandum et pābulandum[5] dīmissī erant T. Mānlius, cōnsulis fīlius, ad castra hostium ēvāsit. Cum equitem Latīnum vidēret, imperī patris oblītus[6] est et cum hoste pugnāre coepit. Quod ubi audīvit cōnsul, statim mīlitēs convocārī iussit. Tum fīliō, "quoniam tū," inquit, "neque imperium cōnsulis neque maiestātem patris 20 veritus, extrā ōrdinem cum hoste pugnāvistī et disciplīnam mīlitārem, quā stetit ad hanc diem Rōmāna rēs,[7] solvistī, trīste exemplum[8] sed salūbre[9] posterīs nostrīs erō. Mē quidem et amor līberōrum et virtūs tua movet; sed tū quoque, sī quid in tē nostrī sanguinis est, volēs disciplīnam mīlitārem poenā tuā restituere." Hōc dictō, imperāvit ut fīlius statim morte 25 afficerētur.

Post hoc Latīnī magnā pugnā superātī sunt.

[1] from Aulus Gellius and Livy. The incident referred to took place in 361 B.C., on the occasion of a second invasion by the Gauls.

[2] *huge*

[3] *struck (the Gaul's) shield with his own*

[4] *collar of gold,* worn by soldiers as a military decoration, like our medals

[5] *forage*

[6] *forgot* (literally, *was forgetful of,* followed by the genitive **imperī**)

[7] = **rēs pūblica**

[8] predicate nominative; *I shall be an example*

[9] *wholesome*

Questions

1. In what ways did the Gaul surpass his comrades?
2. How did he taunt the Romans?
3. How did most of the Romans react to his challenge?
4. What tactic did Manlius use to win the duel?
5. What did Manlius then do and how did it affect him and his family?
6. In what ways were the Latins similar to the Romans, and how did this affect the consul's strategy?
7. What was the consul's son sent to do? What did he end up doing?
8. What lesson did the father's **trīste exemplum** teach?
9. How was the father's action intended to be an **exemplum salūbre** for posterity?

GRAMMAR

Volitive Noun Clauses

Review volitive clauses in Lesson XXII. Find two examples of such clauses in the preceding reading.

The Indefinite Pronouns *Quis, Aliquis,* and *Quīdam*

After **sī, nisi, num,** and **nē, quis** is used as an indefinite pronoun *(some, any)* in place of **aliquis.** Review the declension of **quis, aliquis,** and **quīdam** in Lessons VI and XX.

Practice

Identify the form of **quid, cuidam, aliqua, quoddam, quaedam, alicuius, quōrundam, aliquī.**

Translation

1. The two consuls had warned their (men) to obey (**pareō** + dat.) the order.
2. The consuls had asked that no one fight with the enemy unless ordered.[10]
3. So as to be a wholesome example to the rest the consul ordered his own son to be killed.
4. Certain of the soldiers were sent out to reconnoiter, and the consul's son too had begged to go with them.

[10] Use **iubeō.**

VOCABULARY

Nouns

eques, equitis m. *horseman*   **[equus]**

magnitūdō, -dinis f. *greatness, size*   **[magnus]**

sanguis, -inis m. *blood*   (sanguine, sanguinary)

Adjective

trīstis, -e *sad, severe, bitter*

Verbs

coepī, coeptus *began* (perfect tenses only)

praestō, -āre, -stitī, -stitus   **[stō]**
  stand before, excel (w. dat.)

prōiciō, -ere, -iēcī, -iectus   **[iaciō]**
  throw, thrust (forward)

restituō, -ere, restituī, restitūtus *restore*   **[stō]**

Preposition

extrā (w. acc.) *outside of*   (extraordinary)

Conjunction

quoniam *since*

WORD STUDY

Aviation Terms from Latin The following aviation terms are all derived from Latin.

accelerometer (**ad-, celer**)	jet (**iaciō**)
aileron (**āla**)	motor (**moveō**)
airplane (**āēr, plānus**)	propeller (**pro-, pellō**)
altimeter (**altus**)	retractable (**re-, trahō**)
aviator, aviatrix (**avis**)	stabilizer (**stō**)
compass (**com-, passus**)	supersonic (**super-, sonus**)
contact (**con-, tangō**)	turbo-prop (**turbō, prō-, pellō**)
interceptor (**inter-, capiō**)	visibility (**videō**)

Find other aviation terms derived from Latin.

LESSON OBJECTIVES
- Relative Pronoun as a Sentence Connector
- Accusative of Place to Which without a Preposition

THE PUNIC WARS[1]

[1] First Punic War, 264–241 B.C.; Second Punic War, 218–201 B.C. The word "Punic" is derived from **Poeni,** another name for the Carthaginians, who originally came from Phoenicia.

[2] *was (a battle) fought* (impersonal)

[3] the battle of Lake Trasimene (north-central Italy) in 217 B.C.

Prīmō bellō Pūnicō Rōmānī prīmum in marī pugnāvērunt et hostēs vīcērunt. Neque ūlla victōria Rōmānīs grātior fuit, quod, invictī in terrā, iam etiam in marī plūrimum poterant. Postquam Sicilia capta est et Corsica Sardiniaque vāstātae sunt, bellum in Āfricam trānslātum est. Victī

5 Carthāginiēnsēs pācem ā Rōmānīs petīvērunt. Illō tempore Rēgulus, dūx Rōmānōrum, senātuī persuāsit nē pācem cum Poenīs faceret. Tandem cōnsul Catulus profectus est cum CCC nāvibus in Siciliam; Poenī contrā ipsum CCCC nāvēs parāvērunt. Numquam in marī tantīs cōpiīs pugnātum est.[2] Carthāginiēnsēs superātī sunt.

10 Bellum Pūnicum secundum Rōmānīs ab Hannibale illātum est. Cum magnō exercitū Alpēs trānsiit. Post complūrēs parvās victōriās Hannibal Rōmānōs ad lacum Trasumennum[3] gravissimē vīcit.

Rōmae ad prīmum nūntium proelī populus cum magnō terrōre in Forum concurrit. Mulierēs rogāvērunt omnēs quae fortūna exercitūs esset.

15 Tandem praetor, "Pugnā," inquit, "magnā victī sumus." Posterīs diēbus ad

A Roman warship from imperial times in a battle at sea. The Romans' gradual conquest of the Italian peninsula eventually brought them into conflict with Carthage, the great sea power of the Mediterranean. In the First Punic War, after the loss, from storms or hostile action, of several fleets which they then doggedly rebuilt, the Romans finally gained the experience to prevail over their enemy. From the middle of the third century B.C. onward, it was Rome that ruled the waves, and seapower was to play a vital role in her later history.

Ronald Sheridan/Ancient Art & Architecture Collection

These remains of a Roman villa at Carthage, near modern Tunis, date from the third century A.D. Extensive excavations of Carthage began only late in the nineteenth century because the modern town had overgrown the old and it was mistakenly thought that little remained on the site because it had so often been destroyed. Now many archaeological teams from Europe and America have, in the last half of the twentieth century, uncovered large areas of that ancient and intriguing civilization.

portās maior prope multitūdō mulierum quam virōrum stetit, quae aut suōrum aliquem aut nūntiōs dē eīs exspectābat. Ūnam fēminam in ipsā portā incolumī fīliō[4] subitō occurrentem in complexū[5] eius exspīrāvisse dīcunt; alteram, cui mors fīlī falsō nūntiāta erat, sedentem domī ad prīmum cōnspectum redeuntis fīlī gaudiō mortuam esse dīcunt.   20

Proximō annō Rōmānī ab Hannibale pulsī etiam maius dētrīmentum ad Cannās accēpērunt. Multae Italiae cīvitātēs ad Poenōs dēfēcērunt. Quae tamen rēs Rōmānōs nōn mōvit ut pācis umquam mentiō apud eōs fieret. Servōs mīlitēs[6] fēcērunt, quod[7] numquam ante factum erat. Hannibal trēs modiōs ānulōrum[8] aureōrum Carthāginem mīsit, quōs ex manibus equitum   25
Rōmānōrum mortuōrum dētrāxerat.

Rōmānī tamen post multōs annōs Hannibalem vīcērunt.

[4] dative, depending on **occurrentem**
[5] *embrace, arms*
[6] *they enlisted slaves as soldiers*
[7] *(a thing) which*
[8] *pecks of rings (three-quarters of a bushel). Roman nobles and those who held high office wore golden rings.*

Questions

1. What did their victory at sea in the First Punic War mean to the Romans?
2. What three islands were taken in battle by the Romans?
3. What did the general Regulus persuade the Senate not to do?
4. What, in terms of size, was the significance of the final battle in the First Punic War?
5. From what direction did Hannibal and his army attack Italy?
6. What did the praetor announce? What was its effect?
7. How are two women said to have died?
8. What was the emotional impact of the defeat at Cannae in Italy? At Rome?
9. What new policy for raising troops was introduced?
10. What did Hannibal send back to Carthage as evidence of his victory?
11. How long did it take for the Romans to defeat Hannibal?

GRAMMAR

The Relative as a Sentence Connector

In Latin the relative pronoun or adjective is often used to connect a sentence with a preceding sentence. In English a personal or demonstrative pronoun with or without a conjunction (*and, but* etc.) is more common. You have seen a number of examples of this construction already.

Quae rēs Rōmānīs salūtī fuit... *But the circumstance was (a source*
    (Lesson XXXIII, line 4) *of) salvation for the Romans) . . .*

Quod ubi audīvit cōnsul... *And when the consul heard this . . .*
    (Lesson XXXIV, line 19)

Quae tamen rēs Rōmānōs *This fact did not, however, induce*
    nōn mōvit... *the Romans . . .*
    (Lesson XXXV, lines 22–23)

Place to Which

Ordinarily *place to which* is expressed by the accusative with the preposition **ad** or **in**. The preposition is omitted before names of cities, towns, and a few other words, such as **domus** *(home).*

Pūblius Furiānusque Athēnās *Publius and Furianus went to*
    iērunt. *Athens.*

Trēs modiōs ānulōrum *He sent three modii of gold rings*
    aureōrum Carthāginem *to Carthage.*
    mīsit.

Translation

1. You all know that the Romans received a great loss the next year.
2. Not moved by the words of women and friends, Regulus returned to Carthage.
3. Although terrified by reports of the defeat, nevertheless Rome did not make peace.
4. Regulus, when sent unharmed to Rome, persuaded his country to make war upon the enemy.

Nota•Bene

Just as the names of towns, cities, small islands, and **domus** do not need **ad** in the accusative Place to Which construction, so may these same words use the locative case to express Place *at* or *in* Which, rather than use **in** + ablative.

VOCABULARY

Nouns

dētrīmentum, -ī n. *loss*   (detriment, detrimental)

fēmina, -ae f. *woman*   (feminine, feminist)

multitūdo, -dinis f. *great number*   **[multus]**

Adjectives

complūrēs, -a or **-ia** *several*   **[plūs]**

incolumis, -e *unharmed*

Verbs

exspīrō, 1 *breathe out, die*   **[spīrō]**

īnferō, īnferre, intulī, illātus *bring*   **[ferō]**

Adverbs

prope *almost*

umquam *ever, at any time*

Conjunction

nisi *unless, except*

WORD STUDY

Suffixes The suffix **-idus** (English *-id*) is added chiefly to verb stems to form adjectives: **timidus,** *timid*. When the noun suffix **-tās** (English *-ty*) is added, **-idus** becomes **-idi-: timiditās,** *timidity*.

The suffix **-īnus** (English *-ine*) is added to noun and adjective stems to form adjectives: **equīnus,** *equine*. When the suffix **-tās** is added, **-īnus** becomes **-īni-: vīcīnitās,** *vicinity*.

Similarly, adjectives formed from the suffix **-ānus** (see page 137) become nouns with a change to **-āni-** and the addition of **-tas: urbānitās,** *urbanity;* **humānitās,** *humanity*.

Define the following and give the Latin words from which they are derived: *placid, rapid, valid, vivid, feminine, marine, submarine*. Give additional examples of these suffixes in English words.

Thirteen American states have towns named after *Carthage;* New York and Ohio have a *Sardinia;* Pennsylvania and South Dakota have a *Corsica*.

THE BATTLE OF CANNAE

The battle of Cannae was the greatest defeat the Romans suffered in their long history—and yet they won the war. The Romans had fifty thousand to eighty thousand men in this battle; the Carthaginians only forty thousand, but Hannibal chose his own battlefield and used the plan of encirclement—closing in on the Romans on right and left while his center withdrew. This encircling movement of Cannae has been extensively imitated in modern warfare, on a much larger scale, of course. The Germans used it in Poland in 1939, in Belgium and France in 1940, and in Russia in 1941. The Allied forces won great success with it in capturing the Ruhr district of Germany in 1945.

Of the Romans at Cannae, only ten thousand escaped; most of the rest were killed.

The Carthaginian victory made necessary a strategy which one Roman general, Quintus Fabius Maximus, had advocated against the more aggressive policies of his colleagues: by constantly hounding Hannibal's forces but avoiding pitched battles, Fabius eventually wore down the Carthaginians' strength. This course of action won for him the cognomen **Cunctator** (*Delayer* or *Slowpoke*), which only later came to be used as a mark of respect. The poet Ennius wrote:

> **Ūnus homō nōbīs cūnctandō**   *One man, by delaying, saved our*
> **restituit rem.**   *state for us.*

But it was not only Fabius' very Roman qualities of caution and stubborn courage that saved Rome. Hannibal himself did not follow up his victories, and gradually he lost the support of the war party in Carthage. The morale of the Roman senators and of the ordinary Roman legionaries was unshakable and cannot be praised too highly. Finally, in the last stages of the war, the boldness of the young Scipio and his military genius in reorganizing the army brought victory.

The outcome of this war determined the future of the world. It made certain that Rome, not Carthage, was to rule and transmit its own and Greek civilization to future generations. Life today would be vastly different if the Carthaginians had won the war—whether better or worse is a subject for debate.

LESSON XXXVI

THE ROMANS "LIBERATE" THE GREEKS

LESSON OBJECTIVES
- Forms of the Passive Imperative
- **Quisque** and **Quisquam**
- Review Result Clauses

Post Pūnicum bellum secūtum est Macedonicum[1] quod cum Philippō rēge Rōmānī gessērunt ut Graecās cīvitātēs līberārent. T. Quīnctius Flāminīnus contrā Philippum missus rem bene gessit. Corinthum prōcessit ut ibi in lūdīs Isthmiīs[2] condiciōnēs pācis dēferret. Omnēs ad spectāculum cōnsēderant et praecō,[3] ut[4] mōs erat, in medium prōcessit et, tubā silentiō factō, prōnūntiat senātum Rōmānum et Quīnctium imperātōrem iubēre omnēs gentēs Graeciae līberās esse. Audītā vōce praecōnis, vix quisque satis crēdere potest sē bene audīvisse.[5] Potuitne quisquam suīs auribus crēdere? Tum tantus clāmor est ortus ut facile appārēret nihil omnium bonōrum multitūdinī grātius quam lībertātem esse. Aliī aliīs dīcēbant[6] Rōmānōs esse gentem quae suā pecūniā, suō labōre ac perīculō bella gereret[7] prō lībertāte aliōrum.

5

10

[1] 200–197 B.C. Philip V of Macedon had attempted to counteract the growing Roman influence in the Mediterranean by harassing the Greek states that had leagued themselves with Rome. Finally, under Flamininus, the Romans thwarted Philip's ambitions and declared Greece a free state. Thereafter, most of Greece, though "free," but often unruly, often plundered, and often the site of battles between Roman armies in the Civil War, was under Roman supervision and eventually became a Roman province. This was not the first nor the last time that one country, to protect its own interests, undertook the liberation of another country from the oppression of a tyrant.

[2] *Isthmian;* similar to the Olympic Games. They got their name from being held on the Isthmus of Corinth.

[3] nominative: *public crier, herald*

[4] *as*

[5] *no one could really believe that he had heard correctly*

[6] *one said to another*

[7] Subordinate clauses within indirect statement are in the subjunctive.

Erich Lessing/Art Resource, NY

Seven of the original thirty-eight columns of the magnificent Temple of Apollo still dominate the skyline in the ancient quarter of Corinth. The temple, built in the sixth century B.C., remains one of the best examples of the Doric order of architecture. Its proportions are gigantic, six columns across and fifteen down each side, each twenty-four feet high and six feet in diameter.

[8] Why dative?

[9] conditional: *if you agree (among yourselves)*

[10] Cf. "United we stand, divided we fall."

[11] *flowed for all* (i.e., from the eyes of all)

[12] *threw into confusion*

[13] Flamininus had persuaded a reluctant Senate to ratify his decree. His actions have been compared to the United States' restoration of war-torn Japan and Europe after World War II.

Duōbus annīs posteā Quīnctius in Ītaliam profectūrus Graecōs hōc modō monet: "Concordiae[8] cōnsulite. Contrā vōs cōnsentientēs[9] nec rēx 15 quisquam nec tyrannus satis valēbit.[10] Aliēnīs armīs redditam lībertātem vestrā cūrā servāte, ut populus Rōmānus dignīs datam esse lībertātem sciat." Hās velut parentis vōcēs cum audīrent, omnibus mānāvērunt[11] gaudiō lacrimae, ita ut Quīnctium ipsum quoque cōnfunderent[12] dīcentem.[13]

Questions

1. What was the stated purpose of fighting King Philip?
2. Why did Flamininus go to Corinth?
3. On what occasion did he make an important announcement, and what was that announcement?
4. How did the audience react to it?
5. What were people saying to one another?
6. What advice did Flamininus give before leaving Greece?
7. How did his speech affect the Greeks?
8. How did their response affect Flamininus?

GRAMMAR

The Imperative

Remember that the present active imperative singular is identical to the present stem. The plural is formed by adding **-te.** (In the third conjugation change the **-e** of the stem to **i.**)

	ACTIVE	
SINGULAR	PLURAL	ENGLISH
portā	**portāte**	*carry!*
docē	**docēte**	*teach!*
pōne	**pōnite**	*place!*
cape	**capite**	*take!*
mūnī	**mūnīte**	*build!*

The present passive imperative has the same forms as the second person present passive indicative, except that in the singular only the alternate form ending in **-re** (rather than **-ris**) is used, making it look exactly like the present infinitive. Passive imperatives are rare in this book.

	PASSIVE	
SINGULAR	PLURAL	ENGLISH
portāre	**portāminī**	*be carried!*
docēre	**docēminī**	*be taught!*
pōnere	**pōniminī**	*be placed!*
capere	**capiminī**	*be taken!*
mūnīre	**mūnīminī**	*be built!*

Deponent verbs use the passive imperative forms only, with active meanings.

SINGULAR	PLURAL	ENGLISH
pollicēre	**pollicēminī**	*promise!*

Quisque and *Quisquam*

Quisque, *each,* as a pronoun is declined like **quis,** with **-que** added as an indeclinable suffix. As an adjective, it is declined like **quī,** with **-que** added as an indeclinable suffix.

Quisque is often placed after a reflexive pronoun or a superlative adjective.

Nōn omnia omnibus tribuenda, sed suum cuique.	*All things are not to be granted to everyone, but his own to each.*
optimus quisque	*all the best of men* (literally, *each best man*)

Quisquam, *anyone,* is stronger than **aliquis** and is usually found in sentences containing or implying a negative. It can often be translated as *any at all.*

Potuitne quisquam suīs auribus crēdere?	*Could anyone believe his own ears?*
Estne quisquam fortior?	*Is anyone (at all) braver?*

Practice

1. Practice the present imperatives (singular and plural). Construct various commands (e.g., in Latin, tell a classmate to "carry the book") and see if your fellow students are able to understand and carry them out.
2. Tell the form of **quōque, quendam, aliquod, quicquam, quaeque, quid, cuiquam, quaedam, quidque, alicuius.**

Result Clauses

Review Result Clauses in Lesson XIV. Find two examples in the reading on pages 207 and 208.

Translation

1. "Tell us what he said," each one asked.
2. All were so overcome that they could hardly speak.
3. "Agree among yourselves and no king will be so brave as to attack you."
4. The messenger had spoken, and not a single one could believe his words.

▦ VOCABULARY

Pronouns

quisquam, quicquam *anyone, anything, any*		**[quis]**
quisque, quidque *each, each one*		**[quis]**

Verb

cōnsīdō, -ere, -sēdī, -sessūrus *sit down*	**[sedeō]**

A Roman floor mosaic from the second century A.D. The medallion in the center is said to represent Dionysus, the Greek god of vegetation and wine, known to the Romans as Bacchus. The artist must have been highly skilled in geometry! In the four corners are cups with ivy vines, symbols of the god. This mosaic is now housed in the archaeological museum in Corinth.

Elio Ciol/CORBIS

WORD STUDY

Spanish We have already seen that a few simple principles will enable one to recognize the Latin origin of many Spanish words (Lesson XXII). On the basis of these principles, explain Spanish *campo, útil, vivo; ocurrir; desierto, puente; vida, virtud; mujer.*

Since *d* is sometimes lost between vowels, what must be the Latin words from which Spanish *caer* and *juicio* are derived?

Since an *e* is added before *sc, sp,* and *st* at the beginning of a word, what must be the Latin words from which the following Spanish words are derived: *esperar, especie, escribir, estar, estudio?*

Since Latin *ex* sometimes becomes *ej* in Spanish, what is the Latin for *ejemplo, ejército?*

CIVIL WAR

[1] ablative absolute expressing time: *in the consulship of* (63 B.C.). The Romans used the names of the consuls to date the year. Why did they not say 63 B.C.?

[2] 58–50 B.C. Consult the map on pages 158–159 to see the extent of Caesar's campaigns.

[3] *the die* (one of a pair of dice)

M. Tulliō Cicerōne ōrātōre et C. Antōniō cōnsulibus,[1] L. Sergius Catilīna, vir nōbilissimī generis, ad dēlendam patriam coniūrāvit cum quibusdam clārīs quidem, sed audācibus virīs. Ā Cicerōne urbe expulsus est. Sociī eius comprehēnsī occīsī sunt. Catilīna ipse victus proeliō est et
5 interfectus.

Sed Cicerō Rōmānōs timōre bellī cīvīlis nōn līberāvit. C. Iūlius Caesar, quī Catilīnam iūvisse ā quibusdam dīcitur, cōnsul est factus. Dēcrēta est eī Gallia et Īllyricum cum legiōnibus decem. Annīs novem in potestātem populī Rōmānī prope omnem Galliam redēgit.[2] Britannīs mox bellum
10 intulit, quibus ante eum nē nōmen quidem Rōmānōrum cognitum erat. Eōs victōs, obsidibus acceptīs, stīpendium pendere coēgit. Germānōs trāns Rhēnum aggressus proeliīs vīcit.

Caesar rediēns ex Galliā victor coepit poscere alterum cōnsulātum. Senātū negante, contrā patriam cum exercitū prōcessit, trānsiēns flūmen
15 Rubicōnem et clāmāns, "Ālea[3] iacta est!"

Although he was **novus homō** (a *new man* whose ancestors had never held high office), Cicero (106–43 B.C.) through his remarkable industry and oratorical skill reached the consulship in 63 B.C. As consul he was responsible for the defeat and death of Catiline and his fellow conspirators who advocated revolution. Later, he fled the charge of having put Roman citizens to death without trial by going into exile in Macedonia for a year. In the Civil War between Caesar and Pompey, who took the Senate's side, Cicero wavered badly, finally joining with the Senate against Octavian and Mark Antony, in the vain hope that republican government could be restored. A series of his speeches made a bitter enemy of Antony, who with Octavian's acquiescence, had him put to death.

Deinde in Graeciam trānsiit et contrā Pompeium pugnāvit. Prīmō proeliō victus est, ēvāsit tamen, quod, nocte intercēdente, Pompeius sequī nōluit. Dīxit Caesar Pompeium nōn scīre[4] vincere et illō diē tantum[5] sē potuisse superārī.[6]

Deinde in Thessaliā ad Pharsālum pugnāvērunt. Numquam ante maiōrēs Rōmānae cōpiae in ūnum locum convēnerant neque meliōrēs ducēs habuerant. Tandem Pompeius victus est et Alexandrīam petīvit ut ā rēge Aegyptī auxilia acciperet. Sed rēx occīdit Pompeium et caput eius ad Caesarem mīsit. Caesar lacrimās fūdisse dīcitur, tantī virī vidēns caput et generī[7] quondam suī.[7] Caesar rēgnum Aegyptī Cleopātrae dedit.

Caesar, bellīs cīvīlibus in tōtō orbe terrārum perfectīs, Rōmam rediit. Agere coepit contrā cōnsuētūdinem Rōmānae lībertātis. Cum honōrēs[8] ex[9] suā voluntāte tribueret quī ā populō anteā dēferēbantur aliaque rēgia[10] faceret, coniūrātum est in eum ā LX vel amplius senātōribus equitibusque Rōmānīs, quōrum prīncipēs fuērunt C. Cassius et duo Brūtī. Itaque Caesar, cum Īdibus Mārtiīs[11] in senātum vēnisset, XXIII vulneribus acceptīs, mortuus est.

An idealized portrait bust of Cleopatra (69–30 B.C.) from the first century B.C. Cleopatra was not an Egyptian, but a descendant of Ptolemy, the [20] Greek general who took over Egypt after Alexander the Great's death. Her intelligence, her conversational charm, and her steadfast desire to maintain her own kingdom and authority [25] enabled her to manipulate powerful Romans like Caesar and Mark Antony. Octavian, to raise popular support among the Romans for his campaign against [30] Antony, skillfully portrayed her as a threat to Rome, and finally cornered her at Actium (31 B.C.). Still, she and Antony escaped and fled to Alexandria. But, trapped there, they realized [35] their cause was hopeless and she followed Antony in committing suicide, choosing to die rather than be paraded as a captive in a Roman triumph— **nōn humilis mulier,** as Horace [40] rightly praised her in a brilliant poem (*Odes* I, 38).

Sandro Vannini/CORBIS

Questions

1. What crisis arose during the year of Cicero's consulship?
2. What was Catiline's aim?
3. Into what parts of the Roman world did Caesar bring war?
4. What issue brought Caesar and the Senate into conflict?
5. Where did Caesar and Pompey fight their final battle?
6. Whose help did Pompey seek? What happened to him?
7. What is said to have made Caesar weep?
8. Who gained control of the kingdom of Egypt? How?
9. What actions of Caesar provoked the formation of a conspiracy against him?
10. Can you name three of the principal conspirators?

[4] *know how* (with infinitive)

[5] *only*

[6] *could have been defeated*

[7] *his former son-in-law* (genitive of **gener**); Pompey had married Caesar's daughter Julia in 60 B.C. After her death in 54 B.C. Caesar and Pompey drifted apart.

[8] *offices*

[9] *in accordance with*

[10] *kinglike,* i.e., *as if he were a king.* The Romans' memory of their hardships during the regal period was long and bitter.

[11] *the Ides of March* (March 15)

GRAMMAR

Ablative of Separation

rediēns ex Galliā	*returning from Gaul*
Urbe expulsus est.	*He was driven out of the city.*
Timōre... līberāvit	*He freed from fear . . .*

Separation is usually expressed by the ablative with **ab, dē,** or **ex,** e.g., the ablative of place from which. But with some verbs and adjectives the preposition is regularly omitted; in other cases it is occasionally omitted.

Translation

1. Cicero drove Catiline from Rome after seizing his accomplices.
2. You all read that civil war occurred between Caesar and Pompey.
3. Since Caesar had not driven his personal enemies from the city, sixty or more of them later killed him.
4. Having conquered Gaul, Caesar also attacked the Britons, who were much braver than the Gauls.

Words Easily Confused

Look up and distinguish carefully the following sets of words that are somewhat similar in pronunciation or spelling.

alius, aliquis	**dīcō, dūcō**	**mors, mors, mōs**
at, aut	**equēs, equus**	**opēs, opus**
audeō, audiō	**fors, fortis**	**parō, parcō, pereō**
cadō, caedō, cēdō	**mīles, mīlle**	**passus** (n.), **passus** (p.p.)
cōnsistō, cōnstituo	**moror, morior**	**quīdam, quidem**

VOCABULARY

Nouns

legiō, -ōnis f. *legion*	[**legō**]
obses, obsidis[12] m. *hostage*	
timor, -ōris m. *fear*	[**timeō**]
voluntās, -tātis f. *wish*	[**volō**]

Adjective

audāx, audācis (gen.) *bold*	(audacious, audacity)

---

[12] In those times, a hostage was a person from a conquered territory who was held by the conquerors as a pledge that no unfriendly act would be committed.

Verbs

aggredior, aggredī, aggressus *attack*
dēleō, -ēre, ēvī, -ētus *destroy*
fundō, -ere, fūdī, fūsus *pour, shed*
poscō, -ere, poposcī *demand, call for*

[gradior]
(delete, deletion)
(profound, diffuse)

Adverbs

amplius *more*
anteā *before*
mox *soon*

[amplus]
[ante]

WORD STUDY

Spelling In English, after the prefix *ex-*, a root word beginning with *s* drops the s: **ex-sequor**, ex-ecute; **ex-sistō**, *ex-ist;* **ex-spectō**, *ex-pect.*

Explain *aggression, audacity, confusion, delete, indelible, infusion, legionary, projectile, timorous, voluntary.*

Virginia and twelve other American states, including New Hampshire and Louisiana, have towns named *Alexandria.* Kentucky and Michigan have towns named after *Brutus*, and *Pompey* is in New York.

Latīnum Hodiernum

Medicīna

Mīror cūr medicīna semper amāra[13] necesse sit. Sīc et nunc est apud Rōmānōs fuit. Nunc quidem dulce quiddam in medicīnā liquidā pōnimus vel pilulās dulcī tegimus. Rōmānī quoque hoc fēcērunt. Saepe ōram pōculī melle contingēbant[14] ut puer innocēns tōtum, dulce et amārum, biberet priusquam sentīret gustum maximae partis horribilem esse. Etiam crūstula[15] puerīs puellīsque dabant ut medicīnam libenter sūmerent. Sed sī aeger es, medicīna sūmenda est, cum crūstulīs vel sine crūstulīs. Posteā quandō valēbis banānam fissam vel lac agitātum tibi habēre licēbit.

Fortasse putās hanc fābulam prō crūstulō esse ut Caesaris et aliōrum rēs gestās libentius legās. Sī hoc putās, nōn errās.

---

[13] *bitter*
[14] *they smeared the lip of the cup with honey*
[15] *cookies*

PĀX RŌMĀNA[1]

[1] Under Augustus (31 B.C.–14 A.D.) a long era of peace began.

[2] Actually Octavian was the grandson of Caesar's sister.

[3] *divorced*

[4] *married* (with **uxōrem**)

[5] i.e., Rome

[6] *let an asp* (a poisonous snake) *bite her*

Octāviānus, nepōs[2] Caesaris, ā Caesare adoptātus, posteā Augustus est appellātus. Iuvenis fōrmā praestantī et vultū tranquillō erat. Post mortem Caesaris Octāviānō, adulēscentī XX annōrum, cōnsulātus datur. Nōn multō post cum M. Antōniō contrā Brūtum et Cassium, quī Caesarem
5 interfēcerant, profectus est. Ad Philippōs, Macedoniae urbem, Brūtus et Cassius victī et interfectī sunt.

Antōnius, sorōre Caesaris Augustī repudiātā,[3] Cleopātram, rēgīnam Aegyptī, dūxit[4] uxōrem. Tum ultimum bellum cīvīle commōvit, cōgente uxōre Cleopātrā, quae cupīvit in urbe[5] quoque rēgnāre. Victus est ab
10 Augustō nāvālī pugnā clārā apud Actium, quī locus in Ēpīrō est, ex quā fūgit in Aegyptum et, dēspērātīs suīs rēbus, ipse sē occīdit. Cleopātra sibi aspidem admīsit[6] et venēnō eius exstīncta est. Aegyptus ab Augustō imperiō Rōmānō adiecta est.

Pāce Rōmānā cōnstitūtā, Augustus Rōmānōs timōre bellī līberāvit. Ex
15 eō annō rem pūblicam per XLIIII annōs sōlus obtinuit. In Campō Mārtiō

The emperor Augustus established his government in 27 B.C., rebuilt Rome, restored the economy of Italy, reformed the Senate, made the taxation system more fair, revived the census, and patronized the arts. Rome's utter domination of the Mediterranean world began the two hundred years of peace that came to be called the Pax Romana. He died in A.D. 14 and was buried in this tomb in Rome.

Scala/Art Resource, NY

Syria came under Roman domination in the second century B.C. with the defeat of Antiochus III at Thermopylae in 190 B.C. as he tried to invade Greece. Evidence of the Roman influence can be seen in these ruins at Palmyra, Syria. Note the castle in the background, built by the Crusaders in the thirteenth century.

sepultus est,[7] vir quī meritīs quidem deō similis est putātus. Neque enim quisquam aut in bellīs fēlīcior fuit aut in pāce moderātior. Scythae et Indī, quibus anteā Rōmānōrum nē nōmen quidem cognitum erat, mūnera et lēgātōs ad eum mīsērunt.

Pūblica opera plūrima Rōmae exstrūxit et cēterōs prīncipēs virōs saepe 20
hortātus est ut monumentīs vel novīs vel refectīs urbem adōrnārent.
Spatium urbis in regiōnēs XIV dīvīsit. Contrā incendia vigiliās īnstituit.
Viās et templa refēcit. Annum[8] ā Iūliō Caesare in ōrdinem redāctum, sed
posteā neglēctum, rūrsus ad prīstinam[9] ratiōnem redēgit. Sextīlem mēnsem
ē suō nōmine Augustum nōmināvit. 25

[7] *was buried*
[8] *i.e., the calendar, which was very inexact before Caesar's time*
[9] *former*

Questions

1. Describe Octavian's appearance.
2. At what age did he become chief officer of the Roman state?
3. Who were the combatants at Philippi?
4. Who was Antony's first wife?
5. Who, according to the reading, was also to blame for the civil war besides Antony?
6. Describe the bitter end of Antony and Cleopatra following their defeat at Actium.
7. How far did Roman influence extend under Augustus?
8. Does this passage praise Augustus' accomplishments in war? Explain.
9. What accomplishments of Augustus, once peace had been established, are cited in the reading?

GRAMMAR

Description and Measure of Difference

Review the Genitive and Ablative of Description in the Grammar Appendix (p. 495.2; p. 500.13) and the Ablative of Measure of Difference[10] in Lesson XV. Find one example of each of these three constructions in the reading on pages 216 and 217.

Translation

1. Cleopatra urged Antony not to neglect his own interests ("things").
2. Antony was a man of the greatest courage; Augustus was a youth of twenty years.
3. Augustus constructed monuments and temples of the greatest size in all parts of the Roman Empire.
4. Despairing of victory, Antony killed himself, and not much later all other enemies were defeated.

Etiam and *Quoque; Quidem*

Distinguish carefully the following words: **etiam** and **quoque** both mean *also,* but **etiam** generally precedes the word it emphasizes, **quoque** always follows. In the same way, English *even* generally precedes, like **etiam,** while *too* follows, like **quoque. Quidem** means *certainly, to be sure,* and follows the word it emphasizes. **Nē... quidem** means *not even,* and the emphatic word is placed between **nē** and **quidem. Quidem** alone never means *even,* nor is **nē... etiam** ever used for *not even.*

VOCABULARY

Noun

vultus, -ūs m. *(facial) expression, features*

Verbs

admittō, -ere, admīsī, admissus	[mitto]
let in, admit	
dēspērō, 1 *despair (of)*	[spērō]
exstruō, -ere, exstrūxī, exstrūctus *construct*	
neglegō, -ere, -lēxī, -lectus *neglect*	[legō]

Adverb

rūrsus *again*

---

[10] Also called the Degree of Difference

WORD STUDY

Suffixes The suffix **-ārium** (English *-arium, -ary*) is added chiefly to noun stems. The suffix **-ōrium** (English *-orium, -ory, -or*) is added chiefly to participial stems and so is usually preceded by **-t-.** Both suffixes mean a *place where* or *for:* granary, a *place for grain* (**grānum**), *depository*. The plurals of *-ary* and *-ory* are *-aries* and *-ories.*

Define the following words according to their derivation and give the Latin words from which they come: *aquarium, itinerary, library, laboratory, mirror* (**mīror**), *auditorium, factory, armory.*

Caution: Other Latin suffixes besides **-ārium** and **-ōrium** sometimes take on the English forms mentioned above; e.g., *primary* from **prīmārius,** *honorary* from **honorārius,** and *cursory* from **cursōrius.**

LESSON OBJECTIVE
- Relative Purpose Clauses

ROMAN SCANDALS

[1] A.D. 54–68
[2] *fishing nets*
[3] *singing teacher*
[4] *handkerchief*

Dē Nerōne[1] multa īnfāmia nārrābantur. Nerō erat prīnceps inūsitātae lūxuriae, adeō ut unguentīs lavāret et rētibus[2] aureīs piscārētur. Nūllam vestem bis gessit. Semper mīlle carrīs vel amplius fēcit iter. Soleae mūlārum eius ex argentō factae sunt. Domum ā Palātiō ad Ēsquiliās

5　exstrūxit, quam auream nōmināvit. In eius vēstibulō locāta est imāgō Nerōnis CXX pedēs alta, appellāta "Colossus." Erant lacūs, aedificia, agrī, silvae, cum multitūdine omnis generis animālium. In cēterīs partibus omnia aurō tēcta, ōrnāta gemmīs erant. Cum hanc domum dēdicāret, dīxit: "Tandem quasi homō habitāre coepī."

10　Etiam saltāvit et cantāvit in scaenā. In Graeciam profectus est ut ibi cantāret. Cantante eō, excēdere theātrō nēminī licitum est. Multī, dēfessī audiendō laudandōque, clausīs oppidōrum portīs, aut fūrtim dēsiluērunt dē mūrō aut, morte simulātā, fūnere ēlātī sunt. In Ītaliam reversus studium nōn remīsit. Cōnservandae vōcis grātiā neque mīlitēs umquam appellāvit

15　neque quicquam ēgit nisi prope stante phōnascō[3] quī monēret ut parceret sibi ac sūdārium[4] ad ōs applicāret.

The emperor Nero was born in A.D. 37 and ruled Rome from 54–68. Although his reign began well, he soon became infamous for his excesses, ruthlessly destroying those whom he suspected of intriguing against him, even his own mother. His true passion was for art, drama, and music. When several provincial governors rose up against him and his own bodyguards (the Praetorian Guard) deserted him, he committed suicide. In this painting, a repulsive Nero is signaling the death sentence to a gladiator.

A.K.G. Berlin/SuperStock

Frātrem, uxōrem, sorōrem, mātrem interfēcit. Urbem Rōmam incendit[5] ut spectāculum simile incendiō Troiae antīquae cerneret. Magnam senātūs partem interfēcisse dīcitur.

Tandem ā senātū hostis iūdicātus est. Cum quaererētur ad poenam, 20 fūgit et sē interfēcit. In eō omnis Augustī familia cōnsūmpta est.

[5] This was a false charge, as Nero was not in Rome when the fire started, but at his birthplace, Antium, modern Anzio. The city burned six days and seven nights continuously and then started again.

Questions

1. What do you consider the most notorious or outrageous features of Nero's extravagant lifestyle?
2. What were the shoes of Nero's mules made of?
3. What was Nero's *Domus Aurea?* Describe it.
4. Why was the comment he made in dedicating it offensive?
5. How successful were Nero's musical performances in the theatres of Greece?
6. Do you think most Romans approved of Nero's devotion to song and dance? Why or why not?
7. How well did Nero get along with his family?
8. Describe his relationship with the Roman Senate.
9. What was the alleged reason Nero set Rome on fire? Argue the pros and cons for believing or disbelieving the story.

GRAMMAR

Relative Purpose Clauses

The relative pronoun may be used instead of **ut** to introduce a purpose clause in the subjunctive when there is an antecedent. The pronoun must of course agree with the antecedent in gender and number, but take its case from its use in the relative clause.

prope stante phōnascō quī monēret...	*a singing teacher standing near to warn . . .* (lit., *who might warn*)
Servōs admīsit quī līberōs servārent.	*He let the slaves in (who were) to guard the children.*

Translation

1. Nero built a house covered with gold in which to live.
2. He summoned slaves who were to erect beautiful buildings.
3. He is said to have burned Rome to furnish a spectacle for himself.
4. He led a life of great luxury and cruelty and spent his time in singing.

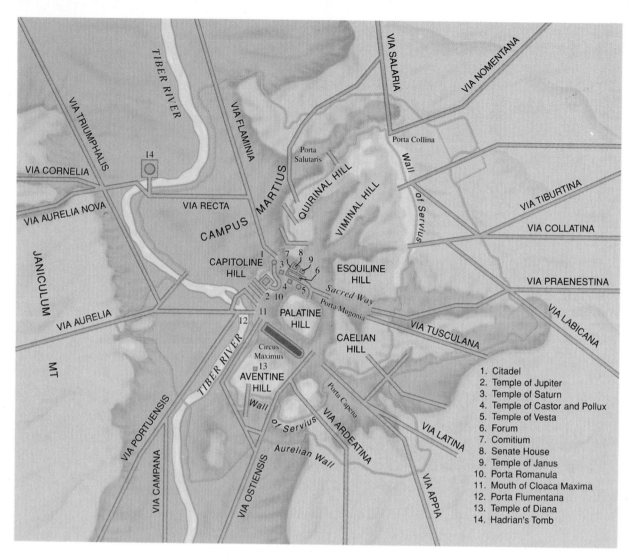

1. Citadel
2. Temple of Jupiter
3. Temple of Saturn
4. Temple of Castor and Pollux
5. Temple of Vesta
6. Forum
7. Comitium
8. Senate House
9. Temple of Janus
10. Porta Romanula
11. Mouth of Cloaca Maxima
12. Porta Flumentana
13. Temple of Diana
14. Hadrian's Tomb

The city of Rome as it was in ancient days

VOCABULARY

Verbs

efferō, efferre, extulī, ēlātus *carry out*	[ferō]
locō, 1 *place*	[locus]
simulō, 1 *pretend*	(dissimulate, simulate)
tegō, -ere, tēxī, tēctus *cover*	(protégé, detect)

Adverbs

adeō *to this extent, so much so*	
bis *twice*	(bicentennial)
quasi (adv. and conj.) *as if*	(quasi-scientific)

WORD STUDY

Prefixes The prefix **sē-** means *apart from* in Latin and English: **sēparō**, *separate*. Define according to the prefix: *secret* **(cernō),** *secede, seclude, secure* **(cūra).**

The Latin adverb **nōn,** meaning *not,* is freely used as a prefix in English: *nonsense, nonpartisan.* Give three other examples.

The preposition **ultrā** (related to **ultimus**) is used as a prefix in English with the meaning *beyond the norm* or *extremely:* *ultrafashionable.* Give two other examples.

Explain *admission, collocation, desperation, detective, negligence, simulated.*

THE ROMAN EMPIRE

The establishment of the extensive Roman Empire was a remarkable achievement at a time when communications were slow and difficult. A glance at the map (pages 158–159) shows that, during the second century A.D., the Roman Empire encircled the Mediterranean and covered parts of three continents. Some of these territories have never recovered the prosperity they had in Roman times.

The Empire brought not only prosperity but also peace and security to Roman citizens. Occasionally foreign wars were fought in remote parts of the Empire, but that meant nothing to most citizens, and sometimes there was a flare-up of civil war.

Political liberty was of course diminished during the Empire, compared with the Republic, but for most citizens this meant merely that the emperor and his officials ran things instead of the nobility who composed the Senate during the Republic. The government was an efficient bureaucracy, and the emperors were, by and large, very capable administrators. Personal liberty was not affected, nor even the self-rule of the many communities scattered throughout the Empire. In the East the emperors did not force the people to give up their Greek language. In the West the people of their own accord gradually abandoned their native languages in favor of Latin, which remained the standard in literary works for many centuries, but in popular speech gradually decayed into the Romance languages.

These Roman ruins in Volubilis, Morocco mark one of the most remote Roman bases of the Empire. Originally a Punic town, it became thoroughly Romanized in the first century A.D. and flourished as an agricultural center, particularly for the cultivation of olives.

Gianni Tortoli/Photo Researchers

Roman influence in Egypt. A Roman pavilion built in the time of Trajan (ca. second century A.D.) sits desolately near the gates of the Temple of Isis, an Egyptian goddess whose worship extended throughout the Roman world. Roman patronage or tolerance of foreign gods and religions, as long as they did not incite rebellion, became typical under the later Roman emperors.

Great freedom was allowed the individual. The Romans did not look upon themselves as a superior race, although there was of course some race prejudice. There was occasional persecution of the Christians, it is true, but that was not due to a desire to suppress individual religious beliefs, but chiefly to the unwillingness of Christians to conform to practices that were considered part of one's duty to the state.

Something is to be said for the claim that the Roman Empire was based on the Stoic doctrine that all men are equal. This was felt by some to be true of slaves, too. Roman slavery is not to be confused with some modern forms of slavery, for many Roman slaves won or bought their freedom. Citizenship was granted to men of the most diverse origins. A real world state, a kind of United Nations, was achieved, in which the chief right relinquished by its members was that of making war on their neighbors. The Empire was not an utterly despotic government that aimed at dominating the private lives of its subjects.

Pliny the Elder (A.D. 23?–79) remarks on the mighty majesty of the Roman peace (**immēnsae Rōmānae pācis maiestāte),** which made the people and places and products of the whole world known to everyone, and prays that this gift of the gods may last forever, for, he says, the Romans are a gift to humanity comparable only to the sun which shines over all the world. In A.D. 400 the poet Claudian praised Rome for being the only nation that ever welcomed to her arms those she conquered, treating the whole human race as sons, not slaves, giving citizenship to the vanquished and uniting the most remote regions by the bonds of loyalty.

Exaggeration? Without doubt. But the reference to Rome's treatment of human beings as sons, not slaves, is of particular significance in estimating the place of the Roman Empire among the empires of history.

Summary of Pronouns
(For their declension, see the Grammar Appendix, pp. 517–519.)

Personal

ego (pl. **nōs**)	*I (we)*
tū (pl. **vōs**)	*you (you)*
is, ea, id (pl. **eī, eae, ea**)	*he, she, it (they)*
(also **hic** and **ille;** see below)	

Reflexive

meī (gen.) (pl. **nostrī**)	*of myself (of ourselves)*
tuī (pl. **vestrī**)	*of yourself (of yourselves)*
suī (pl. **suī**)	*of himself/herself/itself/themselves*

Demonstrative

hic, haec, hoc	*this (here), the latter, he, she, it*
ille, illa, illud	*that (there), the former, he, she, it*
is, ea, id	*this, that, he, she, it*
iste, ista, istud	*that (where you are)*
īdem, eadem, idem	*the same*
ipse, ipsa, ipsum	*-self, the very*

Relative

quī, quae, quod (pron. and adj.)	*who, which, that*

Interrogative

quis? quid? (pron.)	*who? what?*
quī? quae? quod? (adj.)	*which? what?*

LESSONS XXVII–XXXIX

Indefinite

quis, quid (pron.)[1]	*anyone, anything, someone, something*
quī, quae, (qua), quod (adj.)[1]	*any, some*
aliquis, aliquid (pron.)	*someone, something, anyone, anything*
aliquī, aliqua, aliquod (adj.)	*some, any*
quīdam, quaedam, quiddam (pron.)	*a certain one (person or thing)*
quīdam, quaedam, quoddam (adj.)	*a certain*
quisquam, quicquam (quidquam)	*anyone, anything*
quisque, quidque (pron.)	*each one, each thing*
quisque, quaeque, quodque (adj.)	*each*

Indefinite Relative

quīcumque, quaecumque, quodcumque	*whoever, whatever*

[1] indefinite after **sī, nisi, nē,** and **num**

VOCABULARY

Circle the word that best completes each sentence.

1. Pūblium litterās ad patrem ob _____ pecūniae mittere oportet.
   a. stultitiam
   b. inopiam
   c. initium
   d. obsidem

2. "Cum tuum socium ācriter pugnandō servārēs, putō tē _____ esse," mater fīliō dīxit.
   a. audācem
   b. inīquum
   c. vīvum
   d. propinquum

3. Operīs celeriter perfectīs, tribūnus mīlitēs discēdere _____.
   a. implēvit
   b. dēlēvit
   c. pepercit
   d. sīvit

4. Dux locāvit custōdēs quī captīvōs _____ et ipse cum equitibus ad collem mātūrāvit.
   a. circumvenīrent
   b. coniūrārent
   c. neglegerent
   d. postulārent

5. Comitēs Cornēliae ad multitūdinem mulierum in Forō cucurrērunt, sed ipsa vix _____ potuit.
   a. dēferre
   b. mālle
   c. sequī
   d. verērī

GRAMMAR

Complete each sentence with the correct endings.

6. Is quī in magistrātū patr___ suō successit vir tantae stultiti___ erat ut plēbs e___ ēicere vell___.

7. Īnsidi___ apertīs, mūrī et fossae legiōn___ mūniend___ sunt ut urbs tūt___ reman___.

8. "Sequ___ mē, amīc___ nōbil___ (superlative), sī quam spem victōri___ restituere vultis!" inquit tribūnus mīlit___.

9. Cōnsuētūdō Rōmān___ erat ut du___ (number) cōnsul___ exercituum dūcend___ causā ēlēct___ ___.

10. Cum Camillus illam ōrātiōn___ habuit, dīxit sē Rōm___ nāt___ ___, et nūllam ali___ urb___ parem___ e___ esse.

TRANSLATION

Translate the following sentences.

11. Cum rēx nihil malī verērētur, Brūtus dēlēctus est comes quī ōrāculum cum fīliīs rēgis cōnsuleret.

12. Adventus nāvis pectus mercātōris tantō gaudiō implēvit ut cōnsīdere domī nōllet, sed ad portum quam prīmum mātūrāre māllet.

13. "Quisque suā arte praestet." Tālī sententiā omnibus licet persequī suās spēs vel voluntātēs ut successum attingant.

14. Hostis Rōmānīs ad lacum caedem terrōremque intulit et proximō annō, proeliō multō maiōre gestō, Carthāginem multam praedam mīsit.

15. Cum fēminae nūntium dē līberīs incolumibus audīvissent, coepērunt mīrārī in quō locō tot diēs abditī essent, et quō modō alitī essent.

INVESTIGATION

Find the answers to these questions from any lesson in Unit III.

16. Tell the names of the seven kings of Rome in chronological order: _____
_____
_____
_____

17. How did Titus Manlius get the name "Torquatus"?_____
_____
_____

18. Why were the wars between Rome and Carthage called the Punic Wars? _____
_____
_____

19. Against what enemy and for what reason did Q. Fabius Maximus acquire the cognomen **Cunctator?**_____
_____

20. What is the translation of the Latin word **vetō,** and how does that original meaning relate to this word's modern political usage? _____
_____
_____

CULTURE

Vērum aut Falsum? Indicate whether each statement is true or false.

21. The temple of Apollo at Corinth is one of the finest examples of the Corinthian order of architecture.

22. In the Roman Civil War the forces of Pompey defeated those of Caesar, who was murdered in Egypt.

23. Fire departments were established in Rome during Augustus' Pax Romana.

24. A great equestrian statue of the emperor Marcus Aurelius now stands atop the Capitoline Hill in Rome.

25. The office of **tribūnus plēbis,** or tribune, was established during the Republic to help protect the rights of the **Patrēs.**

FROM LATIN TO ENGLISH

Apply your knowledge of Latin roots to determine the best meaning of the italicized words.

26. The new proposal seemed *detrimental* to the conservation policy of the town.
  a. unrelated   **c.** essential
  b. helpful   **d.** damaging

27. Each side defended its position with great *vehemence* in the debate.
  a. hesitancy   **c.** pleasure
  b. force   **d.** hatred

28. The company was considering the *restitution* of the worker's rights.
  a. denial   **c.** restoration
  b. cost   **d.** benefit

29. An article in the journal tried to explain the *insidious* nature of the disease.
  a. mild   **c.** unknown
  b. treacherous   **d.** unusual

30. Many people were astonished by the *iniquity* of the king's actions.
  a. speed   **c.** consequences
  b. fairness   **d.** injustice

THE ARGONAUTS

Unit Objective

Read:

* The Story of *Jason and the Argonauts*

Jason and the Argonauts is a famous story from Greek mythology. It was one of many Greek tales admired and preserved by the Romans. In this painting by Lorenzo Costa (c. 1460–1535), we see Jason and his friends sailing toward Colchis in search of the Golden Fleece.

231

THE STORY OF THE GOLDEN FLEECE

The story of the Trojan War, made famous by the Greek poet Homer, was but one of the many interesting tales, sometimes fact, sometimes fiction, often both, which the Greeks told and retold. Another was that of the Argonauts, those adventurers who sailed unknown seas in search of the Golden Fleece. The story runs as follows:

Aeson (Ēson), king of Thessaly, had a brother Pelias (Pe´lias) and a son Jason. Pelias drove out Aeson, seized the throne, and planned to kill Jason. But Jason escaped with the help of friends, who then told Pelias that his nephew had died.

An oracle told Pelias to beware of a man wearing only one shoe. Some years later Pelias announced a great festival, and crowds came to the city. Among them was Jason, now grown to manhood. On the way to the festival he lost one shoe. When Pelias saw him, he recalled the oracle. To get rid of Jason, he gave him the seemingly impossible task of obtaining the Golden Fleece. Jason asked Argus to build him a ship and gathered about him a group of brave friends. After many adventures they finally reached Colchis on the Black Sea.

From this point on the story becomes chiefly that of the enchantress Medea (Medē´a), daughter of Aeetes (Ēē´tēs), king of Colchis. She fell in love with Jason, and with her help he obtained the Golden Fleece. Jason and the Argonauts returned to Thessaly, taking Medea with them.

Medea now determined to get rid of Pelias so that Jason might be king. Pretending to make Pelias young again, she killed him. But the people were so incensed that they drove out Medea and Jason, who then went to Corinth. Here they quarreled, and Medea killed her own children. She fled to Athens, and Jason was later killed in an accident.

The Argonauts and Latin Grammar

The story of the Argonauts as given in the following pages was published some years ago in a book by Ritchie entitled *Fabulae Faciles*. It is written in simple Latin and is intended to give intensive drill on the subjunctive and other constructions common in Caesar. In the lessons that follow, identify every subjunctive, giving its form and the construction if it is one that has already been covered. Identify also all uses of the future passive participle and gerund, and uses of the infinitive.

Remember that it is one thing to determine what a Latin sentence means, and another, often much more difficult, to put this meaning into good English. You should *understand* Latin as Latin, but *translate* it as English. Two hints for translation: if you can keep the natural English word order close to the Latin, so much the better; if you cannot, turn the whole Latin sentence upside down, if need be, to produce a smooth English version. Second, wherever you easily can, avoid the passive voice in English. The passive is very frequent in Latin, but its constant use in English makes the style flat, weak, and stilted.

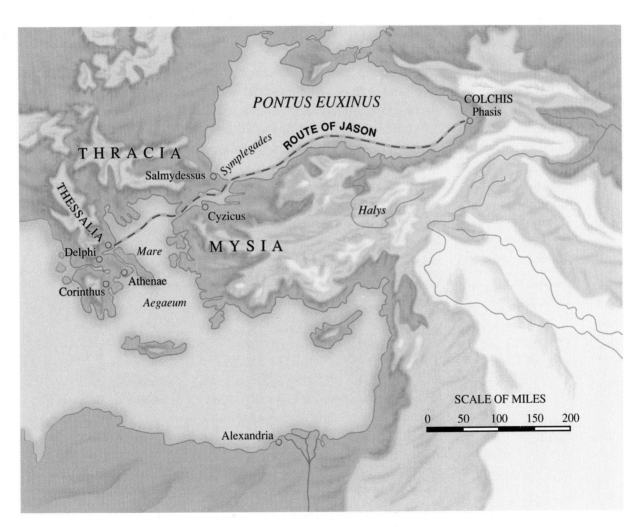

Map of the voyage of the Argonauts

LESSON OBJECTIVE
• Read about Pelias' plot to kill Jason and Jason's return to Thessaly

THE WICKED UNCLE

¹ *planned* (with **in animō**)

² Subject of **audivisset** but placed outside the **cum** clause, because it is also the subject of the following verbs. This is common in Latin.

³ *fearing.* The past participles of many deponent verbs have present force.

⁴ *that.* See the Grammar Appendix under Subjunctive: Clauses of Fear

Erant ōlim in Thessaliā duo frātrēs, quōrum alter Aesōn, alter Peliās appellābātur. Aesōn prīmō rēgnum obtinuerat; at post paucōs annōs Peliās rēgnī cupiditāte adductus nōn modo frātrem suum expulit, sed etiam in animō habēbat¹ Iāsonem, Aesonis fīlium, interficere. Quīdam tamen amīcī
5 Aesonis puerum ē tantō perīculō ēripere cōnstituērunt. Noctū igitur Iāsonem ex urbe abstulērunt, et cum posterō diē ad rēgem rediissent, eī renūntiāvērunt puerum mortuum esse. Peliās² cum hoc audīvisset, speciem dolōris praebuit et quae causa esset mortis quaesīvit. Illī autem cum bene intellegerent dolōrem eius falsum esse, fābulam dē morte puerī fīnxērunt.

Post breve tempus Peliās, veritus³ nē⁴ rēgnum suum āmitteret, amīcum quendam Delphōs mīsit, quī ōrāculum cōnsuleret. Ille igitur quam

Chiron, the wise and just centaur, on a black-figured Greek vase now in the British Museum. The half-man, half-horse Chiron was the teacher of many Greek heroes, including Jason.

On the other side of the same vase depicting Chiron, we see Achilles' father, King Peleus, handing over his small son for instruction. Chiron's dog greets the visitors.

celerrimē Delphōs prōcessit et quam ob causam[5] vēnisset dēmōnstrāvit.
Ōrāculum monuit Peliam ut, sī quis venīret[6] calceum ūnum gerēns, eum
cavēret. Post paucōs annōs accidit ut Peliās magnum sacrificium factūrus
esset. Diē cōnstitūtō magnus numerus hominum undique convēnit; inter
aliōs vēnit etiam Iāsōn, quī ā pueritiā apud centaurum[7] quendam
habitāverat. Dum tamen iter facit,[8] calceum alterum[9] in trānseundō
flūmine āmīsit.

[5] *for what reason*

[6] see Subjunctive by Attraction: Grammar Appendix, p. 505.15 and 506.3

15 [7] *centaur,* a fabulous monster—half man, half horse

[8] A present tense following **dum** has the force of the imperfect, if the main verb is past.

[9] *one* (literally, *the other*)

VOCABULARY

Nouns

cupiditās, -tātis f. *desire*   [cupiō]

dolor, -ōris m. *grief, pain*   [doleō]

Adjective

brevis, -e *short*   (abbreviation, brief)

Verb

renūntiō, 1 *report*   [nūntiō]

Adverbs

noctū *by night*   [nox]

igitur *therefore*

undique *from all sides*

Review **posterus, praebeō, quaerō, quīdam, redeō, tantus, vereor.**

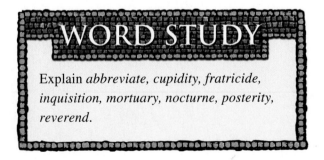

WORD STUDY

Explain *abbreviate, cupidity, fratricide, inquisition, mortuary, nocturne, posterity, reverend.*

THE GOLDEN FLEECE AND THE BUILDING OF THE ARGO

[1] ablative absolute: *with one foot bare*

[2] **Quem** is used for **eum** to connect closely with the preceding sentence; translate as if **cum eum**.

[3] The subjunctive is used in a subordinate clause in indirect statement.

[4] *fleece* (the wooly coat of a sheep)

[5] Phrixus and his sister Helle fled from a cruel stepmother on the back of a winged ram sent by Jupiter. On the way Helle fell into the sea which was from that time on named the Hellespont. Phrixus arrived in Colchis, on the Black Sea. He sacrificed the ram to Jupiter and gave its fleece, which was of gold, to Aeetes, king of Colchis.

[6] The clause is in apposition to **negōtium.**

[7] accusative of extent

Iāsōn igitur, ūnō pede nūdō,[1] in rēgiam pervēnit; quem[2] cum Peliās vīdisset, subitō timōre affectus est; intellēxit enim hunc esse hominem quem ōrāculum dēmōnstrāvisset.[3] Hoc igitur iniit cōnsilium. Rēx erat quīdam nōmine Aeētēs, quī rēgnum Colchidis illō tempore obtinēbat. Huic 5 commissum erat vellus[4] aureum quod Phrixus[5] ōlim ibi relīquerat. Cōnstituit igitur Peliās Iāsonī negōtium dare, ut hoc vellus obtinēret;[6] cum enim rēs esset magnī perīculī eum in itinere peritūrum esse spērābat. Iāsonem igitur ad sē arcessīvit et quid fierī vellet docuit. Iāsōn autem, etsī intellegēbat rem esse difficillimam, negōtium libenter suscēpit.

Cum Colchis multōrum diērum iter[7] ab eō locō abesset, nōluit Iāsōn 10 sōlus proficīscī. Dīmīsit igitur nūntiōs in omnēs partēs, quī causam itineris

This Roman terra-cotta relief shows Athena comfortably seated, helping to rig the sails of the *Argo*. Although the story of the Argonauts is filled with myth and miracle, it probably records some dim memory of the Greeks' first exploration of the Black Sea.

Ronald Sheridan/Ancient Art & Architecture Collection

docērent et diem certum conveniendī dīcerent. Intereā negōtium dedit
Argō[8] ut nāvem aedificāret. In hīs rēbus circiter decem diēs cōnsūmptī
sunt; Argus enim tantam dīligentiam praebēbat ut nē noctū quidem
labōrem intermitteret. Ad multitūdinem hominum trānsportandam nāvis   15
paulō erat lātior quam quibus[9] ūtī cōnsuēvimus.

[8] from **Argus**, a man, not from **Argō**
[9] Supply **eae:** *those which.*

VOCABULARY

Verbs

cōnsuēscō, -ere, -suēvī, -suētus *become*   [**cōnsuētūdō**]
  accustomed; (in perf.) *be accustomed*
ūtor, ūtī, ūsus *use* (with abl.)   (utilize, useful)

Adverbs

intereā *meanwhile*   [**inter + eā**]
paulō *a little*

Review **circiter, cōnsūmō, enim, ineō, pereō, proficīscor, subitō.**

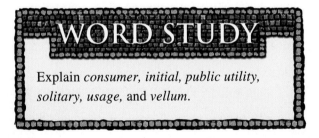

WORD STUDY

Explain *consumer, initial, public utility,
solitary, usage,* and *vellum.*

LESSON
OBJECTIVE
• Read about Jason's
departure and the
predicament of King
Phineus

DINNER UNDER DIFFICULTIES

[1] The relative **quōs** has been put before its antecedent **eōs** (in the next line). Translate as if **eōs quōs**, *those whom.*

[2] *about*

[3] *weather*

[4] *set sail; literally, loosed (ship)*

[5] = **quaesivissent**. Perfects ending in **-vī** often lose the **-v-** and contract the remaining vowels.

[6] *blind*

[7] *his*

Intereā is diēs aderat quem Iāsōn per nūntiōs ēdīxerat, et ex omnibus regiōnibus Graeciae multī undique conveniēbant. Trāditum est autem in hōc numerō fuisse Herculem, Orpheum, Castorem, multōsque aliōs quōrum nōmina nōtissima sunt. Ex hīs Iāsōn, quōs[1] arbitrātus est ad omnia
5 subeunda perīcula parātissimōs esse, eōs ad[2] numerum quīnquāgintā dēlēgit; tum paucōs diēs morātus ut ad omnēs cāsūs subsidia comparāret, nāvem dēdūxit, et tempestātem[3] ad nāvigandum idōneam nactus solvit.[4]

Post haec Argonautae ad Thrāciam cursum tenuērunt et ibi in terram ēgressī sunt. Cum ab incolīs quaesīssent[5] quis rēgnum eius regiōnis
10 obtinēret, certiōrēs factī sunt Phīneum quendam tum rēgem esse. Cognōvērunt hunc caecum[6] esse et suppliciō afficī, quod ōlim sē crūdēlissimum in fīliōs suōs praebuisset. Cuius[7] supplicī hoc erat genus. Missa erant ā Iove mōnstra quaedam speciē horribilī, quae capita

The Mediterranean world, much as Jason would have seen it. The geographical formations are the same today—mountains, forests, islands, and maybe a little mystery.

Luca Tamagnini/Archivio e Studio Folco Quilici

Alinari/Art Resource, NY

Caput virginis, corpus volucris habet. This terra-cotta Harpy once stood on the roof of an Etruscan building in the fifth or sixth century B.C. It is called an antefix, a decorative piece used to conceal the open end of a row of tiles.

virginum, corpora volucrum habēbant. Hae volucrēs, quae Harpȳiae appellābantur, Phīneō summam molestiam afferēbant; quotiēns enim ille accubuerat, veniēbant et cibum appositum statim auferēbant. Quae cum ita essent,[8] Phīneus famē paene mortuus est.

15

[8] *as a result.* What literally?

VOCABULARY

Noun

cursus, -ūs m. *course*   [**currō**]

Adjective

idōneus, -a, -um *suitable, fitting*

Verbs

comparō, 1 *get ready*   [**parō**]
ēgredior, ēgredī, ēgressus *go out, land*   [**gradior**]
nancīscor, nancīscī, nactus *meet with*

Review **arbitror, cāsus, famēs, moror, paene, trādō.**

WORD STUDY

Explain *convention, egress, moratorium, subsidy, tradition.*

LESSON
OBJECTIVE
• Read about how the
Argonauts drove off
the Harpies and their
encounter with the
Symplegades

TWO GOOD TURNS

[1] *that,* used after a negative expression of doubting to introduce a clause in the subjunctive (**ferrent**)

[2] accusative singular of **āēr, āeris,** m. *air*

[3] *dove*

[4] *subjunctive in an anticipatory clause after* **antequam;** *see Grammar Appendix, p. 505.12*

Rēs igitur in hōc locō erant cum Argonautae nāvem appulērunt. Phīneus autem, simul atque audīvit eōs in suōs fīnēs ēgressōs esse, magnopere gāvīsus est. Nōn enim dubitābat quīn[1] Argonautae sibi auxilium ferrent. Nūntium igitur ad nāvem mīsit quī Iāsonem sociōsque ad
5 rēgiam vocāret. Eō cum vēnissent, Phīneus prōmīsit sē magna praemia datūrum esse sī illī remedium repperissent. Argonautae negōtium libenter suscēpērunt et cum rēge accubuērunt; at simul ac cēna apposita est, Harpȳiae cibum auferre cōnābantur. Argonautae prīmum gladiīs volucrēs petīvērunt; cum tamen vidērent hoc nihil prōdesse, Zētēs et Calais, quī ālīs
10 īnstrūctī sunt, in āera[2] sē sublevāvērunt ut dēsuper impetum facerent. Quod cum sēnsissent Harpȳiae, perterritae statim fūgērunt neque posteā umquam rediērunt.

Hōc factō, Phīneus, ut prō tantō beneficiō grātiās referret, Iāsonī dēmōnstrāvit quā ratiōne Symplēgadēs vītāre posset. Symplēgadēs autem
15 duae erant rūpēs ingentī magnitūdine. Hae parvō intervāllō in marī natābant et sī quid in medium spatium vēnerat, incrēdibilī celeritāte concurrēbant. Iāsōn, sublātīs ancorīs, nāvem solvit et mox ad Symplēgadēs appropinquāvit. Tum in prōrā stāns columbam[3] ēmīsit. Illa rēctā viā per medium spatium volāvit et priusquam rūpēs cōnflīxērunt, ēvāsit, caudā
20 tantum āmissā. Tum rūpēs utrimque discessērunt; antequam tamen rūrsus concurrerent,[4] Argonautae summā vī rēmīs contendērunt et nāvem perdūxērunt.

▦ VOCABULARY

Nouns

ratiō, -ōnis f. *manner, reason*	(ration, rationale)
rēmus, -ī m. *oar*	(bireme)

Verbs

appropinquō, 1 *come near to, approach*	[**propinquus**]
cōnflīgō, -ere, -flīxī, -flīctus *dash together*	(conflict)
cōnor, 1 *try*	(conation)
reperiō, -īre, repperī, repertus *find*	(repertoire)
sublevō, 1 *raise;* (with reflex.) *rise*	
tollō, -ere, sustulī, sublātus *raise*	(sublate)
vītō, 1 *avoid*	(inevitable)

Adverbs

magnopere *greatly*	[**magnus**]
simul *at the same time*	(simulcast, simultaneous)
simul atque (ac) *as soon as*	

Review **eō** (adv.), **impetus, rūrsus, statim.**

WORD STUDY

Explain *aerial, conflict, impetuous, repertory, simultaneous, volatile.*

A RISKY JOB

LESSON OBJECTIVE
• Read about King Aeetes' tasks for Jason and Medea's efforts to help him succeed

Brevī intermissō spatiō, Argonautae ad flūmen Phāsim vēnērunt, quod in fīnibus Colchōrum erat. Eō cum in terram ēgressī essent, statim ad rēgem Aeētem prōcessērunt et ab eō postulāvērunt ut vellus aureum sibi trāderētur. Ille īrā commōtus diū negābat sē vellus trāditūrum esse.
5 Tandem tamen, quod sciēbat Iāsonem nōn sine auxiliō deōrum hoc negōtium suscēpisse, prōmīsit sē vellus trāditūrum esse, sī Iāsōn labōrēs duōs difficillimōs perfēcisset;[1] et cum Iāsōn dīxisset sē ad omnia perīcula subeunda parātum esse, quid fierī vellet ostendit.
10 Prīmum iungendī erant duo taurī speciē horribilī, quī flammās ex ōre ēdēbant; tum, hīs iūnctīs, ager arandus erat, et dentēs dracōnis serendī. Hīs audītīs, Iāsōn, nē hanc occāsiōnem reī bene gerendae[2] āmitteret,
15 negōtium suscēpit.

At Mēdēa, rēgis fīlia, Iāsonem amāvit, et ubi audīvit eum tantum perīculum subitūrum esse, rem aegrē ferēbat. Intellegēbat enim patrem suum hunc labōrem prōposuisse eō
20 ipsō cōnsiliō, ut Iāsōn morerētur. Quae cum ita essent, Mēdēa (quae summam scientiam medicīnae habēbat) hoc cōnsilium iniit. Mediā nocte clam ex urbe ēvāsit et herbās quāsdam carpsit; ex hīs unguentum parāvit
25 quod vī suā corpus aleret[3] nervōsque[4] cōnfirmāret. Hōc factō, Iāsonī unguentum dedit; praecēpit autem ut eō diē quō istī[5] labōrēs cōnficiendī essent corpus suum et arma oblineret. Iāsōn, etsī paene omnibus[6]
30 magnitūdine et vīribus corporis praestābat, tamen hoc cōnsilium nōn neglegendum esse cēnsēbat.

[1] *would perform.* This is a subjunctive in a subordinate clause in indirect statement. In direct statement the verb would have been in the future perfect indicative.
[2] *of accomplishing his mission.* What literally?
[3] Translate with "would."
[4] *muscles*
[5] *the above-mentioned*
[6] *dative after a compound verb*

This portrait of Medea, daughter of King Aeetes, comes from a Roman wall painting in a villa in Herculaneum. It was painted sometime before A.D. 79.

C.M. Dixon/Photo Resources

VOCABULARY

Noun

occāsiō, -ōnis f. *opportunity*   [cadō]

Verbs

cēnseō, -ēre, cēnsuī, cēnsus *think, judge*   (censor)
subeō, -īre, -iī, -itūrus *go under, undergo*   [eō]

Adverbs

aegrē *with difficulty*
clam *secretly*
diū *(for) a long time, long*

Review **alō, iungō, neglegō, postulō, praestō.**

WORD STUDY

Explain *dental, conjunction, liniment, postulate.*

SOWING THE DRAGON'S TEETH

¹ ablative absolute: *at daybreak.* What literally?

² modifies **difficultāte.** The order *adjective, preposition, noun,* is sometimes used when the adjective is emphatic.

³ *near*

⁴ *with one another.* What literally?

⁵ *without trouble.* Why ablative?

Ubi is diēs vēnit quem rēx ad arandum agrum ēdīxerat, Iāsōn, ortā lūce,¹ cum sociīs ad locum cōnstitūtum prōcessit. Ibi stabulum ingēns repperit in quō taurī erant inclūsī; tum, portīs apertīs, taurōs in lūcem trāxit, et summā² cum difficultāte iugum imposuit. Tum Iāsōn, omnibus
5 aspicientibus, agrum arāre coepit; quā in rē tantam dīligentiam praebuit ut ante merīdiem tōtum opus cōnficeret. Hōc factō, ad locum ubi rēx sedēbat adiit et dentēs dracōnis postulāvit; quōs ubi accēpit, in agrum sparsit. Hōrum autem dentium nātūra erat tālis ut in eō locō ubi sparsī essent virī armātī mīrō modō gignerentur.
10   Postquam igitur omnēs dentēs in agrum sparsit, Iāsōn lassitūdine exanimātus quiētī sē trādidit, dum virī istī gignerentur. Paucās hōrās dormiēbat; sub³ vesperum tamen ē somnō subitō excitātus rem ita ēvēnisse ut praedictum erat cognōvit; nam in omnibus agrī partibus virī ingentī magnitūdine gladiīs galeīsque armātī mīrō modō ē terrā oriēbantur. Hōc
15 cognitō, Iāsōn cōnsilium quod dedisset Mēdēa nōn omittendum esse putābat. Saxum igitur ingēns in mediōs virōs coniēcit. Illī undique ad locum concurrērunt, et cum sibi quisque id saxum habēre vellet, magna contrōversia orta est. Mox, strictīs gladiīs, inter sē⁴ pugnāre coepērunt, et cum hōc modō plūrimī occīsī essent, reliquī vulneribus cōnfectī ā Iāsone
20 nūllō negōtiō⁵ interfectī sunt.

Jason seizes the horns of a fire-breathing bull. Once he yokes this one with the other, he will plow the field and sow the dragon's teeth.

Erich Lessing/Art Resource, NY

VOCABULARY

Nouns

contrōversia, -ae f. *dispute*   [contrā, vertō]

iugum, -ī n. *yoke*   (jugular)

merīdiēs, -ēī m. *midday, noon*   [diēs]

Pronoun/Adjective

iste, ista, istud *that*

Verbs

aspiciō, -ere, aspexī, aspectus *look on*   (aspect)

exanimō, 1 *exhaust, kill*   [animus]

Review **aperiō, coepī, occīdō, orior, quiēs, saxum, vesper.**

WORD STUDY

Explain *disperse* (from **spargō**), *lassitude, quietus.*

JASON GETS THE FLEECE

At rēx Aeētēs, ubi cognōvit Iāsonem labōrem prōpositum cōnfēcisse, īrā graviter commōtus est; intellegēbat enim Mēdēam auxilium eī tulisse. Mēdēa autem, cum intellegeret sē in magnō esse perīculō, fugā salūtem petere cōnstituit. Omnibus igitur rēbus ad fugam parātīs, mediā nocte cum
5 frātre Absyrtō ēvāsit et quam celerrimē ad locum ubi Argō¹ subducta erat prōcessit. Eō cum vēnisset, ad pedēs Iāsonis sē prōiēcit et multīs cum lacrimīs eum ōrāvit nē in tantō perīculō sē² dēsereret. Ille libenter eam excēpit et hortātus est nē patris īram timēret. Prōmīsit autem sē quam prīmum eam in nāvī suā āvectūrum.³
10   Postrīdiē Iāsōn cum sociīs suīs, ortā lūce, nāvem dēdūxit, et tempestātem idōneam nactī ad eum locum rēmīs contendērunt quō Mēdēa vellus cēlātum esse dēmōnstrāvit. Eō cum vēnissent, Iāsōn in terram ēgressus, ipse cum Mēdēā in silvās contendit. Pauca mīlia passuum per silvam prōgressus vellus quod quaerēbat ex arbore suspēnsum vīdit. Id
15 tamen auferre rēs erat summae difficultātis: nōn modo enim locus ipse ēgregiē et nātūrā et arte mūnītus erat, sed etiam dracō speciē terribilī arborem custōdiēbat. Tum Mēdēa, quae, ut suprā dēmōnstrāvimus,

¹ *Argo* (the ship)
² i.e., Medea
³ *would carry away*

On this red-figured vase in New York City, Jason reaches up to steal the Golden Fleece, while Athena (center) looks on. At the right, one of the Argonauts holds the rail of the *Argo*. We might expect the hero Jason to be a little bigger and less awkward than this.

medicīnae summam scientiam habuit, rāmum quem ex arbore proximā
arripuerat venēnō īnfēcit.[4] Hōc factō, ad locum appropinquāvit et
dracōnem, quī faucibus apertīs eius adventum exspectābat, venēnō sparsit; 20
deinde, dum dracō somnō oppressus dormit, Iāsōn vellus aureum ex arbore
arripuit et cum Mēdēā quam celerrimē pedem rettulit.[5]

[4] Use the derivative.

[5] *withdrew* (with **pedem**). What literally?

VOCABULARY

Noun

difficultās, -tātis f. *difficulty*   [facilis]

Adjective

apertus, -a, -um *open*   [aperiō]

Adverbs

postrīdiē *on the next day*   [diēs]
quam *how, as* (with comp., *than;* with
superl., *as...possible*) (also conjunction)
suprā *above*   (supranational,
                                          supraorbital)

Review **arbor, contendō, excipiō, hortor, passus.**

WORD STUDY

Explain *contention, dragon, hortatory,
infection, projectile, suspension.*

ESCAPE THROUGH MURDER

Postquam Iāsōn et Mēdēa, vellus aureum ferentēs, ad nāvem pervēnissent, omnēs sine morā nāvem rūrsus cōnscendērunt et prīmā vigiliā¹ solvērunt. At rēx Aeētēs, ubi cognōvit fīliam suam nōn modo ad Argonautās sē recēpisse sed etiam ad vellus auferendum auxilium tulisse,
5 nāvem longam² quam celerrimē dēdūcī iussit et fugientēs³ īnsecūtus est. Argonautae omnibus vīribus rēmīs contendēbant; cum tamen nāvis quā vehēbantur ingentī esset magnitūdine, nōn eādem celeritāte quā⁴ Colchī prōgredī poterant. Quae cum ita essent, ā Colchīs sequentibus paene captī sunt. At Mēdēa, cum vīdisset quō in locō rēs essent, nefārium cōnsilium
10 cēpit.

Erat in nāvī Argonautārum fīlius rēgis Aeētae, nōmine Absyrtus, quem, ut suprā dēmōnstrāvimus, Mēdēa fugiēns sēcum abdūxerat. Hunc puerum Mēdēa interficere cōnstituit ut, membrīs eius in mare coniectīs, cursum Colchōrum impedīret;⁵ sciēbat enim Aeētem, cum membra fīlī vīdisset,
15 nōn longius prōsecūtūrum esse. Neque opīniō eam fefellit.⁶ Aeētēs, cum prīmum membra vīdit, ad ea colligenda nāvem dētinērī iussit. Dum tamen ea geruntur, Argonautae mox ex
20 cōnspectū hostium remōtī sunt, neque prius⁷ fugere dēstitērunt quam ad flūmen Ēridanum⁸ pervēnērunt.

Tandem post multa
25 perīcula Iāsōn in eundem locum pervēnit unde ōlim profectus erat. Tum ē nāvī ēgressus ad rēgem Peliam statim prōcessit et, vellere
30 aureō mōnstrātō, ab eō postulāvit ut rēgnum sibi trāderētur. Peliās prīmum nihil respondit, sed diū in

¹ *watch.* The night was divided into four "watches."
² i.e., a *warship*
³ *the fugitives.* What literally?
⁴ *as*
⁵ Understand Medea as the subject.
⁶ From **fallō:** *she was not mistaken.* What literally?
⁷ to be taken with **quam** = **priusquam**
⁸ *the Po,* a river of northern Italy

In this Pompeian wall-painting, Jason, wearing only one shoe, makes his first appearance before an alarmed King Pelias. Seeing the bare foot, Pelias realized that before him stood the man the oracle had warned him to fear.

eādem trīstitiā tacitus permānsit; tandem ita locūtus est: "Vidēs mē aetāte
iam esse cōnfectum; certē diēs suprēmus mihi adest. Liceat[9] igitur mihi,   35 [9] *let it be permitted*
dum vīvam, hoc rēgnum obtinēre; cum autem tandem dēcesserō, tū in
meum locum veniēs." Hāc ōrātiōne adductus Iāsōn respondit sē id
factūrum quod ille rogāvisset.

VOCABULARY

Noun

opīniō, -ōnis f. *opinion*   (opinionated)

Verbs

dēsistō, -ere, dēstitī, dēstitūrus *cease*   [stō]
īnsequor, īnsequī, īnsecūtus *pursue*   [sequor]

Adverb

unde *from which (place)*

Conjunction

cum prīmum *as soon as*

Review **colligō, cōnficiō, cōnspectus, fallō, licet, loquor, mora, ōlim,
priusquam, prōgredior, sequor, vehō**.

WORD STUDY

Explain *circumlocution, detention, fallacy,
infallible, nefarious, opinionated, survivor,
taciturn.*

LESSON
OBJECTIVE
• Read about Medea's
  plot to kill Pelias

BOILED MUTTON

His rēbus cognitīs, Mēdēa rēgnī cupiditāte adducta mortem rēgī per dolum īnferre cōnstituit. Ad fīliās rēgis vēnit atque ita locūta est: "Vidētis patrem vestrum aetāte iam esse cōnfectum neque ad labōrem rēgnandī perferendum[1] satis valēre. Vultisne eum rūrsus iuvenem fierī?" Tum fīliae
5 rēgis ita respondērunt: "Num[2] hoc fierī potest? Quis enim umquam ē sene iuvenis factus est?" At Mēdēa respondit: "Scītis mē medicīnae summam habēre scientiam. Nunc igitur vōbīs dēmōnstrābō quō modō haec rēs fierī possit." Hīs dictīs, cum arietem aetāte iam cōnfectum interfēcisset, membra eius in vāse aēneō[3] posuit et, ignī suppositō,[4] in aquam herbās
10 quāsdam īnfūdit. Tum carmen magicum cantābat. Mox ariēs ē vāse exsiluit et, vīribus refectīs, per agrōs currēbat.

  Dum fīliae rēgis hoc mīrāculum stupentēs intuentur, Mēdēa ita locūta est: "Vidētis quantum valeat medicīna. Vōs igitur, sī vultis patrem vestrum in adulēscentiam redūcere, id quod fēcī ipsae faciētis. Vōs patris membra
15 in vās conicite; ego herbās magicās praebēbō." Quod ubi audītum est, fīliae rēgis cōnsilium quod dedisset Mēdēa nōn omittendum putāvērunt.

[1] Which is the gerund—**rēgnandī** or **perferendum?** How are the gerund and the gerundive to be distinguished?

[2] introduces a question implying a negative answer: *this can't be done, can it?*

[3] *of bronze*

[4] *placed under* (the pot)

White-haired King Pelias watches Medea (center) perform her magic while the ram boils. At the right is one of Pelias' daughters. A slave, or perhaps Jason, tends the fire. Is this vase red-figured or black-figured?

Copyright British Museum

Patrem igitur Peliam necāvērunt et membra eius in vās coniēcērunt. At
Mēdēa nōn eāsdem herbās dedit quibus[5] ipsa ūsa erat. Itaque postquam diū
frūstrā exspectāvērunt, patrem suum rē vērā[6] mortuum esse intellēxērunt.
Hīs rēbus gestīs, Mēdēa spērābat sē cum coniuge suō rēgnum acceptūram   20
esse; sed cīvēs cum intellegerent quō modō Peliās periisset, Iāsone et
Mēdēā ē rēgnō expulsīs, Acastum rēgem creāvērunt.

[5] The ablative is used with **ūtor**.
[6] with **rē**: *in fact, really*

VOCABULARY

Verbs

   coniciō, -ere, -iēcī, -iectus *throw*   **[iaciō]**
   necō, 1 *kill*   (internecine)

Adverb

   frūstrā *in vain*   (frustrate, frustration)

Review **aetās, ignis, ita, quantus, satis, spērō.**

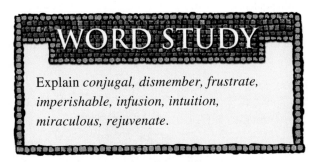

WORD STUDY

Explain *conjugal, dismember, frustrate,
imperishable, infusion, intuition,
miraculous, rejuvenate.*

LESSON
OBJECTIVE
• Read about Jason and
  Medea in Corinth

DEATH AND MORE DEATH

¹ *Creon had* (literally, *there was to Creon*). See Grammar Appendix, p. 497.

² accusative (Greek form)

³ subjunctive by attraction. See Grammar Appendix, pp. 505.15 and 506.3.

Post haec Iāsōn et Mēdēa ad urbem Corinthum vēnērunt, cuius urbis Creōn rēgnum tum obtinēbat. Erat autem Creontī¹ fīlia ūna nōmine Glaucē. Quam cum vīdisset, Iāsōn cōnstituit Mēdēam uxōrem suam repudiāre, ut Glaucēn² in mātrimōnium dūceret. At Mēdēa, ubi intellēxit quae ille in
5 animō habēret, īrā graviter commōta iūre iūrandō cōnfirmāvit sē tantam iniūriam ultūram. Hoc igitur cōnsilium cēpit. Vestem parāvit summā arte contextam; hanc īnfēcit venēnō, cuius vīs tālis erat ut, sī quis eam vestem induisset,³ corpus eius quasi ignī urerētur. Hōc factō, vestem ad Glaucēn mīsit. Illa autem nihil malī suspicāns dōnum libenter accēpit, et vestem
10 novam, mōre fēminārum, sine morā induit.

Statim Glaucē dolōrem gravem per omnia membra sēnsit et post paulum summō cruciātū affecta ē vītā excessit. Tum Mēdēa furōre impulsa fīliōs

Roman ruins from the city of Corinth, showing a temple and acropolis of Corinth. Here is where the final chapter of the story of Jason took place with the death of Glauce and the timely disappearance of Medea.

Ronald Sheridan/Ancient Art & Architecture Collection

suōs necāvit et ex eā regiōne fugere cōnstituit. Sōlem ōrāvit ut in tantō
perīculō auxilium sibi ferret. Sōl autem hīs precibus commōtus currum
mīsit cui dracōnēs ālīs īnstrūctī iūnctī erant. Mēdēa currum cōnscendit,   15
itaque per āera[4] vecta incolumis ad urbem Athēnās pervēnit. Iāsōn autem
post breve tempus mīrō modō occīsus est. Ille enim sub umbrā nāvis suae,
quae in lītus subducta erat, ōlim dormiēbat. At nāvis in eam partem[5] ubi
Iāsōn iacēbat subitō dēlāpsa virum īnfēlīcem oppressit.

[4] *air; a Greek form of the accusative*
[5] *to be taken with* **dēlāpsa**: *falling towards that side*

VOCABULARY

Nouns

cruciātus, -ūs m. *torture*   (cruciform)
iūs iūrandum, iūris iūrandī n. *oath*   [iūs]
prex, precis f. *prayer*   (deprecate, deprecatory)

Verb

suspicor, 1 *suspect*   (suspicion, suspicious)

Review **fēmina, incolumis, opprimō, sentiō, sōl, uxor, vestis.**

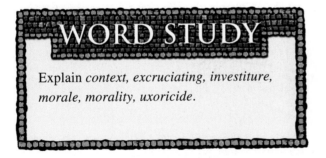

WORD STUDY

Explain *context, excruciating, investiture, morale, morality, uxoricide.*

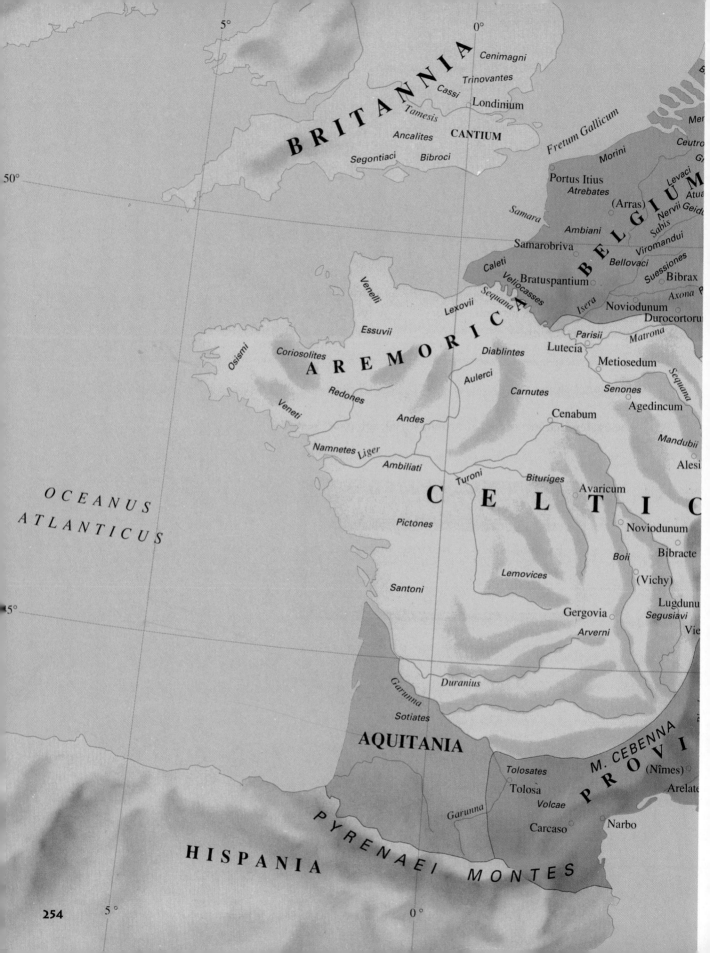

5°

0°

Cenimagni

Trinovantes

Cassi

Londinium

BRITANNIA

Tamesis

Ancalites   **CANTIUM**

Segontiaci   Bibroci

Fretum Gallicum

Mer

Ceutro

Morini

Gi

Levaci

Portus Itius   Atua

Atrebates   Nervii Geidu

(Arras)

Samara   Sabis

Ambiani   Viromandui

Samarobriva   Bellovaci   Suessiones

Caleti   Bibrax

Veliocasses   Bratuspantium   Axona

Venelli   Sequana   Isera   Noviodunum

Lexovii   Sequana   Durocortoru

Essuvii   Parisii

Diablintes   Lutecia   Matrona

Osismi   Coriosolites   Metiosedum   Sequana

A R E M O R I C   Aulerci   Senones

Redones   Carnutes   Agedincum

Veneti   Andes   Cenabum   Mandubii

Namnetes Liger   Alesi

Ambiliati   Turoni   Bituriges   **C E L T I C**

Pictones   Avaricum

O C E A N U S   Noviodunum

A T L A N T I C U S   Boii   Bibracte

Lemovices   (Vichy)

Santoni   Lugdunu

Gergovia   Segusiavi

Arverni   Vie

Duranius

Garunna

Sotiates   M. CEBENNA

AQUITANIA   **P R O V I**

Tolosates   (Nîmes)

Tolosa   Arelate

Garunna   Volcae

Carcaso   Narbo

P Y R E N A E I

H I S P A N I A   **M O N T E S**

50°

5°

5°

5°

0°

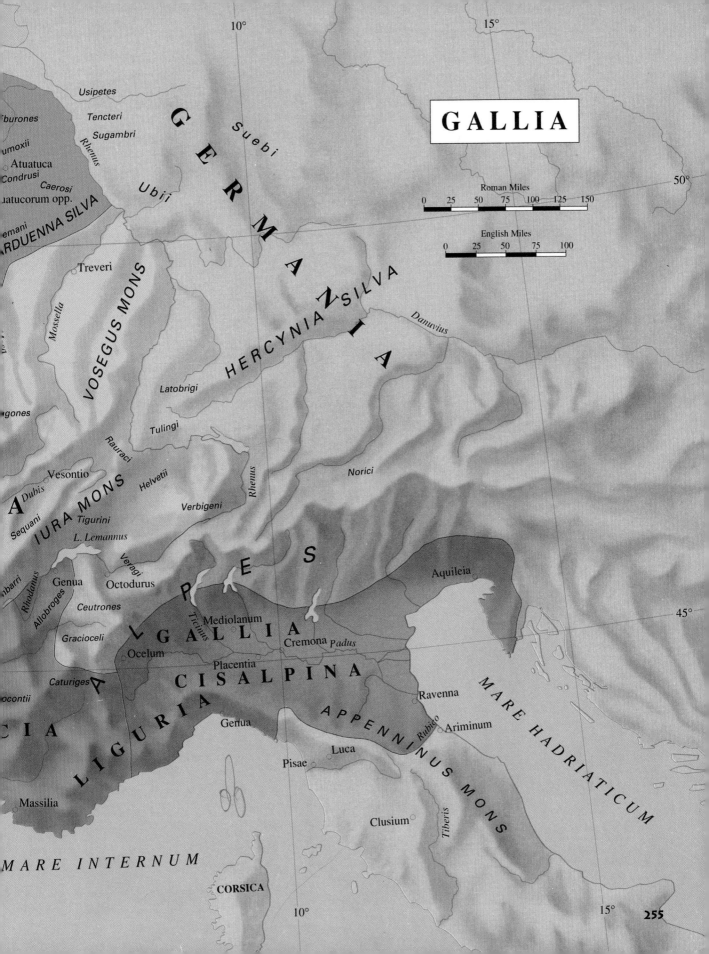

GERMANIA

Usipetes
Tencteri
Sugambri
...burones
...umoxii
Atuatuca
Condrusi
Caerosi
...uatucorum opp.
...emani

ARDUENNA SILVA

Rhenus

Ubii

Suebi

GALLIA

Roman Miles

0   25   50   75   100   125   150

English Miles

0   25   50   75   100

Treveri

VOSEGUS MONS

Mosella

HERCYNIA SILVA

Danuvius

Latobrigi

Tulingi

Norici

...gones

Rauraci

Vesontio

Helvetii

IURA MONS

Dubis

A

Sequani   Tigurini

Verbigeni

Rhenus

L. Lemannus

Veragi

A   L   P   E   S

...nbarri

Genua   Octodurus

Rhodanus

Allobroges

Ceutrones

Aquileia

Gracioceli

L   GALLIA

Mediolanum

Ocelum

Ticinus

Cremona   Padus

Placentia

CISALPINA

Caturiges

...contii

Ravenna

A

...CIA

LIGURIA

Genua

APPENNINUS MONS

Ariminum
Rubico

MARE HADRIATICUM

Luca

Pisae

Massilia

Clusium

Tiberis

MARE INTERNUM

CORSICA

50°

45°

255

DĒ BELLŌ GALLICŌ I

Unit Objective

Read:
- About the career of Julius Caesar and Caesar *Dē Bellō Gallicō,* Book 1

Learn:
- Dative of Possession, Subjunctive in Anticipatory Clauses, Causal Clauses with **Quod** and **Quoniam,** Subordinate Clauses in Indirect Statement

Review:
- Comparative and Superlative Adjectives and Adverbs, Ablative of Respect, Conjugation of **Fīō,** Future Passive Participle with **Ad,** Indicative Clauses with **Ubi** and **Postquam,** Indirect Statements, **Cum** Clauses, Purpose Clauses, Impersonal Verbs, Volitive Clauses, **Iubeō** Construction, Perfect and Future Infinitives in Indirect Statement, Datives of Purpose and Reference, Indirect Question, Volitive Subjunctive

The Senate House in Rome. Originally an advisory group to the early kings, the Senate decreed an end to the kings and thus established the Republic. As Caesar came to power and took up the cause of the general populace against the senatorial clique, he had the Senate House rebuilt and renamed it the **Cūria Jūlia.**

C.M. Dixon/Photo Resources

257

OUR HERITAGE

JULIUS CAESAR

No man is more immediately associated with Rome than is Julius Caesar. To most people, the name Caesar symbolizes the dynamism and greatness of the republic that he did so much to turn into an empire. The word Caesar is preserved in the titles Kaiser and Czar and has come so nearly to be a synonym for royal or dictatorial power that we speak of a minor autocrat as a "little Caesar." Most of us have heard or used many of the phrases that have grown up around him— "crossing the Rubicon," "the Ides of March," "Et tu, Brute," "great Caesar's ghost." No other Roman has been the subject of so much later attention: we have his biography in Latin by Suetonius, one in Greek by Plutarch, plays by Shakespeare and George Bernard Shaw; and several novels and films have celebrated his life and character.

Scala/Art Resource, NY

The Temple of Venus and Rome, in the Roman Forum, was restored by the emperor Maxentius in A.D. 307. It was dedicated to Venus, the supposed ancestor of Julius Caesar's family, and to all the local divinities of Rome.

Gaius Julius Caesar was born in 100 B.C. to a patrician family whose members flattered themselves on being so ancient that they could trace their line all the way back to a divine ancestress— Venus, the mother of Aeneas. But, in spite of their aristocratic lineage, the Julians had, in the early first century B.C., been associated with the political program of the common people. Whether from these connections, or from personal conviction, or from shrewd political insight into the way his ambitions could most easily be realized, and probably from all three, Caesar early adopted the popular cause against the senatorial clique, made up of a small number of noble families who had ruled Rome well but autocratically for centuries. Caesar's stand alarmed the conservative dictator Sulla and nearly cost Caesar his life, but, by a combination of a gambler's daring, great acumen in wooing the favor of the people, and an almost irresistible personal magnetism, he steadily made his way up the political ladder.

Somewhat before 60 B.C. he had allied himself with Crassus, a wealthy politician (who underwrote the enormous debts Caesar had contracted), and in that year he joined Pompey, the greatest military hero of the time, and Crassus in the coalition called the First Triumvirate ("Three-man Rule"). As a result, in 59 B.C., Caesar was elected to the consulship, the highest office in the Roman government. He so dominated his colleague Bibulus that the year was jestingly called, not "the consulship of Caesar and Bibulus," but "the consulship of Julius and Caesar." Many senators, realizing the danger that Caesar presented to their conservative position, tried to restrict the importance of the command he would hold as an ex-consul, but by political maneuvering Caesar won the proconsulship of Gaul and Illyricum. In all he spent nine years (58–50 B.C.) in subjugating and governing Gaul. In the following pages, you will read his own account of that conquest, the *Commentaries* (or *Notes*) *on the Gallic War*.

Caesar is remarkably tight-lipped about his own personal motives. It is apparent, however, that at the start of his command his attitude was a defensive one of simply protecting Italy and the Roman **Prōvincia** in southern France from the barbarian tribes. He then shifted to a more aggressive attitude aimed at reducing all Transalpine Gaul to the status of a Roman province. Possibly he realized that "a good offense is the best defense." He often states that friendly Gallic tribes appealed to him for protection against their more aggressive neighbors. Possibly he was driven farther and farther north by a consuming ambition for military power and glory. It is certain, however, that he used these years to develop his extraordinary military talents and to forge a highly loyal and efficient fighting force. There is also much evidence to show that even while Caesar was away in Gaul, he used his prestige and captured gold to build a strong political party at Rome.

Unquestionably he was a great military commander; his absolute physical courage, self-confidence, iron will, fairness, and generosity with praise and rewards made him an unparalleled leader of men. He was a master tactician, relying on great mobility to surprise his enemies, quick to adapt his maneuvers to the terrain and to press every advantage in the field. He showed no less skill in dealing with the people of Gaul, capitalizing on their failure to unite and on their vacillation, trusting those who became his allies (some would say he trusted them too much), and employing harsh punishments only when the offenders' rebelliousness was incorrigible.

Caesar's successes in Gaul, Britain, and Germany and the growth of his party at Rome led inevitably to conflict with Pompey and the Senate. In 49 B.C., a Civil War began when Caesar crossed the Rubicon, the boundary river between Cisalpine Gaul and Italy proper. The Senatorial army under Pompey's command abandoned Italy and was defeated near Pharsalus (in Greece) in

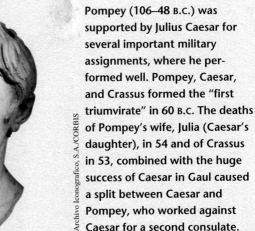

Pompey (106–48 B.C.) was supported by Julius Caesar for several important military assignments, where he performed well. Pompey, Caesar, and Crassus formed the "first triumvirate" in 60 B.C. The deaths of Pompey's wife, Julia (Caesar's daughter), in 54 and of Crassus in 53, combined with the huge success of Caesar in Gaul caused a split between Caesar and Pompey, who worked against Caesar for a second consulate.

Archivo Iconografico, S.A./CORBIS

48 B.C. Within the next three years Caesar had overrun all opposition and become virtually master of the Western world. In the few years before his assassination in 44 B.C., he brought about many reforms in Roman political and economic life, and laid the basis upon which his grandnephew and adopted son Octavian built the Roman Empire.

Caesar was also most expert in public relations. He wrote his *Commentaries* (or *Notes*) *on the Gallic War* not only to provide a record of the campaigns for future historians, but also to keep himself and his victories before the eyes of the Roman voters. Since he regularly refers to himself in the third person (only occasionally using the modest "we"), the work takes on a deceptively impersonal air, and the reader is inclined to forget that the image of this dynamic and unconquerable, yet understanding and merciful, general is being created by the "hero" himself. The style is likewise deceptively straightforward and clear, and the facts apparently so complete that no ancient historian ever needed or dared to rewrite his story. His three-book account of the Civil War is a valuable document of that bloody period, but it is the earlier work on Gaul that assures Caesar a place among the first rank of military historians.

It is, therefore, easy to see why so versatile a man was not only a great general, statesman, and writer, but also one of the best orators of his day, remarkable for the vigor of his speeches. But you might be surprised to know that he was something of a poet and was seriously interested in Latin grammar.

As a military man, Caesar ranks with such geniuses as Alexander, Hannibal, and Napoleon. Like Pericles, Washington, and Churchill, he was a great statesman, one whose military triumphs and political activities profoundly affected the future of the world. Yet, with all we know about him, there remains some of the mystery and controversy that surround all

"Et tū, Brūte, mi fili?" The assassination of Julius Caesar in 44 B.C. brought to a shocking end the life of Rome's best-known military general and genius. It interrupted, and mostly ended, a bold series of financial reforms designed to benefit the people, and reignited the flames of civil war that had plagued Rome for decades. Crowds of supporters, including Caesar's former soldiers, turned out to mourn the great man's death as Marc Antony spoke the eulogy.

Scala/Art Resource, NY

C.M. Dixon/Photo Resources

The cavalry, often recruited from Gallic tribes as an auxiliary force, played a crucial role throughout Caesar's campaign in Gaul. This relief shows an *eques* about to kill a barbarian.

great men. Naturally he had his faults. He was a bit vain about his personal appearance and particularly sensitive about his baldness. Although not especially superstitious about himself, he capitalized on the people's belief that Fortune favored him. Even though "Caesar's wife must be above suspicion," Caesar himself was not. But the gossip that surrounded his personal life served only to spread his reputation and to aid him at the polls. Much more serious is the charge that he was nothing more than a tyrant, bent on destroying the Roman republican form of government to satisfy his own lust for power. This question is still hotly debated, and, as you read his own words in the pages that follow, you will have a chance to decide the answer for yourself.

Caesar's Army and the American Army

Caesar's army (**exercitus,** literally, a body of "trained" men) was composed mainly of Roman citizens who served as foot soldiers (**peditēs),** but it also contained a cavalry force (**equitēs),** which during the Gallic Wars averaged about four thousand men. The cavalry were foreign mercenaries recruited in Spain, Germany, and Gaul. They were used mainly for scouting and surprise attacks, in preliminary skirmishing to test the enemy's strength, or in pursuit of a retreating foe.

Units of the United States Army train with basic drill movements much like that of the Roman army. The advantages are simplicity and maneuverability. The Roman army unit corresponding to a modern company marched in eight ranks or rows; our platoons march in three or four ranks.

The Roman army was organized as follows.

I. Groupings

    A. Infantry (**peditēs**)

        1. Legiō. The average size of one of Caesar's legions during the Gallic War was probably about thirty-two hundred, though the full strength was supposed to be six thousand. It is comparable to a *division* in the United States Army, for, like a division, it was a complete unit, consisting of various types of troops. The wartime strength of a division today ranges from ten to seventeen thousand men and women, divided between three brigades.

        2. Cohortēs. Each legion was divided into ten *cohorts* (**cohortēs**), averaging three hundred sixty men each. The similar grouping in the United States Army is the *brigade* consisting of about two thousand to four thousand men in two companies. Since the possibility of nuclear warfare today requires that combat units be more mobile, more self-sustaining, and capable of wider dispersal than in the past, the latest reorganizations of the United States Army assign to battle groups the various types of troops needed to allow them to operate independently, at least for limited periods. Thus the brigade also is in many respects comparable to the Roman legion. The specialized combat troops which support the infantry, such as combat engineers, field artillerymen, tank personnel, signal corps men, etc., are usually grouped into battalions ranging in size from five hundred to one thousand men.

        3. Manipulī. Each cohort was divided into three *maniples* (**manipulī**) of one hundred twenty men each. This corresponds to our *company,* with nearly two hundred men (four platoons).

        4. Ōrdinēs. Each maniple was divided into two *centuries* (**ōrdinēs**),[1] originally of one hundred men each but averaging sixty in Caesar's army. This corresponds to our *platoon,* with about fifty men.

    B. Cavalry (**equitēs**)

        1. Ālae. The **āla,** or *squadron,* consisted of three hundred or four hundred men commanded by a **praefectus equitum** (*cavalry prefect*).

        2. Turmae. Each **āla** was divided into **turmae,** or *troops,* of about thirty men each.

        3. Decuriae. Each **turma** was divided into **decuriae,** or *squads,* of ten men each.

---

[1] This term is sometimes used in Caesar in the sense of line, position, or rank.

C. Auxiliaries **(auxilia)**

1. **Levis armātūrae peditēs.** *Light-armed troops* recruited from allied or dependent states. Their officers were Romans. Caesar did not depend upon his **auxilia** to win battles but used them mostly for raiding and foraging.

2. **Funditōrēs.** *Slingers,* principally from the Balearic Islands (Majorca, etc.), near the east coast of Spain.

3. **Sagittāriī.** *Bowmen,* or *archers,* from Crete in the eastern Mediterranean and Numidia in Africa.

D. Noncombatants

1. **Cālōnēs.** *Camp servants,* including slaves attached to the officers' quarters. Each legion had about five hundred.

2. **Mūliōnēs.** *Muledrivers* in charge of heavy baggage of the army.

3. **Mercātōrēs.** *Traders* allowed to accompany the army and conduct canteens outside the camp.

II. Personnel

A. Enlisted Men

1. **Mīles legiōnārius.** A *legionary soldier* was usually a citizen volunteer who enlisted for the regular term of twenty years. Roman citizens between the ages of seventeen and forty-six were subject to military draft **(dīlēctus).**

2. **Ēvocātus.** A *volunteer* who had served his full time but had reenlisted. Such men were the flower of Caesar's army.

3. **Signifer.** *Standard bearer* of the maniple, resembling the modern color bearer.

4. **Aquilifer.** *Bearer of the eagle,* emblem of the legion.

5. **Centuriō, decuriō.** Each of the sixty centuries of the legion was in charge of a *centurion,* a noncommissioned officer appointed from the ranks in recognition of brave and efficient service. The centurions correspond in a general way to our sergeants, the first sergeant being called the *first centurion* **(prīmipīlus).** They were fearless officers who fought in the ranks, leading their men in person. Much of the success of an army depended on them. They maintained strict discipline, which they enforced with the **vītis,** similar to a police officer's club (see page 385). The commander of a squad of cavalry was called a *decurion.*

B. Commissioned Officers

1. **Tribūnus mīlitum, praefectus equitum.** Each legion had six *military tribunes,* the lowest commissioned officers. They were usually young men, well educated and of good family, but untrained, and were entrusted with duties of minor importance,

such as the command of a legion in camp or on the march (the modern second lieutenant). These men usually were in the army to get the military experience that was prerequisite to a political career. A *cavalry prefect,* similar in rank to a military tribune, commanded an **āla.**

2. **Quaestor.** Like a *quartermaster,* the **quaestor** supervised the pay of the men and the purchase of supplies; in battle he sometimes commanded a legion.

3. **Lēgātus.** Caesar had a number of *staff officers* (**lēgātī),** who were appointed by the Roman senate with the rank of a modern *lieutenant general* or *major general.* In battle each legion was usually commanded by a **lēgātus,** but the **lēgātī** did not hold permanent command.

4. **Dux, imperātor.** The *general* (**dux**) assumed the title **imperātor** after winning his first important victory. After defeating the Helvetians, Caesar was regularly addressed as **imperātor,** a title which corresponds to that of *commanding general* in a modern army. Any staff officer appointed by the **imperātor** to command a division of troops became temporarily **dux** of that division.

Ronald Sheridan/Ancient Art & Architecture Collection

The Praetorian Guard was a privileged, politically influential bodyguard established in 27 B.C. to attend and protect the emperor. It consisted of sixteen thousand men. The Praetorian Guard was disbanded in A.D. 312 by Constantine I.

Third-century depiction of a wounded Gaul.

C. Specialists Attached to the General Staff

    1. Fabrī. *Engineers* specially trained or detailed from the ranks to build ships, bridges, siege engines, and winter quarters. Such work was in charge of the chief of engineers **(praefectus fabrum).**

    2. Speculātōrēs. *Spies* employed singly by the general to obtain news by going within the enemy's lines, often in disguise.

    3. Explōrātōrēs. Mounted *scouts,* or *patrols,* who scoured the country for information. They usually went out in small parties.

Ancient vs. Modern Warfare

The means of waging war have changed over the last two thousand years. Caesar did not need to worry about effectively combining operations among various branches of the armed services or among other nations; in the field, he was the supreme commander. Air power today has proved devastatingly effective, not just in inflicting physical damage, but also in surveillance and in disrupting communications. Missiles, electronic technology, intelligence gathering, cryptography, and psychological warfare now play major roles in combat operations, and there are now the threats of biological and nuclear warfare. After final victory, soldiers are now expected to act as peacekeepers and help rebuild the defeated nation. Let us hope that a *Pax Americana,* so named from the ancient **Pax Romana,** will come into being and bring the blessings of peace, not just to Americans, but to all peoples of the world.

A GEOGRAPHY LESSON

LESSON OBJECTIVES
- **Read**
  Caesar *Dē Bellō Gallicō* I, 1
- **Review**
  Comparative and Superlative Adjectives and Adverbs
  Ablative of Respect

[1] *as a whole,* i.e., *Greater Gaul. All Gaul* would be **omnis Gallia.** See map of Gaul (pp. 254–255).

[2] predicate adjective: *is divided*

[3] Supply **partem.**

[4] hence modern Belgium's name

[5] *in their own language* (literally, *by*)

[6] Supply **linguā.** What language is meant?

[7] *from one another.* What literally?

[8] Caesar here limits the name *Gauls* to the natives of the central part, and this is the sense in which he usually employs the term.

[9] *Garonne, Marne, Seine*

[10] Look at the map (pp. 254–255) and see whether you can tell why Caesar uses this verb in the singular.

[11] Southern France is still known as *Provence.*

[12] conjunction

[13] Note the emphasis on **suis** and **eōrum.**

[14] ablative of separation

[15] i.e., **Germānōrum**

This Roman aqueduct supplied water to Nîmes (ancient Nemausus) from water sources 31 miles away, crossing over the Gardon River on this masonry bridge, the Pont du Gard, the tallest bridge the Romans ever built and so wide at its base that a modern six-lane highway could pass through a single span of its lowest arches. How the Romans designed and built such a sophisticated system with their almost primitive surveying and calculating instruments still amazes engineers today.

I, **1.** Gallia est omnis[1] dīvīsa[2] in partēs trēs, quārum ūnam[3] incolunt Belgae,[4] aliam Aquītānī, tertiam eī quī ipsōrum linguā[5] Celtae, nostrā[6] Gallī appellantur. Hī omnēs linguā, īnstitūtīs, lēgibus inter sē[7] differunt. Gallōs[8] ab Aquītānīs Garunna[9] flūmen, ā Belgīs Matrona[9] et Sēquana[9]
5 dīvidit.[10]

Hōrum omnium fortissimī sunt Belgae, proptereā quod ā cultū atque hūmānitāte Prōvinciae[11] longissimē absunt, minimēque saepe mercātōrēs ad eōs veniunt atque ea quae ad effēminandōs animōs pertinent important. Proximī sunt Germānīs quī trāns Rhēnum incolunt, quibuscum semper
10 bellum gerunt. Quā dē causā Helvētiī quoque reliquōs Gallōs virtūte superant, quod ferē cotīdiānīs proeliīs cum Germānīs contendunt, cum[12] aut suīs[13] fīnibus[14] eōs prohibent aut ipsī in eōrum[15] fīnibus bellum gerunt.

Wayne Rowe

Maison Carrée. Throughout the Roman provinces small temples were found in the cities. This temple is one of the best preserved examples still in existence today. It is located in Nîmes. An inscription says it was dedicated to Gaius and Lucius Caesar, who were adopted sons of Augustus.

Eōrum[16] ūna pars, quam Gallī obtinent, initium capit ā flūmine Rhodanō; continētur Garunnā flūmine, Ōceanō, fīnibus Belgārum; attingit etiam ab[17] Sēquanīs et Helvētiīs flūmen[18] Rhēnum; vergit ad septentriōnēs.[19] Belgae ab extrēmīs Galliae fīnibus oriuntur, pertinent ad īnferiōrem partem flūminis Rhēnī, spectant in septentriōnēs et orientem sōlem. Aquītānia ā Garunnā flūmine ad Pyrēnaeōs montēs et eam partem Ōceanī quae est ad[20] Hispāniam pertinet; spectat inter occāsum sōlis et septentriōnēs.

[16] Some think that lines 13–20 were not written by Caesar but added later.

15 [17] *on the side of;* literally, *from (the direction of)*

[18] accusative

[19] From the point of view of the Romans in the Province.

[20] *near* what part of the Spanish coast? See map (pp. 254–255).

20

Questions

1. Why were the Helvetians brave?
2. What were three reasons for the bravery of the Belgians?
3. Find the three divisions of Gaul on the map (pp. 254–255) and indicate their boundaries.

GRAMMAR

Review of Adjectives, Adverbs, and the Ablative of Respect

Give the positive of **fortissimus, longissimē;** the comparative of **minimē, saepe;** the superlative of **īnferior, saepe.**

Review the Ablative of Respect in Lesson VII.

Translation

1. The rest of the Gauls were surpassed by the Belgians in courage.
2. In what respects ("things") did the Gauls differ from one another?

Foreign Names

Add English endings to Latin proper nouns wherever possible, as in *Belgians, Aquitanians, Celts.* When the Latin form is kept, use the nominative case and pronounce the letters as in English but keep the Latin accent. Consult the Dictionary. Always give the modern French forms of all Latin names of rivers, mountains, and lakes in Gaul. To find them see the Dictionary.

The word for *east* is the present participle of **orior,** *rising.* The word for *north* literally means *seven plow-oxen,* from the seven stars of the constellation Great Bear, or Big Dipper.

VOCABULARY

Adjective

cotīdiānus, -a, -um *daily*   [diēs]

Adverbs

ferē *almost*
proptereā *on this account*   [propter + eā]

Conjunction

proptereā quod *because*

Review **differō, incolō, initium, mercātor, orior, saepe, sōl.**

WORD STUDY

Spanish To what extent Spanish is like Latin may be seen in the following translation of the beginning and end of the first chapter of the *Gallic War:*

La Galia entera stá dividida en tres partes, de las cuales los belgas habitan una, otra los aquitanos y la tercera los que se llaman celtas en su lengua, galos en la nuestra. Todos estos difieren entre sí en cuanto a lengua, instituciones y leyes. ... Aquitania se extiende desde el río Garona hasta los montes Pirineos y aquella parte del océano que está cerca de España; mira hacia el ocaso y hacia el septentrión.

Explain *culture, differential, effeminate, humanities, mercantile, occident, verge.*

LESSON LI

AN ENTIRE NATION EMIGRATES

LESSON OBJECTIVES
- **Read**
  Caesar *Dē Bellō Gallicō* I, 2–3
- **Review**
  Conjugation of **Fīō**
  Future Passive
  Participle with **Ad**

I, **2.** Apud Helvētiōs longē nōbilissimus fuit Orgetorīx. Is, M. Messālā M. Pīsōne cōnsulibus,[1] rēgnī cupiditāte inductus coniūrātiōnem nōbilitātis fēcit, et cīvibus persuāsit ut[2] dē fīnibus suīs cum omnibus cōpiīs exīrent.

Id[3] facilius eīs persuāsit, quod undique locī nātūrā Helvētiī continentur: ūnā[4] ex parte flūmine Rhēnō lātissimō atque altissimō, quī agrum Helvētium ā Germānīs dīvidit; alterā ex parte monte[5] Iūrā altissimō, quī est inter Sēquanōs et Helvētiōs; tertiā, lacū Lemannō et flūmine Rhodanō, quī prōvinciam nostram ab Helvētiīs dīvidit. 5

Hīs rēbus fīēbat[6] ut et minus lātē vagārentur et minus facile fīnitimīs[7] bellum īnferre possent; quā dē causā hominēs bellandī[8] cupidī magnō dolōre afficiēbantur. Prō[9] multitūdine autem hominum et prō glōriā bellī angustōs sē fīnēs habēre arbitrābantur, quī in longitūdinem mīlia passuum CCXL, in lātitūdinem CLXXX patēbant. 10

3. Hīs rēbus adductī et auctōritāte Orgetorīgis permōtī cōnstituērunt ea quae ad proficīscendum pertinērent[10] comparāre, carrōrum quam maximum 15

[1] 61 B.C.

[2] This clause is direct object of **persuāsit.**

[3] direct object of **persuāsit**

[4] The position of the adjective before the preposition emphasizes the adjective. Translate *on one side.*

[5] *mountain range*

[6] *it happened*

[7] dative with compounds

[8] gerund depending on **cupidī**

[9] *in proportion to*

[10] Translate as if indicative.

Erich Lessing/Art Resource, NY

It is said that an "army travels on its stomach." The same can be said for a whole community. The Helvetians sowed grain and then harvested it for two years before beginning their great journey.

[11] *for*

[12] A historical present, vividly describing a past action, is often followed by a secondary tense. See the Grammar Appendix, p. 501.2. For the case after **persuādeō**, see the Grammar Appendix, p. 496.6.

[13] Dumnorix, who himself led a popular faction among the Haeduans and was a rival for the **rēgnum** held by his pro-Roman brother Diviciacus.

numerum emere, frūmentum quam plūrimum serere, ut in itinere cōpia frūmentī esset, cum proximīs cīvitātibus pācem et amīcitiam cōnfirmāre. Ad eās rēs cōnficiendās biennium sibi satis esse putāvērunt; in[11] tertium annum profectiōnem lēge cōnfirmant.

20   Ad eās rēs cōnficiendās Orgetorīx dēligitur. Is sibi lēgātiōnem ad cīvitātēs suscēpit. In eō itinere persuādet[12] Casticō Sēquanō ut rēgnum in cīvitāte suā occupāret, quod pater ante habuerat; itemque Dumnorīgī Haeduō, frātrī Dīviciācī, quī[13] eō tempore prīncipātum in cīvitāte obtinēbat, ut idem cōnārētur persuādet, eīque fīliam suam in mātrimōnium
25   dat. Dīxit sē ipsum suae cīvitātis imperium obtentūrum esse.

Questions
1. Who was Orgetorix?
2. With whom did Orgetorix conspire?
3. Why did the Helvetians want to migrate?
4. How did the Helvetians prepare for migration?

GRAMMAR

Conjugation of *Fīō* and the Future Passive Participle
Review the conjugation of **fīō** in Lesson XXIV.
Review the future passive participle with **ad** in Lesson XXIII.

In Orange, France, you can still see the well-preserved Roman theater. By 121 B.C., the Romans had established Transalpine Gaul as a Roman province. Even far from home, the Romans expected to retain their important forms of entertainment, such as drama, dance, and music.

S. Fiore/SuperStock

Translation

1. An embassy was sent to other states for the purpose of encouraging their departure.

2. The Helvetians were always ready to carry on war with those who inhabited that part of Gaul.

VOCABULARY

Nouns

lātitūdō, -dinis f. *width*	**[lātus]**
lēgātiō, -ōnis f. *embassy*	**[lēx]**
nōbilitās, -tātis f. *nobility*	**[nōbilis]**
prīncipātus, -ūs m. *first place, leadership*	**[prīnceps]**
profectiō, -ōnis f. *departure*	**[proficīscor]**

Adjective

cupidus, -a, -um desirous	**[cupiō]**

Verbs

pateō, -ēre, patuī, — *stand open, extend*	(patent)
vagor, 1 *wander*	(vagrancy, vague)

Adverb

item *also*	(itemization, itemize)

Idiom: **quā dē causā.**

Review **angustus, arbitror, cōnor, dēligō, dīvidō, persuādeō, proficīscor, undique.**

WORD STUDY

Roots *Item* was once used in English as in Latin, to mean *also* in a list: "2 lbs. sugar, *item* 3 lbs. flour," etc. Then it came to be used wrongly for every article in the list, including the first. *Item* occurs fourteen times in George Washington's will.

Explain *biennial, cupidity, extravagant, itemize, latitude, patent, principate, vagabond, vagary, vagrant.*

A MYSTERIOUS DEATH AND A BONFIRE

LESSON OBJECTIVES

- **Read**
  Caesar *Dē Bellō Gallicō* I, 4–6
- **Review**
  Indicative Clauses with **Ubi** and **Postquam**
  Subjunctive Clauses with **Cum**

[1] *in accordance with*

[2] We say *in*, not *from.*

[3] participle with conditional force: *if condemned*

[4] *household* (including all his slaves)

[5] *about.* **Ad** is an adverb when used with numerals.

[6] Note the different meanings of the word here and in line 2.

[7] with **nihilō**: *nevertheless*

[8] The clause is in apposition with **id.**

[9] The name Boii is preserved in the word "Bohemia."

[10] in apposition to **Boiōs**; supply *as*

[11] *from home*

[12] descriptive relative clause; see the Grammar Appendix, p. 504.10

[13] *where*

[14] *could be drawn.* The Rhone valley for a distance of about 17 miles narrows down to a steep ravine with cliffs 1000 feet high, known as "Mill Race Gorge" (Pas de l'Écluse). One of the largest dams in Europe has been built there. The railway passes under the mountain through a tunnel over 2 miles long. Switzerland is at one end of the pass, France the other.

I, 4. Ea rēs est Helvētiīs ēnūntiāta. Mōribus[1] suīs Orgetorīgem ex[2] vinculīs causam dīcere coēgērunt. Eum damnātum[3] oportēbat ignī cremārī.

Diē cōnstitūtā Orgetorīx ad iūdicium omnem suam familiam,[4] ad[5] hominum mīlia decem, undique coēgit[6] et omnēs clientēs suōs, quōrum magnum numerum habēbat, eōdem condūxit; per eōs sē ēripuit neque causam dīxit.

Cum cīvitās ob eam rem incitāta armīs iūs suum exsequī cōnārētur, multitūdinemque hominum ex agrīs magistrātūs cōgerent, Orgetorīx mortuus est. Helvētiī suspicantur ipsum sē interfēcisse.

5. Post eius mortem nihilō minus[7] Helvētiī id quod cōnstituerant facere cōnantur, ut[8] ē fīnibus suīs exeant. Ubi iam sē ad eam rem parātōs esse arbitrātī sunt, oppida sua omnia, numerō ad duodecim, vīcōs ad quadringentōs, reliqua prīvāta aedificia incendunt. Frūmentum omne, praeter quod sēcum portātūrī erant, combūrunt, ut, reditūs spē sublātā, parātiōrēs ad omnia perīcula subeunda essent.

Persuādent Rauracīs et Tulingīs et Latobrīgīs fīnitimīs ūtī, oppidīs suīs vīcīsque combustīs, ūnā cum eīs proficīscantur. Boiōs,[9] quī trāns Rhēnum incoluerant et in agrum Nōricum trānsierant Nōreiamque oppugnābant, ad sē sociōs[10] recipiunt.

6. Erant omnīnō itinera duo quibus domō[11] exīre possent:[12] ūnum per Sēquanōs, angustum et difficile, inter montem Iūram et flūmen Rhodanum, quā[13] vix singulī carrī dūcerentur;[14] mōns autem altissimus impendēbat, ut

Imagine the difficulty in transporting food, equipment, and other basic necessities through the mountains in all kinds of weather in carts such as these.

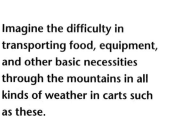

Alinari/Art Resource, NY

ROMAN MILITARY ACCOMPLISHMENTS

F. E. Adcock ends his book[1] with these words:

"The art of war under the Roman Republic was something that belonged to Rome, a plant that grew in Roman soil, something which needed for its application talent, not genius, but in its culmination it did produce a soldier greater than itself, a soldier in whom there was that fusing together of intellect and will that marks off genius from talent."

An interesting manual on the art of war, written in the fourth century A.D. by Vegetius, contains this paragraph:

Nūllā enim aliā rē vidēmus populum Rōmānum orbem subēgisse terrārum nisi armōrum exercitiō,[2] disciplīnā castrōrum, ūsūque mīlitiae. Quid enim adversus[3] Gallōrum multitūdinem paucitās Rōmāna valuisset?[4] Quid adversus Germānōrum prōcēritātem[5] brevitās potuisset audēre? Hispānōs quidem nōn tantum numerō sed et vīribus corporum nostrīs praestitisse manifēstum est; Āfrōrum dolīs atque dīvitiīs semper imparēs fuimus; Graecōrum artibus prūdentiāque nōs vincī nēmō dubitāvit. Sed adversus omnia prōfuit tīrōnem[6] sollerter[7] ēligere, cotīdiānō exercitiō rōborāre, quaecumque ēvenīre in aciē atque proeliīs possunt, omnia in campestrī meditātiōne[8] praenōscere, sevērē in dēsidēs vindicāre.[9] Scientia enim reī bellicae dīmicandī nūtrit audāciam: nēmō facere metuit quod sē bene didicisse cōnfīdit. Etenim[10] in certāmine bellōrum exercitāta paucitās ad victōriam prōmptior est, rudis et indocta multitūdō exposita semper ad caedem.

[1] *The Roman Art of War under the Republic,* Cambridge, Harvard University Press, 1940, p. 124.

[2] from **exercitium,** *training*

[3] prep. w. acc.: *against*

[4] *would have availed*

[5] *tallness*

[6] *recruit*

[7] *skillfully*

[8] *practice in the field*

[9] *to punish the idle*

[10] *for*

LESSON
OBJECTIVES
• **Read**
  Caesar *Dē Bellō*
  Gallicō I, 21–22
• **Review**
  Purpose Constructions

A SURPRISE THAT FAILED

THIS IS A GOOD STORY RIGHT HERE

Summary of Chapters 13–20. After crushing the rearguard of the Helvetians at the Saône, Caesar crosses in pursuit of the main body. The latter now send a deputation to Caesar. The parley fails, and the Helvetians resume their march. Caesar follows; his cavalry is defeated in a skirmish. Meanwhile his supplies give out because the Haeduans, his Gallic allies, fail to furnish grain any longer. Caesar complains to the Haeduan chiefs who are in his camp and is told secretly that Dumnorix, a rich and powerful noble, is responsible; that he has a Helvetian wife and therefore favors the Helvetians; furthermore, that Dumnorix alone is to blame for the recent defeat of the Roman cavalry, for he led the retreat in person. Caesar decides that Dumnorix must be punished but fears to offend his friend Diviciacus, chief magistrate of the Haeduans and brother of Dumnorix. He therefore urges Diviciacus himself to punish him. Diviciacus pleads so earnestly for his brother's life that Caesar pardons him.

[1] indirect question introduced by **quālis,** depending on **cognōscerent**

[2] *on the other side;* literally, *in going around*

[3] appositive to **eis:** *(as) guides*

[4] depends on **peritissimus.** Caesar takes special pains to state the military training and experience of Considius because the latter's later conduct is all the more unaccountable.

[5] *was considered*

[6] *top of the mountain*

[7] ablative of comparison

[8] *with his horse at full speed* (literally, *with horse let go*)

[9] The subject is Caesar.

[10] The verb would be future perfect indicative in direct statement.

I, 21. Eōdem diē ab explōrātōribus certior factus hostēs sub monte cōnsēdisse mīlia passuum ab ipsīus castrīs octō, quālis esset[1] nātūra montis et quālis in circuitū[2] ascēnsus, explōrātōrēs quī cognōscerent mīsit. Renūntiātum est ascēnsum facilem esse. Dē tertiā vigiliā T. Labiēnum

5 lēgātum cum duābus legiōnibus et eīs ducibus[3] quī iter cognōverant, summum iugum montis ascendere iubet; suum cōnsilium ostendit. Ipse dē quārtā vigiliā eōdem itinere quō hostēs ierant ad eōs contendit, equitātumque omnem ante sē mittit. P. Cōnsidius, quī reī[4] mīlitāris perītissimus habēbātur[5] et in exercitū L. Sullae et posteā in M. Crassī

10 fuerat, cum explōrātōribus praemittitur.

22. Prīmā lūce, cum summus[6] mōns ā Labiēnō tenērētur et ipse ab hostium castrīs nōn longius MD passibus[7] abesset, neque (ut posteā ex captīvīs comperit) aut ipsīus adventus aut Labiēnī cognitus esset, Cōnsidius, equō admissō,[8] ad eum accurrit. Dīcit montem quem ab

15 Labiēnō occupārī voluerit[9] ab hostibus tenērī; id sē ā Gallicīs armīs atque īnsignibus cognōvisse. Caesar suās cōpiās in proximum collem subdūcit, aciem īnstruit. Labiēnō imperāverat nē proelium committeret, nisi ipsīus cōpiae prope hostium castra vīsae essent,[10] ut undique ūnō tempore in

Differences in the culture and outlook of Roman and Gallic soldiers (as seen from the Roman point of view) seem to be etched in the facial features and posture of each man. How? In the background, there is a thatched hut dwelling. Clustered together, huts like these formed the Gallic **pagāni** (*village hamlets*).

hostēs impetus fieret. Itaque Labiēnus, monte occupātō, nostrōs exspectābat proeliōque abstinēbat. Multō[11] dēnique[12] diē per explōrātōrēs 20 Caesar cognōvit et montem ab suīs tenērī et Helvētiōs castra mōvisse et Cōnsidium timōre perterritum quod[13] nōn vīdisset prō[14] vīsō sibi renūntiāvisse. Eō diē, quō intervāllō[15] cōnsuēverat, hostēs sequitur et mīlia passuum tria ab eōrum castrīs castra pōnit.

[11] *late in the day*
[12] *finally*
[13] Supply **id** as antecedent.
[14] *as seen*
[15] For **eō intervāllō quō**. The antecedent is sometimes put in the subordinate clause.

Questions

1. What did Caesar tell Labienus to do?
2. What did Caesar tell Considius to do?
3. What was the mistake that Considius made?
4. What was Caesar's purpose in giving these orders?

GRAMMAR

Purpose Constructions

Review purpose constructions in Lessons XI, XXIII, XXVI, and XXXIX.

Translation

1. He ordered (**imperō**) them to wait until he should arrive.
2. He summoned the generals for the sake of showing his plan.
3. The Romans were accustomed to send ahead scouts who were to learn where the enemy were.

Ronald Sheridan/Ancient Art & Architecture Collection

Abstinence

▉VOCABULARY

Nouns

aciēs, aciēī f. *battle line*
equitātus, -ūs m. *cavalry* [equus]
īnsigne, -is n. *ensign, (military) decoration,* [signum]
  signal

Verbs

comperiō, -īre, -perī, -pertus *find out*

Idioms: **castra moveō, castra pōnō, prīmā lūce, rēs mīlitāris,
summus mōns.**
  Review **ascendō, cōnsīdō, cōnsuēscō, perītus.**

WORD STUDY

Derivatives From what Latin words are
the following derived: **abstineō, subdūcō?**
  Explain *abstinence, ascension,
circuitous, insignia.*

LESSON LVII

THE FIGHT IS ON

LESSON OBJECTIVES
- **Read**
  Caesar *Dē Bellō Gallicō* I, 23–25
- **Review**
  Causal Clauses with **Quod** and **Quoniam**

I, 23. Postrīdiē eius diēī,[1] quod omnīnō bīduum supererat[2] cum exercituī frūmentum mētīrī oportēret, reī frūmentāriae prōspiciendum[3] exīstimāvit. Itaque iter ab Helvētiīs āvertit ac Bibracte[4] īre contendit. Hoc oppidum Haeduōrum longē maximum nōn amplius mīlibus passuum XVIII aberat. Ea rēs per fugitīvōs L. Aemilī, decuriōnis[5] equitum Gallōrum, hostibus nūntiātur. Helvētiī, seu quod timōre perterritōs Rōmānōs discēdere ā sē exīstimārent,[6] seu quod rē frūmentāriā interclūdī posse[7] cōnfīderent, mūtātō cōnsiliō atque itinere conversō, nostrōs ab novissimō agmine īnsequī ac lacessere coepērunt.

24. Postquam id animadvertit, cōpiās suās Caesar in proximum collem subdūxit equitātumque quī sustinēret hostium impetum mīsit. Ipse interim in colle mediō[8] triplicem aciem īnstrūxit legiōnum quattuor veterānārum. In summō iugō duās legiōnēs quās in Galliā citeriōre proximē cōnscrīpserat et omnia auxilia[9] collocāvit. Impedīmenta in ūnum locum cōnferrī, et eum locum ab eīs quī in superiōre aciē cōnstiterant mūnīrī[10] iussit. Helvētiī cum omnibus suīs carrīs secūtī, impedīmenta in ūnum locum contulērunt; ipsī[11] cōnfertissimā aciē, reiectō nostrō equitātū, sub prīmam nostram aciem successērunt.

25. Caesar prīmum suum,[12] deinde omnium[13] ex cōnspectū remōvit equōs ut, aequātō omnium perīculō, spem fugae tolleret. Cohortātus suōs proelium commīsit. Mīlitēs, ē locō superiōre pīlīs missīs, facile hostēs disiēcērunt et gladiīs in eōs impetum fēcērunt. Gallīs magnō ad pugnam erat impedīmentō quod,[14] plūribus eōrum scūtīs ūnō ictū[15] pīlōrum trānsfīxīs et colligātīs,[16] neque ēvellere neque, sinistrā manū impedītā,[17] satis commodē pugnāre poterant. Itaque multī scūtum manū ēmīsērunt et nūdō[18] corpore pugnāvērunt.

Ronald Sheridan/Ancient Art & Architecture Collection

[1] *next day;* **eius diēī** *is superfluous*

[2] *from* **supersum:** *two days were left before*

[3] Supply **esse;** *impersonal: he should provide for supplies* (literally, *it should be provided for supplies*). There are constant allusions in Caesar to the problem of feeding his army. He had grain barges on the Saône, but the Helvetians had turned away from the river.

[4] *accusative*

[5] see page 263, II, A, 5.

[6] subjunctive because Caesar assigns these as the reasons of the Helvetians and not as his own

[7] Supply **Rōmānōs** as subject.

[8] *halfway up the hill*

[9] consisting of friendly Gauls and other foreign troops

[10] with a trench. The claim is made that the course of this trench has actually been discovered in excavations made in recent times.

[11] i.e., the fighting men

[12] Supply **equum** from **equōs.**

[13] i.e., all the mounted officers, not the cavalry; **omnium** modifies **equōs.**

[14] The clause introduced by **quod** is subject of **erat;** translate **quod** as *the fact that.*

[15] *volley*

(continued on next page)

Before the arrival of the Romans, the inhabitants of Gaul had their own rites and rituals. These four Celtic death masks were found at Entremont in Provence.

The Gauls overlapped their shields, and so two shields were easily pinned together by one spear. Because of the barbed ends and easily bent iron shafts of the spears, it was hard to draw them out. At first it was probably mere chance that this happened, but the Romans were quick to take advantage of the situation and thus to introduce an element of surprise.

17 i.e., by the shield, now pinned to that of another soldier

18 *unprotected* (by a shield)

Questions

1. Why did Caesar go to Bibracte?
2. How did Caesar place his troops?
3. What advantages did Caesar have?
4. What disadvantages did the Helvetians have?

GRAMMAR

Causal Clauses with *Quod* and *Quoniam*

Causal clauses introduced by **quod** (or **proptereā quod**) and **quoniam** (*since, because*) are in the indicative when they give the writer's or the speaker's reason, the subjunctive when the reason is presented as that of another person.

Amīcō grātiās ēgī quod mihi pecūniam dederat.	*I thanked my friend because he had given me money.*
Rōmānīs bellum intulit quod agrōs suōs vāstāvissent.	*He made war against the Romans because (as he alleged) they had laid waste to his lands.*

Translation

1. The enemy advanced crowded together because they did not have their baggage.
2. The Helvetians began to pursue him because (as they thought) he could be cut off.
3. Meanwhile, since Caesar had noticed this, he stationed his cavalry to check[19] them.

19 Express in three ways.

As soldiers travelled, they either lived off the land or used the grain they brought with them. This detail from Trajan's column shows soldiers reaping grain, possibly from the territory of a conquered tribe.

National Historical Museum, Bucharest/E.T. Archive, London/SuperStock

VOCABULARY

Nouns

agmen, agminis n. *line of march*   [agō]
pīlum, -ī n. *spear, javelin* (for throwing)   (pile)
rēs frūmentāria f. *grain supply*

Adjectives

cōnfertus, -a, -um *crowded together*
frūmentārius, -a, -um *of grain*   [frūmentum]
sinister, -tra, -trum *left*   (sinister, sinistral)

Verbs

aequō, 1 *make equal*   [aequus]
animadvertō, -ere, -vertī, -versus *notice*   [animus + ad + vertō]
collocō, 1 *place, station*   [locus]
cōnferō, -ferre, contulī, collātus   [ferō]
     bring together
cōnfīdō, -ere, cōnfīsus[20] *be confident*   (confidant, confidential)

Adverb

interim *meanwhile*   (interim)

Review **facile, iugum, supersum.**

WORD STUDY

Derivatives The motto of the state of Maryland is a quotation from the *Psalms:* **scuto bonae voluntatis tuae coronasti nos** *(Thou hast encircled us).* The motto of Arkansas is **regnat populus;** of Arizona, **ditat** *(enriches)* **deus.**

From what Latin words are the following derived: **bīduum, convertō?**

Explain *collation, collocation, conference, confidence, conversion, equation, prospective, sinister.*

---

[20] Semideponent, i.e., active forms in the present system, passive in the perfect system, active meanings in both.

THE HELVETIANS SURRENDER

¹ *they fought. What literally?*
² *although*
³ *i.e., in retreat*
⁴ *until late at night*
⁵ *javelins*
⁶ Like **ūtor**, **potior** is followed by the ablative.
⁷ *accusative (Greek form)*
⁸ *a command in indirect discourse*
⁹ *i.e., the ambassadors*
¹⁰ *object of* **convēnissent**

I, 26. Ita diū atque ācriter pugnātum est.¹ Diūtius cum sustinēre nostrōrum impetūs nōn possent, alterī sē in montem recēpērunt, alterī ad impedīmenta et carrōs suōs sē contulērunt. Nam hōc tōtō proeliō, cum² ab hōrā septimā ad vesperum pugnātum sit, āversum³ hostem vidēre nēmō
5 potuit. Ad multam noctem⁴ etiam ad impedīmenta pugnātum est, proptereā quod prō vāllō carrōs obiēcerant et ē locō superiōre in nostrōs venientēs tēla coniciēbant, et nōn nūllī inter carrōs trāgulās⁵ subiciēbant nostrōsque vulnerābant. Diū cum esset pugnātum, impedīmentīs⁶ castrīsque nostrī potītī sunt. Ibi Orgetorīgis fīlia atque ūnus ē fīliīs captus est. Ex eō proeliō
10 circiter hominum mīlia CXXX superfuērunt, eāque tōtā nocte iērunt. In fīnēs Lingonum diē quārtō pervēnērunt, cum et propter vulnera mīlitum et propter sepultūram occīsōrum nostrī eōs sequī nōn potuissent. Caesar ad Lingonas⁷ litterās nūntiōsque mīsit nē eōs frūmentō nēve aliā rē iuvārent.⁸ Ipse, trīduō intermissō, cum omnibus cōpiīs eōs sequī coepit.

15 **27.** Helvētiī omnium rērum inopiā adductī lēgātōs dē dēditiōne ad eum mīsērunt. Quī⁹ cum eum¹⁰ in itinere convēnissent sēque ad pedēs

This detail from a Roman sarcophagus from the first or second century A.D. shows Roman soldiers and a captured barbarian. Notice that the barbarian is wearing **bracchae** *(long pants).*

C.M. Dixon/Photo Resources

prōiēcissent flentēsque pācem petīssent,[11] eōs[12] in eō locō quō tum erant suum adventum exspectāre iussit. Eō[13] postquam Caesar pervēnit, obsidēs, arma, servōs quī ad eōs perfūgerant poposcit.

Dum ea[14] conquīruntur et cōnferuntur, nocte intermissā, circiter hominum mīlia VI eius pāgī quī Verbigenus appellātur, sīve timōre perterritī,[15] sīve spē salūtis inductī, prīmā nocte[16] ē castrīs Helvētiōrum ēgressī ad Rhēnum fīnēsque Germānōrum contendērunt.

[11] for **petivissent**

[12] i.e., the Helvetians, not the ambassadors

[13] adverb

20 [14] neuter plural, referring to **obsidēs, arma, servōs**

[15] While the grammatical subject is **milia**, the logical subject is **hominēs**, with which **perterriti** agrees.

[16] *early in the night*

Questions

1. How long did the battle last?
2. What were Caesar's peace terms?
3. Who refused to accept these terms?
4. How many Helvetians escaped to the Lingones?

GRAMMAR

Impersonal Verbs

Review impersonal verbs in Lesson XXXI.

Translation

1. They were not permitted[17] to keep their arms.
2. They fought[17] six hours before they were compelled to flee.
3. After they arrived[17] in the territory of friends, Caesar ordered them to await his arrival.

VOCABULARY

Nouns

dēditiō, -ōnis f. *surrender*	[**dō**]
trīduum, -ī n. *three days*	[**trēs + diēs**]
vāllum, -ī n. *rampart, wall*	(interval, wall)

Adjective

nōn nūllī (nōnnūllī) -ae, -a *some*	[**nūllus**]

Verbs

conquīrō, -ere, -quīsīvī, -quīsītus *seek for*	[**quaerō**]
obiciō, -ere, obiēcī, obiectus	[**iaciō**]
throw against, oppose	

[17] Use the impersonal construction.

WORD STUDY

Derivatives Some Latin American countries and cities have names ultimately derived from Latin. Ecuador is the Spanish for our word *equator;* both are derived from **aequō,** because the equator divides the earth into *equal* parts. Argentina was so named because it was mistakenly thought to contain *silver* (**argentum);** its capital, Buenos Aires, is Spanish for *good air* (Latin **bonus āēr**). Montevideo, the capital of Uruguay, has properly a longer name, ending in pure Latin, de Montevideo, **dē monte videō,** or, possibly, it stands for **monte(m) videō.** The capital of Bolivia, La Paz, takes its name from **pāx,** *peace.* Honduras is from the Spanish **hondo,** Latin **(pro)fundus,** *deep,* perhaps on account of its deep coastal waters. Costa Rica is *rich coast,* and both Spanish **costa** and English *coast,* come from Latin **costa,** *side* or *rib.* Puerto Rico is *rich port,* from **portus.** Since many of these South American countries were formed as the result of conquest by Spanish Christian **conquistadores,** we find names like Asunción for the capital of Paraguay, named after the Assumption (from **sūmō**), i.e., the taking into Heaven of the Virgin Mary. Rio de Janeiro is from Latin (through Portuguese) **rīvus Ianuārī,** *River of (Saint) January.* Salvador is from **salvātor,** the *Savior.*

THE PRICE OF PEACE

LESSON OBJECTIVES
- **Read**
  Caesar *Dē Bellō Gallicō* I, 28–29
- **Review**
  Iubeō with Infinitive
  Volitive Clauses

I, 28. Quod ubi Caesar comperit, hīs quōrum per fīnēs[1] ierant imperāvit utī eōs conquīrerent et redūcerent; eōs reductōs in hostium numerō habuit;[2] reliquōs omnēs, obsidibus, armīs, perfugīs trāditīs, in dēditiōnem accēpit.

Helvētiōs, Tulingōs, Latobrīgōs in fīnēs suōs, unde erant profectī, revertī iussit; et quod, omnibus frūgibus āmissīs, domī nihil erat quō famem sustinērent,[3] Allobrogibus imperāvit ut eīs frūmentī cōpiam facerent; ipsōs oppida vīcōsque, quōs incenderant, restituere iussit. Id eā maximē ratiōne[4] fēcit, quod nōluit eum locum unde Helvētiī discesserant vacāre, nē propter bonitātem agrōrum Germānī, quī trāns Rhēnum incolunt, ē suīs fīnibus in Helvētiōrum fīnēs trānsīrent et fīnitimī Galliae Prōvinciae Allobrogibusque essent. Boiōs,[5] quod ēgregiā virtūte erant, Haeduī in finibus suīs collocāre voluērunt; hoc Caesar concessit. Eīs illī agrōs dedērunt, eōsque posteā in parem iūris lībertātisque condiciōnem atque[6] ipsī erant recēpērunt.

29. In castrīs Helvētiōrum tabulae repertae sunt litterīs Graecīs[7] cōnfectae et ad Caesarem relātae, quibus in tabulīs nōminātim ratiō cōnfecta erat, quī numerus domō exīsset[8] eōrum quī arma ferre possent,[9] et

[1] = **per quōrum fīnēs**
[2] This is just another way of saying that he killed them or sold them into slavery as prisoners of war.
[3] *they might withstand*
[4] *for this reason;* explained by the **quod** clause
[5] emphatic; direct object of **collocāre**
[6] *as;* so regularly with words implying likeness, as **parem** here
[7] They learned the Greek alphabet through contact with the Greek colony Massilia (Marseilles) in southern Gaul.
[8] indirect question implied in the noun **ratiō** and introduced by **quī numerus**
[9] For the subjunctive see Descriptive Relative Clause in the Grammar Appendix, p. 504.10.

An artist's representation of a Gallic town at the foot of the Alps after the Roman conquest. The Roman soldiers, as well as the civilians who accompanied them, interacted with the Gauls on a regular basis as they went about their daily activities. There were even many intermarriages.

SuperStock

¹⁰ sum total
¹¹ i.e., 25 percent
¹² agrees with the predicate nominative milia

item puerī, senēs mulierēsque. Quārum omnium ratiōnum summa¹⁰ erat Helvētiōrum mīlia CCLXIII, Tulingōrum mīlia XXXVI, Latobrīgōrum XIIII, Rauracōrum XXIII, Boiōrum XXXII; ex hīs quī arma ferre possent, ad mīlia XCII.¹¹ Summa omnium fuērunt¹² ad mīlia CCCLXVIII. Eōrum quī domum rediērunt, cēnsū habitō, ut Caesar imperāverat, repertus est numerus mīlium C et X.

Questions

1. Why did Caesar want the Helvetians to restore their former homes?
2. What proportion of the Helvetians and their allies returned home?
3. What did Caesar do to the canton who tried to escape after the surrender?

GRAMMAR

Volitive Clauses and *Iubeō*

Review volitive clauses in Lesson XXII and in the Grammar Appendix, p. 503.5. Also review the command construction with **iubeō** in the Grammar Appendix, p. 503.5a.

Translation

1. Caesar persuaded the neighbors to give the Helvetians food.
2. He ordered¹³ them to throw down their arms and return¹⁴ the slaves.
3. He ordered¹³ them to return¹⁴ to their own territory and warned them not to flee.

WORD STUDY

Derivatives The original Roman "senate" consisted of **senēs**, *old men*, i.e., men over forty-five, who were considered too old to fight. A "senior" is *older*; he really ought to be addressed as "sir," for "sir" is derived from **senior**.

Explain *circumvallation, exit, famish, incense, restitution, reversion, tabulate*.

---

¹³ Express in two ways.

¹⁴ Distinguish between transitive *return* in the sense of *give back* and intransitive *return* in the sense of *go back*. Two different verbs are used in Latin.

LESSON LX

THE GERMAN THREAT

LESSON OBJECTIVES

- **Read**
Caesar *Dē Bellō Gallicō* I, 31
- **Review**
Perfect and Future Infinitives in Indirect Statement

I, 31. Concilium tōtīus Galliae indictum est. Eō conciliō dīmissō, īdem prīncipēs cīvitātum quī ante fuerant[1] ad Caesarem revertērunt petiēruntque utī sibi sēcrētō in occultō dē suā omniumque salūte cum eō agere licēret. Locūtus est prō hīs Dīviciācus Haeduus:

"Galliae tōtīus factiōnēs sunt duae; hārum alterius prīncipātum tenent Haeduī, alterius Arvernī. Hī cum dē prīncipātū inter sē multōs annōs contenderent, factum est[2] utī ab Arvernīs Sēquanīsque Germānī mercēde[3] arcesserentur. Hōrum prīmō circiter mīlia XV Rhēnum trānsiērunt; posteāquam agrōs et cultum et cōpiās[4] Gallōrum hominēs ferī ac barbarī amāre coepērunt, trāductī sunt plūrēs; nunc sunt in Galliā ad centum et XX mīlium numerum.[5] Cum hīs Haeduī eōrumque clientēs semel atque iterum[6] armīs contendērunt; magnam calamitātem pulsī accēpērunt, omnem nōbilitātem, omnem senātum, omnem equitātum āmīsērunt.[7]

"Sed peius[8] victōribus Sēquanīs quam Haeduīs victīs accidit, proptereā quod Ariovistus, rēx Germānōrum, in eōrum fīnibus cōnsēdit tertiamque partem agrī Sēquanī, quī est optimus tōtīus Galliae, occupāvit, et nunc dē

[1] i.e., with Caesar
[2] *it happened*
[3] *for pay;* cf. "mercenary" troops
[4] *wealth*
[5] The fighting between Caesar and Ariovistus took place in Alsace, which has been a fertile source for trouble between the Germans and the French, the modern inhabitants of once-Roman territory, and which has changed hands repeatedly. In 1870 it became part of Germany, in 1918 it passed to France, in 1940 it again passed into German hands, and now it is once more part of France.
[6] *again and again* (literally, *once and again*)
[7] probably greatly exaggerated
[8] *a worse thing.* Appeasement seems to have been worse than military defeat.

Photo Vatican Museums

Although this may appear to be a battle scene, it actually represents a **dēcursiō**, the military parade that took place when an emperor was deified after his death. In this case, the emperor was Antoninus Pius (A.D. **138–161**). On the relief, a troop of cavalry gallops around two groups of infantrymen, each having its own standard-bearer (both at lower left). Note the many details of military dress.

9 *when*

10 in apposition with **liberōs**

11 from **quisque**: *of all the nobles*

12 *all kinds of cruelties* (with **cruciātūsque**)

13 *prevent a larger number . . . from being brought over*, an example of the subjunctive with a verb of hindering; see the Grammar Appendix, p. 503.6

14 accusative after **trādūcō**; see the Grammar Appendix, p. 497.5

alterā parte tertiā Sēquanōs dēcēdere iubet, proptereā quod, paucīs mēnsibus ante, Harūdum mīlia hominum XXIIII ad eum vēnērunt, quibus locus parātur. Paucīs annīs omnēs Gallī ex Galliae fīnibus pellentur atque 20 omnēs Germānī Rhēnum trānsībunt; neque enim cōnferendus est Gallicus ager cum Germānōrum agrō, neque haec cōnsuētūdō vīctūs cum illā.

"Ariovistus autem, ut[9] semel Gallōrum cōpiās proeliō vīcit, superbē et crūdēliter imperat, obsidēs[10] nōbilissimī cuiusque[11] līberōs poscit, et in eōs omnia exempla[12] cruciātūsque ēdit, sī qua rēs nōn ad nūtum aut ad 25 voluntātem eius facta est. Homō est barbarus et īrācundus; nōn possumus eius imperia diūtius sustinēre. Tū vel auctōritāte tuā atque exercitūs recentī victōriā vel nōmine populī Rōmānī dēterrēre[13] potes nē maior multitūdō Germānōrum Rhēnum[14] trādūcātur, Galliamque omnem ab Ariovistī iniūriā potes dēfendere."

Questions

1. Which were the leading tribes in the Gallic factions?
2. What steps did one of them take to gain the supremacy?
3. What was the result and what did the Gauls want Caesar to do about it?

GRAMMAR

Perfect and Future Infinitives

Review the use of perfect and future infinitives in indirect statement in Lesson VI.

Translation

1. They showed that they themselves would endure tortures and slavery.
2. They said that certain tribes of Gauls had sent for the fierce Germans.
3. They stated that the king of the Germans had seized the best part of all Gaul.

This Roman arena in Arles, France, dates from the early years of colonization, about 45 B.C. It measures 446 by 351 feet and seated 21,000 people. It was restored in 1828.

Nouns

concilium, -lī n. *council*   (conciliate, conciliatory)
factiō, -ōnis f. *faction*   **[faciō]**
victor, -ōris m. *victor;* adj. *victorious*   **[vincō]**

Adjectives

ferus, -a, -um *wild*   (feral, ferocious)
occultus, -a, -um *secret*   **[colō]**
recēns, recentis (gen.) *recent*   (recent)

Verbs

arcessō, -ere, -īvī, -ītus *summon*
indīcō, -ere, indīxī, indictus *announce,*   **[dīcō]**
   proclaim

Adverb

prīmō *at first*   **[prīmus]**

Review **cōnsuētūdō, cruciātus, loquor.**

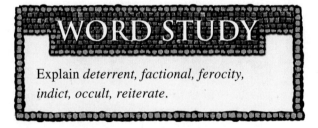

WORD STUDY

Explain *deterrent, factional, ferocity,
indict, occult, reiterate.*

Summary of Chapter 32. Caesar notices that during all the time that
Diviciacus is speaking the Sequanians remain silent. He asks the reason
and is told that the Sequanians are in such fear of the cruelty of Ariovistus
that they do not even dare complain or ask aid because they are so
completely at the mercy of the Germans, who had occupied their towns.

CAESAR PROMISES TO SUPPORT THE GAULS

LESSON OBJECTIVES
- **Read**
  Caesar *Dē Bellō Gallicō* I, 33–34
- **Review**
  Datives of Purpose and Reference

Wayne Rowe

A triumphal arch in Orange, France. Such triumphal arches were freestanding ceremonial gateways erected in honor of a military victory.

[1] Caesar, when consul the year before, had induced the Senate to recognize Ariovistus by conferring upon him the honorary title **amicus populi Rōmānī.**

[2] = ut

[3] an honorary title, like that of **amicus,** conferred upon foreign leaders for diplomatic reasons

[4] *in view of*

[5] *for the Germans,* etc. The infinitive clauses **cōnsuēscere... venire** are the subjects of **esse,** to be supplied with **periculōsum.**

I, 33. Hīs rēbus cognitīs, Caesar Gallōrum animōs verbīs cōnfirmāvit, pollicitusque est sibi eam rem cūrae futūram: magnam sē habēre spem et beneficiō[1] suō et auctōritāte adductum Ariovistum fīnem iniūriīs factūrum. Hāc ōrātiōne habitā, concilium dīmīsit. Et multae rēs eum hortābantur

5 quārē[2] sibi eam rem cōgitandam et suscipiendam putāret: in prīmīs quod Haeduōs, frātrēs[3] cōnsanguineōsque populī Rōmānī saepe ā senātū appellātōs, in servitūte vidēbat Germānōrum tenērī, eōrumque obsidēs esse apud Ariovistum ac Sēquanōs intellegēbat; quod in[4] tantō imperiō populī Rōmānī turpissimum sibi et reī pūblicae esse arbitrābātur. Paulātim autem

10 Germānōs[5] cōnsuēscere Rhēnum trānsīre et in Galliam magnam eōrum multitūdinem venīre, populō Rōmānō perīculōsum vidēbat. Hominēs ferōs ac barbarōs exīstimābat, omnī Galliā occupātā, in Prōvinciam exitūrōs esse atque inde in Italiam contentūrōs, praesertim cum Sēquanōs ā prōvinciā

nostrā Rhodanus[6] dīvideret; quibus rēbus[7] quam mātūrrimē[8] occurrendum putābat. Ipse autem Ariovistus tantam sibi arrogantiam sūmpserat ut ferendus[9] nōn vidērētur.

34. Quam ob rem placuit eī ut ad Ariovistum lēgātōs mitteret, quī ab eō postulārent utī aliquem locum medium[10] utrīusque colloquiō dīligeret: velle[11] sē dē rē pūblicā et summīs utrīusque rēbus cum eō agere. Eī lēgātiōnī Ariovistus respondit:

"Sī quid mihi ā Caesare opus esset, ego ad eum vēnissem;[12] sī quid ille mē vult,[13] illum ad mē venīre oportet. Praetereā neque sine exercitū in eās partēs Galliae venīre audeō quās Caesar tenet, neque exercitum sine magnō commeātū atque difficultāte in ūnum locum contrahere possum. Mihi autem mīrum vidētur quid in meā Galliā, quam bellō vīcī, aut Caesarī[14] aut omnīnō populō Rōmānō negōtī[15] sit."

15

6 (only) the Rhone
7 this situation; dative with **ocurrendum (esse sibi):** he ought to meet
8 irregular superlative form
9 unbearable (with **nōn**)
10 midway between them (literally, both)

20 11 (stating) that he wished (indirect statement). The verb of saying is implied in **postulārent.**
12 "If I needed anything from Caesar, I should have come to him"
13 if he wishes anything of me. **Volō** here is used with two accusatives.

25 14 dative of possession with **sit**
15 genitive of the whole after **quid**

Questions

1. Why did Caesar think he might influence Ariovistus?
2. What reasons led Caesar to promise the Gauls support?
3. What answer did Ariovistus make to Caesar's request for a conference?

GRAMMAR

Datives of Purpose and Reference

Review the datives of purpose and of reference (double dative) in Lesson XXVI.

Translation

1. He decided to choose a place for a conference.
2. "It will be my concern," he said, "to defend you."
3. He said that the Roman army would be a protection to the Gauls.

A Germanic war leader, possibly Ariovistus. This bronze head from the first century A.D. was found in Switzerland.

▉ VOCABULARY

Nouns

colloquium, -quī n. *conference*	**[loquor]**
servitūs, -tūtis f. *slavery*	**[servus]**

Adjective

turpis, -e *disgraceful*	(turpitude)

Verbs

audeō, -ēre, ausus *dare* (semideponent)	**[audāx]**
cōgitō, 1 *think, consider*	**[agō]**

Adverbs

paulātim *little by little*
praesertim *especially*

Idioms: **opus est, quam ob rem.**
Review **placeō, praetereā.**

WORD STUDY

Derivatives The original meaning of **commeātus** was *coming and going*. Its use in the sense of *supplies* shows that supply trains for the Roman army must have been on the go all the time and gives an idea of the importance attached to provisioning the soldiers.

Explain *arrogance, cogitate, colloquium, contract, dividend, servitude*.

Summary of Chapter 35. After receiving Ariovistus' insolent reply, Caesar sends an ultimatum: first, that Ariovistus is not to bring any more Germans into Gaul; second, that he must return the hostages of the Haeduans; third, that he is not to wage war upon the Haeduans and their allies. If Ariovistus will agree to these demands, there will be peace; otherwise Caesar will protect the interest of the Haeduans.

LESSON LXII

ARIOVISTUS' DEFIANT STAND

LESSON OBJECTIVES
• **Read** Caesar *Dē Bellō Gallicō* I, 36, 38, 42
• **Review** Volitive Subjunctive Subjunctive in Indirect Questions

I, **36.** Ad haec Ariovistus respondit:

"Iūs est bellī ut victōrēs victīs quem ad modum velint[1] imperent; item populus Rōmānus victīs nōn ad[2] alterius praescrīptum, sed ad[2] suum arbitrium imperāre cōnsuēvit. Sī ego populō Rōmānō nōn praescrībō quem ad modum suō iūre ūtātur, nōn oportet mē ā populō Rōmānō in meō iūre impedīrī. Haeduī mihi,[3] quoniam bellī fortūnam temptāvērunt et armīs congressī ac superātī sunt, stīpendiāriī sunt factī. Magnam Caesar iniūriam facit quī suō adventū vectīgālia[4] mihi dēteriōra facit. Haeduīs obsidēs nōn reddam, neque hīs neque eōrum sociīs iniūriā[5] bellum īnferam, sī in eō manēbunt[6] quod convēnit stīpendiumque quotannīs pendent; sī id nōn fēcerint, longē hīs frāternum[7] nōmen populī Rōmānī aberit.[8] Quod[9] mihi Caesar dēnūntiat sē Haeduōrum iniūriās nōn neglēctūrum, nēmō mēcum sine suā perniciē[10] contendit. Cum volet, congrediātur;[11] intelleget quid invictī Germānī, exercitātissimī in armīs, quī inter annōs XIIII tēctum nōn subiērunt, virtūte possint."[12]

Summary of Chapter 37. On hearing of further German outrages Caesar advances rapidly against Ariovistus.

38. Cum trīduī viam prōcessisset, nūntiātum est eī Ariovistum cum suīs omnibus cōpiīs ad occupandum Vesontiōnem,[13] quod est oppidum maximum Sēquanōrum, contendere trīduīque viam ā suīs fīnibus prōcessisse. Hūc Caesar magnīs nocturnīs diurnīsque itineribus contendit occupātōque oppidō, ibi praesidium collocat.

Summary of Chapters 39–41. Exaggerated reports about the Germans throw Caesar's army into a panic, and throughout the camp soldiers may be

[1] *as they wish* In lines 4–5 **quem ad modum** means *how* (literally, *according to what manner*).
[2] *according to*
[3] depends on **stipendiārii**
[4] *revenues*
[5] *unjustly*
[6] *if they will abide by that* (with **in eō**)
[7] adj., = **frātrum** (a sneer at the honorary title)
[8] i.e., *will be of little use to them*
[9] *as to the fact that*
[10] *destruction*
[11] *let him come on*
[12] *can (do)*
[13] masculine: *Besançon,* one of the strongest natural fortresses in France

This marble relief of Caesar from the Louvre shows the great man whose name is synonymous with Rome, complete with a laurel leaf crown.

Photo Bulloz, Louvre

seen making their wills. The officers even predict mutiny when Caesar
gives the order to advance. He restores confidence by recalling how
Marius defeated the Germans and by stating that Helvetians, whom they
35 themselves had just defeated, do not fear the Germans, for they have often
beaten them in battle. This speech has a bracing effect and his men clamor
for an immediate advance. Caesar marches against Ariovistus.

42. Cognitō Caesaris adventū, Ariovistus lēgātōs ad eum mittit: quod
anteā dē colloquiō postulāvisset, id per sē[14] fierī licēre,[15] quoniam propius
40 accessisset, sēque id sine perīculō facere posse exīstimāret. Nōn respuit
condiciōnem Caesar iamque eum ad sānitātem revertī arbitrābātur.

[14] *as far as he was concerned*

[15] indirect statement, dependent
on the idea of saying implied
in **legātos mittit**

Questions

1. How did Ariovistus defend his actions?
2. Why did he have such confidence in his Germans?
3. How did he explain his willingness to have a conference?
4. What do you think was the real reason for his changing his mind?

GRAMMAR

Volitive Subjunctive and the Subjunctive in Indirect Questions

Review the volitive subjunctive in Lesson X.
Review the subjunctive in indirect questions in Lesson XIX.

Translation

1. Let us not tempt fortune too often.
2. Let Caesar meet (in battle) with us and learn how Germans conquer.
3. The Germans did not know whether (**utrum**) to kill the prisoner or (**an**)
reserve him for (**in**) another time.

A Gallic warrior fallen in battle.
Many tribes of Gauls and
Germans wore pants to protect
themselves from the elements.

Ronald Sheridan/Ancient Art & Architecture Collection

VOCABULARY

Verbs

congredior, congredī, congressus *meet*
temptō, 1 *try, test*

[gradior]
(tempt, temptation)

Idiom: **quem ad modum.**
Review **hūc, pendō, stīpendium, ūtor.**

WORD STUDY

Derivatives Explain *congress, convention, covenant, denunciation, deteriorate, journal, journey, pernicious, prescription, sanitation.*

Reading Caesar's *Gallic Wars* sometimes gives the impression that every eligible Gallic male fought against the Romans. Men were still needed for building and agricultural occupations. This third-century bronze shows a farmer. The odd way in which he is holding his hands shows us that a wheelbarrow or plow is missing from this piece.

Ronald Sheridan/Ancient Art & Architecture Collection

Summary of Chapters 42–54. Caesar grants the request but guards against treachery. In his speech, Caesar pleads for peace but insists upon his former demands. Ariovistus is as arrogant as before and demands that Caesar withdraw from *his* Gaul before he drives him out of it. Caesar rejects appeasement and replies that he will not forsake his allies. The conference is brought to a sudden end when the German cavalry attacks Caesar's escort. Ariovistus later arrests as spies two Roman envoys whom Caesar sent in response to his request for another conference. Ariovistus then begins actual hostilities by cutting off Caesar's line of communication, but Caesar later reestablishes it by a skillful maneuver. Learning that the superstitious Germans are waiting for a full moon in order to attack, Caesar, like the keen general that he was, takes the initiative and attacks at once. The fighting on both sides is desperate. At the critical moment, Crassus sends up the reserves and the Romans win a decisive victory. Ariovistus escapes across the Rhine in a small boat. After establishing his legions in winter quarters at Vesontio, Caesar returns to Cisalpine Gaul.

Latīnum Hodiernum

"Nucēs"

In Bellō Magnō Secundō nostrōrum temporum Americānī ā Germānīs in Galliā vincēbantur. Tum dux Germānōrum Americānōs monuit ut sē dēderent. Sed dux Americānus respondisse dīcitur: "Nucēs," et Americānī fortiter pugnantēs Germānōs tandem superāvērunt. Dux īnfēlix Germānōrum neque vocābulum[16] "nucēs" comprehendit neque cūr Americānī nōn cēderent. Nunc Dux "Nux" vir īnsignis habētur. Quantum valent parvae nucēs!

[16] *word*

THE GALLIC CONQUEST AND ITS EFFECT ON THE WORLD

The immediate result of Caesar's conquest of Gaul was to free Italy for centuries from the fear of another invasion like that of the Gauls who had swept down from the north and sacked Rome in 390 B.C. "Let the Alps sink," Cicero exclaimed; "the gods raised them to shelter Italy from the barbarians; they are now no longer needed."

The Roman conquest of Gaul likewise relieved Italy from the German menace. Two German tribes, the Teutons and the Cimbri, had annihilated two Roman armies before Marius and his legions succeeded in stopping their advance in the Alpine passes. Caésar not only drove the Germans out of Gaul but bridged the Rhine and pushed the German tribes back into

Everywhere the Romans governed, they established theaters for public entertainment. From the Greeks, the Romans borrowed the dramatic styles of comedy and tragedy. Masks were used so that the audience could identify various characters at a glance. This Roman theater was constructed by Agrippa in A.D. 18 in Merida, Spain. In no province did Roman ways take firmer root outside of Italy than in Spain.

SEF/Art Resource, NY

their own forests. It was Caesar who fixed the frontier of Gaul at the Rhine. Had it not been for Caesar's conquest of Gaul, the country extending from the Rhine to the Pyrenees and from the Alps to the ocean might have become an extension of Germany, embracing the Iberian peninsula as well.

This subjugation of Gaul by the Romans gave the Greco-Italic culture time to become thoroughly rooted, not only in Gaul, but also in Spain, before the breakup of the Roman Empire. Belgium, France, Portugal, and Spain became *Latin* instead of *Teutonic*. The language, customs, and arts of Rome were gradually introduced and the "vulgar," or spoken, Latin of Gaul became early French. Thus the whole history of western Europe was profoundly affected by the Roman conquest of Gaul. We should not forget, moreover, that through the Norman-French language our own English speech became predominantly Latin, though Caesar in his two invasions of the island of Britain (England) had merely, according to Tacitus, "revealed Britain to the Romans." The distinguished historian, T. Rice Holmes, has written that the French nation is the monument of Caesar's conquest of Gaul.

QUESTIONS

1. Can you give ten modern examples of the readiness of English speakers to borrow and use words from other foreign languages, e.g., *Sayonara, Ciao, Hombre?*
2. *Legal, regal,* and *dignity* came into English one way. *Loyal, royal,* and *dainty* came into English another way. *Gendarme, entrepreneur,* and *chauffeur* came into English yet a third way. All of these words ultimately go back to Latin. Distinguish between the three routes these groups took into the English language.
3. What would have been the probable effect upon the history of Europe if the Germans had conquered Gaul?
4. Was Rome, as the possessor of a more advanced culture, justified in imposing her civilization upon the Gauls?

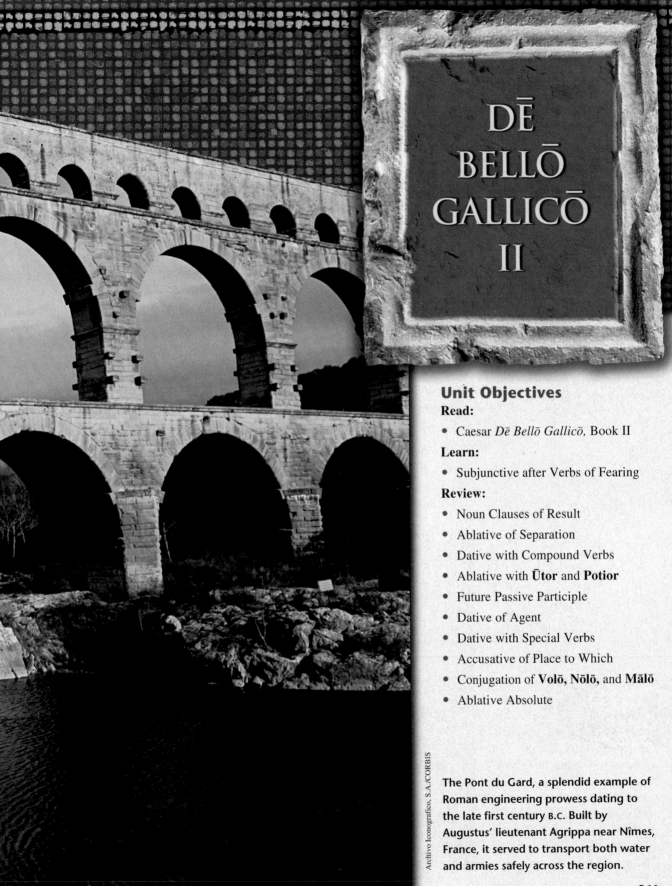

DĒ BELLŌ GALLICŌ II

Unit Objectives

Read:
- Caesar *Dē Bellō Gallicō,* Book II

Learn:
- Subjunctive after Verbs of Fearing

Review:
- Noun Clauses of Result
- Ablative of Separation
- Dative with Compound Verbs
- Ablative with **Ūtor** and **Potior**
- Future Passive Participle
- Dative of Agent
- Dative with Special Verbs
- Accusative of Place to Which
- Conjugation of **Volō, Nōlō,** and **Mālō**
- Ablative Absolute

Archivo Iconografico, S.A./CORBIS

The Pont du Gard, a splendid example of Roman engineering prowess dating to the late first century B.C. Built by Augustus' lieutenant Agrippa near Nîmes, France, it served to transport both water and armies safely across the region.

LESSON OBJECTIVES

- **Read**
  Caesar *Dē Bellō Gallicō* II, 1–3
- **Learn**
  Subjunctive after Verbs of Fearing

THE BELGIANS UNITE TO WIN INDEPENDENCE

[1] Note the tense.

[2] *were exchanging*

[3] in the narrow sense; cf. p. 266, footnote 8

[4] refers to the Belgians

[5] *as . . . so* (with **ita**)

[6] *were displeased that* ("took it hard")

[7] ablative of cause

[8] dative with **studēbant**

[9] *under our rule.* The ablative here expresses the attendant circumstances.

[10] Caesar's nephew, son of his sister Julia

II, 1. Cum esset Caesar in citeriōre Galliā, crēbrī ad eum rūmōrēs afferēbantur,[1] litterīsque item Labiēnī certior fīēbat omnēs Belgās contrā populum Rōmānum coniūrāre obsidēsque inter sē dare.[2] Coniūrandī hae erant causae: prīmum verēbantur nē, omnī pācātā Galliā,[3] ad eōs[4] exercitus noster addūcerētur; deinde ab nōn nūllīs Gallīs sollicitābantur. Multī ex hīs, ut[5] Germānōs diūtius in Galliā versārī nōluerant, ita populī Rōmānī exercitum hiemāre atque manēre in Galliā molestē ferēbant.[6] Aliī mōbilitāte[7] et levitāte animī novīs imperiīs[8] studēbant. Ab nōn nūllīs etiam sollicitābantur, quod in Galliā ā potentiōribus atque eīs quī ad condūcendōs hominēs facultātēs habēbant rēgna occupābantur, quī minus facile eam rem imperiō[9] nostrō cōnsequī poterant.

2. Hīs nūntiīs litterīsque commōtus, Caesar duās legiōnēs in citeriōre Galliā novās cōnscrīpsit et initiō aestātis Q. Pedium[10] lēgātum mīsit quī in

Hadrian's Wall in northern Britain marks the furthest reach of the Roman Empire in the North. Nearly 75 miles in length, it sealed off Scotland from settlements in Roman Britain. Though protected by forts positioned at intervals, it was eventually breached by invading northern tribes in A.D. 197, 296, and 368 and then abandoned entirely.

Ric Ergenbright/CORBIS

The spectacular Trophée des Alpes in the town of La Turbie in southeastern France commemorates an important victory won by Augustus over the Gauls of that region in 7–6 B.C. The word trophy comes from the Greek word **tropē** meaning *turning point* in battle.

ulteriōrem Galliam eās dēdūceret. Ipse, cum[11] prīmum pābulī cōpia esse inciperet, ad exercitum vēnit. Dat negōtium Senonibus reliquīsque Gallīs qui fīnitimī Belgīs erant, utī ea quae apud eōs gerantur[12] cognōscant sēque dē hīs rēbus certiōrem faciant. Hī omnēs nūntiāvērunt manūs cōgī, excercitum in ūnum locum condūcī.[13] Tum vērō exīstimāvit sē dēbēre ad eōs proficīscī. Rē frūmentāriā prōvīsā, castra movet diēbusque circiter XV ad fīnēs Belgārum pervenit.

3. Eō[14] cum dē imprōvīsō celeriusque omnium opīniōne[15] vēnisset, Rēmī[16] ad eum lēgātōs Iccium et Andecombogium, prīmōs cīvitātis, mīsērunt, quī dīcerent:

"Nōs nostraque[17] omnia in fidem atque potestātem populī Rōmānī permittimus; neque cum reliquīs Belgīs cōnsēnsimus neque contrā populum Rōmānum coniūrāvimus, parātīque sumus et obsidēs dare et imperāta facere et in oppida vōs recipere et frūmentō cēterīsque rēbus iuvāre. Reliquī omnēs Belgae in armīs sunt, Germānīque quī citrā Rhēnum incolunt sēsē cum hīs coniūnxērunt; tantusque est eōrum omnium furor ut[18] nē Suessiōnēs[19] quidem, frātrēs cōnsanguineōsque nostrōs, quī eōdem iūre et eīsdem lēgibus ūtuntur, ūnum imperium ūnumque magistrātum nōbīscum habent, coniūrātiōne prohibēre potuerīmus."

[11] with **primum:** *as soon as.* The indicative is more common in such clauses.

[12] subjunctive by attraction

[13] *was being mobilized*

[14] adverb

[15] ablative of comparison: *sooner than anyone expected;* Caesar's usual speed

[16] Reims, standing on the site of their capital, preserves their name.

[17] *our possessions*

[18] introduces **potuerimus** (result)

[19] accusative; emphatic position between **nē... quidem.** Their name survives in Soissons.

Questions

1. Why did the Belgians plan to revolt against the Romans?

2. What steps did Caesar take when he heard of the Belgian plan?

3. What light does the map (pp. 254–255) throw on the reason for the declaration of loyalty of the Rēmī?

GRAMMAR

Subjunctive after Verbs of Fearing

> Verēbantur nē ad eōs
> exercitus noster
> addūcerētur.

*They feared that our army would be
led against them.*

> Verēmur ut veniat.

We fear that he will not come.

After verbs meaning *fear* (**timeō, vereor,** etc.), the conjunction **nē**
introducing a clause in the subjunctive is to be translated as *that,* and **ut** as
that not.

Translation

1. Do you fear that the Remi will not help you with grain?

2. Caesar feared that all Gaul would conspire against the Romans.

3. The Gauls feared that the Roman army would spend the winter in Gaul.

VOCABULARY

Nouns

facultās, -tātis f. *faculty;* pl. *means*   **[facilis]**

fidēs, -eī f. *trust, protection*   (fidelity, confide)

rūmor, -ōris m. *rumor*

Verbs

dēdūcō, -ere, dēdūxī, dēductus *lead*   **[dūcō]**

pācō, 1 *pacify*   **[pāx]**

sollicitō, 1 *stir up*   (solicit, solicitous)

versō, 1 *turn over;* passive, *live*   **[vertō]**

Adverb

prīmum *first*   **[prīmus]**

Review **coniūrō, cōnsentiō, crēber.**

WORD STUDY

Derivatives In Portuguese the first sentence in the first paragraph on page 312 reads:

> Como César estivesse na Galia citerior, freqüentes boatos eram levados para êle e igualmente era certificado por uma carta de Labieno que todos os Belgas conspiravam contra o povo romano e davam entre si reféns.

From what Latin words are the following derived: **cōnsanguineus, imperātum, imprōvīsus, partim?**

Explain *bona fide, infuriate, mobility, versatile.*

CAESAR GETS THE FACTS ABOUT THE BELGIANS

II, **4**. Cum ab hīs quaereret quae cīvitātēs quantaeque in armīs essent et quid in bellō possent, sīc reperiēbat:

"Plērīque Belgae sunt ortī ā Germānīs Rhēnumque ōlim trāductī propter locī fertilitātem ibi cōnsēdērunt Gallōsque quī ea loca incolēbant
5 expulērunt; sōlīque sunt quī patrum nostrōrum memoriā, omnī Galliā vexātā, Teutonōs Cimbrōsque intrā suōs fīnēs ingredī[1] prohibuerint; quā ex rē fit utī eārum rērum memoriā[2] magnam sibi auctōritātem in rē mīlitārī sūmant."

"Plūrimum inter eōs Bellovacī[3] et virtūte et auctōritāte et hominum
10 numerō valent; hī possunt cōnficere armāta mīlia centum; pollicitī sunt ex eō numerō mīlia LX tōtīusque bellī imperium sibi postulant. Suessiōnēs nostrī sunt fīnitimī; fīnēs lātissimōs fertilissimōsque agrōs habent. Apud eōs fuit rēx nostrā etiam memoriā Dīviciācus,[4] tōtīus Galliae potentissimus, quī cum[5] magnae partis hārum regiōnum, tum etiam
15 Britanniae imperium obtinuit. Nunc est rēx Galba; ad hunc propter iūstitiam prūdentiamque summa tōtīus bellī omnium voluntāte dēfertur. Oppida habent numerō XII, pollicentur mīlia armāta L; totidem Nerviī, quī maximē ferī inter ipsōs habentur longissimēque[6] absunt; XV mīlia Atrebātēs,[7] Ambiānī[8] X mīlia, Morinī XXV mīlia, Menapiī VIIII mīlia,
20 Caletī X mīlia, Veliocassēs et Viromanduī totidem, Atuatucī XVIIII mīlia; Condrūsōs, Eburōnēs, Caerōsōs, Paemānōs, quī ūnō nōmine Germānī appellantur, arbitrāmur ad XL mīlia posse cōnficere."

Questions

1. Where was the original home of the Belgians?

2. Which Belgian tribe was the strongest; which was the nearest to Remi; which was the most remote?

---

[1] object of **prohibuerint**: *keep the Teutons from entering*

[2] ablative of cause

[3] The city of Beauvais preserves the name.

[4] not the Haeduan mentioned in Book I and again in the next chapter

[5] with **tum**: *not only . . . but also*

[6] Farthest from where?

[7] They have given their name to the city of Arras.

[8] hence the name of the city of Amiens

Réunion des Musées Nationaux/Art Resource, NY

The Praetorians served in the Republic as bodyguards to protect Rome's generals while on military campaign. Augustus, the first Roman emperor, had them stationed in Rome itself, simultaneously serving to watch over his person and the peace. However, with each succeeding emperor, the Praetorians exercised greater and more dangerous influence, in effect choosing the emperor and making him subject to their will and needs.

VOCABULARY

Adjectives

plērīque, plēraeque, plēraque *most*
potēns, (gen.), **potentis** *powerful*   [possum]
totidem (indeclinable) *the same number*   [tot + īdem]

Review **dēferō, intrā, postulō, propter, reperiō.**

WORD STUDY

Spanish Translate these Spanish sentences.

En la memoria de nuestros padres sólo los belgas han prohibido a los alemanes entrar en su tierra.

Era el rey más poderoso de toda la Galia.

LESSON OBJECTIVES
- **Read**
  Caesar *Dē Bellō Gallicō* II, 5–6
- **Review**
  Noun Clauses of Result

CAESAR CROSSES THE AISNE RIVER

II, 5. Caesar Rēmōs cohortātus līberāliterque ōrātiōne prōsecūtus, omnem senātum ad sē addūcī iussit. Quae omnia ab hīs dīligenter ad diem[1] facta sunt. Ipse Dīviciācum Haeduum magnopere cohortātus docet necesse esse manūs hostium distinērī, nē cum tantā multitūdine ūnō tempore
5 cōnflīgendum sit.[2] Id fierī posse, sī suās cōpiās Haeduī in fīnēs Bellovacōrum intrōdūxerint[3] et eōrum agrōs populārī coeperint. Hīs rēbus mandātīs, eum ā sē dīmittit.

Postquam omnēs Belgārum cōpiās in ūnum locum coāctās ad sē venīre neque iam longē abesse ab eīs quōs mīserat explōrātōribus et ab Rēmīs
10 cognōvit, flūmen Axonam,[4] quod est in extrēmīs Rēmōrum fīnibus, exercitum trādūcere mātūrāvit atque ibi castra posuit. Quae rēs[5] et latus[6] ūnum castrōrum rīpīs flūminis mūniēbat et post eum quae erant[7] tūta ab hostibus reddēbat et commeātūs[8] ab Rēmīs reliquīsque cīvitātibus ut sine perīculō ad eum portārī possent efficiēbat. In eō flūmine pōns erat. Ibi
15 praesidium pōnit et in alterā parte flūminis Q. Titūrium Sabīnum lēgātum cum sex cohortibus relinquit; castra in altitūdinem pedum XII vāllō fossāque XVIII pedum mūnīrī iubet.

[1] *on time.* What literally?

[2] impersonal: *so that the Romans would not have to fight.* Caesar's strategy here, of taking his enemies one at a time, is the same as that attempted by the Germans at the beginning of both World Wars (1914, 1939).

[3] *if the Haeduans should lead,* etc. The perfect subjunctive here represents the future perfect indicative of the direct statement.

[4] now the Aisne. By crossing the river he gained a bridgehead. There was another famous battle of the Aisne in 1914 during World War I. The word is governed by the prefix **trā-** in **trādūcere,** whose direct object is **exercitum.**

[5] *this maneuver*

[6] direct object. The preceding **et** means *both.*

[7] for **ea quae post eum erant:** *the rear*

[8] This and the following words belong to the **ut** clause, which depends on **efficiēbat.**

This fifteenth-century manuscript illustration purporting to show Caesar's landing on Britain would actually seem to show, albeit indistinctly, a naval battle in progress. Can you tell how, in specific terms, the battle is being waged? For part of the answer, read Lesson LXXVI, lines 11–18 on page 356.

Bridgeman-Giraudon/Art Resource, NY

6. Ab hīs castrīs oppidum Rēmōrum nōmine Bibrax[9] aberat mīlia passuum VIII. Id ex itinere[10] magnō impetū Belgae oppugnāre coepērunt. Aegrē eō diē sustentum est.[11] Gallōrum eadem atque[12] Belgārum oppugnātiō est haec: ubi, circumiectā multitūdine hominum, undique in mūrum lapidēs iacī coeptī[13] sunt mūrusque dēfēnsōribus nūdātus est, testūdine[14] factā, propius succēdunt mūrumque subruunt. Quod tum facile fīēbat. Nam cum tanta multitūdō lapidēs ac tēla conicerent,[15] in mūrō cōnsistendī potestās erat nūllī.[16] Cum fīnem oppugnandī nox fēcisset, Iccius Rēmus nūntium[17] ad eum mittit: nisi subsidium sibi submittātur, sēsē diūtius sustinēre nōn posse.

20

9 *Bī´brax,* now supposed to be Bievre

10 *on the march,* i.e., without stopping to make the usual preparations for a siege

11 Use the personal construction in translating.

12 *as*

13 used only in the perfect system

25

14 Locking the shields together to form a **testūdō** (see p. 347) is somewhat like circling the wagons for defense in a Wild West movie.

15 singular subject is plural in thought and so here uses a verb in the plural

16 used instead of the dative of **nēmō**

17 *message (stating that)*

Questions

1. How did the Belgians attack Bibrax?
2. Where did Caesar station Sabinus?
3. What did Caesar ask the Haeduans to do?
4. On what side of the Aisne did Caesar take his position?

GRAMMAR

Review of Noun Clauses of Result

Review noun clauses of result in Lesson XXII and the Grammar Appendix, p. 504.9.

Translation

1. Caesar will cause the supplies to be brought without delay.
2. By his speed he achieved (the result) that the Belgians could not capture the town.
3. It happened that Caesar's camp was (only) a few miles away from the town of the Remi.

WORD STUDY

Derivatives Distinguish **lātus** (adj.), **lātus** (participle of **ferō**), **latus** (noun).

From what Latin words are the following derived: **dēfēnsor, distineō, oppugnātiō?**

Explain *denudation, intramural, introduction, lapidary, lateral.*

Summary of Chapter 7. Caesar sends help to Bibrax, causing the Belgians to abandon the siege and to proceed towards the Roman army.

LESSON OBJECTIVES

- **Read**
  Caesar *Dē Bellō Gallicō* II, 8–9
- **Review**
  Ablative of Separation

FEELING OUT THE ENEMY

[1] ablative absolute with **idōneō**, or ablative of place

[2] depends on **fossam**

[3] See photo p. 347.

[4] with **circumvenīre**

[5] with **suōs**, i.e., Caesar's soldiers

[6] dative of purpose

II, 8. Caesar prīmō et propter multitūdinem hostium et propter magnam opīniōnem virtūtis proeliō abstinēre statuit. Cotīdiē tamen equestribus proeliīs quid hostis virtūte posset et quid nostrī audērent experiēbātur. Ubi nostrōs nōn esse īnferiōrēs intellēxit, locō[1] prō castrīs
5 ad aciem īnstruendam nātūrā idōneō, ab utrōque latere eius collis in quō castra erant trānsversam fossam dūxit circiter passuum[2] CCCC et ad extrēmās fossās castella cōnstituit ibique tormenta[3] collocāvit. Hoc fēcit nē, cum aciem īnstrūxisset, hostēs ab lateribus[4] pugnantēs[5] suōs circumvenīre possent. Hōc factō, duābus legiōnibus quās proximē
10 cōnscrīpserat in castrīs relīctīs, ut, sī opus esset, subsidiō[6] dūcī possent, reliquās VI legiōnēs prō castrīs in aciē cōnstituit. Hostēs item suās cōpiās ex castrīs ēductās īnstrūxerant.

In the Rhone river valley **(Rhodanus flūmen)**, territory of the friendly **Allobrogēs**, Caesar established a base camp to prevent a mass exodus of **Helvētiī** out of modern-day Switzerland into the Roman province beyond the Alps **(Gallia Ulterior)** in 58 B.C. Cf. Unit V, Lessons LI–LIII (pp. 269–278) and the map on page 277.

Paul Almasy/CORBIS

9. Palūs erat nōn magna inter nostrum atque hostium exercitum. Hanc sī[7] nostrī trānsīrent hostēs exspectābant; nostrī autem, sī ab illīs initium trānseundī fieret,[8] ut[9] impedītōs aggrederentur parātī in armīs erant. Interim proeliō equestrī inter duās aciēs contendēbātur.[10] Ubi neutrī trānseundī initium faciunt, secundiōre[11] equitum proeliō nostrīs, Caesar suōs in castra redūxit. Hostēs prōtinus ex eō locō ad flūmen Axonam contendērunt, quod esse post nostra castra dēmōnstrātum est. Ibi, vadīs repertīs, partem cōpiārum suārum trādūcere cōnātī sunt, ut,[12] sī possent, castellum cui praeerat Q. Titūrius lēgātus expugnārent pontemque rescinderent; sī minus potuissent,[13] agrōs Rēmōrum vāstārent, quī magnō nōbīs ūsuī ad bellum gerendum erant, commeātūque nostrōs prohibērent.

[7] *(to see) whether;* subjunctive in an indirect question

[8] *should be made;* subjunctive by attraction

[9] a purpose clause, depending on **parātī erant**

[10] impersonal

[11] *the cavalry battle being rather favorable to our men*

[12] introduces **expugnārent, rescinderent, vāstārent,** and **prohibērent**

[13] *if not;* represents a future perfect, while **possent** represents a future

Questions

1. Was Caesar's failure to attack at once a sign of fear or prudence? Defend your answer.
2. How did the Belgians plan to defeat Caesar?
3. How did Caesar take precautions to prevent being surrounded?

GRAMMAR

Review of the Ablative of Separation

Review the ablative of separation in Lesson XXXVII and the Grammar Appendix, p. 498.1.

Translation

1. At first Caesar wanted to refrain from battle.
2. Caesar saw that it was necessary to keep the enemy from the river.
3. He sent the hostages away from the camp on account of the danger.

VOCABULARY

Adjectives

equester, -tris, -tre *(of) cavalry* [equus]
īnferior, -ius *lower, inferior,* superl. **īnfimus,**
  and **īmus** *lowest*

Verbs

adeō, adīre, adiī, aditūrus *go to, approach* [eō]
experior, experīrī, expertus *try* (experiential, expert)

Adverbs

paulisper *for a little while* [paulō]
prōtinus *immediately*

Idioms: **ex itinere, novissimum agmen.**
Review **collis, cotīdiē, idōneus, moror, palūs, praesum, ūsus.**

WORD STUDY

Derivatives As the firing power of Roman artillery (see
pp. 347–351) was furnished by twisted ropes, the general term for
artillery was **tormenta** (from **torqueō,** *twist*); cf. English *torment,
torture.*

Secundus is from **sequor,** for what *follows* is "second." A wind
is called **secundus** because a *following* wind is a *favorable* one.
So too a battle may be **secundum.** We speak of "seconding," i.e.,
favoring, a motion. See also p. 175.

Explain *experience, experiment, rescind.*

LESSON LXVII

THE BELGIANS WITHDRAW

LESSON OBJECTIVES
- **Read**
  Caesar *Dē Bellō Gallicō* II, 10–11
- **Review**
  Dative with Compound Verbs

II, 10. Caesar, certior factus ab Titūriō, omnem equitātum et levis armātūrae[1] Numidās, funditōrēs sagittāriōsque pontem trādūcit atque ad eōs contendit. Ācriter in eō locō pugnātum est. Hostēs impedītōs nostrī in flūmine aggressī magnum eōrum numerum occīdērunt. Hostēs ubi et dē expugnandō oppidō et dē flūmine trānseundō spem sē fefellisse[2] intellēxērunt, et nostrōs in locum inīquiōrem nōn prōgredī pugnandī causā vīdērunt, atque ipsōs[3] rēs frūmentāria dēficere coepit, concilium convocāvērunt. Cōnstituērunt optimum esse domum suam quemque[4] revertī ut potius in suīs quam in aliēnīs fīnibus dēcertārent et domesticīs cōpiīs reī frūmentāriae ūterentur. Ad eam sententiam cum reliquīs causīs haec quoque ratiō[5] eōs dēdūxit, quod Dīviciācum atque Haeduōs fīnibus Bellovacōrum appropinquāre cognōverant. Hīs[6] persuādērī ut diūtius morārentur neque[7] suīs auxilium ferrent nōn poterat.

10

[1] genitive describing **Numidās**; see the Grammar Appendix, p. 495.2
[2] *that their hope had failed them*
[3] direct object, referring to the enemy
[4] *(for) each man to return (to) his own home*
[5] explained by the **quod** clause
[6] *the latter could not be persuaded;* see the Grammar Appendix, p. 495.6
[7] *and not*

Araldo de Luca/CORBIS

Column of Marcus Aurelius, emperor from 161–180 A.D., shows his successful campaigns against the Germans and Sarmatians—people living in present-day Ukraine and Russia. Standing 100 Roman feet tall, its spiral narrative relief displayed scenes of valor to onlookers in the many buildings that surrounded it.

11. Eā rē cōnstitūtā, secundā vigiliā magnō cum tumultū castrīs ēgressī,
nūllō certō ōrdine[8] neque imperiō, cum sibi quisque prīmum itineris
locum peteret et domum pervenīre properāret, fēcērunt[9] ut similis fugae
profectiō vidērētur. Hāc rē statim Caesar per speculātōrēs cognitā, īnsidiās
veritus, quod quā dē causā discēderent nōndum perspexerat, exercitum
equitātumque castrīs continuit. Prīmā lūce cōnfirmātā rē ab explōrātōribus,
omnem equitātum quī novissimum agmen morārētur praemīsit eīque
Q. Pedium et L. Cottam lēgātōs praefēcit; T. Labiēnum lēgātum cum
legiōnibus tribus subsequī iussit. Hī novissimōs adortī et multa mīlia
passuum prōsecūtī, magnam multitūdinem eōrum fugientium concīdērunt.
Ita sine ūllō perīculō tantam eōrum multitūdinem nostrī interfēcērunt
quantum fuit diēī spatium;[10] sub occāsum sōlis sequī dēstitērunt sēque in
castra, ut erat imperātum, recēpērunt.

8 ablative absolute: *there being*, etc. (line 15)
9 *they made their departure seem*, etc.
10 *as the length of the day allowed*

Questions

1. How did Caesar defeat the plan of the Belgians?
2. What did the Belgians decide to do then? Why?
3. How did Caesar at first interpret the action of the Belgians?

▦ GRAMMAR

Review of the Dative with Compound Verbs

Review the dative with compound verbs in Lesson XXVII and the Grammar
Appendix, p. 496.7.

Translation

1. Cotta was in command of part of the cavalry.
2. Whom did Caesar put in charge of the other part?

▦ VOCABULARY

Noun

tumultus, -ūs m. *uproar*   (tumult, tumultuary)

Verbs

adorior, adorīrī, adortus *rise up to, attack*   **[orior]**
dēcertō, 1 *fight (it out)*
perspiciō, -ere, -spexī, -spectus *see clearly*
subsequor, subsequī, subsecūtus *follow (closely)*   **[sequor]**

Adverb

audācter *boldly*   **[audāx]**

Review **appropinquō, inīquus, īnsidiae.**

WORD STUDY

Derivatives **Adorior** comes from **orior,** *rise up to* with hostile intention, i.e., *attack;* cf. **aggredior** (lit., *step up to*) and its English derivative *aggression.*

From what Latin words are the following derived: **armātūra, concīdo, domesticus, sagittārius?**

Explain *insidious, perspicacity, subsequent, tumultuous.*

THE SUESSIONES AND THE BELLOVACI SURRENDER

LESSON OBJECTIVE
- **Read**
Caesar *Dē Bellō Gallicō* II, 12–13

II, 12. Postrīdiē eius diēī Caesar, priusquam sē hostēs ex terrōre ac fugā reciperent,[1] in fīnēs Suessiōnum, quī proximī Rēmīs erant, exercitum dūxit et, magnō itinere cōnfectō, ad oppidum Noviodūnum[2] contendit. Id ex itinere oppugnāre cōnātus, quod vacuum ab[3] dēfēnsōribus esse audiēbat,
5 propter lātitūdinem fossae mūrīque altitūdinem, paucīs[4] dēfendentibus, expugnāre nōn potuit. Castrīs mūnītīs, vīneās agere quaeque[5] ad oppugnandum ūsuī erant comparāre coepit. Interim omnis ex fugā Suessiōnum multitūdō in oppidum proximā nocte convēnit. Celeriter vīneīs ad oppidum āctīs, aggere iactō turribusque cōnstitūtīs, magnitūdine[6]
10 operum, quae neque vīderant ante Gallī neque audierant,[7] et celeritāte Rōmānōrum permōtī, lēgātōs ad Caesarem dē dēditiōne mittunt et, petentibus Rēmīs ut cōnservārentur, impetrant.

13. Caesar, obsidibus[8] acceptīs prīmīs cīvitātis atque ipsīus Galbae rēgis duōbus fīliīs, armīsque omnibus ex oppidō trāditīs, in dēditiōnem
15 Suessiōnēs accēpit exercitumque in Bellovacōs dūcit. Quī cum sē suaque omnia in oppidum Brātuspantium contulissent, atque ab eō oppidō Caesar

[1] *before the enemy should recover;* see the Grammar Appendix, p. 505.12

[2] now called Soissons, after the Suessiones. It played an important part in World War I (1914–18).

[3] *from.* The phrase depends on **vacuum.**

[4] ablative absolute: *although only,* etc.

[5] i.e., **et quae**

[6] with **permōtī**

[7] contracted form

[8] in apposition with **primis** and **filiis**

A Roman battle sarcophagus of roughly the same date as the Column of Marcus Aurelius (p. 323). Scholars identify the deceased as a prominent general who fought against the Moesians and Pannonians (modern Slovenia, Croatia, and Serbia). At the center he is the victorious commander, larger than life; at the side he stands ready to say a final good-bye to his wife and his life as a soldier.

Scala/Art Resource, NY

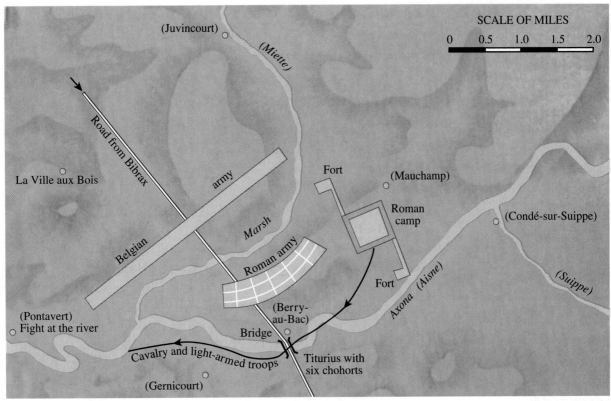

The battle of the Aisne

Mapping Specialists, Ltd.

cum exercitū circiter mīlia passuum V abesset, omnēs maiōrēs nātū[9] ex oppidō ēgressī, manūs ad Caesarem tendere et vōce significāre[10] coepērunt sēsē in eius fidem ac potestātem venīre neque contrā populum Rōmānum armīs contendere. Item, cum ad oppidum accessisset castraque ibi pōneret, 20 puerī mulierēsque ex mūrō passīs[11] manibus suō mōre[12] pācem ab Rōmānīs petīvērunt.

[9] with **maiōrēs**: *older men;* literally, *older in birth;* see the Grammar Appendix, p. 500.16

[10] While they could not speak Latin, they could nevertheless make themselves understood by signs and cries.

[11] *extended*

[12] ablative expressing accordance

Questions

1. Trace Caesar's course on the map above.
2. What led the Suessiones to surrender?
3. Who of the Bellovaci asked for peace first?

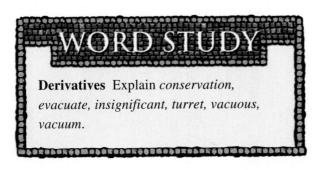

WORD STUDY

Derivatives Explain *conservation, evacuate, insignificant, turret, vacuous, vacuum.*

A PLEA FOR MERCY

II, 14. Prō hīs Dīviciācus facit verba:

"Bellovacī omnī tempore in fidē atque amīcitiā cīvitātis Haeduae fuērunt; impulsī ab suīs prīncipibus, quī dīcēbant Haeduōs ā tē in servitūtem redāctōs omnēs indignitātēs contumēliāsque perferre, et ab
5 Haeduīs dēfēcērunt et populō Rōmānō bellum intulērunt. Quī[1] eius cōnsilī prīncipēs fuerant, quod intellegēbant quantam calamitātem cīvitātī intulissent, in Britanniam profūgērunt. Petunt nōn sōlum Bellovacī, sed etiam prō eīs Haeduī, ut tuā[2] clēmentiā in eōs[3] ūtāris. Quod[4] sī fēceris, Haeduōrum auctōritātem apud omnēs Belgās amplificābis, quōrum auxiliīs
10 atque opibus, sī qua bella incidērunt, sustinēre[5] cōnsuērunt."[6]

15. Caesar, honōris Dīviciācī atque Haeduōrum causā, sēsē eōs in fidem receptūrum et cōnservātūrum dīxit et, quod erat cīvitās magnā inter Belgās auctōritāte atque hominum multitūdine praestābat, DC obsidēs poposcit. Hīs trāditīs omnibusque armīs ex oppidō collātīs, ab eō locō in fīnēs
15 Ambiānōrum pervēnit, quī sē suaque omnia sine morā dēdidērunt. Eōrum fīnēs Nerviī attingēbant; quōrum dē nātūrā mōribusque Caesar cum quaereret, sīc reperiēbat:

[1] for **ei qui**
[2] Note the emphatic position before the noun: *your (well-known)*.
[3] *toward them*
[4] object of **fēceris**
[5] used without object: *hold out*
[6] contracted form

Stonehenge, England. Built in stages between 3100 and 1100 B.C., its function and meaning remain largely a mystery. The alignment of its stones with the sunrise on the longest day of the year suggest a marking of the seasons for agriculture. Its stones, as great as thirty feet long and fifty tons in weight, testify to the engineering prowess of the area inhabitants thousands of years before the first Roman set foot on the island.

Roger Ressmeyer/CORBIS

Nūllus est aditus ad eōs mercātōribus. Nihil patiuntur vīnī reliquārumque rērum ad lūxuriam pertinentium īnferrī, quod hīs rēbus relanguēscere animōs virtūtemque remittī exīstimant. Sunt hominēs ferī 20 magnaeque virtūtis; accūsant reliquōs Belgās, quī[7] sē populō Rōmānō dēdiderint patriamque[8] virtūtem prōiēcerint. Cōnfirmant sē neque lēgātōs missūrōs neque ūllam condiciōnem pācis acceptūrōs.

[7] *because they*
[8] adjective

Questions

1. What did Caesar find out about the Nervii?
2. Who was to blame for the revolt of the Bellovaci?
3. What other tribe surrendered besides the Bellovaci?
4. Why did Diviciacus use the phrase **tuā clēmentiā** (line 8) and why did Caesar quote it?

GRAMMAR

Review of Ablative with *Ūtor* and *Potior*

Review the ablative with **ūtor** and **potior** in the Grammar Appendix, p. 499.10.

Translation

1. Their friends begged that Caesar use mercy.
2. He used towers in order to get possession of the enemy's town.
3. Upon being urged by their leaders, he permitted them to enjoy their liberty and resources.

VOCABULARY

Nouns

aditus, -ūs m. *approach, access*   [adeō]
contumēlia, -ae f. *insult*   (contumely, contumelious)

Verbs

dēdō, dēdere, dēdidī, dēditus *surrender*   [dō]
perferō, -ferre, -tulī, -lātus *endure*   [ferō]

Review **causā, ops, poscō, prōiciō, sīc.**

Summary of Chapters 16–19. Caesar learns that the Nervii and their allies have taken a position on the south side of the Sabis (Sambre) River. Deserting Gauls tell the Nervii that the Roman legions are widely separated on the march by baggage trains and that the first could easily be attacked and defeated before the others come up. But when Caesar comes closer to the enemy, he places his baggage in the rear. Six legions begin building a camp on a hill sloping down to the river, just opposite a wooded hill where the Nervii are encamped. When the latter see the baggage, supposing that only one legion has arrived, they attack the Roman camp. Then begins the most exciting of Caesar's battles in Gaul.

ROMAN SKILL AND EXPERIENCE

LESSON OBJECTIVES
- **Read**
  Caesar *Dē Bellō Gallicō* II, 20–21
- **Review**
  Future Passive Participle
  Dative of Agent

II, **20.** Caesarī omnia ūnō tempore erant agenda: vēxillum[1] prōpōnendum (quod erat īnsigne[2] cum ad arma concurrī[3] oportēret); ab opere revocandī mīlitēs; quī paulō longius aggeris[4] petendī causā prōcesserant arcessendī; aciēs īnstruenda; mīlitēs cohortandī; signum[5] tubā dandum. Quārum rērum magnam partem temporis brevitās et impetus 5 hostium impediēbat.

His difficultātibus duae rēs erant subsidiō, scientia atque ūsus mīlitum, quod superiōribus proeliīs exercitātī quid[6] fierī oportēret ipsī sibi praescrībere poterant; et quod[7] ab opere singulīsque legiōnibus singulōs lēgātōs Caesar discēdere nisi[8] mūnītīs castrīs vetuerat. Hī propter propinquitātem et celeritātem hostium nihil[9] iam Caesaris imperium exspectābant sed per sē quae vidēbantur[10] administrābant.

21. Caesar, necessāriīs rēbus imperātīs, ad cohortandōs mīlitēs dēcucurrit et forte ad legiōnem decimam[11] dēvēnit. Mīlitēs nōn longiōre[12] ōrātiōne cohortātus est quam utī suae prīstinae virtūtis memoriam 15 retinērent neu perturbārentur animō hostiumque impetum fortiter sustinērent. Quod nōn longius hostēs aberant quam quō[13] tēlum adigī

[1] *banner,* a red flag displayed at the general's tent before a battle. Compare the modern practice of "running up the colors."
[2] noun
[3] impersonal
[4] *material for the rampart*
[5] to fall in line
[6] The clause depends on **praescrībere.**
[7] *the fact that;* the second line of **duae rēs**
[8] with **mūnītīs** (ablative absolute): *unless the camp was fortified*
[9] = **nōn iam,** but stronger: *not (a moment) longer*
[10] *seemed best*
[11] *Caesar's favorite*
[12] *in a speech not longer than (this),* i.e., *that they,* etc.
[13] *(the distance) to which*

Roman aqueduct in Segovia, Spain. This amazingly well-preserved structure testifies to the lasting influence the Romans had in Spain, a Roman province from A.D. 133 onwards.

Vanni Archive/CORBIS

posset,[14] proelī committendī signum dedit. Atque in alteram partem item cohortandī causā profectus, pugnantibus[15] occurrit. Temporis tanta fuit
20 exiguitās hostiumque tam parātus ad dīmicandum animus ut nōn modo ad īnsignia[16] accommodanda sed etiam ad galeās induendās[17] scūtīsque[18] tegimenta dētrahenda tempus dēfuerit.[19] Quam[20] quisque ab opere in partem cāsū dēvēnit, quaeque[21] prīma signa cōnspexit, ad haec cōnstitit, nē in quaerendīs suīs pugnandī tempus dīmitteret.

Questions

1. What order did Caesar give first?

2. How was the battle line eventually formed?

3. What factors enabled the Romans to meet the emergency?

GRAMMAR

Review of the Future Passive Participle and the Dative of Agent

Review the future passive participle and the dative of agent in Lesson XXI and the Grammar Appendix, p. 497.9.

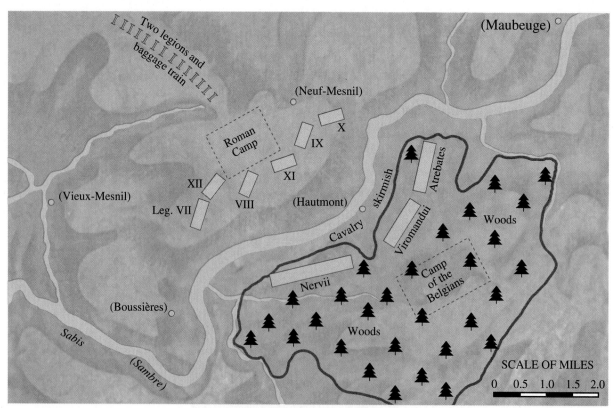

Mapping Specialists, Ltd.

The battle with the Nervii at the Sambre

Translation

1. The time was very short for accomplishing all these things.
2. Caesar had to send certain soldiers for the sake of recalling others.
3. Caesar had to give the signal and recall the soldiers while (**dum**[22]) he drew-up his battle line.

VOCABULARY

[22] with the present indicative; see the Grammar Appendix, p. 501.2a

Adjectives

necessārius, -a, -um *necessary*   [**necesse**]
prīstinus, -a, -um *former*

Verbs

adigō, -ere, adēgī, adāctus *throw (to)*   [**agō**]
administrō, 1 *manage, perform*
dēsum, deesse, dēfuī, dēfutūrus *be lacking*   [**sum**]
dīmicō, 1 *fight*

Conjunction

nēve (neu) *and not, nor*   [**nē**]

Review **cōnspiciō, oportet, perturbō.**

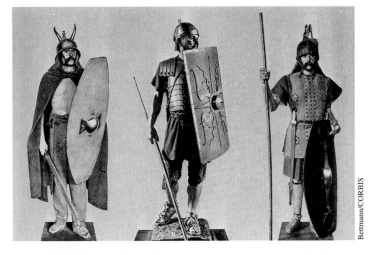

Two Gallic warriors and a Roman legionnaire.

WORD STUDY

Derivatives Distinguish **forte** (noun), **forte** (adjective), and **fortiter** (adverb).

From what Latin words are the following derived: **accommodō, cohortor, exercitō, scientia, tegimentum?**

What does *per se* mean in English? Explain *administration, perturbation, pristine, propinquity, veto.*

LESSON
OBJECTIVES
• **Read**
Caesar *Dē Bellō
Gallicō* II, 22, 24
• **Review**
Dative with Special
Verbs

TENSE MOMENTS

[1] *some in one place, others in
another*

[2] *hedges,* similar to the hedgerows
which hampered the invasion of
Normandy in 1944

[3] All of the infinitives depend on
poterant.

[4] depends on **ēventūs:** *chance
results*

[5] **ūnā cum:** *along with*

[6] *met the enemy face to face*

[7] See page 263 I, D, 1.

[8] *(as) victors;* i.e., the ninth and
tenth legions, mentioned in
Chapter 23

[9] *rushed* (reflexive use of passive)

[10] here used as an adjective; their
name survives in that of the city
Treves (Trier).

[11] introduces **vidissent**

[12] *despairing of our success*

[13] Supply **esse.**

[14] with **potitōs**

II, **22.** Īnstrūctus erat exercitus magis ut locī nātūra et necessitās temporis quam ut reī mīlitāris ratiō atque ōrdō postulābat. Dīversae legiōnēs, aliae[1] aliā in parte, hostibus resistēbant saepibusque[2] dēnsissimīs interiectīs prōspectus impediēbātur. Neque certa subsidia collocārī[3] neque
5 quid in quāque parte opus esset prōvidērī[3] neque ab ūnō omnia imperia administrārī[3] poterant. Itaque in tantā rērum inīquitāte fortūnae[4] quoque ēventūs variī sequēbantur.

Summary of Chapter 23. The ninth and tenth legions, on the left wing, push back the Atrebatians and pursue them across the river. The eighth and
10 eleventh legions also push back the enemy. But the main force of the enemy attacks the exposed front and left sides of the camp.

24. Eōdem tempore equitēs nostrī levisque armātūrae peditēs, quī cum eīs ūnā[5] fuerant (quōs prīmō hostium impetū pulsōs esse dīxerāmus), cum sē in castra reciperent, adversīs[6] hostibus occurrēbant ac rūrsus aliam in
15 partem fugam petēbant. Cālōnēs,[7] quī ab summō iugō collis nostrōs victōrēs[8] flūmen trānsīsse cōnspexerant, praedandī causā ēgressī, cum respexissent et hostēs in nostrīs castrīs versārī vīdissent, praecipitēs fugae sēsē mandābant. Simul eōrum quī cum impedīmentīs veniēbant clāmor oriēbātur, aliīque aliam in partem perterritī ferēbantur.[9] Quibus omnibus
20 rēbus permōtī sunt equitēs Trēverī,[10] quōrum inter Gallōs virtūtis opīniō est singulāris, quī auxilī causā ā cīvitāte missī ad Caesarem vēnerant. Cum[11] multitūdine hostium castra nostra complērī, legiōnēs premī et paene circumventās tenērī, cālōnēs, equitēs, funditōrēs, Numidās dissipātōs in omnēs partēs fugere vīdissent, dēspērātīs[12] nostrīs rēbus, domum
25 contendērunt. Rōmānōs pulsōs superātōsque,[13] castrīs[14] impedīmentīsque eōrum hostēs potītōs cīvitātī renūntiāvērunt.

Questions
1. What did the Treveri do?
2. What did the camp servants do?
3. What happened to the Roman cavalry?
4. What interfered with the Roman view?

GRAMMAR

Review of the Dative with Special Verbs

Review the dative with special verbs in Lesson XXVI and the Grammar Appendix, p. 496.6.

Translation

1. The soldiers were not persuaded to wait.
2. The cavalry could resist no longer and fled to camp.
3. The generals ordered the soldiers not to pursue the enemy.

VOCABULARY

Noun

pedes, peditis m. *foot soldier;* pl., *infantry*　　[**pēs**]

Adjectives

adversus, -a, -um *facing, opposite*　　[**vertō**]

dīversus, -a, -um *different*　　[**vertō**]

Adverb

magis, *more*

The base of a triumphal arch in Carpentras (near Orange, southern France) showing Gallic prisoners.

WORD STUDY

Derivatives From what Latin words are the following derived: **collocō, ēventus, intericiō, necessitās, praedor, singulāris?**

Explain *adverse, complement, diversity, eventual, singularity.*

THE CRISIS PASSES

[1] The chapter resumes Caesar's account of his own part in the battle, interrupted in Chapter 21 (pages 331–332).

[2] *where,* introducing **vidit**

[3] The **-que** connects the two infinitives, **urgērī** and **esse.**

[4] *in the rear*

[5] *did not cease coming up*

[6] *in a tight place*

[7] subjunctive in a descriptive result clause

[8] *seizing a shield from a soldier in the rear ranks;* dative of separation

[9] This reveals one secret of Caesar's success as a leader—he knew every noncommissioned officer by name.

[10] for **ut;** regularly used in a purpose clause containing a comparative

[11] causal

[12] *in the midst of extreme danger to himself*

[13] with **operam:** *to do his best*

II, 25. Caesar[1] ab decimae legiōnis cohortātiōne ad dextrum cornū profectus est, ubi[2] suōs urgērī, signīsque[3] in ūnum locum collātīs, duodecimae legiōnis cōnfertōs mīlitēs sibi ipsōs ad pugnam esse impedīmentō vīdit. Quārtae cohortis omnēs centuriōnēs occīsī erant,
5 signiferque interfectus, signum āmissum, reliquārum cohortium omnēs ferē centuriōnēs aut vulnerātī aut occīsī. Reliquī erant tardiōrēs et nōn nūllī ab novissimīs[4] dēsertōrēs proeliō execēdēbant ac tēla vītābant. Hostēs neque ā fronte ex īnferiōre locō subeuntēs[5] intermittēbant et ab utrōque latere īnstābant. Caesar rem esse in angustō[6] vīdit neque ūllum esse
10 subsidium quod submittī posset.[7] Scūtō[8] ab novissimīs ūnī mīlitī dētrāctō, quod ipse eō sine scūtō vēnerat, in prīmam aciem prōcessit; centuriōnibusque nōminātim appellātīs,[9] reliquōs cohortātus mīlitēs signa īnferre et manipulōs laxāre iussit, quō[10] facilius gladiīs ūtī possent. Cuius adventū spē illātā mīlitibus ac redintegrātō animō, cum[11] prō sē quisque in
15 cōnspectū imperātōris etiam in extrēmīs[12] suīs rēbus operam nāvāre[13] cuperet, paulum hostium impetus tardātus est.

The plain of Alesia, (near present-day Alise-Sainte-Reine, outside Dijon), where Caesar quelled the dangerous rebellion of Vercingetorix and thus put an end to Gallic autonomy for many decades to come (see Lesson XCVII, p. 413 ff.).

Vanni Archive/CORBIS

26. Caesar cum septimam legiōnem, quae iūxtā cōnstiterat, item urgērī ab hoste vīdisset, tribūnōs mīlitum monuit ut paulātim sē legiōnēs coniungerent et conversa[14] signa in hostēs īnferrent. Quō factō, cum alius aliī subsidium ferret neque timērent nē āversī[15] ab hoste circumvenīrentur, 20 audācius resistere ac fortius pugnāre coepērunt. Interim mīlitēs legiōnum duārum quae in novissimō agmine praesidiō impedīmentīs fuerant, proeliō nūntiātō, cursū incitātō,[16] in summō colle ab hostibus cōnspiciēbantur; et Labiēnus castrīs hostium potītus et ex locō superiōre quae rēs in nostrīs castrīs gererentur cōnspicātus, decimam legiōnem subsidiō nostrīs mīsit. 25 Quī, cum ex equitum et cālōnum fugā quō in locō rēs esset quantōque in perīculō et castra et legiōnēs et imperātor versārētur cognōvissent, nihil ad celeritātem sibi reliquī[17] fēcērunt.

[14] *face about and advance,* i.e., to meet the attack on the flanks
[15] *in the rear*
[16] *advancing double-quick;* what literally?
[17] *genitive of the whole; they* came *as fast as they could; literally,* they made nothing of a remainder (in respect) to speed.

Questions

1. What did Caesar do?
2. Which legion suffered most?
3. What three things saved the twelfth legion?

▓VOCABULARY

Nouns

centuriō, -ōnis m. *centurion*   [centum]
cornū, -ūs n. *horn, wing* (of an army)[18]   (cornea, unicorn)

[18] the only fourth declension neuter in this book. All the singular forms except the genitive are identical. (See page 513 in the Grammar Appendix.)

Adjective

dexter, -tra, -trum *right*   (dexterous, ambidextrous)

Verb

tardō, 1 *slow up*   [tardus]

Review **opera, vitō.**

▓WORD STUDY

Derivatives From what Latin words are the following derived: **cohortātiō, dēsertor, duodecimus, nōminātim, redintegrō, signifer?**

Explain *cornucopia, dexterity, invulnerable, relaxation, retardation, urgent.*

THE NERVII AND THE ATUATUCI

II, 27. Hōrum adventū tanta rērum commūtātiō est facta ut nostrī, etiam quī vulneribus cōnfectī prōcubuissent[1] scūtīs[2] innīxī proelium redintegrārent, et cālōnēs perterritōs hostēs cōnspicātī etiam inermēs[3] armātīs occurrerent. Equitēs vērō ut turpitūdinem fugae virtūte dēlērent, omnibus in locīs pugnae sē legiōnāriīs mīlitibus praeferēbant.[4] At hostēs etiam in extrēmā spē salūtis tantam virtūtem praestitērunt ut, cum prīmī eōrum cecidissent, proximī iacentibus[5] īnsisterent atque ex eōrum corporibus pugnārent. Hīs dēiectīs et coacervātīs cadāveribus, quī supererant[6] ut ex tumulō[7] tēla in nostrōs coniciēbant pīlaque intercepta remittēbant. Nōn nēquīquam[8] tantae virtūtis hominēs iūdicārī dēbet[9] ausōs esse trānsīre lātissimum flūmen, ascendere altissimās rīpās, subīre inīquissimum locum; quae facilia[10] ex difficillimīs animī magnitūdō redēgerat.

5

10

[1] attracted into the subjunctive
[2] ablative with **innixi:** *resting on*
[3] in agreement with **cālōnēs** (nominative)
[4] *tried to show themselves superior to.* The legionary, or infantry, soldiers formed the real fighting strength of the Roman army.
[5] *the fallen* (from **iaceō**); dative with compounds
[6] from **supersum**
[7] as (**ut**) *from a mound*
[8] *not in vain;* with **ausōs**
[9] literally, *it ought to be judged that*
[10] predicate accusative: *had rendered easy instead of* (**ex**)

15 **Summary of Chapter 28.** When the noncombatants, who hid in swamps, learn that their army has been almost annihilated, they surrender. Only three out of six hundred senators survive, five hundred out of sixty thousand fighting men. Caesar allows the survivors to return to their homes.

The citadel of Namur, where the **Atuatucī** sought refuge from Caesar's army. Can you locate it on the map on pages 254–255? There it is called **Atuatucōrum opp.** Do you know what **opp.** stands for?

29. Atuatucī, dē quibus suprā dīximus,[11] cum[12] omnibus cōpiīs[13] auxiliō Nerviīs venīrent, hāc pugnā nūntiātā, ex itinere domum revertērunt; omnibus oppidīs castellīsque dēsertīs, sua omnia in ūnum oppidum ēgregiē nātūrā mūnītum contulērunt. Quod cum[14] ex omnibus in circuitū[15] partibus altissimās rūpēs habēret, ūnā ex parte lēniter acclīvis[16] aditus in lātitūdinem nōn amplius[17] pedum CC relinquēbātur; quem locum duplicī altissimō mūrō mūnierant;[18] tum magnī ponderis saxa et praeacūtās trabēs in mūrō collocābant. Ipsī erant ex Cimbrīs Teutonīsque[19] prōgnātī, quī cum iter in prōvinciam nostram atque Italiam facerent, eīs impedīmentīs[20] quae sēcum agere ac portāre nōn poterant citrā flūmen Rhēnum dēpositīs, custōdiam[21] ex suīs[22] ac praesidium sex mīlia hominum relīquērunt. Hī post eōrum[23] mortem multōs annōs ā fīnitimīs vexātī, cum aliās[24] bellum īnferrent, aliās illātum[25] dēfenderent, cōnsēnsū eōrum omnium pāce factā, hunc sibi domiciliō locum dēlēgērunt.

20

25

30

[11] in Chapter 16
[12] the conjunction
[13] ablative of accompaniment
[14] *although this (town).* This is probably Namur, though some favor a hill near Huy.
[15] *all around*
[16] *ascending* (nom.)
[17] for **amplius quam**
[18] contracted form
[19] These two German tribes had been decisively defeated by Marius, Caesar's uncle, in 102 and 101 B.C.
[20] here *live stock* and *goods,* as shown by **agere and portāre**
[21] *(as) a guard*
[22] **ex suis** belongs with **sex milia**
[23] the main group
[24] adverb: *now . . . now*
[25] Supply **bellum.**

Questions

1. Trace Caesar's course on the map (pp. 254–255).
2. What did the camp servants of the Romans do?
3. What did the Nervii do when their first line fell?
4. How did the Atuatuci come to make Belgium their home?

GRAMMAR

Review of the Accusative of Place to Which

Review the accusative of place to which in the Grammar Appendix, p. 497.3.

Translation

1. Caesar proceeded to Noviodunum to destroy that town.
2. After the Atuatuci had arrived at that town, they immediately fortified it.
3. Because Caesar admired the courage of the Nervii, he sent home those who survived.

Réunion des Musées Nationaux/Art Resource, NY

Gallic warrior in green wax by Emmanuel Frémiet from the nineteenth century.

Roots If John and Jane Doe are *otherwise* known as Richard and Mary Roe, the latter names are "aliases." The Latin adverb **aliās** became an English noun, just as happened in the case of *item* (p. 271). Similarly an "alibi" is claimed when one alleges that he or she was *elsewhere*.

From what Latin words are the following derived: **commūtātiō, cōnsēnsus, custōdia, domicilium, inermis, inīquus, legiōnārius, praeferō, turpitūdō?**

Explain *adjacent, cadaver, duplicity, turpitude, vexatious.*

Part of the spiral frieze of Trajan's Column in Rome recording his victories over the Dacians (modern Romania) in A.D. 101–102 and 105–106. Illustrated here is the siege of a town on the Danube River. Note the goddess overseeing Roman success in the top part of the frieze.

Scala/Art Resource, NY

THE ATUATUCI MAKE FUN OF THE ROMAN "TANKS"

LESSON OBJECTIVES
- **Read**
  Caesar *Dē Bellō Gallicō* II, 30–31
- **Review**
  Volō, Nōlō, and **Mālō** Special and Compound Verbs with Dative

II, **30.** Ac prīmō adventū exercitūs nostrī crēbrās ex oppidō ēruptiōnēs faciēbant[1] parvulīsque proeliīs cum nostrīs contendēbant; posteā vāllō pedum XII, in circuitū XV mīlium,[2] crēbrīsque castellīs circummūnītī[3] oppidō[4] sē continēbant. Ubi, vīneīs āctīs, aggere exstrūctō, turrim[5] procul cōnstituī vīdērunt, prīmum irrīsērunt ex mūrō quod tanta māchinātiō ā tantō spatiō īnstituerētur:[6] "Quibusnam[7] manibus aut quibus vīribus vōs, praesertim hominēs[8] tantulae statūrae (nam plērumque omnibus Gallīs, prae magnitūdine corporum suōrum, brevitās Rōmānōrum contemptuī est) tantī oneris turrim in mūrō nostrō vōs posse collocāre cōnfīditis?"

31. Ubi vērō movērī[9] et appropinquāre moenibus vīdērunt, novā atque inūsitātā speciē commōtī lēgātōs ad Caesarem dē pāce mīsērunt, quī ad hunc modum locūtī sunt:

"Nōn exīstimāmus vōs sine ope deōrum bellum gerere, quī[10] tantae altitūdinis māchinātiōnēs tantā celeritāte prōmovēre possītis; nōs nostraque omnia vestrae potestātī permittimus. Ūnum petimus et ōrāmus:

5

10

15

---

[1] Supply **hostēs** as subject.

[2] i.e., **pedum**

[3] *when hemmed in* (i.e., by Caesar's rampart), agreeing with the subject of **continēbant**

[4] ablative of means

[5] third declension **i**-stem

[6] **quod** causal clause

[7] **-nam** is intensive: *with what hands anyway*

[8] in apposition with **vōs**: *(being) men*

[9] Supply **turrim** as subject.

[10] *since you.* A subjunctive relative clause may express cause.

The Bridgeman Art Library

Gauls prepare to defend their homeland. As Caesar points out in the passage on this page (lines 7–8), they did not fear the Romans at first, since the Romans were smaller in stature. They were often fewer in number, too.

sī forte prō tuā clēmentiā, quam ab aliīs audīmus, statueris Atuatucōs esse cōnservandōs, nōlī[11] nōs armīs dēspoliāre. Nōbīs omnēs ferē fīnitimī sunt inimīcī ac nostrae virtūtī[12] invident; ā quibus nōs dēfendere, trāditīs armīs, nōn poterimus. Nōbīs praestat, sī in eum cāsum dēdūcāmur,[13] quamvīs[14]

20 fortūnam ā populō Rōmānō patī quam ab eīs per cruciātum interficī inter quōs dominārī cōnsuēvimus."

Questions

1. Why did the Atuatuci laugh at the Roman preparations?
2. What explanation did their envoys have for Roman ingenuity?
3. What concession did the Atuatuci ask of the Romans?

GRAMMAR

Review of *Volō, Nōlō,* and *Mālō* and Special/Compound Verbs with Dative

Review the conjugation of **volō, nōlō,** and **mālō** in the Grammar Appendix, pp. 529–530.

Find five special and compound verbs with the dative in the passage on pages 341–342 and the passage in Lesson LXXIII.

Translation

1. Our neighbors envy us and will want to kill us all if we surrender our arms.
2. When they saw our army approaching the town, they were unwilling to resist us.

VOCABULARY

Nouns

ēruptiō, -ōnis f. *sally*
onus, oneris n. *weight*
turris, -is f. *tower*

[rumpō]
(exonerate, onerous)
(turret)

Adverbs

plērumque *usually*
procul *far off*

WORD STUDY

Suffixes The suffix **-lus (-ulus, -ellus)** is a *diminutive*, i.e., it means *little:* **castellum** (from **castra**), **parvulus, tantulus.** In English it often becomes *-le: particle* (from **parti-culum**), *corpuscle* (**corpus-culum**). Sometimes the original form is kept: **formula, gladiolus** (literally, *little sword*, from **gladius,** because of the shape of its leaves).

From what Latin words are the following derived: **brevitās, circummūniō, contemptus, dominor, inūsitātus, statūra?**

Explain *despoil, domination, eruption, exonerate, onerous.*

SURRENDER, TREACHERY, PUNISHMENT

[1] *in the case of*

[2] *said they were doing*

[3] Translate this and the following ablative absolute as main clauses.

[4] *piles*

[5] *they observed a truce*

[6] *toward*

[7] *in accordance with a plan.* The adverb **ante** belongs with **initō**, which is from **ineō**.

[8] *because*

[9] *at least*

[10] *where*

[11] *fire signals.* These were in general use among all peoples until more rapid means of communication were invented, such as the telegraph, telephone, and radio. Native Americans "telegraphed" news by means of smoke and fire signals.

[12] Translate actively and personally. Do the same with the next two verbs used impersonally, by making **hostibus** and **viris fortibus** the subjects. The neuter of the perfect participle of intransitive verbs may be used in this construction.

II, **32.** Ad haec Caesar respondit:

"Magis cōnsuētūdine meā quam meritō vestrō cīvitātem cōnservābō, sī, priusquam mūrum ariēs attigerit, vōs dēdideritis; sed dēditiōnis nūlla est condiciō nisi armīs trāditīs. Id quod in[1] Nerviīs fēcī faciam, fīnitimīsque
5 imperābō nē quam dēditīciīs populī Rōmānī iniūriam īnferant." Rē nūntiātā ad suōs, illī sē quae imperārentur facere[2] dīxērunt. Armōrum magnā multitūdine[3] dē mūrō in fossam quae erat ante oppidum iactā, sīc ut prope summam mūrī aggerisque altitūdinem acervī[4] armōrum adaequārent (et tamen circiter parte tertiā, ut posteā perspectum est, cēlātā atque in
10 oppidō retentā), portīs patefactīs, eō diē pāce sunt ūsī.[5]

33. Sub[6] vesperum Caesar portās claudī mīlitēsque ex oppidō exīre iussit, nē quam noctū Atuatucī ā mīlitibus iniūriam acciperent. Illī, ante initō cōnsiliō,[7] quod,[8] dēditiōne factā, nostrōs praesidia dēductūrōs aut dēnique[9] indīligentius servātūrōs crēdiderant, tertiā vigiliā, quā[10] minimē
15 arduus ad nostrās mūnītiōnēs ascēnsus vidēbātur, omnibus cōpiīs repente ex oppidō ēruptiōnem fēcērunt. Celeriter, ut ante Caesar imperāverat, ignibus[11] significātiōne factā, ex proximīs castellīs eō concursum est,[12]

A naval fight between Romans and Gauls from a fourteenth-century Italian manuscript, revealing how little the artist cared (or knew how) to represent Romans of Caesar's time. Note the interest in the animal figureheads, which almost seem to take part in the battle.

A magnificent entrance gate to the Roman colony at Trier (**Augusta Trēvirōrum**), West Germany. Founded under Augustus around 15 B.C., this Roman colony soon became a flourishing capital and trade center for Roman Belgium and the surrounding regions.

pugnātumque ab hostibus ita ācriter est ut ā virīs fortibus in extrēmā spē salūtis pugnārī dēbuit, cum in ūnā[13] virtūte omnis spēs cōnsisteret. Occīsīs ad hominum mīlibus IIII, reliquī in oppidum reiectī sunt. Postrīdiē eius 20 diēī frāctīs portīs, cum iam dēfenderet nemō,[14] atque intrōmissīs mīlitibus nostrīs, sectiōnem[15] eius oppidī ūniversam Caesar vēndidit. Ab eīs quī ēmerant capitum numerus ad eum relātus est mīlium LIII.

[13] *alone*

[14] with **iam**: *no one any longer*

[15] *loot.* Merchants followed Roman armies and purchased the spoils of war. Caesar accepts their count as to the number of slaves they bought. Caesar contrasts the bravery of the Nervii and the treachery of the Atuatuci and his leniency toward the former and the severity toward the latter.

Questions

1. Trace Caesar's course on the map (pp. 254–255).
2. What happened the night after the surrender?
3. How did Caesar punish the Atuatuci for their treachery?

GRAMMAR

Review of Ablative Absolute

Find all the examples of the ablative absolute in the reading on pages 344–345.

Translation

1. If the enemy surrendered[16] their arms, they could not resist the Roman army.
2. After the gates were closed,[16] the enemy concealed[16] their arms and made a sally.
3. Since the enemy had been defeated,[16] Caesar demanded hostages and returned to Italy.

[16] Use the ablative absolute.

Summary of Chapters 34–35. The coast towns are brought under Roman power by Crassus. The Germans across the Rhine offer to submit. Caesar arranges winter quarters and returns to Italy.

Latīnum Hodiernum

Vacca[17] Contenta

Vaccae virtūs est nōbīs lac praebēre ac contenta esse, ut in vāsibus lactis condēnsātī vidērī potest. Fierī quidem saepe potest ut vacca adhūc contenta īram subitō ostendat. Tālis fuit ista quae, lanternā calce[18] ēversā, Chicaginem urbem incendit. Inter fābulās puerīlēs nārrātur dē vaccā quae trāns lūnam trānsiluit. Fuitne īnsāna an cupiditāte altissimē saliendī impulsa est? Dīcī vix potest. Contenta quidem nōn fuit.

Multōs iam annōs mōs ortus est vaccārum māchinā mulgendārum.[19] Hōc modō plūrimae simul mulgērī possunt. Dum haec rēs geritur, vaccae, sī mūsica dulcis phōnographī praebētur, magis contentae stant. Mūsicam classicam mālunt, hodiernam nōn amant. Quod ad nōs pertinet, plūs lactis bibāmus,[20] quod cibus optimus nōbīs est. Ita nōn modo vaccae sed nōs ipsī magis contentī erimus.

17 *cow,* adapted from Norman W. Dewitt in *Classical Journal,* 44 (1948), p.14.
18 *heel, kick*
19 *milk*
20 *let us drink*

WARFARE IN ANCIENT AND MODERN TIMES

Despite revolutionary changes in warfare, from the introduction of firearms and heavy artillery to the invention of submarines, airplanes, atomic bombs, and guided missiles, there still remain many curious parallels between ancient and modern techniques. The Roman soldier dug trenches in order to fortify his camp; the modern soldier sometimes digs him or herself in for protection against high-range guns that can drop explosive shells within an enemy's lines from a distance. In Caesar's day the rampart formed by throwing up the earth taken from a trench around the camp gave sufficient protection from low-range weapons then in use. A Roman army on the march used this means of defense every night. The use of spades, foxholes, and lines of trenches in World War I had their early counterparts (on a smaller scale, of course) in Caesar's siege of Alesia, where he constructed ten miles of earthen ramparts and trenches. The Roman trenches were five-feet deep and obstructed with wolfholes, sharpened stakes, and brush barricades to guard against attacks from the town (cf. p. 423). Similar devices are used today, especially against tanks.

Bettmann/CORBIS

A city under siege, illustrating the various types of weaponry known to Romans of Caesar's time. *From left to right:* the **turris ambulātōria** (movable tower) used to overcome the advantage in height the city walls provided; the **testūdō arietāria** (a battering ram concealed under a shed like the shell of a tortoise) used to dislodge masonry; the **testūdō** (a cover of interlocking shields) and **scālae** (ladders); the **onager** ("donkey," so nicknamed from its "kick") and the **ballista**, machines for throwing heavy and light missiles, stones, or spears.

The Romans showed great adaptability in the development of armor and weapons, steadily altering them to meet different conditions, and often borrowing from their enemies. The metal helmet (**cassis**), of Greek origin, gave protection to the brow and neck and replaced the earlier leather **galea.** Over his tunic the soldier wore a leather breastplate (**lōrīca**), covered with segmented metal plates. The Gallic trousers (**brācae**) gave him mobility and protection from the cold. On his feet were leather sandals (**caligae**), tied on with thongs. The long rectangular shield (**scūtum**) was adopted from the Samnites; the pointed boss (**umbō**) projecting from the center could inflict a wound on its own. The principal offensive weapon was the **pīlum,** a seven-foot spear with a soft iron point which bent on contact and could not be extracted. At his right side, the legionary carried a short double-edged Spanish sword (**gladius**) better for stabbing at close quarters than for slashing; at his left, a dagger (**pūgiō**). Rigorously trained and well led, the Roman legionary was an awesome fighting machine.

Bettmann/CORBIS

Like the Romans, modern soldiers are equipped with steel helmets and occasionally steel breastplates and greaves (shin guards) for hazardous work.

Roman soldiers held their spears (**pīla**) until they got within range of the enemy and then hurled them. Before the enemy could recover from this volley, the Romans attacked with their heavy swords (**gladiī**) held close to the body. Today, long-range artillery fire prepares the way for a charge, while the hand grenade is used in closer quarters, followed at times by a charge of troops with bayonets fixed. Although artillery and rifle fire have superseded the spear-throwing of the Romans, and the bayonet and the grenade have taken the place of the sword, the principle remains the same. The motor-driven tank has taken the place of the old Roman **turris ambulātōria,** "movable tower," which was pushed forward on rollers toward the besieged town. The closest parallel to the tank, however, was the elephant. First used by Rome's enemies, the elephants terrified the Romans, who had never before seen any. Later the Romans themselves used them. Caesar does not mention them in the *Gallic War,* but a later writer says that Caesar scared the Britons at the Thames River with a single "armored" elephant carrying a tower filled with slingers and bowmen.

The Roman troops often advanced under fire protected by lines of movable sheds (**vīneae**) placed end to end, while occasionally smaller barriers, called **pluteī,** were pushed forward covering the advance of a small party under fire. Similarly, modern infantry advance behind the cover of tanks. Smoke screens, now used chiefly by warships, were also used by ancient armies.

In sieges like those at Avaricum and Alesia, Caesar employed the battering-ram (**ariēs**) to break down the enemy's walls. These rams were heavy swinging logs, capped with bronze, which, striking repeated blows at the same spot, would demolish any wall. A ram used by the Romans against Carthage in 148 B.C. was so huge that six thousand men were required to swing it into action. Today tanks and demolition teams are used this way.

The **onager, ballista,** and **catapulta,** which threw stones or arrows, formed the Romans' "heavy" artillery and were largely confined to siege operations. The power of these weapons came from twisted ropes; today children twist rubber bands in the same way to obtain motive power. For light artillery, the Romans used the **scorpiō,** a large bow mounted on a portable frame. A certain Greek of Alexandria, we are told, invented a **scorpiō** with an arrow magazine which shot arrows in rapid succession, resembling in principle the modern machine gun. From Caesar's account of its use at the siege of Avaricum, we know that this weapon was like a quick-firing gun. The Romans also had their **carroballistae,** or field-pieces, so that the modern gun carriage is nothing new. Incendiary bombs and flame throwers have their parallel in fireballs.

Airplanes are, of course, quite modern, but the first mention of a heavier-than-air flying machine is of one made by a Greek from southern Italy, a friend of Plato, who invented a flying machine resembling a dove (**columba**).

Caesar, in conquering Gallic towns and tribes, regularly demanded a certain number of influential persons to be held by him as hostages (**obsidēs**), or "pledges" that the terms of peace agreed upon would be kept. Unfortunately the word hostage is not yet obsolete.

In recent years much attention has been paid to the construction of military roads for the easy movement of troops. Until very recently, no other nation had built as many miles of paved roadway as had Rome. For durability the Roman roads are still unsurpassed; many miles of their military roads are still in existence after two thousand years.

We have heard much in recent years of blitzkrieg, or lightning war. Caesar was one of its earliest and most famous exponents. Before the enemy even knew that he was approaching he had already arrived! By use of technical aids he did things faster than his enemies, thereby surprising and terrifying them. It took the Helvetians twenty days to cross the Saone and even then not all of them got over; Caesar built a bridge and crossed in one day. The Remi surrendered because Caesar arrived before he was expected. He crossed the Cévennes mountains in six feet of snow, which the natives considered an impossible feat, and gathered his scattered legions into one place before the Arverni even knew he was there. From Gergovia, Caesar marched his legions twenty-five miles, settled the Haeduan revolt, gave his soldiers three hours' rest, and marched back again—fifty miles in less than twenty-four hours.

By comparison with modern fighting, ancient warfare does not seem very deadly. Yet Caesar tells us that one hundred and twenty arrows struck the shield of one of his men at Dyrrachium and that not one of his soldiers was unhurt.

Ancient battles are still studied by the military for the lessons they teach. Generals Douglas MacArthur and George Marshall are examples of soldiers thoroughly familiar with ancient strategy and tactics. General Puller, called the "toughest marine in the corps," carried with him and read the *Gallic War* during World War II because he believed its lessons were still valuable.

There are also striking similarities between the military slang of ancient times and that of today. An ancient writer tells us that the men of the Roman army, many of whom had been brought up on farms in Italy, were fond of calling weapons and things about the camp by the names of animals and objects with which they were familiar as boys. The forked sticks on which Marius' soldiers carried their packs (**sarcinae**) were called "Marius' mules" (**mūlī Mariānī**).[21] A certain kind of **ballista** was named **onager,** "wild ass," from that animal's habit of flinging stones at its pursuers with its hind feet. Another type of hurling machine was called **scorpiō,** "scorpion," presumably because it shot arrows that "stung" the enemy. The beam used in battering down the enemy's walls was humorously called **ariēs,** "ram," from that animal's fondness for butting, and, as a matter of fact, it was often capped with a ram's head made of bronze. A defensive formation, when the men stood shoulder to shoulder so that their shields overlapped, while the inner ranks held their shields over their heads, was nicknamed "turtle" (**testūdō).** A large protecting shed, used to shield men while digging toward the walls of a besieged town, was called **mūsculus,** "little mouse," from the burrowing habits of that animal.

The use of animal names by the Roman soldier has its modern parallel in such words as "jeep" (originally the name of a comic-strip animal), "whirlybird" (helicopter), "caterpillar tractor," "weasel" (small caterpillar truck), "duck" (land and water truck), and "grasshoppers" (small planes).

---

[21] According to some, the soldiers themselves received this name.

Even "scorpion" is used but in a different sense: a tank attachment to explode mines.

Country boys serving in the Roman army probably coined the term **vīneae,** "grape arbors," described above. The term "lilies" **(līlia)** was applied to the conelike holes in the center of which sharpened stakes were set. In World War II, the Russians called such devices "asparagus." **Stimulī,** "goads," applied to the barbed pieces of iron set in pieces of wood and implanted in the earth, is another instance of soldier slang. They served the same purpose as the four-pronged iron "crow feet" that the early settlers used to scatter about the frontier forts for prowling Native Americans to step on. The lead slingstones, or bullets, used by the Romans were called "acorns" **(glandēs);** the French call bullets "chestnuts" or "prunes." "Grenade" came through French from Latin **grānātum,** "pomegranate." "Grapeshot" was the name of one kind of artillery ammunition used in earlier years.

QUESTIONS

1. What sort of artillery did the Romans have?
2. How has the introduction of gunpowder affected warfare?
3. What aspects of warfare today are most like and which most unlike those of Caesar's day?

DĒ BELLŌ GALLICŌ III–V

Unit Objectives

Read

Selections from Caesar *Dē Bellō Gallicō*, Books III–V

Review

- Purpose and Result Clauses
- Conjugation of **Ferō**
- Genitive of the Whole
- Volitive Clauses
- Datives of Purpose and Reference
- Ablative of Separation
- Future Passive Participle and Gerund

The Forum of Julius Caesar is located a short distance from the Roman Forum. It was begun in 54 B.C., during the period of Caesar's military campaigns. The Forum contains the Temple of Venus Genetrix, from whom Caesar claimed descent. In this photo, you can see the **tabernae** (*shops*) behind the columns of the double colonnade.

Scala/Art Resource, NY

LESSON
OBJECTIVES
• **Read**
Caesar *Dē Bellō
Gallicō* III, 14
• **Review**
Purpose and Result
Clauses

THE FIRST BATTLE ON THE ATLANTIC

The selections in this and the next lesson are from Book III of Caesar's *Gallic War,* which deals with the campaign against the Veneti. The events described took place in 56 B.C.

Summary of Chapters 1–13. After subduing the Belgians, Caesar decides to make access to their northern country easy and safe for Roman traders by opening a road through the Alps to Italy by way of what we now call the Great St. Bernard Pass. He accordingly sends Servius Galba with a small force to guard this pass and hold the Alpine tribes in check. Galba takes up winter quarters in Octodurus (see map, pp. 254–255). This proves to be a death trap, for the mountaineers, who had pretended to submit, suddenly gather in large numbers on the heights above and attack the Romans before they have completed their fortifications. Galba beats them off, but finding it impossible to get supplies, he burns the village, destroys his camp, and withdraws to the Province.

Caesar had sent Publius Crassus with a legion to establish winter quarters among the coast tribes of what is now Brittany and Normandy. Foremost of these were the Vĕn´etī. They had pretended to submit and had sent hostages to Crassus but later, in order to force him to restore their hostages, they seize some of the officers sent by him to arrange for supplies. All the northwestern seacoast tribes combine to resist the

Julius Caesar spent the years from 58 to 50 B.C. in his military campaigns in the Gallic provinces. This frieze from a sarcophagus shows the Roman soldiers battling the Gauls.

Ronald Sheridan/Ancient Art & Architecture Collection

A large Roman vessel, used for carrying men and goods, usually had two banks of oars. The master at the front of the ship set the cadence, or tempo, for the rowers to follow. This was sometimes done with a drum, with his voice, or with his own oar. This detail is from the Column of Trajan in Rome.

Romans and send an embassy to Crassus, demanding the hostages. Caesar at once orders ships to be built at the mouth of the Liger (Loire) and oarsmen to be procured from the Province, and hastens north in the early spring. He sends Labienus to the Treveri, near the Rhine, to keep the Belgians under control and to prevent the Germans, whom the Belgians had asked for aid, from crossing the Rhine. Crassus is sent to Aquitania to prevent help from being sent from there into Gaul. Brutus is sent to prevent the coast tribes of the north from aiding the Veneti. Decimus Brutus is put in charge of the fleet which is being obtained from the pacified districts.

The towns of the Veneti are almost inaccessible from the land side because high tide cuts them off, and from the sea because low tide causes ships to be stranded in the shallows. In case of extreme danger, the Veneti move from town to town by ship, taking all with them. They have a powerful fleet of seagoing vessels which have every advantage over the Roman galleys, because they have high prows and flat keels and are fitted with sails, being well adapted to fighting in shallow water or to riding out storms at sea.

III, 14. Complūribus expugnātīs oppidīs, Caesar, ubi intellēxit frūstrā tantum labōrem sūmī, neque hostium fugam, captīs oppidīs, reprimī neque eīs nocērī[1] posse, statuit exspectandam classem.[2] Quae ubi convēnit ac prīmum ab hostibus vīsa est, circiter CCXX nāvēs eōrum parātissimae atque omnī genere armōrum ōrnātissimae ex portū profectae nostrīs adversae cōnstitērunt; neque satis Brūtō,[3] quī classī praeerat, vel tribūnīs mīlitum centuriōnibusque, quibus singulae nāvēs erant attribūtae, cōnstābat quid agerent[4] aut quam ratiōnem pugnae īnsisterent. Rōstrō[5] enim nocērī nōn posse cognōverant; turribus autem excitātīs, tamen[6] hās

[1] that they could not be injured

[2] i.e., his own

[3] with **cōnstābat**; this is Decimus Brutus, not the more famous Marcus.

[4] what they should do

[5] ship's beak; ablative not dative; the ships of the Veneti were made of oak.

[6] What does **tamen** show as to the force of the preceding ablative absolute?

7 *on*

8 *those thrown*

9 *long poles*

10 *not unlike that of;* **fōrmā** *is ablative of description*

11 *ablative of means, with* **comprehēnsī**

12 *whenever*

13 *bound to the masts*

14 *i.e., the attacking Roman ship*

15 *in the case of the Gallic ships; dative of reference*

16 *The Gallic ships, unlike those of the Romans, had no oars.*

17 *a little braver (than usual)*

10 altitūdō puppium ex[7] barbarīs nāvibus superābat ut neque ex īnferiōre locō satis commodē tēla adigī possent et missa[8] ā Gallīs gravius acciderent. Ūna erat magnō ūsuī rēs praeparāta ab nostrīs—falcēs praeacūtae īnsertae affīxaeque longuriīs[9] nōn absimilī[10] fōrmā mūrālium falcium. Hīs[11] cum[12]
fūnēs quī antemnās ad mālōs dēstinābant[13] comprehēnsī adductīque erant,
15 nāvigiō[14] rēmīs incitātō, praerumpēbantur. Quibus abscīsīs, antemnae necessāriō concidēbant; ut, cum omnis Gallicīs nāvibus[15] spēs in vēlīs armāmentīsque cōnsisteret, hīs ēreptīs, omnis ūsus nāvium ūnō tempore ēriperētur.[16] Reliquum erat certāmen positum in virtūte, quā nostrī mīlitēs facile superābant atque eō magis, quod in cōnspectū Caesaris atque omnis
20 exercitūs rēs gerēbātur, ut nūllum paulō fortius[17] factum latēre posset; omnēs enim collēs ac loca superiōra, unde erat propinquus dēspectus in mare, ab exercitū tenēbantur.

Questions

1. Who commanded the Roman fleet?

2. Why were the Romans particularly brave?

3. In what three ways did the Roman and Venetan ships differ?

The rocky coast of Brittany, France. Caesar's fleet, with ships powered by oars, defeated the Gallic fleet in this region by pulling down their sails and rigging, rendering them immobile.

Joe Cornish/Stone

GRAMMAR

Review of Purpose and Result Clauses

Review purpose and result clauses in Lessons XI, XII, and XIV.

Translation

1. The ships of the enemy were so high that the Romans could not throw their spears.
2. The soldiers fought with great courage in order not to be beaten in the sight of Caesar.

WORD STUDY

Derivatives **Classis** originally meant a calling out of citizens for military service, or draft. Then it came to mean any group, or *class*. One specialized meaning was that of the naval *class*, or *fleet*.

From what Latin words are the following derived: **abscīdō, absimilis, affīgō, attribuō, concīdō, praerumpō, reprimō?**

Explain *affix, attribution, insertion, latent, repression.*

LESSON
OBJECTIVES
• **Read**
Caesar *Dē Bellō
Gallicō* III, 15–16, 19
• **Review**
Conjugation of **Fērō**
Genitive of the Whole

A DECISIVE VICTORY

[1] *whenever*

[2] *each (Gallic vessel)*

[3] adverb

[4] *was blowing*

[5] loosely attached to the preceding: *the fighting going on,* etc.

[6] The Roman hour was one-twelfth of daylight and therefore varied from 45 to 75 minutes according to the time of year. Roughly, the fourth hour would be about 10 A.M.

[7] with **tum:** *not only . . . but also*

[8] *more advanced.* What literally? Age is thought of as a burden.

[9] depends on **quod:** *all the ships there were anywhere*

III, **15.** Dēiectīs (ut dīximus) antemnīs, cum[1] singulās[2] bīnae ac ternae nāvēs circumsteterant, mīlitēs summā vī trānscendere in hostium nāvēs contendēbant. Quod postquam barbarī fierī animadvertērunt, expugnātīs complūribus nāvibus, cum eī reī nūllum reperīrētur auxilium, 5 fugā salūtem petere contendērunt. Ac iam conversīs in eam partem nāvibus quō[3] ventus ferēbat,[4] tanta subitō tranquillitās exstitit ut sē ex locō movēre nōn possent. Quae quidem rēs ad negōtium cōnficiendum maximē fuit opportūna; nam singulās nostrī cōnsecūtī expugnāvērunt, ut perpaucae ex omnī numerō noctis interventū ad terram pervenīrent, cum[5] ab hōrā ferē 10 quārtā[6] usque ad sōlis occāsum pugnārētur.

16. Quō proeliō bellum Venetōrum tōtīusque ōrae maritimae cōnfectum est. Nam cum[7] omnis iuventūs, omnēs etiam graviōris[8] aetātis, in quibus aliquid cōnsilī aut dignitātis fuit, eō convēnerant, tum nāvium[9] quod ubīque fuerat[9] in ūnum locum coēgerant; quibus āmissīs reliquī neque

Fortasse trans aquam in Britanniam procedemus.
This wall painting from Pompeii shows Roman warships in battle. The soldiers are visible, but the rowers are protected below deck.

Erich Lessing/Art Resource, NY

quō[10] sē reciperent neque quem ad modum oppida dēfenderent habēbant. Itaque sē suaque omnia Caesarī dēdidērunt. In quōs eō[11] gravius Caesar vindicandum[12] statuit, quō dīligentius in reliquum tempus ā barbarīs iūs lēgātōrum cōnservārētur. Itaque omnī senātū necātō, reliquōs sub corōnā[13] vēndidit.

Summary of Chapters 17–19. Caesar sends Sabinus to subdue the northern allies of the Veneti near Avranches in Normandy. Knowing that he must employ strategy to deal with their overwhelming numbers, Sabinus bribes a Gaul to play the role of a deserter and tell the Gauls that Sabinus is going to Caesar's aid. The ruse works, for the Gauls immediately attack Sabinus in his camp, whereupon, having the advantage of position, he orders his trained soldiers to charge them from the right and left gates and sends them flying. The enemy at once surrenders.

19. Sīc ūnō tempore et dē nāvālī pugnā Sabīnus et dē Sabīnī victōriā Caesar est certior factus, cīvitātēsque omnēs sē statim Titūriō dēdidērunt. Nam ut ad bella suscipienda Gallōrum alacer ac prōmptus est animus, sīc mollis ac minimē resistēns ad calamitātēs ferendās mēns eōrum est.

15 [10] *(a place) where they might take refuge or means whereby*

[11] *all the more severely,* looking forward to **quō**, which introduces a purpose clause

[12] *that punishment ought to be inflicted*

20 [13] "under the crown," i.e., as *slaves.* Prisoners of war were crowned with wreaths when offered for sale.

30

Questions
1. What won the sea battle for the Romans?
2. Why did Caesar punish the Veneti more severely than he had punished others?
3. From Caesar's description of the spirit of the Gauls, what do you infer was his idea of Roman spirit?

A Gallic warrior is taken prisoner by the Romans. Compare his weapons and armor to those of the Romans. What differences do you see?

⊞ GRAMMAR

Review of the Conjugation of *Ferō* and the Genitive of the Whole
Review the conjugation of **ferō** in Lesson XIII.

Review the genitive of the whole in Lesson XXXII and the Grammar Appendix, p. 495.3 with Notes.

Translation
1. Two of Caesar's ships surrounded one of the enemy's ships.
2. When Caesar had brought together enough ships, he attacked the enemy.

VOCABULARY

Noun

ōra maritima, ōrae maritimae f. *seacoast* [ōs + mare]

Adjectives

bīnī, -ae, -a *two at a time* (binational, binocular)

maritimus, -a, -um *of the sea* [mare]

opportūnus, -a, -um *opportune,* [portus]
   advantageous

Verb

circumsistō, -ere, -stetī — *surround* [stō]

Adverb

usque *up to*

Review **alacer, expugnō, necō, statim, ventus.**

WORD STUDY

Derivatives From what Latin words are the following derived:
dēiciō, dignitās, interventus, nāvālis, perpaucī?
   Explain *alacrity, binary, combine, coronation, dejection,
dignitary, intervention, maritime, mollify, ventilate.*

Summary of Chapters 20–29. Crassus, who had been sent by Caesar
to subdue Aquitania, is attacked by the Sotiates. He defeats them and
captures their city. Advancing farther, Crassus faces a formidable
Aquitanian army, which fights according to Roman tactics. Since the
enemy's forces are being strengthened daily, Crassus decides to attack
their camp at once. Finding that the rear gate is not well guarded, he makes
a surprise attack and routs the enemy. The various tribes of Aquitania now
surrender and send hostages. In the north, Caesar defeats the Morini and
Menapii, who, avoiding a pitched battle, seek refuge in their forests. The
Romans pursue and attempt to cut their way after them, but are prevented
by storms. After ravaging the enemy's country, Caesar returns to winter in
recently conquered territory.

DESCRIPTION OF THE SUEBI[1]

LESSON OBJECTIVE
- **Read**
  Caesar *Dē Bellō Gallicō* IV, 1

In Book IV of the *Gallic War,* represented by Lessons LXXVIII through LXXXIV, Caesar describes his war with the Suebi, a German tribe, and his first expedition to Britain, made in 55 B.C.

IV, 1. Eā quae secūta est hieme, quī[2] fuit annus Cn. Pompeiō[3] M. Crassō cōnsulibus, Usipetēs Germānī[4] et item Tencterī magnā cum multitūdine hominum flūmen Rhēnum trānsiērunt, nōn longē ā marī quō[5] Rhēnus īnfluit. Causa trānseundī fuit quod ab Suēbīs complūrēs annōs exagitātī bellō premēbantur et agrī cultūrā prohibēbantur.

Suēbōrum gēns est longē maxima et bellicōsissima Germānōrum omnium. Hī centum pāgōs habēre dīcuntur, ex quibus quotannīs singula[6] mīlia armātōrum bellandī causā suīs ex fīnibus ēdūcunt. Reliquī, quī domī mānsērunt, sē atque illōs alunt. Hī rūrsus in vicem annō post in armīs sunt, illī domī remanent. Sīc neque agrī cultūra nec ratiō atque ūsus bellī intermittitur. Sed prīvātī agrī apud eōs nihil est, neque longius annō[7] remanēre ūnō in locō colendī causā licet. Neque multum frūmentō, sed maximam partem[8] lacte atque pecore vīvunt, multumque[9] sunt in vēnātiōnibus; quae rēs[10] et cibī genere et cotīdiānā exercitātiōne et lībertāte vītae, quod ā puerīs[11] nūllō officiō aut disciplīnā assuēfactī[12] nihil omnīnō contrā voluntātem faciunt, et vīrēs alit et immānī corporum magnitūdine hominēs efficit. Atque in eam sē cōnsuētūdinem addūxērunt ut locīs[13] frīgidissimīs neque[14] vestītūs praeter pellēs habeant[15] quicquam, quārum propter exiguitātem magna est corporis pars aperta, et laventur in flūminibus.

Insignienträger (Germane).   Römischer Feldherr.

North Wind Picture Archives

A Roman general in full armor but wearing a laurel crown stands next to a German warrior, possibly one of the Suebi, who holds his tribe's standard.

[1] Ariovistus was a Sueban.

[2] refers to **hieme** *(fem.)* but agrees with **annus** *(masc.)*

[3] Pompey and Crassus had been elected to the consulship for 55 B.C., with Caesar's political support, on the understanding that they would gain for him a five-year extension of his term as proconsular governor of Gaul, giving him the opportunity to complete its conquest.

[4] *the German Usipetes*

[5] adverb

[6] *a thousand each;* What then was their combined military strength?

[7] *than a year*

[8] *for the most part*

[9] *they are much given to*

[10] *this manner of life,* subject of **alit** and **efficit**

[11] *from boyhood*

[12] *accustomed to* (literally, *by*)

[13] *ablative of place*

[14] with **et:** *not only not . . . but even*

[15] When the perfect tense has present perfect force (as **addūxērunt** here), primary sequence may be used.

Questions

1. What were the chief foods of the Suebi?
2. What do you infer was the Romans' chief food?
3. What was the nature of the military system of the Suebi?
4. What modern system of land ownership resembles theirs?
5. Why did the Germans cross the Rhine into Gaul? Where?

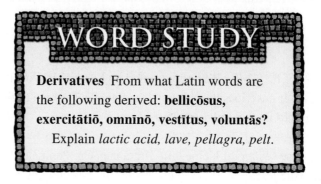

WORD STUDY

Derivatives From what Latin words are the following derived: **bellicōsus, exercitātiō, omnīnō, vestītus, voluntās?** Explain *lactic acid, lave, pellagra, pelt.*

Summary of Chapters 2–12. The Suebi tolerate the presence of traders solely that they may sell what they take in war. They do not allow the importation of wine. They ride bareback, often fighting on foot, making a speedy getaway on horseback if the fighting goes against them. They live in isolation, allowing no one to settle near their borders. They drive out the German Usipetes and Tencteri, who go to the Rhine, where they are held in check by the Menapii, a Gallic tribe, who have settlements on both sides of the river. The Germans, however, make a surprise attack and cross into Gaul. Caesar, knowing the fickle character of the Gauls, fears that they may unite with the Germans against him. He therefore decides to drive out the Germans. When their envoys come to him asking for lands in Gaul, he orders them to leave the country. They plead for a delay and gain a truce, but later make a treacherous attack upon the Roman cavalry.

THE BRIDGING OF THE RHINE

IV, **12.** In eō proeliō ex equitibus nostrīs interficiuntur IIII et LXX; in hīs vir fortissimus, Pīsō Aquītānus, amplissimō genere[1] nātus, cuius avus in cīvitāte suā rēgnum obtinuerat, amīcus ā senātū nostrō appellātus. Hic cum frātrī interclūsō ab hostibus[2] auxilium ferret, illum ex perīculō ēripuit, ipse equō vulnerātō dēiectus quoad potuit fortissimē restitit; cum circumventus, multīs vulneribus acceptīs, cecidisset, atque id frāter, quī iam proeliō excesserat, procul animadvertisset, incitātō equō, sē hostibus obtulit atque interfectus est.

[1] ablative of origin; Grammar Appendix, p. 498.3
[2] with **interclūsō**
[3] *for their own possessions* (**suis** is emphatic). Caesar wanted to give them a taste of their own medicine. Previously they had done their fighting in Gallic territory.

Summary of Chapters 13–15. After this attack, the Germans send some of their chiefs to ask for a truce. Caesar seizes them and then, advancing upon the leaderless force of Germans, annihilates it.

16. Germānicō bellō cōnfectō, multīs dē causīs Caesar statuit sibi Rhēnum esse trānseundum. Quārum illa fuit iūstissima, quod, cum vidēret Germānōs tam facile impellī ut in Galliam venīrent, suīs quoque rēbus[3] eōs

In order to cross rivers efficiently with thousands of **copiae**, **impedīmenta**, and **equī**, the Romans built bridges. This model shows Caesar's bridge over the Rhine according to the description in Book IV of *Dē Bellō Gallicō*.

Photri/AISA

[4] subject of **posse** and **audēre**

[5] predicate genitive of possession: *not in accord with the dignity*, etc. The building of the bridge over the Rhine, which had never been bridged before, was in part a shock tactic, a form of psychological warfare intended to impress the Germans and lower their morale.

[6] *he must make the effort*

15 timēre voluit, cum intellegerent et posse et audēre populī Rōmānī exercitum[4] Rhēnum trānsīre.

17. Caesar hīs dē causīs quās commemorāvimus Rhēnum trānsīre dēcrēverat; sed nāvibus trānsīre neque satis tūtum esse arbitrābātur neque suae neque populī Rōmānī dignitātis[5] esse statuēbat. Itaque, etsī summa
20 difficultās faciendī pontis prōpōnēbātur propter lātitūdinem, rapiditātem, altitūdinemque flūminis, tamen id sibi contendendum[6] aut aliter nōn trādūcendum exercitum exīstimābat.

Questions

1. What single reason does Caesar give for crossing the Rhine?
2. What other reasons can you give?
3. What method of crossing did he use?
4. What were his reasons for using this method?

VOCABULARY

Verbs

commemorō, 1 *mention*	[memoria]
dēcernō, -ere, dēcrēvī, dēcrētus *decide*	[cernō]
offerō, offerre, obtulī, oblātus *offer*	[ferō]
mē offerō *rush against*	

Review **amplus, eques, nāscor, tūtus.**

WORD STUDY

Derivatives From what Latin words are the following derived: **ēripiō, interclūdō, trānseō?**

Explain *amplitude, commemorate, proposition, renaissance.*

Summary of Chapters 18–19. Caesar invades Germany and terrifies the Germans. After eighteen days he returns to Gaul and destroys the bridge.[7]

[7] In World War II American troops were able to cross the Rhine by capturing a bridge at Remagen, about 15 miles north of where Caesar built his bridge. Near Remagen a Roman milestone of A.D. 162 was found, giving the distance to Cologne as **m(īlia) p(assuum) XXX.**

CAESAR'S INVASIONS OF BRITAIN

The Romanization of Britain may be said to begin with Caesar's two invasions of 55 and 54 B.C., although traders in search of tin had gone there for centuries before, and although the final conquest and consequent transformation of British culture began a hundred years later under the emperor Claudius. On August 25, 1946, in recognition of the significance of Caesar's invasion, a tablet "to commemorate the two thousandth anniversary of the landing" was unveiled at Deal (north of Dover), where historians think Caesar first set foot on British soil. It is hard for us to imagine what an adventure it was for the Romans to set sail over strange seas, from a port in a country that they were just conquering, to an entirely unknown land.

Caesar made no attempt at a permanent conquest, perhaps because he saw that it would take too long and he was afraid that the hostile Gallic tribes at his back might cause trouble. He was a long way from home. As the historian Tacitus said a century and a half later, Caesar did not hand Britain over to future generations of Romans but merely revealed it to them. But that in itself was a very important contribution.

Almost exactly a century after Caesar, when all of Gaul, thanks to his efforts, had not only been pacified but also Romanized, the Romans began the serious task of conquering Britain. This was under the emperor Claudius in A.D. 43. By the end of the century most of the island had been thoroughly Romanized.

The historian R. G. Collingwood, quoting Sir Mortimer Wheeler, writes of Roman London:

"Londinium was a civilized city, a comfortable one, with an efficient drainage system and an adequate water-supply. There were probably more buildings of stone and brick than at any subsequent period until after the Great Fire of 1666. There were more adequate and attractive facilities for bathing than ever until the latter part of Queen Victoria's reign."[1]

---

[1] R.G. Collingwood, *Roman Britain* (London, 1953), p. 58.

LESSON OBJECTIVES
- **Read**
  Caesar *Dē Bellō Gallicō* IV, 20–21
- **Review**
  Volitive Clauses

SCARCITY OF INFORMATION ABOUT BRITAIN

[1] *(being) left*

[2] ablative of time. Note that Caesar feels the need of justifying the invasion of Britain by putting the blame on the enemy.

[3] i.e., **ē Britanniā**

[4] Supply **esse.**

[5] = **futūrum esse**

[6] For **adīsset** see the Grammar Appendix, p. 529.

[7] **neque temere,** scarcely

[8] adverb

[9] *although he called*

[10] a series of indirect questions, depending on **reperīre**

[11] *the attempt*

[12] subject of **esse** and object of **praemittit**

[13] *passage*

[14] *to this point* (the modern Boulogne)

[15] The antecedent is **classem.**

[16] *Venetan* (not "Venetian")

[17] But Commius deserted Caesar in 52 B.C.

[18] *was considered great;* literally, *of great (value)*

[19] The antecedent is **civitātēs.**

[20] Supply **ut** before **adeat, hortētur,** and **nūntiet.**

[21] i.e., Caesar

[22] with **quantum:** *as far as opportunity,* etc.

[23] The antecedent is **ei:** *to one who;* descriptive relative clause

IV, 20. Exiguā parte aestātis reliquā,[1] Caesar, etsī in hīs locīs (quod omnis Gallia ad septentriōnēs vergit) mātūrae sunt hiemēs, tamen in Britanniam proficīscī contendit, quod omnibus ferē Gallicīs bellīs[2] hostibus nostrīs inde[3] subministrāta[4] auxilia intellegēbat; et, sī tempus ad
5 bellum gerendum dēficeret, tamen magnō sibi ūsuī fore[5] arbitrābātur, sī modo īnsulam adīsset,[6] genus hominum perspexisset, loca, portūs, aditūs cognōvisset, quae omnia ferē Gallīs erant incognita. Neque enim temere[7] praeter mercātōrēs illō[8] adit quisquam, neque eīs ipsīs quicquam praeter ōram maritimam atque eās regiōnēs quae sunt contrā Galliam nōtum est.
10 Itaque ēvocātīs[9] ad sē undique mercātōribus, neque quanta[10] esset īnsulae magnitūdō, neque quae aut quantae nātiōnēs incolerent, neque quem ūsum bellī habērent aut quibus īnstitūtīs ūterentur, neque quī essent ad maiōrem nāvium multitūdinem idōneī portūs reperīre poterat.

21. Ad haec cognōscenda priusquam perīculum[11] faceret, idōneum esse
15 arbitrātus C. Volusēnum[12] cum nāvī longā praemittit. Huic mandat ut, explōrātīs omnibus rēbus, ad sē quam prīmum revertātur. Ipse cum omnibus cōpiīs in Morinōs proficīscitur, quod inde erat brevissimus in Britanniam trāiectus.[13] Hūc[14] nāvēs undique ex fīnitimīs regiōnibus et quam[15] superiōre aestāte ad Veneticum[16] bellum fēcerat classem iubet
20 convenīre. Interim, cōnsiliō eius cognitō et per mercātōrēs perlātō ad Britannōs, ā complūribus eius īnsulae cīvitātibus ad eum lēgātī veniunt, quī polliceantur obsidēs dare atque imperiō populī Rōmānī obtemperāre. Quibus audītīs, līberāliter pollicitus hortātusque ut in eā sententiā permanērent, eōs domum remittit et cum eīs ūnā Commium, quem ipse,
25 Atrebātibus superātīs, rēgem ibi cōnstituerat, cuius et virtūtem et cōnsilium probābat, et quem sibi fidēlem[17] esse arbitrābātur, cuiusque auctōritās in hīs regiōnibus magnī habēbātur,[18] mittit. Huic imperat quās[19] possit adeat[20] cīvitātēs, hortēturque ut populī Rōmānī fidem sequantur, sēque[21] celeriter eō ventūrum nūntiet. Volusēnus, perspectīs regiōnibus
30 quantum eī facultātis[22] darī potuit quī[23] ex nāvī ēgredī ac sē barbarīs committere nōn audēret, quīntō diē ad Caesarem revertitur quaeque ibi perspexisset renūntiat.

Questions

1. At what time of year did Caesar go to Britain?
2. What were his reasons for crossing into Britain?
3. How did he try to get information about the island?
4. Why did Caesar and his forces set out for the land of the Morini?

GRAMMAR

Review of Volitive Clauses

Review volitive clauses in Lesson XXII.

Translation

1. "Persuade the Britons to send hostages and to refrain from war."
2. He urged his friend to investigate everything and to report as soon as possible.

VOCABULARY

Nouns

classis, -is f. *fleet* (class, classify)

nātiō, -ōnis f. *nation, tribe* **[nāscor]**

Adjective

exiguus, -a, -um small **[agō]**

Adverb

temere *rashly, without reason* (temerity)

Review **brevis, mātūrus.**

Summary of Chapter 22. The Morini submit as Caesar prepares to cross the Channel. He gathers together eighty transports for two legions and eighteen for the cavalry, besides several warships for the officers.

WORD STUDY

Derivatives Motto of the United States Marine Corps: **semper fidelis.**

From what Latin words are the following derived: **ēvocō, fidēlis, incognitus, līberāliter, trāiectus?**

Explain *converge, divergent, fidelity, incognito.*

LESSON LXXXI

MIDNIGHT SAILING

[1] *while they had carried out his order a little too slowly*

[2] *probably near the steep chalk cliffs of Dover*

[3] *chariot fighters*

[4] *ablative of accompaniment*

[5] *Note the imperfect.*

[6] *in deep water*

[7] *dative of agent with* **dēsiliendum, cōnsistendum, pugnandum.** Make it the subject in English.

IV, **23.** Hīs cōnstitūtīs rēbus, nactus idōneam ad nāvigandum tempestātem tertiā ferē vigiliā nāvēs solvit, equitēsque in ulteriōrem portum prōgredī et nāvēs cōnscendere et sē sequī iussit. Ā quibus cum[1] paulō tardius esset administrātum, ipse hōrā diēī circiter quārtā cum prīmīs
5   nāvibus Britanniam[2] attigit atque ibi in omnibus collibus expositās hostium cōpiās armātās cōnspexit. Hunc ad ēgrediendum nēquāquam idōneum locum arbitrātus, dum reliquae nāvēs eō convenīrent ad hōram nōnam in ancorīs exspectāvit. Interim lēgātīs tribūnīsque mīlitum convocātīs, et quae ex Volusēnō cognōvisset et quae fierī vellet ostendit. Hīs dīmissīs et
10   ventum et aestum ūnō tempore nactus secundum, datō signō et sublātīs ancorīs, circiter mīlia passuum VII ab eō locō prōgressus, apertō ac plānō lītore nāvēs cōnstituit.

   24. At barbarī, cōnsiliō Rōmānōrum cognitō, praemissō equitātū et essedāriīs,[3] reliquīs cōpiīs[4] subsecūtī nostrōs nāvibus ēgredī prohibēbant.[5]
15   Erat ob hās causās summa difficultās quod nāvēs propter magnitūdinem nisi in altō[6] cōnstituī nōn poterant; mīlitibus[7] autem, ignōtīs locīs, impedītīs manibus, magnō et gravī onere armōrum pressīs, simul et dē

Caesar was finally able to land in Britain after redeploying his warships. Notice that the standardbearer, holding his eagle aloft, urges on the other soldiers.

North Wind Picture Archives

nāvibus dēsiliendum et in flūctibus cōnsistendum et cum hostibus erat pugnandum; cum illī[8] aut ex āridō aut paulum in aquam prōgressī, omnibus membrīs expedītīs, nōtissimīs locīs, audācter tēla conicerent et equōs īnsuēfactōs[9] incitārent. Quibus rēbus nostrī perterritī atque huius omnīnō generis[10] pugnae imperītī nōn eādem alacritāte ac studiō quō in pedestribus[11] ūtī proeliīs cōnsuēverant ūtēbantur.

25. Quod ubi Caesar animadvertit, nāvēs[12] longās, quārum speciēs erat barbarīs inūsitātior, paulum removērī ab onerāriīs nāvibus et rēmīs incitārī et ad latus apertum[13] hostium cōnstituī, atque inde fundīs, sagittīs, tormentīs[14] hostēs prōpellī ac submovērī iussit. Quae rēs magnō ūsuī nostrīs fuit. Nam et nāvium figūrā et rēmōrum mōtū et inūsitātō genere tormentōrum permōtī barbarī cōnstitērunt ac paulum pedem rettulērunt. At nostrīs mīlitibus cūnctantibus, maximē propter altitūdinem maris, quī[15] decimae legiōnis aquilam[16] ferēbat obtestātus deōs ut ea rēs legiōnī fēlīciter ēvenīret, "Dēsilīte," inquit, "commīlitōnēs, nisi vultis aquilam hostibus prōdere; ego certē meum reī pūblicae atque imperātōrī officium praestiterō." Hoc cum magnā vōce dīxisset, sē ex nāvī prōiēcit atque in hostēs aquilam ferre coepit. Tum nostrī cohortātī inter sē[17] nē tantum dēdecus admitterētur, ūniversī ex nāvī dēsiluērunt. Hōs item ex proximīs nāvibus[18] cum cōnspexissent, subsecūtī hostibus appropinquāvērunt.

20

25

30

35

[8] *while they,* i.e., the Britons

[9] *trained*

[10] genitive with **imperiti;** see the Grammar Appendix, p. 495.4

[11] i.e., *on land*

[12] subject of **removērī, incitārī, cōnstituī.** Note change of subject in **hostēs... submovērī.**

[13] Which side—right or left? Why?

[14] *artillery*

[15] supply the antecedent: *the one who*

[16] The Roman *eagle* or ensign, like our flag, was regarded with patriotic, almost religious, respect; its loss was considered a great disgrace.

[17] *one another*

[18] Supply **ei:** *the men on the nearest ships* (used as subject of **cōnspexissent** and **appropinquāvērunt**).

Questions

1. Why did Caesar not land immediately?
2. What were the difficulties faced by the Romans?
3. With what types of troops did the Britons keep the Romans from landing?
4. What was Caesar's motive in telling the story of the standard-bearer?

GRAMMAR

Review of the Datives of Purpose and Reference

Review the datives of purpose and reference in Lesson XXVI.

Translation

1. Do you think that the ships will be any protection to us?
2. The shields were of no help to the soldiers struggling in the water.

VOCABULARY

Nouns

aestus, -ūs m. *tide*	(estuarine)
aquila, -ae f. *eagle*	(aquiline)
mōtus, -ūs m. *motion*	**[moveō]**
sagitta, -ae f. *arrow*	(Sagittarius, sagittate)

Adjective

ūniversus, -a, -um *all together*	**[ūnus + vertō]**

Verbs

expōnō, -ere, exposuī, expositus *put out, draw up*	**[pōnō]**
prōdō, -ere, -didī, -ditus *give (forth), betray*	**[dō]**

Idioms: **nāvis longa, nāvis onerāria**

WORD STUDY

Derivatives From what Latin words are the following derived: **alacritās, commīlitō, flūctus, ignōtus, inūsitātus, onerārius, praefectus?**

Explain *aquiline, arid, dismember, estuary, expository, fluctuate.*

Latīnum Hodiernum
Aquila[1]

Mīlitēs Rōmānī aquilam ante legiōnem ferēbant et nummī nostrī imāginem aquilae habent, sed paucī aquilam feram vīdērunt. In hortīs pūblicīs saepe vidērī potest. Ibi in caveā[2] sordidā trīstis sedet, velut rēx in exsiliō. Ō miseram captīvam![3]

Dēmocratica nōn est. Lībertātem amat sed modo suam. Aliās avēs contemnit, etiam aliās aquilās atque pullōs[4] suōs, sī fāma vēra est. In rūpibus excelsīs vel in summīs arboribus ex rāmulīs nīdum[5] turpem aedificat. Ibi, sī Plīniō, auctōrī optimō, crēdimus, usque ad merīdiem sedet. Post merīdiem cibum petit.

Ex caelō in terrā serpentem vidēre potest, quod oculōs optimōs habet. Nōn numquam dīcitur in saxum dē caelō testūdinem dēmittere ut frangātur. Quondam aquila in caput calvum[6] poetae clārissimī, ut fāma est, testūdinem dēmīsit. Ō miserum poētam!

[1] adapted from Norman W. DeWitt in *Classical Journal,* 49 (1954), p. 273.

[2] *cage*
[3] accusative of exclamation
[4] *young*
[5] *nest*
[6] *bald*

LESSON LXXXII

DIFFICULT FIGHTING

LESSON OBJECTIVE
- **Read**
Caesar *Dē Bellō Gallicō* IV, 26–27

IV, **26.** Pugnātum est ab utrīsque ācriter. Nostrī tamen, quod neque ōrdinēs servāre neque firmiter īnsistere neque signa subsequī poterant, atque alius[1] aliā ex nāvī quibuscumque signīs occurrerat sē aggregābat, magnopere perturbābantur; hostēs vērō, nōtīs omnibus vadīs, ubi ex lītore aliquōs singulārēs ex nāvī ēgredientēs cōnspexerant, incitātīs equīs, impedītōs adoriēbantur, plūrēs[2] paucōs circumsistēbant, aliī ab latere apertō in ūniversōs tēla coniciēbant. Quod cum animadvertisset Caesar, scaphās[3] longārum nāvium, item speculātōria nāvigia[4] mīlitibus complērī iussit, et quōs labōrantēs cōnspexerat hīs[5] subsidia submittēbat. Nostrī simul[6] in āridō cōnstitērunt, suīs omnibus cōnsecūtīs,[7] in hostēs impetum fēcērunt atque eōs in fugam dedērunt; neque longius prōsequī potuērunt, quod equitēs cursum tenēre atque īnsulam capere[8] nōn potuerant. Hoc ūnum ad prīstinam fortūnam[9] Caesarī dēfuit.

27. Hostēs proeliō superātī, simul[6] atque sē ex fugā recēpērunt, statim ad Caesarem lēgātōs dē pāce mīsērunt. Ūnā cum hīs lēgātīs Commius Atrebās vēnit, quem suprā dēmōnstrāverāmus ā Caesare in Britanniam praemissum. Hunc illī ē nāvī ēgressum, cum[10] ad eōs ōrātōris modō[11]

[1] *one from one vessel, another from another would join whatever standard he met*

[2] *several*

[3] *boats*

5 [4] *scout boats,* i.e., patrol craft

[5] *antecedent of* **quōs**

[6] *as soon as* (**atque** or **ac** is understood)

[7] *and their fellow soldiers caught up with them* (ablative absolute)

[8] *reach.* They and their ships were 10 still at the **ulterior portus**; see Lesson LXXXI, 23.

[9] *recognized by the Romans as an important factor in a general's success*

[10] *although*

15 [11] *as an envoy; What literally?*

The remains of a Roman theater in St. Albans, England. Since the Romans knew that the people who were garrisoned so far away would miss the comforts of home, they felt it was important to ensure that sports and dramatic entertainment were available. A single column stands on what used to be the stage. Remains of the semicircular seating area can be seen in the foreground.

Robert Estall/Stone

Caesaris mandāta dēferret, comprehenderant atque in vincula coniēcerant.
Tum, proeliō factō, remīsērunt[12] et in petendā pāce eius reī culpam in
20 multitūdinem contulērunt, et propter imprūdentiam ut ignōscerētur[13]
petīvērunt. Caesar questus quod,[14] cum ultrō, in continentem lēgātīs missīs,
pācem ab sē petīssent, bellum sine causā intulissent, ignōscere[15]
imprūdentiae[16] dīxit obsidēsque imperāvit. Quōrum illī partem statim
dedērunt, partem ex longinquiōribus locīs arcessītam paucīs diēbus sēsē
25 datūrōs dīxērunt. Intereā suōs in agrōs remigrāre iussērunt, prīncipēsque
undique convenīre et sē cīvitātēsque suās Caesarī commendāre coepērunt.

Questions

1. What advantage did the Britons have?
2. What caused confusion among the Romans?
3. Why did Caesar have no cavalry to pursue the enemy?
4. How did Caesar come to the aid of those in difficulty?
5. What two things did Caesar complain about to the Britons?

▣ VOCABULARY

Pronoun

quīcumque, quaecumque, quodcumque   [quī]
whoever, whatever

Verb

queror, querī, questus *complain*   (quarrel, querulous)

Adverb

ultrō *voluntarily*

WORD STUDY

Derivatives Distinguish carefully the forms and derivatives of
quaerō and **queror.** Derivatives of **quaerō** include *conquest,
query, quest, question;* of **queror,** *quarrel, querulous.*

From what Latin words are the following derived: **commendō,
comprehendō, continēns, imprūdentia, longinquus,
mandātum, remigrō, speculātōrius?**

Explain *aggregation, comprehension, mandate,
recommendation.*

STORM AND TIDE CAUSE TROUBLE

IV, **28.** Hīs rēbus pāce cōnfirmātā, diē quārtō postquam est in Britanniam ventum,[1] nāvēs XVIII dē quibus suprā dēmōnstrātum est, quae equitēs sustulerant, ex superiōre portū lēnī ventō solvērunt. Quae cum appropinquārent Britanniae et ex castrīs vidērentur, tanta tempestās subitō coorta est ut nūlla eārum cursum tenēre posset sed aliae eōdem unde erant 5 profectae referrentur,[2] aliae ad īnferiōrem partem īnsulae, quae est propius sōlis occāsum, magnō suō[3] cum perīculō dēicerentur. Quae[4] tamen, ancorīs iactīs, cum fluctibus complērentur, necessāriō adversā nocte[4] in altum prōvectae continentem petīvērunt.

29. Eādem nocte accidit ut esset lūna plēna,[5] quī diēs[6] maritimōs aestūs 10 maximōs in Ōceanō efficere cōnsuēvit, nostrīsque id erat incognitum. Ita ūnō tempore et longās nāvēs, quibus Caesar exercitum[7] trānsportandum cūrāverat quāsque in āridum subdūxerat, aestus complēbat, et onerāriās, quae ad ancorās erant dēligātae, tempestās afflīctābat, neque ūlla nostrīs facultās aut administrandī aut auxiliandī dabātur. Complūribus nāvibus 15 frāctīs, reliquae cum essent ad nāvigandum inūtilēs, magna tōtīus exercitūs perturbātiō facta est. Neque enim nāvēs erant aliae quibus reportārī possent,[8] et omnia deerant quae ad reficiendās nāvēs erant ūsuī; et, quod omnibus cōnstābat hiemārī in Galliā oportēre, frūmentum in hīs locīs[9] in hiemem prōvīsum nōn erat. 20

30. Quibus rēbus cognitīs, prīncipēs Britanniae, quī post proelium ad ea quae iusserat Caesar facienda convēnerant, inter sē collocūtī, cum et

[1] *they came* literally, *it was come*

[2] still part of the **ut** clause

[3] *to themselves*

[4] *Nevertheless, when after anchoring they were filling with water, in the face of the night,* etc.

[5] This statement has enabled astronomers to compute the date exactly, August 30 (55 B.C.).

[6] *time*

[7] Only part of the army had been transported in the warships.

[8] For the subjunctive see the Grammar Appendix, p. 504.10.

[9] i.e., in Britain. For **in hiemem** cf. our colloquial use of "against."

These roof tiles are from a first-century Roman villa in Fishbourne, England. The Romans constructed many buildings in the English countryside, expecting their occupation to be permanent. Parts of homes, municipal buildings, walls, and fortifications are not only visible but also in use today.

C.M. Dixon/Photo Resources

equitēs et nāvēs et frūmentum Rōmānīs deesse intellegerent, et paucitātem mīlitum ex castrōrum exiguitāte cognōscerent—quae hōc[10] erant etiam
25 angustiōra quod sine impedīmentīs Caesar legiōnēs trānsportāverat—optimum esse dūxērunt,[11] rebelliōne factā, frūmentō commeātūque nostrōs prohibēre et rem in hiemem prōdūcere; quod, hīs[12] superātīs aut reditū interclūsīs, nēminem posteā bellī īnferendī causā in Britanniam trānsitūrum cōnfīdēbant. Itaque rūrsus coniūrātiōne factā, paulātim ex
30 castrīs discēdere et suōs clam ex agrīs dēdūcere[13] coepērunt.

Questions

1. What became of the cavalry?
2. What happened to the main fleet?
3. What three things did the Romans lack?

GRAMMAR

Review of the Ablative of Separation

Review the ablative of separation in Lesson XXXVII.

Translation

1. Caesar was unwilling to depart from Britain until he received hostages.
2. The Britons thought that they could keep the Romans from their supplies.
3. "Let us cut these Romans off from (the possibility of) return; no one will cross the sea again to attack us."

VOCABULARY

Verbs

colloquor, colloquī, collocūtus	**[loquor]**
talk with, confer	
cōnstat *it is evident*	**[stō]**
cūrō, 1 *care for, cause (to be done)*	**[cūra]**

Review **clam, compleō, prope, subitō.**

WORD STUDY

Derivatives The moon was thought to have an effect not merely on the tide, as Caesar discovered, but also on the human mind: "lunatic" means *moonstruck*.

From what Latin words are the following derived: **auxilior, exiguitās, inūtilis, perturbātiō, prōvehō, rebelliō, reditus, reportō?**

Explain *colloquy, curative, lunacy, lunar, plenipotentiary.*

Lunatic

Latīnum Hodiernum
Scarabaeī

Mēnse Februāriō Annō Dominī MCMLXIV appāruērunt in scaenā Americānā quattuor iuvenēs Britannī (rē vērā Liverpolitānī), nōmine Jōhannes, Paulus, Georgius (trēs citharistae), cum tympanistā Ringō Stellā. Numquam posteā mūsica Americāna idem fuit.

Cantibus vel mollibus dē cruciātū amōris frustrātī, vel simplicibus dē auxiliō grātō amīcōrum, quantum stūdī apud adulēscentēs (praesertim apud puellās) excitāvērunt!

Prīmō seniōrēs frontem contrahēbant, mox tamen paulātim animōs remittēbant, tōta tandem nātiō Scarabaeomaniā capta est. Num quis hōdiē nōn memoriā tenet *Herī,* vel *Manum tuam prehendere velim,* vel *Succurite!* vel *Quantum requīrās, omnīnō amor est*?

Caesar Britannōs vīcit, Scarabaeī tōtum orbem terrārum.

Nōnne intelligitis nunc quid verbum "Scarabaeī" Latīnē significet, etiamsī Anglicē hoc verbum trēs litterās "e" contineat?

LESSON OBJECTIVES
- **Read**
  Caesar *Dē Bellō Gallicō* IV, 31, 34, 36
- **Review**
  Future Passive
  Participle and Gerund

NEW DIFFICULTIES

¹ *accident to his ships*. What literally?

² *from the fact that* (explained by the **quod** clause)

³ for **futūrum esse**. Its subject is **id**.

⁴ Translate as if **eārum nāvium quae**.

⁵ Supply **ea**.

⁶ impersonal

⁷ *he made it possible to sail well enough in the others;* **nāvigari** is used impersonally.

⁸ dative with **auxilium tulit**

⁹ *in a favorable position*. What literally?

¹⁰ i.e., Britons, to join the revolt

¹¹ descriptive relative clause

¹² *of freeing themselves forever*

¹³ *if they should drive*

¹⁴ *by this means*

¹⁵ *for them*

¹⁶ We say *as*.

¹⁷ *reach*

¹⁸ i.e., down the coast

IV, **31.** At Caesar, etsī nōndum eōrum cōnsilia cognōverat, tamen et ex ēventū¹ nāvium suārum et ex eō² quod obsidēs dare intermīserant, fore³ id quod accidit suspicābātur. Itaque ad omnēs cāsūs subsidia comparābat. Nam et frūmentum ex agrīs cotīdiē in castra cōnferēbat et quae⁴ gravissimē
5 afflīctae erant nāvēs, eārum māteriā atque aere ad reliquās reficiendās ūtēbātur, et quae⁵ ad eās rēs erant ūsuī ex continentī comportārī iubēbat. Itaque cum summō studiō ā mīlitibus administrārētur,⁶ XII nāvibus āmissīs, reliquīs ut nāvigārī satis commodē posset effēcit.⁷

Summary of Chapters 32–33. The Britons attack the seventh legion
10 while it is collecting grain. They use chariots, which give them the mobility of cavalry. Caesar comes to the rescue.

34. Quibus rēbus perturbātīs nostrīs⁸ tempore opportūnissimō Caesar auxilium tulit. Namque eius adventū hostēs cōnstitērunt, nostrī sē ex timōre recēpērunt. Quō factō, ad lacessendum hostem et committendum
15 proelium aliēnum esse tempus arbitrātus, suō sē locō⁹ continuit et, brevī tempore intermissō, in castra legiōnēs redūxit. Dum haec geruntur, nostrīs omnibus occupātīs, quī erant in agrīs reliquī discessērunt.¹⁰ Secūtae sunt continuōs complūrēs diēs tempestātēs quae et nostrōs in castrīs continērent¹¹ et hostem ā pugnā prohibērent. Interim barbarī nūntiōs in
20 omnēs partēs dīmīsērunt paucitātemque nostrōrum mīlitum suīs praedicāvērunt, et quanta praedae faciendae atque in perpetuum suī līberandī¹² facultās darētur, sī Rōmānōs castrīs expulissent,¹³ dēmōnstrāvērunt. Hīs rēbus¹⁴ celeriter magnā multitūdine peditātūs equitātūsque coāctā, ad castra vēnērunt.
25 **36.** Lēgātī ab hostibus missī ad Caesarem dē pāce vēnērunt. Hīs¹⁵ Caesar numerum obsidum quem ante imperāverat duplicāvit, eōsque in continentem addūcī iussit. Ipse idōneam tempestātem nactus paulō post mediam noctem nāvēs solvit; quae omnēs incolumēs ad continentem pervēnērunt; sed ex eīs onerāriae duae eōsdem portūs quōs¹⁶ reliquae
30 capere¹⁷ nōn potuērunt et paulō īnfrā¹⁸ dēlātae sunt.

Questions

1. What led Caesar to expect trouble?
2. What preparations did Caesar make?
3. How did he use the ships that could not be repaired?
4. What postponed the final battle?

GRAMMAR

Review of the Future Passive Participle and Gerund

Review the future passive participle and gerund in Lessons XXI and XXIII.

Translation

1. The men were sent to fight.
2. There was no chance of attacking.
3. Caesar was occupied in repairing the ships.
4. They went out for the purpose of collecting grain.

VOCABULARY

Adjective

continuus, -a, -um *successive*   [teneō]

Verbs

lacessō, -ere, -īvī, -ītus *attack*

praedicō, 1 *announce*   [dīcō, -āre]

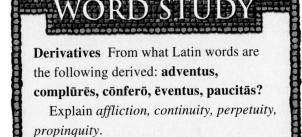

WORD STUDY

Derivatives From what Latin words are the following derived: **adventus, complūrēs, cōnferō, ēventus, paucitās?**

Explain *affliction, continuity, perpetuity, propinquity.*

Summary of Chapters 37–38. Three hundred soldiers from the two transports are attacked by the Morini. The Romans fight bravely and are rescued by reinforcements. Caesar then sends Labienus to pacify the Morini. Winter quarters are established among the Belgians. The Roman Senate decrees a thanksgiving of twenty days for Caesar's victories.

OUR HERITAGE

AMPHIBIOUS WARFARE— THEN AND NOW

Perhaps no aspect of Caesar's campaigns in Gaul illustrates more strikingly the similarity between the principles of ancient and modern warfare than does his account of the amphibious assault upon the British coast. The means and methods of warfare have changed very greatly in two thousand years, but the principles which underlie them theoretically remain the same. Caesar's neglect or ignorance of several of these principles very nearly brought disaster to the expedition.

Amphibious warfare, in which land troops are moved overseas and debark onto hostile territory, has always been one of the most hazardous and difficult operations of war. Its first requirement is that the attacker be able to maintain secure lines of communication from his bases to the area of operations. Since upon his return from Germany Caesar had forced the submission of most of the Morini, who occupied the coast from which he planned to sail, since troops had been dispatched to neutralize the remainder of the neighboring tribes, and finally since a force adequate to hold the harbor was to be left in Gaul, Caesar could be reasonably confident that his ships could move across the Channel unmolested.

The second necessity for a successful amphibious assault is command of the sea (and, today, command of the air) in the combat zone. It would appear that Caesar's defeat in 56 B.C. of the Venetans, the most powerful maritime nation in northern Gaul, and the large number of warships and transports which he had constructed for that campaign and which had now assembled for the British expedition, assured him that he would receive no serious challenge from hostile naval forces.

Another major consideration in amphibious warfare is the gathering of sufficient intelligence to enable the attacker to do three things: by knowledge of the enemy's location and concealment of his own, to deceive the enemy about the time and place of the intended landing; by assembling information about the enemy's coastline and beaches, to determine which spot is most favorable for landing heavily armed men from boats of shallow draft; and, finally, by having enough information about the tide and weather, to insure that the troops can be landed in calm water and that the invasion fleet will not be wrecked by storms. It was in the area of intelligence that Caesar most seriously failed. He admits that his interrogations of traders were unsatisfactory; instead, the traders themselves gave news of his plans to the Britons. The embassy of Commius likewise was unsuccessful, and Volusenus' exploratory survey of the coast could scarcely have revealed much about landing conditions on the coast, since he himself did not dare disembark. The originally intended landfall was but a narrow strip of beach, easily defended from the cliffs behind it, and Caesar was forced to move seven miles up the coast to a smoothly sloping beach free of obstacles.

A much more serious predicament arose when Caesar's men were set ashore in water too deep and waves too heavy to allow them to fight. Allied troops had similar difficulties in the landings in North Africa in 1942, although special landing craft had been designed to bring the troops almost up to dry land in France in 1944. In the emergency Caesar quickly improvised a method for landing the men from the warships of shallower draft, and rapidly discovered for himself the principle of clearing the beaches by naval shore bombardment. Caesar frankly admits that his legionaries were inexperienced in this type of warfare.

We could not expect Caesar to be familiar with all of the modern methods of weather prediction, but it seems strange that he and his staff were so unaware of the tides and the effect of the full moon upon them that they allowed a great part of the fleet to be swamped or wrecked. Of course, the English Channel is a notoriously treacherous body of water and subject to violent storms, like the one which so imperiled the Allied invasion of Normandy in 1944. So perhaps Caesar's failure to allow for this may be partially excused.

Once the first waves of attacking troops are landed, it is imperative that they advance far enough inland to seize the high ground surrounding the landing area, so that they can control the beachhead until their reinforcements and supplies are unloaded, and until all forces are ready to break out together, converting the action from amphibious to land warfare. It is very dangerous to be pinned down on a narrow beach by enemy infantry and artillery. If this happens, as it did when the Allies were on the Anzio beach in Italy in 1943, the enemy can concentrate all his forces against a very limited area. When Caesar's troops appeared, the Britons, perhaps unwittingly, adopted the proper defensive maneuver: while they could, they engaged the Romans in close combat at the shoreline. Furthermore, when the Britons finally did retire, Caesar was unable to extend his beachhead to any great distance, because his means of pursuit, the cavalry, had not been able to reach the scene of battle in time. Caesar openly admits his lack of success in this respect. When the cavalry did arrive four days later, it enabled him to inflict a decisive defeat upon the natives and to prevent their interference with his plans for returning to the continent.

In the light of modern amphibious warfare, this first expedition to Britain was not an unqualified success. The second expedition in 54 B.C. went better; Caesar had more troops, a larger fleet, and specially designed landing craft. Although he still underestimated the important part played by weather and was seriously hampered by storms before his departure and by the desertion of Dumnorix and the Haeduan cavalry, the whole fleet arrived as a unit at the undefended beach. The convoy was so large that its mere appearance had caused the natives to retreat to higher ground. The landing was unopposed, the movement of the troops inland almost immediate, and the cavalry effective in driving the defenders inland.

BRITAIN AND ITS PEOPLE

LESSON
OBJECTIVE
• **Read**
Caesar *Dē Bellō
Gallicō* V, 12–14

Book V of the *Gallic War,* from which Lessons LXXXV through LXXXVII are taken, gives an account of Caesar's second invasion of Britain (54 B.C.) and of the Gallic uprisings he faced upon his return.

Summary of Chapters 1–11. The winter following the first expedition to Britain is spent in preparation for a second invasion. After issuing orders for a large fleet to be ready early the next spring, Caesar sets out for Illyricum because he hears that the Pirustae are raiding the country adjoining his province. After subduing them, he sets out for Gaul, where he finds the ships ready. First, however, he decides to subdue the Treveri, among whom an anti-Roman spirit has developed. Caesar's appearance with an army is sufficient to quell the revolt. He then gives orders for his fleet to assemble at Portus Itius. He decides to take Dumnorix, the crafty and ambitious Haeduan, to Britain, for he fears that in his absence Dumnorix will cause trouble. While the troops are embarking and there is confusion in the Roman camp, Dumnorix escapes. He is soon captured and is killed while resisting arrest.

Caesar, leaving Labienus in charge in Gaul with three legions, takes five legions and two thousand cavalry with him in more than eight hundred ships. After some difficulty with the tide, he lands in Britain without opposition. He afterwards learns that the Britons, frightened by the number of ships, had taken to the hills. Leaving a force under Quintus Atrius sufficient to guard the ships, Caesar advances inland against the Britons and captures one of their forest strongholds. On the following day, while preparing

The Roman lighthouse at Dover, England, 380 feet high, as it appears today. The solidity of its construction (during the first century A.D.) is an indication of the Romans' interest in a permanent conquest and colonization of Britain.

Robert Estall/Stone

[1] *originated*, i.e., the natives of the interior claim to be the aboriginal inhabitants of Britain

[2] *as those from which they originated and from which they migrated to this place*

[3] *bars*

[4] *instead of*

[5] *tin* (literally, *white lead*). Today "white lead" is a different substance. The mines of Cornwall from early times furnished a large supply of tin, which was carried to all parts of the ancient world.

[6] *bronze*, a composition of copper and tin. Its widespread use at one period of history accounts for the name Bronze Age, immediately preceding the Iron Age. Earliest humans belonged to the Stone Age, when all tools were made of stone.

[7] *beech and fir*

[8] *hare*

[9] *chicken*

[10] *goose.* The origin of these taboos is uncertain.

[11] *for pastime and pleasure* (as pets)

[12] This chapter, while not geographically accurate, is interesting in that it describes Britain as the Romans imagined it to be, not one of whom at this time had ever sailed around it or explored its interior.

[13] *three-cornered*

[14] not from **appellō, -āre**

[15] *as it is from*

[16] *in mid-channel*

[17] Supply **esse**: *are thought to lie off the coast*; literally *opposite (the coast).*

[18] *winter solstice.* Caesar's source was incorrect on this point.

[19] *with a water (glass),* resembling in principle the sand or hourglass

[20] *the side of Britain facing Ireland*

[21] *as their opinion goes*

[22] Supply **latus.**

[23] Actually it is over twice as great, though the measurement of coast lines is difficult, and we do not know how Caesar arrived at his estimate. See the map on pages 158–159.

[24] *woad* (a plant). Compare the war paint of Native Americans.

[25] three different ablatives. What are they?

to pursue them, he learns that a great storm has destroyed about forty of his ships and damaged many others. These are repaired and beached. The Britons put Cassivellaunus in charge of their army.

V, 12. Britanniae pars interior ab eīs incolitur quōs nātōs[1] in īnsulā ipsī dīcunt; maritima pars ab eīs quī praedae ac bellī īnferendī causā ex Belgiō trānsiērunt (quī omnēs ferē eīs nōminibus cīvitātum appellantur quibus[2] ortī ex cīvitātibus eō pervēnērunt) et, bellō illātō, ibi remānsērunt atque
5 agrōs colere coepērunt. Hominum est īnfīnīta multitūdō crēberrimaque aedificia ferē Gallicīs cōnsimilia, pecoris magnus numerus. Ūtuntur aut aere aut nummō aureō aut tāleīs[3] ferreīs ad certum pondus exāmīnātīs prō[4] nummō. Nāscitur ibi plumbum[5] album in mediterrāneīs regiōnibus, in maritimīs ferrum, sed eius exigua est cōpia; aere[6] ūtuntur importātō.
10 Māteria cuiusque generis ut in Galliā est praeter fāgum atque abietem.[7] Leporem[8] et gallīnam[9] et ānserem[10] gustāre fās nōn putant; haec tamen alunt animī voluptātisque causā.[11] Loca sunt temperātiōra quam in Galliā, remissiōribus frīgoribus.

13.[12] Īnsula nātūrā triquetra,[13] cuius ūnum latus est contrā Galliam.
15 Huius lateris alter angulus, quī est ad Cantium, quō ferē omnēs ex Galliā nāvēs appelluntur,[14] ad orientem sōlem, īnferior ad merīdiem spectat. Hoc latus pertinet circiter mīlia passuum D. Alterum vergit ad Hispāniam atque occidentem sōlem; quā ex parte est Hibernia, īnsula dīmidiō minor (ut exīstimātur) quam Britannia, sed parī spatiō atque[15] ex Galliā est in
20 Britanniam. In hōc mediō cursū[16] est īnsula quae appellātur Mona; complūrēs praetereā minōrēs obiectae[17] īnsulae exīstimantur; dē quibus īnsulīs nōn nūllī scrīpsērunt diēs continuōs XXX sub brūmam[18] esse noctem. Nōs nihil dē eō reperiēbāmus, nisi certīs ex aquā[19] mēnsūrīs breviōrēs esse quam in continentī noctēs vidēbāmus. Huius[20] est longitūdō
25 lateris, ut[21] fert illōrum opīniō, DCC mīlium. Tertium est contrā septentriōnēs, cui partī nūlla est obiecta terra; sed eius angulus lateris maximē ad Germāniam spectat. Hoc[22] mīlia passuum DCCC in longitūdinem esse exīstimātur. Ita omnis īnsula est in circuitū vīciēs centum mīlium passuum.[23]

14. Ex hīs omnibus longē sunt hūmānissimī quī Cantium incolunt (quae
30 regiō est maritima omnis), neque multum ā Gallicā differunt cōnsuētūdine. Interiōrēs plērīque frūmenta nōn serunt, sed lacte et carne vīvunt pellibusque sunt vestītī. Omnēs vērō sē Britannī vitrō[24] īnficiunt, quod caeruleum efficit colōrem, atque hōc[25] horridiōrēs sunt in pugnā aspectū;[25] capillōque[25] sunt prōmissō.

Questions

1. What was the origin of the Britons?
2. What did the natives do with chickens?
3. What metals were once found in Britain?
4. Draw a map of Britain as described by Caesar.
5. Describe the inhabitants of Britain.

VOCABULARY

Nouns

ferrum, -ī n. *iron*   (ferroconcrete, ferrous)

pecus, pecoris n. *cattle*   [cf. **pecūnia**]

Adjective

interior, -ius *interior*   [inter]

WORD STUDY

Derivatives Believe it or not, *goose* and **ānser** are derived from the same word. Latin, English, and most European languages are descended from a language called Indo-European, which we know only from the common elements in its descendants. The masculine of goose is *gander,* which looks a bit more like **ānser.**

Brūma is from **brevima (diēs),** the *shortest day* of the year; **brevima** is a variant of **brevissima.** From what Latin words are the following derived: **cōnsimilis, importō, īnfīnītus, mediterrāneus?**

Explain *album, albumen, angular, commensurate, disgust, gustatory, gusto, oriole, plumber, ponderous, voluptuous.*

Summary of Chapters 15–43. The Romans on their march are attacked by British charioteers and cavalry, but beat them off. The Britons, by retreating, induce the Roman cavalry to pursue. Then, leaping down from their chariots, they fight on foot, relieving one another at intervals. Later, when Caesar sends out a detachment to forage, the Britons attack his scattered troops and drive them to seek the protection of the legions who are standing guard. The latter charge and drive the Britons off. Caesar leads his army to the Tamesis (Thames) River, which he fords, and again routs the enemy. Cassivellaunus, the British leader, avoiding a general engagement, confines himself to guerrilla tactics. Meanwhile the Trinovantes, the strongest British tribe of that region, surrender and send hostages to Caesar. Other tribes do the same. After an unsuccessful attack on the Roman camp, Cassivellaunus surrenders. Caesar returns to Gaul with his army and prisoners. During the two invasions of Britain, not a single ship carrying troops was lost.

Caesar finds it necessary, on account of the scarcity of provisions, to distribute his legions in six divisions among various Gallic tribes. The Gauls seize this opportunity to revolt. The Carnutes kill Tasgetius, whom Caesar had made king over them. Ambiorix, leader of the Eburones, attacks the camp of Sabinus and Cotta. In a conference, Ambiorix, assuming the role of friend, urges Sabinus to leave his camp and join either Cicero or Labienus. Sabinus and Cotta call a council of war. Sabinus favors acting upon the advice given by Ambiorix, but Cotta opposes. In the end Cotta yields. The army then leaves camp, loaded down with baggage, and is ambushed in a valley. Though the Romans fight bravely, they are gradually worn down. After Cotta is wounded, Sabinus has a conference with Ambiorix, at which he is treacherously murdered. The Romans then fight on until they are killed or commit suicide. Only a few escape; not one surrenders. Ambiorix then stirs up the Atuatuci and the Nervii. All proceed to attack Quintus Cicero, brother of the famous orator, in his winter quarters. All the Romans, including the sick and wounded, work day and night on the fortifications. At a conference with Cicero, the Nervii promise to let him and his army withdraw unharmed if Caesar will refrain from quartering his troops in their territory. Cicero is not deceived and refers them to Caesar. The Gauls then begin a siege. They set fire to the Roman camps with fire bombs and burning arrows.

LESSON LXXXVI

TWO RIVAL HEROES

LESSON OBJECTIVE
- **Read**
Caesar *Dē Bellō Gallicō* V, 44–45

V, 44. Erant in eā legiōne fortissimī virī, centuriōnēs, quī iam prīmīs ōrdinibus appropinquārent, T. Pullō et L. Vorēnus. Hī perpetuās inter sē contrōversiās habēbant uter alterī anteferrētur, omnibusque annīs[1] dē locō contendēbant. Ex hīs Pullō, cum ācerrimē ad mūnītiōnēs pugnārētur,

"Quid dubitās," inquit, "Vorēne, aut quem locum probandae virtūtis tuae exspectās? Hic diēs dē nostrīs contrōversiīs iūdicābit."

Haec cum dīxisset, prōcēdit extrā mūnītiōnēs quaeque pars hostium cōnfertissima est vīsa in eam irrumpit. Nē Vorēnus quidem sēsē tum vāllō continet, sed omnium veritus opīniōnem subsequitur. Mediocrī spatiō relictō, Pullō pīlum in hostēs immittit atque ūnum ex multitūdine prōcurrentem trāicit; quō[2] percussō exanimātōque, hunc scūtīs dēfendunt hostēs, in illum ūniversī tēla coniciunt neque dant prōgrediendī facultātem. Trānsfīgitur scūtum Pullōnī[3] et iaculum in balteō dēfīgitur. Āvertit hic cāsus vāgīnam[4] et gladium ēdūcere cōnantī[5] dextram morātur manum, impedītumque hostēs circumsistunt. Succurrit inimīcus illī Vorēnus et labōrantī subvenit. Ad hunc sē cōnfestim ā Pullōne omnis multitūdō convertit. Vorēnus gladiō rem gerit atque, ūnō interfectō, reliquōs paulum prōpellit; dum cupidius īnstat, in locum dēiectus īnferiōrem concidit. Huic rūrsus circumventō subsidium fert Pullō, atque ambō incolumēs, complūribus interfectīs, summā cum laude intrā mūnītiōnēs sē recipiunt. Sīc fortūna in certāmine utrumque versāvit[6] ut alter alterī inimīcus auxiliō salūtīque esset, neque diiūdicārī posset uter[7] virtūte anteferendus vidērētur.

45. Erat ūnus in castrīs Nervius nōmine Verticō, locō[8] nātus honestō, quī ad Cicerōnem perfūgerat suamque eī fidem praestiterat. Hic servō spē lībertātis magnīsque persuādet praemiīs ut litterās ad Caesarem dēferat. Hās ille in iaculō illigātās[9] effert, et Gallus inter Gallōs sine ūllā suspīciōne versātus ad Caesarem pervenit. Ab eō dē perīculīs Cicerōnis legiōnisque cognōscitur.

---

[1] *every year.* They were rivals for promotion (**locō**).

[2] the wounded Gaul (ablative absolute). Contrary to rule, **hunc** refers to the same person.

[3] dative of reference. In English a genitive is used.

[4] *scabbard.* It was pushed to one side and hard to get at.

[5] Supply ei: *when he tried.*

[6] *dealt with*

[7] *which seemed superior*

[8] ablative of origin

[9] Perhaps concealed in the shaft, which may have been wrapped as if mended.

Marcus Favonius Facilis was a centurion with the twentieth legion of the Pollian tribe. He fought with Caesar in Britain. Notice that he carries a **gladius**, a **pugiō**, and a **vītis** as a symbol of his rank.

Questions

1. Who quarreled and why?
2. Which attacked the enemy first?
3. What difficulty did he run into?
4. Which of the two soldiers was the braver?
5. How did Caesar get word of Cicero's situation?

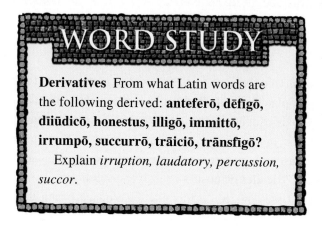

WORD STUDY

Derivatives From what Latin words are the following derived: **anteferō, dēfīgō, diiūdicō, honestus, illigō, immittō, irrumpō, succurrō, trāiciō, trānsfīgō?**

Explain *irruption, laudatory, percussion, succor.*

Summary of Chapters 46–47. Caesar immediately advances with two legions to relieve Cicero. The Treveri, elated by their recent victory over Sabinus, now menace Labienus, preventing him from joining Caesar.

A CODED MESSAGE AND A CLEVER TRICK

LESSON OBJECTIVE
• **Read**
Caesar *Dē Bellō Gallicō* V, 48, 52

V, **48.** Caesar vēnit magnīs itineribus in Nerviōrum fīnēs. Ibi ex captīvīs cognōscit quae apud Cicerōnem gerantur quantōque in perīculō rēs sit. Tum cuidam ex equitibus Gallīs magnīs praemiīs persuādet utī ad Cicerōnem epistulam dēferat. Hanc Graecīs[1] cōnscrīptam litterīs mittit, nē, interceptā epistulā, nostra ab hostibus cōnsilia cognōscantur. Sī adīre nōn 5 possit, monet ut trāgulam cum epistulā dēligātā intrā mūnītiōnēs castrōrum abiciat. In litterīs scrībit sē cum legiōnibus profectum celeriter adfore;[2] hortātur ut prīstinam virtūtem retineat. Gallus perīculum veritus, ut erat praeceptum, trāgulam mittit. Haec cāsū ad turrim adhaesit, neque ā nostrīs bīduō animadversa, tertiō diē ā quōdam mīlite cōnspicitur; ad Cicerōnem 10 dēfertur. Ille perlēctam[3] in conventū mīlitum recitat maximāque omnēs laetitiā afficit. Tum fūmī incendiōrum[4] procul vidēbantur, quae rēs omnem dubitātiōnem adventūs legiōnum expulit.

[1] probably Latin written in Greek letters. In effect the message was in code.

[2] for **adfutūrum esse**

[3] *read through (silently);* supply **epistulam.**

[4] not of campfires but of flaming villages fired by the Romans as they advanced

GAULS.

North Wind Picture Archives

The Romans were not the only army with a cavalry. These two horsemen are Gauls. Do you notice anything different about them, compared with the Romans?

Summary of Chapters 49–51. The Gauls rush to meet Caesar, who is
15 warned by a message from Cicero. By pretending fear, Caesar induces the
enemy to attack him on his own ground and defeats them with great loss.

52. Longius prōsequī veritus, quod silvae palūdēsque intercēdēbant,
omnibus suīs incolumibus, eōdem diē ad Cicerōnem pervēnit. Īnstitūtās
turrēs, testūdinēs mūnītiōnēsque hostium admīrātur; prōductā legiōne,
20 cognōscit nōn decimum quemque[5] esse reliquum mīlitem sine vulnere. Ex
hīs omnibus iūdicat rēbus quantō cum perīculō et quantā virtūte rēs sint
administrātae. Cicerōnem prō eius meritō legiōnemque collaudat;
centuriōnēs singillātim tribūnōsque mīlitum appellat, quōrum ēgregiam
fuisse virtūtem testimōniō Cicerōnis cognōverat.

[5] *not one soldier in ten*

Questions

1. How did Cicero get the message from Caesar?
2. What confirmation of the message did he get?
3. What percentage of Cicero's men were wounded?

Summary of Chapters 53–58. Despite this victory, the spirit of revolt
spreads fast among the Gauls, and Caesar decides to spend the winter with
his army. The leader of the Treveri prepares to attack the camp of
Labienus, but the latter, feigning fear, lures the enemy to the very walls of
his camp; then, by a surprise attack, he routs the Gauls, and the leader is
killed. After that, Caesar states that he "found Gaul a little more peaceful."

WORD STUDY

Derivatives From what Latin words are the following derived:
admīror, conventus, dubitātiō, intercēdō, praecipiō, singillātim?

Explain *adhesive, cohesive, conspicuous, epistolary, indubitable.*

Adhesive Tape

DĒ BELLŌ GALLICŌ VI–VII

Unit Objective
Read:

- Selections from Caesar *Dē Bellō Gallicō*, Books VI–VII

After spending nine years (58–50 B.C.) conquering and governing Gaul, Julius Caesar crossed the Rubicon River into Italy proper in 49 B.C., precipitating a Civil War. Within three years, he had overpowered his opposition and had become ruler of the Western world. In the next few years, he brought about many reforms in Roman political and economic life. Caesar has been painted, sculpted, and drawn throughout the ages. In this painting by Andrea del Sarto (c. 1487–1530), various conquered tribes bring tribute to their conqueror, Julius Caesar. Notice the variety of animals in this scene.

Scala/Art Resource, NY

391

GALLIC LEADERS

Coinage was used throughout the Roman world. This gold coin was minted by the Parisii, a tribe which settled in the area of modern-day Paris around 250–200 B.C. Horses, wild boars, and other animals are common motifs on Celtic coins.

Photo Bulloz, St. Germain en Laye

T he readings in Lessons LXXXVIII through XCIV, selected from Book VI of the *Gallic War,* are devoted to Caesar's comparison of the way of life of the Gauls with that of the Germans.

Summary of Chapters 1–10. Caesar, expecting a more serious revolt in Gaul, increases his force by three legions, one of which is supplied by Pompey. Ambiorix and the Treveri are plotting against him. The Nervii, Atuatuci, Menapii, and all the Germans on the Gallic side of the Rhine are in arms against the Romans, and the Senones are conspiring with the Carnutes and other states. Accordingly, before the winter is over, Caesar leads a strong force against the Nervii and compels them to surrender. He next marches against the Senones, and they, as well as the Carnutes, surrender. Caesar, now free to attack Ambiorix, proceeds to cut him off from allied aid. He first crushes the Menapii. Meanwhile, with reinforcements received from Caesar, Labienus defeats the Treveri. Caesar again builds a bridge and crosses the Rhine, partly to prevent the Germans from sending aid to the Treveri, partly to prevent Ambiorix from finding refuge in Germany. He learns that the Suebi have sent aid to the Treveri and are now mobilizing in a large forest.

VI, 11. Quoniam ad hunc locum[1] perventum est, nōn aliēnum esse vidētur dē Galliae Germāniaeque mōribus et quō[2] differant hae nātiōnēs inter sē prōpōnere. In Galliā nōn sōlum in omnibus cīvitātibus atque in omnibus pāgīs partibusque, sed paene etiam in singulīs domibus
5 factiōnēs sunt, eārumque factiōnum sunt prīncipēs quī summam auctōritātem eōrum[3] iūdiciō habēre exīstimantur, quōrum[4] ad arbitrium iūdiciumque summa omnium rērum cōnsiliōrumque redeat.[5]

12. Cum Caesar in Galliam vēnit, alterius factiōnis prīncipēs erant Haeduī, alterius Sēquanī. Hī cum per sē minus valērent, quod summa
10 auctōritās antīquitus erat in Haeduīs magnaeque eōrum erant clientēlae, Germānōs atque Ariovistum sibi adiūnxerant eōsque ad sē magnīs iactūrīs pollicitātiōnibusque perdūxerant. Proeliīs vērō complūribus factīs secundīs atque omnī nōbilitāte Haeduōrum interfectā, tantum potentiā antecesserant ut magnam partem clientium ab Haeduīs ad sē trādūcerent obsidēsque[6] ab

---

[1] i.e., in the story
[2] *in what respect*
[3] i.e., the Gauls
[4] The antecedent is **prīncipēs**, not **eōrum**: *so that to their decision.*
[5] *is referred*
[6] *(as) hostages*

eīs prīncipum fīliōs acciperent, et pūblicē iūrāre cōgerent nihil sē contrā
Sēquanōs cōnsilī[7] initūrōs,[8] et partem fīnitimī agrī per vim occupātam
possidērent[9] Galliaeque tōtīus prīncipātum obtinērent. Quā necessitāte
adductus Dīviciācus auxilī petendī causā Rōmam ad senātum profectus,
īnfectā rē, redierat. Adventū Caesaris factā commūtātiōne rērum, obsidibus
Haeduīs redditīs, veteribus clientēlīs restitūtīs, novīs per Caesarem
comparātīs, quod eī quī sē ad eōrum amīcitiam aggregāverant meliōre
condiciōne atque aequiōre imperiō sē ūtī[10] vidēbant, reliquīs rēbus[11] eōrum
grātiā dignitāteque amplificātā, Sēquanī prīncipātum dīmīserant. In eōrum
locum Rēmī successerant; quōs quod adaequāre apud Caesarem grātiā
intellegēbātur[12] eī[13] quī propter veterēs inimīcitiās nūllō modō cum
Haeduīs coniungī poterant, sē Rēmīs in clientēlam dicābant.[14] Hōs illī
dīligenter tuēbantur; ita et novam et repente collēctam auctōritātem
tenēbant. Eō tum statū[15] rēs erat ut longē prīncipēs habērentur Haeduī,
secundum locum dignitātis Rēmī obtinērent.

15
[7] depends upon **nihil**
[8] Supply **esse**; indirect statement depending upon **iūrāre**.
[9] *kept;* coordinate with **trādūcerent, acciperent, cōgerent** (lines 14–15)
20 [10] *that they were enjoying*
[11] *in all other respects*
[12] used impersonally: *because it was understood that these* (**quōs**) *equaled (the Haeduans)*
[13] *those (other tribes)*
[14] with **in clientēlam:** *they attached*
25 *themselves*
[15] *situation*

Questions

1. How were the Gallic leaders chosen?
2. Which tribe had the most power before Caesar came?
3. Which tribe was first after Caesar's arrival? Which was second?

▓ VOCABULARY

Adjective

vetus, (gen.) **veteris** *old*   (veteran, inveterate)

Verbs

iūrō, 1 *swear*   **[iūs]**
tueor, tuērī, tūtus *guard*   (tutelage, intuition)

Adverb

repente *suddenly*

Review **colligō, nōn sōlum... sed etiam, redeō.**

WORD STUDY

Derivatives From what Latin words are the following derived:
adaequō, antīquitus, arbitrium, clientēla, commūtātiō, iactūra, īnfectus, iūdicium, necessitās, pollicitātiō, potentia, status?

Explain *adjunct, dedicate, inveterate, status, tutor, veteran.*

THE DRUIDS

[1] *of some account* (with **aliquō**)

[2] = **plēbs**

[3] *over them* (the enslaved plebeians)

[4] *as*

[5] *religious questions*

[6] the Druids

[7] all the Gauls

[8] *likewise*

[9] *did not abide by;* **dēcrētō** is ablative

[10] dative; the antecedent is **hi**

[11] *from these;* see the Grammar Appendix, p. 496.4

[12] genitive

[13] old form of **honor**

[14] for the more usual **quis**

[15] Chartres preserves the name of the *Car´nutēs.* Perhaps the annual Council on the Isle of Man is a survival of such meetings.

[16] They met in groves of oak trees, which were sacred, as was the mistletoe which grew on them. Our use of mistletoe at Christmas is an inheritance from the Druids.

[17] *system* of Druidism

[18] adverb

Among the ancient Celts, the Druids were priests and learned individuals. They were held in high esteem and enjoyed enormous prestige in the community. Druid cults were found in Gaul, Britain, and Ireland. Much of what we know about the Druids comes from Roman texts, since the Druids themselves preferred to pass on their knowledge orally rather than by writing it down.

VI, 13. In omnī Galliā eōrum hominum quī aliquō sunt numerō[1] atque honōre genera sunt duo. Nam plēbēs[2] paene servōrum habētur locō, quae nihil audet per sē, nūllī adhibētur cōnsiliō. Plērīque, cum aut aere aliēnō aut magnitūdine tribūtōrum aut iniūriā potentiōrum premuntur, sēsē in
5 servitūtem dant nōbilibus; quibus in hōs[3] eadem omnia sunt iūra quae[4] dominīs in servōs. Sed dē hīs duōbus generibus alterum est Druidum, alterum equitum. Illī rēbus dīvīnīs intersunt, sacrificia pūblica ac prīvāta prōcūrant, religiōnēs[5] interpretantur. Ad hōs magnus adulēscentium numerus disciplīnae causā concurrit, magnōque hī[6] sunt apud eōs[7] honōre. Nam ferē
10 dē omnibus contrōversiīs pūblicīs prīvātīsque cōnstituunt; et, sī quod est facinus admissum, sī caedēs facta, sī dē hērēditāte, dē fīnibus contrōversia est, īdem[8] dēcernunt; praemia poenāsque cōnstituunt; sī quī aut prīvātus aut populus eōrum dēcrētō nōn stetit,[9] sacrificiīs prohibent. Haec poena apud eōs est gravissima. Quibus[10] ita est prohibitum, hī numerō impiōrum
15 habentur, hīs[11] omnēs dēcēdunt, aditum eōrum sermōnemque dēfugiunt, nē quid ex contāgiōne incommodī[12] accipiant, neque hīs petentibus iūs redditur neque honōs[13] ūllus commūnicātur. Hīs autem omnibus Druidibus praeest ūnus, quī summam inter eōs habet auctōritātem. Hōc mortuō, aut, sī quī[14] ex reliquīs praestat dignitāte, succēdit, aut, sī sunt parēs plūrēs, suffrāgiō
20 Druidum dēligitur; nōn numquam etiam armīs dē prīncipātū contendunt. Hī

Ancient Art & Architecture

certō annī tempore in fīnibus Carnutum,[15] quae regiō tōtīus Galliae media habētur, cōnsīdunt in locō cōnsecrātō,[16] hūc omnēs
25 undique quī contrōversiās habent conveniunt eōrumque dēcrētīs iūdiciīsque pārent. Disciplīna[17] in Britanniā reperta atque inde in Galliam trānslāta exīstimātur; et
30 nunc quī dīligentius eam rem cognōscere volunt plērumque illō[18] discendī causā proficīscuntur.

S. Vidler/SuperStock

Stonehenge, located on Salisbury Plain in southern England, is just one of hundreds of ancient stone circles found in Europe. The ring of stones, which are thought to have been transported all the way from Wales, is 108 feet in diameter. Of the original thirty upright stones, all once capped by a continuous circle of lintels, only seventeen remain. See also page 328.

Questions

1. What three classes were there among the Gauls?
2. What were the functions and powers of the Druids?
3. What business did the Druids transact at their annual meetings?

VOCABULARY

Noun

religiō, -ōnis f. *religion, superstition*

Verbs

adhibeō, -ēre, adhibuī, adhibitus *hold toward, admit to*	[habeō]
commūnicō, 1 *share*	[commūnis]
pāreō, -ēre, pāruī, pāritūrus *obey* (with dative)	

Review **admittō, adulēscēns, caedēs, hūc, morior.**

WORD STUDY

Derivatives *Proxy* is shortened from *procuracy* and therefore means *taking care* of something *for* someone.

From what Latin words are the following derived: **cōnsecrātus, dēfugiō, sacrificium, tribūtum?**

Explain *consecration, heredity, interpretation, suffrage.*

DRUIDS AND KNIGHTS

LESSON OBJECTIVE
- **Read**
  Caesar *Dē Bellō Gallicō* VI, 14–15

[1] *to be exempt from*

[2] Note the force of the prefix.

[3] *these principles*

[4] *although*

[5] like the Egyptian priests and their hieroglyphs ("sacred writing")

[6] *pay less attention to the memory*

[7] *prove*

[8] *souls;* they believed in reincarnation

[9] Supply **hominēs** as subject. Some of our Halloween customs are thought to go back to the Druids.

[10] *whenever*

[11] noun: *need*

[12] *and this,* explained by the **uti** clauses

[13] *warded off injuries inflicted (by others)*

[14] *(in proportion) as*

[15] *retainers (a Gallic word)*

VI

14. Druidēs ā bellō abesse[1] cōnsuērunt neque tribūta ūnā cum reliquīs pendunt. Tantīs excitātī praemiīs et suā sponte multī in disciplīnam conveniunt et ā parentibus propinquīsque mittuntur. Magnum ibi numerum versuum ēdiscere[2] dīcuntur. Itaque annōs nōn nūllī vīcēnōs in

5 disciplīnā permanent. Neque fās esse exīstimant ea[3] litterīs mandāre, cum[4] in reliquīs ferē rēbus, pūblicīs prīvātīsque ratiōnibus, Graecīs ūtantur litterīs. Id mihi duābus dē causīs īnstituisse videntur; quod neque in vulgus disciplīnam efferrī velint[5] neque eōs quī discunt litterīs cōnfīsōs minus memoriae studēre[6]—quod ferē plērīsque accidit ut praesidiō litterārum

10 dīligentiam in perdiscendō ac memoriam remittant. In prīmīs hoc volunt persuādēre,[7] nōn interīre animās,[8] sed ab aliīs post mortem trānsīre ad aliōs; atque hōc maximē ad virtūtem excitārī[9] putant, metū mortis neglēctō. Multa praetereā dē sīderibus atque eōrum mōtū, dē mundī ac terrārum magnitūdine, dē rērum nātūrā, dē deōrum immortālium vī ac potestāte

15 disputant et iuventūtī trādunt.

Ancient Art & Architecture

15. Alterum genus est equitum. Hī cum[10] est ūsus[11] atque aliquod bellum incidit (quod[12]

20 ante Caesaris adventum ferē quotannīs accidere solēbat, utī aut ipsī iniūriās īnferrent aut illātās prōpulsārent),[13]

25 omnēs in bellō versantur, atque eōrum ut[14] quisque est genere cōpiīsque amplissimus, ita plūrimōs circum sē

30 ambactōs[15] clientēsque habet. Hanc ūnam grātiam potentiamque nōvērunt.

Druids were in charge of educating the sons of chiefs and guarding the sacred traditions. Oak trees and mistletoe figured heavily in their rituals, as did human sacrifice. They resisted the Latin culture and were eventually suppressed by the Romans.

Questions

1. What exemptions did the Druids have?
2. What were the teaching methods of the Druids?
3. What was their belief about the souls of the dead?
4. Why did the Druids not put their teachings in writing?

VOCABULARY

Nouns

metus, -ūs m. *fear*

vulgus, -ī n. *common people*   (vulgar, divulge)

Verb

intereō, -īre, -iī, -itūrus *perish*   [eō]

Review **efferō, neglegō, suā sponte.**

WORD STUDY

Suffixes The suffix **-tō (-sō, -itō)** is added to the stems of past participles to form verbs expressing the idea of *keeping on* ("frequentative" verbs): **prōpulsō** (from **prōpulsus**), *keep on warding off.*

From what Latin words are the following derived: **disputō, immortālis?**

Explain *disciple, disputant, divulge, immortality, mundane, sidereal, spontaneity, vulgarity, Vulgate.*

The great Gallic Hammer-God. The hammer associates him with the heavens and the Underworld, and the rustic panpipe links him with the woodlands. The Romans appear to have identified him with their own Jupiter, Diespiter, and Silvanus. By the Gauls he was variously called Sucellus or Taranis. About two hundred of his images have been found.

LESSON OBJECTIVE

- **Read**
  Caesar *Dē Bellō Gallicō* VI, 16–18

RELIGION

¹ *(as) ministers*

² *figures (of men)*

³ *twigs*

⁴ = **deis**

⁵ Instead of their Gallic names, Caesar assigns to the deities of the Gauls the names of Roman gods on the basis of supposed resemblances. This was the Roman way of dealing with the Greek gods; with them Zeus was merely the Greek name for Jupiter, Hera for Juno, etc.

⁶ *they say*

⁷ Supply **colunt.**

⁸ *as*

⁹ *crafts*

¹⁰ subjunctive in implied indirect statement, representing a future perfect

¹¹ *they vow*

¹² because Dis (Pluto) was god of Hades, i.e., of Darkness; A trace of a similar custom of reckoning time by nights has survived from Anglo-Saxon days in the expression "fortnight" ("fourteen nights").

¹³ For holidays beginning in the evening we may compare Christmas Eve. All Jewish holidays begin and end at sunset. The phases of the moon probably had a great deal to do with this, for it is comparatively easy to mark time by full moons, each marking the lapse of a *month* (related to "moon" and Latin **mēnsis**).

VI, **16.** Nātiō est omnis Gallōrum admodum dēdita religiōnibus; atque ob eam causam quī sunt affectī graviōribus morbīs, quīque in proeliīs perīculīsque versantur, aut prō victimīs hominēs immolant aut sē immolātūrōs vovent, administrīsque¹ ad ea sacrificia Druidibus ūtuntur,
5 quod, prō vītā hominis nisi hominis vīta reddātur, nōn posse deōs immortālēs plācārī arbitrantur; pūblicēque eiusdem generis habent īnstitūta sacrificia. Aliī immānī magnitūdine simulācra² habent, quōrum contexta vīminibus³ membra vīvīs hominibus complent; quibus incēnsīs, circumventī flammā exanimantur hominēs. Supplicia eōrum quī in fūrtō
10 aut latrōciniō aut aliquā noxiā sint comprehēnsī grātiōra dīs⁴ immortālibus esse arbitrantur; sed, cum eius generis cōpia dēficit, etiam ad innocentium supplicia dēscendunt.

17. Deōrum maximē Mercurium⁵ colunt. Huius sunt plūrima simulācra; hunc omnium inventōrem artium ferunt,⁶ hunc viārum atque itinerum
15 ducem, hunc ad quaestūs pecūniae mercātūrāsque habēre vim maximam arbitrantur; post hunc⁷ Apollinem et Mārtem et Iovem et Minervam. Dē hīs eandem ferē quam⁸ reliquae gentēs habent opīniōnem: Apollinem morbōs dēpellere, Minervam operum atque artificiōrum⁹ initia trādere, Iovem imperium deōrum tenēre, Mārtem bella regere. Huic, cum proelium
20 committere cōnstituērunt, ea quae bellō cēperint¹⁰ plērumque dēvovent;¹¹ cum superāvērunt, animālia capta immolant, reliquās rēs in ūnum locum cōnferunt. Multīs in cīvitātibus hārum rērum exstrūctōs cumulōs locīs cōnsecrātīs cōnspicārī licet.

18. Gallī sē omnēs ab Dīte patre prōgnātōs praedicant idque ab
25 Druidibus prōditum dīcunt. Ob eam causam spatia omnis temporis nōn numerō diērum sed noctium¹² fīniunt; diēs nātālēs et mēnsium et annōrum initia sīc observant ut noctem¹³ diēs subsequātur.

Questions

1. Who was chief god of the Gauls?

2. Why did the Gauls sacrifice human beings?

3. Which god did they consider their ancestor?

WORD STUDY

Derivatives From what Latin words are the following derived: **artificium, inventor, noxa, prōgnātus?**

Explain *accumulate, artificial, cumulative, furtive, immolate, implacable, mercantile, morbid, noxious, victimize, votive*.

MARRIAGES AND FUNERALS; CENSORSHIP

[1] *property,* as the plural shows

[2] *they combine with*

[3] *profits, income*

[4] *survives* (with **vitā**)

[5] *over.* Cf. page 2 for the similar Roman **patria potestās.**

[6] *ablative of origin*

[7] *What does the plural prove?*

[8] *as is done in the case of slaves,* i.e., by torture

[9] *if (their guilt),* etc.

[10] *before our time*

[11] *those states which*

[12] *have it ordained by law,* explained by the **uti** clauses

[13] *if anyone has heard anything*

[14] *anyone*

[15] *rash*

[16] *whatever seems best;* this is the practice of many totalitarian states today.

[17] *of advantage*

VI, **19.** Virī, quantās pecūniās[1] ab uxōribus dōtis nōmine accēpērunt, tantās ex suīs bonīs, aestimātiōne factā, cum dōtibus commūnicant.[2] Huius omnis pecūniae coniūnctim ratiō habētur frūctūsque[3] servantur; uter eōrum vītā superāvit,[4] ad eum pars utrīusque cum frūctibus superiōrum temporum
5 pervenit. Virī in[5] uxōrēs sīcutī in līberōs vītae necisque habent potestātem; et cum pater familiae illūstriōre locō[6] nātus dēcessit, eius propinquī conveniunt et dē morte, sī rēs in suspīciōnem vēnit, dē uxōribus[7] in servīlem modum[8] quaestiōnem habent, et sī[9] compertum est, ignī atque omnibus tormentīs excruciātās interficiunt. Fūnera sunt prō cultū Gallōrum
10 magnifica; omniaque quae vīvīs cāra fuisse arbitrantur in ignem īnferunt, etiam animālia; ac paulō suprā hanc memoriam[10] servī et clientēs quōs ab eīs amātōs esse cōnstābat, iūstīs fūneribus cōnfectīs, ūnā cremābantur.

20. Quae cīvitātēs[11] commodius suam rem pūblicam administrāre exīstimantur habent lēgibus sānctum,[12] sī quis quid[13] dē rē pūblicā ā
15 fīnitimīs rūmōre ac fāmā accēperit, utī ad magistrātum dēferat nēve cum quō[14] aliō commūnicet, quod saepe hominēs temerāriōs[15] atque imperītōs falsīs rūmōribus terrērī et ad facinus impellī et dē summīs rēbus cōnsilium capere cognitum est. Magistrātūs quae
20 vīsa sunt[16] occultant, quaeque esse ex ūsū[17] iūdicāvērunt multitūdinī prōdunt. Dē rē pūblicā nisi per concilium loquī nōn concēditur.

A bronze statue of a Gallic divinity. This is possibly Cernunnos, a Celtic god whose significance is unknown but whose cult was widespread from northern Italy, throughout Romano-Celtic Gaul, and into Britain.

Photo Bulloz, St. Germain en Laye

Questions

1. What rights did the Gallic women have?
2. What power did the husband have over his wife?
3. What was an individual required to do if he or she got information about public matters?

WORD STUDY

Derivatives From what Latin words are the following derived: **coniūnctim, cultus, dēcēdō, falsus, magnificus, quaestiō, servīlis, temerārius?**

Explain *cremate, crematory, decease, excruciating, funereal, inquest.*

DESCRIPTION OF THE GERMANS[1]

[1] Compare with the description of the Suebi (Lesson LXXVIII).

[2] *from childhood*

[3] *for a single year*

[4] with **quantum**

[5] *elsewhere*

[6] *captivated by fixed habits (of life);* see the Grammar Appendix, p. 498.3

[7] *for agriculture*

[8] object of **expellant**

[9] *contentment*

[10] Similar yet different is Tacitus' remark, put in the mouth of a Briton criticizing the Romans: **ubi sōlitūdinem faciunt pācem appellant.**

[11] explained by **cēdere** and **audēre**

[12] *a sign of*

VI, **21.** Germānī multum ab hāc cōnsuētūdine differunt. Nam neque Druidēs habent quī rēbus dīvīnīs praesint neque sacrificiīs student. Deōrum numerō eōs sōlōs dūcunt quōs cernunt et quōrum apertē opibus iuvantur, Sōlem et Vulcānum et Lūnam; reliquōs nē fāmā quidem
5 accēpērunt. Vīta omnis in vēnātiōnibus atque in studiīs reī mīlitāris cōnsistit; ā parvīs[2] labōrī ac dūritiae student.

22. Agrī cultūrae nōn student, maiorque pars eōrum vīctūs in lacte, cāseō, carne cōnsistit. Neque quisquam agrī modum certum aut fīnēs habet propriōs; sed magistrātūs ac prīncipēs in annōs singulōs[3] gentibus
10 cognātiōnibusque hominum quantum et quō locō vīsum est agrī[4] attribuunt, atque annō post aliō[5] trānsīre cōgunt. Eius reī multās afferunt causās: nē assiduā cōnsuētūdine captī[6] studium bellī gerendī agrī cultūrā[7] commūtent; nē lātōs fīnēs parāre studeant potentiōrēsque humiliōrēs[8] possessiōnibus expellant; nē accūrātius ad frīgora atque aestūs vītandōs
15 aedificent; nē qua oriātur pecūniae cupiditās, quā ex rē factiōnēs dissēnsiōnēsque nāscuntur; ut animī aequitāte[9] plēbem contineant, cum suās quisque opēs cum potentissimīs aequārī videat.

23. Cīvitātibus maxima laus est quam lātissimē circum sē, vāstātīs fīnibus, sōlitūdinēs habēre.[10] Hoc[11] proprium[12] virtūtis exīstimant, expulsōs

The baths from the fourth century A.D. at Trier, Germany, are just some of the remains from the Roman occupation. Trier, founded by Augustus in 15 B.C. as Augusta Treverorum, was named after the Treveri, an eastern Gallic people who had inhabited the area.

Ronald Sheridan/Ancient Art & Architecture Collection

agrīs fīnitimōs[13] cēdere neque quemquam prope sē audēre cōnsistere. Simul 20
hōc sē fore tūtiōrēs arbitrantur, repentīnae incursiōnis timōre sublātō. Cum
bellum cīvitās aut illātum dēfendit aut īnfert,[14] magistrātūs quī eī bellō
praesint et vītae necisque habeant potestātem dēliguntur. In pāce nūllus est
commūnis magistrātus, sed prīncipēs regiōnum atque pāgōrum inter suōs iūs
dīcunt[15] contrōversiāsque minuunt. Latrōcinia nūllam habent īnfāmiam quae 25
extrā fīnēs cuiusque cīvitātis fīunt, atque ea[16] iuventūtis exercendae ac
dēsidiae[17] minuendae causā fierī praedicant. Hospitem violāre fās nōn
putant; quī quācumque dē causā ad eōs vēnērunt ab iniūriā prohibent
sānctōsque habent hīsque omnium domūs patent vīctusque commūnicātur.

Questions

1. What were the chief German foods?
2. How did the Gauls and Germans differ?
3. What was the German attitude toward robbery?
4. How did the government differ in war and peace?
5. What advantages were claimed for the German system of public ownership of land?

WORD STUDY

Derivatives Cognātiō is from **co-** and **gnātus,** whose later form was **nātus.** Cf. English *cognate. Cheese* comes from **cāseus,** through the French. When you are "assiduous" you *sit by* (**ad-sedeō**) a job.

Assiduous

From what Latin words are the following derived: **accūrātus, aequitās, dissēnsiō, dūritia, īnfāmia, possessiō, sōlitūdō, vīctus?**

Explain *casein, diminutive, hospital, hospitality, infamy, inviolate, victuals, volcano, vulcanize.*

Summary of Chapter 24. The Gauls had once been powerful enough to invade and seize the most fertile districts of Germany; but now, as a result of their contact with civilization, they have deteriorated to such an extent that they have grown accustomed to defeat at the hands of the Germans.

THE HERCYNIAN FOREST AND ITS ANIMALS

[1] *for one unencumbered* (with baggage)

[2] i.e., by miles

[3] *stag*

[4] Reindeer have two horns, which they shed yearly. Caesar, or his informant, must have seen one when it had just shed one horn.

[5] *than those horns*

[6] *elk*

[7] *goats*

[8] *spotted appearance*

[9] *legs*

[10] *joints.* Such "nature faking" is known even today; see the "Hodong" story on p. 406.

[11] *beds*

[12] *whenever*

[13] *hunters*

[14] *modifies* **arborēs**

[15] i.e., the trees

[16] *against these*

VI, **25.** Hercyniae silvae lātitūdō VIIII diērum iter expedītō[1] patet; nōn enim aliter fīnīrī potest, neque mēnsūrās[2] itinerum nōvērunt. Multa in eā genera ferārum nāscī cōnstat quae reliquīs in locīs vīsa nōn sint; ex quibus quae maximē differant ā cēterīs et memoriae prōdenda videantur
5 haec sunt.

26. Est bōs cervī[3] figūrā, cuius ā mediā fronte inter aurēs ūnum[4] cornū exsistit excelsius magisque dērēctum hīs[5] quae nōbīs nōta sunt cornibus. Ab eius summō sīcut palmae rāmīque lātē diffunduntur. Eadem est fēminae marisque nātūra, eadem fōrma magnitūdōque cornuum.

27. Sunt item quae appellantur alcēs.[6] Hārum est cōnsimilis caprīs[7]
10 figūra et varietās[8] pellium; sed magnitūdine paulō antecēdunt mutilaeque sunt cornibus et crūra[9] sine articulīs[10] habent; neque quiētis causā prōcumbunt neque, sī quō afflīctae cāsū concidērunt, ērigere sēsē possunt. Hīs sunt arborēs prō cubīlibus;[11] ad eās sē applicant atque ita paulum modo
15 reclīnātae quiētem capiunt. Quārum ex vēstigiīs cum[12] est animadversum ā vēnātōribus[13] quō sē recipere cōnsuērint, omnēs[14] eō locō aut ab rādīcibus subruunt aut accīdunt arborēs, tantum ut speciēs eārum[15] stantium relinquātur. Hūc[16] cum sē cōnsuētūdine reclīnāvērunt, īnfirmās arborēs pondere afflīgunt atque ūnā ipsae concidunt.

Animals always played a significant role for the Romans. This mosaic shows Orpheus, the Thracian musician who could charm not only animals but also trees, rivers, and stones with his lyre. How many of these animals can you identify?

Giraudon/Art Resource, NY

28. Tertium est genus eōrum quī ūrī[17] appellantur. Hī sunt magnitūdine 20
paulō īnfrā elephantōs; speciē et colōre et figūrā taurī. Magna vīs eōrum
est et magna vēlōcitās; neque hominī neque ferae quam cōnspexērunt
parcunt. (Hōs foveīs[18] captōs interficiunt. Hōc sē labōre dūrant
adulēscentēs atque hōc genere vēnātiōnis exercent; et quī plūrimōs ex hīs
interfēcērunt, relātīs in pūblicum cornibus quae[19] sint testimōniō, magnam 25
ferunt laudem.) Sed assuēscere ad hominēs nē parvulī[20] quidem exceptī
possunt. Amplitūdō cornuum et figūra et speciēs multum ā nostrōrum
boum[21] cornibus differt. Haec[22] conquīsīta ab labrīs[23] argentō
circumclūdunt atque in amplissimīs epulīs[24] prō pōculīs[25] ūtuntur.

[17] Some believe that here Caesar is describing the almost extinct aurochs (the European cousin of the American buffalo), now found only in zoos and game preserves; others hold that he means the broad-horned "wild ox," the ancestor of the domesticated cattle. The last of these wild oxen, the true aurochs, died in Poland in 1627.
[18] *pits*
[19] *to serve as proof*
[20] *i.e., ūrī*
[21] *genitive plural of* **bōs**
[22] *supply* **cornua**
[23] *at the edges*
[24] *feasts*
[25] *cups*

Questions

1. How was the "urus" trapped?
2. What were its chief characteristics?
3. What was peculiar about the elk described by Caesar?

VOCABULARY

Noun

laus, laudis f. *praise* [**laudō**]

Verbs

dērigō (dīrigō), -ere, dērēxī, dērēctus *direct;* [**regō**]
  dērēctus *straight*
fīniō, -īre, -īvī, -ītus *limit, determine* [**fīnis**]

Adverb

sīcut (sīcutī) *as if, as it were* [**sīc + ut/utī**]

Review **cōnstat, cornū, parcō, quiēs.**

WORD STUDY

Derivatives The motto of the state of Maine is **Dirigo.**
  To "caper" is to act like a *goat* (**capra**). The old-fashioned
"cab" bounced around like a *goat;* some taxicabs still do.
  From what Latin words are the following derived: **accīdō,
amplitūdō, cōnsimilis, diffundō, varietās?**
  Explain *aural, bovine, Capricorn, eradicate, excelsior, finite,
inarticulate, mutilate, radical, ramification, toreador, vestige.*

Summary of Chapters 29–44. Caesar, finding it impossible to pursue the Suebi in their forests, decides to return to Gaul. As a constant threat to the Germans, he leaves a large part of the bridge standing, protected by a garrison. Ambiorix is still at large, and Caesar devotes all his energy toward his capture. He divides his army into four divisions to prevent the escape of Ambiorix, but that wily chieftain always eludes capture. At last Caesar gives up the pursuit and, after placing his legions in winter quarters, returns to Italy.

Latīnum Hodiernum
Damma Imparicrūs[1]

[1] *deer with unequal legs;* adapted from Norman W. DeWitt in *Classical Journal,* 47 (1952), p. 149.
[2] *annihilation*
[3] *sideways*

Virī perītī nōs certiōrēs faciunt omnium animālium ea tantum quae ad loca ubi vīvant aptissima sint perniciem[2] vītāre posse. Aut Nātūra benigna, ut vidētur, aut quaedam fortūna animālia ad loca aptē accommodāvit.

Cuius reī exemplum mīrum est quod linguā Americānā *Sidehill Hodong,* Latīnē *damma imparicrūs* appellātur. Gignitur, sī fāmae crēdī potest, in Arizōnā tantum. Cuius cīvitātis lātē patet pars ubi montēs continuī sunt, plānitiēs nūlla, arborēs paucissimae. Quae ad loca hoc animal mīrō modō idōneum est. Nam crūra alterius partis breviōrēs sunt quō celerius loca dēclīvia per trānsversum[3] trānscurrat. Sī in plānum forte venit, in circulōs frūstrā circumcursat. Huius animālis summa fēlīcitās est numquam plānitiem vidēre. Nōnne Nātūra mīrābilis est?

Sī dīcēs illōs quī huic fābulae crēdant stultōs esse equidem hoc nōn negābō.

LESSON XCV

VERCINGETORIX TAKES CHARGE

LESSON OBJECTIVE
- **Read**
Caesar *Dē Bellō Gallicō* VII, 4, 8

Vercingetorix, the Gallic leader who heads the final desperate revolt against the Romans in 52 B.C., is the dominant figure of Book VII (Lessons XCV through C) of the *Gallic War*.

Summary of Chapters 1–3. The Gauls, learning of political unrest at Rome, feel that the hour for freedom has come. This is the third and greatest of the Gallic revolts (the first was that of the Veneti and their allies; the second, that of Ambiorix). At a secret council a general uprising is planned. The Carnutes strike the first blow by massacring the Romans in Cenabum (Orléans).

VII, 4. Similī ratiōne ibi Vercingetorīx, Celtillī fīlius, Arvernus, summae potentiae adulēscēns, cuius pater prīncipātum tōtīus Galliae obtinuerat et ob eam causam, quod rēgnum appetēbat, ā cīvitāte erat interfectus, convocātīs suīs clientibus, facile incendit.[1] Cognitō eius cōnsiliō, ad arma concurritur. Prohibētur ā patruō[2] suō reliquīsque prīncipibus, quī hanc temptandam fortūnam nōn exīstimābant; expellitur ex oppidō Gergoviā. Nōn dēsistit tamen atque in agrīs habet dīlēctum[3] egentium ac perditōrum.[4] Hāc coāctā manū, quōscumque adit ex cīvitāte, ad suam sententiam perdūcit; hortātur ut commūnis lībertātis causā arma capiant, magnīsque coāctīs cōpiīs, adversāriōs suōs, ā quibus paulō ante erat ēiectus, expellit ex cīvitāte. 10

Rēx ab suīs appellātur. Dīmittit quōqueversus[5] lēgātiōnēs; obtestātur ut in fidē maneant. Celeriter sibi omnēs quī Ōceanum 15 attingunt adiungit; omnium cōnsēnsū ad eum dēfertur imperium. Quā oblātā potestāte, omnibus hīs cīvitātibus obsidēs imperat, certum numerum mīlitum 20 ad sē celeriter addūcī iubet, armōrum quantum quaeque cīvitās

[1] i.e., the clients
[2] *uncle* 5
[3] *levy*
[4] *of the needy and desperate*
[5] *in every direction*

The Romans were not the only ones who honored their leaders on their coinage. Here is Vercingetorix, the first hero of Gaul, on a coin that dates from the first century B.C.

Ronald Sheridan/Ancient Art & Architecture Collection

6 *how many arms each state should produce and by what time*

7 *Cévennes*

8 *all alone;* One man had a better chance of getting across than an army. "It can't be done," they said—and so Caesar did it.

9 *paths*

domī quodque ante tempus efficiat[6] cōnstituit; in prīmīs equitātuī studet. Summae dīligentiae summam imperī sevēritātem addit; magnitūdine
25 supplicī dubitantēs cōgit. Nam maiōre commissō dēlictō, ignī atque omnibus tormentīs necat, leviōre dē causā, auribus dēsectīs aut singulīs effossīs oculīs, domum remittit, ut sint reliquīs documentō et magnitūdine poenae perterreant aliōs.

Summary of Chapters 5–7. The Bituriges join the revolt. Caesar
30 hastens from Italy to Gaul on receipt of the news. He reinforces his troops at Narbo (Narbonne) in the Province, which is threatened with invasion. Caesar's problem is to reach his scattered legions through possibly hostile tribes. As usual, he depends on speed.

8. Etsī mōns Cebenna,[7] quī Arvernōs ab Helviīs disclūdit, dūrissimō
35 tempore annī altissimā nive iter impediēbat, tamen, discussā nive sex in altitūdinem pedum atque ita viīs patefactīs, summō mīlitum labōre ad fīnēs Arvernōrum pervēnit. Quibus oppressīs inopīnantibus, quod sē Cebennā ut mūrō mūnītōs exīstimābant, ac nē singulārī[8] quidem umquam hominī eō tempore annī sēmitae[9] patuerant, equitibus imperat ut quam lātissimē
40 possint vagentur, ut quam maximum hostibus terrōrem īnferant.

Questions
1. How did Vercingetorix raise an army?
2. How did he become leader of all the Gauls?
3. How did he keep the various tribes faithful?
4. Why did Caesar catch the Arvernians unprepared?

In the Hautes Alpes region of Provence, France, the mountains are covered with snow all year, even in the summer. Crossing this region was therefore treacherous at any time.

Hubertus Kanus/Photo Researchers

WORD STUDY

Derivatives From what Latin words are the following derived: **adversārius, appetō, cōnsēnsus, disclūdō, documentum?**

Explain *corpus delicti, dissect, document, perdition.*

Summary of Chapters 9–16. Caesar gathers together his scattered troops before the Gauls are aware of what is going on. In rapid succession he captures several towns and then advances against Avaricum (Bourges). This place the Gauls had considered impregnable and had therefore spared, while following a "scorched earth" policy in the rest of the country in their effort to check Caesar's advance by cutting off his supplies. Though harassed in the rear by Vercingetorix, who concentrates on attacking the Romans' foraging parties, Caesar begins the siege of Avaricum.

ROMAN SPIRIT

VII

17. Summā difficultāte reī frūmentāriae affectō exercitū, usque eō ut[1] complūrēs diēs frūmentō mīlitēs caruerint,[2] et, pecore ex longinquiōribus vīcīs adāctō, extrēmam famem sustinuerint, nūlla tamen vōx est ab eīs audīta populī Rōmānī maiestāte[3] et superiōribus victōriīs[3]
5 indigna. Quīn etiam Caesar cum in opere singulās legiōnēs appellāret, et, sī[4] acerbius[5] inopiam ferrent, sē dīmissūrum oppugnātiōnem dīceret, ūniversī ab eō nē id faceret petēbant sīc sē complūrēs annōs, illō imperante, meruisse[6] ut nūllam ignōminiam acciperent, numquam, īnfectā rē, discēderent; hoc sē ignōminiae locō lātūrōs,[7] sī inceptam
10 oppugnātiōnem relīquissent; praestāre omnēs perferre acerbitātēs quam nōn cīvēs Rōmānōs quī perfidiā Gallōrum interīssent ulcīscī.

Summary of Chapters 18–56. Vercingetorix tempts Caesar to attack him, but Caesar, finding him too well entrenched, resumes the siege of Avaricum. The Gauls then accuse Vercingetorix of treason because he did
15 not attack the Romans when he was in a position to do so. He successfully defends himself against this charge. The Gauls with renewed determina-

[1] *so much so that*

[2] *were without,* with ablative

[3] ablative with **indigna,** *unworthy*

[4] The clause depends upon **dimissūrum.**

[5] with **ferrent:** *suffer too severely (from)*

[6] depends (with **sē** as subject) on the idea of saying in **petēbant**

[7] *that they would regard as* (literally, *in the place of*)

Paris has come a long way in the past two thousand years since the Île de la Cité, a tiny island in the middle of the Seine River, was first inhabited by the Parisii tribe. You can see the even smaller Île St. Louis just behind the Île de la Cité and the cathedral of Notre Dame de Paris, begun in the twelfth century, on the right.

MOPY/Rapho Agence/Photo Researchers

tion resolve to hold Avaricum at any cost. Vercingetorix sends a strong
reinforcement. The besieged manage to set fire to the Roman siege works
and display marked heroism. At length, however, Avaricum falls, and
most of the inhabitants are killed. Vercingetorix consoles his troops for 20
the loss of the town by stating that he had from the beginning opposed
the defense of the place as untenable. He raises fresh troops. Caesar now
marches along the Elaver (Allier) River, passing, no doubt, the site of
Vichy (the hot springs of Vichy were known in antiquity). Vercingetorix
anticipates Caesar in seizing the hillside near Gergovia, and Caesar can 25
only follow. At this point the Haeduans, who were on their way to join
Caesar, mutiny at the instigation of their leader, who had been bribed, but
Caesar, making a forced march, meets them and wins them back to his
cause. He returns to Gergovia just in time to save his camp from capture
by Vercingetorix. Later the Romans attack the town but are badly 30
defeated. In spite of the critical situation, Caesar does not, as his enemies
might expect, retreat to the Province but goes north to protect his supplies
at his headquarters on the River Loire.

57. Dum haec apud Caesarem geruntur, Labiēnus cum quattuor
legiōnibus Luteciam[8] proficīscitur. Id est oppidum Parīsiōrum positum 35
in īnsulā flūminis Sēquanae. Cuius adventū ab hostibus cognitō, magnae
ex fīnitimīs cīvitātibus cōpiae convēnērunt. Summa imperī trāditur
Camulogenō Aulercō. Is cum animadvertisset perpetuam esse palūdem
quae īnflueret in Sēquanam atque illum omnem locum magnopere
impedīret, hīc cōnsēdit. 40

[8] the capital of the **Parisii** (the
original "Parisians"), on the site of
modern Paris. The spelling **Lutecia**,
in place of the more usual **Lutetia**,
is that of most of the best
manuscripts.

Questions
1. Whom did Caesar send to Paris?
2. Where was ancient Paris situated?
3. What was the greatest hardship for the Romans?

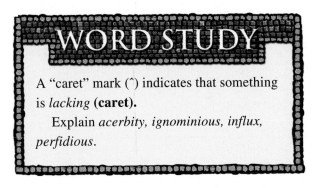

WORD STUDY

A "caret" mark (^) indicates that something
is *lacking* (**caret**).
    Explain *acerbity, ignominious, influx,
perfidious.*

Summary of Chapters 58–68. Labienus retires to Metlosedum (Melun), which he captures. He then again marches toward Lutecia, which he finds in flames. He then learns of Caesar's defeat at Gergovia and receives alarming reports of a general Gallic uprising. Labienus decides to join Caesar and reaches him on the third day. The Haeduans now openly revolt and demand the supreme command, but at a council of the Gauls the command is given to Vercingetorix, who orders the Gauls to furnish hostages and troops, especially cavalry. Caesar sends to Germany for cavalry. The Gallic cavalry attack but are defeated. Vercingetorix heads for Alesia and occupies it. Caesar follows and plans to shut up the Gauls in that town by a series of trenches around it.

LESSON XCVII

THE SIEGE OF ALESIA

LESSON OBJECTIVE
- **Read**
Caesar *Dē Bellō Gallicō* VII, 69, 76

VII, **69.** Ipsum erat oppidum in colle summō admodum ēditō locō, ut nisi obsidiōne expugnārī nōn posse vidērētur. Ante oppidum plānitiēs circiter mīlia passuum tria in longitūdinem patēbat; reliquīs ex omnibus partibus collēs, mediocrī interiectō spatiō, oppidum cingēbant. Sub mūrō, quae pars collis ad orientem sōlem spectābat, hunc omnem locum[1] cōpiae Gallōrum complēverant fossamque et māceriam[2] sex in altitūdinem pedum praedūxerant. Eius mūnītiōnis quae ab Rōmānīs īnstituēbātur circuitus X mīlia passuum tenēbat.[3] Castra opportūnīs locīs erant posita ibique castella[4] XXIII facta, quibus in castellīs interdiū[5] statiōnēs pōnēbantur, nē qua subitō ēruptiō fieret; haec eadem noctū firmīs praesidiīs tenēbantur.

Summary of Chapters 70–75. The Gauls attempt to interfere with Caesar's operations but are repulsed in a great slaughter. Vercingetorix sends his cavalry to get reinforcements. Food runs short and is rationed. Caesar constructs an inner and an outer line of siege works, the former to hem Vercingetorix in Alesia, the latter to defend his own army from attack from without, for Caesar had already learned that the Gauls were raising a great army for the relief of Alesia.

76. Operā Commī fidēlī atque ūtilī superiōribus annīs erat ūsus in Britanniā Caesar; prō quibus meritīs cīvitātem[6] eius immūnem[7] esse iusserat, iūra lēgēsque reddiderat atque ipsī[8] Morinōs attribuerat. Tanta tamen ūniversae Galliae cōnsēnsiō fuit lībertātis vindicandae[9] et prīstinae bellī laudis recuperandae ut neque beneficiīs neque amīcitiae memoriā movērentur,[10] omnēsque et animō et opibus in id bellum incumberent.[11] Coāctīs equitum mīlibus VIII et peditum circiter CCL, haec in Haeduōrum fīnibus recēnsēbantur, et praefectī cōnstituēbantur.[12] Omnēs alacrēs et fīdūciae plēnī ad Alesiam proficīscuntur; neque erat omnium quisquam quī aspectum modo tantae multitūdinis sustinērī posse arbitrārētur, praesertim ancipitī[13] proeliō, cum ex oppidō ēruptiōne pugnārētur, forīs[14] tantae cōpiae equitātūs peditātūsque cernerentur.

[1] **hunc omnem locum**, i.e., **eam partem (quae... spectābat)**
[2] *wall*
[3] *extended*
[4] Eight of these have been found. Alesia is now Mont Auxois, near Dijon. During a recent drought crops were found to be growing in certain places. It was concluded that they were drawing moisture from the walls of the ancient town, which lay underneath.
[5] *in the daytime*
[6] i.e., the Atrebatians
[7] *free from tribute*
[8] Commius, as ruler. In 50 B.C. Commius, who had once been a prisoner in Britain (see Lessons LXXX and LXXXII), escaped to that island and there became a powerful king.
[9] *agreement to claim*
[10] Supply **Galli**, including Commius.
[11] *lent their efforts*
[12] The representatives of the different states formed a war council, thus producing further division of authority, when what was needed was one commander in chief with supreme power.
[13] *on two fronts*
[14] *outside*

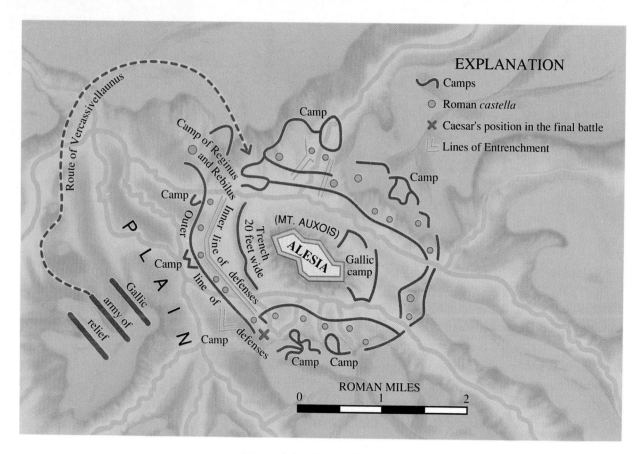

Plan of the siege of Alesia

Questions

1. Describe the location of Alesia.
2. What two things led the Gauls to forget Caesar's previous kindnesses?
3. How many Gallic soldiers came to the rescue of Alesia?

VOCABULARY

Nouns

fīdūcia, -ae f. *confidence* (fiduciary)

plānitiēs, -ēī f. *plain* [**plānus**]

Adjective

mediocris, -e *moderate* [**medius**]

Verb

recuperō, 1 *get back, recover*　　　　　　[capiō]

Adverb

admodum *very (much)*　　　　　　　　　　[modus]

Review **ēditus, opportūnus, praesertim, prīstinus.**

WORD STUDY

Derivatives From what Latin words are the following derived: **ēruptiō, fidēlis, interdiū, intericiō?**

Explain *fidelity, fiduciary, immunity, incumbent, infidel, recuperate, replenish, vindication.*

A Roman army camp included towers, walls, and trenches to help protect it against invaders, especially in a potentially hostile territory. Any invading force would be slowed down by the outerworks, giving those in the towers the opportunity to better defend themselves.

Wayne Rowe

A HORRIBLE SUGGESTION

LESSON
OBJECTIVE
• **Read**
Caesar *Dē Bellō Gallicō* VII, 77

[1] *voted for*

[2] *should not, it seems (to me), be passed over*

[3] *Let my speech deal with those.*

[4] for **istud**; *it is the subject and is explained by* **posse.**

[5] *(men) who*

[6] *I might approve, if I saw*

[7] *the standing (of its backers) has so much weight with me*

[8] depends on **Quid**

[9] *do not* (literally, *be unwilling to),* the three infinitives depend on it

VII, **77.** At eī quī Alesiae obsidēbantur, praeteritā diē quā auxilia suōrum exspectāverant, cōnsūmptō omnī frūmentō, ignōrantēs quid in Haeduīs gererētur, conciliō coāctō, dē exitū suārum fortūnārum cōnsultābant. Apud quōs variīs dictīs sententiīs, quārum pars dēditiōnem,
5 pars, dum vīrēs essent, ēruptiōnem cēnsēbat,[1] nōn praetereunda[2] vidētur ōrātiō Critognātī propter eius singulārem ac nefāriam crūdēlitātem.

Hic summō in Arvernīs ortus locō et magnae habitus auctōritātis, "Nihil," inquit, "dē eōrum sententiā dictūrus sum quī turpissimam servitūtem dēditiōnis nōmine appellant, neque hōs habendōs cīvium locō
10 neque adhibendōs ad concilium cēnseō. Cum hīs mihi rēs sit[3] quī ēruptiōnem probant; quōrum in cōnsiliō omnium vestrum cōnsēnsū prīstinae residēre virtūtis memoria vidētur. Animī est ista[4] mollitia, nōn virtūs, paulisper inopiam ferre nōn posse. Quī[5] sē ultrō mortī offerant facilius reperiuntur quam quī dolōrem patienter ferant. Atque ego hanc
15 sententiam probārem[6] (tantum apud mē dignitās potest[7]), sī nūllam praeterquam vītae nostrae iactūram fierī vidērem; sed in cōnsiliō capiendō omnem Galliam respiciāmus, quam ad nostrum auxilium concitāvimus. Quid, hominum mīlibus LXXX ūnō locō interfectīs, propinquīs cōnsanguineīsque 20 nostrīs animī[8] fore exīstimātis, sī paene in ipsīs cadāveribus proeliō dēcertāre cōgentur? Nōlīte[9] hōs vestrō auxiliō spoliāre quī vestrae salūtis causā suum 25 perīculum neglēxērunt; nec stultitiā ac temeritāte vestrā aut animī imbēcillitāte omnem Galliam prōsternere et 30 perpetuae servitūtī subicere.

The inland waterways connecting many of the long rivers in France provided transportation for the various Gallic tribes. Trade goods could be moved much more economically from one region to another in barges, such as the one in this relief. It looks as if even the dog will be going along for the ride.

Ronald Sheridan/Ancient Art & Architecture Collection

"Quid[10] ergō meī cōnsilī est? Facere quod nostrī maiōrēs nēquāquam parī bellō Cimbrōrum Teutonumque fēcērunt; quī in oppida compulsī ac similī inopiā subāctī, eōrum corporibus quī aetāte ad bellum inūtilēs vidēbantur vītam sustinuērunt, neque sē hostibus trādidērunt. Cuius reī sī exemplum nōn habērēmus, tamen lībertātis causā īnstituī et posterīs prōdī pulcherrimum iūdicārem.[11] Nam quid illī simile bellō fuit? Vāstātā Galliā, Cimbrī, magnāque illātā calamitāte, fīnibus quidem nostrīs aliquandō[12] excessērunt atque aliās terrās petīvērunt; iūra, lēgēs, agrōs, lībertātem nōbīs relīquērunt. Rōmānī vērō quid petunt aliud aut quid volunt, nisi invidiā adductī, quōs[13] fāmā nōbilēs potentēsque bellō cognōvērunt, hōrum in agrīs cīvitātibusque cōnsīdere atque hīs aeternam iniungere servitūtem? Neque enim umquam aliā condiciōne bella gessērunt. Quod sī ea quae in longinquīs nātiōnibus geruntur ignōrātis, respicite fīnitimam Galliam, quae in prōvinciam redācta, iūre et lēgibus commūtātīs, secūribus[14] subiecta perpetuā premitur servitūte!"

35
40
45

[10] *What is my plan?*
[11] *I should consider*
[12] *at last*
[13] Supply **esse;** the antecedent is **hōrum.**
[14] Freely, *authority.* The lictors accompanying the consul carried bundles of rods **(fascēs)** enclosing an ax **(secūris)** the former representing the consul's power to flog a criminal and the latter, his right to put him to death.

Questions

1. What three suggestions were made in the council of the Gauls?
2. What was the objection of Critognatus to fighting their way out?
3. In what way, according to Critognatus, were the Romans worse than the Cimbri?

WORD STUDY

Derivatives From what Latin words are the following derived: **cōnsultō, ignōrō, patienter, praetereō, resideō, subiciō, subigō, temeritās?**

Explain *consultative pact, eternity, ignoramus, imbecile, nefarious, prostrate, residence.*

Yet another dog is immortalized. This Roman pot with a hunting dog was found in Alesia.

Ronald Sheridan/Ancient Art & Architecture Collection

INNOCENT VICTIMS OF WAR

VII, **78.**

Sententiīs dictīs, cōnstituunt ut eī quī valētūdine aut
aetāte inūtilēs sint bellō oppidō excēdant, atque omnia prius experiantur
quam[1] ad Critognātī sententiam dēscendant; illō tamen potius ūtendum[2]
cōnsiliō, sī rēs cōgat atque auxilia morentur, quam aut dēditiōnis aut pācis
5 subeundam condiciōnem. Mandubiī, quī eōs oppidō recēperant, cum
līberīs atque uxōribus exīre cōguntur. Hī cum ad mūnītiōnēs Rōmānōrum
accessissent, flentēs omnibus precibus ōrābant ut sē in servitūtem receptōs
cibō iuvārent. At Caesar, dispositīs in vāllō custōdiīs, recipī[3] prohibēbat.

79. Intereā Commius reliquīque ducēs, quibus summa imperī permissa
10 erat, cum omnibus cōpiīs ad Alesiam perveniunt, et, colle exteriōre
occupātō, nōn longius mīlle passibus ā nostrīs mūnītiōnibus cōnsīdunt.
Posterō diē, equitātū ex castrīs ēductō, omnem eam plānitiem quae in
longitūdinem mīlia passuum III patēbat, complent; pedestrēsque cōpiās
paulum ab eō locō abductās in locīs superiōribus cōnstituunt. Erat ex

[1] Translate with **prius:** *before*

[2] *but that plan was to be used*

[3] Supply **eōs;** these innocent townspeople perished of starvation between the lines. Parallels are not lacking in recent times.

A detail from the painting *Thusnelda in the Triumphal Procession of Germanicus* by Karl Theodor von Piloty (1826–1886). Germanicus Caesar was an immensely popular commander in Germany and Gaul. He was able to suppress a mutiny of the legions after the death of Augustus. He crossed the Rhine to fight the Germans several times and returned to a triumph in A.D. 17 in Rome. Were it not for his early death in A.D. 19, he would have been emperor. He was the brother of Claudius and the father of Caligula.

oppidō Alesiā dēspectus[4] in[5] campum. Concurrunt, hīs auxiliīs vīsīs; fit   15
grātulātiō inter eōs atque omnium animī ad laetitiam excitantur. Itaque,
prōductīs cōpiīs, ante oppidum cōnsīdunt, sēque ad ēruptiōnem atque
omnēs cāsūs comparant.

Summary of Chapters 80–81. Caesar sends his cavalry out of camp to
engage that of the enemy; after a long struggle the enemy is finally   20
defeated. The Gallic relief army, under cover of night, makes a second
attack upon the outer works, while Vercingetorix leads an attack upon the
inner lines.

82. Dum longius ā mūnītiōne aberant Gallī, plūs multitūdine tēlōrum
prōficiēbant; posteāquam propius successērunt, aut sē ipsī stimulīs[6]   25
inopīnantēs induēbant aut in scrobēs[7] dēlātī trānsfodiēbantur aut ex vāllō
ac turribus trāiectī pīlīs mūrālibus[8] interībant. Multīs undique vulneribus
acceptīs, nūllā mūnītiōne perruptā, cum lūx appeteret, veritī nē ab latere
apertō ex superiōribus castrīs ēruptiōne circumvenīrentur, sē ad suōs
recēpērunt. At interiōrēs,[9] dum ea quae ā Vercingetorīge ad ēruptiōnem   30
praeparāta erant prōferunt, priōrēs fossās explent: diūtius in hīs rēbus
administrandīs morātī prius suōs discessisse cognōvērunt quam[10]
mūnītiōnibus appropinquārent. Ita, rē īnfectā, in oppidum revertērunt.

Questions
1. What plan did the Gauls adopt?
2. What happened to the Mandubii?
3. Why did the night attack of the Gauls fail?

[4] A statue of Vercingetorix was erected by Napoleon III near the spot from which the relief army was seen. See page 423.
[5] *over*
[6] *spurs* (pointed iron stakes)
[7] *wolf-holes*
[8] *heavy wall javelins*
[9] *the army within Alesia*
[10] with **prius:** *before*

▦ VOCABULARY

Adjective

prior, prius *former, first*   (prior, prioritize)

Verbs

expleō, -ēre, explēvī, explētus *fill up*   (expletive)
prōficiō, -ere, -fēcī, -fectus *accomplish*   **[faciō]**

Review **cibus, fleō, posteāquam, posterus, prex, turris.**

WORD STUDY

Derivatives From what Latin words are the following derived: **appetō, custōdia, dēspectus, dispōnō, grātulātiō, mūrālis, perrumpō?**

Explain *appetite, priority, stimulation, trajectory, translucent.*

Summary of Chapters 83–87. The Gauls send out scouts and find that the Roman camp on the north is in a weak position. So Vercassivellaunus makes a surprise march by night and attacks the camp the next noon. Vercingetorix attacks from Alesia, and the Romans are forced to fight on all sides. Caesar, perceiving that his men are weakening under the attack of Vercassivellaunus, sends Labienus with six cohorts to reinforce them. He then addresses his troops, reminding them that the reward of all their struggles depends upon that day and hour. Vercingetorix attempts a diversion from Alesia. Caesar sends reinforcements and finally goes to the rescue himself.

NEAR DISASTER FOLLOWED BY VICTORY

LESSON OBJECTIVE
• **Read**
Caesar *Dē Bellō Gallicō* VII, 88–90

VII

, 88. Eius[1] adventū ex colōre vestītūs cognitō, quō īnsignī in proeliīs ūtī cōnsuēverat, turmīsque equitum et cohortibus vīsīs quās sē sequī iusserat, ut dē locīs superiōribus haec dēclīvia cernēbantur, hostēs proelium committunt. Utrimque, clāmōre sublātō, excipit[2] rūrsus ex vāllō atque omnibus mūnītiōnibus clāmor. Nostrī, omissīs pīlīs, gladiīs rem gerunt. Repente post tergum[3] equitātus cernitur; cohortēs aliae appropinquant. Hostēs terga vertunt; fugientibus equitēs occurrunt; fit magna caedēs. Signa mīlitāria LXXIV ad Caesarem referuntur; paucī ex tantō numerō incolumēs sē in castra recipiunt. Cōnspicātī ex oppidō caedem et fugam suōrum, dēspērātā salūte, cōpiās ā mūnītiōnibus   10
redūcunt. Fit prōtinus, hāc rē audītā, ex castrīs Gallōrum fuga. Quod[4] nisi crēbrīs subsidiīs ac tōtīus diēī labōre mīlitēs essent dēfessī, omnēs hostium cōpiae dēlērī potuissent.[5] Dē mediā nocte missus equitātus novissimum agmen cōnsequitur; magnus numerus capitur atque interficitur; reliquī ex fugā in cīvitātēs discēdunt.   15

89. Posterō diē Vercingetorīx, conciliō convocātō, id bellum sē suscēpisse nōn suārum necessitātum sed commūnis lībertātis causā

[1] Caesar wore a scarlet uniform.
[2] *answers*
[3] of the enemy; the cavalry is Roman.
[4] *and*
5 [5] *might have been*

Bettmann/CORBIS

The Gauls, shown here surrendering to Caesar, fought long and hard for their homeland under many leaders, especially Vercingetorix, but finally succumbed to the more powerful Roman troops.

dēmōnstrat; et quoniam sit fortūnae cēdendum,[6] ad utramque[7] rem sē illīs offerre,[8] seu morte suā Rōmānīs satisfacere seu vīvum trādere velint.

20 Mittuntur dē hīs rēbus ad Caesarem lēgātī. Iubet arma trādī, prīncipēs prōdūcī. Ipse in mūnītiōne prō castrīs cōnsīdit; eō ducēs prōdūcuntur. Vercingetorīx dēditur; arma prōiciuntur. Reservātīs Haeduīs atque Arvernīs, sī per eōs cīvitātēs recuperāre posset, ex reliquīs captīvīs tōtī exercituī capita singula[9] praedae nōmine distribuit.

25 **90.** Huius annī rēbus ex Caesaris litterīs cognitīs Rōmae diērum vīgintī supplicātiō redditur.

Questions

1. What led the enemy to begin the attack?

2. What changed the situation and made the enemy flee?

3. What offer did the defeated Vercingetorix make to his soldiers?

WORD STUDY

Developing "Word Sense" **Tollō** is a good word to know well, both for its irregular principal parts and for its basic meaning, *raise up or away from a lower position*. Thus, in the proper contexts, **tollō** can mean: *weigh anchor, cheer up a friend, praise someone highly,* or, on the other hand, *plunder booty, get rid of something,* or *"do away" with a man,* i.e., *murder him.*

After the death of the dictator Caesar, his nineteen-year-old adopted son and heir, Octavian (later the Emperor Augustus), began to seize power for himself. The orator Cicero, fearful of what might happen to the Roman Senate, suggested that: **laudandum (esse) adulēscentem, ornandum, tollendum.** Octavian, who had a good sense of humor, was not exactly pleased by the pun.

VERCINGETORIX AND ALESIA

In strategic skill, organizing ability, and leadership, Vercingetorix was by far the ablest foreign opponent that Caesar faced, but he was unable in a short time to give the Gauls the discipline and military knowledge that the Romans had acquired through centuries of experience. He did succeed for a time in producing Gallic unity, and for that he has been considered the first national hero of France.

After his surrender, Vercingetorix was sent to Rome and remained in prison there for six years. In 46 B.C. he was led through the streets before Caesar's chariot in a triumphal procession and then executed as part of the ceremony.

Historians agree that the fall of Alesia constitutes a turning point in the history of northern Europe, for it settled the question of Roman supremacy in Gaul. The striking contrast between Roman efficiency and Gallic inefficiency is here seen most clearly. With all their courage and physical strength, the Gauls were defeated in their own territory by an army scarcely one-seventh the size of their own.

The military operations of the two years (51–50 B.C.) following the capture of Alesia were not included by Caesar in his *Commentaries,* but we are indebted to one of his generals, Aulus Hirtius, for a full account, which he added as an eighth book. The military strength of the Gauls had been broken forever, and there remained only the task of subduing certain states that had not yet been fully reduced and of garrisoning the country. Caesar's term as proconsular governor expired in 49 B.C. Thus the conquest of Gaul, with its momentous results, occupied nine years in all.

Ronald Sheridan/Ancient Art & Architecture Collection

Vercingetorix is a national hero in the history of France. In 52 B.C. he led a coalition of tribes against the encroaching Romans. Caesar besieged Vercingetorix at Alesia and finally won as famine overcame them. Vercingetorix was taken to Rome and executed in 46 B.C.

Persōnae

C. Iūlius Caesar

Babidus, *scrība senex*

Frontō, *scrība adulēscēns*

M. Terentius Varrō

Sōsigenēs, *astronomus*

M. Flāvius, *amīcus Sōsigenis*

Senātōrēs I *et* II

Aedīlis

Būbulō, *frāter pistōris*[1] *Caesaris*

Syphāx, *margarītārius*

Calpurnia, *uxor Caesaris*

Rhoda, *serva*

[1] *baker*

[The scene is a room in Caesar's house. The time is somewhere between 49 and 44 B.C. The Civil War with Pompey and his followers has ended victoriously for Caesar. Established in Rome as dictator, Caesar is putting into effect his plans for the reorganization of the war-torn state.]

(Intrant Babidus et Frontō. Tabulās, libellōs, stilōs ferunt.)

Babidus: Dēpōne libellōs, Frontō.

Frontō: Aderuntne hodiē multī salūtātōrēs?

Babidus: Multī. Caesarī dictātōrī omnis rēs pūblica cūrae est.

Frontō: Labōrat magis quam servus.

Babidus: Prō eō saepe timeō. Semper labōrat; cibum nōn capit. Valētūdine minus commodā iam ūtitur. Aliquandō animō quidem linquitur.[2]

[2] *Sometimes he even faints.*
[3] *nonsense!*

Frontō: Rūmōrem in urbe audīvī—Caesarem cupere rēgem esse.

Babidus: Nūgās![3] Caesar pācem, concordiam, tranquillitātem in urbe et orbe terrārum cōnfirmāre vult.

Frontō: Candidātōs magistrātuum certē ipse nōminat.

Babidus: Aliōs nōminat Caesar, aliōs populus. Rēs pūblica antīqua autem mortua est.

Frontō: Suntne libellī bene parātī? Memoriā teneō Caesarem quondam interfēcisse scrībam suum Philēmonem.

Babidus: Philēmon erat nefārius. Servus Caesaris inimīcīs Caesaris prōmīserat sē dominum per venēnum necātūrum esse. Tū es neque nefārius neque servus. Nōlī timēre.

Frontō: Audī! Appropinquat Caesar. *(Intrat C. Iūlius Caesar.)*

COMPRIX WHAT'S UP!

Caesar: Salvēte.

Babidus et Frontō: Salvē, imperātor.

Caesar: Prīmum, acta diurna senātūs populīque. Suntne parāta?

Frontō: Ecce, imperātor. *(Caesarī dat libellum, quem Caesar legit.)*

Caesar: Bene! Bene scrīpta! Nunc ad commentāriōs meōs Dē Bellō Cīvīlī animadvertāmus.

Babidus: Ecce, Caesar. *(Caesarī libellum dat.)*

Caesar: Pauca verba addere volō.

Babidus: Parātus sum. *(Cōnsīdit Babidus; notās[4] scrībere parat. Frontō exit.)*

Caesar *(dictat):* "Caesar, omnibus rēbus relīctīs, persequendum sibi Pompeium exīstimāvit, quāscumque in partēs sē ex fugā recēpisset, nē rūrsus cōpiās comparāre aliās et bellum renovāre posset."

Babidus: Scrīptum est.

Caesar: Estne scrīpta epistula mea ad Mārcum Cicerōnem, quam herī dictāvī? *(Intrat Frontō.)*

Babidus: Ecce, Caesar. *(Caesarī epistulam dat.)*

Caesar: Mūtā litterās. Scrībe D prō A, et deinceps.[5]

Babidus: Intellegō.

Frontō: Adsunt salūtātōrēs, imperātor.

Caesar: Intret Varrō. *(Exit Frontō, tum intrat cum Varrōne.)* Salvē, Varrō.

Varrō: Salvē, imperātor.

Caesar: Varrō, tū es vir doctus. Mihi in animō est maximam bibliothēcam, Graecam Latīnamque, aedificāre. Pūblica erit bibliothēca. Tē bibliothēcae praefectum facere volō.

Varrō: Mē?

Caesar: Tē certē.

Varrō: Ego autem Pompeiī, inimīcī tuī, eram lēgātus.

Caesar: Nōlī timēre, Varrō. Dictātor sum—nōn autem tālis dictātor quālis erat Sulla. Prōscrīptiōnēs neque dē capite neque dē bonīs Caesarī placent.

Varrō: Imperātor, quō modō tibi grātiam referre possum?

Caesar: Dē grātiā loquī necesse nōn est. Optimus eris bibliothēcae praefectus. Valē, Varrō.

Varrō: Dī bene vertant! Valē. *(Exit.)*

Caesar: Intrent astronomī. *(Exit Frontō. Intrat cum Sōsigene et Flāviō.)* Salvēte, Sōsigenēs et Flāvī.

Sōsigenēs et Flāvius: Salvē, imperātor.

Caesar: Quid effēcistis?

Sōsigenēs: Nostrā sententiā, annus ad cursum sōlis accommodandus est. Necesse est annum trecentōrum sexāgintā quīnque diērum esse; necesse est quoque ūnum diem quārtō quōque[6] annō intercalārī.[7]

[4] *shorthand notes*

[5] *and so on;* Caesar used a simple cipher in writing important letters.

[6] *every*

[7] *insert* (Caesar had the calendar revised to approximately its present form. The insertion of the leap-year day was a feature of his revision.)

Caesar: Rēctam viam capitis, meā quidem sententiā.

Flāvius: Sī Caesarī placet, mēnsis nātālis Caesaris, nunc Quīnctīlis, nōminētur Iūlius.

Caesar: Dē hāc rē posteā loquāmur. Intereā, prōcēdite ut incēpistis. Valēte.

Sōsigenēs et Flāvius: Valē, imperātor. *(Exeunt.)*

Caesar: Intrent nunc senātōrēs. *(Exit Frontō. Intrat cum senātōribus.)* Salvēte.

Senātōrēs: Salvē, Caesar.

Caesar: Quid est in animō?

Senātor I: Nōbīs sunt magnae cūrae, Caesar. Audīvimus tē sine auctōritāte senātūs mīlitēs Rōmānōs ad rēgēs per orbem terrārum submittere ut eīs auxiliō sint; tē pecūniā pūblicā urbēs Asiae, Graeciae, Hispāniae, Galliae operibus ōrnāre.

Senātor II: Tū cīvitātem Rōmānam medicīs et grammaticīs et aliīs dōnāvistī. In senātum Gallōs sēmibarbarōs cōnscrīpsistī. Mīlitēs tuī domōs cīvium ingressī sunt et cibum abstulērunt.[8] Ipse dirēmistī[9] nūptiās cīvium Rōmānōrum.

Senātor I: Rūmōrēs malī per urbem eunt. Quid agis, Caesar?

Caesar: Dictātor sum. Rem pūblicam, bellō dēiectam, restituō.

Senātor II: Rem pūblicam dēlēs, Caesar.

Caesar: Omnia bene erunt. Nōlīte īram meam concitāre. Valēte, amīcī.

Senātōrēs: Valē, Caesar. *(Exeunt.)*

Caesar: Ad rēs fēlīciōrēs animum advertāmus. Intret aedīlis. *(Exit Frontō. Intrat cum aedīle.)* Salvē.

Aedīlis: Salvē, imperātor. Omnia parāta sunt, ut imperāvistī—mūnus gladiātōrum, vēnātiō, naumachia, lūdī scaenicī, lūdī circēnsēs.

Caesar: Bene.

Aedīlis: Spectācula erunt omnium maxima.

Caesar: Optimē factum. Tibi grātiās agō.

Aedīlis: Mihi est honōrī Caesarem iuvāre. Valē.

Caesar: Valē. *(Exit Aedīlis. Intrat Rhoda. Cibum et epistulās fert. Epistulās Babidō dat.)*

Rhoda: Domina ōrat ut dominus cibum recipiat.

Caesar: Abī, abī! *(Rhoda, cibum ferēns, exit.)* Quae sunt illae epistulae?

Babidus: Architectus scrīpsit dē Forō Iūliō, dē templō novō, dē statuā equī tuī.[10]

Caesar: Ita, ita.

Babidus: Alius scrīpsit dē viā novā mūniendā, dē Isthmō perfodiendō,[11] dē palūdibus Pomptīnīs siccandīs.

Caesar: Dā mihi hanc epistulam.

[8] In an attempt to reduce inflation, Caesar forbade the sale of certain luxurious foods. He sent soldiers to markets and even to private houses to seize such luxuries.

[9] *annul*

[10] Caesar had a horse of which he was very fond; to it he set up a statue in his own Forum.

[11] *digging (a canal through) the Isthmus (of Corinth); this project was not completed until 1893 and the draining of the Pontine Marshes was not completed until the first half of the twentieth century.*

Babidus: Veterānus tibi grātiās ēgit prō praedā, servīs, agrīs quōs eī
dedistī. Pauper vir Rōmānus tibi grātiās ēgit, aurō et frūmentō receptō.

Caesar: Illās epistulās iam legam. Quis in vēstibulō manet?

Frontō: Vir magnus—Būbulō. Et margarītārius.

Caesar: Būbulōne?

Frontō: Frāter est pistōris tuī.

Caesar: Quid petit? Intret. *(Exit Frontō. Intrat cum Būbulōne.)*

Būbulō: Caesar imperātor, tē ōrō, tē ōrō!

Caesar: Quid petis?

Būbulō: Līberā frātrem meum, pistōrem tuum, in vincula coniectum.

Caesar: Alium pānem mihi, alium amīcīs meīs in trīclīniō meō dedit.[12]

Būbulō: Tū autem es Caesar.

Caesar: Īdem cibus erit mihi et amīcīs meīs. Frāter tuus autem poenās iam
solvit. Eum līberābō. *(In tabulā scrībit; tabulam Būbulōnī dat.)*

Būbulō: Ōh, dī tē ament, Caesar! *(Exit. Caesar rīdet.)*

Caesar: Intret Syphāx margarītārius. *(Exit Frontō. Intrat cum Syphāce.)*

Syphāx: Avē, imperātor. Margarītam habeō—maximam. *(Margarītam
Caesarī mōnstrat.)*

Caesar: Quid dīcis? Haec margarīta nōn est magna. *(Intrat Calpurnia.)*
Haec margarīta est parva. Volō rēgīnam margarītārum—prō uxōre meā.

Calpurnia: Quid audiō?

Caesar: Calpurnia!

Calpurnia: Mihi margarītam mōnstrā.—Est pulcherrima.

Caesar: Placetne tibi? Maiōrem tibi dare voluī.

Calpurnia: Certē placet. Pulchra est—et satis magna.

Caesar: Tua erit. *(Scrībīs dīcit.)* Cūrāte omnia.

Syphāx: Tibi grātiās agō, imperātor. *(Exit cum scrībīs.)*

Calpurnia: Utinam tē aequē ac mē cūrārēs!

Caesar: Ego valeō.

Calpurnia: Cibum reicis; nōn satis quiētem capis; etiam per somnum
terrērī solēs.

Caesar: Nihil est.

Calpurnia: Vītam prō rē pūblicā dēdis. Ōmina quoque mala sunt.

Caesar: Ōmina nōn mē terrent. *(Intrat Babidus. Margarītam Caesarī dat.)*
Ecce! Pulcherrimae uxōrī pulcherrimam gemmam dō. Nunc ad
prandium eāmus.

(Exeunt Caesar et Calpurnia, tum Babidus.)

[12] Some rich Romans had special foods served to themselves and fewer fine foods to their guests. Of this practice Caesar violently disapproved.

Now that you have read this play, choose roles and act it out in Latin.

PLINY'S LETTERS

Unit Objectives

Read:

• Selections from Pliny's Letters

Learn:

• About the Life and Times of Pliny the Younger

Ancient Pompeii was a thriving metropolis when it was snuffed out in A.D. 79. Though it had suffered heavy damage from an earthquake in A.D. 62, some of the buildings had been rebuilt and there were plans to redo many others. This view of a main street shows how the practical Romans constructed their roads. The stepping stones allowed pedestrians to cross without getting their feet wet, while chariots and wagons could still pass their wheels between the stones without being hindered.

C.M. Dixon/Photo Resources

429

AN ANCIENT LETTER WRITER

Pliny the Younger, whose name distinguishes him from his uncle and adoptive father, Pliny the Elder, was born at Comum (Como) in northern Italy in A.D. 62 during the reign of Nero. His famous teacher Quintilian filled him with admiration of Cicero, whom he tried to imitate in many ways. Like Cicero he became consul and governor of a province. But his highest ambition was to rival Cicero as an orator; yet only one of his many speeches has survived—and no one reads that.

The fact that many of Cicero's letters were collected and published by his secretary and others gave Pliny the idea of selecting for publication some of his own more polished and less personal letters. These have survived and make fascinating reading for the light they throw on Pliny himself and on life in his day.

Among Pliny's most interesting letters are two that give a vivid account of the famous eruption of Mt. Vesuvius near Naples in A.D. 79. The author was seventeen years old at the time and was living with his mother and uncle near Naples, at Misenum, where the elder Pliny was stationed as admiral of the fleet. Many years later Pliny wrote the letters describing the eruption.

An excavated street in ancient Herculaneum. Located on the Bay of Naples, Herculaneum was known as a resort town. It was much smaller than Pompeii but was destroyed by the same eruption of Vesuvius in A.D. 79. Herculaneum was covered by a layer of hot mud from fifty to sixty-five feet thick that filled the buildings and eventually solidified, preserving much of the contents.

Scala/Art Resource, NY

This great disaster has been a blessing for us, since it preserved as if in a huge plaster cast the towns of Pompeii and Herculaneum. The excavation of these two towns during the last two centuries has made it possible for us to walk into the houses and shops of the people who once lived there and has given us an intimate view of their daily life.

Pliny was a man of fine character, a good representative of the honest and efficient officials who developed and governed the Roman Empire. He was generous and kind, and for these reasons we can forgive him his conceit and overseriousness.

THE ERUPTION OF VESUVIUS

This letter is a reply to a request by Pliny's great friend, the historian Tacitus, who was gathering eyewitness material for his *Histories*. Though part of this work has survived, the section dealing with the eruption has unfortunately been lost, and we are unable to tell how Tacitus used the information furnished by Pliny.

Petis ut tibi dē avunculī meī morte scrībam ut hoc trādere posterīs possīs. Grātiās agō; nam videō mortī eius immortālem glōriam esse prōpositam. Quamquam ipse opera plūrima et mānsūra scrīpsit, multum tamen eius librōrum aeternitātī[1] tuōrum aeternitās addet. Beātōs eōs putō quibus deōrum mūnere datum est aut facere scrībenda[2] aut scrībere legenda,[2] beātissimōs vērō eōs quibus utrumque.[3] Hōrum in numerō avunculus meus et suīs librīs[4] et tuīs erit.

Erat Mīsēnī.[5] Hōrā ferē septimā māter mea ostendit eī nūbem inūsitātā magnitūdine et speciē. Ille ascendit locum ex quō optimē mīrāculum illud cōnspicī poterat. Nūbēs ex monte Vesuviō oriēbātur. Fōrmam pīnūs[6] habēbat.

Iubet nāvēs parārī; mihi cōpiam eundī[7] facit. Respondī studēre mē mālle. Tum accipit litterās cuiusdam mulieris perīculō territae. Nāvem ascendit ut nōn illī mulierī modo sed multīs auxilium ferret. Properat illūc unde aliī fugiunt rēctumque cursum in perīculum tenet, tam solūtus timōre ut omnia vīsa ēnotāret.

Iam nāvibus cinis dēnsior incidēbat, iam pūmicēs[8] etiam nigrīque lapidēs. Cum gubernātor monēret ut retrō flecteret, "Fortēs," inquit, "fortūna iuvat."[9] Ubi ad lītus vēnit, amīcum vīdit. Eum territum hortātur. Tum in balneum it et posteā ad cēnam, aut hilaris aut similis hilarī.

Interim ē Vesuviō monte lātissimās flammās vīdērunt. Ille, nē cēterī timērent, dīcēbat ignēs ab agricolīs relictōs esse. Tum sē quiētī dedit. Sed nōn multō post servī eum excitāvērunt nē exitus ob cinerem negārētur. Domus crēbrīs tremōribus nunc hūc nunc illūc movērī vidēbātur. Itaque placuit ēgredī in lītus. Cervīcālia[10] capitibus impōnunt. Sed ille recubāns[11] aquam poposcit et hausit. Tum surrēxit et statim concidit. Cēterī fugiunt. Posterō diē corpus inventum est integrum. Similior erat dormientī quam mortuō.

Interim Mīsēnī ego et māter—sed nihil ad[12] historiam, nec tū aliud quam dē exitū eius scīre voluistī. Fīnem ergō faciam.

[1] dative with **addet**; supply **librōrum** with **tuōrum**.

[2] *(things) to be* (i.e., *worthy of being*), etc.

[3] Supply **datum est**.

[4] *because of*, etc.; see the Grammar Appendix, p. 499.11

[5] *at Misenum*

[6] (the "umbrella") *pine*

[7] i.e., with him; gerund of **eō**

[8] *pumice stones*

[9] a common Roman proverb

[10] *cushions* (used by his slaves as a protection against falling stones)

[11] *lying down.* His death was evidently due to some such cause as heart disease rather than to the eruption.

[12] *(this has) nothing (to do) with*

FLIGHT FROM DISASTER

Taking the hint given in the last sentence in the reading on page 431 Tacitus asked about Pliny the Younger's own adventures during the eruption. Pliny replied as follows.

Dīcis tē adductum litterīs quās tibi dē morte avunculī meī scrīpsī cupere cognōscere quōs timōrēs et cāsūs ego pertulerim. "Quamquam animus meminisse horret, incipiam."[1]

Profectō[2] avunculō, ipse reliquum tempus studiīs dedī. Tum balneum,
5 cēna, somnus brevis. Praecesserat per multōs diēs tremor terrae. Illā vērō nocte ita crēvit[3] ut nōn movērī omnia sed vertī[4] vidērentur. Māter et ego in āream domūs iimus et cōnsēdimus. Dubitō utrum[5] cōnstantiam vocāre an imprūdentiam dēbeam (nātus enim eram XVII annōs), sed poscō librum T. Līvī et legō.

10 Iam hōra diēī prīma erat. Magnus et certus erat ruīnae timor. Tum dēmum[6] excēdere oppidō placuit. Multī nōs sequuntur. Ēgressī cōnsistimus. Multa ibi mīranda, multōs timōrēs patimur. Nam carrī quōs prōdūcī iusserāmus, quamquam in plānissimō campō, in contrāriās partēs agēbantur. Ab alterō latere nūbēs ātra et horrenda appārēbat. Paulō post,
15 illa nūbēs dēscendit in terrās. Tum māter ōrat, hortātur, iubet mē fugere. "Tū potes," inquit; "ego et annīs et corpore gravis bene moriar sī tibi causa mortis nōn erō." Ego vērō dīcō mē nōn incolumem nisi cum eā futūrum esse. Deinde eam prōcēdere cōgō. Pāret aegrē. Iam cinis cadit. Tum nox, nōn quālis sine lūnā est, sed quālis in locīs clausīs, lūmine exstīnctō.
20 Audiuntur ululātūs[7] fēminārum, īnfantium quirītātūs[8], clāmōrēs virōrum. Aliī parentēs, aliī līberōs, aliī coniugēs vōcibus quaerēbant, vōcibus nōscēbant. Quīdam timōre mortis mortem ōrābant. Multī ad deōs manūs tollēbant, plūrēs nōn iam deōs ūllōs esse aeternamque illam et ultimam noctem dīcēbant. Cinis multus et gravis. Hunc identidem surgentēs
25 excutiēbāmus[9] nē pondus nōbīs nocēret. Possum dīcere mē nōn gemitum in tantīs perīculīs ēdidisse. Tandem nūbēs discessit. Tum diēs vērus. Omnia mūtāta erant altōque cinere tamquam nive tēcta.

[1] a quotation from Vergil
[2] from **proficiscor**
[3] from **crēscō**
[4] to be turning upside down
[5] whether, introducing **dēbeam**
[6] at length
[7] shrieks
[8] wails
[9] shook off

The Metropolitan Museum of Art, Rogers Fund, 1903. (03.14.13) Photography by Schecter Lee. Copyright © 1986 by The Metropolitan Museum of Art.

This **cubiculum** (bedroom) from a villa in Boscoreale near ancient Pompeii shows the elaborate wall paintings and floor mosaics that mark it as an upper-class home during the first century B.C.

THE SECRET OF SUCCESS

This letter and the next are interesting revelations of the Romans'
genius for organization, even of their personal lives.

Mīrāris quō modō tot librōs avunculus meus, homō occupātus, scrībere
potuerit. Magis mīrāberis sī scīveris illum causās ēgisse, vīxisse LV annōs,
medium[1] tempus impedītum esse officiīs maximīs et amīcitiā prīncipum.
Sed erat ācre ingenium, incrēdibile studium. Studēre incipiēbat hieme ab
hōrā septimā noctis. Erat somnī[2] parātissimī, nōn numquam[3] etiam inter   5
ipsa studia īnstantis[4] et dēserentis.[4] Ante lūcem ībat ad Vespasiānum
imperātōrem (nam ille quoque noctibus ūtēbātur),[5] inde ad officium datum.
Reversus domum, reliquum tempus studiīs reddēbat. Post levem cibum
saepe aestāte iacēbat in sōle; liber legēbātur,[6] ille ēnotābat. Dīcere solēbat
nūllum esse librum tam malum ut nōn aliquā parte ūtilis esset. Post sōlem   10
plērumque frīgidā aquā lavābātur;[7] deinde dormiēbat minimum. Tum quasi
aliō diē studēbat in cēnae tempus.

Meminī quendam ex amīcīs, cum lēctor quaedam verba male
prōnūntiāvisset, eum revocāvisse et iterum prōnūntiāre coēgisse. Huic
avunculus meus dīxit, "Nōnne intellēxerās?" Cum ille nōn negāret, "Cūr   15
revocābās? Decem versūs hōc modō perdidimus."

Etiam dum lavātur audiēbat servum legentem. In itinere, quasi solūtus
cēterīs cūrīs, huic ūnī reī vacābat; ad latus servus erat cum librō et tabulīs,
cuius manūs hieme manicīs[8] mūniēbantur, nē ūllum tempus studī
āmitterētur. Perīre omne tempus nōn studiīs datum arbitrābātur.   20

[1] *time in between*

[2] *(a man) of.* Napoleon also had the
habit of taking short naps at any
time or place.

[3] *not never,* i.e., *sometimes*

[4] modifies **somni:** *which came
and went*

[5] The ablative is used with **ūtor.**

[6] i.e., to him by a slave

[7] *bathed (himself).* The passive is
used reflexively.

[8] *gloves*

HOW TO KEEP YOUNG

[1] take place
[2] ball

Spūrinna senex omnia ōrdine agit. Hōrā secundā calceōs poscit, ambulat mīlia passuum tria nec minus animum quam corpus exercet. Sī adsunt amīcī, sermōnēs explicantur;[1] sī nōn, liber legitur dum ambulat. Deinde cōnsīdit et liber rūrsus aut sermō. Tum vehiculum ascendit cum

5 uxōre vel aliquō amīcō. Cōnfectīs septem mīlibus passuum iterum ambulat mīlle, iterum cōnsīdit. Ubi hōra balneī nūntiāta est (est autem hieme nōna, aestāte octāva), in sōle ambulat. Deinde pilā[2] lūdit vehementer et diū; nam hōc quoque exercitātiōnis genere pugnat cum senectūte. LXXVII annōs ēgit sed aurium et oculōrum et corporis vigor adhūc est integer.

THE GOOD DIE YOUNG

In addition to being a touching expression of grief, this letter lists the qualities which the Romans appreciated most in women.

Trīstissimus haec tibi scrībō, Fundānī nostrī fīliā minōre mortuā. Nihil umquam fēstīvius[1] aut amābilius quam illam puellam vīdī. Nōndum annōs XIII complēverat, et iam illī[2] anūs[3] prūdentia, mātrōnae gravitās erat et tamen suāvitās puellae.[4] Ut[5] illa patris cervīcibus[6] haerēbat! Ut nōs, amīcōs patris, et amanter et modestē complectēbātur![7] Ut magistrōs amābat! Quam studiōsē, quam intellegenter legēbat! Ut parcē lūdēbat! Quā patientiā, quā etiam cōnstantiā ultimam valētūdinem tulit! Medicīs pārēbat, sorōrem, patrem adhortābātur, ipsamque sē vīribus animī sustinēbat. Hae vīrēs nec spatiō valētūdinis nec timōre mortis frāctae sunt. Itaque plūrēs graviōrēsque causās dolōris nōbīs relīquit. Iam spōnsa erat ēgregiō iuvenī, iam ēlēctus nūptiārum diēs, iam nōs vocātī.

Nōn possum exprimere verbīs quantum animō vulnus accēperim, cum audīvī Fundānum ipsum imperantem ut illa pecūnia quam in vestēs et gemmās impēnsūrus esset in unguenta et odōrēs impenderētur.[8] Āmīsit fīliam quae nōn minus mōrēs eius quam vultum referēbat.

[1] *more charming*

[2] *dative of possession with* **erat**

[3] *of an old woman*

[4] The urn containing the girl's ashes was actually found in 1881 in the family tomb three miles north of Rome. The inscription on it reads: **d(is) m(ānibus) Miniciae Mārcellae Fundāni f(iliae). V(ixit) a(nnis) xii, m(ēnsibus) xi, d(iēbus) vii.** The parts in parentheses complete the abbreviations found in the inscription. The first two words mean "to the deified shades (of)."

[5] *how*

[6] *neck*

[7] *embraced*

[8] *giving orders that the money which . . . be spent on perfumes* (for the funeral)

Erich Lessing/Art Resource, NY

This wall painting from the first century A.D. shows a young girl wearing a laurel wreath. Perhaps the artist was inspired by someone like the daughter of Fundanus.

A GHOST STORY

¹ *with a bad reputation*
² *advertised.* What literally?
³ *threshold*
⁴ *beckoned*
⁵ *are buried*

Erat Athēnīs magna domus sed īnfāmis.¹ Per silentium noctis sonus vinculōrum, longius prīmō, deinde ē proximō audiēbātur. Tum appārēbat lārva, senex horrentī capillō. Vincula gerēbat. Deinde malae noctēs erant eīs quī ibi habitābant; mors sequēbātur. Domus dēserta est et illī lārvae
5 relīcta. Prōscrībēbātur² tamen, sed nēmō vel emere vel condūcere voluit.

Vēnit Athēnās philosophus Athēnodōrus, lēgit titulum, audītōque pretiō, quaesīvit cūr tam vīlis esset. Omnia cognōscit sed tamen condūcit. Ubi nox vēnit, poposcit tabulās, stilum, lūmen; servōs suōs omnēs dīmīsit, ipse ad scrībendum animum, oculōs, manum intendit nē mēns timōrēs
10 fingeret. Prīmō silentium, deinde vincula audiuntur. Ille nōn tollit oculōs. Tum sonus vinculōrum crēscit, propius venit. Iam in līmine,³ iam intrā līmen audītur. Ille respicit, videt lārvam. Stābat innuēbatque⁴ digitō similis vocantī. Sed philosophus rūrsus studiīs sē dat. Iterum sonus vinculōrum audītur. Ille rūrsus respicit lārvam innuentem. Nōn morātus tollit lūmen et
15 sequitur. Postquam lārva dēflexit in āream domūs, eum dēserit; is signum in locō pōnit. Posterō diē philosophus adit magistrātūs et monet ut illum locum effodī iubeant. Inveniuntur ossa et vincula. Haec collēcta sepeliuntur.⁵ In eō aedificiō numquam posteā lārva vīsa est.

DON'T BE A
HARSH FATHER

Castīgābat quīdam fīlium suum quod paulō sūmptuōsius equōs et canēs
emeret. Huic ego: "Heus[1] tū, numquamne fēcistī quod ā patre tuō culpārī
posset? Nōn etiam nunc facis quod fīlius tuus, sī pater tuus esset, parī
gravitāte culpet?"

Haec tibi admonitus magnae sevēritātis exemplō scrīpsī nē tū quoque
fīlium acerbius dūriusque tractārēs.[2] Cōgitā et illum puerum esse et tē
fuisse atque hominem esse tē et hominis patrem.

[1] *Say!*

[2] *handle*

5

GRADED FRIENDSHIP IS DEGRADED FRIENDSHIP

Longum est altius repetere¹ quō modō acciderit ut cēnārem apud
quendam, ut sibi vidēbātur, lautum et dīligentem, ut mihi, sordidum simul
et sūmptuōsum. Nam sibi et paucīs opīma² quaedam, cēterīs vīlia pōnēbat.
Vīnum etiam parvulīs lagunculīs³ in tria genera dīvīserat, nōn ut potestās
5 ēligendī, sed nē iūs esset recūsandī, aliud sibi et nōbīs, aliud minōribus
amīcīs (nam gradātim⁴ amīcōs habet), aliud suīs nostrīsque lībertīs.
Animadvertit⁵ quī mihi proximus accumbēbat et an probārem interrogāvit.
Negāvī. "Tū ergō," inquit, "quam cōnsuētūdinem sequeris?" "Eadem
omnibus pōnō; ad cēnam enim, nōn ad contumēliam invītō omnibusque
10 rēbus aequō quōs mēnsā aequāvī." "Etiamne lībertōs?" "Etiam: amīcōs
enim tum, nōn lībertōs putō." Et ille, "Magnō⁶ tibi cōnstat?" "Minimē."
"Quō modō fierī potest?" "Quia lībertī meī nōn idem quod ego bibunt, sed
idem ego quod lībertī."

WANTED, A TEACHER

Note the exquisite courtesy that turns a chore into a pleasure.

Quid ā mē grātius potuistī petere quam ut magistrum frātris tuī līberīs
quaererem? Nam beneficiō tuō in scholam redeō et illam dulcissimam
aetātem quasi resūmam. Sedeō inter iuvenēs, ut solēbam, atque etiam
experior quantum apud illōs auctōritātis ex studiīs meīs habeam. Nam
proximē inter sē iocābantur: intrāvī, silentium factum est. Hoc ad illōrum   5
laudem magis quam ad meam pertinet.

Cum omnēs professōrēs audīverō, quid dē quōque sentiam scrībam.
Dēbeō enim tibi, dēbeō memoriae frātris tuī hanc fidem, hoc studium,
praesertim in tantā rē.

The Pierpont Morgan Library/Art Resource, NY

The oldest manuscript of Pliny's
letters in existence. It dates from
about A.D. 500 and is in the
Pierpont Morgan Library, New
York City. What words can you
identify?

A COURAGEOUS WIFE

Pliny gives three examples of Arria's devotion to her husband.

Aeger erat Paetus, marītus Arriae, aeger etiam fīlius. Fīlius dēcessit.
Huic illa ita fūnus parāvit ut ignōrāret marītus. Cum¹ cubiculum eius
intrāret, vīvere fīlium atque etiam commodiōrem esse dīcēbat, ac saepe
marītō interrogantī quid ageret puer respondēbat, "Bene quiētem cēpit et

5 cibum sūmpsit." Deinde, cum lacrimae vincerent, ēgrediēbātur. Tum sē
dolōrī dabat. Compositō vultū redībat.

Paetus cum Scrībōniānō arma in Īllyricō contrā Claudium mōverat.
Occīsō Scrībōniānō, Rōmam Paetus trahēbātur.² Erat ascēnsūrus nāvem;
Arria mīlitēs ōrābat ut simul impōnerētur. "Datūrī estis," inquit, "marītō

10 meō, cōnsulārī virō, servōs aliquōs quōrum ē manū cibum capiat³ et
vestem et calceōs. Omnia haec ego sōla faciam." Hōc negātō, illa condūxit
parvum nāvigium et magnam nāvem secūta est.

Postquam Rōmam pervēnērunt, illa gladium strīnxit, in corde suō
dēfīxit, extrāxit, marītō dedit, addidit vōcem immortālem ac paene
dīvīnam: "Paete, nōn dolet."⁴

TWO LOVE LETTERS

Written by Pliny to his third wife, who was much younger than he.

Numquam magis dē occupātiōnibus meīs sum questus,[1] quae mē nōn sunt passae sequī tē proficīscentem in Campāniam valētūdinis causā. Nunc enim maximē tēcum esse cupiō ut oculīs meīs videam quid vīrium cōnsecūta sīs. Et absentia et īnfirmitās tua mē terrent. Vereor omnia, fingō omnia, ea maximē quae maximē timeō. Itaque rogō ut cotīdiē singulās vel etiam bīnās[2] epistulās scrībās. Sine cūrā erō dum legō statimque timēbō cum lēgerō. Valē.   5

Scrībis tē absentiā meā magnopere afficī ūnumque habēre sōlācium, quod prō mē librōs meōs teneās. Grātum est quod mē requīris. Ego epistulās tuās legō atque identidem in manūs quasi novās sūmō. Tū quam frequentissimē scrībe. Valē.   10

[1] from **queror,** *complain*
[2] *two*

A FISH STORY

To judge from modern parallels, we consider this story a true one. From New Zealand comes the report that Opo, a thousand-pound dolphin, or porpoise, which was a favorite at a beach resort, died in 1956. It would frolic with the bathers and permit children to ride on its back. Similar stories come from California and elsewhere.

Est in Āfricā colōnia marī proxima. Hīc omnis aetās[1] piscandī,[2] nāvigandī, atque etiam natandī studiō tenētur, maximē puerī, quī ōtium habent et lūdere cupiunt. Hīs glōria et virtūs est longissimē natāre; victor ille est quī longissimē lītus et aliōs natantēs relīquit. Puer quīdam
5 audācior[3] in ulteriōra tendēbat.[4] Delphīnus occurrit et nunc praecēdit puerum, nunc sequitur, tum subit,[5] dēpōnit, iterum subit territumque puerum perfert prīmum in altum, deinde flectit ad lītus redditque terrae.

Concurrunt omnēs, ipsum puerum tamquam mīrāculum spectant, rogant, audiunt. Posterō diē rūrsus natant puerī, rūrsus delphīnus ad
10 puerum venit. Fugit ille cum cēterīs. Delphīnus, quasi revocāns, exsilit et mergitur.[6] Hoc plūribus diēbus facit. Tandem puerī accēdunt, appellant, tangunt etiam. Crēscit audācia. Maximē puer quī prīmus expertus est natat ad eum, īnsilit tergō, fertur referturque.[7] Amārī sē putat, amat ipse. Neuter timet, neuter timētur.

Veniēbant omnēs magistrātūs ad 15 spectāculum, quōrum adventū et morā parva rēs pūblica novīs sūmptibus[8] cōnficitur. Posteā locus ipse quiētem suam 20 āmittēbat. Placuit delphīnum interficī ad quem videndum omnēs veniēbant.

Ancient coin of a dolphin and rider. The Greeks and Romans were just as fascinated with dolphins as we are today.

Boltin Picture Library

ADVICE TO A PROVINCIAL GOVERNOR

This letter indicates not only Pliny's respect for Greek culture, but also his belief that, though men and women are born free, they must preserve their right to freedom by the way they live.

Cōgitā tē missum in prōvinciam Achaiam, illam vēram Graeciam, in quā prīmum hūmānitās, litterae, etiam frūgēs inventae esse crēduntur; missum ad hominēs vērē hominēs, ad līberōs[1] vērē līberōs, quī iūs ā nātūrā datum virtūte et meritīs tenuērunt. Reverēre glōriam veterem. Sint antīquitās et magna facta in magnō honōre apud tē. Habē ante oculōs hanc 5 esse terram quae nōbīs mīserit iūra, quae lēgēs nōn victīs sed petentibus dederit, Athēnās esse quās adeās, Lacedaemonem esse quam regās. Plūs potest amor ad obtinendum quod[2] velīs quam timor.

[1] from **liber**, not **liberi**. He means that true manhood and true freedom had their beginnings in Greece.

[2] Supply **id** as antecedent.

A HUMANE MASTER

Cōnfēcērunt mē īnfirmitātēs servōrum meōrum, mortēs etiam. Sōlācia
duo sunt, nōn paria tantō dolōrī: ūnum, cōpia manūmittendī (videor enim
nōn omnīnō perdidisse quōs iam līberōs[1] perdidī); alterum, quod permittō
servīs quoque quasi[2] testāmenta facere. Mandant rogantque in hīs id quod
5 volunt; pāreō ut[3] iussus. Dīvidunt, dōnant, relinquunt, dumtaxat[4] intrā
domum; nam servīs rēs pūblica quaedam et quasi cīvitās domus est.

Nōn ignōrō aliōs[5] eius modī cāsūs nihil amplius vocāre quam damnum.[6]
Fortasse[7] sunt magnī sapientēsque, ut sibi videntur; hominēs nōn sunt.
Homō enim dēbet afficī dolōre.

10 Dīxī dē hīs plūra fortasse quam dēbuī, sed pauciōra quam voluī. Est
enim quaedam etiam dolendī voluptās.

[1] from **liber**
[2] *as it were*
[3] *as*
[4] *only, however*
[5] *other men*
[6] *loss* (of property)
[7] *perhaps*

Household slaves pouring and serving wine. As Roman slaves were by law merely so much property, they could not legally own money or make wills. In actual practice, however, most Roman slaves had these and other privileges.

Ronald Sheridan/Ancient Art & Architecture

A BUSY HOLIDAY

Omne hoc tempus inter tabulās ac librōs grātissimā quiēte ēgī. "Quō modō," inquis, "in urbe potuistī?" Circēnsēs lūdī erant, quō genere spectāculī minimē teneor. Nihil novum, nihil varium, nihil quod nōn semel spectāvisse sufficiat. Mīror tot mīlia virōrum tam puerīliter cupere identidem vidēre currentēs equōs, īnsistentēs curribus[1] hominēs. Nōn vēlōcitāte equōrum aut hominum arte trahuntur.[2] Favent pannō,[3] pannum amant. Sī in ipsō cursū hic color illūc, ille hūc trānsferātur,[4] studium favorque trānsferētur,[5] et statim aurīgās illōs, equōs illōs quōs procul nōscunt, quōrum clāmant nōmina, relinquent. Tanta grātia, tanta auctōritās in ūnā vīlissimā tunicā, nōn modo apud vulgus sed apud quōsdam gravēs hominēs. Capiō aliquam voluptātem quod hāc voluptāte nōn capior. Et ōtium meum in litterīs per hōs diēs collocō, quōs aliī perdunt. Valē.

[1] *standing in chariots*
[2] *they are attracted*
[3] *the cloth,* referring to the different colors worn by the drivers of the various racing clubs (cf. **tunicā** below). We may compare the colors of high school, college, and professional athletic teams. The point is that the spectators are not interested in the skill of the drivers, but in the side they represent.
[4] *should be transferred*
[5] singular because the two subjects represent one idea

5

10

Chariot races were major entertainment for the Romans—so much so that they built a **circus** to hold the shows in many major provincial cities.

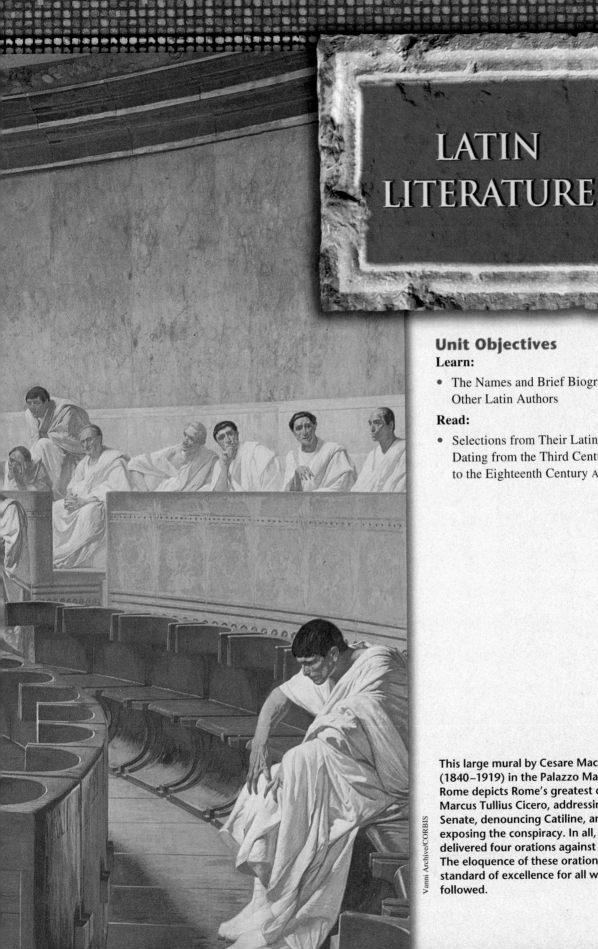

LATIN
LITERATURE

Unit Objectives

Learn:

- The Names and Brief Biographies of Other Latin Authors

Read:

- Selections from Their Latin Writings, Dating from the Third Century B.C. to the Eighteenth Century A.D.

This large mural by Cesare Maccari (1840–1919) in the Palazzo Madama in Rome depicts Rome's greatest orator, Marcus Tullius Cicero, addressing the Senate, denouncing Catiline, and exposing the conspiracy. In all, Cicero delivered four orations against Catiline. The eloquence of these orations set the standard of excellence for all who followed.

Vanni Archive/CORBIS

TWO THOUSAND YEARS OF LATIN

Latin literature, as we have it, extends from the third century B.C. to the present time. It contains material of almost every description: fine poetry, absorbing history and biography, amusing stories, moral essays, pithy sayings, passionate oratory, comic and tragic drama, scientific treatises, and much that is pertinent to life today. In this unit you will find a few samples of that literature down to the eighteenth century.

Ennius

Ennius (239–169 B.C.) has been called the father of Latin poetry. His *Annals,* an epic poem dealing with the history of Rome down to his own time, remained the chief epic of Rome until it was supplanted by Vergil's *Aeneid.* Only fragments of the *Annals* and his plays have survived, preserved in quotations by later authors. Ennius was a bold experimenter with verse. One of his experiments in alliteration reminds one of "Peter Piper picked a peck of pickled peppers."

Ō, Tite, tūte,[1] Tatī, tibi tanta[2] tyranne, tulistī.

This is addressed to Titus Tatius, the Sabine king, by the man who killed him.

Like many Roman writers, Ennius stressed patriotic and moral qualities.

Mōribus[3] antīquīs stat rēs[4] Rōmāna virīsque.[3]

[1] = an emphatic **tū**
[2] neut. pl. acc.; i.e., misfortunes
[3] *because of*
[4] = **rēs pūblica**

Roman Comedy

As early as the third century B.C. the Romans had begun to borrow and adapt from the Greeks a type of comedy based on the manners (or bad manners) of middle-class citizens. Its themes were general: thwarted but eventually successful love, paternal strictness versus the frivolity of an ungovernable teenaged son, the cleverness of a slave who outwits his master to make everything come out right at the end. The plots are complicated, with all sorts of mistaken identities and surprise twists. Much of

Plautus and Terence were Rome's most famous dramatic comedians. This mosaic from Pompeii shows masked actors in a comedy playing a magician and clients.

the humor consists of clever puns, of constant involvement of the characters in embarassing and humiliating situations, and of the wildest sort of slapstick comedy.

Rome's two masters of comedy were Plautus (ca. 254–184 B.C.), twenty of whose plays survive, and Terence (ca. 190–159 B.C.), who has left us six plays. Terence is much the milder, and, if we consider that originally he was a slave born in Africa, the purity of his Latin is truly remarkable. The following selection is taken from the more boisterous Plautus.

The Boastful Soldier

The title of the play, *Miles Gloriosus (The Boastful Soldier),* describes the subject of the play. The soldier, Pyrgopolinices (whose name means "tower-city-conqueror" in Greek) has a good imagination in recounting his deeds, but his sponging friend Artotrogus ("bread-eater") has an even better one, inventing fantastic tales about his companion.

AR: Meminī centum in Ciliciā
et quīnquāgintā, centum in Scytholatrōniā,[1]
trīgintā Sardōs, sexāgintā Macedonēs—
sunt hominēs quōs tū—occīdistī ūnō diē.
PY: Quanta istaec[2] hominum summa est? AR: Septem mīlia.
PY: Tantum esse oportet. Rēctē ratiōnem tenēs.
AR: Quid in Cappadociā, ubi tū quīngentōs simul,
nī hebes machaera foret,[3] ūnō ictū[4] occīderās?
Quid tibi ego dīcam, quod omnēs mortālēs sciunt,
Pyrgopolinīcem tē ūnum in terrā vīvere
virtūte et fōrmā et factīs invictissimīs?

[1] a nonexistent place: "Scythia-robber-land." Cilicia and Cappadocia are in Asia minor, the Sardinians are west of Italy, and the Macedonians north of Greece.
[2] = ista
[3] if your sword had not been dull; ni = nisi
[4] blow

5

10

Amant tē omnēs mulierēs neque iniūriā,[5]
quī sīs tam pulcher; vel[6] illae quae herī palliō
mē reprehendērunt.[7] PY: Quid eae dīxērunt tibi?

15 AR: Rogitābant: "Hicine[8] Achillēs est?"
"Immō[9] eius frāter," inquam, "est."

Lucretius

Almost nothing certain is known about the life of this great poet, who lived during the first half of the first century B.C. His one poem, the *De Rerum Natura (On the Nature of Things),* is a poetic exposition of the theories of the Greek philosopher Epicurus. It is important because it is an attempt to explain the universe in the scientific terms of an atomic theory often surprisingly similar to our own and to dispel our superstitious fears about death and terrifying natural phenomena, such as thunder, lightning, and earthquakes, which were commonly attributed to the actions of the gods. It also anticipates modern notions of biological and social evolution.

Knowledge Produces a Tranquil Mind

Suāve,[1] marī[2] magnō turbantibus aequora[3] ventīs,
ē terrā magnum alterius spectāre labōrem,
nōn quia vexārī quemquam est iūcunda voluptās,
sed quibus ipse malīs careās[4] quia cernere[5] suāve est.

5 Sed nīl dulcius est, bene quam mūnīta tenēre
ēdita doctrīnā sapientum templa[6] serēnā,
dēspicere unde queās[7] aliōs passimque[8] vidēre
errāre atque viam pālantēs[9] quaerere vītae,
certāre ingeniō, contendere nōbilitāte,

10 noctēs atque diēs nītī[10] praestante labōre
ad summās ēmergere opēs rērumque potīrī.
Ō miserās hominum mentēs,[11] ō pectora caeca![12]

The Greek philosopher Epicurus (341–270 B.C.) founded his own school in Athens. Called the Garden, it was one of the few that accepted women and slaves. The followers of Epicurus focused heavily on sense perceptions and enjoyed much pleasure; many thought the Epicureans were hedonistic.

Ronald Sheridan/Ancient Art & Architecture

Two features of Lucretius' scientific explanation of the universe are that nothing is produced from nothing and that the universe consists only of matter and empty space.

Nīl posse creārī dē nīlō.[13]
Corpora[14] sunt et ināne.

Men are like relay racers; they pass on the torch of life to the next generation.

Sīc rērum summa novātur
semper, et inter sē mortālēs mūtua[15] vīvunt.
Augēscunt aliae gentēs, aliae minuuntur,
inque brevī spatiō mūtantur saecla animantum[16]
et quasi cursōrēs vītāī[17] lampada trādunt.

[13] from **nil** (ablative)
[14] i.e., of matter
[15] *in turn*
[16] = **animantium**, *of living beings*
[17] = **vitae**

Cornelius Nepos

Nepos wrote biographies of famous Greeks and Romans. He lived in the first century B.C. In this selection he tells about an honest politician who could not be bought.

Phōcion Athēniēnsis saepe exercitibus praefuit summōsque magistrātūs cēpit, sed tamen multō nōtior est ob prīvātam vītam quam ob glōriam reī mīlitāris. Fuit enim semper pauper, quamquam dītissimus esse poterat propter honōrēs dēlātōs potestātēsque summās quae eī ā populō dabantur. Cum magna mūnera pecūniae ā lēgātīs rēgis Philippī dēlāta reiceret, lēgātī dīxērunt: "Sī ipse haec nōn vīs,[1] līberīs tamen tuīs prōspicere tē oportet, quibus difficile erit in summā inopiā tantam patris glōriam servāre." Hīs ille, "Sī meī[2] similēs erunt," inquit, "īdem hic parvus ager illōs alet quī mē ad hanc dignitātem perdūxit; sī dissimilēs sunt futūrī, nōlō meā pecūniā illōrum lūxuriam alī augērīque." 5 ... 10

[1] from **volō**
[2] genitive of **ego**, with **similis**: *like me*

Catullus

Catullus, a younger contemporary of Caesar, Cicero, and Nepos, was Rome's most inspired lyric poet. Many of his poems are addressed to his sweetheart Lesbia. His love affair had its ups and downs, but it did not end happily. Other short poems of his are written to friends and enemies, including Caesar, who at different times was a friend and foe. Other poems include marriage songs, a short epic, and a lament for his dead brother.

Scala/Art Resource, NY

Passer, dēliciae meae puellae. This detail from a wall painting in a Roman villa shows the Romans' fondness for birds.

"Poor Little Sparrow"

In the following poem, Catullus mourns the death of the pet sparrow **(passer)** of his sweetheart Lesbia.

Lūgēte, ō Venerēs Cupīdinēsque[1]
et quantum est hominum venustiōrum![2]
Passer mortuus est meae puellae,
passer, dēliciae[3] meae puellae,
quem plūs illa oculīs[4] suīs amābat;
nam mellītus[5] erat, suamque nōrat[6]
ipsam tam bene quam puella mātrem,
nec sēsē ā gremiō[7] illius movēbat,
sed circumsiliēns modo[8] hūc modo illūc
ad sōlam dominam usque pīpiābat.[9]
Quī nunc it per iter tenebricōsum[10]
illūc unde negant redīre quemquam.
At vōbīs male sit, malae tenebrae
Orcī, quae omnia bella[11] dēvorātis;
tam bellum mihi passerem abstulistis.
Ō factum male! Iō miselle[12] passer!
Tuā nunc operā meae puellae
flendō turgidulī rubent ocellī.[13]

[1] i.e., all the gods of love and beauty

[2] *all of the handsome men there are*

[3] *pet;* nominative

[4] ablative of comparison; see the Grammar Appendix, p. 498.5

[5] *sweet as honey*

[6] for **nōverat.** With **suam** supply **dominam** (Lesbia); **ipsam** modifies **mātrem:** *as the girl (knew) her own mother.*

[7] *lap*

[8] *now . . . now*

[9] *chirped.* The word imitates the sound ("peep") made by the bird.

[10] *shadowy;* to Hades. See **tenebrae,** *darkness* (line 13).

[11] adjective, from **bellus,** *beautiful;* cf. English *belle*

[12] diminutive of **miser:** *poor little.*

[13] The diminutives (**ocellus** from **oculus, turgidulus** from **turgidus,** *swollen*) are used, like **miselle** above, for pathetic effect, as they heighten the tenderness and affection of the expression. **Rubent** means *are red.*

Counting Kisses

Vīvāmus, mea Lesbia, atque amēmus,
rūmōrēsque senum sevēriōrum
omnēs ūnius aestimēmus assis.[1]
Sōlēs occidere et redīre possunt;
nōbīs cum semel occidit brevis lūx,[2]
nox est perpetua ūna dormienda.
Dā mī[3] bāsia[4] mīlle, deinde centum,
dein mīlle altera, dein secunda centum,
deinde usque altera mīlle, deinde centum.
Dein, cum mīlia multa fēcerīmus,
Conturbābimus illa, nē sciāmus
aut nē quis malus invidēre[5] possit,
cum tantum sciat esse bāsiōrum.

5

10

[1] *at one penny* (genitive of value)
[2] i.e., life
[3] = **mihi**
[4] from **bāsium**, *kiss*
[5] i.e., cast the evil eye

Cicero

You have already become slightly acquainted with M. Tullius Cicero in Lessons XIII and XXXVII. Now you will get to know him a little better.

Cicero (106–43 B.C.) was Rome's greatest prose writer. He was the leading public speaker at a time when the ability to make an effective speech was even more important than it is today. Many of his orations still exist, including those against Catiline and Mark Antony, and the one for Archias the poet, in which he shows his appreciation of poetry. He wrote fine essays on moral and philosophical subjects: on friendship, on old age, on one's duties, etc. He also wrote on the history and technique of oratory. A large number of his letters, which he himself had no intention of publishing, have been preserved. Many are addressed to his intimate friend Atticus. They cover all sorts of subjects, from bathtubs to politics, from

Photri

A fifteenth-century manuscript page from Cicero's treatise *Dē Officiīs*. Cicero's essays deal with a wide range of subjects, from oratorical training, to Greek philosophy, to practical behavior.

the birth of a son to the divorce and death of his daughter. He died while vainly attempting to defend constitutional government against Mark Antony.

The Regulation of War

Adapted from Cicero's treatise ***Dē Officiīs,*** which was written for his son.

In rē pūblicā maximē cōnservanda sunt iūra bellī. Nam sunt duo genera dēcertandī, ūnum per disputātiōnem, alterum per vim. Illud proprium est hominis, hoc animālium. Itaque nōn fugiendum est[1] ad vim et bellum nisi ūtī nōn licet disputātiōne.[2] Suscipienda quidem bella sunt ut sine iniūriā in
5 pāce vīvāmus; post autem victōriam cōnservandī sunt eī quī nōn crūdēlēs in bellō fuērunt, ut maiōrēs nostrī Tusculānōs, Volscōs, Sabīnōs in cīvitātem etiam accēpērunt. At Carthāginem omnīnō sustulērunt; etiam Corinthum (et hoc vix probō), sed crēdō eōs hoc fēcisse nē locus[3] ipse ad bellum faciendum hortārī[4] posset. Nam pāx quae nihil habitūra sit
10 īnsidiārum semper est petenda. Sed eī quī, armīs positīs, ad imperātōrum fidem fugiunt recipiendī sunt. In quō magnopere apud nostrōs iūstitia culta est. Nūllum bellum est iūstum nisi quod[5] aut, rēbus repetītīs, gerātur aut dēnūntiātum ante sit. Bellum autem ita suscipiātur ut nihil nisi pāx quaerī videātur.

Good Citizenship

Adapted from various works of Cicero, primarily the ***Dē Officiīs.***

Nec locus tibi ūllus dulcior esse dēbet patriā.[1]

Omnium societātum[2] nūlla est gravior, nūlla cārior quam ea quae cum rē pūblicā est ūnī cuique[3] nostrum. Cārī sunt parentēs, cārī līberī, propinquī, familiārēs, sed omnēs omnium cāritātēs patria ūna continet, prō quā nēmō
5 bonus dubitet[4] mortem petere. Quō[5] est dētestābilior istōrum immānitās[6] quī lacerāvērunt omnī scelere patriam et in eā dēlendā occupātī et sunt et fuērunt.

Est proprium mūnus[7] magistrātūs intellegere sē gerere persōnam[8] cīvitātis dēbēreque eius dignitātem sustinēre, servāre lēgēs, iūra
10 discrībere,[9] ea[10] fideī suae commissa meminisse. Prīvātum[11] autem oportet aequō et parī iūre cum cīvibus vīvere, atque in rē pūblicā ea velle quae tranquilla et honesta sint: tālem enim solēmus et sentīre bonum cīvem et dīcere.

Sī pecūniam aequam omnibus esse nōn placet, sī ingenia omnium paria
15 esse nōn possunt, iūra certē paria dēbent esse eōrum quī sunt cīvēs in eādem rē pūblicā.

Mēns et animus et cōnsilium et sententia cīvitātis posita est in lēgibus. Ut corpora nostra sine mente, sīc cīvitās sine lēge suīs partibus ūtī nōn potest.

Fundāmentum iūstitiae est fidēs.

[1] impersonal; translate: *we must not resort to*
[2] ablative with **ūti**
[3] *site*
[4] Supply as object "the inhabitants of Corinth."
[5] *except (one) which.* War should be started only if restitution of stolen property (**rēbus**) is sought or if there is a formal declaration beforehand.

[1] ablative of comparison; see the Grammar Appendix, p. 498.5
[2] *associations*
[3] from **quisque:** *which each one of us has with,* etc. **Nostrum** is from **ego,** not **noster.**
[4] *would hesitate*
[5] *therefore*
[6] *ferocity*
[7] *it is the special duty*
[8] *represents;* literally, *wears the mask of (plays the part of)*
[9] *administer justice*
[10] neuter plural, object of **meminisse.** It is modified by **commissa.**
[11] *a private citizen,* in contrast to **magistrātūs**

Quotations from Cicero

1. Aliae nātiōnēs servitūtem patī possunt; populī Rōmānī rēs est propria lībertās.
2. Cavēte, patrēs cōnscrīptī, nē spē praesentis pācis perpetuam pācem āmittātis.
3. Cēdant arma togae.[1]
4. Cōnsuētūdinis magna vīs est.
5. Ō tempora, ō mōrēs!
6. Parēs cum paribus facillimē congregantur.[2]
7. Salūs populī suprēma lēx estō.[3]

[1] The toga represents *civil life,* as contrasted with *military.* Motto of the state of Wyoming.
[2] *gather.* What is the modern form of this proverb?
[3] *let . . . be.* Motto of the state of Missouri.

Sallust

Sallust (86–34 B.C.) was a politician and officer who held important commands under Caesar during the Civil War. With the fortune he amassed, supposedly from plundering the province of Numidia, he bought a palatial estate in Rome, with magnificent gardens which are still famous. Two of his works which have survived are the *Catiline* and the *Jugurtha,* the former dealing with the conspiracy of Catiline, the latter with a war against an African king. Sallust claimed impartiality, but he is bitterly critical of the old Roman aristocracy and the decadence for which he thinks they are responsible.

The Good Old Days of Early Rome

Igitur domī mīlitiaeque[1] bonī mōrēs colēbantur; concordia maxima, minima avāritia erat; iūs bonumque apud eōs nōn lēgibus magis quam nātūrā valēbat. Iūrgia,[2] discordiās, simultātēs[3] cum hostibus exercēbant, cīvēs cum cīvibus dē virtūte certābant. In suppliciīs deōrum magnificī, domī parcī, in amīcōs fidēlēs erant. Duābus hīs artibus, audāciā in bellō, 5
ubi pāx ēvēnerat aequitāte, sēque remque pūblicam cūrābant. Quārum rērum ego maxima documenta haec habeō, quod in bellō saepius vindicātum est[4] in eōs quī contrā imperium in hostem pugnāverant[5] quīque tardius[6] revocātī proeliō[7] excesserant, quam[8] quī signa relinquere aut pulsī locō[7] cēdere ausī erant; in pāce vērō quod beneficiīs magis quam metū 10
imperium agitābant et, acceptā iniūriā, ignōscere quam persequī mālēbant.

[1] *abroad* (locative)
[2] *quarrels*
[3] *hatreds*
[4] *punishment was inflicted* (on)
[5] cf. the story of Manlius in Lesson XXXIV
[6] *too slowly* (with **excesserant**)
[7] ablative; see the Grammar Appendix, p. 498.1
[8] To be taken with **saepius;** supply **in eōs.**

Publilius Syrus and His Proverbs

Publilius Syrus was a writer of a type of comedy which was very popular when he wrote, in the time of Caesar. One reason why he won so much favor was his use of many proverbial expressions. The plays themselves have disappeared, but someone made a collection of the proverbs in them, and these have been preserved. Many are as fresh and applicable today as they were two thousand years ago.

1. Ab aliīs exspectēs¹ alterī² quod³ fēcerīs.
2. Aliēna⁴ nōbīs, nostra plūs aliīs placent.
3. Aliēnum aes hominī ingenuō⁵ acerba est servitūs.
4. Aut amat aut ōdit mulier; nihil est tertium.
5. Avārus ipse miseriae causa est suae.
6. Avārus, nisi cum moritur, nihil rēctē facit.
7. Bis vincit quī sē vincit in victōriā.
8. Comes fācundus⁶ in viā prō vehiculō est.
9. Cui⁷ plūs licet quam pār est plūs vult quam licet.
10. Discordiā fit cārior concordia.
11. Effugere cupiditātem rēgnum est vincere.
12. Etiam capillus ūnus habet umbram suam.
13. Inopī bis dat quī cito dat.
14. Male imperandō summum imperium āmittitur.
15. Necesse est minima⁸ maximōrum esse initia.
16. Paucōrum improbitās est multōrum calamitās.
17. Perīcula timidus etiam quae nōn sunt videt.
18. Quicquid fit cum virtūte fit cum glōriā.
19. Spīna etiam grāta est ex quā spectātur rosa.
20. Stultī timent fortūnam, sapientēs ferunt.
21. Stultum facit fortūna quem vult perdere.
22. Taciturnitās stultō hominī prō sapientiā est.

Livy

Cato and the Women¹

Inter bellōrum magnōrum cūrās intercessit rēs parva sed quae² in magnum certāmen excesserit.³ In mediō Pūnicī bellī lēx lāta erat nē qua mulier plūs quam sēmunciam⁴ aurī habēret nec veste versicolōrī ūterētur nec vehiculō in urbe veherētur. Post bellum mulierēs voluērunt hanc lēgem
5 abrogārī. Nec auctōritāte nec imperiō virōrum continērī poterant; omnēs viās urbis obsidēbant; etiam audēbant adīre cōnsulēs. Sed cōnsul, M. Porcius Catō, haec verba fēcit: "Sī in⁵ suā quisque uxōre, cīvēs, iūs virī retinēre īnstituisset,⁶ minus negōtī cum omnibus fēminīs habērēmus.⁷ Quia singulās nōn continuimus, omnēs timēmus. Maiōrēs nostrī voluērunt
10 fēminās agere nūllam rem, nē prīvātam quidem, sine parentibus vel frātribus vel virīs; nōs, sī deīs placet, iam etiam rem pūblicam capere eās patimur. Hāc rē expugnātā, quid nōn temptābunt? Sī eās aequās virīs esse patiēminī, tolerābilēs vōbīs eās futūrās esse crēditis? Simul ac parēs esse coeperint, superiōrēs erunt. Nūlla lēx satis commoda omnibus est; id
15 modo⁸ quaeritur, sī maiōrī partī prōsit."⁹ Tum ūnus ex tribūnīs contrā lēgem locūtus est, et lēx abrogāta est. Mulierēs vīcerant.

At several points in the course of costly wars, Roman women came to the aid of a depleted state treasury by depositing their own money and jewels and the legacies of widows and orphans to the cause, so that religious ceremonies could continue during the crisis. Temples such as this one housed the state treasuries.

Bettmann/CORBIS

Horace

Horace (65–8 B.C.) was one of the greatest of Roman poets. He was a friend of Augustus and Vergil. His *Odes, Satires,* and *Epistles* are delightful reading. As his poems are not always easy to read, only quotations are given here. They often tell much in very brief but exquisitely phrased language (cf. No. 3 and note 2).

1. Aequam mementō[1] rēbus in arduīs servāre mentem.
2. Aurea mediocritās.
3. Carpe diem.[2]
4. Crēscentem sequitur cūra pecūniam.
5. Est modus[3] in rēbus.
6. Levius fit patientiā quicquid[4] corrigere est nefās.
7. Magnās inter opēs inops.
8. Nīl mortālibus arduī[5] est.
9. Nīl sine magnō vīta labōre dedit mortālibus.
10. Permitte dīvīs cētera.
11. Rāra avis.
12. Rīdentem dīcere vērum.
13. Vīxēre[6] fortēs ante Agamemnona.[7]

[1] imperative: *remember.* **Aequam** modifies **mentem.** In poetry the word order is freer than in prose.

[2] *Seize the (present) day.* It really means: "The day is like a rose that fades fast; pluck it while you may."

[3] in the same sense as **mediocritās** in No. 2

[4] *whatever.* The clause is the subject of **fit.**

[5] with **nil**: *nothing hard*

[6] for **vixērunt**

[7] accusative. Agamemnon led the Greeks in the Trojan War.

Sulpicia

Sulpicia is the only known Latin female poet. She was of aristocratic birth and was the niece of Messalla, a prominent citizen and supporter of the arts. She was welcome in Tibullus' literary circle and probably wrote around 30 B.C. Her contributions indicate the more prominent role women were beginning to play in fashionable society. Only six of her love poems, written to Cerinthus, have survived.

A scene from a series of frescoes in a Pompeian farmhouse called the Villa of the Mysteries, showing an initiation rite into a religious cult. A boy reads passages from the ritual as it goes forward.

Scala/Art Resource, NY

Here, Sulpicia complains to her uncle of having to spend her birthday away from Rome and Cerinthus.

[1] hateful country(side)

[2] to be spent

[3] (the land near modern) Arezzo

[4] river (with **frigidus**)

[5] at the right time, convenient (with **nōn**)

[6] my heart and soul; **meōs** goes with both **animum** and **sēnsūs**

[7] i.e., (ego) quam vīs (I) whom (your) pressure

[8] does not allow

Invīsus nātālis adest, quī rūre molestō[1]
    et sine Cērinthō trīstis agendus erit.[2]
Dulcius urbe quid est? An vīlla sit apta puellae
    atque Arrētīnō[3] frīgidus amnis[4] agrō?
5 Iam, nimium Messalla meī studiōse, quiēscās:
    nōn tempestīvae[5] saepe, propinque, viae.
Hīc animum sēnsūsque[6] meōs abducta relinquō,
    arbitriō quam vīs[7] nōn sinit[8] esse meō.

In the poem that follows, it appears that the trip was, at last, called off.

[1] unexpected

Scīs iter ex animō sublātum trīste puellae?
    nātālī Rōmae iam licet esse meō.
Omnibus ille diēs nōbīs nātālis agātur,
    quī nec opīnātā[1] nunc tibi sorte vēnit.

Vergil and Ovid

You have already met Vergil. You will have a chance to read some selections of his work in some of the chapters that follow. Ovid too is known to you. You may read some more parts of his poems in the next unit.

Roman Elegy

The Greeks had used the elegiac meter for drinking and military songs, for historical and political subjects, for inscriptions on tombstones and laments for the dead, and even for love poetry. It was this last category that the three most famous Roman elegists, Tibullus, Propertius, and Ovid, particularly developed into an extremely personal and sensitive form. Each immortalized the sweetheart to whom he addressed his verse, Tibullus' Delia, Propertius' Cynthia, and Ovid's Corinna. The following selection from Ovid exemplifies elegy's traditional role of mourning for the dead. Ovid here laments the loss of Tibullus, who had joined the earlier elegists in the Elysian Fields.

Sī tamen ē nōbīs[1] aliquid nisi nōmen et umbra
    restat, in Ēlysiā[2] valle Tibullus erit.
Obvius huic veniās[3] hederā iuvenālia cīnctus
    tempora[4] cum Calvō, docte Catulle, tuō.
Hīs comes umbra tua est. Sī qua est modo corporis umbra,
    auxistī numerōs, culte Tibulle, piōs.
Ossa quiēta, precor,[5] tūtā requiēscite in urnā,[6]
    et sit humus cinerī nōn onerōsa tuō.

[1] i.e., poets
[2] The Roman underworld was divided into sections. The Elysian Fields correspond to paradise.
[3] *come to meet him;* obvius is an adjective; literally, *in the way.*
[4] *your temples crowned with ivy*
[5] *I pray*
[6] At this time, cremation was the norm in Rome. A variant of the phrase found on hundreds of Roman tombstones: **sit tibi terra levis.**

Phaedrus

The fable is a very old form of literature in which animals generally speak and act like human beings. Usually a moral is attached. The most famous of all fabulists was the Greek writer Aesop, and his stories are still much read in many languages. In Rome during the age of Augustus, Phaedrus put these fables into simple Latin verse. Here are three of them, rewritten in prose.

The Wolf and the Lamb

Ad rīvum eundem lupus et agnus vēnerant; superior stābat lupus, longēque īnferior agnus. Tum lupus famē incitātus contrōversiae causam intulit. "Cūr," inquit, "turbulentam fēcistī mihi aquam bibentī?" Agnus timēns respondit: "Quō modō possum hoc facere, lupe? Ā tē dēcurrit aqua ad mē." Repulsus ille vēritātis vīribus: "Ante sex mēnsēs," ait, "male dīxistī[1] mihi." Respondit agnus: "Equidem nātus nōn eram." "Pater certē tuus," ille inquit, "male dīxit mihi." Atque ita raptum lacerat iniūstā nece.

Haec propter illōs scrīpta est hominēs fābula quī fictīs causīs innocentēs opprimant.

[1] with **male**: *swore at*

Several Pompeian houses have a mosaic like this on the floor of the vestibulum. Do you get the message?

Ronald Sheridan/Ancient Art & Architecture

The Greedy Dog

Āmittit meritō[1] suum quī aliēnum appetit. Canis dum per flūmen carnem ferret natāns, in aquā vīdit simulācrum suum, aliamque praedam ab aliō cane ferrī putāns ēripere voluit; sed dēceptus avidus, quem tenēbat ōre dīmīsit cibum nec quem petēbat potuit attingere.

[1] *deservedly*

Sour Grapes

[1] *fox*

[2] *grapes, bunch of grapes*

[3] *make light of*

Famē coācta vulpes[1] in altā vīneā ūvam[2] petēbat, summīs vīribus saliēns. Quam ubi tangere nōn potuit, discēdēns, "Nōndum mātūra est," inquit; "nōlō acerbam sūmere."

Eī quī verbīs ēlevant[3] quae nōn facere possunt hoc exemplum sibi
5 ascrībere dēbent.

Valerius Maximus

In the first century A.D. Valerius Maximus compiled a book of well-known stories from history, both Roman and foreign, to illustrate various human qualities and conditions such as courage, superstition, cruelty. The purpose of the book was to provide material for public speakers who wanted to illustrate their points by means of examples from history, just as today many speakers make use of jokebooks.

Damon and Pythias

[1] *(as) bail*

[2] i.e., Dionysius

Cum Dionȳsius, rēx Syrācūsārum, Pythiam philosophum interficere vellet, hic ā Dionȳsiō petīvit ut sibi licēret domum proficīscī rērum suārum dispōnendārum causā. Amīcus eius Dāmōn erat. Tanta erat amīcitia inter Dāmōnem et Pythiam ut Dāmōn sē vadem[1] prō reditū alterīus rēgī dare nōn
5 dubitāret. Appropinquante cōnstitūtō diē nec illō redeunte, ūnus quisque stultitiam Dāmōnis damnāvit. At is nihil sē dē amīcī fidē timēre dīcēbat. Hōrā cōnstitūtā Pythiās vēnit. Admīrātus utrīusque animum Dionȳsius supplicium remīsit et eōs rogāvit ut sē[2] socium amīcitiae reciperent.

A Costly Joke

[1] *aedileship,* a public office

[2] = **Hoc;** see the Grammar Appendix, p. 494.4c

[3] *defeat*

P. Scīpiō Nāsīca, cum aedīlitātem[1] adulēscēns peteret, mōre candidātōrum manum cuiusdam agricolae rūsticō opere dūrātam prehendit. Iocī causā rogāvit agricolam num manibus solitus esset ambulāre. Quod[2] dictum ā circumstantibus audītum ad populum allātum est causaque fuit
5 repulsae[3] Scīpiōnis. Nam omnēs agricolae paupertātem suam ab eō rīdērī iūdicantēs īram suam contrā eius iocum ostendērunt.

Seneca

Seneca, who wrote many books on philosophy, was the tutor and later the adviser of the emperor Nero (A.D. 54–68), who eventually forced him to commit suicide. His books preach Stoic philosophy.

[1] for **nōvisse**

[2] Translate as if indicative.

1. Magna rēs est vōcis et silentī tempora nōsse.[1]

2. Maximum remedium īrae mora est.

3. Nōn est in rēbus vitium, sed in ipsō animō.

4. Nōn sum ūnī angulō nātus; patria mea tōtus hic mundus est.

5. Omnis ars imitātiō est nātūrae.

6. Optimum est patī quod ēmendāre nōn possīs.[2]

7. Ōtium sine litterīs mors est.

8. Quī beneficium dedit taceat: nārret quī accēpit.

9. Sī vīs amārī, amā.

10. Ubicumque homō est, ibi beneficī locus est.

Petronius

Nothing in Latin literature is quite so zany and ludicrous as the *Satiricon* of Petronius. It is a kind of novel, containing a wild medley of prose and poetry, dealing mostly with the escapades of three lower-class rogues who must live by their wits and who are constantly in trouble with the authorities. Best known of their adventures is the account of a fantastic dinner party at the house of an ex-slave named Trimalchio, who was so illiterate that he thought Hannibal took part in the Trojan War and so enormously wealthy that he bought the whole west coast of Italy so that, when he sailed to Sicily, he would not have to sail past anyone else's coastline! The following selection should give you still more indications of the size of Trimalchio's fortune.

Petronius is thought to have lived in the first century A.D. and has been identified with the Petronius who was called the **Arbiter ēlegantiae** of Nero's court because of his exquisite refinement.

Guildhall Art Gallery, Corporation of London, UK/Bridgeman Art Library

Arbiter ēlegantiae. A sumptuous Roman banquet (King Herod's birthday feast) as imagined by Edward A. Armitage in the nineteenth century. Extravagance in dining reached its zenith under the emperor Nero (A.D. 55–64), whose court poet Petronius advised him in all matters of good and bad taste.

¹ *newsman, secretary*
² *doings, news*
³ *the estate at Cumae*
⁴ *barn*
⁵ *500,000 pecks of wheat, enough to feed 10,000 people for a year*
⁶ *tamed, broken in*
⁷ *vault*
⁸ *10,000,000 sesterces (more than $500,000)*
⁹ *therefore*
¹⁰ *estates*
¹¹ = **scīverō**

In this selection, Trimalchio has his own newspaper read aloud to the guests at his dinner party.

Āctuārius¹ tamquam urbis ācta² recitāvit: "Hōc diē in praediō Cūmānō³ quod est Trimalchiōnis, nātī sunt puerī XXX, puellae XL; sublāta in horreum⁴ trīticī mīlia modium quīngenta;⁵ bovēs domitī⁶ quīngentī. Eōdem diē: in arcam⁷ relātum est quod collocārī nōn potuit sēstertium centiēs.⁸ Eōdem diē: incendium factum est in hortīs Pompeiānīs." "Quid," inquit Trimalchiō, "quandō mihi Pompeiānī hortī ēmptī sunt?" "Annō priōre," inquit āctuārius, "et ideō⁹ in ratiōnem nōndum vēnērunt." Trimalchiō, "Quīcumque," inquit, "mihi fundī¹⁰ ēmptī fuerint, nisi intrā sextum mēnsem scierō,¹¹ in ratiōnēs meās īnferrī vetō."

Quintilian

Possibly the most famous schoolteacher of all time is Quintilian (ca. A.D. 35–96), who was appointed the first state-paid professor of rhetoric (oratory) by the emperor Vespasian. After a lifetime of teaching and practice at the bar, at the request of his devoted pupils he put his theories of education into twelve books called the ***Īnstitūtiō Ōrātōria*** *(Introduction to Public Speaking),* which carry the training of the orator from the cradle to the grave, for he believed in beginning education when the child was born and continuing it all one's life. So the nursery school and the kindergarten are not new, nor is adult education. Quintilian's favorite orator was Cicero, although he does not hesitate to criticize even him. The basic principle of his teaching was that a man could not be a great orator, whatever his skill, unless he were first of all a good man.

¹ *nurses*
² *a Greek philosopher and teacher*
³ *with* **haud**: *undoubtedly*
⁴ *form*
⁵ *according as*
⁶ *at any time*
⁷ *he should not accustom himself*
⁸ *with* **nē**: *not even*
⁹ *must be unlearned*
¹⁰ *I could wish*
¹¹ **Gāī**
¹² *i.e., to get an education*

Ante omnia nē sit vitiōsus sermō nūtrīcibus,¹ quās, sī fierī posset, sapientēs Chrysippus² optāvit, certē quantum rēs paterētur, optimās ēligī voluit. Et mōrum quidem in hīs haud dubiē³ prior ratiō est; rēctē tamen etiam loquantur. Hās prīmum audiet puer, hārum verba effingere⁴
5 imitandō cōnābitur. Et nātūrā tenācissimī sumus eōrum quae rudibus animīs percēpimus. Et haec ipsa magis pertināciter haerent quō⁵ dēteriōra sunt. Nam bona facile mūtantur in peius; num quandō⁶ in bonum vertēris vitia? Nōn adsuēscat⁷ ergō, nē dum īnfāns quidem⁸ est, sermōnī quī dēdiscendus sit.⁹

10 In parentibus vērō quam plūrimum esse ērudītiōnis optāverim,¹⁰ nec dē patribus tantum loquor, nam Gracchōrum ēloquentiae multum contulisse accēpimus Cornēliam mātrem, cuius doctissimus sermō in posterōs quoque est epistulīs trāditus; et Laelia C.¹¹ fīlia reddidisse in loquendō paternam ēlegantiam dīcitur; et Hortēnsiae Q. fīliae ōrātiō legitur. Nec tamen iī
15 quibus discere¹² ipsīs nōn contigit minōrem cūram docendī līberōs habeant, sed sint propter hoc ipsum ad cētera magis dīligentēs.

Martial and His Wit

Like Seneca and Quintilian, Martial was born in Spain but moved to Rome. He is the writer who gave the word *epigram* its present meaning. It is generally a short poem which makes fun of someone. Its clever and often unexpected point is at the end, at times in the last word.

An Unfair Exchange
1. Cūr nōn mittŏ meōs tibi, Pontiliāne, libellōs?
      Nē mihi tū mittās, Pontiliāne, tuōs.

A Friend and His Faults
2. Difficilis, facilis, iūcundus, acerbus es īdem.
      Nec tēcum possum vīvere nec sine tē.

"Fifty-Fifty"
3. Nūbere[1] vīs Prīscō: nōn mīror, Paula; sapīstī.[2]
      Dūcere[1] tē nōn vult Prīscus: et[3] ille sapit.

Rich Wives
4. Uxōrem quārē locuplētem[4] dūcere nōlim
      quaeritis? Uxōrī nūbere[5] nōlō meae.
  Īnferior mātrōna suō sit, Prīsce, marītō;
      nōn aliter fīunt fēmina virque parēs.

The Plagiarist
5. Quem recitās meus est, ō Fīdentīne, libellus,
      sed, male cum recitās, incipit esse tuus.

A Good Match
6. Cum sītis similēs parēsque vītā,
  uxor pessima, pessimus marītus,
  mīror nōn bene convenīre[6] vōbīs.

[1] marry, literally, *take the veil for*, and hence followed by the dative; used of a woman, whereas the word used of a man is **dūcere (domum)**

[2] for **sapivisti:** *you are wise*

[3] *also*

[4] *rich*

[5] A man who marries a rich wife becomes the "lady" of the house.

[6] impersonal: *that you are not well suited*

Tacitus

Last of the great Roman historians was Cornelius Tacitus (ca. A.D. 55–120). His two most extensive works are the *Annals* and the *Histories,* which between them originally covered the period of Roman history from the death of Augustus through the reign of Domitian, i.e., from A.D. 14 to A.D. 96. He also wrote monographs on oratory, on Germany, and on the deeds of his father-in-law, Agricola. He was a distinguished orator and public figure, rising to the consulship in 97. His cynical tone, his austerity, and his intense brevity have made him a favorite of students of Latin style, while his bitter senatorial prejudice against the imperial regime has been chiefly responsible for our present impression, largely incorrect, of the corruption and cruelty of Roman emperors. The *Agricola,* from which the following selection is taken, deals largely with Britain, because Tacitus' father-in-law was a successful general there.

Agricola Brings Roman Culture to Britain

Iam vērō prīncipum fīliōs līberālibus artibus ērudīre,[1] et ingenia Britannōrum studiīs Gallōrum anteferre,[2] ut quī modo[3] linguam Rōmānam abnuēbant,[4] ēloquentiam concupīscerent.[5] Inde etiam habitūs[6] nostrī honor et frequēns toga. Paulātimque dēscēnsum ad dēlēnimenta[7] vitiōrum,
5 porticūs et balineās[8] et convīviōrum[9] ēlegantiam. Idque apud imperītōs hūmānitās vocābātur, cum pars servitūtis esset.

[1] The infinitives are used instead of a past tense of the indicative.
[2] *put ahead of* (with dative)
[3] *recently*
[4] *were rejecting*
[5] *were eager for*
[6] *clothing*
[7] *enticements*
[8] = **balnea.** The Roman baths at Bath are still one of the great tourist attractions of England.
[9] *banquets*

Juvenal

Juvenal was a satirist who lived at the beginning of the second century A.D. He was a contemporary of Pliny the Younger. The vices of his times are the themes of his poems.

1. Probitās laudātur et alget.[1]
2. Pānem et circēnsēs.[2]
3. Nēmō malus fēlīx.
4. Quis custōdiet ipsōs custōdēs?
5. Mēns sāna in corpore sānō.

[1] *shivers,* i.e., the honest man is usually too poor to buy warm clothing
[2] *bread and circus games*—all that the degenerate Romans of his day are interested in, according to Juvenal.

Suetonius

Rome's most important writer of biography was Suetonius, who wrote the lives of the first twelve emperors, down to the end of the first century A.D. Much of the gossip that is still passed around about these emperors comes from his *Lives of the Caesars*. The story of Nero in Lesson XXXIX is based on his account.

Aulus Gellius

The two stories that follow are adapted from Aulus Gellius, a writer of the second century A.D., who tells many curious and interesting anecdotes. His *Noctes Atticae,* or *Attic Nights,* is a sort of literary scrapbook, written during winter evenings in Attica, Greece, to amuse and instruct his children.

A Lesson in Voting

Fabricius[1] magnā glōriā vir magnīsque rēbus gestīs fuit. P. Cornēlius Rūfīnus imperātor bonus et fortis et mīlitāris disciplīnae perītus[2] fuit, sed avārus erat. Hunc Fabricius nōn probābat et eī inimīcus ob mōrēs fuit. Sed cum tempore difficillimō reī pūblicae cōnsulēs creandī essent et Rūfīnus peteret cōnsulātum competītōrēsque eius nōn essent bellī perītī, summā ope[3] Fabricius labōrāvit ut Rūfīnō cōnsulātus dēferrētur. Eam rem quibusdam mīrantibus, "Mālō," inquit, "ā cīve spoliārī quam ab hoste vēnīre."[4] M. Cicerō refert hoc esse dictum, nōn aliīs, sed ipsī Rūfīnō, cum hic Fabriciō ob opem[5] grātiās ageret.

Hunc Rūfīnum, postquam bis cōnsul et dictātor fuit, cēnsor[6] Fabricius ob lūxuriam ē senātū ēiēcit.

[1] Fabricius was the hero of the war with Pyrrhus, who admired him so much that he offered him part of his kingdom.
[2] with the genitive
5 [3] *effort*
[4] *to be sold* (from **vēneō**)
[5] *help*
[6] The censor had the right to expel senators who committed offenses or whose manner of living was not in accord with the best Roman 10 tradition.

Androclus[1] and the Lion

In Circō Maximō vēnātiō[2] populō dabātur. Multae ibi ferae erant, sed praeter aliās omnēs ūnus leō magnitūdine corporis animōs oculōsque omnium in sē converterat.

Inductus erat servus inter complūrēs aliōs ad pugnam ferārum. Eī servō[3] Androclus nōmen fuit. Hunc ille leō ubi vīdit procul, statim quasi admīrāns stetit ac deinde lēniter, quasi cognōscēns ad hominem accēdit.

[1] generally called Androcles
[2] *hunt,* i.e., a fight between men and wild beasts
[3] dative of possession

5

Erich Lessing/Art Resource, NY

Vēnātiō *(the hunt),* **or combat between man and animals in the arena. Spectators watch from their boxes as one gladiator, already under attack, faces another lion that is being prodded out of its cage. A second fighter has been badly mauled. The seven "eggs" are to mark the number of events in the spectacles or the laps in the chariot races.**

Tum caudam mōre canis movet hominisque manūs linguā lēniter dēmulcet. Androclus, prīmum territus, nunc leōnem spectat. Tum quasi leōne cognitō, homō gaudēre vīsus est.

10   Eā rē tam mīrā maximī clāmōrēs populī excitātī sunt. Caesar[4] Androclum vocāvit et quaesīvit causam cūr illī ūnī ferōcissimus leō pepercisset. Tum Androclus rem mīrandam nārrat.

"Cum prōvinciae," inquit, "Āfricae dominus meus imperāret, ego iniūstē verberātus fugere coāctus sum. Specum[5] quendam remōtum inveniō
15   et eum ingredior. Neque multō post ad eundem specum venit hic leō, vulnerātō ūnō pede, gemitūs ob dolōrem ēdēns. Prīmō quidem cōnspectū leōnis territus sum. Sed postquam leō ingressus mē vīdit, lēniter accessit et pedem ostendere mihi quasi opis petendae grātiā vīsus est. Ibi ego spīnam magnam, pedī eius haerentem, ēripuī et saniem[6] expressī. Ille tum, pede in
20   manibus meīs positō, quiētem cēpit. Ex eō diē trēs annōs ego et leō in eōdem specū vīximus. Membra ferārum leō mihi ferēbat, quae ego, ignis cōpiam nōn habēns, sōle torrēbam. Sed tandem specum relīquī et ā mīlitibus prehēnsus ad dominum ex Āfricā Rōmam dēductus sum. Is mē statim ad ferās mīsit. Intellegō autem hunc quoque leōnem, posteā captum,
25   grātiam mihi referre."

Haec dīxit Androclus. Omnibus petentibus, dīmissus est et leō eī dōnātus. Posteā Androclus et leō, lōrō[7] ligātus, circum tabernās ībant. Androclus pecūniam accipiēbat, leō flōrēs. Omnēs dīcēbant: "Hic est leō hospes hominis; hic est homō medicus leōnis."

[4] probably Tiberius
[5] cave
[6] pus
[7] strap

Miscellaneous Quotations

No. 1 is from a treatise on farming written by Varro, a contemporary of Cicero. No. 2 is from Sallust. Nos. 3, 4, and 5 are from Ovid. No. 6 is from Livy. No. 7 is attributed to the emperor Tiberius. No. 8 is from Quintilian. No. 9 is from Tacitus. Nos. 10 and 11 are from the poet Claudian (about A.D. 400). No. 12 is from St. Jerome. No. 13 is from the *Vulgate* (Jerome's translation of the Bible). No. 14 is from Vegetius (fourth century). Nos. 15 and 16 are from the *Corpus Iuris Civilis,* the sixth-century law code, even now the basis of law in many countries. No. 17 is from Cassiodorus (sixth century). No. 18 is from Pseudo-Isidore (ninth century). Nos. 19 and 20 are from Thomas à Kempis (fifteenth century). Nos. 21 and 22 are from two seventeenth-century philosophers, Francis Bacon and René Descartes. No. 23 was applied to Benjamin Franklin by A.R.J. Turgot, the eighteenth-century French philosopher-statesman.

[1] Supply **pūblicae.**
[2] fall
[3] even
[4] Supply **itinere.**

1. Dīvīna nātūra dedit agrōs, ars hūmāna aedificāvit urbēs.

2. Concordiā parvae rēs[1] crēscunt, discordiā maximae dīlābuntur.[2]

3. Est deus in nōbīs.

4. Fās est et[3] ab hoste docērī.

5. Mediō[4] tūtissimus ībis.

6. Externus[5] timor maximum concordiae vinculum.

7. In cīvitāte līberā linguam mentemque līberās esse (dīcēbat).

8. Damnant quod nōn intellegunt.

9. Omne ignōtum prō magnificō.[6]

10. Ipsa quidem virtūs pretium sibi.

11. Omnia mors aequat.

12. Facis dē necessitāte virtūtem.

13. Magna est vēritās et praevalet.

14. Quī dēsīderat pācem praeparet bellum.

15. Cōgitātiōnis poenam nēmō patitur.

16. Iūris praecepta sunt haec: honestē vīvere, alterum nōn laedere, suum cuique tribuere.

17. Glōriōsa est scientia litterārum, quia, quod prīmum est, in homine mōrēs pūrgat; quod secundum, verbōrum grātiam subministrat.

18. Necessitās nōn habet lēgem.

19. Dē duōbus malīs, minus est semper ēligendum.

20. Ō quam cito trānsit glōria mundī!

21. Ipsa scientia potestās est.

22. Ego cōgitō, ergō sum.

23. Ēripuit[7] caelō fulmen,[8] mox scēptra tyrannīs.

24. Crocodīlī lacrimae.

25. Vestis virum facit.

26. Festīnā lentē.[9]

27. Nōlī dīcere[10] omnia quae scīs; nōlī crēdere omnia quae audīs; nōlī scrībere omnia quae facis; nōlī facere omnia quae potes.

[5] of a foreigner (literally, external)
[6] Supply is taken for, i.e., is regarded as.
[7] The subject is Benjamin Franklin.
[8] lightning
[9] make haste slowly.
[10] Do not tell

In the Louvre, part of a relief from the Altar of Domitius Ahenobarbus (ca. 122 B.C.). It depicts the census, when the Roman population was counted and the men enrolled for military service. Are the couple to the right the fearful or proud parents of the young man whose name the scribe has just written down?

Photo Bulloz, Louvre

Later and Medieval Latin

Teaching School[1]

Ēgistī[2] ergō mēcum ut mihi persuādērētur Rōmam pergere[3] et potius ibi docēre quod docēbam Carthāginī.[4] Nōn ideō[5] Rōmam pergere[3] voluī, quod maiōrēs quaestūs maiorque mihi dignitās ab amīcīs quī hoc suādēbant prōmittēbātur (quamquam et ista dūcēbant animum tunc meum), sed illa
5 erat causa maxima et paene sōla, quod audiēbam quiētius ibi studēre adulēscentēs et disciplīnā sēdārī, nē in scholam protervē[6] irrumpent. Contrā apud Carthāginem intemperāns est licentia scholasticōrum: irrumpunt impudenter et perturbant ōrdinem.

A Palace Full of Tricks[1]

Est Cōnstantīnopolī domus palātiō proxima, mīrae magnitūdinis et pulchritūdinis. Aerea[2] sed aurō tēcta arbor ante imperātōris solium[3] stābat, cuius rāmōs aereae et aurō tēctae avēs explēbant, quae dīversārum avium vōcēs ēmittēbant. Imperātōris vērō solium huius modī erat arte
5 compositum ut nunc humile, tum excelsius, posteā excelsissimum vidērētur. Leōnēs (incertum est utrum ex aere an lignō[4] factī) aurō tēctī solium custōdiēbant, quī caudā terram percutientēs, apertō ōre, rugītum[5] ēmittēbant.

Ante imperātōris praesentiam sum dēductus. Cum in adventū meō
10 rugītum leōnēs ēmitterent et avēs cantārent, nūllō sum terrōre commōtus, quoniam omnia eī quī bene nōverant mē docuerant. Prōnus imperātōrem adōrāns, caput sustulī, et quem prius moderātā mēnsūrā ā terrā ēlevātum sedēre vīdī, mox aliīs indūtum vestibus ad domūs laquear[6] sedēre prōspexī; quod quō modō fieret cōgitāre nōn potuī, nisi forte sit māchinā hydraulicā
15 sublevātus.

The Norse Discovery of America[1]

Rēx Dāniae[2] īnsulam recitāvit in eō repertam ōceanō[3] quae dīcitur Wīnland quod ibi vītēs[4] sponte nāscantur vīnum optimum ferentēs. Item nōbīs rettulit beātae memoriae pontifex Adalbertus quōsdam nōbilēs virōs in septentriōnēs nāvigāvisse ad ōceanum explōrandum. Relinquentēs
5 Britanniam et glaciālem Īsland[5] subitō in cālīginem[6] cecidērunt quae vix oculīs penetrārī posset. Et iam perīculum cālīginis ēvadentēs appulērunt ad quandam īnsulam altissimīs saxīs mūnītam. Hūc videndōrum grātiā locōrum ēgressī, repperērunt hominēs in antrīs[7] subterrāneīs merīdiē latentēs; prō quōrum iānuīs īnfīnīta iacēbat cōpia vāsōrum aureōrum.
10 Itaque sūmptā parte quam sublevāre poterant, laetī ad nāvēs rēmigant, cum subitō venientēs vīdērunt hominēs mīrae altitūdinis. Ā quibus raptus est ūnus dē sociīs; reliquī vērē ēvāsērunt perīculum.

An illumination of the self-portrait of Hildegard von Bingen (1098–1179). Here, she receives the divine light from heaven.

Hildegard von Bingen

Hildegard von Bingen (1098–1179) was a poet, mystic, composer, scholar, and herbalist. She was also the abbess of a Benedictine convent in Germany. She wrote religious treatises and songs, and at least one musical play, the *Ordō Virtūtum,* which catalogued the virtues and their roles in the battle between good and evil. The following are excerpts from that work.

PATRIĀRCHE ET PROPHETE[1]:	Nōs sumus rādicēs[2] et vōs rāmī,[3] fructūs viventis oculī,[4] et nōs umbrā[5] in illā fuimus.
HUMILITĀS:	Ego, Humilitās, rēgina Virtūtum, dīcō: venīte ad mē, Virtūtēs, et enūtriam[6] vōs ad requīrendam perditam dragmam[7] et ad coronandum in persevērantiā fēlicem.
MISERICORDIA:	Ō quam amara[8] est illa duricia[9] quae nōn cēdit in mentibus misericorditer[10] dolōrī succurrēns![11] Ego autem omnibus dolentibus manum porrigere[12] volō.
DISCRETIŌ:	Ego Discretiō sum lux et dispensatrix[13] omnium creātūrārum in differentiā Deī,[14] quam Adam ā sē fugāvit[15] per lasciviam morum.[16]

[1] *patriarchs,* e.g., Seth, Noah, Abraham, etc., and *prophets,* e.g., Isaiah, Daniel, etc., of the Hebrew Old Testament

[2] *roots*

[3] *branches*

[4] the *eye* or *bud* of a graft that produces fruit

[5] i.e., the *shade* of the tree whose roots the prophets were

[6] *nurture,* i.e., *help*

[7] *coin (drachma)*

[8] *bitter*

[9] *hardness*

[10] *mercifully*

[11] *easing;* for the dative **dolōri,** see the Grammar Appendix, p. 496.7

[12] *to reach out*

[13] i.e., *Discernment is the (guiding) light and steward (or moderator) that distinguishes between good and evil*

[14] *in (their) God-created difference(s)*

[15] *drove away*

[16] *wicked behavior*

Medieval Songs and Hymns

This Crazy World[1]

[1] This and the next two poems are from the *Carmina Burana* (twelfth and thirteenth centuries), a collection of songs by the poor wandering students of medieval Europe called Goliards. The Goliards were disposed to the secular life, conviviality, and the composition of ribald Latin songs. The composer Carl Orff (1895–1982) set many poems in the collection to music.

[2] *like*

Iste mundus
furibundus
falsa praestat gaudia,
quae dēfluunt
et dēcurrunt
ceu[2] campī līlia.

Rēs mundāna,
vīta vāna
vēra tollit praemia:
nam impellit
et submergit
animās in Tartara.

Spring Song

[1] *spring*

[2] *meadow*

Ecce grātum
et optātum
vēr[1] redūcit gaudia.
Purpurātum
flōret prātum,[2]

sōl serēnat omnia.
Iam iam cēdant trīstia.
Aestās redit,
nunc recēdit
hiemis saevitia.

In the Tavern

[1] *game,* i.e., of dice

[2] *perspire, work hard*

[3] *waiter,* i.e., money brings service

[4] *there is need that*

[5] *sacks,* put on by those who lose their shirts in gambling, contrasted with the winners of the preceding line

[6] *wine*

[7] *cast lots,* i.e., in throwing dice

1. In tabernā quandō sumus,
  nōn cūrāmus quid sit humus,
  sed ad lūdum[1] properāmus,
  cui semper īnsūdāmus.[2]
  Quid agātur in tabernā,
  ubi nummus est pincerna,[3]
  hoc est opus[4] ut quaerātur,
  sīc quid loquar audiātur.

2. Quīdam lūdunt, quīdam bibunt,
  quīdam indiscrētē vīvunt.
  Sed in lūdō quī morantur,
  ex hīs quīdam dēnūdantur;
  quīdam ibi vestiuntur,
  quīdam saccīs[5] induuntur.
  Ibi nūllus timet mortem,
  sed prō Bacchō[6] mittunt sortem.[7]

Stābat Māter[1]

[1] A famous hymn by Iacopone of Todi (thirteenth century). The Virgin Mary stands by the Cross, mourning over Jesus. With the conversion of the Roman Empire to Christianity (313 A.D.), Latin became the vehicle of the gradual transmission to Western Europe of its culture and traditions, e.g., the Crucifixion, Judgment Day, the ecclesiastical hierarchy, and the founding of the monasteries which did so much to preserve Latin and Greek literature.

1. Stābat māter dolōrōsa
  iūxtā crucem lacrimōsa
    dum pendēbat fīlius;
  cuius animam gementem,
  contrīstantem et dolentem
    pertrānsīvit gladius.

5. Pia māter, fōns amōris,
  mē sentīre vim dolōris
    fac ut tēcum lūgeam,
  fac ut ārdeat cor meum
  in amandō Christum Deum,
    ut sibi complaceam.

3. Quis est homō quī nōn flēret,
  mātrem Christī sī vidēret
    in tantō suppliciō?
  Quis nōn posset contrīstārī
  piam mātrem contemplārī
    dolentem cum fīliō?

10. Fac mē cruce custōdīrī,
  morte Christī praemūnīrī,
    cōnfovērī grātiā;
  quandō corpus moriētur,
  fac ut animae donētur
    Paradīsī glōria.

Themes from Christianity, such as the crucifixion of Jesus Christ shown here, inspired medieval painters, writers, and poets, who usually wrote their works in Latin, the official language of the Roman Catholic Church.

M. Magliani/SuperStock

Diēs Īrae[1]

1. Diēs īrae, diēs illa
solvet saeclum in favillā,[2]
teste Dāvīd cum Sibyllā.[3]

2. Quantus tremor est futūrus
quandō iūdex est ventūrus,
cūncta strictē[4] discussūrus!

3. Tuba mīrum spargēns sonum
per sepulchra regiōnum
cōget omnēs ante thronum.

4. Mors stupēbit et nātūra
cum resurget creātūra[5]
iūdicantī respōnsūra.

5. Liber scrīptus prōferētur,
in quō tōtum continētur
unde mundus iūdicētur.

11. Iūstae iūdex ultiōnis,[6]
dōnum fac remissiōnis
ante diem ratiōnis.

18. Lacrimōsa diēs illa,
quā resurget ex favillā

19. iūdicandus homō reus,
huic ergō parce, Deus.

20. Pie Iēsū Domine,
dōnā eīs requiem.

[1] Thomas of Celano (thirteenth century) wrote this famous hymn about the Judgment Day, when each individual will face the final judgment as to his salvation or damnation.

[2] *ashes*

[3] i.e., in both biblical and Roman prophecy

[4] *completely*

[5] *(every) creature*

[6] *vengeance*

Gesta Rōmānōrum

The "Hanging Tree"[1]

Homō quīdam flēns dīxit omnibus vīcīnīs suīs: "Heu, heu![2] Habeō in hortō[3] meō arborem īnfēlīcem, in quā uxor mea prīma sē suspendit, posteā secunda, nunc tertia, et dolōre afficior." Ūnus ex vīcīnīs, "Mīror," inquit, "tē in tantīs successibus lacrimās ēmīsisse. Dā mihi, rogō tē, trēs surculōs[4] illīus arboris, quod volō hōs inter vīcīnōs dīvidere ut habeāmus arborēs ad uxōrēs nostrās suspendendās."

[1] Adapted from the *Gesta Rōmānōrum*, a collection of curious stories, some gathered from ancient sources. The collection was probably made about the fourteenth century in England. Most of these stories have fanciful "morals" attached to them. Shakespeare and other later writers made use of this collection. This story is also told by Cicero.

5 [2] *alas!*

[3] *garden*

[4] *sprouts*

Scholars of the Renaissance

Petrarch: *Petrarch and Cicero*

Ab ipsā pueritiā, ubi cēterī Aesōpō sē dant, ego librōs Cicerōnis lēgī. Et illā quidem aetāte nihil intellegere poteram, sōla dulcia quaedam verba mē dētinēbant.

Posteā variās amīcitiās contrāxī, quod concursus ex omnī regiōne factus 5 est in locō in quō eram. Amīcīs abeuntibus et petentibus quid vellem ē patriā suā mittī, respondēbam nihil praeter librōs Cicerōnis. Et saepe litterās, saepe pecūniam mīsī, nōn per Italiam modo, ubi eram nōtior, sed per Galliam atque Germāniam et usque ad Hispāniam atque Britanniam. Etiam in Graeciam mīsī, et ē locō ē quō Cicerōnem exspectābam habuī 10 Homērum. "Labor omnia vincit," inquit Vergilius. Multō studiō multāque cūrā multōs librōs collēgī. Sōlus Cicerō mihi[2] sapiēns erat. Dē quō Quīntiliānus dīxit: "Bene dē sē spēret[3] cui Cicerō placēbit."

Posteā, cum Leodium[4] pervēnissem, invēnī duās ōrātiōnēs Cicerōnis; ūnam meā manū scrīpsī,[5] alteram amīcus scrīpsit. Et, ut rīdeās, in tam 15 bonā urbe aliquid ātrāmentī[6] (et id crocō[7] simillimum) reperīre difficillimum erat.

[1] Petrarch (1304–1374) has been called the first modern man. He was largely responsible for initiating the movement known as the *Renaissance*. He had an intense interest in the ancient classics, especially in Cicero. This letter tells of his attempts to secure Cicero's works. If it had not been for the activity of Petrarch and some of his followers, many ancient works would have been lost forever.

[2] *in my eyes*

[3] *let him hope.* The subject is the antecedent of **cui**.

[4] *Liège,* in Belgium

[5] *copied*

[6] *ink*

[7] *saffron, yellow*

Petrarch (1304–1374) was an Italian Renaissance poet, scholar, and humanist. Born in Arezzo, he moved to Avignon, France, when he was eight and grew up there. He studied law, but without much interest in it, and his fame rests less upon his humanistic studies and an epic poem in Latin called *Āfrica* than upon the love sonnets he wrote to a woman he called Laura. In 1341, he was named poet laureate in Rome.

Et dē librīs quidem *Reī Pūblicae*[8] iam dēspērāns, librum *Dē Cōnsōlātiōne* quaesīvī, nec invēnī. Magnum librum epistulārum[9] manū propriā scrīpsī, adversā tum valētūdine; sed valētūdinem magnus amor operis et gaudium et habendī cupiditās vincēbant. Hunc librum, ut mihi semper ad manum esset, ad iānuam pōnere solēbam.   20

[8] Only Book VI has survived complete.

[9] Cicero's letters to his friend Atticus

Poggio Bracciolini: *The Shrewd Priest*[1]

Erat quīdam sacerdōs rūsticus admodum dīves. Hic canem sibi cārum, cum mortuus esset, sepelīvit in coemētēriō. Sēnsit hoc episcopus et in eius pecūniam animum intendēns,[2] sacerdōtem pūniendum ad sē vocat. Sacerdōs, quī animum episcopī satis nōverat, quīnquāgintā aureōs[3] sēcum dēferēns ad episcopum dēvēnit. Quī sepultūram canis graviter accūsāns   5
iussit ad carcerēs[4] sacerdōtem dūcī. Hic vir callidus: "Ō pater," inquit, "sī nōscerēs quā prūdentiā canis fuit, nōn mīrārēris[5] sī sepultūram inter hominēs meruit. Fuit enim plūs quam hūmānus, et in vītā et maximē in morte." "Quidnam hoc est?" ait episcopus. "Testāmentum," inquit sacerdōs, "in fīne vītae condēns sciēnsque paupertātem tuam tibi   10
quīnquāgintā aureōs ex testāmentō relīquit, quōs mēcum tulī." Tum episcopus et testāmentum et sepultūram probāns, acceptā pecūniā, sacerdōtem solvit.

[1] from the *Facetiae* (joke book) of Poggio, a secretary of the Pope (fifteenth century). When he and his colleagues had nothing to do they got together and told stories in what he called a "Lie Factory."

[2] casting his thoughts towards

[3] gold pieces

[4] prison

[5] if you knew . . . you would not wonder

Pietro Bembo: *An Alarm Clock*[1]

Hōrologiō[2] ē meā bibliothēcā tibi allātō, ā quō expergēfierī,[3] quā hōrā volēs, possīs, tē libenter ūtī nōn molestē[4] ferō. Modo tē id nōn intemperātē[5] ā somnō āvocet. Valētūdinis enim tuae cūram tē habēre in prīmīs volō. Dē tuōrum studiōrum ratiōne nihil tibi mandō nunc quidem nisi ūnum: fac ut in tuīs quās ad mē dās litterīs Cicerōnem accūrātius exprimās mōremque   5
illīus scrībendī, verba, numerōs,[6] gravitātem, dīligentius imitēre. Hoc sī fēceris, omnia tē cōnsecūtum putābō. Magistrō tuō multam salūtem. Valē. MDXLIIII. Rōma.

[1] Pietro Bembo, an Italian man of letters (1470–1547), wrote this letter to his young son.

[2] clock

[3] be awakened

[4] with **ferō:** I don't mind

[5] too early

[6] rhythm

UNIT
XI

OVID AND VERGIL

Unit Objectives

- Read Selections from the Roman Poets Ovid and Vergil
- Learn to Scan and Read Dactylic Hexameter
- Develop an Understanding and Appreciation of Poetic Word Order in Latin Verse

In Greek mythology, Medusa was a Gorgon and the daughter of the sea god Phorcys. She had been beautiful in her youth, but when she bragged of her beauty, the goddess Athena became so jealous that she transformed Medusa into an ugly woman with protruding eyes and snakes for hair. Medusa was so ugly that anyone who looked at her was immediately turned into stone. She was eventually killed by Perseus. A portion of Ovid's story of Medusa is in this unit. This painting by Caravaggio (1573–1610) is in a museum in Florence, Italy.

Scala/Art Resource, NY

475

OVID'S
METAMORPHŌSĒS

Ovid (Publius Ovidius Naso) was born in 43 B.C. Trained for the law and public life, he abandoned his career to devote himself to his great passion, the writing of poetry. In A.D. 8 he incurred the displeasure of the Emperor Augustus and was banished to a little town, Tomi (now Constanza, Romania), on the Black Sea. Here he died in A.D. 17.

Ovid was a very facile poet and left us many poems. The greatest of these is the *Metamorphōsēs.* This consists of a series of mythical tales dealing with the transformation (that is what the title means) of humans, animals, and things into different forms. The tales are loosely joined together with considerable cleverness and reveal Ovid's great ability as a storyteller. They cover so much of Greek and Roman mythology that they are now our chief source of information about it. The work, from which several selections are given here, has always been a favorite and has had great influence on art and literature throughout the ages.

Ronald Sheridan/Ancient Art & Architecture Collection

Orpheus and Eurydice, in a painting by French artist Nicolas Poussin (1594–1665).

Poetic Word Order

The word order of Latin poetry is freer than that of prose. Adjectives often are widely separated from their nouns. Words are often taken out of subordinate clauses and precede the introductory words (**quī, ut,** etc.). Subjects often come at or near the end of sentences.

Reading Latin Verse

The rhythm of Latin verse does not depend on word accent as does that of English, but on the length of syllables. The rules for determining the *length of syllables* are:

1. A syllable is *naturally* long if it contains a long vowel or a diphthong.
2. A syllable is long *by position* if it contains a short vowel followed by two or more consonants or the consonant **x (= cs).**

But a mute (**p, b, t, d, c, g**) followed by a liquid (**l, r**) does not make a syllable long. There are occasional exceptions. The syllable may be counted long *or* short, as the meter requires.

H is disregarded entirely. The combinations **qu** and **gu** (before a vowel) constitute one consonant; the **u** is disregarded.

In poetry, a long syllable is treated as twice the length of a short syllable. Since a line of poetry is considered one long word, in a case like **in mē** the first word is a long syllable because the (short) vowel is followed by two consonants (**n, m**). Even if the first consonant ends a word, and the second consonant begins the next, the rule of "position" applies.

Several syllables are combined to form a foot. The *dactyl* is a foot consisting of a long syllable followed by two short syllables, written — ˘ ˘.[1] The *spondee* consists of two long syllables, — —. When a line contains six feet, it is called a hexameter. The *Metamorphōsēs* and *Aeneid* (p. 485) are written in the *dactylic hexameter*. A spondee may be substituted for a dactyl in every foot except the fifth. The sixth foot is always a spondee.[2] The beat is on the first syllable of each foot.

If a word ends in a vowel or a vowel plus **m** and the next word begins with a vowel (or **h**), the first vowel disappears entirely (called "elision"; the vowel is said to be "elided"): **mar(e) et,** pronounced **maret; iacer(e) (h)ōs,** pronounced **iacerōs; cūnctant(em) et,** pronounced **cūnctantet.**

---

[1] Do not confuse this marking of syllables with the identical signs used in marking vowels.
[2] The last syllable is often short, but the "rest" at the end of the line fills out the foot.

The Flood—Deucalion and Pyrrha

Because of the wickedness of human beings, Jupiter sends a flood to destroy the earth. Only Deucālion (*Doo kay´ li ohn*, the Greek Noah) and his wife Pyrrha survive, landing from their boat on Mt. Parnassus (corresponding to Mt. Ararat of the Bible). The first five lines are "scanned" (marked) to show the meter.

The Flood at Its Height—a Topsy-Turvy World

Iamque ma|r(e) et tel|lūs nūl|lum dis|crīmen ha|bēbant. |

Omnia | pontus e|rant; dee|rant quoque | lītora | pontō. |

Occupat | hīc¹ col|lem, cum|bā sedet | alter ad|uncā² |

et dū|cit³ rē|mōs il|līc ubi | nūper a|rārat, |

295 ille¹ su|prā sege|tēs⁴ aut | mersae | culmina⁵ | vīllae |
nāvigat, hic summā piscem dēprēndit in ulmō.⁶
Fīgitur in viridī,⁷ sī fors tulit, ancora prātō
aut subiecta terunt⁸ curvae vīnēta carīnae;⁹
et, modo quā¹⁰ gracilēs grāmen carpsēre¹¹ capellae,¹²
300 nunc ibi dēfōrmēs pōnunt sua corpora phōcae.¹³
Mīrantur sub aquā lūcōs¹⁴ urbēsque domōsque
Nēreidēs, silvāsque tenent delphīnes¹⁵ et altīs
incursant rāmīs agitātaque rōbora¹⁶ pulsant.
Nat¹⁷ lupus inter ovēs,¹⁸ fulvōs¹⁹ vehit unda leōnēs,
305 unda vehit tigrēs.

¹ *one man*
² with **cumbā:** *in a curved boat*
³ *plies*
⁴ *crops*
⁵ *top;* (poetic plural for singular)
⁶ with **summā:** *on top of an elm*
⁷ with **prātō:** *green meadow*
⁸ *scrape*
⁹ *keels, i.e., ships;* subject
¹⁰ = **quā modo**
¹¹ = **carpsērunt**
¹² *goats*
¹³ *seals*
¹⁴ *groves*
¹⁵ = **delphini** (Greek form)
¹⁶ *oaks*
¹⁷ *swims*
¹⁸ *sheep*
¹⁹ *tawny*

Stones thrown by Deucalion and Pyrrha "grow" into people; from a 1589 edition of Ovid.

When the waters recede, Deucalion seeks dry land. He laments the fact that Pyrrha and he are the only two people left in the world: **Nōs duo turba sumus,** *We two are a crowd,* he says, for two are a crowd in a world which consists of only two persons. He finds the temple of Themis, goddess of prophecy, and prays for aid and advice.

Deucalion Interprets a Strange Oracle

Mōta dea est sortemque dedit: "Discēdite templō
et vēlāte caput cīnctāsque²⁰ resolvite vestēs
ossaque post tergum magnae iactāte parentis."²¹
Obstupuēre²² diū, rumpitque silentia vōce
Pyrrha prior iussīsque deae parēre recūsat,   385
detque²³ sibī veniam pavidō rogat ōre pavetque
laedere iactātīs māternās ossibus umbrās.²⁴   387
Inde Promēthīdēs²⁵ placidīs Epimēthida²⁶ dictīs   390
mulcet²⁷ et "aut fallāx," ait, "est sollertia²⁸ nōbīs²⁹
aut pia sunt nūllumque nefās ōrācula suādent.
Magna parēns terra est, lapidēs in corpore terrae
ossa reor³⁰ dīcī: iacere hōs post terga iubēmur."

The Stones Come to Life

Coniugis auguriō³¹ quamquam Tītānia³² mōta est,   395
spēs tamen in dubiō est; adeō caelestibus ambō
diffīdunt monitīs.³³ Sed quid temptāre nocēbit?
Discēdunt vēlantque caput tunicāsque recingunt
et iussōs lapidēs sua post vēstīgia mittunt.
Saxa (quis hoc crēdat,³⁴ nisi sit prō teste vetustās?)³⁵ 400
pōnere³⁶ dūritiem coepēre³⁷ suumque rigōrem
mollīrīque morā³⁸ mollītaque dūcere³⁹ fōrmam.   402
Inque brevī spatiō superōrum nūmine saxa   411
missa virī manibus faciem trāxēre⁴⁰ virōrum,
et dē fēmineō reparāta est fēmina iactū.
Inde genus dūrum sumus experiēnsque⁴¹ labōrum
et documenta damus quā sīmus orīgine nātī.   415
(*Met.* I, 291–415)

²⁰ *girt up.* In religious services the head was covered and the tunic allowed to hang down ungirdled.

²¹ modifies **ossa**

²² *they were astounded*

²³ Supply **ut:** *asks that (Themis) grant her pardon.*

²⁴ *to offend her mother's ghost by throwing her bones*

²⁵ *son of Promētheus (Proh meeˊ thoos),* i.e., Deucalion

²⁶ accusative singular: *daughter of Epimētheus (Epi meeˊ thoos),* i.e., Pyrrha

²⁷ *calms*

²⁸ *skill*

²⁹ for **mihi;** = **mea.**

³⁰ *I think that the bones are meant to be*

³¹ *interpretation*

³² *the Titan's daughter,* i.e., Pyrrha

³³ *advice;* dative with special verbs; see the Grammar Appendix, p. 496.6

³⁴ *would believe;* see the Grammar Appendix, p. 506.3

³⁵ *if antiquity were not a witness.* What do you think of the argument that the age of a story proves it to be true?

³⁶ for **dēpōnere**

³⁷ = **coepērunt**

³⁸ *gradually*

³⁹ *take on*

⁴⁰ = **trāxērunt**

⁴¹ *used to* (with genitive)

Echo and Narcissus

Juno punishes the nymph Echo for her talkativeness by curtailing her power of speech. Thereafter, Echo can merely echo what others say. She falls in love with the handsome but cold youth Narcissus (Nar sis´ sus).

Echo Falls in Love with Narcissus

Corpus adhūc Ēchō, nōn vōx erat et tamen ūsum
360 garrula nōn alium quam nunc habet ōris[1] habēbat,
361 reddere dē multīs ut verba novissima[2] posset.
370 Ergō ubi Narcissum per dēvia rūra[3] vagantem
vīdit et incaluit,[4] sequitur vēstīgia fūrtim,
372 quōque magis[5] sequitur, flammā propiōre calēscit.
375 Ō quotiēns voluit blandīs accēdere dictīs
et mollēs adhibēre precēs! Nātūra repugnat
nec sinit[6] incipiat; sed, quod[7] sinit, illa parāta est
exspectāre sonōs ad quōs sua verba remittat.

[1] with **ūsum alium**: *no other use of speech.* She was still a living being.
[2] *(only) the last of many;* see the Grammar Appendix, p. 495.36
[3] *trackless countryside*
[4] *fell in love*
[5] *the more . . . the hotter* (literally, *the nearer*) *the flame (with which) she is inflamed*
[6] *permits.* Supply **ut** with **incipiat**.
[7] *a thing which.* The main clause is the antecedent.

Narcissus Calls to His Companions and Echo Answers

Forte puer comitum sēductus ab agmine fīdō
380 dīxerat "ecquis[8] adest?" et "adest" responderat Ēchō.
Hic stupet, utque aciem[9] partēs dīmittit in omnēs,
vōce "venī!" magnā clāmat; vocat illa vocantem.
Respicit et rūrsus, nūllō veniente, "quid," inquit,
"mē fugis?" et totidem quot dīxit verba recēpit.

[8] *is there anyone?*
[9] *glance*

Mythological scenes were a favorite of Nicolas Poussin (1594–1665). Here he has painted his interpretation of Echo and Narcissus. The poet Milton called Echo a "nymph that liv'st unseen."

Giraudon/Art Resource, NY

Perstat et alternae[10] dēceptus imāgine vōcis   385
"hūc coeāmus," ait, nūllīque[11] libentius umquam
respōnsūra sonō "coeāmus" rettulit Ēchō,
et verbīs favet[12] ipsa suīs ēgressaque silvā
ībat ut iniceret spērātō bracchia collō.
Ille fugit fugiēnsque "manūs complexibus[13] aufer.   390
Ante," ait, "ēmoriar[14] quam[15] sit tibi cōpia nostrī."[16]
Rettulit illa nihil nisi "sit tibi cōpia nostrī."

Echo Wastes Away to a Mere Voice

Sprēta[17] latet silvīs pudibundaque[18] frondibus ōra
prōtegit et sōlīs ex illō[19] vīvit in antrīs.
Sed tamen haeret amor crēscitque dolōre repulsae,[20]   395
et tenuant vigilēs corpus miserābile cūrae,
addūcitque cutem[21] maciēs et in āera[22] sūcus[23]
corporis omnis abit. Vōx tantum atque ossa supersunt—
vōx manet; ossa ferunt[24] lapidis trāxisse figūram.
Inde latet silvīs nūllōque in monte vidētur,   400
omnibus[25] audītur; sonus est quī vīvit in illā.
(*Met.* III, 359–401)

[10] *answering*
[11] Modifies **sonō**.
[12] i.e., she suits the action to the words
[13] *from embraces*
[14] *may I die*
[15] with **ante**: *before*
[16] = **mei**: *a chance at me*
[17] *spurned*
[18] *ashamed*
[19] Supply **tempore**.
[20] *refusal*
[21] *skin*
[22] *air (accusative singular)*
[23] *life, strength*
[24] *they say*
[25] *by all*

Perseus and Atlas

Medusa was a maiden with snaky locks—one look at her turned a person into stone. Perseus, son of Jupiter, is commissioned to bring back her head. With the help of the gods he does this without injury to himself. On his way back he stops at the home of the giant Atlas, in northwest Africa. Atlas is the owner of the famous golden apples. When Atlas refuses hospitality to Perseus, the latter turns Atlas into a mountain of stone by means of Medusa's head.

Themis Predicts the Loss of the Golden Apples

Mīlle gregēs[1] illī[2] totidemque armenta[3] per herbās   635
errābant, et humum vīcīnia[4] nūlla premēbant.
Arboreae frondēs aurō radiante nitentēs[5]
ex aurō rāmōs, ex aurō pōma[6] tegēbant.
"Hospes," ait Perseus illī, "seu glōria tangit
tē generis[7] magnī, generis mihi Iuppiter auctor;   640
sīve es mīrātor rērum,[8] mīrābere nostrās.
Hospitium requiemque petō." Memor ille[9] vetustae
sortis erat (Themis hanc dederat Parnassia[10] sortem):
"Tempus, Atlās, veniet tua quō spoliābitur aurō
arbor, et hunc praedae titulum[11] Iove nātus[12] habēbit."   645
Id metuēns solidīs pōmāria clauserat Atlās

[1] *flocks*
[2] i.e., Atlas, dative of reference; see the Grammar Appendix, p. 496.3
[3] *herds*
[4] *no neighbors hemmed in his land,* i.e., he had vast tracts of land
[5] *gleaming,* modifying **frondēs**
[6] *apples of gold;* **ex aurō** modifies **pōma**. These are the golden apples of the Hesperides. It is thought that the mythical apples were really oranges, unknown to Europe in antiquity.
[7] i.e., of Perseus
[8] *deeds,* referring to his defeat of Medusa. Perseus is rather arrogant.
[9] i.e., Atlas
[10] with Themis
[11] *the glory for this prize*
[12] *a son of Jupiter.* Hercules was meant, but when Atlas hears that Perseus is the son of Jupiter, he thinks that he is the one mentioned in the oracle and refuses to admit him.

David Lees/CORBIS

Crēvit in immēnsum... et omne cum tot sīderibus caelum requiēvit in illō. The story of the giant Atlas holding up the universe is a popular Greek myth dating back as far as the poet Hesiod (ca. 700 B.C.). In this much later treatment by Ovid, he is turned into the Atlas mountain range in North Africa by Perseus as penalty for failing to receive him kindly as his guest.

[13] *shut out* (with ablative)

[14] *i.e., Perseus*

[15] *which you falsely claim*

[16] *be far from you,* i.e., *be of no help to you*

[17] *threats*

[18] *could be*

[19] *of little value*

[20] *on his left side*

[21] *i.e., turning his face away, so as not to look at Medusa's head*

[22] *as huge as he had been* (in life)

[23] *beard and hair*

[24] *his shoulders become* (**sunt**)

[25] *to an immense size.* Perseus next flies past Ethiopia, where he rescues the beautiful Andromeda from a sea monster and marries her.

[26] = **dei** (vocative)

montibus et vāstō dederat servanda dracōnī
arcēbatque[13] suīs externōs fīnibus omnēs.
Huic[14] quoque "vade procul, nē longē glōria rērum
650 quam mentīris,"[15] ait, "longē tibi Iuppiter absit."[16]
Vimque minīs[17] addit manibusque expellere temptat
cūnctantem et placidīs miscentem fortia dictīs.
Vīribus īnferior (quis enim pār esset[18] Atlantis
vīribus?) "at quoniam parvī[19] tibi grātia nostra est,
655 accipe mūnus," ait, laevāque ā parte[20] Medūsae,
ipse retrō versus,[21] squālentia prōtulit ōra.
Quantus[22] erat, mōns factus Atlās; nam barba comaeque[23]
in silvās abeunt, iuga sunt umerīque[24] manūsque,
quod caput ante fuit summō est in monte cacūmen.
660 Ossa lapis fīunt; tum partēs altus in omnēs
crēvit in immēnsum[25] (sīc, dī,[26] statuistis), et omne
cum tot sīderibus caelum requiēvit in illō.
(*Met.* IV, 636–662)

Orpheus and Eurydice

Orpheus (*Or´ fee oos*) was such a fine musician that he could make even the trees and stones listen to and follow him. When his wife Eurydice (*You rid´ i see*) died, he followed her to Hades and by his wonderful singing persuaded the king of Hades to let her go back to the land of the living. But there was one condition, that Orpheus should not look back until he had come out of Hades. At the last moment Orpheus looked back to see whether Eurydice was following, and she disappeared forever. There is an opera by Gluck on this theme.

"Omnia dēbēmus vōbīs,[1] paulumque morātī
sērius aut citius sēdem properāmus ad ūnam.
Tendimus hūc omnēs, haec est domus ultima, vōsque
hūmānī generis[2] longissima rēgna tenētis.   35
Haec[3] quoque, cum iūstōs mātūra perēgerit annōs,
iūris erit vestrī; prō mūnere poscimus ūsum.[4]
Quod sī fāta negant veniam[5] prō coniuge, certum est
nōlle[6] redīre mihī; lētō[7] gaudēte duōrum."
Tālia dīcentem[8] nervōsque[9] ad verba moventem   40
exsanguēs flēbant animae.[10]   41
Hanc simul et lēgem[11] Rhodopēius[12] accipit Orpheus,   50
nē flectat retrō sua lūmina, dōnec[13] Avernās[14]
exierit vallēs; aut irrita[15] dōna futūra.
Carpitur acclīvis per mūta silentia trāmes,[16]
arduus, obscūrus, cālīgine[17] dēnsus opācā.
Nec procul āfuerunt tellūris margine summae.   55
Hic nē dēficeret[18] metuēns avidusque videndī,
flexit amāns oculōs; et prōtinus illa relāpsa est,
bracchiaque intendēns prēndīque et prēndere captāns
nīl nisi cēdentēs īnfēlīx arripit aurās.[19]
(*Met.* X, 32–59)

[1] Orpheus is speaking to Pluto and Proserpina, king and queen of Hades.

[2] *over the human race*

[3] Eurydice

[4] i.e., not for a permanent gift but as a temporary loan

[5] *boon,* of longer life

[6] Supply the subject from **mihi**: *I have resolved that I,* etc.

[7] *death;* ablative of cause; see the Grammar Appendix, p. 499.11

[8] modifies **eum** understood, object of **flēbant**

[9] *strings* (of the lyre)

[10] Pluto and Proserpina are so moved that they allow Eurydice to return.

[11] *condition.* The **nē** clause is in apposition with **lēgem**.

[12] *Thracian*

[13] *until*

[14] adjective modifying **vallēs**: *of Avernus,* the entrance of Hades

[15] *void*

[16] with **acclivis**: *ascending path* (to the upper world)

[17] *mist*

[18] The subject is Eurydice.

[19] *breezes*

This marble relief from the Louvre shows Orpheus and Eurydice with the messenger god, Hermes.

Pygmalion

The sculptor Pygmalion of Cyprus carved an ivory statue of a woman so beautiful that he fell in love with it. Venus gave it life, and Pygmalion married the girl. George Bernard Shaw borrowed the name for his play in which he has a professor turn an uneducated young woman into a fine lady; Lerner and Loewe's musical comedy *My Fair Lady* is based on that play.

[1] *ivory*

[2] *in which*

[3] *you could believe*

[4] *cf. "the art that conceals art"*

[5] *the fires (of love)*

[6] *he admits*

[7] *kisses*

[8] *sink in, dent*

[9] *bruise*

[10] *now*

[11] *shells and smooth pebbles*

[12] *colored*

[13] *tears of the Heliades, fallen from. The daughters of the Sun, the Heliades, are said to have been changed to trees and their tears to amber, which is actually the hardened resin of certain trees.*

[14] *necklaces*

[15] *in Cyprus (feminine)*

[16] *incense*

[17] *having performed (with ablative)*

[18] = dei

[19] *of ivory*

[20] *i.e., home from the altar*

[21] *couch*

[22] *thumb. He felt her pulse.*

Intereā niveum mīrā fēlīciter arte
sculpsit ebur[1] fōrmamque dedit quā[2] fēmina nāscī
nūlla potest; operisque suī concēpit amōrem.
250 Virginis est vērae faciēs, quam vīvere crēdās[3]
et, sī nōn obstet reverentia, velle movērī;
ars adeō latet arte suā.[4] Mīrātur et haurit
pectore Pygmaliōn simulātī corporis ignēs.[5]
Saepe manūs operī temptantēs admovet an sit
255 corpus an illud ebur; nec adhūc ebur esse fatētur.[6]
Ōscula[7] dat reddīque putat; loquiturque tenetque
et crēdit tactīs digitōs īnsīdere[8] membrīs;
et metuit, pressōs veniat nē līvor[9] in artūs.
Et modo[10] blanditiās adhibet, modo grāta puellīs
260 mūnera fert illī, conchās teretēsque lapillōs,[11]
et parvās volucrēs et flōrēs mīlle colōrum,
līliaque pictāsque[12] pilās et ab arbore lāpsās
Hēliadum lacrimās.[13] Ōrnat quoque vestibus artūs.
Dat digitīs gemmās, dat longa monīlia[14] collō.
270 Fēsta diēs Veneris tōtā celeberrima Cyprō[15] vēnerat,
273 tūraque[16] fūmābant, cum mūnere fūnctus[17] ad ārās
cōnstitit et timidē "sī, dī,[18] dare cūncta potestis,
sit coniūnx, optō," nōn ausus, "eburnea[19] virgō,"
dīcere Pygmaliōn, "similis mea," dīxit, "eburnae."
280 Ut rediit,[20] simulācra suae petit ille puellae,
incumbēnsque torō[21] dedit ōscula. Vīsa tepēre est.
289 Corpus erat; saliunt temptātae pollice[22] vēnae,
292   dataque ōscula virgō
sēnsit et ērubuit.
(*Met.* X, 247–293)

VERGIL'S *AENEID*

Vergil (Publius Vergilius Maro) was born in 70 B.C. Two thousand years later, in 1930, the entire western world celebrated his birthday, for he is one of the world's greatest and best loved poets. His earlier works were the *Bucolics,* or *Eclogues,* about shepherds, and the *Georgics,* dealing with farming. His chief work, the *Aeneid,* is an epic poem in twelve books which tell the legend of the Trojan Aeneas *(Ee nee´as):* the capture of Troy by the Greeks in the twelfth century B.C., his wanderings to find a new home and eventual arrival in Italy, where he battled to establish his kingdom and where, three centuries later, his descendants founded Rome. Thus Vergil provided a background for Roman history and it is no wonder that the Roman people greeted the *Aeneid* as a national poem glorifying Rome and the Roman Empire.

Vergil was planning to spend three years in giving the finishing touches to the *Aeneid* when he died in 19 B.C. He left word to have the poem

This fifth-century-A.D. illustrated manuscript of Vergil from the Vatican Library in Rome has its letters written in majuscules *(capital letters)*. This manuscript here ends *Eclogue V* and begins *Eclogue VI.* In its next-to-last line, Vergil excuses himself from writing an epic about **rēgēs et proelia** *(epic poetry)* because **Cynthius** (= Apollo) told him to stick to pastoral, telling of the lives, loves, and poetry of shepherds. Later, of course, he did write the *Aeneid,* leaving it slightly unfinished on his early death.

burned but Augustus insisted that it be published—and the world has been grateful to him ever since.

In one of his *Eclogues* Vergil prophesied the birth of a child. In the Middle Ages this was interpreted as a reference to the birth of Jesus, and Vergilius began to be spelled Virgilius, as if derived from *Virgō,* the Virgin Mary. That is why the traditional English spelling is Virgil. In recent years many have preferred the spelling Vergil, newly formed from the ancient name.

So popular was Vergil in the Middle Ages that he was called a magician, and all sorts of tales were told about his deeds.

Book I

Juno's anger causes the Trojans under Aeneas to be wrecked off the coast of Africa. They make their way to the place where Dido, a refugee from Tyre in Phoenicia, is building the new city of Carthage. They are cordially welcomed. The poem opens with the poet's statement of his theme.

> Arma virumque canō, Trōiae quī prīmus ab ōrīs
> Ītaliam[1] fātō profugus[2] Lāvīniaque[3] vēnit
> lītora,[1] multum ille et terrīs[4] iactātus et altō[4]
> vī superum,[5] saevae memorem Iūnōnis ob īram,
> multa quoque et[6] bellō passus, dum conderet[7] urbem   5
> īnferretque deōs[8] Latiō,[9] genus unde Latīnum
> Albānīque patrēs atque altae moenia Rōmae.

Venus goes to Jupiter to complain that the great destiny of her son Aeneas is not being fulfilled. Jupiter's predictions reassure her.

[1] poetic usage without **ad**; see the Grammar Appendix, p. 497.3. The first **"I"** in **Italia** is often counted long in poetry.

[2] *a fugitive by fate*

[3] adjective: *of Lavinium.* In scanning, treat the second **"i"** as a consonant, i.e., **Lāvinyă** (only three syllables). Similarly, in line 1, **Trōiae = Trōjae.**

[4] For the case see the Grammar Appendix, p. 500.14; **altō** is used as a noun for **mari.**

[5] = **superōrum**

[6] *also*

[7] *until he could found;* see the Grammar Appendix, p. 505.12

[8] *his gods,* statues of which he had brought along

[9] = **in Latium,** to *Lay´shium,* poetic use of the dative

A painting by the English artist William Turner (1775–1851) shows Dido building Carthage after fleeing Tyre with many followers and much treasure.

Bridgeman/Art Resource, NY

"Bellum ingēns geret Ītaliā[10] populōsque ferōcēs   263
contundet[11] mōrēsque virīs et moenia pōnet.
At puer Ascanius,[12] cui nunc cognōmen Iūlō[13]   267
additur,

             longam multā vī mūniet Albam.[14]

Rōmulus excipiet gentem et Māvortia[15] condet   276
moenia Rōmānōsque suō dē nōmine dīcet.
Hīs ego nec mētās[16] rērum nec tempora pōnō;
imperium sine fīne dedī. Quīn[17] aspera Iūnō,
quae mare nunc terrāsque metū[18] caelumque fatīgat, 280
cōnsilia in melius referet[19] mēcumque fovēbit
Rōmānōs rērum dominōs gentemque togātam.[20]
Nāscētur pulchrā Trōiānus orīgine Caesar,[21]   286
imperium Ōceanō, fāmam quī terminet[22] astrīs
Iūlius,[21] ā magnō dēmissum nōmen Iūlō.[23]
Aspera tum positīs[24] mītēscent saecula[25] bellīs;   291
cāna[26] Fidēs et Vesta, Remō cum frātre Quirīnus[27]
iūra dabunt; dīrae ferrō et compāgibus artīs[28]
claudentur bellī portae; Furor impius intus[29]
saeva sedēns super arma et centum vīnctus aēnīs[30]   295
post tergum nōdīs fremet[31] horridus ōre cruentō."

Book IV

In Books II and III, at a banquet Dido gives for him, Aeneas relates the
story of the Fall of Troy and his adventures thereafter. The Trojan War
was caused by the elopement of Helen, the wife of the Greek Menelaus,
with the Trojan Paris. As Book IV opens, Dido, wounded by Cupid's
arrow on Venus' orders, has fallen deeply in love with Aeneas.

At rēgīna gravī iam dūdum[1] saucia[2] cūrā
vulnus alit vēnīs et caecō[3] carpitur ignī.
Multa virī virtūs animō multusque recursat
gentis honōs;[4] haerent īnfīxī pectore vultūs[5]
verbaque, nec placidam membrīs dat cūra quiētem.   5
Postera Phoebēā[6] lūstrābat[7] lampade terrās
ūmentemque[8] Aurōra polō[9] dīmōverat umbram,
cum sīc ūnanimam alloquitur male[10] sāna sorōrem:
"Anna soror, quae mē suspēnsam īnsomnia[11] terrent!
Quis novus hic nostrīs successit sēdibus hospes,[12]   10
quem sēsē ōre ferēns,[13] quam fortī pectore[14] et armīs!
Crēdō equidem, nec vāna fidēs, genus esse deōrum.
Dēgenerēs animōs timor arguit.[15] Heu, quibus ille
        iactātus fātīs! Quae bella exhausta canēbat!"

Dido and Aeneas fall in love, but Jupiter (representing Aeneas' conscience) sends Mercury to remind Aeneas of his duty to establish the Trojans in a new country of their own. Aeneas' reaction is immediate.

At vērō Aenēās aspectū obmūtuit āmēns,[16]
280 arrēctaeque horrōre comae,[17] et vōx faucibus haesit.
Ārdet abīre fugā dulcīsque relinquere terrās,
attonitus[18] tantō monitū imperiōque deōrum.
Heu quid agat?[19] Quō nunc rēginam ambīre[20] furentem
audeat affātū? Quae prīma exōrdia[21] sūmat?

Aeneas orders his men to prepare the ships secretly, hoping to sail away without Dido's knowing it.

296 At rēgīna dolōs (quis fallere possit[22] amantem?)
praesēnsit mōtūsque excēpit prīma futūrōs,
omnia tūta[23] timēns; eadem impia Fāma furentī[24]
dētulit armārī classem cursumque parārī.
304 Tandem hīs Aenēān[25] compellat[26] vōcibus ultrō:
305 "Dissimulāre etiam spērāstī,[27] perfide, tantum
posse nefās tacitusque meā dēcēdere terrā?
Nec tē noster amor nec tē data dextera[28] quondam
nec moritūra tenet crūdēlī fūnere Dīdō?"
393   At pius Aenēās, quamquam lēnīre dolentem
sōlandō[29] cupit et dictīs āvertere cūrās,
395 multa[30] gemēns magnōque animum labefactus[31] amōre,
iussa tamen dīvum exsequitur classemque revīsit.
Tum vērō Teucrī[32] incumbunt[33] et lītore celsās
dēdūcunt tōtō nāvīs.

Book VI

After consulting the Sibyl at Cumae (near Naples), Aeneas descends to Hades, where he sees the shades of his father, Dido, and many other famous persons and learns about the great future of the new country he is about to establish.

Tālibus ōrābat dictīs ārāsque[1] tenēbat,
125 cum sīc ōrsa[2] loquī vātēs:[3] "Sate[4] sanguine dīvum,
Trōs Anchīsiadē,[5] facilis dēscēnsus Avernō[6]
(noctēs atque diēs patet ātrī iānua Dītis);
sed revocāre gradum superāsque ēvādere ad aurās,[7]
hoc opus, hic labor est. Paucī, quōs aequus amāvit
130 Iuppiter aut ārdēns ēvexit ad aethera[8] virtūs,
dīs genitī[9] potuēre."[10]

Side notes (left margin):

[16] confused, he becomes silent
[17] with **arrēctae**: hair (stood) on end
[18] astounded
[19] What should he do? **Heu** is one long syllable.
[20] get around, approach
[21] beginnings

[22] would be able
[23] (even if) safe
[24] i.e., Dido
[25] acc.: Aeneas
[26] addresses
[27] contracted form; see the Grammar Appendix, p. 531
[28] = **dextra**, i.e., pledge
[29] by consoling (her)
[30] much, a great deal
[31] his heart overcome (literally, overcome as to his heart)
[32] Trojans
[33] get to work (literally, bend to)

[1] altar
[2] Supply **est**: began.
[3] prophetess (referring to the Sibyl)
[4] voc.: sprung from
[5] voc.: Trojan son of Anchises
[6] to Hades. Lake Avernus was considered the entrance.
[7] air
[8] acc. sing.: sky
[9] from **gignō**: descended from the gods; **dis** = **deis**
[10] i.e., to do so

Aeneas and the Sibyl come to the entrance of Hades.

Ībant obscūrī[11] sōlā sub nocte per umbram
perque domōs Dītis vacuās[12] et inānia rēgna
quāle[13] per incertam lūnam sub lūce malignā[14]   270
est iter in silvīs, ubi caelum condidit umbrā
Iuppiter et rēbus[15] nox abstulit ātra colōrem.
Vēstibulum ante ipsum prīmīsque in faucibus Orcī
Lūctus[16] et ultrīcēs posuēre cubīlia[17] Cūrae
pallentēsque[18] habitant Morbī trīstisque Senectūs   275
et Metus et malesuāda[19] Famēs ac turpis Egestās,[20]
terribilēs vīsū[21] fōrmae, Lētumque[22] Labōsque,[23]
tum cōnsanguineus Lētī Sopor et mala[24] mentis
Gaudia mortiferumque adversō in līmine Bellum
ferreīque Eumenidum thalamī[25] et Discordia dēmēns. 280

Aeneas meets the shade of his father, who points out to him the souls of
various notables.

"Hūc geminās[26] nunc flecte aciēs, hanc aspice gentem
Rōmānōsque tuōs; hīc Caesar et omnis Iūlī
prōgeniēs magnum caelī ventūra sub axem.[27]   790
Hic vir, hic est tibi quem prōmittī saepius audīs,
Augustus Caesar, Dīvī[28] genus, aurea condet
saecula quī rūrsus Latiō[29] rēgnāta per arva[30]
Sāturnō[31] quondam; super et Garamantăs[32] et Indōs
prōferet imperium (iacet extrā sīdera tellūs,   795
extrā annī sōlisque viās,[33] ubi caelifer Atlās[34]
axem umerō torquet stēllīs ārdentibus aptum)."[35]

Anchises tells Aeneas that the great contribution of the Romans will be
good government and peace.

"Excūdent[36] aliī spīrantia[37] mollius[38] aera
(crēdō equidem), vīvōs dūcent dē marmore vultūs;
ōrābunt causās melius caelīque meātūs[39]
dēscrībent radiō[40] et surgentia sīdera dīcent.   850
Tū regere imperiō populōs, Rōmāne, mementō[41]
(hae tibi erunt artēs) pācīque impōnere mōrem,[42]
parcere subiectīs et dēbellāre superbōs."

[11] in the dark

[12] Because only ghosts lived there.

[13] just as one goes (literally, as is the way)

[14] stingy

[15] dative of separation; see the Grammar Appendix, p. 496.4

[16] Grief. The various feelings and causes of death are personified.

[17] couches. The worries of conscience are there to stay.

[18] pale

[19] urging to do wrong

[20] Need

[21] to look at

[22] Death

[23] = Labor

[24] wicked

[25] chambers of the Furies

[26] with aciēs: both eyes

[27] with sub: up to the vault of heaven

[28] Julius Caesar, deified after his death

[29] in Latium

[30] lands

[31] by Saturn (dat. of agent). Saturn was a god in the mythical "Golden Age," when life was peaceful.

[32] the Garaman´tēs, an African tribe

[33] i.e., beyond the constellations of the zodiac through which the sun seems to travel in the course of a year

[34] heaven-carrying Atlas

[35] with axem: the sky studded with

[36] will mold. The Greeks are meant.

[37] breathing, lifelike

[38] more delicately

[39] movements (of the stars)

[40] with the rod—with which the movements of the stars were traced in sand

[41] remember (imperative)

[42] i.e., to make peace customary

[43] *(to be) of horn*

[44] *dreams*

[45] abl.: *white*

[46] *gleaming*

[47] *the spirits*

[48] with **dictis**, referring to Anchises' speech

[49] *of ivory*

[50] *makes (literally, cuts)*

[51] *Caiē´ta, a town on the coast near Formiae*

[52] *straight along the shore*

Aeneas returns to the upper world through the gate of false dreams.

Sunt geminae somnī portae; quārum altera fertur
cornea,[43] quā vērīs facilis datur exitus umbrīs,[44]
895 altera candentī[45] perfecta nitēns[46] elephantō,
sed falsa ad caelum mittunt īnsomnia[44] Mānēs.[47]
Hīs[48] ibi tum nātum Anchīsēs ūnāque Sibyllam
prōsequitur dictīs portāque ēmittit eburnā.[49]
Ille viam secat[50] ad nāvīs sociōsque revīsit;
900 tum sē ad Caiētae[51] rēctō[52] fert lītore portum.
Ancora dē prōrā iacitur; stant lītore puppēs.

This mosaic portrait depicts Publius Vergilius Maro, author of the *Aeneid.* Notice the laurel wreath with which master poets were crowned. He and his writings were so highly esteemed in later times that lines from them have been selected by chance and used to predict one's future. This sort of fortune telling was called **Sortēs Vergiliānae.**

Dagli Orti/Museo della Civilta Romana, Rome/The Art Archive

Quotations from Vergil

Some of Vergil's famous lines are given in the preceding selections. Here are a few more.

1. Forsan[1] et[2] haec ōlim meminisse iuvābit.
2. Hīc domus, haec patria est.
3. Mēns cōnscia rēctī.[3]
4. Nōn omnia possumus omnēs.
5. Pedibus timor addidit ālās.
6. Quōrum[4] pars magna fuī.
7. Ūna salūs victīs, nūllam spērāre salūtem.
8. Varium et mūtābile[5] semper fēmina.

[1] *perhaps*

[2] *even.* **Haec** refers to the misfortunes of Aeneas.

[3] *right,* with **cōnscia.** This quotation plays a part in a famous story of two rival English shoemakers whose shops adjoined each other. One of them put out a sign with the Vergilian quotation on it. Not to be outdone, his rival, who did not know Latin, promptly hung out a sign reading "Mens and Womens Conscia Recti."

[4] neuter, referring to the destruction of Troy, as seen by Aeneas

[5] Supply **est.** Used as nouns in the predicate nominative.

APPENDIX

Important Dates and Events

B.C.

753	(Traditional date) Rome founded
753–509	Legendary kings
509	Republic established
496	Battle of Lake Regillus
494	Secession of the plebs
451–450	Laws of the Twelve Tables
390	Gauls capture Rome
343–290	Samnite Wars
280–275	War with Pyrrhus
264–241	First Punic War
218–201	Second Punic War
200–197	War with Philip
171–168	War with Perseus
157?–86	Marius, general
149–146	Third Punic War
146	Capture of Corinth
111–106	War with Jugurtha
106–48	Pompey, general
106–43	Cicero, orator, statesman
102	Marius defeats Cimbri and Teutons
100–44	Caesar, general, statesman
88–63	Mithridatic Wars
86	Sulla captures Athens
80–78	Caesar in Asia
63	Cicero consul; conspiracy of Catiline
63–A.D. 14	Augustus
62	Caesar praetor (propraetor in Spain in 61)
60	First triumvirate (Caesar, Crassus, Pompey)
59	Caesar consul (proconsul in Gaul and Illyricum, 58–50)
55 and 54	Caesar invades Britain
55 and 53	Caesar invades Germany
52	Fall of Alesia
49	Caesar crosses the Rubicon, thus precipitating civil war
48	Caesar consul; Battle of Pharsalus—Pompey defeated
48–46	Caesar dictator
46	Caesar consul and dictator, reforms calendar
45	Caesar sole consul
44	Caesar assassinated, March 15
42	Battle of Philippi
31	Battle of Actium
31–A.D. 14	Reign of Augustus

A.D.

9	Defeat of Varus
14–37	Reign of Tiberius
37–41	Reign of Caligula
41–54	Reign of Claudius
54–68	Reign of Nero
68–69	Reigns of Galba, Otho, Vitellius
69–79	Reign of Vespasian
79	Eruption of Mt. Vesuvius
79–81	Reign of Titus
81–96	Reign of Domitian
96–98	Reign of Nerva
98–117	Reign of Trajan
117–138	Reign of Hadrian
138–161	Reign of Antoninus Pius
161–180	Reign of Marcus Aurelius

Life Spans of Major Latin Authors

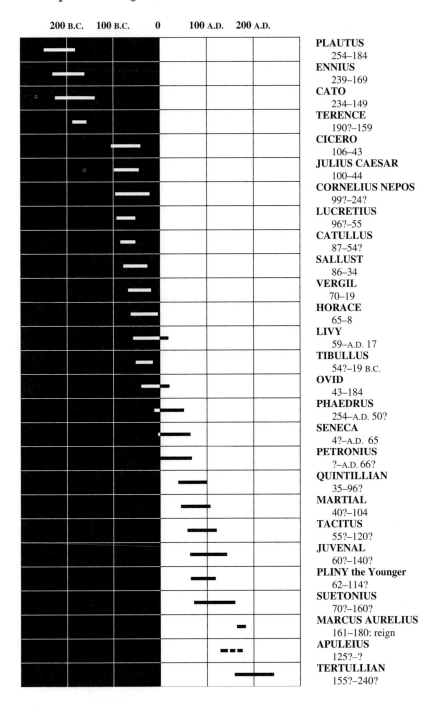

200 B.C.	100 B.C.	0	100 A.D.	200 A.D.

PLAUTUS
254–184

ENNIUS
239–169

CATO
234–149

TERENCE
190?–159

CICERO
106–43

JULIUS CAESAR
100–44

CORNELIUS NEPOS
99?–24?

LUCRETIUS
96?–55

CATULLUS
87–54?

SALLUST
86–34

VERGIL
70–19

HORACE
65–8

LIVY
59–A.D. 17

TIBULLUS
54?–19 B.C.

OVID
43–184

PHAEDRUS
254–A.D. 50?

SENECA
4?–A.D. 65

PETRONIUS
?–A.D. 66?

QUINTILLIAN
35–96?

MARTIAL
40?–104

TACITUS
55?–120?

JUVENAL
60?–140?

PLINY the Younger
62–114?

SUETONIUS
70?–160?

MARCUS AURELIUS
161–180: reign

APULEIUS
125?–?

TERTULLIAN
155?–240?

GRAMMAR APPENDIX

Syntax[1]

Agreement

1. *Adjectives.* Adjectives and participles agree in number, gender, and case with the nouns which they modify.

2. *Adjectives as Nouns (substantives).* Often adjectives are used as nouns: **nostrī,** *our (men);* **malum,** *evil.*

3. *Verbs.* Verbs agree in person and number with their subjects. When two subjects are connected by **aut, aut... aut, neque... neque,** the verb agrees with the nearer subject.

Note: A plural verb may be used with a singular subject which is plural in thought.

4. *Relative Pronoun.* The relative pronoun agrees in gender and number with its antecedent but its case depends upon its use in its own clause.

Note:
    a. The antecedent of the relative pronoun is often omitted.
    b. Sometimes the antecedent is represented by an entire clause, in which case the pronoun is best translated *a thing which.*
    c. In Latin a relative pronoun is often used at the beginning of a sentence to refer to the thought of the preceding sentence. The English idiom calls for a demonstrative or personal pronoun.

        quā dē causā   *for this reason*

5. *Appositives.* Appositives agree in case.

Note: It is often best to supply *as* in translating the appositive.

        eōdem homine magistrō ūtī   *to use the same man as teacher*

Noun Syntax

Nominative

1. *Subject.* The subject of a finite verb is in the nominative case.

2. *Predicate.*
    a. A noun or adjective used in the predicate with a linking verb (*is, are, seem,* etc.) is in the nominative.

        Īnsula est magna.   *The island is large.*
        Sicilia est īnsula.   *Sicily is an island.*

---

[1] In this summary only those constructions are included which are relatively more important and which recur repeatedly in the text, or are referred to in the book.

b. Predicate nouns and adjectives are used not only with **sum** but also with **fīō** and the passive voice of verbs meaning *call, choose, appoint, elect,* and the like.

Caesar dux factus est.	*Caesar was made leader.*
Cicerō Pater Patriae appellātus est.	*Cicero was called the Father of his Country.*

Note: With the active voice of these verbs, two accusatives are used.

Senātus Caesarem dictātōrem fēcit.	*The Senate made Caesar dictator.*

Genitive

1. *Possession.* Possession is expressed by the genitive.

viae īnsulae	*the roads of the island*

2. *Description.* The genitive, if modified by an adjective, may be used to describe a person or thing.

virī magnae virtūtis	*men of great courage*

Note: The descriptive genitive is largely confined to permanent qualities such as measure and number.

spatium decem pedum	*a space of ten feet*

3. *Of the Whole.* The genitive of the whole (also called partitive genitive) represents the whole to which the part belongs.

hōrum omnium fortissmī	*the bravest of all these*
nihil praesidī	*no guard (nothing of a guard)*

Note:

    a. The genitive of the whole is similar to the English idiom except when the genitive is used with such words as **nihil, satis, quid.**

    b. Instead of the genitive of the whole, the ablative with **ex** or **dē** is regularly used with cardinal numerals (except **mīlia**) and **quīdam,** often also with other words, such as **paucī** and **complūrēs.**

quīnque ex nostrīs	*five of our men*
quīdam ex mīlitibus	*certain of the soldiers.*

4. *With Adjectives.* The genitive is used with certain adjectives. In many cases the English idiom is the same; in others, it is not.

bellandī cupidus	*desirous of waging war*
reī mīlitāris perītus	*skilled in warfare*

Dative

1. *Indirect Object.* The indirect object of a verb is in the dative. It is used with verbs of *giving, reporting, telling,* etc.

Nautae pecūniam dōnō.   *I give money to the sailor.*

2. *Purpose.* The dative is sometimes used to express purpose.

Locum castrīs dēlēgit.   *He chose a place for a camp.*

3. *Reference.* The dative of reference shows the person concerned or referred to.

sī mihi dignī esse vultis   *if you wish to be worthy in my sight (lit., for me)*

4. *Separation.* The dative of separation (really reference) is usually confined to persons and occurs chiefly with verbs compounded with **ab, dē,** and **ex.**

scūtō ūnī mīlitī dētrācto   *having seized a shield from a soldier*

5. *With Adjectives.* The dative is used with certain adjectives, as **amīcus, idōneus, pār, proximus, similis, ūtilis,** and their opposites. In many cases the English idiom is the same.

Hic liber est similis illī.   *This book is similar to that.*

6. *With Special Verbs.* The dative is used with a few intransitive verbs, such as **cōnfīdō, crēdō, dēsum, faveō, ignōscō, imperō, invideō, noceō, parcō, pāreō, persuādeō, placeō, praestō, resistō,** and **studeō.**

Tibi pāret sed mihi resistit.   *He obeys you but resists me.*

a. Some of these verbs become impersonal in the passive and the dative is retained. The perfect passive participle of such verbs is used only in the neuter.

Eī persusāsum est.   *He was persuaded.*

b. A neuter pronoun or adjective or an **ut** clause may be used as a direct object with **imperō** and **persuādeō.**

Hoc mihi persuāsit.   *He persuaded me of this.*

7. *With Compounds.* The dative is often used with certain compound verbs, especially when the noun goes closely with the prefix of the verb. No general rule can be given. Sometimes both an accusative and a dative are used when the main part of the verb is transitive.

Gallīs bellum intulit.   *He made war against the Gauls.*

8. *Possession.* With forms of **sum,** the possessor may be expressed by the dative. Generally, the dative of possession emphasizes the owner, the genitive the thing owned.

      Liber mihi est.   *I have a book.*

9. *Agent.* The dative of agent is used with the future passive participle to indicate the person upon whom the obligation rests. (*See also* **Future Passive Participle.**)

      Hoc opus vōbīs faciendum est.   *This work is to be done by you.* i.e.,
                                         This work must be done by you.

Accusative

1. *Direct Object.* The direct object of a transitive verb is in the accusative.

      Viam parāmus.   *We are preparing a way.*

2. *Extent.* Extent of time or space is expressed by the accusative.

      Duōs annōs remānsit.   *He remained two years.*
      Flūmen decem pedēs altum est. *The river is ten feet deep.*

3. *Place to Which.* The accusative with **ad** *(to)* or **in** *(into)* expresses *place to which.* These prepositions, however, are omitted before **domum** and names of towns and cities.

      Lēgātōs ad eum mittunt.   *They send envoys to him.*
      Rōmam eunt.   *They go to Rome.*

Note: When the preposition **ad** is used with names of towns, it means *to the vicinity of.*

4. *Subject of Infinitive.* The subject of an infinitive is in the accusative.

      Puerōs esse bonōs volumus. *We want the boys to be good.*

5. *Two Accusatives.* With **trādūcō** and **trānsportō** two accusatives are used. In the passive the word closely connected with the prefix remains in the accusative.

      Cōpiās Rhēnum trādūcit.   *He leads his forces across the Rhine.*
      Cōpiae Rhēnum trādūcuntur. *The forces are led across the Rhine.*

Note: For two accusatives with verbs meaning *call, choose,* etc., see **Nominative, 2, b,** *Note.*

6. *With Prepositions.* The accusative is used with prepositions (except those listed under **Ablative, 19**). When **in** and **sub** show the direction toward which a thing moves, the accusative is used.

Ablative

Summary. The uses of the ablative may be grouped under three heads:

  I. The *true* or *"from" ablative* (**ab,** *from,* and **lātus,** *carried*), used with the prepositions **ab, dē,** and **ex**—if any preposition is used.

 II. The *associative* or *"with" ablative,* used with the preposition **cum**—if any preposition is used.

III. The *place* or *"in" ablative,* used with the prepositions **in** and **sub**—if any preposition is used.

1. *Separation.* Separation may be expressed by the ablative without a preposition, always so with **careō** and **līberō,** often also with **abstineō, dēsistō, excēdō,** and other verbs.

Note:

  a. Caesar uses **prohibeō,** *keep from,* usually without a preposition, but occasionally with it.

Suīs fīnibus eōs prohibent.	*They keep them from their own territory.*

  b. Other verbs expressing separation regularly require the prepositions **ab, dē,** or **ex.**

2. *Place from Which.* The ablative with **ab, dē,** or **ex** expresses *place from which.*

ex agrīs	*out of the fields*

Note: The preposition is regularly omitted before **domō** as well as before names of towns and cities. When it is used with such names, it means *from the vicinity of.*

3. *Origin.* The ablative without or with a preposition (**ab, dē, ex**) expresses origin.

amplissimō genere nātus	*born of most illustrious family*

4. *Agent.* The ablative with **ā** or **ab** is used with a passive verb to show the person (or animal) by whom something is done.

Amāmur ab amīcīs.	*We are loved by our friends.*

5. *Comparison.* After a comparative the ablative is used when **quam** *(than)* is omitted.

amplius pedibus decem	*more than ten feet*
Nec locus tibi ūllus dulcior esse dēbet patriā.	*No spot ought to be dearer to you than your native land.*

6. *Accompaniment.* The ablative with **cum** expresses accompaniment.

> **Cum servō venit.**   *He is coming with the slave.*

    a. When **cum** is used with a personal, reflexive, or relative pronoun, it is attached to it as an enclitic: **vōbīscum,** *with you;* **sēcum,** *with himself;* **quibuscum,** *with whom.*

    b. Cum may be omitted in military phrases indicating accompaniment, if modified by an adjective other than a numeral.

> **omnibus suīs cōpiīs**   *with all his forces*
> **cum tribus legiōnibus**   *with three legions*

7. *Manner.* The ablative of manner with **cum** describes how something is done. **Cum** is sometimes omitted if an adjective modifies the noun.

> **(Cum) magnō studiō labōrat.**   *He labors with great eagerness (very eagerly).*

8. *Absolute.* A noun in the ablative used with a participle, adjective, or other noun and having no grammatical connection with any other word in its clause is called an ablative absolute.

    In translating, an ablative absolute should, as a rule, be changed to a clause expressing *time, cause, condition, means,* or *concession,* according to the context. At times it may best be rendered by a coordinate clause.

> **Servō accūsātō, dominus discessit.**
> *After accusing the slave* (lit., *the slave having been accused*), *the master departed.*

> **Oppidīs nostrīs captīs, bellum gerēmus.**
> *If our towns are captured* (lit., *our towns captured*), *we shall wage war.*

9. *Means.* The means by which a thing is done is expressed by the ablative without a preposition.

> **Ratibus trānsībant.**   *They were trying to cross by means of rafts.*

10. *With Special Verbs.* The ablative is used with a few verbs, notably **fruor, fungor, potior, ūtor,** and **vescor,** whose English equivalents govern a direct object.

> **Castrīs potītī sunt.**   *They got possession of the camp.*

11. *Cause.* The ablative of cause is used chiefly with verbs and adjectives expressing feeling.

> **labōrāre iniūriā**   *to suffer because of the wrong*
> **vīribus cōnfīsī**   *relying on their strength*

12. *Measure of Difference.* The ablative without a preposition expresses the measure of difference.

tribus annīs ante	*three years ago* (lit., *before by three years*)
multō maior	*much larger* (lit., *larger by much*)

13. *Description.* The ablative, like the genitive, is used with an adjective to describe a noun. It is regularly used of temporary qualities, such as personal appearance.

hominēs inimīcā faciē	*men with an unfriendly appearance*

14. *Place Where.* The ablative with **in** or **sub** expresses *place where*. The preposition may be omitted, however, with certain words like **locō**, **locīs**, and **parte**, also in certain fixed expressions like **tōtō orbe terrārum**, *in the whole world*. In poetry the omission of the preposition is more frequent. (*See also* **Locative.**)

15. *Time When. Time when* or *within which* is expressed by the ablative without a preposition.

aestāte	*in summer*
paucīs diēbus	*within a few days*

16. *Respect.* The ablative tells in what respect the statement applies.

Nōs superant numerō.	*They surpass us in number.*

17. *Accordance.* The ablative is used with a few words to express the idea *in accordance with.*

mōre suō	*in accordance with his custom*

18. *With Dignus.* The ablative is used with **dignus** and **indignus.**

dignus patre	*worthy of his father*

19. *With Prepositions.* The ablative is used with the prepositions **ab, cum, dē, ex, prae, prō, sine;** sometimes with **in** and **sub** (see 14).

Locative

Domus and the names of towns and cities require a separate case, called the locative, to express *place where*. The locative has the same ending as the genitive in the singular of nouns of the first and second declensions; it has the same ending as the ablative in the plural of these declensions and in the third declension, singular and plural.

domī	*at home*
Rōmae	*at Rome*
Athēnīs	*at Athens*

Vocative

The vocative is used in addressing a person. Unless emphatic it never stands first.

> **Quid facis, amīce?**   *What are you doing, my friend?*

Verb Syntax

Tenses

The tenses of the indicative in Latin are in general used like those in English, but the following points are to be noted.

1. *Present.* The Latin present has the force of the English simple present and of the progressive present.

> **Vocat.**   *He calls.* or *He is calling.*

2. *Historical Present.* The historical present is used for vivid effect instead of a past tense in Latin as in English.

> **Rōmam proficīscuntur.**   *They depart(ed) for Rome.*

   a. In clauses introduced by **dum** meaning *while,* the historical present is always used. In translating use the English past. For **dum** meaning *as long as* or *until* see **Indicative Mood, 2** and **Subjunctive Mood, 12.**

> **dum haec geruntur**   *while these things were going on*

3. *Imperfect.* The Latin imperfect expresses repeated, customary, or continuous action in the past and is usually best translated by the English progressive past, sometimes by the auxiliary *would,* or by a phrase, such as *used to, kept on,* or *kept on trying to.*

> **Pugnābant.**   *They were fighting.*

4. *Perfect.* The Latin perfect is generally equivalent to the English past, occasionally to the present perfect.

> **Vīcī.**   *I conquered.* or *I have conquered.*

5. *Sequence of Tenses.* The subjunctive mood is used chiefly in subordinate clauses, in which its tenses are determined by the principle of "sequence of tenses," as shown in the following summary and examples:

   a. PRIMARY TENSES   (referring to the present or future)
   Indicative: present, future, future perfect
   Subjunctive: present, perfect

> **Venit ut mē videat.**   *He is coming to see me (that he may see me).*
>
> **Veniet ut mē videat.**   *He will come to see me (that he may see me).*

Excesserō priusquam veniat.	*I shall have departed before he comes.*
Rogō quid crās faciās (or factūrus sīs).	*I ask what you will do tomorrow.*
Rogō quid herī fēcerīs.	*I ask what you did yesterday.*

b. SECONDARY TENSES   (referring to the past)
Indicative: imperfect, perfect, pluperfect
Subjunctive: imperfect, pluperfect

Vēnit ut mē vidēret.	*He came to see me (that he might see me).*
Rogābam quid facerēs.	*I kept asking what you were doing.*
Rogābam quid anteā fēcissēs.	*I kept asking what you had done before.*
Excesseram priusquam venīret.	*I had departed before he came.*

Primary indicative tenses are followed by primary subjunctive tenses, secondary by secondary.

Note:

a. The "historical" present (see 2), used for vivid effect in describing a past action, is often followed by a secondary tense.

b. In result clauses, the perfect subjunctive sometimes follows a secondary tense.

Indicative Mood

The indicative mood is generally used in Latin as in English to state what have been, are, or will be facts. The following points are to be noted.

1. *Relative Clauses.* Most relative clauses are in the indicative, as in English.

2. *Adverbial Clauses.* Clauses introduced by **postquam, posteāquam** *(after),* **ubi, ut** *(when),* **cum prīmum, simul ac** *(as soon as),* **dum** *(while, as long as),* **quamquam, etsī** *(although)* are in the indicative.

Postquam id cōnspexit, signum dedit.	*After he noticed this, he gave the signal.*

3. *Noun Clauses.* A clause introduced by **quod** *(the fact that, that)* is in the indicative and may be used as subject or object of the main verb or in apposition with a demonstrative.

Grātum est quod mē requīris.	*It is gratifying that you miss me.*

Subjunctive Mood

1. *Volitive.* The volitive (**volō**) subjunctive represents an act as *willed* and is translated by *let.* The negative is **nē.**

| **Patriam dēfendāmus.** | *Let us defend our country.* |
| **Nē id videat.** | *Let him not see it.* |

2. *Purpose Clauses.* The subjunctive is used in a subordinate clause with **ut** or **utī** (negative **nē**) to express the purpose of the act expressed by the principal clause.

Venīmus ut videāmus.	*We come that we may see.* or
	We come to see.
Fugit nē videātur.	*He flees that he may not be seen.*

3. *Relative Purpose Clauses.* If the principal clause contains (or implies) a definite antecedent, the purpose clause may be introduced by the relative pronoun **quī** (= **ut is** or **ut eī**) instead of **ut.**

| **Mīlitēs mīsit quī hostem impedīrent.** | *He sent soldiers to hinder the enemy.* |

4. *Quō Purpose Clauses.* If the purpose clause contains an adjective or adverb in the comparative degree, **quō** is generally used instead of **ut.**

| **Accēdit quō facilius audiat.** | *He approaches in order that he may hear more easily.* |

(For other ways to express purpose see **Dative, Future Passive Participle, Gerund.**)

5. *Volitive Noun Clauses.* Clauses in the subjunctive with **ut** (negative **nē**) are used as the objects of such verbs as **moneō, rogō, petō, hortor, persuādeō,** and **imperō.**

| **Mīlitēs hortātus est ut fortēs essent.** | *He urged the soldiers to be brave.* |
| **Helvētiīs persuāsit ut exīrent.** | *He persuaded the Helvetians to leave.* |

Note:

    a. With **iubeō** *(order),* unlike **imperō,** the infinitive is used. The subject of the infinitive is in the accusative.

| **Iussit eōs venīre.** | *He ordered them to come.* |
| **Imperāvit eīs ut venīrent.** | *He ordered them to come.* |

    b. **Vetō** *(forbid)* and **cupiō** *(desire)* are used like **iubeō.**

6. *Clauses with Verbs of Hindering.* With verbs of *hindering* and *preventing,* as **impediō** and **dēterreō,** the subjunctive introduced by **nē** or **quō minus** is used if the main clause is affirmative, by **quīn** if negative.

    Tū dēterrēre potes nē maior multitūdō trādūcātur.
    You can prevent a greater number from being brought over.

Note:

The infinitive is often used with **prohibeō** (*prevent*).

7. *Clauses of Fear.* With verbs of *fearing,* clauses in the subjunctive introduced by **nē** (*that*) and **ut** (*that not*) are used.

> **Verēbātur nē tū aeger essēs.** *He feared that you were sick.*
> **Timuī ut venīrent.** *I was afraid that they would not come.*

8. *Result Clauses.* The result of the action or state of the principal verb is expressed by a subordinate clause with **ut (utī),** negative **ut nōn (utī nōn),** and the subjunctive.

> **Tantum est perīculum ut paucī veniant.**
> *So great is the danger that few are coming.*

> **Ita bene erant castra mūnīta ut nōn capī possent.**
> *So well had the camp been fortified that it could not be taken.*

Note: Result clauses are usually anticipated by some word in the main clause meaning *so* or *such* (**ita, tantus, tot, tam,** etc.).

9. *Noun Clauses of Result.* Verbs meaning to happen (**accidō**) or to cause or effect (**efficiō**) require clauses of result in the subjunctive with **ut (utī)** or **ut (utī) nōn,** used as subject or object of the main verb:

> **Accidit ut mē nōn vidēret.** *It happened that he did not see me.*
> **Efficiam ut veniat.** *I shall cause him to come.*

10. *Descriptive Relative Clauses.* A relative clause with the subjunctive may be used to describe an indefinite antecedent. Such clauses are called relative clauses of description (characteristic) and are especially common after such expressions as **ūnus** and **sōlus, sunt quī** (*there are those who*), and **nēmō est quī** (*there is no one who*).

Note: Sometimes a descriptive clause expresses cause, result, or concession.

11. *Cum Clauses.* In secondary sequence **cum** (*when*) is used with the imperfect of the pluperfect subjunctive to describe the circumstances under which the action of the main verb occurred.

> **Cum mīlitēs redīssent, Caesar ōrātiōnem habuit.**
> *When the soldiers returned, Caesar made a speech.*

a. In some clauses **cum** with the subjunctive is best translated *since.*

> **Quae cum ita sint, nōn ībō.** *Since this is so, I shall not go* (literally, *When this is so*).

b. In some clauses **cum** with the subjunctive is best translated *although*.

Cum ea ita sint, tamen nōn ībō. *Although this is so, yet I shall not go* (literally, *When*, etc.).

When **ut** means *although, granted that*, its clause is in the subjunctive.

12. *Anticipatory Clauses.* **Dum** *(until),* **antequam,** and **priusquam** *(before)* introduce clauses (a) in the indicative to indicate *an actual fact,* (b) in the subjunctive to indicate an act *as anticipated.*

Silentium fuit dum tū vēnistī.	*There was silence until you came.*
Caesar exspectāvit dum nāvēs convenīrent.	*Caesar waited until the ships should assemble.*
Priusquam tēlum adigī posset, omnēs fūgērunt.	*Before a weapon could be thrown, all fled.*

13. *Indirect Questions.* In a question indirectly quoted or expressed after some introductory verb such as *ask, doubt, learn, know, tell, hear,* etc., the verb is in the subjunctive.

Rogant quis sit. *They ask who he is.*

14. *Subordinate Clauses in Indirect Discourse.* An indicative in a subordinate clause becomes subjunctive in indirect discourse. If the clause is not regarded as an essential part of the quotation but is merely explanatory or parenthetical, its verb may be in the indicative.

Dīxit sē pecūniam invēnisse quam āmīsisset.
He said that he found the money which he had lost.

15. *Attraction.* A verb in a clause dependent upon a subjunctive or an infinitive is frequently "attracted" to the subjunctive, especially if its clause is an essential part of the statement.

Dat negōtium hīs utī ea quae apud Belgās gerantur cognōscant.
He directs them to learn what is going on among the Belgians.

16. *Quod Causal Clauses.* Causal clauses introduced by **quod** (or **proptereā quod**) and **quoniam** *(since, because)* are in the indicative when they give the writer's or speaker's reason, the subjunctive when the reason is presented as that of another person.

Amīcō grātiās ēgī quod mihi pecūniam dederat.
I thanked my friend because he had given me money.

Rōmānīs bellum intulit quod agrōs suōs vāstāvissent.

He made war against the Romans because (as he alleged) they had laid waste his lands.

Outline of Conditions

a. Subordinate clause ("condition") introduced by **sī, nisi,** or **sī nōn.**

b. Principal clause ("conclusion").

1. *Simple* (nothing implied as to truth). Any possible combination of tenses of the indicative, as in English.

> **Sī mē laudat, laetus sum.**　　*If he praises me, I am glad.*

2. *Contrary to Fact.*

a. *Present:* imperfect subjunctive in both clauses.

> **Sī mē laudāret, laetus essem.**　　*If he were praising me* (but he isn't), *I should be glad (now).*

b. *Past:* pluperfect subjunctive in both clauses.

> **Sī nē laudāvisset, laetus fuissem.**　　*If he had praised me* (but he didn't), *I should have been glad* (then).

c. *Mixed:* past condition and present conclusion.

> **Sī mē laudāvisset, laetus essem.**　*If he had praised me* (but he didn't), *I should be glad* (now).

3. *Future Less Vivid* ("should," "would"). Present subjunctive in both clauses.

> **Sī mē laudet, laetus sim.**　　*If he should praise me, I should be glad.*

Imperative Mood

Affirmative commands are expressed by the imperative; negative commands by the present imperative of **nōlō (nōlī, nōlīte)** plus the infinitive. The imperative with **nē** is used in poetry.

> **Amā inimīcōs tuōs.**　　*Love your enemies.*
> **Nōlīte īre.**　　*Do not go* (lit., *Be unwilling to go*).

Note: Exhortations and commands, though main clauses, become subjunctive in indirect discourse.

> (Direct) **Īte!**　　*Go!*
> (Indirect) **Dīxit īrent.**　　*He said that they should go.*

Reflexive Use of the Passive

Occasionally the passive form of a verb or participle is used in a reflexive sense: **armārī,** *to arm themselves.*

Participle

1. The tenses of the participle (present, perfect, future) indicate time *present, past,* or *future* from the standpoint of the main verb.
2. **a.** Perfect participles are often used simply as adjectives: **nōtus,** *known.*
   b. Participles, like adjectives, may be used as nouns: **factum,** "having been done," *deed.*
3. The Latin participle is often a *one-word substitute* for a subordinate clause in English introduced by *who* or *which, when* or *after, since* or *because, although,* and *if.*

Future Passive Participle

The future passive participle (gerundive) is a verbal adjective, having thirty forms. It has two distinct uses:

1. As a predicate adjective with forms of **sum**[1] when it naturally indicates, as in English, *what must be done.* The person upon whom the obligation rests is in the dative. (*See* **Dative, 9.**)

   Caesarī omnia erant agenda.   *Caesar had to do all things* (lit., *all things were to be done by Caesar*).

2. As modifier of a noun or pronoun in various constructions, with no idea of obligation:

   dē Rōmā cōnstituendā   *about founding Rome* (lit., *about Rome to be founded*)

Note: With phrases introduced by **ad** and the accusative or by **causā** (or **grātiā**) and the genitive it expresses purpose. **Causā** and **grātiā** are always placed after the participle.

   Ad eās rēs cōnficiendās Mārcus dēligitur.
   Marcus is chosen to accomplish these things (lit., *for these things to be accomplished*).

   Caesaris videndī causā (or **grātiā**) **vēnit.**
   He came for the sake of seeing Caesar (lit., *for the sake of Caesar to be seen*).

---

[1] The so-called passive periphrastic, a term not used in this book.

Gerund

The gerund is a verbal noun of the second declension with only four forms—genitive, dative, accusative, and ablative singular.

The uses of the gerund are similar to some of those of the future passive participle:

cupidus bellandī	*desirous of waging war*
Ad discendum vēnī.	*I came for learning* (i.e., *to learn*).
Discendī causā (or **grātiā**) **vēnī.**	*I came for the sake of learning.*

Note: The gerund usually does not have an object. Instead, the future passive participle is used, modifying the noun.

Infinitive

1. The infinitive is an indeclinable neuter verbal noun, and as such it may be used as the subject of a verb.

Errāre hūmānum est.	*To err is human.*
Vidēre est crēdere.	*To see is to believe.*

2. With many verbs the infinitive, like other nouns, may be used as a direct object. (Sometimes called the complementary infinitive.)

Cōpiās movēre parat.	*He prepares to move the troops.*

3. The infinitive object of some verbs, such as **iubeō, volō, nōlō,** and **doceō,** often has a noun or pronoun subject in the accusative.

4. Statements that give indirectly the thoughts or words of another, used as the objects of verbs of *saying, thinking, knowing, hearing, perceiving,* etc., have verbs in the infinitive with their subjects in the accusative.

(Direct) **Dīcit, "Puerī veniunt."**	*He says, "The boys are coming."*
(Indirect) **Dīcit puerōs venīre.**	*He says that the boys are coming.*

Note: With the passive third singular (impersonal) of these verbs the infinitive is the subject.

Caesarī nūntiātur eōs trānsīre.	*It is reported to Caesar that they are crossing.*

5. a. The present infinitive represents time or actions as going on, from the standpoint of the introductory verb:

Dīcit } **eōs pugnāre.** *He* { *says* / *said* } *(that) they* { *are* / *were* } *fighting.*
Dīxit

b. The future infinitive represents time or actions as subsequent to that of the introductory verb:

Dīcit ⎱
⎰ **eōs pugnātūrōs esse.** *He* ⎰ *says* ⎱ *(that) they* ⎰ *will* ⎱ *fight.*
Dīxit ⎰ ⎱ *said* ⎰ ⎱ *would* ⎰

c. The perfect infinitive represents time or action as completed before that of the introductory verb:

Dīcit ⎱
⎰ **eōs pugnāvisse.** *He* ⎰ *says* ⎱ *(that) they* ⎰ *have* ⎱ *fought.*
Dīxit ⎰ ⎱ *said* ⎰ ⎱ *had* ⎰

Summary of Prefixes and Suffixes

Prefixes

Many Latin words are formed by joining prefixes (**prae,** *in front;* **fīxus,** *attached*) to *root* words. These same prefixes, most of which are prepositions, are also those used most often in English, and by their use many new words are continually being formed.

Some prefixes change their final consonants to make them like the initial consonants of the words to which they are attached. This change is called assimilation (**ad,** *to;* **similis,** *like*).

Many prefixes in Latin and English may have intensive force, especially **con-, ex-, ob-, per-.** They are then best translated either by an English intensive, such as *up* or *out,* or by an adverb, such as *completely, thoroughly, deeply.* Thus **commoveō** means *move greatly,* **permagnus,** *very great,* **obtineō,** *hold on to,* **concitō,** *rouse up,* **excipiō,** *catch, receive.*

1. **ab (abs, ā),** *from:* **abs-tineō;** *ab-undance, abs-tain, a-vocation.*
2. **ad,** *to, toward:* **ad-iciō;** *ac-curate, an-nounce, ap-paratus, ad-vocate.*
3. **ante,** *before:* **ante-cēdō;** *ante-cedent.*
4. **bene,** *well:* **bene-dīcō;** *bene-factor.*
5. **bi-, bis-,** *twice, two:* **bi-ennium;** *bi-ennial.*
6. **circum,** *around:* **circum-eō;** *circum-ference.*
7. **con-,** *with, together:* **con-vocō;** *con-voke, col-lect, com-motion, cor-rect.*
8. **contrā,** *against:* *contra-dict.*
9. **dē,** *from, down from, not:* **dē-ferō;** *de-ter.*
10. **dis-,** *apart, not:* **dis-cēdō;** *dis-locate, dif-fuse, di-vert.*
11. **ex (ē),** *out of, from:* **ex-eō;** *ex-port, e-dit, ef-fect.*
12. **extrā,** *outside:* *extra-legal.*
13. **in,** *in, into, against:* **in-dūcō;** *in-habit, im-migrant, il-lusion, en-chant.*
14. **in-,** *not, un-:* **im-mēnsus;** *il-legal, im-moral, ir-regular.*
15. **inter,** *between, among:* **inter-clūdō;** *inter-class.*
16. **intrā,** *within, inside:* *intra-collegiate.*

17. **intrō-,** *within: intro-duce.*

18. **male,** *ill: male-factor, mal-formation.*

19. **multi-,** *much, many: multi-graph.*

20. **nōn,** *not: non-sense.*

21. **ob,** *against, toward:* **ob-tineō;** *oc-cur, of-fer, o-mit, op-pose, ob-tain.*

22. **per,** *through, thoroughly:* **per-moveō;** *per-fect.*

23. **post,** *after: post-pone.*

24. **prae,** *before, in front of:* **prae-ficiō;** *pre-cede.*

25. **prō,** *for, forward:* **prō-dūcō;** *pro-mote.*

26. **re- (red-),** *back, again:* **re-dūcō, red-igō;** *re-fer.*

27. **sē-,** *apart from:* **sē-cēdō;** *se-parate.*

28. **sēmi-,** *half, partly:* **sēmi-barbarus;** *semi-annual.*

29. **sub,** *under, up from under:* **suc-cēdō;** *suf-fer, sug-gest, sup-port, sub-let.*

30. **super (sur-),** *over, above:* **super-sum;** *super-fluous, sur-mount.*

31. **trāns (trā-),** *through, across:* **trā-dūcō;** *trans-fer.*

32. **ultrā,** *extremely: ultra-fashionable.*

33. **ūn- (ūni-),** *one: uni-form.*

Suffixes

Particles that are attached to the ends of words are called suffixes (**sub,** *under, after;* **fīxus,** *attached*). Like the Latin prefixes, the Latin suffixes play a very important part in the formation of English words.

The meaning of suffixes is often far less definite than that of prefixes. In many cases they merely indicate the part of speech.

Suffixes are often added to words that already have suffixes. So, *functionalistically* has six suffixes, all of Latin or Greco-Latin origin except the last. A suffix often combines with a preceding letter or letters to form a new suffix. This is especially true of suffixes added to perfect participles whose base ends in **-s-** or **-t-.** In the following list no account is taken of such English suffixes as *-ant,* derived from the ending of the Latin present participle.

1. **-ālis** *(-al), pertaining to:* **līber-ālis;** *annu-al.*

2. **-ānus** *(-an, -ane, -ain), pertaining to:* **Rōm-ānus;** *capt-ain, hum-ane.*

3. **-āris** *(-ar), pertaining to:* **famili-āris;** *singul-ar.*

4. **-ārium** *(-arium, -ary), place where: aqu-arium, gran-ary.*

5. **-ārius** *(-ary), pertaining to:* **frūment-ārius;** *ordin-ary.*

6. **-āticum** *(-age): bagg-age.*

7. **-āx** *(-ac-ious), tending to:* **aud-āx;** *rap-acious.*

8. **-faciō, -ficō** *(-fy), make:* **cōn-ficiō;** *satis-fy.*

9. **-ia** *(-y),* **-cia, -tia** *(-ce),* **-antia** *(-ance, -ancy),* **-entia** *(-ence, -ency), condition of:* **memor-ia, grā-tia, cōnst-antia, sent-entia;** *memor-y, provin-ce, gra-ce, const-ancy, sent-ence.*

10. **-icus** *(-ic), pertaining to:* **pūbl-icus;** *civ-ic.*

11. **-idus** *(-id), having the quality of:* **rap-idus;** *flu-id.*

12. **-ilis** *(-ile, -il)*, **-bilis** *(-ble, -able, -ible)*, *able to be:* **fac-ilis, laudā-bilis;** *fert-ile, no-ble, compar-able, terr-ible.*

13. **-īlis** *(-ile, -il)*, *pertaining to:* **cīv-īlis;** *serv-ile.*

14. **-īnus** *(-ine)*, *pertaining to:* **mar-īnus;** *div-ine.*

15. **-iō** *(-ion)*, **-siō** *(-sion)*, **-tiō** *(-tion)*, *act or state of:* **reg-iō, mān-siō, ōrā-tiō;** *commun-ion, ten-sion, rela-tion.*

16. **-ium** *(-y)*, **-cium, -tium** *(-ce):* **remed-ium, sōlā-cium, pre-tium;** *stud-y, edifi-ce.*

17. **-īvus** *(-ive)*, *pertaining to:* **capt-īvus;** *nat-ive.*

18. **-lus, -ellus, -ulus** *(-lus, -le) little* ("diminutive"): **parvu-lus, castel-lum;** *gladio-lus, parti-cle.*

19. **-men** *(-men, -min, -me):* **lū-men;** *cri-min-al, cri-me.*

20. **-mentum** *(-ment)*, *means of:* **im-pedī-mentum;** *comple-ment.*

21. **-or** *(-or)*, *state of:* **tim-or;** *terr-or.*

22. **-or, -sor, -tor** *(-sor, -tor)*, *one who:* **scrīp-tor;** *inven-tor.*

23. **-ōrium** *(-orium, -ory, -or) place where:* *audit-orium, fact-ory, mirr-or.*

24. **-ōsus** *(-ous, -ose)*, *full of:* **ōti-ōsus;** *copi-ous.*

25. **-ōx** *(-ocity)*, *tending to:* **ferōx;** *fer-ocity.*

26. **-tās** *(-ty)*, *state of:* **līber-tās;** *integri-ty.*

27. **-tō, -sō, -itō,** *keep on* ("frequentative"): **dic-tō, prēn-sō, vent-itō.**

28. **-tūdō** *(-tude)*, *state of:* **magni-tūdō;** *multi-tude.*

29. **-tūs** *(-tue)*, *state of:* **vir-tūs;** *vir-tue.*

30. **-ūra, -sūra, -tūra** *(-ure, -sure, -ture):* **fig-ūra, mēn-sūra, agricul-tūra;** *proced-ure, pres-sure, na-ture.*

Basic Forms

Nouns

	First Declension			**Second Declension**	
	SINGULAR	PLURAL		SINGULAR	PLURAL
NOM.	via	viae		servus	servī
GEN.	viae	viārum		servī	servōrum
DAT.	viae	viīs		servō	servīs
ACC.	viam	viās		servum	servōs
ABL.	viā	viīs		servō	servīs
(VOC.)				serve	

Vocative forms have been omitted unless they differ from the nominative. Second declension nouns in **-ius** have **-ī** in the genitive and vocative singular: **fīlī, Cornēlī**. The accent does not change.

Second Declension

	SING.	PL.	SING.	PL.	SING.	PL.
NOM.	ager	agrī	puer	puerī	signum	signa
GEN.	agrī	agrōrum	puerī	puerōrum	signī	signōrum
DAT.	agrō	agrīs	puerō	puerīs	signō	signīs
ACC.	agrum	agrōs	puerum	puerōs	signum	signa
ABL.	agrō	agrīs	puerō	puerīs	signō	signīs

Nouns in **-ium** have **-ī** in the genitive singular: **cōnsilī**. The accent does not change.

Third Declension

	SING.	PL.	SING.	PL.	SING.	PL.
NOM.	mīles	mīlitēs	lēx	lēgēs	corpus	corpora
GEN.	mīlitis	mīlitum	lēgis	lēgum	corporis	corporum
DAT.	mīlitī	mīlitibus	lēgī	lēgibus	corporī	corporibus
ACC.	mīlitem	mīlitēs	lēgem	lēgēs	corpus	corpora
ABL.	mīlite	mīlitibus	lēge	lēgibus	corpore	corporibus

Third Declension I-Stems

	SING.	PL.	SING.	PL.
NOM.	cīvis	cīvēs	mare	maria
GEN.	cīvis	cīvium	maris	marium
DAT.	cīvī	cīvibus	marī	maribus
ACC.	cīvem	cīvēs (-īs)	mare	maria
ABL.	cīve	cīvibus	marī	maribus

Turris and a few proper nouns have **-im** in the accusative singular. **Turris, ignis, nāvis,** and a few proper nouns sometimes have **-ī** in the ablative singular.

(a) The classes of masculine and feminine **i**-stem nouns are:

    1. Nouns ending in **-is** and **-ēs** having no more syllables in the genitive than in the nominative: **cīvis, nūbēs.**

    2. Nouns of one syllable whose base ends in two consonants: **pars** (gen. **part-is**), **nox** (gen. **noct-is**).

3. Nouns whose base ends in **-nt** or **-rt: cliēns** (gen. **client-is**).

(b) Neuter **i**-stem nouns ending in **-e, -al, -ar: mare, animal, calcar.**

Fourth Declension

	SING.	PL.	SING.	PL.
NOM.	cāsus	cāsūs	cornū	cornua
GEN.	cāsūs	cāsuum	cornūs	cornuum
DAT.	cāsuī	cāsibus	cornū	cornibus
ACC.	cāsum	cāsūs	cornū	cornua
ABL.	cāsū	cāsibus	cornū	cornibus

Fifth Declension

	SING.	PL.	SING.	PL.
NOM.	diēs	diēs	rēs	rēs
GEN.	diēī	diērum	reī	rērum
DAT.	diēī	diēbus	reī	rēbus
ACC.	diem	diēs	rem	rēs
ABL.	diē	diēbus	rē	rēbus

Irregular Nouns

	SING.	PL.	SING.	SING.	PL.
NOM.	vīs	vīrēs	nēmō	domus	domūs
GEN.	——	vīrium	(nūllīus)	domūs (-ī)	domuum (-ōrum)
DAT.	——	vīribus	nēminī	domuī (-ō)	domibus
ACC.	vim	vīrēs (-īs)	nēminem	domum	domōs (-ūs)
ABL.	vī	vīribus	(nūllō)	domō (-ū)	domibus
(LOC.)				(domī)	

Adjectives and Adverbs

First and Second Declensions

	SINGULAR			PLURAL		
	M.	F.	N.	M.	F.	N.
NOM.	magnus	magna	magnum	magnī	magnae	magna
GEN.	magnī	magnae	magnī	magnōrum	magnārum	magnōrum
DAT.	magnō	magnae	magnō	magnīs	magnīs	magnīs
ACC.	magnum	magnam	magnum	magnōs	magnās	magna
ABL.	magnō	magnā	magnō	magnīs	magnīs	magnīs
(VOC.)	(magne)					

	SINGULAR			SINGULAR		
NOM.	līber	lībera	līberum	noster	nostra	nostrum
GEN.	līberī	līberae	līberī	nostrī	nostrae	nostrī
DAT.	līberō	līberae	līberō	nostrō	nostrae	nostrō
ACC.	līberum	līberam	līberum	nostrum	nostram	nostrum
ABL.	līberō	līberā	līberō	nostrō	nostrā	nostrō

Plural, **līberī, līberae, lībera,** etc.   Plural, **nostrī, -ae, -a,** etc.

Third Declension[1]

(a) THREE ENDINGS

	SINGULAR			PLURAL		
	M.	F.	N.	M.	F.	N.
NOM.	ācer	ācris	ācre	ācrēs	ācrēs	ācria
GEN.	ācris	ācris	ācris	ācrium	ācrium	ācrium
DAT.	ācrī	ācrī	ācrī	ācribus	ācribus	ācribus
ACC.	ācrem	ācrem	ācre	ācrēs (-īs)	ācrēs (-īs)	ācria
ABL.	ācrī	ācrī	ācrī	ācribus	ācribus	ācribus

(b) TWO ENDINGS

	SINGULAR		PLURAL	
	M., F.	N.	M., F.	N.
NOM.	fortis	forte	fortēs	fortia
GEN.	fortis	fortis	fortium	fortium
DAT.	fortī	fortī	fortibus	fortibus
ACC.	fortem	forte	fortēs (-īs)	fortia
ABL.	fortī	fortī	fortibus	fortibus

(c) ONE ENDING

	SINGULAR		PLURAL	
	M., F.	N.	M., F.	N.
NOM.	pār	pār	parēs	paria
GEN.	paris	paris	parium	parium
DAT.	parī	parī	paribus	paribus
ACC.	parem	pār	parēs (-īs)	paria
ABL.	parī	parī	paribus	paribus

Present Participle

	SINGULAR		PLURAL	
	M., F.	N.	M., F.	N.
NOM.	portāns	portāns	portantēs	portantia
GEN.	portantis	portantis	portantium	portantium
DAT.	portantī	portantī	portantibus	portantibus
ACC.	portantem	portāns	portantēs (-īs)	portantia
ABL.	portante (-ī)	portante (-ī)	portantibus	portantibus

The ablative singular regularly ends in **-e,** but **-ī** is used wherever the participle is used simply as an adjective.

Irregular Adjectives and Numerals

	M.	F.	N.	M., F.	N.
NOM.	ūnus	ūna	ūnum	trēs	tria
GEN.	ūnīus	ūnīus	ūnīus	trium	trium
DAT.	ūnī	ūnī	ūnī	tribus	tribus
ACC.	ūnum	ūnam	ūnum	trēs	tria
ABL.	ūnō	ūnā	ūnō	tribus	tribus

	M.	F.	N.	M., F., N. (*adj.*)	N. (*noun*)
NOM.	duo	duae	duo	mīlle	mīlia
GEN.	duōrum	duārum	duōrum	mīlle	mīlium
DAT.	duōbus	duābus	duōbus	mīlle	mīlibus
ACC.	duōs	duās	duo	mīlle	mīlia
ABL.	duōbus	duābus	duōbus	mīlle	mīlibus

[1] Most third declension adjectives are **i**-stems, but **iuvenis** and **vetus** have **-e** in the abl. sing. and **-um** in the gen. pl.

Like **ūnus** are **alius, alter, ūllus, nūllus, sōlus, tōtus, uter, neuter, uterque;** plural regular. The nom. and acc. sing. neuter of **alius** is **aliud;** for the genitive sing., **alterius** is generally used. **Ambō** is declined like **duo.**

Comparison of Regular Adjectives and Adverbs

POSITIVE		COMPARATIVE		SUPERLATIVE	
ADJ.	ADV.	ADJ.	ADV.	ADJ.	ADV.
alt**us**	alt**ē**	alt**ior**	alt**ius**	alt**issimus**	alt**issimē**
fort**is**	fort**iter**	fort**ior**	fort**ius**	fort**issimus**	fort**issimē**
līber	līber**ē**	līber**ior**	līber**ius**	līber**rimus**	līber**rimē**
ācer	ācr**iter**	ācr**ior**	ācr**ius**	ācer**rimus**	ācer**rimē**
facil**is**	facil**e**	facil**ior**	facil**ius**	facil**limus**	facil**limē**

Like **facilis** are **difficilis, similis, dissimilis, gracilis, humilis,** but their adverbs (not used in this book) vary in the positive degree. Adjectives in **-er** are like **līber** or **ācer.**

Comparison of Irregular Adjectives

POSITIVE	COMPARATIVE	SUPERLATIVE
bon**us**	mel**ior**	opt**imus**
mal**us**	pe**ior**	pess**imus**
magn**us**	ma**ior**	max**imus**
parv**us**	min**or**	min**imus**
mult**us**	——, plūs	plūr**imus**
īnfer**us**	īnfer**ior**	īnf**imus** *or* **īmus**
super**us**	super**ior**	suprē**mus** *or* sum**mus**
——	pr**ior**	prī**mus**
——	prop**ior**	prox**imus**
——	ulter**ior**	ult**imus**

Comparison of Irregular Adverbs

ben**e**	mel**ius**	opt**imē**
mal**e**	pe**ius**	pess**imē**
(magnopere)	mag**is**	max**imē**
——	min**us**	min**imē**
mult**um**	plūs	plūr**imum**
diū	diūt**ius**	diūt**issimē**
prop**e**	prop**ius**	prox**imē**

Declension of Comparatives

	SINGULAR		PLURAL		SINGULAR	PLURAL	
	M., F.	N.	M., F.	N.	N.	M., F.	N.
NOM.	altior	altius	altiōr**ēs**	altiōr**a**	plūs[1]	plūr**ēs**	plūr**a**
GEN.	altiōr**is**	altiōr**is**	altiōr**um**	altiōr**um**	plūr**is**	plūr**ium**	plūr**ium**
DAT.	altiōr**ī**	altiōr**ī**	altiōr**ibus**	altiōr**ibus**	——	plūr**ibus**	plūr**ibus**
ACC.	altiōr**em**	altius	altiōr**ēs**	altiōr**a**	plūs	plūr**ēs**	plūr**a**
ABL.	altiōr**e**	altiōr**e**	altiōr**ibus**	altiōr**ibus**	plūr**e**	plūr**ibus**	plūr**ibus**

[1] Masculine and feminine lacking in the singular.

Numerals

	ROMAN NUMERALS	CARDINALS	ORDINALS
1	I	ūnus, -a, -um	prīmus, -a, -um
2	II	duo, duae, duo	secundus (alter)
3	III	trēs, tria	tertius
4	IIII *or* IV	quattuor	quārtus
5	V	quīnque	quīntus
6	VI	sex	sextus
7	VII	septem	septimus
8	VIII	octō	octāvus
9	VIIII *or* IX	novem	nōnus
10	X	decem	decimus
11	XI	ūndecim	ūndecimus
12	XII	duodecim	duodecimus
13	XIII	tredecim	tertius decimus
14	XIIII *or* XIV	quattuordecim	quārtus decimus
15	XV	quīndecim	quīntus decimus
16	XVI	sēdecim	sextus decimus
17	XVII	septendecim	septimus decimus
18	XVIII	duodēvīgintī	duodēvīcēsimus[1]
19	XVIIII *or* XIX	ūndēvīgintī	ūndēvīcēsimus
20	XX	vīgintī	vīcēsimus
21	XXI	vīgintī ūnus *or* ūnus et vīgintī	vīcēsimus prīmus *or* ūnus et vīcēsimus
30	XXX	trīgintā	trīcēsimus
40	XXXX *or* XL	quadrāgintā	quadrāgēsimus
50	L	quīnquāgintā	quīnquāgēsimus
60	LX	sexāgintā	sexāgēsimus
70	LXX	septuāgintā	septuāgēsimus
80	LXXX	octōgintā	octōgēsimus
90	LXXXX *or* XC	nōnāgintā	nōnāgēsimus
100	C	centum	centēsimus
101	CI	centum (et) ūnus	centēsimus (et) prīmus
200	CC	ducentī, -ae, -a	ducentēsimus
300	CCC	trecentī, -ae, -a	trecentēsimus
400	CCCC	quadringentī, -ae, -a	quadringentēsimus
500	D	quīngentī, -ae, -a	quīngentēsimus
600	DC	sescentī, -ae, -a	sescentēsimus
700	DCC	septingentī, -ae, -a	septingentēsimus
800	DCCC	octingentī, -ae, -a	octingentēsimus
900	DCCCC	nōngentī, -ae, -a	nōngentēsimus
1000	M	mīlle	mīllēsimus
2000	MM	duo mīlia	bis mīllēsimus

[1] The forms in **-ēsimus** are sometimes spelled **-ēnsimus.**

Pronouns

Personal

	SING.	PL.		SING.	PL.		M.	F.	N.
NOM.	ego	nōs		tū	vōs		is	ea	id
GEN.	meī	nostrum (nostrī)		tuī	vestrum (-trī)		(used as a third		
DAT.	mihi	nōbīs		tibi	vōbīs		personal pronoun. For		
ACC.	mē	nōs		tē	vōs		full declension see		
ABL.	mē	nōbīs		tē	vōbīs		**Demonstrative**		
							below.)		

Reflexive

	FIRST PERSON		SECOND PERSON		THIRD PERSON	
	SING.	PL.	SING.	PL.	SING.	PL.
GEN.	meī	nostrī	tuī	vestrī	suī	suī
DAT.	mihi	nōbīs	tibi	vōbīs	sibi	sibi
ACC.	mē	nōs	tē	vōs	sē (sēsē)	sē (sēsē)
ABL.	mē	nōbīs	tē	vōbīs	sē (sēsē)	sē (sēsē)

Not being used in the nominative, reflexives have no nominative form.

Demonstrative

	SINGULAR			PLURAL		
	M.	F.	N.	M.	F.	N.
NOM.	hic	haec	hoc	hī	hae	haec
GEN.	huius	huius	huius	hōrum	hārum	hōrum
DAT.	huic	huic	huic	hīs	hīs	hīs
ACC.	hunc	hanc	hoc	hōs	hās	haec
ABL.	hōc	hāc	hōc	hīs	hīs	hīs
NOM.	is	ea	id	eī (iī)	eae	ea
GEN.	eius	eius	eius	eōrum	eārum	eōrum
DAT.	eī	eī	eī	eīs (iīs)	eīs (iīs)	eīs (iīs)
ACC.	eum	eam	id	eōs	eās	ea
ABL.	eō	eā	eō	eīs (iīs)	eīs (iīs)	eīs (iīs)

	SINGULAR			PLURAL		
	M.	F.	N.	M.	F.	N.
NOM.	īdem	eadem	idem	eīdem (īdem)	eaedem	eadem
GEN.	eiusdem	eiusdem	eiusdem	eōrundem	eārundem	eōrundem
DAT.	eīdem	eīdem	eīdem	eīsdem (īsdem)	eīsdem (īsdem)	eīsdem (īsdem)
ACC.	eundem	eandem	idem	eōsdem	eāsdem	eadem
ABL.	eōdem	eādem	eōdem	eīsdem (īsdem)	eīsdem (īsdem)	eīsdem (īsdem)

	SINGULAR			SINGULAR		
	M.	F.	N.	M.	F.	N.
NOM.	**ille**	**illa**	**illud**	**ipse**	**ipsa**	**ipsum**
GEN.	**illīus**	**illīus**	**illīus**	**ipsīus**	**ipsīus**	**ipsīus**
DAT.	**illī**	**illī**	**illī**	**ipsī**	**ipsī**	**ipsī**
ACC.	**illum**	**illam**	**illud**	**ipsum**	**ipsam**	**ipsum**
ABL.	**illō**	**illā**	**illō**	**ipsō**	**ipsā**	**ipsō**

(Plural regular like **magnus**)   (Plural regular)

Iste is declined like **ille**.

Relative   Interrogative

	SINGULAR			PLURAL			SINGULAR	
	M.	F.	N.	M.	F.	N.	M., F.	N.
NOM.	**quī**	**quae**	**quod**	**quī**	**quae**	**quae**	**quis?**	**quid?**
GEN.	**cuius**	**cuius**	**cuius**	**quōrum**	**quārum**	**quōrum**	**cuius?**	**cuius?**
DAT.	**cui**	**cui**	**cui**	**quibus**	**quibus**	**quibus**	**cui?**	**cui?**
ACC.	**quem**	**quam**	**quod**	**quōs**	**quās**	**quae**	**quem?**	**quid?**
ABL.	**quō**	**quā**	**quō**	**quibus**	**quibus**	**quibus**	**quō?**	**quō?**

Plural of **quis** like **quī**. Interrogative adjective **quī** like relative **quī**.

Indefinite

	SINGULAR		PLURAL		
	M., F.	N.	M.	F.	N.
NOM.	**aliquis**	**aliquid**	**aliquī**	**aliquae**	**aliqua**
GEN.	**alicuius**	**alicuius**	**aliquōrum**	**aliquārum**	**aliquōrum**
DAT.	**alicui**	**alicui**	**aliquibus**	**aliquibus**	**aliquibus**
ACC.	**aliquem**	**aliquid**	**aliquōs**	**aliquās**	**aliqua**
ABL.	**aliquō**	**aliquō**	**aliquibus**	**aliquibus**	**aliquibus**

The adjective form is **aliquī, -qua, -quod,** etc.

	SINGULAR		
	M.	F.	N.
NOM.	**quīdam**	**quaedam**	**quiddam**
GEN.	**cuiusdam**	**cuiusdam**	**cuiusdam**
DAT.	**cuidam**	**cuidam**	**cuidam**
ACC.	**quendam**	**quandam**	**quiddam**
ABL.	**quōdam**	**quādam**	**quōdam**

	PLURAL		
NOM.	**quīdam**	**quaedam**	**quaedam**
GEN.	**quōrundam**	**quārundam**	**quōrundam**
DAT.	**quibusdam**	**quibusdam**	**quibusdam**
ACC.	**quōsdam**	**quāsdam**	**quaedam**
ABL.	**quibusdam**	**quibusdam**	**quibusdam**

The adjective has **quoddam** for **quiddam**.

	SINGULAR		SINGULAR	
	M., F.	N.	M., F.	N.
NOM.	**quisquam**	**quicquam (quidquam)**	**quisque**	**quidque**
GEN.	**cuiusquam**	**cuiusquam**	**cuiusque**	**cuiusque**
DAT.	**cuiquam**	**cuiquam**	**cuique**	**cuique**
ACC.	**quemquam**	**quicquam (quidquam)**	**quemque**	**quidque**
ABL.	**quōquam**	**quōquam**	**quōque**	**quōque**
	(Plural lacking)		(Plural rare)	

The adjective form of **quisque** is **quisque, quaeque, quodque,** etc.

The indefinite pronoun **quis** (declined like the interrogative) and adjective **quī** (declined like the relative, but in the nom. fem. sing. and the nom. and acc. neut. plur. **qua** may be used for **quae**) are used chiefly after **sī**, **nisi**, **num**, and **nē**.

Verbs

First Conjugation

PRINCIPAL PARTS: **portō, portāre, portāvī, portātus**

ACTIVE		PASSIVE	

INDICATIVE

PRESENT

I carry, etc.

portō	portāmus
portās	portātis
portat	portant

I am carried, etc.

portor	portāmur
portāris (-re)	portāminī
portātur	portantur

IMPERFECT

I was carrying, etc.

portābam	portābāmus
portābās	portābātis
portābat	portābant

I was (being) carried, etc.

portābar	portābāmur
portābāris (-re)	portābāminī
portābātur	portābantur

FUTURE

I shall carry, etc.

portābō	portābimus
portābis	portābitis
portābit	portābunt

I shall be carried, etc.

portābor	portābimur
portāberis (-re)	portābiminī
portābitur	portabuntur

PERFECT

I carried, have carried, etc.

portāvī	portāvimus
portāvistī	portāvistis
portāvit	portāvērunt (-ēre)

I was carried, have been carried, etc.

portātus (-a, -um)	sum / es / est	portātī (-ae, -a)	sumus / estis / sunt

PLUPERFECT

I had carried, etc.

portāveram	portāverāmus
portāverās	portāverātis
portāverat	portāverant

I had been carried, etc.

portātus (-a, -um)	eram / erās / erat	portātī (-ae, -a)	erāmus / erātis / erant

	ACTIVE		PASSIVE	
FUTURE	*I shall have carried,* etc.		*I shall have been carried,* etc.	

PERFECT	portāv**erō**	portāv**erimus**					
	portāv**eris**	portāv**eritis**		erō			erimus
	portāv**erit**	portāv**erint**	portātus	eris	portātī	eritis
			(-a, -um)	erit	(-ae, -a)	erunt

SUBJUNCTIVE

PRESENT	port**em**	port**ēmus**	porter	portēmur
	port**ēs**	port**ētis**	port**ēris (-re)**	port**ēminī**
	port**et**	port**ent**	port**ētur**	port**entur**

IMPERFECT	portā**rem**	portā**rēmus**	portā**rer**	portā**rēmur**
	portā**rēs**	portā**rētis**	portā**rēris (-re)**	portā**rēminī**
	portā**ret**	portā**rent**	portā**rētur**	portā**rentur**

PERFECT	portāv**erim**	portāv**erīmus**					
	portāv**erīs**	portāv**erītis**		sim			sīmus
	portāv**erit**	portāv**erint**	portātus	sīs	portātī	sītis
			(-a, -um)	sit	(-ae, -a)	sint

PLUPERFECT	portāv**issem**	portāv**issēmus**					
	portāv**issēs**	portāv**issētis**		essem			essēmus
	portāv**isset**	portāv**issent**	portātus	essēs	portātī	essētis
			(-a, -um)	esset	(-ae, -a)	essent

PRESENT IMPERATIVE

2ND SING.	portā, *carry*	portā**re**, *be carried*
2ND PLUR.	portā**te**, *carry*	portā**minī**, *be carried*

INFINITIVE

PRESENT	portā**re**, *to carry*	portā**rī**, *to be carried*
PERFECT	portāv**isse**, *to have carried*	portā**tus esse**, *to have been carried*
FUTURE	portāt**ūrus esse**, *to be going to carry*	

PARTICIPLE

PRESENT	portā**ns**, *carrying*	
PERFECT		portā**tus** *(having been) carried*
FUTURE	portāt**ūrus**, *going to carry*	porta**ndus**, *(necessary) to be carried*

GERUND

GEN.   porta**ndī**   DAT.   porta**ndō**   ACC.   porta**ndum**   ABL.   porta**ndō**, *of carrying,* etc.

Second, Third, and Fourth Conjugations

2nd Conj.	*3rd Conj.*	*4th Conj.*	*3rd Conj.* (*-iō*)

PRINCIPAL PARTS

2nd Conj.	3rd Conj.	4th Conj.	3rd Conj. (-iō)
doceō	**pōnō**	**mūniō**	**capiō**
docēre	**pōnere**	**mūnīre**	**capere**
docuī	**posuī**	**mūnīvī**	**cēpī**
doctus	**positus**	**mūnītus**	**captus**

	2nd Conj.	3rd Conj.	4th Conj.	3rd Conj. (*-iō*)
		INDICATIVE ACTIVE		
PRESENT	doceō	pōnō	mūniō	capiō
	docēs	pōnis	mūnīs	capis
	docet	pōnit	mūnit	capit
	docēmus	pōnimus	mūnīmus	capimus
	docētis	pōnitis	mūnītis	capitis
	docent	ponunt	mūniunt	capiunt
IMPERFECT	docēbam	pōnēbam	mūniēbam	capiēbam
	docēbās	pōnēbās	mūniēbās	capiēbās
	docēbat	pōnēbat	mūniēbat	capiēbat
	docēbāmus	pōnēbāmus	mūniēbāmus	capiēbāmus
	docēbātis	pōnēbātis	mūniēbātis	capiēbātis
	docēbant	pōnēbant	mūniēbant	capiēbant
FUTURE	docēbō	pōnam	mūniam	capiam
	docēbis	pōnēs	mūniēs	capiēs
	docēbit	pōnet	mūniet	capiet
	docēbimus	pōnēmus	mūniēmus	capiēmus
	docēbitis	pōnētis	mūniētis	capiētis
	docēbunt	pōnent	mūnient	capient
PERFECT	docuī	posuī	mūnīvī	cēpī
	docuistī	posuistī	mūnīvistī	cēpistī
	docuit	posuit	mūnīvit	cēpit
	docuimus	posuimus	mūnīvimus	cēpimus
	docuistis	posuistis	mūnīvistis	cēpistis
	docuērunt	posuērunt	mūnīvērunt	cēpērunt
	(-ēre)	(-ēre)	(-ēre)	(-ēre)
PLUPERFECT	docueram	posueram	mūnīveram	cēperam
	docuerās	posuerās	mūnīverās	cēperās
	docuerat	posuerat	mūnīverat	cēperat
	docuerāmus	posuerāmus	mūnīverāmus	cēperāmus
	docuerātis	posuerātis	mūnīverātis	cēperātis
	docuerant	posuerant	mūnīverant	cēperant

	2nd Conj.	3rd Conj.	4th Conj.	3rd Conj. (*-iō*)
FUTURE	docuerō	posuerō	mūnīverō	cēperō
PERFECT	docueris	posueris	mūnīveris	cēperis
	docuerit	posuerit	mūnīverit	cēperit
	docuerimus	posuerimus	mūnīverimus	cēperimus
	docueritis	posueritis	mūnīveritis	cēperitis
	docuerint	posuerint	mūnīverint	cēperint

SUBJUNCTIVE ACTIVE

	2nd Conj.	3rd Conj.	4th Conj.	3rd Conj. (*-iō*)
PRESENT	doceam	pōnam	mūniam	capiam
	doceās	pōnās	mūniās	capiās
	doceat	pōnat	mūniat	capiat
	doceāmus	pōnāmus	mūniāmus	capiāmus
	doceātis	pōnātis	mūniātis	capiātis
	doceant	pōnant	mūniant	capiant
IMPERFECT	docērem	pōnerem	mūnīrem	caperem
	docērēs	pōnerēs	mūnīrēs	caperēs
	docēret	pōneret	mūnīret	caperet
	docērēmus	pōnerēmus	mūnīrēmus	caperēmus
	docērētis	pōnerētis	mūnīrētis	caperētis
	docērent	pōnerent	mūnīrent	caperent
PERFECT	docuerim	posuerim	mūnīverim	cēperim
	docuerīs	posuerīs	mūnīverīs	cēperīs
	docuerit	posuerit	mūnīverit	cēperit
	docuerīmus	posuerīmus	mūnīverīmus	cēperīmus
	docuerītis	posuerītis	mūnīverītis	cēperītis
	docuerint	posuerint	mūnīverint	cēperint
PLUPERFECT	docuissem	posuissem	mūnīvissem	cēpissem
	docuissēs	posuissēs	mūnīvissēs	cēpissēs
	docuisset	posuisset	mūnīvisset	cēpisset
	docuissēmus	posuissēmus	mūnīvissēmus	cēpissēmus
	docuissētis	posuissētis	mūnīvissētis	cēpissētis
	docuissent	posuissent	mūnīvissent	cēpissent

PRESENT IMPERATIVE ACTIVE

	2nd Conj.	3rd Conj.	4th Conj.	3rd Conj. (*-iō*)
2ND SING.	docē	pōne[1]	mūnī	cape[1]
2ND PLUR.	docēte	pōnite	mūnīte	capite

[1] **Dīcō, dūcō,** and **faciō** have **dīc, dūc, fac** in the imperative singular.

	2nd Conj.	*3rd Conj.*	*4th Conj.*	*3rd Conj. (-iō)*
		INFINITIVE ACTIVE		
PRESENT	docēre	pōnere	mūnīre	capere
PERFECT	docuisse	posuisse	mūnīvisse	cēpisse
FUTURE	doctūrus esse	positūrus esse	mūnītūrus esse	captūrus esse
		PARTICIPLE ACTIVE		
PRESENT	docēns	pōnēns	mūniēns	capiēns
FUTURE	doctūrus	positūrus	mūnītūrus	captūrus
		GERUND		
GEN.	docendī	pōnendī	mūniendī	capiendī
DAT.	docendō	pōnendō	mūniendō	capiendō
ACC.	docendum	pōnendum	mūniendum	capiendum
ABL.	docendō	pōnendō	mūniendō	capiendō
		INDICATIVE PASSIVE		
PRESENT	doceor	pōnor	mūnior	capior
	docēris (-re)	pōneris (-re)	mūnīris (-re)	caperis (-re)
	docētur	pōnitur	mūnītur	capitur
	docēmur	pōnimur	mūnīmur	capimur
	docēminī	pōniminī	mūnīminī	capiminī
	docentur	pōnuntur	mūniuntur	capiuntur
IMPERFECT	docēbar	pōnēbar	mūniēbar	capiēbar
	docēbāris (-re)	pōnēbāris (-re)	mūniēbāris (-re)	capiēbāris (-re)
	docēbātur	pōnēbātur	mūniēbātur	capiēbātur
	docēbāmur	pōnēbāmur	mūniēbāmur	capiēbāmur
	docēbāminī	pōnēbāminī	mūniēbāminī	capiēbāminī
	docēbantur	pōnēbantur	mūniēbantur	capiēbantur
FUTURE	docēbor	pōnar	mūniar	capiar
	docēberis (-re)	pōnēris (-re)	mūniēris (-re)	capiēris (-re)
	docēbitur	pōnētur	mūniētur	capiētur
	docēbimur	pōnēmur	mūniēmur	capiēmur
	docēbiminī	pōnēminī	mūniēminī	capiēminī
	docēbuntur	pōnentur	mūnientur	capientur
PERFECT	doctus sum	positus sum	mūnītus sum	captus sum
	doctus es	positus es	mūnītus es	captus es
	doctus est	positus est	mūnītus est	captus est

	2nd Conj.	3rd Conj.	4th Conj.	3rd Conj. (-iō)
	doctī **sumus**	positī **sumus**	mūnītī **sumus**	captī **sumus**
	doctī **estis**	positī **estis**	mūnītī **estis**	captī **estis**
	doctī **sunt**	positī **sunt**	mūnītī **sunt**	captī **sunt**
PLUPERFECT	doctus **eram**	positus **eram**	mūnītus **eram**	captus **eram**
	doctus **erās**	positus **erās**	mūnītus **erās**	captus **erās**
	doctus **erat**	positus **erat**	mūnītus **erat**	captus **erat**
	doctī **erāmus**	positī **erāmus**	mūnītī **erāmus**	captī **erāmus**
	doctī **erātis**	positī **erātis**	mūnītī **erātis**	captī **erātis**
	doctī **erant**	positī **erant**	mūnītī **erant**	captī **erant**
FUTURE	doctus **erō**	positus **erō**	mūnītus **erō**	captus **erō**
PERFECT	doctus **eris**	positus **eris**	mūnītus **eris**	captus **eris**
	doctus **erit**	positus **erit**	mūnītus **erit**	captus **erit**
	doctī **erimus**	positī **erimus**	mūnītī **erimus**	captī **erimus**
	doctī **eritis**	positī **eritis**	mūnītī **eritis**	captī **eritis**
	doctī **erunt**	positī **erunt**	mūnītī **erunt**	captī **erunt**

SUBJUNCTIVE PASSIVE

	2nd Conj.	3rd Conj.	4th Conj.	3rd Conj. (-iō)
PRESENT	doce**ar**	pōn**ar**	mūni**ar**	capi**ar**
	doce**āris (-re)**	pōn**āris (-re)**	mūni**āris (-re)**	capi**āris (-re)**
	doce**ātur**	pōn**ātur**	mūni**ātur**	capi**ātur**
	doce**āmur**	pōn**āmur**	mūni**āmur**	capi**āmur**
	doce**āminī**	pōn**āminī**	mūni**āminī**	capi**āminī**
	doce**antur**	pōn**antur**	mūni**antur**	capi**antur**
IMPERFECT	docē**rer**	pōne**rer**	mūnī**rer**	cape**rer**
	docē**rēris (-re)**	pōne**rēris (-re)**	mūnī**rēris (-re)**	cape**rēris (-re)**
	docē**rētur**	pōne**rētur**	mūnī**rētur**	cape**rētur**
	docē**rēmur**	pōne**rēmur**	mūnī**rēmur**	cape**rēmur**
	docē**rēminī**	pōne**rēminī**	mūnī**rēminī**	cape**rēminī**
	docē**rentur**	pōne**rentur**	mūnī**rentur**	cape**rentur**
PERFECT	doctus **sim**	positus **sim**	mūnītus **sim**	captus **sim**
	doctus **sīs**	positus **sīs**	mūnītus **sīs**	captus **sīs**
	doctus **sit**	positus **sit**	mūnītus **sit**	captus **sit**
	doctī **sīmus**	positī **sīmus**	mūnītī **sīmus**	captī **sīmus**
	doctī **sītis**	positī **sītis**	mūnītī **sītis**	captī **sītis**
	doctī **sint**	positī **sint**	mūnītī **sint**	captī **sint**

	2nd Conj.	3rd Conj.	4th Conj.	3rd Conj. (-iō)
PLUPERFECT	doctus essem	positus essem	mūnītus essem	captus essem
	doctus essēs	positus essēs	mūnītus essēs	captus essēs
	doctus esset	positus esset	mūnītus esset	captus esset
	doctī essēmus	positī essēmus	mūnītī essēmus	captī essēmus
	doctī essētis	positī essētis	mūnītī essētis	captī essētis
	doctī essent	positī essent	mūnītī essent	captī essent

PRESENT IMPERATIVE PASSIVE

	2nd Conj.	3rd Conj.	4th Conj.	3rd Conj. (-iō)
2ND SING.	docēre	pōnere	mūnīre	capere
2ND PLUR.	docēminī	pōniminī	mūnīminī	capiminī

INFINITIVE PASSIVE

	2nd Conj.	3rd Conj.	4th Conj.	3rd Conj. (-iō)
PRESENT	docērī	pōnī	mūnīrī	capī
PERFECT	doctus esse	positus esse	mūnītus esse	captus esse

	2nd Conj.	3rd Conj.	4th Conj.	3rd Conj. (-iō)

PARTICIPLE PASSIVE

	2nd Conj.	3rd Conj.	4th Conj.	3rd Conj. (-iō)
PERFECT	doctus	positus	mūnītus	captus
FUTURE	docendus	pōnendus	mūniendus	capiendus

Deponent Verbs[1]

	1st Conj.	2nd Conj.	3rd Conj.	4th Conj.	3rd Conj. (-iō)

PRINCIPAL PARTS

1st Conj.	2nd Conj.	3rd Conj.	4th Conj.	3rd Conj. (-iō)
arbitror	vereor	loquor	orior	gradior
arbitrārī	verērī	loquī	orīrī	gradī
arbitrātus	veritus	locūtus	ortus	gressus

INDICATIVE

	1st Conj.	2nd Conj.	3rd Conj.	4th Conj.	3rd Conj. (-iō)
PRESENT	arbitror, *I think*	vereor, *I fear*	loquor, *I talk*	orior, *I rise*	gradior, *I walk*
IMPERFECT	arbitrābar	verēbar	loquēbar	oriēbar	gradiēbar
FUTURE	arbitrābor	verēbor	loquar	oriar	gradiar
PERFECT	arbitrātus sum	veritus sum	locūtus sum	ortus sum	gressus sum
PLUPERFECT	arbitrātus eram	veritus eram	locūtus eram	ortus eram	gressus eram
FUT. PERF.	arbitrātus erō	veritus erō	locūtus erō	ortus erō	gressus erō

[1] See p. 110.

	1st Conj.	*2nd Conj.*	*3rd Conj.*	*4th Conj.*	*3rd Conj. (-iō)*
PRESENT	arbitr**er**	ver**ear**	loqu**ar**	ori**ar**	gradi**ar**
IMPERFECT	arbitrā**rer**	verē**rer**	loque**rer**	orī**rer**	grade**rer**
PERFECT	arbitrā**tus** **sim**	veri**tus** **sim**	locū**tus** **sim**	or**tus** **sim**	gress**us** **sim**
PLUPERFECT	arbitrā**tus** **essem**	veri**tus** **essem**	locū**tus** **essem**	or**tus** **essem**	gress**us** **essem**

PRESENT IMPERATIVE

2ND SING.	arbitrā**re**	verē**re**	loque**re**	orī**re**	grade**re**
2ND PLUR.	arbitrā**minī**	verē**minī**	loqui**minī**	orī**minī**	gradi**minī**

INFINITIVE

PRESENT	arbitrā**rī**	verē**rī**	loqu**ī**	orī**rī**	grad**ī**
PERFECT	arbitrā**tus** **esse**	veri**tus** **esse**	locū**tus** **esse**	or**tus** **esse**	gress**us** **esse**
FUTURE	arbitrāt**ūrus** **esse**	verit**ūrus** **esse**	locūt**ūrus** **esse**	ort**ūrus** **esse**	gress**ūrus** **esse**

PARTICIPLE

PRESENT	arbitrā**ns**	verē**ns**	loquē**ns**	ori**ēns**	gradi**ēns**
PERFECT	arbitrā**tus**	veri**tus**	locū**tus**	or**tus**	gress**us**
FUT. ACT.	arbitrāt**ūrus**	verit**ūrus**	locūt**ūrus**	ort**ūrus**	gress**ūrus**
FUT. PASS.	arbitra**ndus**	vere**ndus**	loque**ndus**	ori**endus**	gradi**endus**

GERUND

GEN.	arbitra**ndī,** etc.	vere**ndī,** etc.	loque**ndī,** etc.	ori**endī,** etc.	gradi**endī,** etc.

A few verbs (called "semideponent") are active in the present system and deponent in the perfect system, as **audeō, audēre, ausus.**

Irregular Verbs

PRINCIPAL PARTS: **sum, esse, fuī, futūrus**

	INDICATIVE		SUBJUNCTIVE		
PRESENT	su**m**, *I am*	su**mus**, *we are*	PRESENT	si**m**	sī**mus**
	e**s**, *you are*	es**tis**, *you are*		sī**s**	sī**tis**
	es**t**, *he is*	su**nt**, *they are*		si**t**	si**nt**
IMPERFECT	*I was*, etc.				
	er**am**	er**āmus**	IMPERFECT	es**sem**	es**sēmus**
	er**ās**	er**ātis**		es**sēs**	es**sētis**
	er**at**	er**ant**		es**set**	es**sent**
FUTURE	*I shall be*, etc.				
	er**ō**	er**imus**			
	er**is**	er**itis**			
	er**it**	er**unt**			
PERFECT	*I was*, etc.				
	fu**ī**	fu**imus**	PERFECT	fu**erim**	fu**erīmus**
	fu**istī**	fu**istis**		fu**erīs**	fu**erītis**
	fu**it**	fu**ērunt (-ēre)**		fu**erit**	fu**erint**
PLUPERFECT	*I had been*, etc.				
	fu**eram**	fu**erāmus**	PLUPERFECT	fu**issem**	fu**issēmus**
	fu**erās**	fu**erātis**		fu**issēs**	fu**issētis**
	fu**erat**	fu**erant**		fu**isset**	fu**issent**
FUTURE PERFECT	*I shall have been*, etc.				
	fu**erō**	fu**erimus**			
	fu**eris**	fu**eritis**			
	fu**erit**	fu**erint**			

	INFINITIVE		IMPERATIVE			
PRESENT	es**se**, *to be*		2ND SING.	e**s**, *be*	2ND PLUR.	es**te**, *be*
PERFECT	fu**isse**, *to have been*					

			PARTICIPLE	
FUTURE	fut**ūrus esse,** *to be going to be*	FUTURE	fut**ūrus,** *going to be*	

PRINCIPAL PARTS: **possum, posse, potuī, ——**

	INDICATIVE		SUBJUNCTIVE		
PRESENT	*I am able, I can* etc.				
	pos**sum**	pos**sumus**	PRESENT	pos**sim**	pos**sīmus**
	pot**es**	pot**estis**		pos**sīs**	pos**sītis**
	pot**est**	pos**sunt**		pos**sit**	pos**sint**
IMPERFECT	*I was able, I could* etc.				
	pot**eram,** etc.		IMPERFECT	pos**sem,** etc.	
FUTURE	*I shall be able,* etc.				
	pot**erō,** etc.				
PERFECT	*I was able, I could,* etc.				
	potu**ī,** etc.		PERFECT	pot**erim,** etc.	
PLUPERFECT	*I had been able,* etc.				
	potu**eram,** etc.		PLUPERFECT	potu**issem,** etc.	
FUTURE PERFECT	*I shall have been able,* etc.				
	potu**erō,** etc.				

	INFINITIVE	PARTICIPLE	
PRESENT	pos**se,** *to be able*	PRESENT	pot**ēns** *(adj.), powerful*
PERFECT	potu**isse,** *to have been able*		

PRINCIPAL PARTS: **ferō, ferre, tulī, lātus**

	ACTIVE		PASSIVE	
		INDICATIVE		
PRESENT	**ferō**	**ferimus**	**feror**	**ferimur**
	fers	**fertis**	**ferris (-re)**	**feriminī**
	fert	**ferunt**	**fertur**	**feruntur**
IMPERFECT	**ferēbam,** etc.		**ferēbar,** etc.	
FUTURE	**feram, ferēs,** etc.		**ferar, ferēris,** etc.	
PERFECT	**tulī,** etc.		**lātus sum,** etc.	
PLUPERFECT	**tuleram,** etc.		**lātus eram,** etc.	
FUTURE PERFECT	**tulerō,** etc.		**lātus erō,** etc.	

	ACTIVE	PASSIVE
SUBJUNCTIVE		
PRESENT	**feram, ferās,** etc.	**ferar, ferāris,** etc.
IMPERFECT	**ferrem,** etc.	**ferrer,** etc.
PERFECT	**tulerim,** etc.	**lātus sim,** etc.
PLUPERFECT	**tulissem,** etc.	**lātus essem,** etc.

PRESENT IMPERATIVE

2ND PERS.	**fer**	**ferte**	**ferre**	**feriminī**

INFINITIVE

PRESENT	**ferre**		**ferrī**
PERFECT	**tulisse**		**lātus esse**
FUTURE	**lātūrus esse**		

PARTICIPLE

PRESENT	**ferēns**	
PERFECT		**lātus**
FUTURE	**lātūrus**	**ferendus**

GERUND

GEN.	**ferendī**	DAT.	**ferendō**	ACC.	**ferendum**	ABL.	**ferendō**

PRINCIPAL PARTS: **eō, īre, iī, itūrus**

	INDICATIVE		SUBJUNCTIVE	INFINITIVE
PRESENT	**eō**	**īmus**	**eam,** etc.	**īre**
	īs	**ītis**		
	it	**eunt**		
IMPERFECT	**ībam,** etc.		**īrem,** etc.	
FUTURE	**ībō**	**ībimus**		**itūrus esse**
	ībis	**ībitis**		
	ībit	**ībunt**		
PERFECT	**iī (-īrī)**	**iimus**	**ierim,** etc.	**īsse**
	īstī	**īstis**		
	iit	**iērunt (-ēre)**		
PLUPERFECT	**ieram,** etc.		**īssem,** etc.	
FUTURE PERFECT	**ierō,** etc.			

	PARTICIPLE	IMPERATIVE		GERUND	
PRESENT	**iēns,** GEN. **euntis**	**ī**	**īte**	GEN.	**eundī**
				DAT.	**eundō**
FUTURE	**itūrus** (PASSIVE **eundus**)			ACC.	**eundum**
				ABL.	**eundum**

PRINCIPAL PARTS

volō	**nōlō**	**mālō**
velle	**nōlle**	**mālle**
voluī	**nōluī**	**māluī**

INDICATIVE

PRESENT	volō	volumus	nōlō	nōlumus	mālō	mālumus
	vīs	vultis	nōn vīs	nōn vultis	māvīs	māvultis
	vult	volunt	nōn vult	nōlunt	māvult	mālunt
IMPERFECT	volēbam, etc.		nōlēbam, etc.		mālēbam, etc.	
FUTURE	volam, volēs, etc.		nōlam, nōlēs, etc.		mālam, mālēs, etc.	
PERFECT	voluī, etc.		nōluī, etc.		māluī, etc.	
PLUPERFECT	volueram, etc.		nōlueram, etc.		mālueram, etc.	
FUT. PERF.	voluerō, etc.		nōluerō, etc.		māluerō, etc.	

SUBJUNCTIVE

PRESENT	velim	velīmus	nōlim	nōlīmus	mālim	mālīmus
	velīs	velītis	nōlīs	nōlītis	mālīs	mālītis
	velit	velint	nōlit	nōlint	mālit	mālint
IMPERFECT	vellem, etc.		nōllem, etc.		māllem, etc.	
PERFECT	voluerim, etc.		nōluerim, etc.		māluerim, etc.	
PLUPERFECT	voluissem, etc.		nōluissem, etc.		māluissem, etc.	

PRESENT IMPERATIVE

2ND PERS.	——	——	nōlī	nōlīte	——	——

INFINITIVE

PRESENT	velle		nōlle		mālle	
PERFECT	voluisse		nōluisse		māluisse	

PARTICIPLE

PRESENT	volēns		nōlēns		——	——

PRINCIPAL PARTS: fīō, fierī, (factus)

	INDICATIVE		SUBJUNCTIVE	IMPERATIVE	INFINITIVE
PRESENT	fīō	——	fīam, etc.		fierī
	——	——		fī fīte	
	fit	fīunt			
IMPERFECT	fīēbam, etc.		fierem, etc.		
FUTURE	fīam, fīēs, etc.				

Defective Verbs

Coepī is used only in the perfect system. For the present system **incipiō** is used. With a passive infinitive the passive of **coepī** is used: **Lapidēs iacī coeptī sunt,** *Stones began to be thrown.* **Meminī** and **ōdī** likewise are used only in the perfect system, but with present meaning. The former has an imperative **mementō, mementōte.**

Contracted Forms

Verbs having perfect stems ending in **-āv-** or **-ēv-** are sometimes contracted by dropping **-ve-** before **-r-** and **-vi-** before **-s-: amārunt, cōnsuēsse.** Verbs having perfect stems ending in -īv- drop **-vi-** before -s- but only **-v-** before **-r-: audīsset, audierat.**

DICTIONARY

Latin–English

Verbs of the first conjugation whose parts are regular (i.e., like **portō**) are indicated by the figure 1 in parentheses. Words from Level 1 are indicated by the lesson number (in Level 1) in lightface type. Words from Level 2 are indicated by the lesson number in boldface type. Proper names are not included unless they are spelled differently in English or are difficult to pronounce in English. Their English pronunciation is indicated by a simple system. The vowels are as follows: **ā** as in *hate,* **ă** as in *hat,* **ē** as in *feed,* **ĕ** as in *fed,* **ī** as in *bite,* **ĭ** as in *bit,* **ō** as in *hope,* **ŏ** as in hop, **ū** as in *cute,* **ŭ** as in *cut.* In the ending **ēs** the *s* is soft as in *rose.* When the accented syllable ends in a consonant, the vowel is short; otherwise it is long.

A

A., *abbreviation for* **Aulus, -ī,** m., Aulus

ā, ab, abs, *(prep. w. abl.)* away from, from, by 13

abdō, -ere, abdidī, abditus, put away, hide **30**

abdūcō, -ere, abdūxī, abductus, lead or take away

abeō, abīre, abiī, abitūrus, go away, depart; change (into)

abiciō, -ere, abiēcī, abiectus, throw away

abrogō, (1) repeal

abscīdō, -ere, -cīdī, -cīsus, cut away

absēns, *(gen.)* **absentis,** absent

absentia, -ae, *f.,* absence

abstineō, -ēre, -tinuī, -tentus, hold away; refrain

abstulī, *(see* **auferō)**

absum, -esse, āfuī, āfutūrus, be away, be absent 30

abundō, (1) be well supplied

ac, *(see* **atque)**

Acadēmīa, -ae, *f.* a grove near Athens

accēdō, -ere, accessī, accessūrus, approach *(impers.)* 19, **6**

accidō, -ere, accidī, —, *(w. dat.)* fall to, befall, happen 63, **8**

accīdō, -ere, accīdī, accīsus, cut into

accipiō, -ere, accēpī, acceptus, receive 20

accommodō, (1) fit (on)

accumbō, -ere, accubuī, accubitūrus, recline (at the table)

accūrātē, *(adv.)* carefully

accurrō, -ere, accurrī, accursūrus, run

accūsō, (1) blame, criticize 21

ācer, ācris, ācre, sharp, keen, fierce 60, **2;**

ācriter, *(adv.)* fiercely; *(comp.)* **ācrius,** fiercer; *(superl.)* **ācerrimē,** fiercest

acerbitās, -tātis, *f.,* bitterness; suffering

acerbus, -a, -um, sour, bitter; **acerbē,** *(adv.)* severely

Achaia, -ae, *f.,* Achaia (Akāya), Greece

aciēs, aciēī, *f.,* battle line **56**

Actium, -tī, *n.,* Actium (Akshĭum), *a promontory in Epirus*

acūtus, -a, -um, sharp 16

ad, *(prep. w. acc.)* to, toward, for, near; *(adv., w. numbers)* about 6

adāctus, *perf. part. of* **adigō**

adaequō, (1) equal

addō, -ere, addidī, additus, add

addūcō, -ere, addūxī, adductus, lead (to), influence 43, **9**

adeō, adīre, adiī, aditūrus, go to, approach **66**

adeō, *(adv.)* so, so much **39**

adfore, *fut. inf. of* **adsum**

adhaereō, -ēre, adhaesī, adhaesus, stick (to), cling (to) **12**

adhibeō, -ēre, adhibuī, adhibitus, hold toward; admit to, use **89**

adhūc, *(adv.)* up to this time, still **28**

adiciō, -ere, adiēcī, adiectus, add

adigō, -ere, adēgī, adāctus, bring (to), bring near, throw (to) **70**

aditus, -ūs, *m.,* approach, access **69**

adiungō, -ere, adiūnxī, adiūnctus, join to **28**

adiuvō, -āre, -ūvī, -ūtus, help

administrō, (1) manage, perform **70**

admīrātiō, -ōnis, *f.,* admiration

admīror, (1) wonder (at), admire

admittō, -ere, admīsī, admissus, send to, let in, commit, admit **38**

admodum, *(adv.)* very (much) **97**

admoneō, -ēre, admonuī, admonitus, remind, advise

admoveō, -ēre, admōvī, admōtus, move (to)

adoptiō, -ōnis, *f.,* adoption

adoptō, (1) adopt

adorior, adorīrī, adortus, rise up to, attack **67**

adornō, (1) to get ready, prepare; to make arrangements for; **adōrnātus, -a, -um,** decorated

adōrō, (1) worship

adsum, -esse, adfuī, adfutūrus, be near, be present **34, 6**

adulēscēns, -entis, *m.,* young man **21**

adulēscentia, -ae, *f.,* youth

adulēscentulus, -ī, *m.,* young man

adveniō, -īre, advēnī, adventūrus, approach

adventus, -ūs, *m.,* arrival, approach **32**

adversārius, -rī, *m.,* opponent

adversus, -a, -um, facing, opposite, unfavorable **71**

aedificium, -cī, *n.,* building **12**

aedificō, (1) build

aedīlis, -is, aedilium, *m.,* aedile *(an official)*

aeger, aegra, aegrum, sick, ill **15; aegrē,** *(adv.)* with difficulty, reluctantly **44;** *(w.* **ferre***)* be indignant (at)

Aegyptiī, -ōrum, *m. pl.* the Egyptians

Aegyptus, -ī, *f.,* Egypt

Aenēās, -ae, *m.,* Aeneas (Enē´as)

aēneus, -a, -um, (of) bronze, copper

Aeolus, -ī, *m.,* Aeolus (E´olus)

aequālis, -e, equal **26**

Aequī, -ōrum, *m.,* the Aequians (Ēquians), *a people of Italy*

aequitās, -tātis, *f.,* fairness

aequō, (1) make equal **57**

aequus, -a, -um, even, just, calm, equal **18**

āēr, āeris, *m.,* air

aes, aeris, *n.,* copper, bronze, money, bronze statue **31; aes aliēnum,** *(another's money),* debt

Aesculāpius, -pī, *m.,* Aesculapius (Esculāpius), god of healing

Aesōpus, -ī, *m.,* Aesop (Ēsop), writer of fables

aestās, -ātis, *f.,* summer **51**

aestimātiō, -ōnis, *f.,* estimate

aestimō, (1) estimate

aestus, -ūs, *m.,* heat; tide **81**

aetās, -ātis, *f.,* age, time **61**

aeternitās, -tātis, *f.,* immortality

aeternus, -a, -um, eternal

Aethiopēs, -um, *m. pl.,* the Ethiopians, *a people of Africa*

Aetna, -ae, *f.,* (Mt.) Etna

affātus, -ūs, *m.,* speech

afferō, afferre, attulī, allātus, bring (to), assign, report

afficiō, -ere, affēcī, affectus, affect, afflict with, move **23, 3**

affīgō, -ere, affīxī, affīxus, fasten to

afflīctō, wreck

afflīgō, -ere, afflīxī, afflīctus, throw down, afflict, damage

Āfrī, -ōrum, *m. pl,* the Africans, Carthaginians; **Āfricānus, -a, -um,** African; *(as noun) m.,* an African; **Āfricānus,** *an honorary name of Scipio*

ager, agrī, *m.,* field **14;** farm, territory

agger, aggeris, *m.,* mound, rampart

aggredior, aggredī, aggressus, attack **37**

aggregō, (1) attach

agitō, (1) carry on; shake

agmen, -minis, *n.,* line of march, column **57; novissimum agmen,** rear; **prīmum agmen,** front

agnōscō, -ere, agnōvī, agnitus, recognize

Agora, -ās, *f.* (Greek) agora (ăgŏrah´), assembly place

agnus, -ī, *m.,* lamb

agō, -ere, ēgī, āctus, do, drive, discuss, live, spend time **19, 3; grātiās agō,** thank; **vītam agō,** lead a life

agricola, -ae, *m.,* farmer **3**

ait, (he) says

āla, -ae, *f.,* wing **17;** squadron

alacer, -cris, -cre, eager **21**

alacritās, -tātis, *f.,* eagerness

Albānus, -a, -um, Alban; *m.,* an Alban

albus, -a, -um, white

alces, -is, *f.,* elk

Alesia, -ae, *f.,* Alēsia, *now* Alise-Sainte-Reine

Alexander, -drī, *m.,* Alexander

Alexandrīa, -ae, *f.,* Alexandria, *a city in Egypt*

aliēnus, -a, -um, another's, unfavorable 57

aliquandō, *(adv.)* sometimes

aliquī, aliqua, aliquod, *(adj.)* some(one), any **20**

aliquis, aliquid, someone, some, any, something, anyone, anything **20**

aliter, *(adv.)* otherwise

alius, alia, aliud, other, another; **alius... alius,** one . . . another; **aliī... aliī,** some . . . others 56; **quid aliud,** what else

allātus, *perf. part. of* **afferō**

Allobrogēs, -um, *m. pl.,* the Allobroges (Allŏb´rojēs), *a people of SW Gaul*

alloquor, alloquī, allocūtus, address

alō, -ere, aluī, alitus, support, feed, nourish, raise 31

Alpēs, -ium, *f. pl.,* the Alps

alter, altera, alterum, the other; **alter... alter,** the one . . . the other 56

altitūdō, -dinis, *f.,* height, depth **53**

altus, -a, -um, high, deep, tall 12; **altē,** *(adv.)* high, deeply

amābilis, -e, lovely, lovable

amanter, *(adv.)* lovingly

ambō, -ae, -ō, both

ambulō, (1) walk

Americānus, -a, -um, American; **Americānus, -ī,** *m.,* an American

amīcitia, -ae, *f.,* friendship 11

amīcus, -a, -um, friendly 14, **4; amīcus, -ī,** *m.,* **amīca, ae,** *f.,* friend 7

āmittō, -ere, āmīsī, āmissus, let go, lose 29, **5**

amō, (1) love, like 3

amor, -ōris, *m.,* love

amphitheātrum, -ī, *n.,* amphitheater

amplificō, (1) increase

amplitūdō, -dinis, *f.,* size

amplus, -a, -um, great; distinguished, magnificent 12; **amplē,** *(adv.)* fully; *(comp.)* **amplius,** more 37

an, *(conj.)* or *(introducing the second part of a double question)* **25**

ancīle, -is, *n.,* shield

ancora, -ae, *f.,* anchor

Anglicus, -a, -um, English

anguis, -is, *m. and f.,* snake, serpent

angulus, -ī, *m.,* corner, little place

angustiae, -ārum, *f. pl.,* narrowness, narrow pass

angustus, -a, -um, narrow, small **12**

anima, -ae, *f.,* breath, spirit, soul

animadvertō, -ere, -vertī, -versus, turn attention, notice **57**

animal, -ālis, *n.,* animal **8**

animus, -ī, *m.,* mind, courage, spirit 15; **in animō est,** intend; **in animō habeō,** plan

Aniō, Aniēnis, *m.,* the Anio river

annus, -ī, *m.,* year 16, **5**

ante, *(adv.)* before *(prep. w. acc.)* before *(of time or place)* 39; *see* **antequam**

anteā, *(adv.)* before **37**

antecēdō, -ere, -cessī, -cessūrus, go before, go earlier 41; surpass

anteferō, -ferre, -tulī, -lātus, prefer

antemna, ae, *f.,* yardarm *(of a ship; the spar to which sails are fastened)*

antequam (ante... quam), *(conj.)* before

anterior, -ius, *(comp. adj.)* earlier

antīquitās, -tātis, *f.,* antiquity

antīquitus, *(adv.)* long ago

antīquus, -a, -um, old, ancient

Antōnius, -nī, *m.,* Antony

antrum, -ī, *n.,* cave

ānxius, -a, -um, troubled

aperio, -īre, -uī, -tus, open, reveal **30; apertus, -a, -um,** open, exposed; **apertē,** *(adv.)* openly, manifestly

Apollō, -inis, *m.,* Apŏllo, *god of music, prophecy, and medicine*

appāreō, -ēre, appāruī, appāritūrus, appear

appellō (1) call, name 28, **1**

appellō, -ere, appulī, appulsus, land, drive to, bring up

appetō, -ere, appetīvī, appetītus, seek; approach

Appius, -a, -um, *(adj.)* of Appius, Appian; **Appius, -pī,** *m.,* Appius

applaudō, -ere, applausī, applausus, (1) applaud

applicō, (1) apply (to); lean against

appōnō, -ere, apposuī, appositus, set before, serve

appropinquō, (1) come near to **43;** approach *(w. dat.)*

aptus, -a, -um, fit, suitable *(w. dat.)* 62; **aptē,** *(adv.)* suitably

apud, *(prep. w. acc.)* among, in the presence of 70

aqua, -ae, *f.,* water 1

aquaeductus, -ūs, *m.,* aqueduct

aquila, -ae, *f.,* eagle **81; aquilifer, -erī,** *m.,* standard bearer

Aquilēia, -ae, *f.,* Aquilēia, *a town of Cisalpine Gaul*

Aquītānia, -ae, *f.,* Aquitānia; **Aquītānus, -ī,** *m.,* an Aquitā´nian

āra, -ae, *f.,* altar

Arar, -aris, *(acc.)* **-im,** *(abl.)* **-ī,** *m.,* Arar river, *now the Saône*

arbitrium, -trī, *n.,* decision, judgment

arbitror, (1) think **18**

arbor, -is, *f.,* tree **20**

arboreus, -a, -um, of a tree

Arcadia, -ae, *f.,* Arcadia, *a region in S. Greece*

arcessō, -ere, -īvī, -ītus, summon, send for **60**

architectus, -ī, *m.,* architect

arcus, -ūs, *m.,* arch, bow

ārdeō, -ēre, ārsī, ārsūrus, burn, be eager

arduus, -a, -um, steep, hard

ārea, -ae, *f.,* courtyard

arēna, -ae, *f.,* arena, sand, desert, seashore

argentum, -ī, *n.,* silver

āridus, -a, -um, dry; **āridum, -ī,** *n.,* dry land

ariēs, -ietis, *m.,* ram, battering-ram

Aristotelēs, -is, *m.,* Aristŏtle, *a Greek philosopher*

arma, -ōrum, *n. pl.,* arms, weapons **17, 9**

armāmenta, -ōrum, *n. pl.,* equipment

armātūra, -ae, *f.,* armor; *(gen of descr.)* **levis armātūrae,** light-armed

armō, (1) arm, equip

arō, (1) plow

arripiō, -ere, arripuī, arreptus, seize

arrogantia, -ae, *f.,* insolence

ars, artis, artium, *f.,* skill, art

artus, -ūs, *m.,* limb

Arvernus, -ī, *m.,* an Arvernian

arx, arcis, arcium, *f.,* citadel **32**

ascendō, -ere, ascendī, ascēnsus, climb (up), ascend **70**

ascēnsus, -ūs, *m.,* ascent

ascrībō, -ere, ascrīpsī, ascrīptus, add to (in writing), apply

aspectus, -ūs, *m.,* appearance, sight

asper, -era, -erum, harsh

aspiciō, -ere, aspexī, aspectus, look on *or* at **45**

assistō, -ere, astitī, —, stand

assuēscō, -ere, assuēvī, assuētus, become accustomed

astronomus, -ī, *m.,* astronomer

astrum, -ī, *n.,* star

at, *(conj.)* but **23**

āter, ātra, ātrum, black, gloomy

Athēna, -ae, *f.,* *a Greek goddess* = Minerva

Athēnae, -ārum, *f. pl.,* Athens

Athēniēnsis, -is, *(adj. and n.)* Athenian

atomus, -ī, *f.,* atom

atque (ac), *(conj.)* and, and even **38**

Atrebās, -ātis, *m.,* an Atrebatian *(Atrebāshian)*

ātrium, ātrī, *n.,* atrium, entry hall **10**

attingō, -ere, attigī, attāctus, touch, reach, border **23**

attribuō, -ere, attribuī, attribūtus, assign

auctor, -ōris, *m.,* maker, author, writer **48, 4**

auctōritās, -ātis, *f.,* authority, influence **49, 5**

audācia, -ae, *f.,* boldness

audāx, audācis, *(gen.)* bold, daring **37; audācter,** *(adv.)* boldly **67**

audeō, -ēre, ausus, *(semideponent)* dare **61**

audiō, -īre, -īvī, -ītus, hear **24, 5**

auferō, auferre, abstulī, ablātus, take away

augeō, -ēre, auxī, auctus, increase **10**

augēscō, -ere, —, —, increase

augustus, -a, -um, magnificent; *(cap.),* of Augustus; August; *m.,* Augustus, *the emperor*

Aulercus, -ī, *m.,* an Aulercan

aureus, -a, -um, golden

aurīga, -ae, *m.,* charioteer

auris, -is, aurium, *f.,* ear

aurum, -ī, *n.,* gold

auspicium, -cī, *n.,* auspices

aut, or; **aut... aut,** either . . . or **28**

autem, *(conj.)* however, moreover, now *(never first word)* **67, 4**

autumnus, -ī, *m.,* autumn, fall

auxilior, (1) help

auxilium, -lī, *n.,* aid, help **17, 6;** *pl.,* reinforcements

avāritia, -ae, *f.,* greed

avārus, -a, -um, avaricious, greedy

Aventīnus (mōns), -ī, *m.,* *the* Aventīne Hill

āvertō, -ere, āvertī, āversus, turn away **65**

avidus, -a, -um, desirous, greedy

avis, avis, avium *f.,* bird **8**

āvocō, (1) call away

avunculus, ī, *m.,* uncle

avus, -ī, *m.,* grandfather

Axona, -ae, *m.,* Axona *river, now the* Aisne

B

balneum, -ī, *n.,* bath **10**

balteus, -ī, *m.,* belt

barbarus, -a, -um, *(adj.),* foreign; **barbarus, -ī,** *(noun) m.,* foreigner, barbarian **16**

beātus, -a, -um, happy

Belgae, -ārum, *m. pl.,* the Belgians; the Belgian people; **Belgium, -iī,** *n.,* Belgium

bellicōsus, -a, -um, warlike

bellicus, -a, -um, of war

bellō, (1) carry on war

bellum, -ī, *n.,* war **17; bellum gerō,** carry on war; *(with dat.)* **bellum īnferō,** make war upon

bene, *(adv.)* well **64;** *(comp.)* **melius,** better; *(superl.)* **optimē,** best, very well

beneficium, -cī, *n.,* kindness, benefit **33**

benignus, -a, -um, kind

bibliothēca, -ae, *f.,* library

bibō, -ere, bibī, —, drink

Bibracte, -actis, *n.,* Bibrăcte, *now* Mont Beauvray *near Autun*

bīduum, -ī, *n.,* two days

biennium, -nī, *n.,* two years

bīnī, -ae, -a, two at a time **77**

bis, *(adv.)* twice **39**

blanditia, -ae, *f.,* caress

blandus, -a, -um, caressing

bonitās, -tātis, *f.,* goodness, fertility

bonus, -a, -um, good **2;** *(comp.)* **melior, melius,** better; *(superl.)* **optimus, -a, -um,** best; **bona, -ōrum,** *n.,* possessions

bōs, bovis, *(gen. pl.)* **boum,** *m.,* ox, bull

bracchium, bracchī, *n.,* arm

brevis, -e, short, brief, small **40**

brevitās, -tātis, *f.,* shortness

Britannia, -ae, *f.,* Britain; **Britannus, -ī,** *m.,* a Briton

Brundisium, -sī, *n.,* Brundisium (Brundizhium), a *town in Italy, now* Brindisi

bulla, -ae, *f.,* bulla, *an ornament worn on the neck by children*

C

C., *abbreviation for* **Gāius**

cacūmen, -minis, *n.,* peak

cadāver, -eris, *n.,* corpse

cadō, -ere, cecidī, cāsūrus, fall **63, 7**

Caecilius, -lī, *m.,* Caecilius (Sēsil´ius); **Caecilia, -ae,** *f.,* Caecilia; **Caecilius, -a, -um,** Caecilian (Sēsil´ian);

caecus, -a, -um, blind

caedēs, -is, *f.,* slaughter, murder **32**

caedō, -ere, cecīdī, caesus, cut (down), beat, kill **21**

caelestis, -e, heavenly

Caelius (mōns), -ī, *m.,* the Caelian (Sēlian) Hill

caelum, -ī, *n.,* sky

caeruleus, -a, -um, blue

Caesar, -aris, *m.,* Caesar

calamitās, -tātis, *f.,* disaster, defeat **55**

calceus, -ī, *m.,* shoe

calidus, -a, -um, hot

callidus, -a, -um, clever

cālō, -ōnis, *m.,* camp servant

campus, -ī, *m.,* plain, field **22; campus Mārtius, campī Mārtiī,** *m.,* Campus Martius (Mar´shius), *the drill field and voting area in Rome*

candidātus, -ī, *m.,* candidate

canis, -is, *m. or f.,* dog

Cannae, -ārum, *f. pl.,* Cannae (Canē), *a town in Italy*

canō, -ere, cecinī, cantus, sing (about), tell **10**

Cantium, -tī, *n.,* Kent, *a district in Britain*

cantō, (1) sing

Capēna (porta), porta Capena (Capē´na), *a gate in the wall of Rome*

caper, -rī, *m.,* goat

capillus, -ī, *m.,* hair

capiō, -ere, cēpī, captus, take, seize **20, 8; cōnsilium capiō,** adopt a plan

Capitōlium, -lī, *n.,* the Capitol, *temple of Jupiter at Rome;* the Capitoline Hill

captīvus, -ī, *m.;* **captīva, -ae,** *f.,* prisoner **13**

captō, (1) strive

caput, capitis, *n.,* head **45**

careō, -ere, caruī, caritūrus, be without *(w. abl.)*

cāritās, -tātis, *f.,* affection

carmen, -minis, *n.,* song **45**

Carneadēs, -is, *m.,* Carnēadēs, *a Greek philosopher*

carō, carnis, *f.,* meat

carpō, -ere, carpsī, carptus, pick; take; consume

carrus, -ī, *m.,* cart, wagon **4**

Carthāginiēnsēs, -ium, *m. pl.,* the Carthaginians (Carthajin´ians)

Carthāgō, -ginis, *f.,* Carthage, *a city in Africa;* **Carthāgō Nova,** New Carthage *(in Spain)*

cārus, -a, -um, dear, expensive, esteemed **18**

casa, -ae, *f.,* house 12

cāseus, -ī, *m.,* cheese

Castalius, -a, -um, Castālian

castellum, -ī, *n.,* fort **53**

castīgō, (1) punish

castra, -ōrum, *n. pl.,* camp 16

cāsus, -ūs, *m.,* downfall, accident, chance, misfortune 68

Catilīna, -ae, *m.,* Cătilīne

cauda, -ae, *f.,* tail

causa, -ae, *f.,* cause, reason, case 18; **causā,** for the sake of *(w. gen. preceding)*

caveō, -ēre, cāvī, cautūrus, beware (of), take precautions against

cecīdī, *(see* **caedō***)*

cēdō, -ere, cessī, cessūrus, move (away from), retreat, yield, give way 19

celeber, -bris, -bre, celebrated

celebrō, (1) celebrate, honor

celer, celeris, celere, swift, quick 47, **7; celeriter** *(adv.),* swiftly, quickly

celeritās, -tātis, *f.,* swiftness, speed 49

cēlō, (1) hide, conceal

celsus, -a, -um, high

Celtae, -ārum, *m. pl.,* Celts, *a people of Gaul*

cēna, -ae, *f.,* dinner 13

cēnō, (1) dine

cēnseō, -ēre, cēnsuī, cēnsus, think, appraise, give an opinion 44

cēnsus, -ūs, *m.,* census

centum, *(indeclinable)* hundred 66

centuriō, -ōnis, *m.,* centurion **72**

cēra, -ae, *f.,* wax

Cerēs, -eris, *f.,* Ceres (Sē´rēs), *goddess of agriculture*

cernō, -ere, crēvī, crētus, discern, see 42

certāmen, -minis, *n.,* contest, struggle

certō, (1) strive

certus, -a, -um, fixed, sure, certain 42; **certiōrem eum faciō dē,** inform him about; **certior fīō,** be informed; **certē,** *(adv.)* certainly, at least

cervus, -ī, *m.,* deer, stag

cēterī, -ae, -a, the other(s), the rest **16**

Christus, -ī, *m.,* Christ

cibus, -ī, *m.,* food 5

Cicerō, -ōnis, *m.,* Cicero (Sis´ero)

cingō, -ere, cīnxī, cīnctus, surround

cinis, cineris, *m.,* ashes

Circē, -ae, *f.,* Circe (Sir´se), *a sorceress*

circēnsis, -e, of the circus

circiter, *(adv.)* about **22**

circuitus, -ūs, *m.,* distance around

circulus, -ī, *m.,* circle

circum, *(prep. w. acc.)* around **67**

circumclūdō, -ere, -clūsī, -clūsus, surround

circumcursō, (1) run around

circumdō, -dare, -dedī, -datus, put around, surround **30**

circumiciō, -ere, -iēcī, -iectus, throw around

circumsiliō, -īre, -siluī, —, hop around

circumsistō, -ere, -stetī, —, surround **77**

circumstō, -āre, -stetī, —, stand around

circumveniō, -īre, -vēnī, -ventus, surround **26;** cheat

circus, -ī, *m.,* circle, circus *(esp. the Circus Maximus at Rome)*

citerior, -ius, nearer

cito, *(adv.)* quickly; *(comp.)* **citius,** sooner

citrā, *(prep. w. acc.)* on this side of

cīvīlis, -e, civil

cīvis, cīvis, cīvium, *m. or f.,* citizen 46, **9**

cīvitās, -ātis, *f.,* citizenship, state 48, **3**

clam, *(adv.)* secretly **44**

clāmō, (1) shout, cry out, exclaim 40, **4**

clāmor, -ōris, *m.,* noise, shouting 45

clārus, -a, -um, clear, famous 5, **5**

classis, -is, *f.,* fleet **80**

claudō, -ere, clausī, clausus, close 45, **6**

clēmentia, -ae, *f.,* clemency, mercy

cliēns, -entis, clientium, *m.,* client **15**

clientēla, -ae, *f.,* clientship

cloāca, -ae, *f.,* sewer

Cn., *abbreviation for* **Gnaeus, -ī,** *m.,* Gnaeus (Nē´us)

Cnidiī, -ōrum, *m. pl.,* the Cnidians (Nĭ´dians)

coacervō, (1) pile up

coctus, -a, -um, cooked

coemētērium, -rī, *n.,* cemetery

coeō, coīre, coiī, coitūrus, meet

coepī, coeptus *(perf. tenses only),* began, have begun **34**

cōgitātiō, -ōnis, *f.,* thought

cōgitō, (1) think, consider **61**

cognātiō, -ōnis, *f.,* related group

cognōmen, -minis, *n.,* surname, nickname

cognōscō, -ere, -nōvī, -nitus, learn; have learned, *(perf.)* know **39, 5**

cōgō, -ere, coēgī, coāctus, drive together, collect, compel **38, 3**

cohors, cohortis, *f.,* cohort, one tenth of a legion

cohortātiō, -ōnis, *f.,* encouragement

cohortor, (1) encourage

Colchī, -ōrum, *m. pl.,* the Colchians (Kolkians)

colligō, (1) fasten together

colligō, -ere, -lēgī, -lēctus, collect, acquire **13**

collis, -is, *m.,* hill **33**

collocō, (1) place, invest, station **57**

colloquium, -quī, *n.,* conference **61**

colloquor, colloquī, collocūtus, talk with, confer **83**

collum, -ī, *n.,* neck

colō, -ere, coluī, cultus, till, cultivate, worship, inhabit **54**

colōnia, -ae, *f.,* colony

colōnus, -ī, *m.,* settler, colonist **15**

color, -ōris, *m.,* color

Colossēum, -ī, *n.,* the Colossē´um (also Colisē´um), *an amphitheater in Rome*

columna, -ae, *f.,* column

combūrō, -ere, -ussī, -ustus, burn up

comes, -itis, *m. and f.,* companion **29**

Comitium, -tī, *n.,* Comitium (Comishium), *the assembly place of the Romans;* **comitia, -ōrum,** *n. pl.,* assemblies, election

commeātus, -ūs, *m.,* (going to and fro), supplies

commemorō, (1) mention **79**

commendō, (1) entrust

commentārius, -rī, *m.,* commentary, notes

commīlitō, -ōnis, *m.,* fellow soldier

committō, -ere, -mīsī, -missus, join together, commit, entrust **27; proelium committō,** begin battle **27**

commodus, -a, -um, suitable, convenient **22; commodē,** *(adv.)* well, suitably, effectively

commoveō, -ēre, -mōvī, -mōtus, disturb, alarm **42**

commūnicō, (1) share **89**

commūniō, -īre, -īvī, -ītus, fortify on all sides

commūnis, -e, common **52**

commūtātiō, -ōnis, *f.,* change

commūtō, change wholly, exchange

comparō, (1) prepare, get ready; procure **42**

compellō, -ere, -pulī, -pulsus, drive (together), collect

comperiō, -īre, -perī, -pertus, find out **56**

competītor, -ōris, *m.,* competitor

complaceō = placeō

compleō, -ēre, -ēvī, -ētus, fill, complete **20**

complexus, -ūs, *m.,* embrace

complūrēs, -a *or* **-ia,** several, many **35**

compōnō, -ere, -posuī, -positus, put together, compose

comportō, (1) collect

comprehendō, -ere, -hendī, -hēnsus, understand; grab

cōnātus, -ūs, *m.,* attempt

concēdō, -ere, -cessī, -cessūrus, yield, withdraw, grant, permit **21**

concidō, -ere, -cidī, —, fall down, collapse

concīdō, -ere, -cīdī, -cīsus, cut up, kill

concilium, -lī, *n.,* meeting, council **60**

concipiō, -ere, -cēpī, -ceptus, conceive

concitō, (1) rouse

concordia, -ae, *f.,* harmony **17**

concurrō, -ere, -currī, -cursūrus, run *or* dash together, rush, flock

concursus, -ūs, *m.,* running together, gathering, onset

condēnsātus, -a, -um, condensed

condiciō, -ōnis, *f.,* condition, terms **61, 2**

condīmentum, -ī, *n.,* seasoning

condō, -ere, -didī, -ditus, found, establish, make; conceal

condūcō, -ere, -dūxī, -ductus, bring together; hire, rent

cōnferō, cōnferre, contulī, collātus, bring together, collect, compare **57;** give, place; **mē cōnferō,** proceed

cōnfertus, -a, -um, crowded together, dense **57**

cōnfestim, *(adv.)* immediately, at once

cōnficiō, -ere, -fēcī, -fectus, complete, exhaust, do thoroughly, do in, accomplish **46, 4**

cōnfīdō, -ere, cōnfīsus sum, *(semi-deponent)* have confidence in, be confident **57**

cōnfirmō, (1) make firm, encourage, establish **49, 9**

cōnfīsus, *perf. part. of* **cōnfīdō**

cōnflīgō, -ere, -flīxī, -flīctus, dash together **43**

cōnfoveō = foveō

cōnfundō, -ere, -fūdī, -fūsus, confuse

congredior, congredī, congressus, meet (in battle) 62

coniciō, -ere, -iēcī, -iectus, throw, conjecture 48

coniūnctim, (adv.) jointly

coniungō, -ere, -iūnxī, -iūnctus, join (with), unite

coniūnx, -iugis, m. and f., husband, wife

coniūrātiō, -ōnis, f., conspiracy

coniūrō, (1) swear together, conspire 31

cōnor, (1) try, attempt 43

conquīrō, -ere, -quīsīvī, -quīsītus, seek for 58

cōnsanguineus, -ī, m., (blood) relative

cōnscendō, -ere, -scendī, -scēnsus, climb (in); embark (in)

cōnscius, -a, -um, conscious

cōnscrībō, -ere, -scrīpsī, -scrīptus, write, enroll, levy 54; patrēs cōnscrīptī, senators

cōnsecrātus, -a, -um, sacred

cōnsecūtus, perf. part. of cōnsequor

cōnsēnsiō, -ōnis, f., agreement

cōnsentiō, -īre, -sēnsī, -sēnsus, agree, conspire 16; cōnsēnsus, -ūs, m., agreement

cōnsequor, cōnsequī, cōnsecūtus, follow, reach, attain

cōnservō, (1) save, preserve 37

cōnsīdō, -ere, -sēdī, -sessūrus, sit down, encamp, settle 36

cōnsilium, -lī, n., plan, advice 16, 6

cōnsimilis, -e, very similar

cōnsistō, -ere, cōnstitī, cōnstitūrus, stand still, stop 58

cōnsōlātiō, -ōnis, f., consolation

cōnspiciō, -ere, -spexī, -spectus, catch sight of, see, spot 65; cōnspectus, -ūs, m., sight 28

cōnspicor, (1) catch sight of, see

cōnstantia, -ae, f., steadfastness

cōnstat, it is evident 83

cōnstitī, (see cōnsistō)

cōnstituō, -ere, -stituī, -stitūtus, determine, decide, establish 10

cōnsto, -āre, -stitī, -stātūrus, stand together; cōnstat, it is evident, it is clear, it is certain

cōnsuēscō, -ere, -suēvī, -suētus, become accustomed 41; (in perf.) be accustomed 41

cōnsuētūdō, -dinis, f., custom, habit 27

cōnsul, -ulis, m., consul, the highest Roman elected official

cōnsulāris, -e, of consular rank

cōnsulātus, -ūs, m., consulship

cōnsulō, -ere, -suluī, -sultus, consult 43, 8

cōnsultō, (1) consult

cōnsūmō, -ere, -sūmpsī, -sūmptus, use up, spend 18

contāgiō, -ōnis, f., contact

contemnō, -ere, -tempsī, -temptus, despise 16

contemplor, (1) look at

contemptus, -ūs, m., contempt

contendō, -ere, -tendī, -tentus, struggle, hasten 57

contentus, -a, -um, contented

contexō, -ere, -texuī, -textus, weave (together)

continēns, -entis, f., mainland

contineō, -ēre, -uī, -tentus, hold (together), contain 24, 4

contingō, -ere, -tigī, -tāctus, touch; happen 29

continuus, -a, -um, successive, continuous 84

contrā, (prep. w. acc.) against, opposite 65; (adv.) on the other hand

contrahō, -ere, -trāxī, -trāctus, draw or bring together, contract

contrārius, -a, -um, opposite

contrīstō, (1) sadden

contrōversia, -ae, f., dispute 45

contumēlia, -ae, f., insult 69

conturbō, (1) confuse, mix up

conveniō, -īre, -vēnī, -ventūrus, come together 25; convenit, it is agreed upon; conventus, -ūs, m., meeting

convertō, -ere, -vertī, -versus, turn

convocō, (1) call together 25

coorior, coorīrī, coortus, arise

cōpia, -ae, f., supply, abundance 5; opportunity; pl. forces, troops; resources

cor, cordis, n., heart 51

Corinthus, -ī, f., Corinth, a Greek city

corium, corī, n., skin, leather

cornū, -ūs, n., horn; wing (of an army) 72

corōna, -ae, f., crown

corōnō, (1) crown

corpus, corporis, n., body 45

corrigō, -ere, -rēxī, -rēctus, correct

cotīdiānus, -a, -um, daily 50

cotīdiē, (adv.) daily 15

crās, *(adv.)* tomorrow 6, **6**

crātēr, -is, *m.,* large bowl

creātūra, -ae, *f.* creature, creation

crēber, -bra, -brum, frequent, numerous

crēditor, -ōris, *m.,* creditor

crēdō, -ere, -didī, -ditus, *(w. dat.)* believe, entrust 65

cremō, (1) burn

creō, (1) elect, appoint

crēscō, -ere, crēvī, crētus, grow, increase

Crēta, -ae, *f.,* Crete

crocodīlus, -ī, *m.,* crocodile

cruciātus, -ūs, *m.,* torture **49**

crūdēlis, -e, cruel; **crūdēliter,** *(adv.)* cruelly

crūdēlitās, -tātis, *f.,* cruelty

cruentus, -a, -um, bloody

crūs, crūris, *n.,* leg

crux, crucis, *f.,* cross

cubiculum, -ī, *n.,* bedroom

culmen, -minis, *n.,* top, roof

culpa, -ae, *f.,* blame, fault **18**

culpō, (1) blame

cultūra, -ae, *f.,* cultivation

cultus, -a, -um, cultured; **cultus, -ūs,** *m.,* way of living, civilization

cum, *(prep. w. abl.)* with 23

cum, *(conj.)* when **16**; whenever, since, although; **cum prīmum,** as soon as **47; cum... tum,** not only . . . but also

cumulus, -ī, *m.,* heap, pile

cūnctor, (1) hesitate

cūnctus, -a, -um, all

cupiditās, -tātis, *f.,* desire **40**

Cupīdō, -inis, *m.,* Cupid, the god of love

cupidus, -a, -um, eager, desirous **51; cupidē,** *(adv.)* eagerly

cupiō, -ere, cupīvī, cupītus, desire, wish, want 31, **4**

cūr, *(adv.)* why 36

cūra, -ae, *f.,* worry, care, concern 5

cūria, -ae, *f.,* senate house; **Cūria Iūlia,** *the senate house built by Julius Caesar*

cūriōsitās, -tātis, *f.,* curiosity

cūrō, (1) care for, cure, cause (to be done) **83**

currō, -ere, cucurrī, cursūrus, run 50, **7**

currus, -ūs, *m.,* chariot

cursor, -ōris, *m.,* runner

cursus, -ūs, *m.,* running, course, voyaging **42; cursus honōrum,** course of offices, career

curvus, -a, -um, curved

custōdia, -ae, *f.,* guard

custōdiō, -īre, -īvī, -ītus, guard

custōs, -ōdis, *m.,* guard **33**

D

damnō, (1) condemn

dē, *(prep. w. abl.)* from, down from, about, concerning 13

dea, -ae, *f.,* goddess 22

dēbellō, (1) crush (in war)

dēbeō, -ēre, dēbuī, dēbitus, owe, ought 17, **6**

dēbitum, -ī, *n.,* debt

dēcēdō, -ere, dēcessī, dēcessūrus, depart, go away, die

decem, ten

decemvirī, -ōrum, *m. pl.,* decemvirs, *a board of ten men*

dēcernō, -ere, dēcrēvī, dēcrētus, decide, vote **79**

dēcertō, (1) fight (it out), contend **67**

decimus, -a, -um, tenth **11**

dēcipiō, -ere, dēcēpī, dēceptus, deceive

dēclīvis, -e, sloping (downward); **dēclīvia, -um,** *n. pl.,* slopes

dēcrētum, -ī, *n.,* decree, decision

decuria, -ae, *f.,* squad; **decuriō, -ōnis,** *m.,* squad leader

dēcurrō, -ere, dēcucurrī, dēcursūrus, run down or off

dēdecus, -coris, *n.,* disgrace

dēdicō, (1) dedicate

dēditīcius, -cī, *m.,* prisoner

dēditiō, -ōnis, *f.,* surrender **58**

dēdō, dēdere, dēdidī, dēditus, surrender, devote **69**

dēdūcō, -ere, dēdūxī, dēductus, lead, withdraw, bring, launch **63**

dēfendō, -ere, dēfendī, dēfēnsus, defend 19; repel

dēfēnsor, -ōris, *m.,* defender

dēferō, dēferre, dētulī, dēlātus, carry, bestow, offer, enroll, report **28;** *(passive)* fall

dēfessus, -a, -um, tired **17**

dēficiō, -ere, dēfēcī, dēfectus, fail, revolt **33**

dēfīgō, -ere, dēfīxī, dēfīxus, drive in

dēflectō, -ere, dēflexī, dēflexus, turn aside

dēfluō, -ere, dēflūxī, dēflūxus, flow away

dēfōrmis, -e, unshapely

dēfugiō, -ere, dēfūgī, dēfugitūrus, avoid

dēiciō, -ere, dēiēcī, dēiectus, throw (down), dislodge, drive **33**

dein, deinde, *(adv.)* then **12**

dēlātus, *perf. part. of* **dēferō**

dēlecto, (1) please

dēlēctus, *part. of* **dēligō**

dēleō, -ēre, -ēvī, -ētus, destroy, wipe out **37**

dēlīberō, (1) consider

dēlīctum, -ī, *n.,* crime

dēligō, (1) fasten

dēligō, -ere, dēlēgī, dēlēctus, select **24**

Delphī, -ōrum, *m. pl.,* Delphi

delphīnus, -ī, *m.,* dolphin, porpoise

dēmēns, *(gen.)* **dēmentis,** mad

dēmittō, -ere, dēmīsī, dēmissus, let *or* drop down, send down, derive

dēmocraticus, -a, -um, democratic *(neo-Latin)*

dēmōnstrō, (1,) point out, show, mention **68**

Dēmosthenēs, -is, *m.,* Dēmŏs´ thenēs, *a Greek orator*

dēmulceō, -ēre, dēmulsī, dēmulctus, lick

dēns, dentis, *m.,* tooth

dēnsus, -a, -um, thick

dēnūdō, (1) strip

dēnūntiō, (1) declare

dēpellō, -ere, dēpulī, dēpulsus, drive away

dēpōnō, -ere, dēposuī, dēpositus, put *or* lay aside, put down, leave with **17**

dēprēndō, -ere, dēprēndī, dēprēnsus, catch

dērigō (dīrigō), -ere, dērēxī, dērēctus, direct **94**; **dērēctus, -a, -um,** straight **94**

dēscendō, -ere, dēscendī, dēscēnsus, descend **11**; **dēscēnsus, -ūs,** *m.,* descent

dēscrībō, -ere, dēscrīpsī, dēscrīptus, write down, copy, describe

dēsecō, -āre, dēsecuī, dēsectus, cut off

dēserō, -ere, dēseruī, dēsertus, desert **68**

dēsertor, -ōris, *m.,* deserter

dēsīderō, (1) long for **26**

dēsiliō, -īre, dēsiluī, dēsultūrus, jump down, dismount

dēsistō, -ere, dēstitī, dēstitūrus, stand away, cease **47**

dēspērō, (1) despair (of) **38**

dēspiciō, -ere, dēspexī, dēspectus, look down on, despise **68**; **dēspectus, -ūs,** *m.,* view

dēstitī, *see* **dēsistō**

dēsum, deesse, dēfuī, dēfutūrus, be lacking **70**

dēsuper, *(adv.)* from above

dēterior, -ius, poorer, less, worse

dētestābilis, -e, detestable

dētineō, -ēre, dētinuī, dētentus, detain

dētrahō, -ere, dētrāxī, dētrāctus, draw off, take (off)

dētrīmentum, -ī, *n.,* loss **35**

deus, -ī, *m.,* god **22**

dēveniō, -īre, dēvenī, dēventūrus, come

dēvorō, (1) devour

dexter, -tra, -trum, right (hand), right *(as opposed to left)* **72**

dī (diī) = *(nom. and voc.)* **deī**

dīcō, -ere, dīxī, dictus, say, tell, speak **22, 4**; **salūtem dīcō,** pay respects; **causam dīcō,** plead a case

dictātor, -ōris, *m.,* dictator

dictō, (1) dictate

dictum, -ī, *n.,* word

didicī, *see* **discō**

diēs, diēī, *m. and f.* day **69**

differō, differre, distulī, dīlātus, spread; differ **25**

difficilis, -e, difficult **63**

difficultās, -tātis, *f.,* difficulty **46**

diffīdō, -ere, diffīsus, *(semideponent)* distrust

diffundō, -ere, -fūdī, -fūsus, spread out

digitus, -ī, *m.,* finger

dignitās, -tātis, *f.,* worth, rank, position

dignus, -a, -um, worthy **10**

dīiūdicō, (1) determine

dīligēns, *(gen.)* **-entis,** careful, diligent **24**; **dīligenter,** *(adv.)* carefully

dīligentia, -ae, *f.,* diligence **35**

dīmicō, (1) fight **70**

dīmidium, -dī, *n.,* half

dīmittō, -ere, dīmīsī, dīmissus, let go, send (away *or* out), dismiss **31, 6**

dīmoveō, -ēre, dīmōvī, dīmōtus, move away

dīrigō, *see* **dērigō**

dīripiō, -ere, dīripuī, dīreptus, plunder **32**

dīrus, -a, -um, horrible

Dīs, Dītis, *m.,* Pluto, *god of Hades*

discēdō, -ere, -cessī, -cessūrus, go away, depart, draw back **32**

disciplīna, -ae, *f.,* training, instruction **10**

discipulus, -ī, *m.,* **discipula, -ae,** *f.,* student learner, pupil

disclūdō, -ere, -clūsī, -clūsus, separate

discō, -ere, didicī, —, learn **23**

discordia, -ae, *f.,* discord

discrīmen, -minis, *n.,* difference

discutiō, -ere, -cussī, -cussus, push aside, destroy

disiciō, -ere, -iēcī, -iectus, scatter

dispergō, -ere, dispersī, dispersus, scatter

dispōnō, -ere, -posuī, -positus, put here and there, arrange

disputātiō, -ōnis, *f.,* discussion

disputō, (1) discuss

dissēnsiō, -ōnis, *f.,* dissension

dissimilis, -e, unlike *(w. dat.)* **63**

dissimulō, (1) conceal

dissipō, (1) scatter

distineō, -ēre, -tinuī, -tentus, keep apart

distribuō, -ere, -tribuī, -tribūtus, distribute, divide, assign

dītissimus, *(see* **dīves)**

diū, *(adv.)* (for) a long time, long; *(comp.)* **diūtius;** *(superl.)* **diūtissimē**

diurnus, -a, -um, (by) day; *(n.pl.)* **acta diurna,** journal, newspaper

dīversus, -a, -um, different **71**

dīves, *(gen.)* **dīvitis,** rich; *(comp.)* **dītior;** *(superl.)* **dītissimus**

Dīviciācus, -ī, *m.,* Diviciacus (Divishiā´cus)

dīvidō, -ere, dīvīsī, dīvīsus, divide **70**

dīvīnus, -a, -um, divine

dīvitiae, -ārum, *f. pl.,* riches

dīvus, -ī *(gen. pl.)* **dīvum,** *m.,* god

dō, dare, dedī, datus, give **35, 3; poenam dō,** pay the penalty; **in fugam dō,** put to flight

doceō, -ēre, docuī, doctus, teach **10, 1; doctus,** skilled

doctrīna, -ae, *f.,* teaching

documentum, -ī, *n.,* proof, warning

doleō, -ēre, doluī, dolitūrus, grieve, be sorry **13**

dolor, -ōris, *m.,* grief, pain, suffering **40**

dolōrōsus, -a, -um, grieving

dolus, -ī, *m.,* treachery, deceit, trick(ery)

domesticus, -a, -um, one's own

domicilium, -lī, *n.,* home

dominor, (1) be master

dominus, -ī, *m.,* master **18; domina, -ae,** *f.,* mistress

domus, -ūs, *f.,* house, home **68**

dōnō, (1) give, present to *(as a gift)* **7**

dōnum, -ī, *n.,* gift

dormiō, -īre, -īvī, -ītus, sleep

dōs, dōtis, *f.,* dowry

dracō, -ōnis, *m.,* dragon

Druidēs, -um, *m. pl.,* druids

dubitātiō, -iōnis, *f.,* doubt

dubitō, (1) hesitate, doubt **31**

dubium, -bī, *n.,* doubt

dūcō, -ere, dūxī, ductus, lead, draw **21**

dulcis, -e, sweet; *(as noun, n. pl.)* cakes

dum, *(conj.)* while **52,** until

duo, -ae, -o, two **66**

duodecim, twelve; **duodecimus, -a, -um,** twelfth

duplex, *(gen.)* **duplicis,** double

duplicō, (1) double

dūritia, -ae, *f.,* hardship

dūritiēs, -ēī, *f.,* hardness

dūrō, (1) harden

dūrus, -a, -um, hard, harsh **2, 1; dūrē,** *(adv.)* harshly

dux, ducis, *m.,* leader, general **40, 2**

Dyrrachium, -chī, *n.,* Dyrrachium, *now* Durazzo, *a city on the east coast of the Adriatic*

E

ē, ex, *(prep. w. abl.)* out from, from, out of **13**

ea, *see* **is**

ecce, *(interj.)* look, here!

ēdīcō, -ere, ēdīxī, ēdictus, appoint

ēdiscō, -ere, ēdidicī, —, learn by heart

ēditus, -a, -um, elevated **13**

ēdō, ēdere, ēdidī, ēditus, give out, publish, inflict, utter **15**

edō, esse, ēdī, ēsus, eat

ēducō, (1) bring up, educate

ēdūcō, -ere, ēdūxī, ēductus, lead out **34**

effēminō, (1) weaken

efferō, efferre, extulī, ēlātus, carry out, make known **39**

efficiō, -ere, effēcī, effectus, bring about, produce, effect, cause **21, 8**

effodiō, -ere, effōdī, effossus, dig up

effugiō, -ere, effūgī, effugitūrus, escape

ego, meī, *m.,* or *f.,* I **31**

ēgredior, ēgredī, ēgressus, go or march out, leave, land **42**

ēgregiē, (adv.) excellently

ēgregius, -a, -um, distinguished, excellent 33, **3**

ēheu! (interj.) alas!

eī, eae, ea, they

ēiciō, -ere, ēiēcī, ēiectus, throw (out), stick out, expel 12

eius, his, her, its; eōrum, their, (see is) 52

ēlegantia, -ae, f., elegance, style

elephantus, -ī, m., elephant, ivory

Eleusis, -is, f., Eleusis, a city near Athens

ēlevō, (1) raise

ēligō, -ere, -ēlēgī, ēlēctus, pick out, choose

ēloquentia, -ae, f., eloquence, rhetoric

ēmendō, (1) correct

ēmergō, -ere, ēmersī, ēmersus, emerge

ēmittō, -ere, ēmīsī, ēmissus, let drop, let or send out, shed

emō, -ere, ēmī, ēmptus, take, buy 66

enim, (conj.) for (never first word) 12

ēnotō, (1) take notes (on)

ēnūntiō, (1) announce, report

eō, īre, iī (īvī), itūrus, go, come 20

eō, (adv.) there, to that place 24

eōdem, (adv.) to the same place 52

eōrum, eārum, eōrum, (gen. pl. of is) their

Ēpīrus, -ī, f., Ēpī´rus, a province in Greece

episcopus, -ī, m., bishop

epistula, -ae, f., letter

eques, -itis, m., horseman, knight; pl., cavalry 34

equester, -tris, -tre, (of) cavalry 66

equidem, (adv.) to be sure

equitātus, -ūs, m., cavalry 56

equus, -ī, m., horse 4

ergō, (adv.) therefore

ērigō, -ere, ērēxī, ērēctus, raise up

ēripiō, -ere, ēripuī, ēreptus, snatch away, remove, save

errō, (1) wander; be mistaken

ērubēscō, -ere, ērubuī,—, blush

ērudiō, -īre, -īvī, -ītus, instruct

ērudītiō, -ōnis, f., learning

ērumpō, -ēre, ērūpī, ēruptus, burst forth

ēruptiō, -ōnis, f., sally, attack, a bursting forth 74

Ēsquiliae, -ārum, f. pl., Ēsquilīnus (mōns), the Esquilīne Hill

et, (conj.) and, even 1; et... et, both . . . and 28

etiam, (adv.) also, even, too 32

Etrūscī, -ōrum, m. pl., the Etruscans

etsī, (conj.) although 22

Eumaeus, -ī, m., Eumaeus (Ūmē´us)

Eurōpa, -ae, f., Europe

ēvādō, -ere, ēvāsī, ēvāsūrus, go out, escape 33

ēvehō, -ere, ēvexī, ēvectus, carry up

ēvellō, -ere, ēvellī, ēvulsus, pull out

ēveniō, -īre, ēvēnī, ēventūrus, turn out, happen

ēventus, -ūs, m., outcome, result

ēvertō, -ere, ēvertī, ēversus, overturn

ēvocō, (1) call out, summon 16; ēvocātus, -ī, m., reenlisted volunteer

ex (ē), (prep. w. abl.) from, out of, of, as a result of, in accordance with

exāctus, perf. part. of exigō

exagitō, (1) weigh, harass, drive about

exanimō, (1) exhaust, kill 45

excēdō, -ere, excessī, excessūrus, depart 19

excelsus, -a, -um, high

excipiō, -ere, excēpī, exceptus, receive, capture, sense 13

excitō, (1) arouse, erect

exclāmō, (1) shout, exclaim

excruciō, (1) torture

exemplum, -ī, n., example 33

exeō, exīre, exiī, exitūrus, go out (from) 20

exerceō, -ēre, exercuī, exercitus, keep busy, train, exercise, make use of 67; exercitus, -ūs, m., (trained) army 68

exercitātiō, -ōnis, f., exercise

exercitātus, -a, -um, trained

exhauriō, -īre, exhausī, exhaustus, draw out, endure

exigō, -ere, exēgī, exāctus, drive out, demand

exiguitās, -tātis, f., scantiness, shortness, smallness

exiguus, -a, -um, small 80; exiguē, (adv.) scarcely

existimō, (1) think 16

exitus, -ūs, m., outlet, outcome, departure, death 10

expediō, -īre, -īvī, -ītus, set free 44; expedītus, -a, -um, unencumbered; free, easy 52

expellō, -ere, expulī, expulsus, drive out 50, **7**

experior, experīrī, expertus, try 66; expertus, -a, -um, experienced

expleō, -ēre, explēvī, explētus, fill up 99

explicō, (1) unfold, explain 63

explōrātor, -ōris, m., scout 55

explōrō, (1) investigate, explore, reconnoiter 70; **explōrātus, -a, -um,** assured

expōnō, -ere, -posuī, expositus, put out, draw up, expose 81

exprimō, -ere, expressī, expressus, press out, express, portray, imitate 26

expugnō, (1) capture by assault 53

exsanguis, -e, bloodless

exsequor, exsequi, execūtus, follow up, enforce

exsiliō, -īre, exsiluī, —, leap up or out

exsilium, -lī, *n.,* exile

exsistō, -ere, exstitī, —, stand out, arise

exspectō, (1) look out for, wait, await 19, **6**

exspīrō, (1) breathe out, expire 35

exstinguō, -ere, exstīnxī, exstīnctus, extinguish

exstruō, -ere, exstrūxī, exstrūctus, pile up, build, erect 38

exterus, -a, -um, outside; **exterior, -ius,** outer; **extrēmus, -a, -um,** outermost, farthest, last, end of 64

externus, -ī, *m.,* stranger

extrā, *(prep. w. acc.)* outside (of), beyond 34

extrahō, -ere, extrāxī, extrāctus, draw out

extraōrdinārius, -a, -um, (out of order), extraordinary

extrēmus, -a, -um, *see* **exterus**

F

faber, -brī, *m.,* workman, engineer

fābula, -ae, *f.,* story

faciēs, -ēī, *f.,* face, appearance 21

facile, *(adv.)* easily 63

facilis, -e, easy, doable 47, **3**

facinus, facinoris, *n.,* crime

faciō, -ere, fēcī, factus, do, make 20, **3; verba faciō,** speak, make a speech; **certiōrem eum faciō dē,** inform him about; **iter faciō,** march, travel

factiō, -ōnis, *f.,* faction 60

factum, -ī, *n.,* deed 42

facultās, -tātis, *f.,* faculty, opportunity 63; *pl.,* means 63

fallāx, *(gen.)* **-ācis,** false

fallō, -ere, fefellī, falsus, deceive 65

falsus, -a, -um, false; **falsō,** *(adv.)* falsely

falx, falcis, *f.,* hook

fāma, -ae, *f.,* report, fame 2

famēs, -is, *(abl.)* **famē** *f.,* hunger 21

familia, -ae, *f.,* family 2; household

familiāris, -e, *(adj.)* (of the family), friendly 49; *(noun) m.,* friend (familiar);

fāmōsus, -a, -um, famous, notorious

fās, *(indeclinable) n.,* (what is) right (by divine law)

fatīgō, (1) weary, wear out

fātum, -ī, *n.,* fate; *(often personified)* the Fates

faucēs, -ium, *f. pl.,* throat, jaws

faveō, -ēre, fāvī, fautūrus, be favorable to, favor

favor, -ōris, *m.,* favor

fefellī, *see* **fallō**

fēles, -is, fēlium, *m.* or *f.,* cat

fēlīcitās, -tātis, *f.,* happiness

fēlīx, *(gen.)* **fēlīcis,** happy, fortunate, successful, lucky 18; **fēlīciter,** *(adv.)* fortunately, successfully; (interj.) good luck!

fēmina, -ae, *f.,* woman, wife 35; **fēmineus, -a, -um,** womanly

ferē, *(adv.)* almost, about, generally **50**

fēriae, -ārum, *f. pl.,* festival, holidays 22; **fēriae Latīnae,** festival of the allied Latins

feriō, -īre, -īvī, -ītus, hit, strike

ferō, ferre, tulī, lātus, bear, endure, carry, bring, receive, report, propose (of a law) 13

ferōx, *(gen.)* **ferōcis,** bold, fierce

ferrum, -ī, *n.,* iron 85; *(adj.)* **ferreus, -a, -um,** iron

fertilis, -e, fertile

fertilitās, -tātis, *f.,* fertility

ferus, -a, -um, wild, fierce 60; **fera, -ae,** *f.,* wild beast

festīnō, (1) hurry

fēstus, -a, -um, festal

fidēs, -eī, *n.,* faith, trust, loyalty 63; *(adj.)* **fidēlis, -e** *and* **fīdus, -a, -um,** faithful, loyal

fidūcia, -ae, *f.,* confidence

fīgō, -ere, fīxī, fīxus, fix 30

figūra, -ae, *f.,* figure, shape

fīlius, -lī, *m.,* son 14; **filia, -ae,** *f.,* daughter 9, **1**

fingō, -ere, fīnxī, fictus, form, invent, imagine

fīniō, -īre, -īvī, -ītus, limit, determine **94**

fīnis, fīnis, fīnium, *m.* end; *pl.,* borders, territory 46

fīnitimus, -a, -um, *(adj.)* neighboring 27; **fīnitimus, -ī,** *m.,* neighbor 27

fīō, fieri, —, (factus), be made, become, be done, happen 24; **certior fīō,** be informed (*literally,* be made more certain) 24

firmus, -a, -um, strong, firm 23; **firmiter,** *(adv.)* firmly

fissus, -a, -um, split

flagellum, -i, *n.,* whip

flamma, -ae, *f.,* flame

flectō, -ere, flexī, flexus, bend, turn

fleō, flēre, flēvī, flētus, weep (for) 11

flōreō, -ēre, flōruī, —, bloom

flōs, flōris, *m.,* flower

flūctus, -ūs, *m.,* wave

flūmen, flūminis, *n.,* river 45, **8**

fluō, -ere, flūxī, flūxus, flow 52

focus, -ī, *m.,* hearth

fōns, fontis, *m.,* spring, source 20

fore = futūrum esse, *from* **sum**

fōrma, -ae, *f.,* shape 5

fors, fortis, *f.,* chance 27

fortasse, *(adv.)* perhaps 41

forte, *(adv.)* by chance

fortis, -e, strong, brave 47; **fortiter,** *(adv.)* bravely

fortūna, -ae, *f.,* fortune, luck 2; *pl.,* property

forum, -ī, *n.,* market place; Forum *(at Rome)*

fossa, -ae, *f.,* trench 28

foveō, -ēre, fōvī, fōtus, cherish

frangō, -ere, frēgī, frāctus, break 54

frāter, frātris, *m.,* brother 54, **2**

fraus, fraudis, *f.,* fraud, wrong

frequēns, *(gen.)* **frequentis,** frequent, numerous; **frequenter,** *(adv.)* often

frīgidus, -a, -um, cold

frīgus, frīgoris, *n.,* cold

frōns, frondis, frondium, *f.,* leaf

frōns, frontis, frontium, *f.,* forehead, front 70

frūctus, -ūs, *m.,* fruit

frūgēs, -um, *f. pl.,* crops

frūmentārius, -a, -um, of grain; fertile 57; **rēs frūmentāria,** grain supply 57

frūmentum, -ī, *n.,* grain 16; *pl.,* ears of grain, crops

fruor, fruī, frūctus, enjoy

frūstrā, *(adv.)* in vain 48

fuga, -ae, *f.,* flight 43, **3; in fugam dō,** put to flight, cause to run away, make run 43

fugiō, -ere, fūgī, fugitūrus, run away, flee, escape 22, **3**

fugitīvus, -ī, *m.,* deserter

fulmen, -minis, *n.,* lightning

fūmō, (1) smoke

fūmus, -ī, *m.,* smoke

funda, -ae, *f.,* sling, slingshot

fundāmentum, -ī, *n.,* foundation

funditor, -ōris, *m.,* slinger

fundō, -ere, fūdī, fūsus, pour, shed 37

fūnis, -is, *m.,* rope

fūnus, -eris, *n.,* funeral

Furiae, -ārum, *f. pl.,* the Furies, *avenging and tormenting spirits*

furibundus, -a, -um, mad

furō, -ere, —, —, rage

furor, -ōris, m., madness

fūrtim, *(adv.)* secretly

furtum, -ī, *n.,* theft

futūrus, *see* **sum**

G

Gāius, -ī, *m.,* Gā´ius

galea, -ae, *f.,* helmet

Gallia, -ae, *f.,* Gaul, ancient France; **Gallicus, -a, -um,** Gallic; **Gallus, -a, -um,** Gallic (from Gaul); *(noun)* **Gallus, -ī,** *-m.,* a Gaul

garrulus, -a, -um, talkative

gaudeō, -ēre, gāvīsus, *(semideponent)* rejoice, be glad

gaudium, -dī, *n.,* joy, gladness 18

gāvīsus, *perf. part. of* **gaudeō**

geminus, -a, -um, twin

gemitus, -ūs, *m.,* groan

gemma, -ae, *f.,* precious stone

gemō, -ere, gemuī, —, groan

Genava, *see* **Genua**

genius, -nī, *m.,* inborn spirit

gēns, gentis, gentium, *f.,* people, nation, tribe 62, **9**

Genua, -ae, *f.,* Geneva

genus, generis, *n.,* birth, kind 53, **8**

Germānia, -ae, *f.,* Germany; **Germānicus, -a, -um,** German; **Germānus, -a, -um,** German; *(noun)* **Germānus, -ī,** *m.,* a German

gerō, gerere, gessī, gestus, carry on, wage 23, **3;** *(passive)* go on; **mē gerō,** act; *(noun, nom. pl.)* **rēs gestae,** deeds

gignō, -ere, genuī, genitus, produce; *(passive)* be born

gladiātor, -ōris, *m.,* gladiator

gladiātōrius, -a, -um, gladiatorial

gladius, -dī, *m.,* sword

glōria, -ae, *f.,* glory 11

glōriōsus, -a, -um, glorious

gracilis, -ē, slender, graceful

gradior, gradī, gressus, step, walk 22

gradus, -ūs, *m.,* step

Graecia, -ae, *f.,* Greece; **Graecus, -a, -um,** Greek; **Graecus, -ī,** *m.,* a Greek

grāmen, grāminis, *n.,* grass

grammaticus, -ī, *m.,* school teacher

grātia, -ae, *f.,* gratitude, influence 11; **grātiam habeō,** feel grateful; **grātiās agō,** thank *(w. dat.); (as prep.)* **grātiā,** for the sake of *(w. gen. preceeding)*

grātulātiō, -ōnis, *f.,* congratulation

grātus, -a, -um, pleasing, grateful 7, **4**

gravis, -e, heavy, severe 57, **5; graviter,** *(adv.)* heavily, seriously, severely, decisively

gravitās, -tātis, *f.,* weight, dignity, seriousness

gubernātor, -ōris, *m.,* pilot, helmsman 12

gustō, (1) taste

gustus, -ūs, *m.,* taste

H

ha! *(interj.)* ha!

habeō, -ēre, habuī, habitus, have, hold 10, **1; grātiam habeō,** feel grateful *(w. dat.);* **ōrātiōnem habeō,** deliver an oration

habitō, (1) live, dwell 15

Haeduus, -a, -um, Haeduan (Hĕduan); **Heduus, -ī,** *m.,* a Haeduan

haereō, -ēre, haesī, haesus, stick, cling 60

Hamburgiēnsis, -e, of Hamburg

Hannibal, -alis, *m.,* Hannibal, *a Carthaginian general*

Harpȳiae, -ārum, *f. pl.,* the Harpies

haud, *(adv.)* by no means

hauriō, -īre, hausī, haustus, drain, drink

Helvētius, -a, -um, Helvetian (Helvēshian); **Helvētius, -ī,** *m.* a Helvetian

herba, -ae, *f.,* herb, plant, grass

Herculēs, -is, *m.,* Herculēs

hērēditās, -tātis, *f.,* inheritance

herī, *(adv.)* yesterday **6**

heu! *(interj.)* alas!

hīberna, -ōrum *(i.e.,* **castra),** *n. pl.,* winter quarters 54

Hibernia, -ae, *f.,* Ireland

hic, haec, hoc, this, these, the latter; *(pron.)* he, she, it 50

hīc, *(adv.)* here, in this place **18**

hiemō, (1) spend the winter

hiems, hiemis, *f.,* winter 51

hilaris, -e, gay, cheerful

Hispānia, -ae, *f.,* Spain; **Hispānus, -a, -um,** Spanish

historia, -ae, *f.,* story, history

hodiē, *(adv.)* today **6**

hodiernus, -a, -um, of today

Homērus, -ī, *m.,* Homer, *a Greek poet*

homō, hominis, *m.,* man, person, human being; *pl.,* people 40, **4**

honestās, -tātis, *f.,* honor, honesty

honestus, -a, -um, honorable; **honestē,** *(adv.)* honorably

honor, -ōris, *m.,* honor, office **23**

hōra, -ae, *f.,* hour 9

Horātius, -tī, *m.,* Horace, *a Roman poet; and* Horatius (Horāshius) Cocles, *an ancient hero*

horrēns, *(gen.)* **horrentis,** shaggy

horreō, -ēre, horruī, —, shudder, dread

horribilis, -e, horrible

horridus, -a, -um, frightful

horror, -ōris, *m.,* horror

hortor, (1) urge, encourage **21**

hortus, -ī, *m.,* garden, park

hospes, -itis, *m.,* stranger, guest, guest-friend, host 11; **hospita, -ae,** *f.,* guest/hostess

hospitium, -tī, *n.,* hospitality

hostis, hostis, hostium, *m.,* enemy *(usually pl.)* 46, **5**

hūc, *(adv.)* to this side, here, to this place **25**

hūmānitās, -tātis, *f.,* culture

hūmānus, -a, -um, human, civilized

humilis, -e, low, humble 62, **2**

humus, -ī, *f.,* ground, earth

hydraulicus, -a, -um, hydraulic, water-powered

I

iaceō, -ēre, iacuī, —, lie (down)

iaciō, -ere, iēcī, iactus, throw, hurl, cast 45; build

iactō, (1) throw, toss

iactūra, -ae, *f.,* (throwing), loss, expense, sacrifice

iactus, -ūs, *m.,* throw

iaculum, -ī, *n.,* dart, javelin

iam, *(adv.)* already, now, 30; by this time, at last, *(w. future)* soon; **nōn iam,** no longer

iānua, -ae, *f.,* door

ibi, *(adv.)* there 11

id, *(see* **is***)*

īdem, eadem, idem, *(adj.)* the same 53, **8;** *(pron.)* the same man, woman, thing

identidem, *(adv.)* again and again

idōneus, -a, -um, suitable, fitting **42**

igitur, *(adv.)* therefore **40**

ignis, -is, ignium, *sing. (abl.)* **igne** *or* **ignī** *m.,* fire 63

ignōminia, -ae, *f.,* disgrace

ignōrō, (1) not know

ignōscō, -ere, ignōvī, ignōtus, pardon

ignōtus, -a, -um, unknown, strange **26**

illātus, *perf. part. of* **īnferō**

ille, illa, illud, that, those the former; *(pron.)* he, she, it 50; **ille... hic,** the former . . . the latter

illigō, (1) tie to

illō, *(adv.)* there, to that place

illūc, *(adv.)* to that place or side

illūstris, -e, noble

Illyricum, -ī, *n.,* Illyricum, *a region along the east coast of the Adriatic*

imāgō, imāginis, *f.,* statue, likeness, echo

imbecillitās, -tātis, *f.,* weakness

imitātiō, -ōnis, *f.,* imitation

imitor, (1) imitate

immānis, -e, huge, savage

immittō, -ere, immīsī, immissus, let go, throw

immolō, (1) sacrifice

immortālis, -e, undying, immortal

impār, *(gen.)* **imparis,** unequal

impedīmentum, -ī, *n.,* hindrance 44; **impedīmenta, -ōrum,** *n. pl.,* baggage

impediō, -īre, -īvī, -ītus, hinder, obstruct 44; **impedītus, -a, -um,** burdened

impellō, -ere, impulī, impulsus, drive on, influence, incite, impel, urge

impendeō, -ēre, —, —, hang over

impendō, -ere, impendī, impēnsus, spend

imperātor, -ōris, *m.,* commander, general, emperor **23**

imperātum, -ī, *n.,* order

imperītus, -a, -um, inexperienced, ignorant

imperium, -rī, *n.,* command, power, empire 66; *pl.* **nova imperia,** revolution

imperō, (1) command, order, rule, demand 70

impetrō, (1) gain or obtain (one's request) **54**

impetus, -ūs, *m.,* attack 68; **impetum facio in** *(w. acc.)* make an attack against

impius, -a, -um, impious

impleō, -ēre, implēvī, implētus, fill **29**

impōnō, -ere, imposuī, impositus, put on, impose

importō, (1) bring in, import

improbitās, -tātis, *f.,* dishonesty

imprōvīsus, -a, -um, unforeseen; **dē imprōvīsō,** suddenly

imprūdentia, -ae, *f.,* poor sense

impudenter, *(adv.)* impudently

impulsus, *part. of* **impellō**

īmus, *(see* **inferus***)*

in, *(prep. w. acc.)* into, onto, to, against 15; *(prep. w. abl.)* in, on 11

inānis, -e, empty

incēdō, -ere, incessī, incessus, enter

incendium, -dī, *n.,* fire, burning

incendō, -ere, incendī, incēnsus, set on fire, burn; rouse 15

incertus, -a, -um, uncertain 52

incidō, -ere, incidī, —, fall (into or upon), happen

incipiō, -ere, incēpī, inceptus, take on, begin 23

incitō, (1) excite, stir up, incite, arouse 8

inclūdō, -ere, inclūsī, inclūsus, shut up

incognitus, -a, -um, unknown

incola, -ae, *m.,* inhabitant

incolō, -ere, incoluī, —, live, inhabit 66

incolumis, -e, unharmed, safe **35**

incommodum, -ī, *n.,* harm

incrēdibilis, -e, unbelievable

incumbō, -ere, incubuī, incubitūrus, lean over

incursiō, -ōnis, *f.,* raid

incursō, (1) run against

inde, *(adv.)* then, from there, thereafter, therefore

Indī, -ōrum, *m. pl.,* the Indians, inhabitants of India

indīcō, -ere, indīxī, indictus, call **60**

indignitās, -tātis, *f.,* outrage

indīligenter, *(adv.)* carelessly

indiscrētē, *(adv.)* indiscreetly

indoctus, -a, -um, untrained

indūcō, -ere, indūxī, inductus, lead in, bring in; influence

induō, -ere, induī, indūtus, put on, dress, impale

ineō, inīre, iniī, initūrus, enter in or upon **26; cōnsilium ineō,** form a plan

inermis, -e, unarmed

īnfāmia, -ae, *f.,* dishonor

īnfāmis, -e, notorious

īnfāns, -fantis, *m.,* infant

īnfectus, -a, -um, not done

īnfēlīx, *(gen.)* **īnfēlīcis,** unfortunate, unlucky, unhappy

īnferō, īnferre, intulī, illātus, bring **35;** bring in, to, or against; place upon, inflict, enter; **signa īnferō,** charge

īnferus, -a, -um, low; **īnferior, -ius,** lower; **īmus** *or* **īnfimus, -a, -um,** lowest; *(noun)* **īnferī, -ōrum,** *m.,* inhabitants of the Underworld

īnficiō, -ere, īnfēcī, īnfectus, stain, infect

īnfimus, *see* **īnferus**

īnfīnītus, -a, -um, endless, countless

īnfirmitās, -tātis, *f.,* illness

īnfirmus, -a, -um, weak

īnfīxus, -a, -um, fixed

īnfluō, -ere, īnfūxī, īnfūxus, flow (in)

īnfrā, *(adv.)* below, farther on; *(prep. w. acc.)* below

īnfundō, -ere, īnfūdī, īnfūsus, pour in

ingeniōsus, -a, -um, clever, ingenious

ingenium, -nī, *n.,* ability

ingēns, *(gen.)* **ingentis,** huge

ingredior, ingredī, ingressus, step into, enter **19**

iniciō, -ere, iniēcī, iniectus, throw into, inspire

inimīcitia, -ae, *(f.)* enmity, feud

inimīcus, -a, -um, *(adj.)* unfriendly, hostile **30, 8; inimīcus, -ī,** *m.,* (personal) enemy

inīquitās, -tātis, *f.,* unfavorableness

inīquus, -a, -um, uneven, unfavorable, unjust **33**

initium, -tī, *n.,* beginning **27**

iniungō, -ere, iniūnxī, iniūnctus, join to, impose on

iniūria, -ae, *f.,* injustice, wrong, injury **8**

iniūriōsus, -a, -um, harmful

iniūstus, -a, -um, unjust; **iniūstē,** *(adv.)* unjustly

innocēns, *(gen.)* **innocentis,** innocent

inopia, -ae, *f.,* lack, scarcity, poverty **30**

inopīnāns, *(gen.)* **inopīnantis,** unsuspecting

inops, *(gen.)* **inopis,** poor, helpless

inquit, he/she said *(never first word)* **28; inquis,** you say

īnsānia, -ae, *f.,* madness

īnsānus, -a, -um, mad

īnsciēns, *(gen.)* **īnscientis,** not knowing

īnscrībō, -ere, īnscrīpsī, īnscrīptus, inscribe

īnsequor, īnsequī, īnsecūtus, follow up, pursue **47**

īnserō, -ere, īnseruī, īnsertus, insert

īnsidiae, -ārum, *f. pl.,* plot, ambush, treachery **30**

īnsignis, -e, remarkable, noted, conspicuous **16; īnsigne, -is,** *n.,* ensign, (military) decoration, signal **56**

īnsiliō, -īre, īnsiluī, —, leap upon

īnsistō, -ere, īnstitī, —, adopt, stand (on)

īnstituō, -ere, īnstituī, īnstitūtus, establish, decide upon; begin, train; build, provide **21**

īnstitūtum, -ī, *n.,* custom

īnstō, -āre, īnstitī, —, threaten **60** press on

īnstrūmentum, -ī, *n.,* instrument

īnstruō, -ere, īnstrūxī, īnstrūctus, arrange, *set up,* draw up, provide **62**

īnsula, -ae, *f.,* island **1**

integer, -gra, -grum, fresh, whole, untouched **31**

intellegenter, *(adv.)* intelligently

intellegō, -ere, -lēxī, -lēctus, realize, understand **67**

intemperāns, *(gen.)* **-antis,** intemperate

intendō, -ere, intendī, intentus, stretch out, direct

inter, *(prep. w. acc.)* between, among **35; inter sē,** with each other, between one another

intercēdō, -ere, -cessī, -cessūrus, go between, intervene

intercipiō, -ere, -cēpī, -ceptus, intercept, cut off, catch **53**

interclūdō, -ere, -clūsī, -clūsus, cut off **69**

intereā, *(adv.)* meanwhile **41**

intereō, -īre, -iī, -itūrus, perish **90**

interest, *see* **intersum**

interficiō, -ere, -fēcī, -fectus, kill **34, 6**

intericiō, -ere, -iēcī, -iectus, throw between, intervene

interim, *(adv.)* meanwhile **57**

interior, -ius, interior **85; interiōrēs, -um,** *m.,* those in the interior; **infimus, -a, -um,** in most

intermittō, -ere, -mīsī, -missus, stop, interrupt, let go **37**

interpōnō, -ere, -posuī, -positus, present

interpretor, (1) explain

interrogō, (1) ask, question **23**

intersum, -esse, -fuī, -futūrus, be between, take part (in); **interest,** it makes a difference

intervāllum, -ī, *n.,* interval, distance

interventus, -ūs, *m.,* coming on, arrival

intrā, *(prep. w. acc.)* within **30**

intrō, (1) enter

intrōmittō, -ere, -mīsī, -missus, let in

intueor, intuērī, intuitus, look at

inūsitātus, -a, -um, unusual, strange

inūtilis, -e, useless

inveniō, -īre, invēnī, inventus, find, come upon 20, **5**

inventor, -ōris, *m.,* discoverer

invictus, -a, -um, unconquered

invideō, -ēre, invīdī, invīsus, envy, hate

invidia, -ae, *f.,* envy

invītō, (1) invite

invītus, -a, -um, unwilling **54**

iō, *(interj.)* hurrah!

iocor, (1) joke

iocus, -ī, *m.,* joke

Iovis, *see* **Iuppiter**

ipse, ipsa, ipsum, -self, the very 54, **8**

īra, -ae, *f.,* anger 60

īrācundus, -a, -um, hot-tempered, quick-tempered

īrātus, -a, -um, angry

irrīdeō, -ēre, irrīsī, irrīsus, laugh at, jeer

irrumpō, -ere, irrūpī, irruptus, break in, rush in

is, ea, id, *(pron.)* he, she, it 31, **8;** *(adj.)* this, that 52

iste, ista, istud, that **45**

ita, *(adv.)* so, yes 22; in such a way, thus **14; ita ut(ī),** just as

Italia, -ae, *f.,* Italy

Italus, -a, -um, Italian; **Italī, -ōrum,** *m.,* the Italians

itaque, *(adv.)* and so, therefore, and as a result

item, *(adv.)* also, likewise **51**

iter, itineris, *n.,* journey, route, march, road 46, **8; iter faciō,** march, travel

iterum, *(adv.)* again, a second time **10**

iubeō, -ēre, iussī, iussus, order 32, **3**

iūcundus, -a, -um, pleasant

iūdex, iūdicis, *m.,* judge

iūdicium, -cī, *n.,* trial, investigation, judgment

iūdicō, (1) judge **62**

iugum, -ī, *n.,* yoke, ridge **45**

Iūlius, -a, -um, *m.,* Julius; **Iūlia, -ae,** *f.,* Julia

iungō, -ere, iūnxī, iūnctus, join (to), harness **63**

iūnior, -ius, *(comp. of* **iuvenis***)* younger

Iūnō, -ōnis, *f.,* Juno, *a goddess, wife of Jupiter*

Iuppiter, Iovis, *m.,* Jupiter, *king of the gods*

Iūra, -ae, *m.,* Jura, *a mountain range*

iūrō, (1) swear **88**

iūs, iūris, *n.,* right 47, **5; iūs iūrandum, iūris iūrandī,** *n.,* oath **49**

iussum, -ī, *n.,* order

iūstitia, -ae, *f.,* justice

iūstus, -a, -um, just 59, proper, regular

iuvenis, -is, *m.,* young man **12; iuvenālis, -e,** youthful

iuventūs, -tūtis, *f.,* youth, young people

iuvō, -āre, iūvī, iūtus, help, aid, please **27**

iūxtā, *(adv.)* close by

L

L., *abbreviation for* **Lūcius, Lūcī,** *m.,* Lucius (Lū´shius)

labor, -ōris, *m.,* work, hardship 59

labōrō, (1) work 3

lac, lactis, *n.,* milk

Lacedaemon, -onis, *f.,* Sparta, *a region in Greece*

lacerō, (1) tear to pieces

lacessō, -ere, -īvī, -ītus, attack **84**

lacrima, -ae, *f.,* tear; **lacrimōsus, -a, -um,** tearful

lacrimō, (1) weep

lacus, -ūs, *m.,* lake

laetitia, -ae, *f.,* joy

laetus, -a, -um, joyful

lampas, -adis, *f.,* lamp, torch

lanterna, -ae, *f.,* lantern

lapis, lapidis, *m.,* stone

Lār, Laris, *m.,* Lar, *a household god*

lārva, -ae, *f.,* ghost

lassitūdō, -dinis, *f.,* weariness

lateō, -ēre, -uī, —, hide, escape notice

later, lateris, *m.,* brick, tile

Latīnus, -a, -um, Latin, belonging to Latium; **Latīnī, -ōrum,** *m.,* the Latins

Latīnus, -ī, *m.,* Latī´nus, *king of Latium*

lātitūdō, -dinis, *f.,* width **51**

latrō, -ōnis, *m.,* robber, bandit

latrōcinium, -nī, *n.,* robbery

latus, lateris, *n.,* side, flank

lātus, -a, -um, wide 18; **lātē,** *(adv.)* widely

lātus, *(see* **ferō***)*

laudō, (1) praise 4

laus, laudis, *f.,* praise **94**

lautus, -a, -um, magnificent

lavō, -āre, lāvī, lautus, wash, bathe

laxō, (1) open out

lēctor, -ōris, *m.,* reader

lēgātiō, -ōnis, *f.,* embassy **51**

lēgātus, -ī, *m.,* ambassador, envoy, staff officer, governor **60**; general

legiō, -ōnis, *f.,* legion **37**

legiōnārius, -a, -um, legionary

legō, -ere, lēgī, lēctus, gather, choose, read **26, 4**

Lemannus, -ī, *m.,* (*w.* **lacus**) Lake Geneva

lēniō, -īre, -īvī, -ītus, soothe

lēnis, -e, gentle; **lēniter,** *(adv.)* gently

leō, -ōnis, *m.,* lion

Leōnidās, -ae, *m.,* Leōnidas

levis, -e, light (in weight) **58**

levitās, -tātis, *f.,* lightness, inconstancy

lēx, lēgis, *f.,* law **40, 5**

libellus, -ī, *m.,* little book

libenter, *(adv.)* willingly, gladly

līber, -era, -erum, *(adj.)* free **14**

liber, librī, *m.,* book **24**

līberālis, -e, liberal; **līberāliter,** *(adv.)* liberally, courteously

līberātor, -ōris, *m.,* liberator

līberī, -ōrum, *m. pl.,* children **34, 1**

līberō, (1) set free **12**

lībertās, -tātis, *f.,* freedom, liberty **47**

lībertus, -ī, *m.,* freedman

librārius, -rī, *m.,* bookseller

licentia, -ae, *f.,* license

licet, -ēre, licuit *or* **licitum est,** it is permitted *or* allowed, one may **31**

ligō, (1) bind, tie **44**

līlium, līlī, *n.,* lily

līmen, līminis, *n.,* threshold

lingua, -ae, *f.,* tongue, language **10**

liquidus, -a, -um, liquid

littera, -ae, *f.,* letter (of the alphabet), *pl.* a letter (epistle), letters (*if modified by an adjective such as* **multae**) **7**, literature

lītus, lītoris, *n.,* shore **23**

Līvius, -vī, *m.,* Livy, *a Roman historian*

locō, (1) place **39**

locus, -ī, *m., pl.* **loca, locōrum,** *n.,* place **21**

longē, *(adv.)* far away, far, by far; **longē lātēque,** far and wide

longinquus, -a, -um, distant

longitūdō, -dinis, *f.,* length

longus, -a, -um, long **3**

loquor, loquī, locūtus, talk, speak **18**

lūdificō, (1) make sport of

lūdō, -ere, lūsī, lūsus, play **7**

lūdus, -ī, *m.,* game, play, show, school **35**

lūgeō, -ēre, lūxī, lūctus, mourn for

lūmen, lūminis, *n.,* light, lamp; glory; eye

lūna, -ae, *f.,* moon

lupus, -ī, *m.,* wolf

Lūsitānia, -ae, *f.,* Portugal

lūx, lūcis, *f.,* light **69, 2**; **prīmā** *or* **ortā lūce,** at dawn

luxuria, -ae, *f.,* luxury

Lycurgus, -ī, *m.,* Lycurgus, *a Spartan king*

M

M., *abbreviation for* **Mārcus**

Macedonia, -ae, *f.,* Macedonia, a country northeast of Greece; **Macedonicus, -a, -um,** Macedonian

māceria, -ae, *f.,* wall

māchina, -ae, *f.,* machine

māchinātiō, -ōnis, *f.,* engine

maciēs, -ēī, *f.,* thinness

mactē, *(interj.)* well done!

magicus, -a, -um, magic

magis, *(adv.)* more, rather **71**; *(superl.)* **maximē,** most, very, very greatly, especially, very hard

magister, -trī, *m.,* **14**; **magistra, -ae,** *f.,* teacher

magistrātus, -ūs, *m.,* magistrate, official, magistracy, office **31**

magnificus, -a, -um, magnificent, generous

magnitūdō, -dinis, *f.,* greatness, size **34**

magnopere, *(adv.)* greatly **43**

magnus, -a, -um, large, great, big **2**; *(comp.)* **maior, maius,** greater; *(superl.)* **maximus, -a, -um,** greatest, very great; *(w.* **iter***)* forced; **maiōrēs, -um,** older men, ancestors **15**

maiestās, -tātis, *f.,* dignity, honor

maior, (*see* **magnus**)

mālō, mālle, māluī, —, prefer **28**

mālum, -ī, *n.,* apple

malus, -a, -um, bad **4**; *(comp.)* **peior, peius,** worse; *(superl.)* **pessimus, -a, -um,** very bad, worst; **male,** *(adv.)* badly; **malum, -ī,** *n.,* trouble

mandātum, -ī, *n.,* order

mandō, (1) entrust, give to (to keep safe) 7, **5;**
   fugae mē mandō, take to flight

maneō, -ēre, mānsī, mānsūrus, remain 11, **4**

manifēstus, -a, -um, obvious

manipulus, -ī, *m.,* maniple, part of a cohort

manūmittō, -ere, -mīsī, -missus, make free

manus, -ūs, *f.,* hand 68

Mārcius, -cī, *m.,* Marcius (Mar´shus)

mare, maris, *n.,* sea 46

margarīta, -ae, *f.,* pearl

margarītārius, -rī, *m.,* pearl dealer

margō, marginis, *m.,* edge

maris, *genitive of* **mare** *and* **mās**

maritimus, -a, -um, of the sea, near the sea 77; **ōra**
   maritima, ōrae maritimae, *f.,* seacoast 77

marītus, -ī, *m.,* husband

Marius, -rī, *m.,* the Roman general Marius

marmor, -oris, *n.,* marble

marmoreus, -a, -um, of marble

Mārs, Mārtis, *m.,* Mars, *god of war*

Mārtius, -a, -um, of Mars; of March; *(noun) m.,*
   Martius (Mar´ shius)

mās, maris, *m.,* male

māter, mātris, *f.,* mother 50, **2; māterfamiliās,**
   mātrisfamiliās, *f.,* mother of the household

māteria, -ae, *f.,* matter, timber 11, **7**

mātrimōnium, -nī, *n.,* marriage; **in mātrimōnium**
   dō, give in marriage; **in mātrimōnium dūcō,**
   marry

mātrōna, -ae, *f.,* wife, married woman

mātūrō, (1) hasten 17

mātūrus, -a, -um, ripe, early, mature, quick **12;**
   mātūrē, *(adv.)* soon, quickly

maximē, *see* **magis; maximus,** *see* **magnus**

mēcum = cum mē

medicīna, -ae, *f.,* medicine

medicus, -ī, *m.,* doctor

mediocris, -e, short, moderate **97**

mediocritās, -tātis, *f.,* mean

Mediterrāneum (Mare), Mediterranean Sea

mediterrāneus, -a, -um, inland

medius, -a, -um, middle, middle of 25

mel, mellis, *n.,* honey

melior, *see* **bonus; melius,** *see* **bene**

membrum, -ī, *n.,* member, part of the body, limb

meminī *(perf. translated as pres.)* remember

memor, *(gen.)* **memoris,** mindful, unforgetting

memoria, -ae, *f.,* memory 8; **memoriā teneō,**
   remember

mēns, mentis, mentium, *f.,* mind 33

mēnsa, -ae, *f.,* table

mēnsis, -is, -ium, *m.,* month 58, **7**

mēnsūra, -ae, *f.,* measurement

mentiō, -ōnis, *f.,* mention

mercātor, -ōris, *m.,* merchant **13**

mercātūra, -ae, *f.,* trade

Mercurius, -rī, *m.,* Mercury

mereō, -ēre, meruī, meritus, deserve, earn 12

merīdiēs, -ēī, *m.,* midday, noon **45;** south

meritum, -ī, *n.,* merit, service

mersus, -a, -um, submerged

mētior, -īrī, mēnsus, measure (out)

metuō, -ere, -uī, —, fear

metus, -ūs, *m.,* fear **90**

meus, -a, -um, my, mine 9; *(voc.)* **mi**

migrō, (1) depart, migrate, move 15

mīles, mīlitis, *m.,* soldier 40, **8**

mīlitāris, -e, military **32**

mīlitia, -ae, *f.,* military service

mīlle, *(indeclinable adj.)* thousand 66; **mīlia,**
   mīlium, *n. (pl. noun)* thousands 66; **mīlle passūs,**
   mile **17**

Minerva, -ae, *f.,* a goddess

minimē, *(adv.)* not at all, no 3; *see* **minus**

minimus, minor, *see* **parvus**

minuō, -ere, minuī, minūtus, lessen, settle

minus, *(adv.)* less; *(superl.)* **minimē,** least, by no
   means

mīrābilis, -e, wonderful

mīrāculum, -ī, *n.,* wonderful thing

mīrātor, -ōris, *m.,* admirer

mīror, (1) wonder, wonder at, admire **19**

mīrus, -a, -um, wonderful, strange **16**

misceō, -ēre, -uī, mixtus, mix

miser, -era, -erum, unhappy, poor 29

miserābilis, -e, wretched

miseria, -ae, *f.,* wretchedness

Mithridātēs, -is, *m.,* Mithridates, *king of Pontus*

mittō, -ere, mīsī, missus, let go, send 19, **5**

mixta, *see* **misceō**

mōbilis, -e, moving

mōbilitās, -tātis, *f.,* changeableness

moderātus, -a, -um, moderate

modernus, -a, -um, modern

modestē, *(adv.)* modestly

modo, *(adv.)* only, merely, even; **nōn modo ...sed etiam,** not only . . . but also

modus, -ī, *m.,* manner, way 38, **5; quem ad modum,** how

moenia, -ium, *n. pl.,* (city) walls, fortifications

molestia, -ae, *f.,* annoyance

molliō, -īre, -īvī, -ītus, soften

mollis, -e, tender

mollitia, -ae, *f.,* weakness

Mona, -ae, *f.,* the Isle of Man, *between England and Ireland*

moneō, -ēre, -uī, -itus, remind, warn 38, **8**

monitus, -ūs, *m.,* warning

mōns, montis, montium, *m.,* mountain 46, **9**

mōnstrō, (1) point out, show to 7

mōnstrum, -ī, *n.,* monster

monumentum, -ī, *n.,* monument

mora, -ae, *f.,* delay, stay **12**

morbus, -ī, *m.,* disease

morior, morī, mortuus, die **22; mortuus, -a, -um,** dead, having died; **moritūrus,** about to die

moror, (1) delay, stay **24**

mors, mortis, mortium, *f.,* death **51**

mortālis, -e, mortal

mortifer, -fera, -ferum, deadly

mortuus, *see* **morior**

mōs, mōris, *m.,* custom **27;** *pl.,* character **27**

mōtus, -ūs, *m.,* motion, movement **81**

moveō, -ēre, mōvī, mōtus, move 13

mox, *(adv.)* soon **37**

mūla, -ae, *f.,* mule

mulier, mulieris, *f.,* woman, wife **10**

muliō, -ōnis, *m.,* muledriver

multitūdō, -dinis, *f.,* multitude, (great) number **35**

multō, *(adv.)* (by) much

multum, *(adv.)* much, great; *(comp.)* **plūs,** more **2;** *(superl.)* **plūrimum,** most, very much, great deal

multus, -a, -um, much 3; *pl.,* many; *(comp.)* **plus,** *pl.* **plūrēs, plūra,** more; *(superl.)* **plūrimus, -a, -um,** most

mundānus, -a, -um, of the world

mundus, -ī, *m.,* world

mūniō, -īre, -īvī, -ītus, fortify 20, **3; viam mūniō,** build a road

mūnītiō, -ōnis, *f.,* fortification, defenses **53**

mūnus, mūneris, *n.,* duty, service, gift 59, **7;** *pl.,* shows (of gladiators), games

mūrālis, -e, *(adj.)* wall

mūrus, -ī, *m.,* wall **28**

Mūsae, -ārum, *f. pl.,* the Muses

mūtābilis, -e, changeable, fickle

mutilus, -a, -um, broken

mūtō, (1) change; **mūtātus, -a, -um,** changed

mūtus, -a, -um, mute

N

nactus, *perf. part. of* **nancīscor**

nam, *(conj.)* for 38; **namque,** for **13**

nancīscor, nancīscī, nactus, gain, obtain, find, meet with **42**

narrō, (1) tell, relate **21**

nāscor, nāscī, nātus, be born, be found **33; duōs annōs nātus,** two years old; **nātus, -ī,** *m.,* son

nātālis, -e, of birth; **diēs nātālis,** birthday

nātiō, -ōnis, *f.,* nation, tribe **80**

natō, (1) swim

nātūra, -ae, *f.,* nature **36**

nātus, *perf. part. of* **nāscor**

naumachia, -ae, *f.,* sea fight

nauta, -ae, *m.,* sailor **6**

nāvālis, -e, naval

nāvigium, -gī, *n.,* boat

nāvigō, (1) sail 6, **1**

nāvis, nāvis, nāvium, *f.,* ship 46; **nāvis longa,** warship; **nāvis onerāria,** transport

-ne, *(introduces questions)* 18; indirect questions, whether

nē, *(conj.)* not, (so) that . . . not, lest, in order that . . . not, that **11;** *(adv.)* not; **nē... quidem** *(emphatic word between)* not even

nec, *see* **neque**

necessāriō, *(adv.)* necessarily

necessārius, -a, -um, necessary **70**

necesse, *(adj.) (indeclinable)* necessary **18**

necessitās, -tātis, *f.,* necessity

necō, (1) kill **48**

nefārius, -a, -um, unspeakable

nefās, *n., (indeclinable)* sin, wrong

neglegentia, -ae, *f.,* negligence

neglegō, -ere, -lēxī, -lēctus, disregard, neglect **38**

negō, (1) say no, deny, say . . . not **21**

negōtium, -tī, *n.,* business 67, **1**

nēmō, *(dat.)* **nēminī,** *(acc.)* **nēminem** *(no other forms)* no one 62, **7**

nepōs, nepōtis, *m.,* grandson, nephew, descendant

Neptūnus, -ī, *m.,* Neptune, *god of the sea*

nēquāquam, *(adv.)* by no means

neque (or **nec**), and not, nor 28; **neque... neque,** neither . . . nor 28; **neque quisquam,** not a single one

nescio, -īre, -īvī, -ītus, not know

neu, *see* **nēve**

neuter, -tra, -trum, neither (of two) 56

nēve (neu), *(conj.)* and not, nor **70**

nex, necis, *f.,* death

niger, -gra, -grum, black

nihil, nīl, *n.,* nothing *(indeclinable),* not 51

nimis (or **nimium**), *(adv.)* too, too much

nisi, *(conj.)* unless, except **35**

niveus, -a, -um, snow-white

nix, nivis, *f.,* snow

nōbilis, -e, noble 53, **2**

nōbilitās, -tātis, *f.,* nobility **51**

nōbīscum = cum nōbīs

noceō, -ēre, nocuī, nocitūrus, *(w. dat.)* do harm to 69

noctū, *(adv.)* by night **40**

nocturnus, -a, -um, of night, night

nōlō, nōlle, nōluī, —, not want, not wish, be unwilling **25**

nōmen, nōminis, *n.,* name 45, **2**

nōminātim, *(adv.)* by name

nōminō, (1) name

nōn, *(adv.)* not 1; **nōn iam,** no longer 43; **nōn nūllī (nōnnūllī), -ae, -a,** some 58; **nōn numquam,** sometimes 53; **nōn sōlum... sed etiam,** not only . . . but also **23**

nōndum, *(adv.)* not yet **17**

nōnus, -a, -um, ninth **10**

Nōreia, -ae, *f.,* Norēia, *a city of the Norici*

Nōricus, -a, -um, Norican, of the Norici

nōs, nostrum, we *(pl. of* **ego***)* 31

nōscō, -ere, nōvī, nōtus, learn; *(perf.)* have learned, know 30, **4**

noster, -tra, -trum, our 14

nōtus, -a, -um, known, familiar 42

novem, nine

novō, (1) renew

novus, -a, -um, new, strange 3, **4; novissimum agmem** or **novissimī,** the rear; *(w.* **rēs** *or* **imperia**) revolution

nox, noctis, noctium, *f.,* night

noxia, -ae, *f.,* crime

nūbēs, -is, nūbium, *f.,* cloud

nūdō, (1) strip, expose

nūgae, -ārum, *f.,* nonsense

nūllus, -a, -um, no, none 56; *(noun) m.,* no one; **nōn nūllī,** some

num, *(adv.) (introduces questions expecting negative answer); (conj.)* whether **25**

nūmen, nūminis, *n.,* divinity, will

numerus, -ī, *m.,* number 5, **7**

Numidae, -ārum, *m. pl.,* the Numidians

nummus, -i, *m.,* coin, money

numquam, *(adv.)* never 26

nunc, *(adv.)* now 4

nūntiō, (1) announce, report to 7, **6**

nūntius, -tī, *m.,* messenger, report 17

nūper, *(adv.)* recently

nūptiae, -ārum, *f. pl.,* wedding

nūtriō, -īre, -īvī, -ītus, nourish, foster

nūtus, -ūs, *m.,* nod

nux, nucis, *f.,* nut

nympha, -ae, *f.,* nymph

O

ō, *(interj.)* O!

ob, (prep. w. acc.) facing toward, on account of, for, because of 35

obiciō, -ere, obiēcī, obiectus, throw to or against, put in the way, oppose **58**

oblinō, -ere, oblēvī, oblitus, smear

obscūrus, -a, -um, dark

observō, (1) observe, watch

obses, obsidis, *m.,* hostage **37**

obsideō, -ēre, obsēdī, obsessus, besiege, blockade **30**

obsidiō, -ōnis, *f.,* siege

obstō, -āre, obstitī, obstātūrus, (1) prevent

obtemperō, (1) submit to

obtestor, (1) entreat, pray

obtineō, -ēre, obtinuī, obtentus, hold, obtain 37, **1**

occāsiō, -ōnis, *f.,* opportunity **44**

occāsus, -ūs, *m.,* setting; **occāsus sōlis,** sunset, west

occidō, -ere, occidī, occāsūrus, set

occīdō, -ere, occīdī, occīsus, kill, cut down **23**

occultō, (1) conceal

occultus, -a, -um, secret **60**

occupātiō, -ōnis, f., business

occupō, (1) seize hold of 8, **3**

occurrō, -ere, occurrī, occursūrus, run against, meet, occur **33**

Ōceanus, -ī, m., ocean

Octāviānus, -ī, m., Octāvian, *later called Augustus*

octāvus, -a, -um, eighth **11**

octō, eight

oculus, -ī, m., eye **13**

ōdī, ōsūrus (perf. translated as pres.) hate

offerō, offerre, obtulī, oblātus, offer **79**; mē offerō, rush against **79**

officium, -cī, n., duty 19, **1**

ōh, (interj.) oh!

ōlim, (adv.) formerly, once (upon a time) **31**

Olympia, -ae, f., Olympia, *a Greek city*; Olympicus, -a, -um, Olympic

Olympiēum, -ī, n., Olympiēum, *temple of the Olympian Jupiter*

ōmen, ōminis, n., omen, sign **19**

omittō, -ere, omīsī, omissus, let go, drop, disregard

omnīnō, (adv.) altogether, in all **52**

omnis, omne, all, every 47, **2**

onerārius, -a, -um, for freight; nāvis onerāria, transport ship

onerōsus, -a, -um, heavy

onus, oneris, n., weight **74**

opācus, -a, -um, gloomy

opera, -ae, f., work, effort **15**

opēs, see ops

opīniō, -ōnis, f., opinion, expectation; reputation **47**

oportet, -ēre, -tuit, it is fitting, it is necessary (w. acc. of person + inf.) **31**

oppidum, -ī, n., town **18**

opportūnus, -a, -um, opportune, convenient, advantageous **77**

opprimō, -ere, oppressī, oppressus, overcome, crush, surprise, oppress 57, **6**;

oppugnātiō, -ōnis, f., siege, method of attack

oppugnō, (1) attack, besiege **31**

ops, opis, f., aid; pl., wealth, resources **20**

optimē, (see bene)

optimus, (see bonus)

optō, (1) desire

opus, operis, n., work, labor 63, **5**

opus, n., (indeclinable) need; necessary

ōra, -ae, f., coast, edge

ōrāculum, -ī, n., oracle, prophesy

ōrātiō, -ōnis, f., speech **62**; ōrātiōnem habeō, deliver a speech

ōrātor, -ōris, m., orator

orbis, -is, -ium, m., world, circle, ring; *(esp. w. terrārum)* the world (i.e., *the circle of lands around the Mediterranean)*

Orcus, -ī, m., Orcus, *god of Hades*; Hades

ōrdō, ōrdinis, m., order, rank, row 45, platoon

oriēns, -entis, m., east

orīgo, originis, f., origin

orior, orīrī, ortus, rise, arise, begin, be descended from **19**

ōrnāmentum, -ī, n., jewel, costume

ōrnō, (1) adorn; ōrnātus, fitted out

ōrō, (1) beg, ask, pray (for), plead **24**

Orpheus, -ī, m., Orpheus (Orfūs), *a legendary musician*

ōs, ōris, n., mouth, face, expression **23**

os, ossis, n., bone

ōsculum, -ī, n., kiss

ostendō, -ere, ostendī, ostentus, show, stretch out before, present 58, **7**

ōtiōsus, -a, -um, leisurely, idle

ōtium, ōtī, n., leisure, peace **22**

Ovidius, -dī, m., Ovid

ōvum, -ī, n., egg

P

P., *abbreviation for* Pūblius

pābulor, (1), to graze, feed, forage

pābulum, -ī, n., food (for cattle), fodder

pācō, (1) pacify, subdue **63**

paedagōgus, -ī, m., an escort for children

paene, (adv.) almost **9**

Paestum, -ī, n., Paestum (Pĕs´ tum), *a town in southern Italy*

pāgus, -ī, m., district, canton **55**

Palātīnus (mōns), -ī, m., Palātium, -tī, n., the Palatine Hill; palace

palma, -ae, f., hand

palūs, palūdis, f., marsh, swamp **11**

pānis, -is, -ium, m., bread

pār, *(gen.)* **paris,** equal, equal to 47, **2;** *(noun)* n., pair

parcō, -ere, pepercī, parsūrus, spare, save **32**

parcus, -a, -um, sparing, economical; **parcē,** *(adv.)* sparingly

parēns, -entis, m. and f., parent

pāreō, -ēre, pāruī, pāritūrus, (appear), obey *(w. dat.)* **89**

pariō, -ere, peperī, partus, gain

Parnassius, -a, -um, Parnassian

parō, (1) get, get ready, prepare 3; **parātus, -a, um,** prepared, ready **42**

pars, partis, partium, f., part, direction, side 52, **4**

parum, *(indecl. n. and adv.),* little

parvulus, -a, -um, very small, little

parvus, -a, -um, small, little 2; *(comp.)* **minor, minus,** less; *(superl.)* **minimus, -a, -um,** least

passus, -ūs, m., step, pace *(about five feet);* **mīlle passūs,** mile **17**

passus, *perf. part. of* **patior**

pāstor, -ōris, m., herdsman, shepherd 46

patefaciō, -ere, -fēcī, -factus, open

patēns, *(gen.)* **patentis,** open

pateō, -ēre, patuī, —, stand open, extend **51**

pater, patris, m., father 48, **2; patrēs cōnscrīptī,** senators; **paterfamiliās, patrisfamiliās,** m., father of the household

paternus, -a, -um, of the father

patienter, *(adv.)* patiently

patientia, -ae, f., patience

patior, patī, passus, suffer, permit **54**

patria, -ae, f., fatherland, country 10

patriciī, -ōrum, m. patricians

patrius, -a, -um, of a father, ancestral

patrōnus, -ī, m., patron

patruus, -ī, m., uncle

paucī, -ae, -a, a few, few 27, **1**

paucitās, -tātis, f., small number

paulātim, *(adv.)* little by little; a few at a time **61**

paulisper, *(adv.)* for a little while **66**

paulō and **paulum,** *(adv.)* shortly, a little **41**

pauper, *(gen.)* **pauperis,** poor **2**

paupertās, -tātis, f., poverty, humble circumstances

paveō, -ēre, pāvī, —, fear

pavidus, -a, -um, trembling

pāx, pācis, f., peace 40, **3**

pectus, pectoris, n., breast, heart **29**

pecūnia, -ae, f., money 6

pecus, pecoris, n., cattle **85**

pedes, peditis, m., foot soldier; *pl.,* infantry **71**

pedester, -tris, -tre, (of) infantry; on foot

peditātus, -ūs, m., infantry

peior, *see* **malus**

pellis, -is, f., skin

pellō, -ere, pepulī, pulsus, beat, drive, defeat, drive out 48

Penātēs, -ium, m., the Penā´tēs, household gods

pendeō, -ēre, pependī, —, hang

pendō, -ere, pependī, pēnsus, hang, weigh, pay **33**

Pēnelopē, -ae, f., Penĕl´ope, wife of Ulysses

penetrō, (1) penetrate

per, *(prep. w. acc.)* through, by, during **33**

peragō, -ere, -ēgī, -āctus, complete

percipiō, -ere, -cēpī, -ceptus, feel, learn

percurrō, -currerre, -(cu)currī, -cursum, to run, move quickly over *or* through

percutiō, -ere, -cussī, -cussus, strike

perdiscō, -ere, -didicī, —, learn thoroughly

perdō, -ere, -didī, -ditus, lose, destroy, waste

perdūcō, -ere, -dūxī, -ductus, lead or bring through, extend, win over

pereō, -īre, -iī (-īvī), -itūrus, perish, be lost **21**

perferō, -ferre, -tulī, -lātus, carry (through), report, endure **69**

perficiō, -ere, -fēcī, -fectus, finish **66**

perfidia, -ae, f., faithlessness, treachery **25**

perfidus, -a, -um, treacherous

perfuga, -ae, m., deserter

perfugiō, -ere, -fūgī, —, flee

perīculōsus, -a, -um, dangerous

perīculum, -ī, n., danger 29, **9**

perītus, -a, -um, skilled, experienced **14**

perlegō, -ere, -lēgī, -lēctus, read through

permaneō, -ēre, -mānsī, -mānsūrus, remain

permittō, -ere, -mīsī, -missus, let go through, allow, permit, entrust *(w. dat.)* **34**

permoveō, -ēre, -mōvī, -mōtus, move (deeply), upset **37**

permūtātiō, -ōnis, f., exchange

perpaucī, -ae, -a, very few

perpetuus, -a, -um, constant **23**

perrumpō, -ere, -rūpī, -ruptus, break through

Persae, -ārum, m. pl., the Persians

persequor, -sequī, -secūtus, pursue, punish

persōna, -ae, *f.,* character

perspiciō, -ere, -spexī, -spectus, see (clearly), examine **67**

perstō, -āre, -stitī, -stātūrus, persist

persuādeō, -ēre, -suāsī, -suāsūrus, persuade **26**

perterreō, -ēre, -terruī, -territus, scare thoroughly, alarm **14**

pertināciter, *(adv.)* persistently

pertineō, -ēre, -tinuī, -tentūrus, extend (to), pertain to

pertrānseō, -īre, -īvī, -itūrus, pass through

perturbātiō, -ōnis, *f.,* confusion

perturbō, (1) disturb, throw into confusion **10**

perveniō, -īre, -vēnī, -ventūrus, (come through), arrive **60**

pēs, pedis, *m.,* foot **44, 7; pedibus,** on foot

pessimus, *see* **malus**

petō, -ere, petīvī, petītus, seek, ask, beg **36, 5**

Pharsālus, -ī, *f.,* Pharsā' lus, *a town in Thessaly*

Philippī, -ōrum, *m. pl.,* Philippi (Filĭp' ī), *a city in Macedonia*

Philippus, -ī, *m.,* Philip

philosophia, -ae, *f.,* philosophy

philosophus, -ī, *m.,* philosopher

Phrygia, -ae, *f.,* Phrygia (Frij´ia) *a country of Asia Minor*

pictūra, -ae, *f.,* picture

pila, -ae, *f.,* ball

pilula, -ae, *f.,* pill

pīlum, -ī, *n.,* spear (for throwing), javelin **57**

piscis, -is, *m.,* fish

piscor, (1) fish

pius, -a, -um, loyal, dutiful

placeō, -ēre, placuī, placitūrus, *(w. dat.)* be pleasing to, please **26; placet,** it pleases (him), *i.e.,* (he) decides, be decided

placidus, -a, -um, gentle

plācō, (1) please, calm

plānitiēs, -ēī, *f.,* plain **97**

plānus, -a, -um, level, flat **5**

Platō, -ōnis, *m.,* Plātō, *a Greek philosopher*

plēbs, plēbis, *f.,* common people, plebeians **31**

plēnus, -a, -um, full **24**

plērīque, -aeque, -aque, most **64**

plērumque, *(adv.)* usually **74**

plicō, (1) fold **39**

plūrēs, plūra, more *see* **multus**

plūrimum, *see* **multum**

plūrimus, *see* **multus**

plūs, *see* **multus, multum**

Plūtō, -ōnis, *m.,* Plū´tō, *god of the underworld*

poena, -ae, *f.,* punishment, penalty **8, 6; poenam dō,** pay the penalty

Poenī, -ōrum, *m. pl.,* the Carthaginians

poēta, -ae, *m.,* poet **26**

polliceor, pollicērī, pollicitus, promise **18**

pollicitātiō, -ōnis, *f.,* promise

Polyphēmus, -ī, *m.,* Polyphē´mus, *a man-eating giant*

pōmārium, -rī, *n.,* orchard

pompa, -ae, *f.,* parade, procession

Pompeiānus, -a, -um, at Pompeii

Pompeius, -peī, *m.,* Pompey

Pomptīnae palūdēs, Pŏn' tīne Marshes, *south of Rome*

pondus, ponderis, *n.,* weight

pōnō, -ere, posuī, positus, put, place **19, 5;** *(passive)* be situated, depend upon; **castra pōnō,** pitch camp

pōns, pontis, pontium, *m.,* bridge **54**

pontifex, -ficis, *m.,* priest **19**

Pontus, -ī, *m.,* Pontus *a country in Asia Minor*

pontus, -ī, *m.,* sea

poposcī, *see* **poscō**

populor, (1) destroy **55**

populus, -ī, *m.,* people **18, 1;** *pl.,* peoples, nations

porta, -ae, *f.,* gate *(of a city or a camp)* **32**

porticus, -ūs, *f.,* colonnade

portō, (1) carry **3**

portus, -ūs, *m.,* harbor, port **13**

poscō, -ere, poposcī, —, demand, call for **37**

possessiō, -ōnis, *f.,* possession

possum, posse, potuī, —, can, be able **42, 7; multum (plūs, plūrimum) possum,** be very (more, most) powerful

post, *(adv. and prep. w. acc.)* behind *(of place);* after *(of time)* **48;** later; **paulō post,** a little later

posteā, *(adv.)* afterwards **48;** later; **posteāquam,** *(conj.)* after **13**

posterus, -a, -um, following, next **14;** *m. pl.,* posterity, descendants; *(comp.)* **posterior, -ius,** later; *(superl.)* **postrēmus, -a, -um,** last

postquam, *(conj.)* after **67**

postrēmō, *(adv.)* finally

postrīdiē, *(adv.)* on the next day **46**

postulō, (1) demand **31**

potēns, *(gen.)* **potentis,** powerful **64**

potentia, -ae, *f.,* power

potestās, -tātis, *f.,* power **54, 2**

potior, potīrī, potītus, gain possession of *(w. gen. or abl.)*

potius, *(adv.)* rather

prae, *(prep. w. abl.)* in front of, before **67**

praeacūtus, -a, -um, pointed

praebeō, -ēre, -uī, -itus, hold forth, furnish, present, show **20**

praecēdō, -ere, -cessī, -cessūrus, go before, precede

praeceps, praecipitis, *(gen.)* headfirst, steep, straight (down) **50**

praeceptum, -ī, *n.,* rule, instruction

praecipiō, -ere, -cēpī, -ceptus, instruct

praecō, praecōnis, *m.,* announcer

praeda, -ae, *f.,* loot, booty **7**

praedicō, (1) announce, declare **84**

praedīcō, -ere, -dīxī, -dictus, predict

praedor, (1) loot

praedūcō, -ere, -dūxī, -ductus, extend

praefectus, -ī, *m.,* commander, prefect

praeficiō, -ere, -fēcī, -fectus, put in charge of **69**

praemittō, -ere, -mīsī, -missus, send ahead **67**

praemium, -mī, *n.,* reward **16**

praemūniō = mūniō

praenōscō, -ere, -nōvī, -nōtus, learn beforehand

praeparō, (1) prepare

praerumpō, -ere, -rūpī, -ruptus, break off

praescrībō, -ere, -scrīpsī, -scrīptus, direct

praescrīptum, -ī, *n.,* order

praesēns, *(gen.)* **praesentis,** present

praesentiō, -īre, -sēnsī, -sēnsus, foresee

praesertim, *(adv.)* especially **61**

praesidium, -dī, *n.,* guard, protection **28**

praestāns, *(gen.)* **praestantis,** outstanding

praestō, -āre, -stitī, -stitūrus, stand before, excel **34;** offer, perform, show; **praestat,** it is better

praesum, -esse, -fuī, -futūrus, be in charge of, be in command of **69**

praeter, *(prep. w. acc.)* besides, except, beyond **52**

praetereā, *(adv.)* besides **16**

praetereō, -īre, -iī, -itus, go by, pass

praeterquam, *(adv.)* other than

praetextus, -a, -um, (woven in front), bordered; **toga praetexta,** crimson-bordered toga

praetor, -ōris, *m.,* praetor *(an official),* judge

praevaleō, -ēre, -valuī, -valitūrus, prevail

prandium, -dī, *n.,* lunch

prātum, -ī, *n.,* meadow

prehendō, -ere, -hendī, -hēnsus, grasp, seize, catch **14**

premō, -ere, pressī, pressus, press, press hard **40, 6**

prēndō = prehendō

pretium, -tī, *n.,* price **21**

prex, precis, *f.,* prayer, entreaty **49**

prīdiē, *(adv.)* on the day before **19**

prīmō, *(adv.)* at first **60**

prīmum, *(adv.)* for the first time **63; quam prīmum,** as soon as possible

prīmus, -a, -um, first **34; in prīmīs,** especially

prīnceps, -cipis, first; *(noun) m.,* leader, chief **69, 5**

prīncipātus, -ūs, *m.,* first place, leadership **51**

prior, prius, *(comp.)* former, first **99**

prīstinus, -a, -um, former **70**

prius, *(adv.)* before, first; **priusquam (prius ... quam),** *(conj.)* before **31**

prīvātus, -a, -um, private **52;** *m.,* private citizen

prō, *(prep. w. abl.)* in front of, before, for, in behalf of **29**

probitās, -tātis, *f.,* honesty

probō, (1) test, prove, approve **7, 6**

prōcēdō, -ere, -cessī, -cessūrus, go forward, advance, proceed **30, 9**

procul, *(adv.)* at a distance, far off **74**

prōcumbō, -ere, -cubuī, -cubitūrus, lie down, sink down

prōcūrō, (1) take care of

prōcurrō, -ere, -currī, -cursūrus, run forward

prōdō, -ere, -didī, -ditus, give (forth), hand down, betray **81**

prōdūcō, -ere, -dūxī, -ductus, lead out **30**

proelium, -lī, *n.,* battle **27; proelium committō,** *begin battle* **27**

profectiō, -ōnis, *f.,* departure **51**

prōferō, prōferre, prōtulī, prōlātus, bring out, extend

professor, -ōris, *m.,* professor

prōficiō, -ere, -fēcī, -fectus, accomplish **99**

proficīscor, proficīscī, profectus, set out, start **18**

profugiō, -ere, -fūgī, -fugitūrus, flee

prōgeniēs, -iēī, *f.,* descendants

prōgnātus, -a, -um, descended

prōgredior, prōgredī, prōgressus, step forward, advance **22**

prohibeō, -ēre, -hibuī, -hibitus, prevent, keep from **58**

prōiciō, -ere, -iēcī, -iectus, throw, thrust (forward), abandon **34**

prōlabor, -ī, prōlāpsus, slip

prōmittō, -ere, -mīsī, -missus, let go; promise; **prōmissus,** long

prōmoveō, -ēre, -mōvī, -mōtus, move forward

prōmptus, -a, -um, ready

prōnūntiō, (1) announce, recite **23**

prōnus, -a, -um, flat (face down)

prope, *(adv.*and *prep. w. acc.)* near, nearby, almost **35**

prōpellō, -ere, -pulī, -pulsus, drive away, dislodge

properō, (1) hasten, hurry **27, 7**

propinquitās, -tātis, *f.,* nearness

propinquus, -a, -um, near **33;** *m.,* relative

propior, -ius, *(comp. adj.)* nearer; *(superl.)* **proximus, -a, -um,** next

propitius, -a, -um, favorable

prōpōnō, -ere, -posuī, -positus, put forward, offer, present **33**

proprius, -a, -um, (one's) own **63**

propter, *(prep. w. acc.)* because of, on account of **20**

proptereā, *(adv.)* on this account **50; proptereā quod,** because **50**

prōpugnō, (1) fight (on the offensive)

prōra, -ae, *f.,* prow

prōscrīptiō, -ōnis, *f.,* proscription, list of condemned

prōsequor, prōsequī, prōsecūtus, pursue, address

prōspectus, -ūs, *m.,* view

prōspiciō, -ere, -spexī, -spectus, look out for, see

prōsternō, -ere, -strāvī, -strātus, overthrow

prōsum, prōdesse, prōfuī, —, benefit, help

prōtegō, -ere, -tēxī, -tēctus, cover

prōtinus, *(adv.)* immediately **66**

prōvehō, -ere, -vexī, -vectus, carry forward

prōvideō, -ēre, -vīdī, -vīsus, foresee, see ahead **43**

prōvincia, -ae, *f.,* province **8**

proximē, *(adv.)* recently

proximus, -a, -um, nearest, next *(w. dat.)* **64**

prūdēns, *(gen.)* **prūdentis,** sensible **25**

prūdentia, -ae, *f.,* foresight, good sense

pūblicē, *(adv.)* publicly

pūblicus, -a, -um, *m.,* public **18**

Pūblius, -lī, *m.,* Pub´lius

puella, -ae, *f.,* girl **2**

puer, puerī, *m.,* boy **14**

puerīlis, -e, boyish, childish; **puerīliter,** *(adv.)* childishly

pueritia, -ae, *f.,* childhood, boyhood

pugna, -ae, *f.,* battle, fight **8**

pugnō, (1) fight **8**

pulcher, -chra, -chrum, beautiful **20**

pulchritūdō, -dinis, *f.,* beauty

pulsō, (1) dash against

pulsus, *perf. part. of* pellō

Pūnicus, -a, -um, Punic, Carthaginian

pūniō, -īre, -īvī, -ītus, punish

pūpa, -ae, *f.,* doll, little girl

puppis, -is, *f.,* stern

pūrgō, (1) cleanse

purpurātus, -a, -um, purple

putō, (1) think, suppose **59, 6**

Pyrēnaeī montēs, Pyrenees Mountains

Pyrrhus, -ī, *m.,* Pyr´rhus, *king of Epirus*

Q

Q., *abbreviation for* **Quīntus**

quā, *(adv.)* where **52**

quadringentī, -ae, -a, four hundred

quaerō, -ere, quaesīvī, quaesītus, seek (from), inquire (of) **22**

quaestiō, -ōnis, *f.,* investigation

quaestor, -ōris, *m.,* quaestor, *a Roman official* **26**

quaestus, -ūs, *m.,* gain

quālis, -e, what kind of, what, such as

quam, *(conj.)* than **61;** *(adv. and conj.)* how, as **46;** *(adv. w. superl.)* as . . . as possible **63;** *(w. comp.)* than; **quam prīmum,** as soon as possible **17**

quamquam, *(conj.)* although **25**

quandō, *(conj.)* when

quantus, -a, -um, how great, how much, what, as (great *or* much as) **19**

quārē, *(interrog. and rel. adv.)* why

quārtus, -a, -um, fourth **11; quārtus decimus,** fourteenth

quasi, *(adv. and conj.)* as if, like, as it were **39**

quattuor, four

-que, *(conj., joined to second word),* and 26

quī, quae, quod, *(rel. pron.)* who, which, what, that 36; *(interrog. adj.)* what, which 38; **quī, qua, quod,** *(indef. adj.)* any

quia, *(conj.)* because

quīcumque, quaecumque, quodcumque, whoever, whatever 82

quid?, *(adv.)* why?

quīdam, quaedam, quiddam and *(adj.)* **quoddam,** a certain one *or* thing 20; *(adj.)* certain, some, a, one 20

quidem, *(adv.) (follows emphasized word)* at least, to be sure 16; **nē... quidem,** not even 16

quidnam, *see* **quis?**

quiēs, quiētis, *f.,* rest, sleep, quiet 15

quiēsco, -ere, quiēvī, quiētus, sleep, rest, be quiet

quiētus, -a, -um, quiet 18; **quiētē,** *(adv.)* quietly

quīn, *(conj.)* that; **quīn etiam,** moreover

Quīnctīlis, -e, (of) July

quīndecim, fifteen

quīngentī, -ae, -a, five hundred

quīnquāgintā, fifty

quīnque, five

Quīntiliānus, -ī, *m.,* Quintilian, *a professor of rhetoric*

quīntus, -a, -um, fifth 9

Quirīnālis (mōns), -is, *m.,* Quir´īnal Hill

quis? quid?, *(interrog, pron.)* who? what? 18, 38; *(indef. pron.)* anyone, anything; *(emphatic)* **quisnam? quidnam?** who/what in the world?

quisquam, quicquam, anyone, anything, any 36; **neque quisquam,** not a single one

quisque, quidque, each one, each thing, each 36

quō, *(adv.)* where, to which; **quō modō,** how (in what manner)

quō, *(conj.)* in order that; **quō minus (quōminus),** that not

quoad, *(conj.)* as long as

quod, *(conj.)* because, since 4; **quod sī,** but if

quondam, *(adv.)* once (upon a time) 53

quoniam, *(conj.)* since, because 34

quoque, *(adv.)* too *(follows the word it emphasizes)* 21

quot, *(indeclinable adj.)* how many; as (many as) 24

quotannīs, *(adv.)* every year

quotiēns, *(adv.)* as often as, how often

R

radiō, (1) shine

rādīx, -dīcis, *f.,* root

raeda, -ae, *f.,* carriage, bus

rāmulus, -ī, *m.,* branch

rāmus, -ī, *m.,* branch

rāna, -ae, *f.,* frog

rapiditās, -tātis, *f.,* swiftness

rapiō, -ere, rapuī, raptus, carry off, steal 61, 7

rārus, -a, -um, rare

ratiō, -ōnis, *f.,* account, reason 70; manner 43

ratis, -is, *f.,* raft

rebelliō, -ōnis, *f.,* rebellion

recēdō, -ere, recessī, recessūrus, withdraw

recēns, *(gen.)* **recentis,** new, recent 60

recēnseō, -ēre, recēnsuī, recēnsus, count again, review

recingō, -ere, recīnxī, recīnctus, loosen

recipiō, -ere, recēpī, receptus, take back, recover 32; receive; **mē recipiō,** withdraw, recover, retire 32

recitō, (1) recite, read aloud

reclīnō, (1) bend back; passive, lean

rēctus, *(see* **regō***);* **rēctē,** *(adv.)* rightly 13

recuperō, (1) get back, recover 97

recursō, (1) run back and forth

recūsō, (1) refuse

reddō, -ere, reddidī, redditus, give back, restore 68

redeō, -īre, rediī, reditūrus, go back, return 20

redigō, -ere, redēgī, redāctus, drive back, reduce 32

redimō, -ere, redēmī, redēmptus, buy back, ransom

redintegrō, (1) renew

reditus, -ūs, *m.,* return

redūcō, -ere, redūxī, reductus, lead back 25

referō, referre, rettulī, relātus, bring or carry back, report, reproduce 24; **pedem referō,** withdraw; **grātiam referō,** show gratitude

reficiō, -ere, refēcī, refectus, repair, refresh, restore 15

rēgia, -ae, *f.,* palace

rēgīna, -ae, *f.,* queen 5

regiō, -ōnis, *f.,* region 62

rēgnō, (1) reign, rule

rēgnum, -ī, *n.,* kingdom, realm 44

regō, -ere, rēxī, rēctus, rule, guide 20; **rēctus,** straight

reiciō, -ere, reiēcī, reiectus, drive back, reject

relābor, relābī, relāpsus, slip back

relanguēscō, -ere, -languī, —, become weak

religiō, -ōnis, *f.,* religion, superstition **89**

relinquō, -ere, relīquī, relictus, leave (behind), abandon 41

reliquus, -a, -um, remaining, rest (of) 26; (*w.* **tempus**) the future

remaneō, -ēre, remānsī, remānsūrus, stay behind, remain 34

remedium, -dī, *n.,* remedy

rēmigō, -āre, —, —, row

remigrō, (1) go back

remissiō, -ōnis, *f.,* forgiveness

remittō, -ere, remīsī, remissus, relax, send back, (let back) 52; **remissus,** mild

removeō, -ēre, remōvī, remōtus, remove, move back 32; **remōtus,** remote

rēmus, -ī, *m.,* oar 43

Rēmī, -ōrum, *m. pl.,* the Rēmans, *a N. Gallic tribe*

renūntiō, (1) report **40**

reparō, (1) restore

repellō, -ere, reppulī, repulsus, drive back, repulse 62

repente, (*adv.*) suddenly **88**

repentīnus, -a, -um, sudden **55**

reperiō, -īre, repperī, repertus, find **43**

repetō, -ere, -īvī, -ītus, seek back

reportō, (1) carry or bring back

reprimō, -ere, repressī, repressus, stop

repudiō, (1) divorce

repugnō, (1) oppose

requiēs, -ētis, *f.,* rest

requiēscō, -ere, -ēvī, -ētus, rest

requīrō, -ere, requīsīvī, requīsītus, miss, seek

rēs, reī, *f.,* thing, matter, affair, situation, circumstance 69; **rēs pūblica,** public affairs, government; **novae rēs, novārum rerum,** *f. pl.,* revolution; **rēs frūmentāria, reī frūmentāriae,** *f.,* grain supply **57**; **rēs mīlitāris,** military affairs, art of war; **rēs gestae,** deeds, history

rescindō, -ere, rescidī, rescissus, cut down

reservō, (1) reserve

resideō, -ēre, resēdī, —, remain

resistō, -ere, restitī, —, stand against; resist

resolvō, -ere, resolvī, resolūtus, loosen

respiciō, -ere, respexī, respectus, look back, consider

respondeō, -ēre, respondī, respōnsus, answer, reply 49, **2**; **respōnsum, -ī,** *n.,* answer

respuō, -ere, respuī, —, reject

restituō, -ere, restituī, restitūtus, restore **34**

restō, -āre, restitī, —, remain

resūmō, -ere, resūmpsī, resūmptus, take up again, resume

resurgō = surgō

retineō, -ēre, retinuī, retentus, hold back, keep **30**

retrahō, -ere, retrāxī, retrāctus, drag back

retrō, (*adv.*) back

rettulī, *see* **referō**

reus, -ī, *m.,* defendant

reverentia, -ae, *f.,* respect

revereor, reverērī, reveritus, respect

revertō, -ere, revertī, reversūrus, (*sometimes deponent*) turn back, return **26**

revīsō, -ere, —, —, revisit

revocō, (1) recall, call back

rēx, rēgis, *m.,* king **44**

Rhēnus, -ī, *m.,* the Rhine river

rhētor, -ōris, *m.,* rhetorician

Rhodanus, -ī, *m.,* Rhone river

rideō, -ēre, rīsī, rīsus, laugh (at) **14**

rīdiculus, -a, -um, funny, ridiculous

rigor, -ōris, *m.,* stiffness

rīpa, -ae, *f.,* bank (of a river)

rōborō, (1) strengthen

rogitō, (1) keep on asking

rogō, (1) ask, ask for 42, **2**

Rōma, -ae, *f.,* Rome

Rōmānus, -a, -um, (*adj.*) Roman; **Rōmānus, -ī,** *m.,* a Roman

rosa, -ae, *f.,* rose

rostrum, -ī, *n.,* prow (of a ship); beak

rotundus, -a, -um, round

rudis, -e, untrained, ignorant

ruīna, -ae, *f.,* downfall, collapse; *pl.* ruins

rūmor, -ōris, *m.,* rumor **63**

rumpō, -ere, rūpī, ruptus, break **13**

rūpēs, -is, *f.,* cliff, rock

rūrsus, (*adv.*) again **38**

rūsticus, -a, -um, rustic

S

Sabīnus, -a, -um, Sabine; **Sabīna, -ae,** *f.,* a Sabine woman; *pl.,* the Sābīnes, a people of Italy

saccus, -ī, *m.,* sack, bag

sacer, sacra, sacrum, sacred **14**

sacerdōs, -ōtis, *m.,* or *f.,* priest, priestess

sacrificium, -cī, *n.,* sacrifice

sacrificō, (1) sacrifice, sacrifice to (+ *dat.*)

saeculum (saeclum), -ī, *n.,* age

saepe, *(adv.)* often **14; saepius,** more often; **saepissime,** most often

saevitia, -ae, *f.,* fierceness

saevus, -a, -um, cruel

sagitta, -ae, *f.,* arrow **81**

sagittārius, -rī, *m.,* bowman

Saliī, -ōrum, *m. pl.,* the Sāliī or "Jumpers," *priests of Mars*

saliō, -īre, saluī, saltūrus, jump, beat

saltō, (1) dance

salūbris, -e, wholesome, healthy

salūs, salūtis, *f.,* health, safety **40, 2**

salūtātor, -ōris, *m.,* greeter, visitor

salūtō, (1) greet

salvē, *sing.,* **salvēte,** *pl.,* (good) health to you, hail, hello

sānctus, -a, -um, sacred

sanguis, sanguinis, *m.,* blood **34**

sānitās, -tātis, *f.,* sanity

sānus, -a, -um, sound, sane

sapiēns, *(gen.)* **sapientis,** wise **20; sapienter,** wisely

sapientia, -ae, *f.,* wisdom

satis, *(adv.* and *indeclinable adj.)* enough, rather **14**

satisfaciō, -ere, -fēcī, -factus, satisfy

Sāturnālia, -ōrum, *n. pl.,* Saturnalia *a winter festival in honor of the god Saturn*

Sāturnus, -ī, *m.,* the god Saturn

saucius, -a, -um, wounded, hurt

saxum, -ī, *n.,* rock, stone **20**

scaena, -ae, *f.,* stage

scaenicus, -a, -um, of the theater; *(w.* **lūdī)** stage plays

scelus, sceleris, *n.,* crime

scēptrum, -ī, *n.,* scepter

schola, -ae, *f.,* school

scholasticus, -a, -um, scholastic; *m.,* student

scientia, -ae, *f.,* knowledge, science

sciō, -īre, scīvī, scītus, know **59, 5**

Scīpiō, -ōnis, *m.,* Scipio (Sip´io)

scrība, -ae, *m.,* secretary

scrībō, -ere, scrīpsī, scrīptus, write **26, 4**

sculpō, -ere, sculpsī, sculptus, carve

scūtum, -ī, *n.,* shield **24**

Scythae, -ārum, *m. pl.,* the Scythians (Síth´ ians), *people beyond the Black Sea*

sē, *acc.* and *abl. of* **suī**

sēcēdō, -ere, sēcessī, sēcessūrus, secede, withdraw

sēcrētō, *(adv.)* in private, secretly

sēcum = cum sē

secundus, -a, -um, second **59**

sēcūrus, -a, -um, free of care, safe

sed, *(conj.)* but **1**

sedeō, -ēre, sēdī, sessūrus, sit **54**

sēdēs, -is, *f.,* abode, home

sēdō, (1) quiet

sēductus, -a, -um, separated

sella, -ae, *f.,* chair, seat, stool

semel, *(adv.)* once

sēmibarbarus, -a, -um, half-barbarian

semita, -ae, *f.,* path, footpath

semper, *(adv.)* always **9, 7**

senātor, -ōris, *m.,* senator

senātus, -ūs, *m.,* senate **68**

senectūs, -tūtis, *f.,* old age

senex, senis, *m.,* old man **27;** *(adj.)* old **27;** *(comp.)* senior **27**

sententia, -ae, *f.,* feeling, opinion, motto **25, 6**

sentiō, -īre, sēnsī, sēnsus, feel, realize **60, 6**

sēparō, (1) separate

sepeliō, -īre, -īvī, sepultus, bury

septem, seven

septentriōnēs, -um, *m. pl.,* seven plow-oxen *(the seven stars of the constellation Great Bear or Big Dipper), north*

septimus, -a, -um, seventh **11**

sepulchrum, -ī, *n.,* tomb

sepultūra, -ae, *f.,* burial

Sēquana, -ae, *m.,* the Seine river

Sēquanus, -a, -um, Sequānian; *m. pl.,* the Sequanians

sequor, sequī, secūtus, follow, pursue, seek **27**

serēnō, (1) clear up

serēnus, -a, -um, quiet

sērius, *(comp. adv.)* later

sērius, -a, -um, *(adj.)* serious, grave

sermō, -ōnis, *m.,* talk, conversation

serō, -ere, sēvī, satus, plant, sow

serpēns, -entis, *f.,* snake

serva, -ae, *f.,* slave

servīlis, -e, of a slave

servitūs, -tūtis, *f.,* slavery **61**

servō, (1) save, guard, preserve 8, **2**

servus, -ī, *m.;* **serva, -ae,** *f.,* slave 4, **1**

sēsē, -sē *(acc. and abl. of* **suī)**

seu, *(see* **sīve)**

sevēritās, -tātis, *f.,* severity

sevērus, -a, -um, stern; **sevērē,** *(adv.)* severely

sex, six; **sexāgintā,** sixty

Sextīlis, -e, August

sextus, -a, -um, sixth **11**

sī, *(conj.)* if 59

Sibylla, -ae, *f.,* the Sibyl, *a prophetess*

sīc, yes, thus, so 3

siccō, (1) dry up

Sicilia, -ae, *f.,* Sicily (Sis´ily)

sīcut (sīcutī), *(adv.)* just as, as if, as it were **94**

sīdus, sīderis, *n.,* star

signifer, -ferī, *m.,* standard bearer

significātiō, -ōnis, *f.,* signal

significō, (1) indicate, mean **21**

signum, -ī, *n.,* sign, standard, signal 16, **8**

silentium, -ī, *n.,* silence **10**

silva, -ae, *f.,* forest, woods 1

similis, -e, like, similar (to) *(w. dat.)* 63, **7**

simul, *(adv.)* at the same time **43; simul atque (ac)** as soon as **43**

simulācrum, -ī, *n.,* figure, image

simulō, (1) pretend **39**

sine, *(prep. w. abl.)* without 30

singillātim, *(adv.)* one by one, individually

singulāris, -e, one by one, remarkable

singulī, -ae, -a, *(always pl.)* one at a time, one by one 13

sinister, -tra, -trum, left **57**

sinō, -ere, sīvī, situs, allow **29**

sīve (seu), *(conj.)* or if **55; sīve (seu)... sīve (seu),** whether . . . or, either . . . or **55**

socius, -cī, *m.,* ally, comrade, accomplice **12**

sōl, sōlis, *m.,* sun 63

sōlācium, -cī, *n.,* comfort

solea, -ae, *f.,* sandal, shoe

soleō, -ēre, solitus, *(semideponent)* be used to, be accustomed

solidus, -a, -um, solid

sōlitūdō, -dinis, *f.,* wilderness

sollicitō, (1) stir up **63**

sōlus, -a, -um, alone 56; **sōlum** *(adv.)* only

solvō, -ere, solvī, solūtus, loosen, break, free 59; set sail; *(w.* **poenam)** pay

somnus, -ī, *m.,* sleep **14**

sonus, -ī, *m.,* sound

sopor, -ōris, *m.,* sleep

sordidus, -a, -um, dirty, mean, disreputable **12**

soror, -ōris, *f.,* sister 54, **2**

sors, sortis, *f.,* lot, prophecy

spargō, -ere, sparsī, sparsus, scatter, sprinkle

Sparta, -ae, *f.,* Sparta, a Greek city

Spartacus, -ī, *m.,* Spartacus, *leader in a revolt of gladiators*

Spartānus, -ī, *m.,* a Spartan

spatium, -tī, *n.,* space, time **43**

speciēs, speciēī, *f.,* appearance **69**

spectāculum, -ī, *n.,* spectacle, show

spectō, (1) look (at), watch 3, **7**

speculātor, -ōris, *m.,* spy

spērō, (1) hope for, hope that 52, **9**

spēs, speī, *f.,* hope **69**

spīna, -ae, *f.,* thorn

spīrō, (1) breathe **52**

spoliō, (1) rob

spondeo, -ēre, spopondi, spōnsus, promise, pledge, engage **19**

spōnsa, -ae, *f.,* a betrothed woman

spōnsus, -i, *m.,* a betrothed man

sponte, *(w.* **suā)** of his/her/their own accord, by his/her/their own influence, voluntarily **54**

sportula, -ae, *f.,* small gift basket

squālēns, *(gen.)* **squālentis,** foul

st, *(interj.)* hush!

stabulum, -ī, *n.,* stable

statim, *(adv.)* at once, immediately **17**

statiō, -ōnis, *f.,* outpost, guard, picket

statua, -ae, *f.,* statue

statuō, -ere, statuī, statūtus, establish, determine, arrange **61**

statūra, -ae, *f.,* stature

stēlla, -ae, *f.,* star

stetī, *see* **stō**

stilus, -ī, *m.,* stylus *instrument used in writing on wax tablets*

stīpendiārius, -a, -um, tributary

stīpendium, -dī, *n.,* pay, tribute **30**

stō, stāre, stetī, statūrus, stand, stand up **41, 5**

stringō, -ere, strīnxī, strictus, draw

studeō, -ēre, studuī, —, be eager (for), study **19**

studiōsus, -a, -um, eager, studious; **studiōsē,** *(adv.)* eagerly

studium, -dī, *n.,* eagerness, interest, studies **22, 9**

stultitia, -ae, *f.,* stupidity, folly **29**

stultus, -a, -um, foolish

stupeō, -ēre, -uī, —, be amazed

suādeō, -ēre, suāsī, suāsūrus, urge

suāvis, -e, sweet

suāvitās, -tātis, *f.,* sweetness

sub, *(prep. w. acc. with verbs of motion; w. abl. with verbs of rest or position)* under, close up to **33**

subdūcō, -ere, -dūxī, -ductus, lead up; draw up

subeō, -īre, -iī, -itūrus, go under, enter, come up, undergo

subiciō, -ere, -iēcī, -iectus, throw from below, subject, conquer; **subiectus,** lying beneath

subigō, -ere, -ēgī, -āctus, force, subdue

subitō, *(adv.)* suddenly **19**

sublātus, *perf. part. of* **tollō**

sublevō, (1) lighten, raise **43;** *(w. reflex.)* rise **43**

submergō, -ere, -mersī, -mersus, submerge, plunge

subministrō, (1) furnish

submittō, -ere, -mīsī, -missus, let down, furnish **35**

submoveō, -ēre, -mōvī, -mōtus, drive back

subruō, -ere, -ruī, -rutus, undermine

subsequor, subsequī, subsecūtus, follow (closely) **67**

subsidium, -dī, *n.,* aid, military reserves

subterrāneus, -a, -um, subterranean

subveniō, -īre, -vēnī, -ventūrus, come to help

succēdō, -ere, -cessī, -cessūrus, come up, succeed (w. dat.) **27**

successus, -ūs, *m.,* success

succurrō, -ere, -currī, -cursūrus, run to help

Suēbī, -ōrum, *m. pl.,* the Suē´ bans, *or* Suē´ bī

sufficiō, -ere, -fēcī, -fectus, suffice

suffrāgium, -gī, *n.,* vote

suī, *(reflex. pron.)* of himself, herself, itself, themselves **65**

sum, esse, fuī, futūrus, be **15**

summa, -ae, *f.,* sum; leadership; **summa imperī,** supreme command

summus, -a, -um, highest, top of, greatest **64; summum, -ī,** *n.,* top

sūmō, -ere, sūmpsī, sūmptus, take **65**

sūmptuōsus, -a, -um, extravagant; **sūmptuōsē,** *(adv.)* extravagantly

super, *(prep. w. acc.)* over, above **67**

superbia, -ae, *f.,* pride, arrogance **34**

superbus, -a, -um, proud, arrogant **34; superbē,** *(adv.)* arrogantly

superior, -ius, higher, upper, superior; previous

superō, (1) excel, overcome, surpass, conquer, beat, defeat **49**

supersum, -esse, -fuī, -futūrus, be left (over), survive **67**

superus, -a, -um, upper; *m. pl.,* gods (above)

supplex, *(gen.)* **supplicis,** begging

supplicātiō, -ōnis, *f.,* thanksgiving

supplicium, -cī, *n.,* punishment **53**

suprā, *(adv. and prep. w. acc.)* above **46**

suprēmus, -a, -um, highest, last

surgō, -ere, surrēxī, surrēctūrus, rise **15**

suscipiō, -ere, -cēpī, -ceptus, undertake, take up, start **33**

suspendō, -ere, -pendī, -pēnsus, hang; **suspēnsus,** in suspense

suspīciō, -ōnis, *f.,* suspicion

suspicor, (1) suspect **49**

sustineō, -ēre, -tinuī, -tentus, hold up, maintain, endure **36;** check

sustulī, *see* **tollō**

suus, -a, -um, *(reflex.)* his, her, its, their; his own, her own, its own, their own **65**

Syrācūsae, -ārum, *f. pl.,* Syracuse, *a city in Sicily*

T

T., *abbreviation for* **Titus**

taberna, -ae, *f.,* shop, tavern

tablīnum, -ī, *n.,* study, den

tabula, -ae, *f.,* table, tablet (of the law); writing tablet

taceō, -ēre, tacuī, tacitus, be silent; **tacitus,** silent

taciturnitās, -tātis, *f.,* silence

tālis, -e, such

tam, *(adv.)* so, such *(with adjectives and adverbs)* **14**

tamen, *(adv.)* nevertheless **34**

tamquam, *(adv.)* as if

tandem, *(adv.)* at last, finally **17**

tangō, -ere, tetigī, tāctus, touch **53**

tantulus, -a, -um, so small

tantum, *(adv.)* only

tantus, -a, -um, so great, so much, so large, such **14**

tardō, (1) slow up **72**

tardus, -a, -um, late, slow **24, 6; tardē,** slowly

Tarentīnī, -ōrum, *m. pl.,* the people of Tarentum

Tarquinius, -nī, *m.,* Tarquin' ius, Tarquin

Tartarus, -ī, *m.* or **Tartara, -ōrum,** *n. pl.,* Hades

taurus, -ī, *m.,* bull

tēctum, -ī, *n.,* roof, house

tēcum = cum tē

tegimentum, -ī, *n.,* cover

tegō, -ere, tēxī, tēctus, cover **39**

Tēlemachus, -ī, *m.,* Telĕm´achus

tellus, -ūris, *f.,* earth

tēlum, -ī, *n.,* weapon **53**

temere, *(adv.,)* rashly, without reason **80**

temeritās, -tātis, *f.,* rashness

temperātus, -a, -um, temperate

tempestās, -tātis, *f.,* weather, storm **12**

templum, -ī, *n.,* temple **20**

temptō, (1) test, try, attempt, tempt **62**

tempus, -oris, *n.,* time **45, 7**

tenāx, *(gen.)* **tenācis,** tenacious

tendō, -ere, tetendī, tentus, stretch **47**

tenebrae, -ārum, *f. pl.,* darkness

teneō, -ēre, tenuī, tentus, hold, keep **12, 1;**
  memoriā teneō, remember

tenuō, (1) make thin

tepeō, -ēre, —, —, be warm

ter, *(adv.)* three times

tergum, -ī, *n.,* back

terminus, -ī, *m.,* end, boundary **21**

ternī, -ae, -a, three at a time

terra, -ae, *f.,* earth, land **2**

terreō, -ēre, terruī, territus, scare, frighten **10, 8**

terribilis, -e, frightful

terror, -ōris, *m.,* terror

tertius, -a, -um, third **42**

testāmentum, -ī, *n.,* will

testimōnium, -nī, *n.,* testimony, proof

testis, -is, *m.,* witness

testūdō, -dinis, *f.,* shed, turtle, testudo

Teutonī, -ōrum, *m. pl.,* the Teutons

texō, -ere, texuī, textus, weave

theātrum, -ī, *n.,* theater, amphitheater

Thēbae, -ārum, *f. pl.,* Thebes, *a Greek city*

thermae, -ārum, *f. pl.,* hot baths

Thessalia, -ae, *f.,* Thessaly, *part of Greece*

Thrācia, -ae, *f.,* Thrace, *a country north of Greece*

Thrāx, -ācis, *m.,* a Thracian

thronus, -ī, *m.,* throne

Ti., *abbreviation for* **Tiberius**

Tiberis, -is, *m.,* the Tī´ber (a river in Italy)

Tiberius, -rī, *m.,* Tībē´rius

Tigurīnus, -ī, *m.,* Tigurīnus, *a Helvetian district*;
  pl., the Tigurīnī

timeō, -ēre, timuī, —, fear, be afraid of **51, 1**

timidus, -a, -um, shy **43; timidē,** *(adv.)* timidly

timor, -ōris, *m.,* fear **37**

Tīrō, -ōnis, *m.,* Tī´rō, *Cicero's freedman*

titulus, -ī, *m.,* title, sign

toga, -ae, *f.,* toga (cloak) **1**

tolerābilis, -e, endurable

tollō, -ere, sustulī, sublātus, raise, carry, remove,
  destroy **43**

tormentum, -ī, *n.,* torture; artillery

torqueō, -ēre, torsī, tortūs, twist, turn, torture

torreō, -ēre, torruī, tostus, roast, scorch

tot, *(indeclinable adj.)* so many **15**

totidem, *(indeclinable adj.)* just as many, the same
  number **64**

totiēns, *(adv.)* as *or* so often

tōtus, -a, -um, whole, entire **56**

trabs, trabis, *f.,* beam

trādō, -ere, -didī, -ditus, give/hand over, surrender,
  relate **66**

trādūcō, -ere, -dūxī, -ductus, lead across **41**

trāgula, -ae, *f.,* javelin

trahō, -ere, trāxī, trāctus, draw, drag **24**

trāiciō, -ere, -iēcī, -iectus, strike through

trānō, (1) swim across

tranquillitās, -tātis, *f.,* calm

tranquillus, -a, -um, peaceful

trāns, *(prep. w. acc.)* across **39**

trānscendō, -ere, -cendī, —, board, climb over

trānscurrō, -ere, -currī, -cursūrus, traverse

trānseō, -īre, -iī, -itūrus, cross, pass, go **52**

trānsferō, trānsferre, trānstulī, trānslātus,
carry over

trānsfīgō, -ere, -fīxī, -fīxus, pierce through

trānsfodiō, -ere, -fōdī, -fossus, pierce through

trānsiliō, -īre, -siluī, —, jump across

trānsportō, (1) transport, carry across **41**

trānsversus, -a, -um, cross

trecentī, -ae, -a, three hundred

tremor, -ōris, _m.,_ shaking

trēs, tria, three **66**

tribūnus, -ī, _m.,_ tribune, a Roman official **24;**
tribūnus mīlitum, junior officer

tribuō, -ere, tribuī, tribūtus, grant **65**

tribūtum, -ī, _n.,_ tax, tribute

trīclīnium, -nī, _n.,_ dining room

trīduum, -ī, _n.,_ three days **58**

trīgintā, thirty

triplex, _(gen.)_ triplicis, threefold, triple

trīstis, -e, sad, severe **34**

trīstitia, -ae, _f.,_ sadness

triumphō, (1) triumph

triumphus, -ī, _m.,_ triumph

Trōia, -ae, _f.,_ Troy

Trōiānus, -a, -um, _(adj.)_ Trojan; **Trōiānus, -i, _m.,_**
a Trojan

tū, tuī, you, of you _(sing.)_ **31**

tuba, -ae, _f.,_ trumpet **36**

tueor, tuērī, tūtus, look, guard **88**

tulī, _see_ ferō

tum, _(adv.)_ then, next **6**

tumultus, -ūs, _m.,_ uproar **67**

tunc, _(adv.)_ then

tunica, -ae, _f.,_ tunic

turbō, (1) _throw into disorder, confuse_

turbulentus, -a, -um, muddy

turma, -ae, _f.,_ troop (of cavalry)

turpis, -e, disgraceful, ugly **61**

turpitūdō, -dinis, _f.,_ disgrace

turris, -is, _f.,_ tower **74**

Tusculānī, -ōrum, _m. pl.,_ the Tusculans, _people of_
Tusculum, a town in Italy

tūtus, -a, -um, safe, guarded **31**

tuus, -a, -um, your, yours _(referring to one person)_ **9**

tyrannus, -ī, _m.,_ tyrant

U

ubi, _(adv.)_ where? 4; when? 18, **5**

ubicumque, _(adv.)_ wherever

ulcīscor, ulcīscī, ultus, avenge

Ulixēs, -is, _m.,_ Ūlys´sēs

ūllus, -a, -um, any **56**

ulterior, ulterius, farther **64**

ultimus, -a, -um, farthest, last **43**

ultrā, _(prep. w. acc.)_ beyond

ultrīx, _(gen.)_ ultrīcis, avenging

ultrō, _(adv.)_ voluntarily, actually **82**

ultus, _part. of_ ulcīscor

umbra, -ae, _f.,_ shade, shadow

umquam, _(adv.)_ ever, at any time **35**

ūnā, _(adv.)_ at the same time, **ūnā cum,** along
with **52**

ūnanimus, -a, -um, of one mind, sympathetic

unda, -ae, _f.,_ wave **6**

unde, _(adv.)_ from which (place), by which **47**

undique, _(adv.)_ from _or_ on all sides **40**

unguentum, -ī, _n.,_ ointment, salve

ūniversus, -a, -um, all (together) **81**

ūnus, -a, -um, one **56**

Uranus, -ī, _m.,_ Ū´ranus god of the Sky

urbs, urbis, urbium, _f.,_ city **60**

urgeō, urgēre, ursī, —, press hard

urna, -ae, _f.,_ urn

ūrō, -ere, ussī, ustus, burn

usque, _(adv.)_ up to, continuously, still **77**

ūsus, -ūs, _m.,_ use, custom

ut, _(conj.)_ (in order) that, to, so that **11;** as, when;
ut... nōn, that . . . not _(in result clauses)_

uter, -ra, -rum, which (of two)

uterque, utraque, utrumque, each (of two)

utī = ut, 52

ūtilis, -e, useful **61, 8**

ūtilitās, -tātis, _f.,_ usefulness

ūtor, ūtī, ūsus, use, make use of _(w. abl.)_ **41;** enjoy

utrimque, _(adv.)_ on both sides

utrum... an, _(conj.)_ whether... or

uxor, -ōris, _f.,_ wife **47**

V

vacō, (1) be uninhabited, have leisure

vacuus, -a, -um, empty, free

vādō, -ere, —, —, go

vadum, -ī, *n.,* ford, shallow place **53**

vagor, (1) wander **51**

valeō, -ēre, valuī, valitūrus, be well, be strong **22, 8;** *(impv.)* **valē** *(sing.),* **valēte** *(pl.),* farewell, good-bye

valētūdō, -dinis, *f.,* health; illness

vallēs, -is, -ium, *f.,* valley

vāllum, -ī, *n.,* wall **58**

vānus, -a, -um, empty, false

varius, -a, -um, changing, various **22**

vās, vāsis, *(pl.)* **vāsa, -ōrum,** *n.,* kettle, pot, vessel

vāstō, (1) destroy, ruin

vāstus, -a, -um, huge

vehemēns, *(gen.)* **vehementis,** vigorous **33**

vehiculum, -ī, *n.,* carriage

vehō, -ere, vēxī, vectus, carry **12;** *(passive)* sail, ride

Veiī, -ōrum, *m. pl.,* Veii (Vē´ī), *an Etruscan city*

vel, *(conj.)* or **55; vel... vel,** either . . . or **55**

vellus, -eris, *n.,* fleece, wool

vēlō, (1) cover

vēlōcitās, -tātis, *f.,* swiftness

vēlum, -ī, *n.,* sail

velut, velutī, *(adv.)* just as, as

vēna, -ae, *f.,* vein

vēnātiō, -ōnis, *f.,* hunting, hunt

vendō, -ere, -didī, -ditus, sell

venēnum, -ī, *n.,* poison

Venetī, -ōrum, *m. pl.,* the Vĕn´ etī

veniō, -īre, vēnī, ventūrus, come **20, 3**

venter, -tris, *m.,* belly, stomach

ventus, -ī, *m.,* wind **27**

Venus, -eris, *f.,* Vēnus, *goddess of love and beauty*

vēr, vēris, *n.,* spring

verberō, (1) beat, strike

verbōsus, -a, -um, wordy

verbum, -ī, *n.,* word **24; verba faciō,** make a speech

Vercingetorīx, -īgis, *m.,* Vercingetorix, *a Gallic leader,* (Versinjet´ orix)

vērē, *(adv.)* truly

vereor, verērī, veritus, fear, respect **32**

Vergilius, -lī, *m.,* Vergil (Virgil)

vergō, -ere, —, —, slope, lie

vēritās, -tātis, *f.,* truth

versicolor, *(gen.)* **-ōris,** of various colors

versō, (1) turn over **63;** *(passive)* live **63**

versor, (1) move about, be engaged, live, be

versus, -ūs, *m.,* line, verse

vertō, -ere, vertī, versus, turn **44;** *(passive)* turn (oneself); *(sometimes deponent)*

vērus, -a, -um, true, real, not false **18, 7; vērē** *(adv.)* truly; **vērō** *(adv.)* in truth, but, however

Vespasiānus, -ī, *m.,* the emperor Vespasian (Vespā´ zhian)

vesper, -erī, *m.,* evening **19; vesperī,** in the evening *(loc.)* **19**

Vesta, -ae, *f.,* Vesta *goddess of the hearth;* **Vestālis, -e,** of Vesta

vester, -tra, -trum, your, yours *(referring to two or more persons)* **18**

vēstibulum, -ī, *n.,* entrance

vēstīgium, -gī, *n.,* footprint, foot

vestiō, -īre, -īvī, -ītus, clothe

vestis, -is, -ium, *f.,* garment, clothes **46, 7**

vestītus, -ūs, *m.,* clothing

veterānus, -a, -um, veteran, experienced

vetō, -āre, vetuī, vetitus, forbid **28**

vetus, *(gen.)* **veteris,** *(gen. pl.)* **veterum,** old **88**

vetustus, -a, -um, old, ancient

vexō, (1) disturb

via, -ae, *f.,* road, way, street **1**

viātor, -ōris, *m.,* traveler

vīcēnī, -ae, -a, twenty (each)

vīciēs, *(adv.)* twenty times

vīcīnus, -a, -um, neighboring; *m.,* neighbor

—, *(gen.)* **vicis,** *f. (defective),* change; **in vicem,** in turn

victima, -ae, *f.,* victim

victor, -ōris, *m.,* conqueror, victor **60;** *(adj.)* victorious **60**

victōria, -ae, *f.,* victory **8**

vīctus, -ūs, *m.,* living, food

vīcus, -ī, *m.,* village **52**

videō, -ēre, vīdī, vīsus, see **11, 4; videor,** *(passive)* be seen, seem, seem best **4**

vigil, *(gen.)* **vigilis,** wakeful; *(noun) m.,* watchman, fireman

vigilia, -ae, *f.,* watchman, watch (a fourth part of the night)

vīgintī, *(indeclinable)* twenty **18**

vigor, -ōris, *m.,* vigor

vīlis, -e, cheap, worthless

vīlla, -ae, *f.,* country home

Vīminālis (mōns), -is, *m.,* the Vĭminal Hill

vincō, -ere, vīcī, victus, conquer, defeat, overcome 61, **8**

vinculum, -ī, *n.,* bond, chain

vindicō, (1) claim, appropriate

vīnea, -ae, *f.,* grape arbor, shed

vīnētum, -ī, *n.,* vineyard

vīnum, -ī, *n.,* wine

violēns, -ntis, violent, vehement; **violenter** *(adv.),* with (needless) force, violently

violō, (1) injure

vir, virī, *m.,* man, hero 14, **1**

virgō, -ginis, *f.,* virgin, maiden

virīlis, -e, of a man

virtūs, -tūtis, *f.,* manliness, courage 49

vīs, —, F., force, power, violence; *pl.* **vīrēs, virium,** strength 58

vīta, -ae, *f.,* life 2

vitiōsus, -a, -um, full of faults

vitium, -tī, *n.,* fault

vītō, (1) avoid **43**

vīvō, -ere, vīxī, vīctus, live, be alive 41

vīvus, -a, -um, alive, living **27**

vix, *(adv.)* scarcely, hardly **36**

vōbīscum = cum vōbīs

vocō, (1) call, invite 13, **6**

volō, (1) fly

volō, velle, voluī, —, want, wish, be willing **25**

Volscī, -ōrum, *(m. pl.,)* the Volscians (Vŏl´ shians)

volucris, -ris, *f.,* bird

voluntās, -tātis, *f.,* wish, consent **37**

voluptās, -tātis, *f.,* pleasure

volvō, -ere, volvī, volūtus, roll (up); turn over **14;** *(passive)* (be) toss(ed) about

vōs, vestrum, you, of you *(pl.)* 31

voveō, -ēre, vōvī, vōtus, vow, promise

vōx, vōcis, *f.,* voice, remark 57, **6**

Vulcānus, -ī, *m.,* Vulcan, *god of fire*

vulgus, -ī, *n.,* common people **90**

vulnerō, (1) wound 40

vulnus, vulneris, *n.,* wound 45

vultus, -ūs, *m.,* expression, features **38**

DICTIONARY

English–Latin

For proper nouns and proper adjectives not given in this vocabulary, see the Latin-English Dictionary or the text. Verbs of the first conjugation whose parts are regular are indicated by the figure 1 in parentheses. Lightface numbers following an entry indicate the number of the lesson in Level 1 where the word is a vocabulary entry. Boldface numbers indicate the number of the lesson in this book where the word is vocabulary entry.

A

abandon, relinquō, -ere, relīquī, relictus 41

able (be), possum, posse, potuī, — 42, **7**

about, dē, *(w. abl.)* 13; *(adv.)* circiter **22**

above, super *(w. acc.)* 67; suprā **46**

absent (be), absum, abesse, āfuī, āfutūrus 30

abundance, cōpia, -ae, *f.* 5

access, aditus, -ūs, *m.* **69**

accident, cāsus, -ūs, *m.* 68

accomplice, socius, -cī, *m.*

accomplish, cōnficiō, -ere, -fēcī, -fectus; prōficiō, -ere, -fēcī, -fectus **99**

account, ratiō, -ōnis, *f.* 70

account of (on), *(see* **on***)*

accustomed (be), cōnsuēscō, -ere, -suēvī, -suētus **41**

achieve, efficiō, -ere, effēcī, effectus 21, **8**

across, trāns, *(w. acc.)* 39

add, adiciō, -ere, adiēcī, adiectus

admire, admīror, (1); mīror, (1) **19**

admit, admittō, -ere, admīsī, admissus **38; admitto,** adhibeō, -ēre, adhibuī, adhibitus **89**

adopt, adoptō, (1)

adorn, ōrnō, (1)

advance, prōcēdō, -ere, -cessi, -cessūrus 30; prōgredior, prōgredī, prōgressus **22**

advantageous, opportūnus, -a, -um **77**

advice, cōnsilium, -lī, *n.* 16, **6**

affair, rēs, reī, *f.* 69

affect, afficiō, -era, affēcī, affectus 23, **3**

afflict with, afficiō, -ere, affēcī, affectus 23, **3**

afraid (be), timeō, -ēre, timuī, — 51, **1**

after, post *(w. acc.)* 48; *(conj.)* postquam 67; posteāquam **13** *or use perf. part. or abl. abs.*

afterwards, *(adv.)* posteā 48

again, iterum **10;** rūrsus **38**

against, contrā, *(w. acc.)* 65

age, aetās, ātis, *f.* 61

agree, cōnsentiō, -īre, -sēnsī, -sēnsus **16**

aid, auxilium, -lī, *n.* 17, **6;** ops, opis, *f.* **20;** *(verb)* iuvō, iuvāre, iūvī, iūtus **27**

alarm, commoveō, -ēre, -mōvī, -mōtus **42**

all, omnis, -e 47, **2;** tōtus, -a, -um 56; **all other,** cēterī, -ae, -a **16; all together,** ūniversus, -a, -um **81**

allow, licet, -ēre, licuit *or* licitum est **31;** sinō, -ere, sīvī, situs **29**

ally, socius, -cī, *m.* 12

almost, paene 9; ferē *(adv.)* **50;** prope **35**

alone, sōlus, -a, -um 56

along with, ūnā cum *(with abl.)* **52**

already, iam 30

also, etiam 32; item **51**

although, cum; quamquam; *(use participle or abl. abs.)* 25; etsī **22**

altogether, omnīnō **52**

always, semper 9

ambassador, lēgātus, -ī, *m.* 60

ambush, īnsidiae, -ārum, *f. pl.* **29**

among, inter, *(w. acc.)* 35; apud *(w.acc.)* 70

ancestors, maiōrēs, -um, *m. pl.* **15**

and, et 1; -que 26; atque (ac) 38; **and not,** neque (nec) 28; nēve (neu) **70**

anger, īra, -ae, *f.* 60

announce, nūntiō (1) 7; praedicō, (1) **84**

another, alius, alia, aliud 56

another's, aliēnus, -a, -um 57

answer, respondeō, -ēre, respondī, respōnsus 49

any, aliquī, aliqua, aliquod **20; any(one),** ūllus, -a, -um **56;** quis, quid *(after* sī*)*; **anyone, anything, any,** quisquam, quicquam **36; anyone, anything,** aliquis, aliquid **20**

appear, appāreō, -ēre, appāruī, appāritūrus

appearance, speciēs, speciēī, *f.* **69;** faciēs, faciēī, *f.* **21**

approach *(noun)* adventus, -ūs, *m.;* aditus, -ūs, *m.* **69, 32;** *(verb)* accēdō, -ere, accessī, accessūrus *(w.* ad*)* **19;** adeō, adīre, adiī, aditūrus **66;** appropinquō, (1) *(w. dat.)* **43;**

approve, probō, (1) **7**

arena, arēna, -ae, *f.*

arise, orior, orīrī, ortus **19**

arm, armō, (1)

arms, arma, -ōrum, *n. pl.* **17**

army, exercitus, -ūs, *m.* **68**

around, circum *(w. acc.)* **67**

arouse, incitō, (1) **8**

arrange, statuō, -ere, statuī, statūtus **61;** īnstruō, -ere, īnstrūxi, īnstrūctus **62**

arrival, adventus, -ūs, *m.* **32**

arrive, perveniō, -īre, -vēnī, -ventūrus **60**

arrogance, superbia, -ae, *f.* **34**

arrogant, superbus, -a, -um **34**

arrow, sagitta, -ae, *f.* **81**

art, ars, artis, *f.*

as, quam **46; as... as possible,** quam, *(w. superl.)* **63; as soon as possible,** quam prīmum **17; as to,** ut **11; as (many as),** quot **24; as soon as,** simul atque (ac) **43;** cum prīmum **47; as if,** *(adv. and conj.)* quasi **39; as if, as it were,** sīcut (sīcutī) **94**

ascend, ascendō, -ere, ascendī, ascēnsus **70**

ask, rogō, (1) **42, 2;** interrogō, (1) **23**

at (near), ad *w. acc.;* Use abl. of time or place; *locative (see p. 500);* **at once,** statim **17; at last,** tandem **17**

Athens, Athēnae, -ārum, *f. pl.*

atrium, ātrium, -ī, *n.* **10**

attack, impetus, -us, *m.,* **68;** *(verb)* oppugnō, (1) **31;** aggredior, aggredī, aggressus **37;** adorior, adorīrī, adortus **67;** lacessō, -ere, -īvī, -ītus **84**

author, auctor, -ōris, *m.* **48, 4**

authority, auctōritās, -ātis, *f.* **49, 5**

avoid, vītō, (1) **43**

await, exspectō, (1) **19, 6**

away (be), absum, -esse, āfuī, āfutūrus **30**

B

bad, malus, -a, -um **4**

baggage, impedīmenta, -ōrum, *n. pl.*

bandit, latrō, -ōnis, *m.*

banish, expellō, -ere, expulī, expulsus **50, 7**

barbarian, barbarus, -i, *m.* **16**

bath, balneum, -ī, *n.* **10**

battle, pugna, -ae, *f.* **8,** proelium, -lī, *n.* **27**

battle line, aciēs, aciēī, *f.* **56**

be, sum, esse, fuī, futūrus **15**

bear, ferō, ferre, tulī, lātus **13**

beat, superō, (1) **49;** caedō, -ere, cecīdī, caesus **21**

beautiful, pulcher, -chra, -chrum **20**

because, quod **4;** quoniam; proptereā quod **50;** *(use participle or abl. abs.)*

become, fīō, fierī, (factus) **24**

befall, accidō, -ere, accidī, — *(w. dat.)* **63, 3**

before, *(adv. and prep.)* ante, *(w. acc.)* **39;** *(adv.)* anteā **37;** *(conj.)* priusquam **31**

beg, ōrō, (1) **24;** petō, -ere, petīvī, petītus **36, 5**

begin, incipiō, -ere, incēpī, inceptus **23; began,** coepī, coeptus **34**

beginning, initium, -tī, *n.* **27**

behind, post *(w. acc.)* **48**

believe, crēdō, -ere, crēdidī, crēditus *(w. dat.)* **65**

benefit, beneficium, -cī, *n.* **33**

besides, praeter *(w. acc.)* **52;** *(adv.)* praetereā **16**

besiege, obsideō, -ēre, obsēdī, obsessus **30**

best, optimus, -a, -um

betray, prōdō, -ere, -didī, -ditus **81**

better, melior, melius

between, inter *(w. acc.)* **35; between each other,** inter sē

big, magnus, -a, -um **2**

bind, ligō, -āre, -āvī, -ātus **44**

birth, genus, generis, *n.* **53, 8**

bitter, tristis, -e **34**

blame, accūsō, (1) **21;** culpa, -ae, *f.* **18**

blood, sanguis, -inis, *m.* **34**

body, corpus, corporis, *n.* **45**

bold, audāx, *(gen.)* -ācis **37; boldly,** *(adv.)* audācter **67**

book, liber, librī, *m.* **24**

booty, praeda, -ae, *f.* **7**

border, fīnis, fīnis, fīnium, *m.* **46**

born (be), nāscor, nāscī, nātus **33**

both. . . and, et... et **28**

boundary, terminus, -ī, *m.* **21**

boy, puer, puerī, *m.* **14**

brave, fortis, -e **47; bravely,** fortiter

break, frangō, -ere, frēgī, frāctus **54;** rumpō, -ere, rūpī, ruptus **13**

breast, pectus, pectoris, *n.* **29**

breathe, spīrō, (1) **52; breathe out,** exspīrō, (1) **35**

bridge, pōns, pontis, *m.* **54**

bring, ferō, ferre, tulī, lātus **13;** īnferō, īnferre, intulī, illātus **35; bring together,** condūcō, -ere, -dūxī, -ductus; cōnferō, -ferre, contulī, collātus **57; bring about,** efficiō, -ere, effēcī, effectus **21, 8; bring back,** referō, referre, rettulī, relātus **24**

Britons, Britannī, -ōrum, *m. pl.*

bronze, aes, aeris, *n.* **31**

brother, frāter, frātris, *m.* **54, 2**

build, exstruō, -ere, exstrūxī, exstrūctus **38;** aedificō, (1)

building, aedificium, -cī, *n.* **12**

burn, incendō, -ere, incendī, incēnsus **15**

business, negōtium, -tī, *n.* **67, 1**

but, sed 1; at **23**

buy, emō, -ere, -ēmī, emptus **66**

by, ā, ab, *(w. abl.)* 13

C

call, vocō, (1) 13; appellō, (1) 28; **call out,** ēvocō 16; **call together,** convocō 25; indīcō, -ere, indīxī, indictus **60; call for,** poscō, -ere, poposcī, — **37**

calm, aequus, -a, -um 18

camp, castra, -ōrum, *n. pl.* 16

can, possum, posse, potuī, — 42, **7**

cannot, nōn possum

canton, pāgus, -ī, *m.* **55**

capture, expugnō, (1) 53; capiō, -ere, cēpī, captus 20, **8**

care for, cūrō, (1) **83**

careful, dīligēns, *(gen.)* -entis **24**

carry, portō, (1) 3; vehō, -ere, vēxī, vectus 12; ferō, ferre, tulī, lātus **13; carry on war,** bellum gerō; **carry back,** referō, referre, rettulī, relātus **24; carry out,** efferō, efferre, extulī, ēlātus **39**

cart, carrus, -i *m.* 4

case, causa, -ae, *f.* 18

cast, iaciō, -ere, iēcī, iactus, 45

catch, intercipiō, -ere, -cepī, -ceptus 53

catch sight of, cōnspiciō, -ere, -spexī, -spectus 65

cattle, pecus, pecoris, *n.* **85**

cause, causa, -ae, *f.* 18; *(verb)* efficiō, -ere, effēcī, effectus *(w. ut and subjunct.)* 21; **cause (to be done),** cūrō, (1) **83**

cavalry, equitātus, -ūs, *m.* **56;** equitēs, -um, *m. pl.;* **cavalry,** *(adj.)* equester, -tris, -tre **66**

cease, dēsistō, -ere, dēstitī, dēstitūrus **47**

centurion, centuriō, -ōnis, *m.* **72**

certain, certus, -a,-um 42; **certainly,** *(adv.)* certē; **a certain one,** *(demon.)* quīdam, quaedam, quiddam **20**

chain, vinculum, -ī, *n.*

chance, cāsus, -ūs, *m.* 68 ; fors, fortis, *f.* **27**

changing, varius, -a, -um 22

charge of, (be in) praesum, -esse, -fuī, -futūrus 69; **(put in),** praeficiō, -ere, -fēcī, -fectus 69

check, sustineō, -ēre, -tinuī, -tentus

chief, prīnceps, -cipis, *m.* 69, **5**

children, līberī, -ōrum, *m. pl.* 34, **1**

choose, ēligō, -ere, ēlēgī, ēlēctus; dēligō, (1)

circumstance, rēs, reī, *f.* 69

citadel, arx, arcis, arcium, *f.* **32**

citizen, cīvis, -is, *m.* 46

citizenship, cīvitās, -ātis, *f.* 48

city, urbs, urbis, urbium, *f.* 60

civil, cīvīlis, -e

clear, clārus, -a, -um 5

client, cliēns, -entis, -entium, *m.* 15

climb (up), ascendō, -ere, ascendī, ascēnsus 70; ēvādō, -ere, ēvāsī, ēvāsūrus **33**

cling, haereō, -ēre, haesī, haesus 60; adhaereō, -ēre, -haesī, -haesus **12**

close up to, *(prep.)* sub *(w. acc or abl.)* 33

close, claudō, -ere, clausī, clausus 45, **6**

clothes, vestis, -is, -ium, *f.* 46, **7**

collect, conferō, conferre, contulī, collātus; cōgō, -ere, -ēgī, -āctus 38; colligō, -ere, -lēgī, -lēctus **12**

colonist, colōnus, -ī, *m.* 15

come, veniō, -īre, vēnī, ventūrus 20; eō, īre, iī (īvī), itūrus **20; come near to,** appropinquō (1) **43 come through,** perveniō, -īre, -vēnī, -ventūrus 60; **come together,** conveniō 25; **come upon,** inveniō 20

command (be in), praesum, -esse, -fuī, -futūrus *(w. dat.)* 69; **command** *(noun)* imperium, -rī, *n.* 66; *(verb)* imperō, (1) *(w. dat.)* 70

commander, imperātor, -ōris, *m.* **23**

commit, committō, -ere, -mīsī, -missus 27

common, commūnis, -e 52

common people, plēbs, plēbis, *f.* **31;** vulgus, -ī, *n.* **90**

companion, comes, -itis, *m. or f.* 29

compel, cōgō, -ere, coēgī, coāctus 38

complain, queror, querī, questus **82**

complete, cōnficiō, -ere, -fēcī, -fectus 46, **4**

comrade, socius, -cī, *m.* 12

conceal, cēlō, (1)

concern, cūra, -ae, *f.* 5

concerning, dē *(w. abl.)* 13

condemn, damnō, (1)

condition, condiciō, -ōnis, *f.* 61, **2**

confer, colloquor, colloquī, collocūtus **83**

conference, colloquium, -quī, *n.* **61**

confidence, fīdūcia, -ae, *f.* **97; confident (be),** cōnfīdō, -ere, cōnfīsus *(semi-deponent)* **57**

conquer, vincō, -ere, vīcī, victus 61, **8;** superō, (1) **49**

consider, cōgitō, (1) **61**

conspire, coniūrō, (1) 31

constant, perpetuus, -a, -um 23

construct, exstruō, -ere, exstrūxī, exstrūctus 38

consul, cōnsul, -ulis, m.

consult, cōnsulō, -ere, -suluī, -sultus 43, 8

contain, contineō, -ēre, -uī, -tentus 24, 4

convenient, commodus, -a, -u 22

council, concilium, -lī, n. 60

country, patria, -ae, f. 10

courage, virtūs, -tūtis, f. 49

course, cursus, -ūs, m. 42

cover, tegō, -ere, tēxī, tectus 39

creditor, crēditor, -ōris, m.

criticize, accūsō, (1) 21

cross, trānseō, -īre, -iī, -itūrus 52

crowded together, cōnfertus, -a, -um 57

cruel, crūdēlis, -e

cruelty, crūdēlitās, -tātis, f.

cry out, clāmō, (1) 40, 4

cultivate, colō, -ere, coluī, cultus 54

custom, mōs, mōris, m. 27; cōnsuētūdō, -dinis, f. 27

cut, caedō, -ere, cecīdī, caesus 21; cut off, interclūdō, -ere, -clūsī, -clūsus 69; cut down, occīdō, -ere, occīdī, occīsus 23

D

daily, (adj.) cotīdiānus, -a, -um 50; (adv.) cotīdiē 15

danger, perīculum, -ī, n. 29, 9

dare, audeō, -ēre, ausus (semideponent) 61

dash together, cōnflīgō, -ere, -flīxī, -flīctus 43

daughter, fīlia, -ae, f. 9, 1

day, diēs, diēī, m. and f. 69; on the next day, (adv.) postrīdiē 46; three days, trīduum, -ī 58; on the day before, (adv.) prīdiē 19

dear, cārus, -a, -um 18

death, mors, mortis, mortium, f. 51

deceive, fallō, -ere, fefellī, falsus 65

decide, dēcernō, -ere, dēcrēvī, dēcrētus 79; cōnstituō, -ere, cecinī, cantus 10

decided (be), placet, -ēre, placuit

decorated, adōrnātus, -a, -um

deed, factum, -ī, n. 42

deep, altus, -a, -um 12

defeat, (noun) calamitās, -tātis, f.; (verb) superō, (1) 49; pellō, -ere, pepulī, pulsus 48; vincō, -ere, vīcī, victus 61

defend, dēfendō, -ere, dēfendī, dēfēnsus 19

defenses, mūnītiō, -ōnis, f.

delay, mora, -ae, f. 12; moror, (1) 24

demand, postulō, (1) 31; poscō, -ere, poposcī, — 37

deny, negō, (1) 21

depart, excēdō, -ere, excessī, excessūrus 19

departure, exitus, -ūs, m. 10; profectiō, -ōnis, f. 51

depth, altitūdō, -dinis, f. 53

descend, dēscendō, -ere, dēscendī, dēscēnsus 11

desert, dēserō, -ere, dēseruī, dēsertus 68

deserve, mereō, -ēre, meruī, meritus 12

desire, cupiō, -ere, -īvī, -ītus 31, 4; (noun) cupiditās, -tātis, f. 40; desirous, cupidus, -a, -um 51

despair (of), dēspērō, (1) 38

despise, dēspiciō, -ere, dēspexī, dēspectus 68; contemnō, -ere, -tempsī, -temptus 16

destroy, dēleō, -ēre, -ēvī, -ētus 37; populor, (1) 55

determine, cōnstituō, -ere, -stituī, -stitūtus 10; fīniō, -īre, -īvī, -ītus 94

die, morior, morī, mortuus 22; exspīrō, (1) 35

differ, differō, differre, distulī, dīlātus 25

different, dīversus, -a, -um 71

difficult, (adj.) difficilis, -e 63; difficulty, (noun) difficultās, -tātis, f. 46; with difficulty, (adv.) aegrē 44

diligence, dīligentia, -ae, f. 35

dinner, cēna, -ae, f. 13

direct, dērigō, (dīrigō), -ere, dērēxī, dērēctus 94

direction, pars, partis, partium, f. 52

dirty, sordidus, -a, -um 12

disaster, calamitās, -tātis, f. 55

discern, cernō, -ere, crēvī, crētus 42

discipline, disciplīna, -ae, f. 10

discuss, agō, -ere, ēgī, āctus 19, 3

disgraceful, turpis, -e 61

dislodge, dēiciō, -ere, dēiēcī, dēiectus 33

dismiss, dīmittō, -ere, dīmīsī, dīmissus 31, 6

dispute, contrōversia, -ae, f. 45

disreputable, sordidus, -a, -um 12

distinguished, ēgregius, -a, -um 33, 3

district, pāgus, -ī, m. 55

disturb, commoveō, -ēre, -mōvī, -mōtus 42; perturbō, (1) 10

divide, dīvidō, -ere, dīvīsī, dīvīsus 70

do, faciō, -ere, fēcī, factus 20; agō, -ere, ēgī, āctus 19, 3; do harm to, noceō, -ēre, nocuī, nocitus (w. dat.) 69; do in, cōnficiō, -ere, fēcī, -fectus 46

doable, facilis, -e 47

doubt, dubitō, (1) 31

downfall, cāsus, -ūs, m. 68

drag, trahō, -ere, trāxī, tractus 24

draw, dūcō, -ere, dūxī, ductus 21; trahō, -ere, trāxī, trāctus 24

draw up, īnstruō, -ere, īnstrūxī, īnstrūctus 62; expōnō, -ere, exposuī, expositus 81

drive, agō, -ere, ēgī, āctus 19; pellō, -ere, pepulī, pulsus 48; **drive back,** redigō 32; **drive out,** expellō, -ere, expulī, expulsus 50; **drive together,** cōgō, -ere, -ēgī, āctus 38, **3**

during, per *(w. acc.)* 33

dutiful, pius, -a, -um

duty, officium, -cī, *n.* 19, **1;** mūnus, mūneris, *n.* 59, **7**

dwell, habitō, (1) 15

E

each (of two), uterque, utraque, utrumque

each one, quisque, quidque 36

eager, *(adj.)* alacer, -cris, -cre **21; eager for (be),** *(verb)* studeō, -ēre, studuī, — *(w. dat.)* 19

eagerness, studium, -dī, *n.* 22, **9**

eagle, aquila, -ae, *f.* **81**

early, matūrus, -a, -um **12**

earn, mereō, -ēre, meruī, meritus 12

earth, terra, -ae, *f.* 2

easy, facilis, -e 47; **easily,** facile 63; expedītus, -a, -um **52**

effect, efficiō, -ere, effēcī, effectus 21, **8**

effort, opera, -ae, *f.* **15**

eighth, octāvus, -a, -um **11**

either . . . or, aut... aut 28; vel... vel **55**

elect, creō, (1)

elevated, ēditus, -a, -um **13**

embassy, lēgātiō, -ōnis, *f.* **51**

empire, imperium, -rī, *n.* 66

encourage, cōnfirmō, (1) 49, **9**

end, fīnis, fīnis, fīnium, *m.* 46; terminus, -ī, *m.* 21

endure, ferō, ferre, tulī, lātus **13;** sustineō, -ēre, -tinuī, -tentus 36; perferō, -ferre, -tulī, -lātus **69**

enemy, *(personal)* inimīcus, -ī, *m.; (national)* hostis, -is, *m.* 46

engage, spondeō, -ēre, spopondī, spōnsus **19**

enjoy, ūtor, ūtī, ūsus *(w. abl.)* **41;** fruor, fruī, fructus *(w. abl.)*

enlist, cōnscrībō, -ere, scrīpsī, -scrīptus **54**

enough, satis 14

enroll, dēferō, dēferre, dētulī, dēlātus **28**

enter, ingredior, ingredī, ingressus **19; enter in** *or* **upon,** ineō, -īre, iniī, initūrus **26**

entire, tōtus, -a, -um 56

entrust, mandō, (1) 7; committō, -ere, -mīsī, -missus 27; permittō 34; crēdō, -ere, -didī, -ditus 65

envoy, lēgātus, -ī, *m.* 60

envy, invideō, -ēre, invīdī, invīsus *(w. dat.)*

equal, pār, *(gen.)* paris 47, **2;** aequus, -a, -um 18; aequālis, -e **26; make equal,** *(verb)* aequō (1) **57**

erect, exstruō, -ere, exstrūxī, exstrūctus

escape, fugiō, -ere, fūgī, fugitūrus 22; ēvādō, -ere, ēvāsī, ēvāsūrus **33**

especially, praesertim *(adv.)* **61**

establish, cōnstituō, -ere, -stituī, -stitūtus **10;** īnstituō, -ere, īnstituī, īnstitūtus **21**

esteemed, cārus, -a, -um **18**

even, *(adj.)* aequus, -a, -um 18; *(adv.)* etiam 32

evening, vesper, vesperī, *m.* **19; in the evening,** vesperī *(loc.)* 19

ever, umquam 35

every, omnis, -e 47, **2**

everything, omne or omnia

evident (it is), cōnstat **83**

example, exemplum, -ī, *n.* 33

excel, praestō, -āre, -stitī, -stitūrus *(w. dat.)* **34**

excellent, ēgregius, -a, -um 33, **3**

except, nisi **35;** *(prep. w. acc.)* praeter **52**

excite, incitō, (1) 8

exclaim, (ex)clāmō, (1)

exhaust, cōnficiō, -ere, -fēcī, -fectus 46; exanimō, (1) 45

expensive, cārus, -a, -um **18**

explain, explicō, (1) 63

explore, explōrō, (1) 70

express, exprimō, -ere, -pressī, expressus 26

expression (facial), vultus, -ūs, *m.* 38

extend, pateō, -ēre, patuī, — **51**

eye, oculus, -ī, *m.* **13**

F

face, faciēs, faciēī, *f.* 21

facing (toward), ob *(w. acc.)* 35; *(adj.)* adversus, -a, -um **71**

faction, factiō, -ōnis, *f.* **60**

faculty, facultās, -tātis, *f.* **63**

fail, dēficiō, -ere, dēfēcī, dēfectus 33

fall, cadō, -ere, cecidī, cāsūrus 63, **7**

fame, fāma, -ae, *f.* 2

familiar, nōtus, -a, -um 42

family, familia, -ae, *f.* 2

famous, clārus, -a, -um 5, **5**

far (off), *(adv.)* procul **74**

farm, ager, agrī, *m.*

farmer, agricola, -ae, *m.* 3

farther, ulterior, ulterius 64

farthest, extrēmus, -a, -um 64; ultimus, -a, -um 43

father, pater, patris, *m.* 48, **2**

fatherland, patria, -ae, *f.* 10

fault, culpa, -ae 18

fear, timeō, -ēre, timuī, — 51, **1;** vereor, verērī, veritus **32;** *(noun)* timor, -ōris, *m.* 37; metus, -ūs, *m.* **90**

features, vultus, -ūs, *m.* **38**

feed, alō, -ere, aluī, alitus **31**

feel, sentiō, -īre, sēnsī, sēnsus **60; feel grateful,** grātiam habeō

feeling, sententia, -ae, *f.* **25**

festival, fēriae, -ārum, *f.* **22**

few, paucī, -ae, -a **27, 1**

field, ager, agrī, *m.* **14**

fierce, ferus, -a, -um

fifth, quīntus, -a, -um **9**

fight, *(verb)* pugnō, (1) **8;** *(noun)* pugna, -ae, *f.* **8;** proelium, -lī, *n.* **27; fight (it out),** dēcertō, (1) **67;** dīmicō, (1) **70**

fill, compleō, -ēre, -ēvī, -ētus **20;** impleō, -ēre, implēvī, implētus **29; fill up,** expleō, -ēre, explēvī, explētus **99**

finally, tandem **17**

find, inveniō, -īre, invēnī, inventus **20, 5;** reperiō, -īre, repperī, repertus **43; find out,** comperiō, -īre, -perī, -pertus **56**

finish, perficiō, -ere, -fēcī, -fectus **66**

fire, ignis, -is, -ium, *m.* **63**

firm, firmus, -a, -um **23**

first, *(adv.)* prīmum **63; at first,** prīmō **60;** *(adj.)* prior, prius **99; first place,** *(noun)* prīncipātus, -ūs, *m.* **51**

fit, aptus, -a, -um **62; fitting,** idōneus, -a, -um **42**

fix, figō, -ere, fīxī, fīxus **30; fixed,** certus, -a, -um **42**

flat, plānus, -a, -um **5**

flame, flamma, -ae, *f.*

flee, fugiō, -ere, fūgī, fugitūrus **22, 3**

fleet, classis, -is, *f.* **80**

flight, fuga, -ae, *f.* **43, 3**

flow, fluō, -ere, flūxī, flūxus **52**

fold, plicō, (1) **39**

follow, sequor, sequī, secūtus **27; follow closely,** subsequor, subsequī, subsecūtus **67; following,** *(adj.)* posterus, -a, -um **14**

food, cibus, -ī, *m.* **5**

foot, pēs, pedis, *m.* **44, 7; on foot,** pedibus; **foot soldier,** pedes, peditis, *m.* **71**

for *(conj.)* nam **38;** namque **13;** *(prep.)* ad **6;** ob, *(w. acc.)* **35;** prō, *(w. abl.)* **29;** *(often expressed by dative);* **for the purpose or sake of,** causā *or* grātiā *(preceded by gen.);*

forbid, vetō, vetāre, vetuī, vetitus **28**

force, provideō, -ēre, -vīdī, -vīsus

ford, vadum, -ī, *n.* **53**

foreign, barbarus, -a, -um **16**

foreigner, barbarus, -ī, *m.* **16**

foresee, prōvideō, -ēre, -vīdī, -vīsus **43**

forest, silva, -ae, *f.* **1**

former, prīstinus, -a, -um **70;** prior, prius **99; former (the),** ille **50; the former . . . the latter,** ille... hic

formerly, ōlim **31**

fort, castellum, -ī, *n.* **53**

fortification, mūnītiō, -ōnis, *f.* **53**

fortify, mūniō, -īre, -īvī, -ītus **20, 3**

fortunate, fēlīx, -īcis **18**

fortune, fortūna, -ae, *f.* **2**

four, quattuor; **fourth,** quārtus, -a, -um **11**

free, *(adj.)* līber, -era, -erum **14;** *(verb)* līberō, (1) **12;** expediō, -īre, -īvī, -ītus **44**

freedom, lībertās, -tātis, *f.* **47**

fresh, integer, -gra, -grum **31**

friend, amīcus, -ī; *m.;* **(girl) friend,** amīca, -ae, *f.* **7**

friendly, amīcus, -a, -um **14, 4**

frighten, terreō, -ēre, terruī, territus **10, 8**

frog, rāna, -ae, *f.*

from, ē, ex, ā, ab, dē, *(w. abl.)* **13; away from,** ā, ab *(w. abl.)* **13; down from,** dē *(w. abl.)* **13; from all sides,** *(adv.)* undique **40; from which (place)** *(adv.)* unde **47**

full, plēnus, -a, -um **24**

furnish, praebeō, -ēre, -uī, -itus **20;** submittō, -ere, -mīsī, -missus **35**

G

gain one's request, impetrō (1) **54**

game, lūdus, -i, *m.* **35**

garment, vestis, -is, -ium, *f.* **46, 7**

gate, porta, -ae, *f.* **32**

gather, legō, -ere, lēgī, lēctus **26, 4**

Gaul, Gallia, -ae, *f.;* **Gauls,** Gallī, -ōrum, *m. pl.*

general, dux, ducis, *m.* **40;** lēgātus, -ī, *m.* **26;** imperātor, -ōris, *m.* **23**

get, get ready, parō, (1) **3; get (possession of),** potior, potiri, potītus *(w. abl.);* parō, (1) **3;** comparō, (1) **42; get back,** recuperō, (1) **97**

gift, mūnus, mūneris, *n.* **59, 7**

girl, puella, -ae, *f.* **2**

give, dō, dare, dedī, datus **35; (as a gift),** dōnō, (1) **7; (to keep safe),** mandō, (1) **7; give back,** reddō, -ere, reddidī, redditus **68; give (forth),** prōdō, -ere, -didī, -ditus **81; give out,** ēdō, -ere, ēdidī, ēditus **15**

gladiator, gladiātor, -ōris, *m.;* **gladiatorial,** gladiātōrius, -a, -um

glory, glōria, -ae, *f.* **11**

go, eō, īre, iī, itūrus **20; go away,** discēdō, -ere, -cessī, -cessūrus **32; go before,** antecēdō **41; go forward,** prōcēdō **30, 9; go out,** ēgredior, ēgredī, ēgressus **42;** exeō, exīre, exiī, exitūrus **20;** ēvādō, -ere, ēvāsī, ēvāsūrus **33; go to,** adeō, adīre, adiī, aditūrus **66; go back,** redeō, -īre, rediī, reditūrus **20**

god, deus, -ī, *m.;* **goddess,** dea, -ae, *f.* **22**

gold, aurum, -ī, *n.*

good, bonus, -a, -um **2**

good-bye, valē *(sing.),* valēte *(pl.)*

grain, frūmentum, -ī, *n.* **16; of grain,** frūmentārius, -a, -um **57; grain supply,** rēs frūmentāria **57**

grant, tribuō, -ere, tribuī, tribūtus **65;** concēdō, -ere, -cessī-cessūrus **21**

grasp, prehendō, -ere, -hendī, -hēnsus **14**

grateful, grātus, -a, -um **7; (be** *or* **feel)** grātiam habeō

gratitude, grātia, -ae, *f.* **11**

great, *(adj.)* magnus, -a, -um **2;** amplus, -a, -um **12; greater,** maior, maius; **greatest,** maximus, -a, -um; summus, -a, -um **64; greatness,** *(noun)* magnitūdō, -dinis, *f.* **34; great deal,** *(adv.)* plūrimum; **so great,** *(adj.)* tantus, -a, -um **14; great number,** multitūdō, -dinis, *f.* **35; greatly,** *(adv.)* magnopere **43**

Greece, Graecia, -ae, *f.;* **Greek,** *(adj.)* Graecus, -a, -um

grief, dolor, -ōris, *m.* **40**

grieve, doleō, -ēre, doluī, dolitūrus **13**

guard, *(noun)* praesidium, -dī, *n.* **28;** *(adj.)* custōs, -ōdis, *m.* **33;** *(verb)* servō, (1) **8;** tueor, tuērī, tūtus **88; guarded,** tūtus, -a, -um **31**

guest, guest-friend, hospes, -itis, *m.* **11**

guide, regō, -ere, rēxī, rēctus **20**

H

hall, ātrium, -ī, *n.* **10**

hand, *(noun)* manus, -ūs, *f.* **68; hand over,** *(verb)* trādō, -ere, -didī, -ditus **66**

hang, pendō, -ere, pependī, pēnsus **33**

happen (to), accidō, -ere, accidī, — *(w. dat.)* **63, 3**

happy, fēlīx, *(gen.)* -īcis **18**

harbor, portus, -ūs, *m.* **13**

hard, dūrus, -a, -um **2, 1**

hardly, vix

hardship, labor, -ōris, *m.* **59**

harm, do harm to, noceō, -ēre, nocuī, nocitus *(w. dat.)* **69**

harmony, concordia, -ae, *f.* **17**

harness, iungō, -ere, iūnxī, iūnctus **63**

harsh, dūrus, -a, -um **2, 1**

hasten, properō, (1) **27, 7;** contendō, -ere, -tendī, -tentus **57;** mātūrō, (1) **17**

have, habeō, -ēre, habuī, habitus **10; have to,** *(use fut. pass. part.)*

he, is **31;** hic **50;** ille **50;** *often not expressed*

head, caput, capitis, *n.* **45**

headfirst, praeceps, *(gen.)* praecipitis **50**

health, salūs, salūtis, *f.* **40, 2**

hear, audiō, -īre, -īvī, -ītus **24, 5**

heart, cor, cordis, *n.* **51;** pectus, pectoris, *n.* **29**

heavy, gravis, -e **57, 5**

height, altitūdō, -dinis, *f.* **53**

helmsman, gubernātor, *m.* **12**

help, auxilium, -lī **17, 6**

her *(poss.)* eius **52;** *(reflex.)* suus, -a, -um **65; herself** *(reflex.)* suī **65**

herdsman, pāstor, -ōris, *m.* **46**

here, hīc **18;** hūc **25**

hero, vir, virī, *m.* **14, 1**

hesitate, dubitō, (1) **31**

hide, abdō, -ere, abdidī, abditus **30**

high, altus, -a, -um **12; highest,** summus, -a, -um **64**

hill, mōns, montis, montium, *m.* **46, 9;** collis, -is, *m.* **33**

himself *(reflex.)* —, suī **65;** *(intens.)* ipse **54, 8**

hinder, impediō, -īre, -īvī, -ītus **44**

hindrance, impedīmentum, -ī, *n.* **44**

his *(poss.)* eius **52; his own** *(reflex.)* suus, -a, -um **65**

hold, habeō, -ēre, habuī, habitus **10, 1;** teneō, -ēre, tenuī, tentus **12, 1;** obtineō **37, 1; hold back,** retineō **30; hold together,** contineō **24, 4; hold up,** sustineō **36; hold toward,** adhibeō, -ēre, adhibuī, adhibitus **89**

holidays, fēriae, -ārum, *f.* **22**

home, domus, -ūs, *f.* **68**

honor, honor, -ōris, *m.* **23**

hope, *(noun)* spēs, speī, *f.* **69; hope for/that,** *(verb)* spērō, (1) **52**

Horace, Horātius, -tī, *m.*

horn, cornū, -ūs, *n.* **72**

horse, equus, -ī, *m.* **4**

horseman, eques, equitis, *m.* **34**

host, hospes, hospitis, *m.* **11**

hostage, obses, obsidis, *m.* **37**

hostile, inimīcus, -a, -um **30, 8**

hour, hōra, -ae, *f.* **9**

house, casa, -ae, *f.* **12;** domus, -ūs, *f.* **68**

how, *(adv.)* quō modō; quam **46; how great, how much,** *(adj.)* quantus, -a, -um **19; how many,** *(adj.)* quot **24**

however, autem *(never first word)* **67, 4**

human being, homō, hominis, *m.* **40, 4**

humble, humilis, -e **62, 2**

hundred, centum **66**

hunger, famēs, -is *(abl.* famē*)* **21**

hurl, iaciō, -ere, iēcī, iactus **45**

hurry (on), properō, (1) **27, 7**

I

I, ego, meī; *(often not expressed)* 31

if, sī 59; sīve (seu) 55

immediately, statim 17; prōtinus *(adv.)* 66

impel, impellō, -ere, impulī, impulsus

in, in *(w. abl. or acc.)* 11; **in front of,** prō *(w. abl.)* 29; prae *(w. abl.)* 67; **in the presence of,** apud *(w. acc.)* 70; **in order to** or **that,** ut *(w. subjunctive)* 11; **in order not to,** *(conj.)* nē 11; **in such a way,** *(adv.)* ita 14; **in all,** *(adv.)* omnīnō 52

incite, incitō, (1) 8

increase, augeō, -ēre, auxī, auctus 10

inferior, īnferior, -ius 66

inflict, ēdō, -ere, ēdidī, ēditus 15

influence *(verb)* addūcō, -ere, addūxī, adductus 43; *(noun)* grātia, -ae, *f.* 11; auctōritās, -tātis, *f.* 49

inform, certiōrem faciō, -ere, fēcī, factus; **be informed,** certior fīō, fierī 24

inhabit, incolō, -ere, incoluī, — 66

injury, iniūria, -ae, *f.* 8

injustice, iniūria, -ae, *f.* 8

inquire (of), quaerō, -ere, quaesīvī, quaesītus 22

inspire, iniciō, -ere, iniēcī, iniectus *(w. acc. and dat.)*

instruction, disciplīna, -ae, *f.* 10

insult, contumēlia, -ae, *f.* 69

intercept, intercipiō, -ere, -cēpī, -ceptus 53

interest, studium, -dī, *n.* 22, 9

interior, *(adj.)* interior, -ius 85

interrupt, intermittō, -ere, -mīsī, -missus 37

into, in *(w. acc.)* 15

investigate, explōrō, (1) 70

invite, vocō, (1) 13

iron, ferrum, -ī, *n.* 85

island, īnsula, -ae, *f.* 1

it, is, ea, id 31, 8; hic, haec, hoc 50; ille, illa, illud 50; *(often not expressed)*

its (own), *(reflex.)* suus, -a, -um 65

itself, *(intens.)* ipsum 54, 8; *(reflex.)* suī 65

J

javelin, pīlum, -ī 57

join, iungō, -ere, iūnxī, iūnctus 63; **join together,** committō, -ere, -mīsī, -missus 27; **join to,** adiungō, -ere, adiūnxī, adiūnctus 28

journey, iter, itineris, *n.* 46, 8

joy, gaudium, -i, *n.* 18

judge, (1) 62

just, aequus, -a, -um 18; iūstus, -a, -um 59

K

keen, ācer, ācris, ācre 60, 2

keep, retineō, -ēre, retinuī, retentus 30; **keep from,** prohibeō, -ēre, -hibuī, -hibitus 58

kill, interficiō, -ere, -fēcī, -fectus 34; caedō, -ere, cecīdī, caesus 21; occīdo, -ere, occīdi, occīsus 23; exanimō, (1) 45; necō, (1) 48

kind, genus, generis, *n.* 53, 8

kindness, beneficium, -cī, *n.* 33

king, rēx, rēgis, *m.* 44

kingdom, regnum, -ī, *n.* 44

know, sciō, scīre, scīvī, scītus 59, 5; *(perf. of)* nōscō, -ere, nōvī, nōtus 30, 4; *or of* cognōscō, -ere, -nōvī, -nitus 39, 5

known, nōtus, -a, -um 42

L

labor, opus, operis, *n.* 63, 5

lack, inopia, -ae, *f.* 30; **lacking (be),** *(verb)* dēsum, deesse, dēfuī, dēfutūrus 70

land, terra, -ae, *f.* 2; **native land,** patria, -ae, *f.* 10; **(disembark)** *(verb)* ēgredior, ēgredī, ēgressus 42

language, lingua, -ae, *f.* 10

large, magnus, -a, -um 2; **so large,** tantus, -a, -um 14

last, ultimus, -a, -um 43; extrēmus, -a, -um 64

late, tardus, -a, -um 24, 6

later, post *(adv. and prep. with acc.)* 48; *(adv.)* posteā 48

latter, hic

laugh (at), rideō, ridēre, rīsī, rīsus 14

law, lēx, lēgis, *f.* 40, 5

lay aside, dēpōnō, -ere, dēposuī, dēpositus 17

lead, dūcō, -ere, dūxī, ductus 21; dēdūcō, -ere, dēdūxī, dēductus 63; **lead across,** trādūcō 41; **lead a life,** vītam agō; **lead back,** redūcō 25; **lead out,** ēdūcō 34, prōdūcō 30; **lead to,** addūcō 43, 9

leader, dux, ducis, *m.* 40, 2; prīnceps, prīncipis, *m.* 69, 5

leadership, prīncipātus, -ūs, *m.* 51

learn, cognōscō, -ere, -nōvī, -nitus 39, 5; nōscō, -ere, nōvī, nōtus 30, 4; discō, -ere, didicī, — 23

least (at) quidem *(follows the word it emphasizes)* 16

leave (behind), relinquō, -ere, relīquī, relictus 41

left, sinister, -tra, trum 57

left over (be), supersum, -esse, -fuī, -futūrus 67

legion, legiō, -ōnis, *f.* 37

leisure, ōtium, otī, *n.* 22

lest, nē 11

let down, submittō, -ere, -mīsī, -missus 35; **let go,** mittō, -ere, mīsī, -missus 19, 5; amittō 29, 5; dīmittō 31, 6; intermittō 37; **let in,** admittō, -ere, admīsī, admissus 38; **let to,** admittō, -ere, admīsī, admissus 38; **let through,** permittō, -ere, -mīsī, -missus 34

letter (epistle), litterae, -ārum, *f.* 7; **(of the alphabet),** littera, -ae, *f.* 7

level, plānus, -a, -um 5

liberty, lībertās, -tātis, *f.* 47

life, vīta, -ae, *f.* 2

light, lūx, lūcis, *f.* 69, **2**

light (in weight), levis, -e 58

like, *(verb)* amō, (1) 3; **(similar)** *(adj.)*, similis, -e 63

limit, fīniō, -īre, -īvī, -ītus **94**

little, parvus, -a, -um 2; **a little,** *(adv.)* paulō **41; little by little,** *(adv.)* paulātim **61**

little later, paulō post

live, vīvō, -ere, vīxī, vīctus 41; incolō, -ere, incoluī, incultus 66; **(a life),** agō, -ere, ēgī, āctus 19, **6; (dwell),** habitō, (1) 15; *(passive)* versō, (1) **63**

living, vīvus, -a, -um **27**

long, longus, -a, -um 3; **long** *(adv.)* **(for) a long time,** diū; **long for,** dēsīderō, (1) **26**

look at *or* **on,** spectō, (1) 3, **7; look down on,** despiciō, -ere, dēspexī, dēspectus 68; **look on,** aspiciō, -ere, aspexī, aspectus **45; look out for,** exspectō, (1) 19, **6**

loosen, solvō, -ere, solvī, solūtus 59

loot, praeda, -ae, *f.* 7

lose, āmittō, -ere, āmīsī, āmissus 29, **5; perdō, -ere, -didī, -ditus**

loss, dētrīmentum, -ī, *n.* **35**

love, *(noun)* amor, amōris, *m.; (verb)* amō, (1) 3

low, humilis, -e 62, **2**

lower, īnferior, īnferius 64; *(superl.)* **lowest,** īnfimus *and* īmus **66**

luck, fortūna, -ae, *f.* 2

luxury, luxuria, -ae, *f.*

M

magistracy, magistrātus, -ūs, *m.* **31**

magnificent, amplus, -a, -um **12**

maintain, sustineō, -ēre, -tinuī, -tentus 36

make, faciō, -ere, fēcī, factus 20, **3; make firm,** cōnfirmō, (1) 49, **9; make war upon,** bellum īnferō *(w. dat.)*

maker, auctor, -ōris 48, **4**

man, vir, virī, *m.* 14, **1; homō, hominis,** *m.* 40, **4**

manage, administrō, (1) **70**

manliness, virtūs, -tūtis, *f.* 49

manner, modus, -ī, *m.* 38, **5; ratiō, -ōnis,** *f.* **43**

many, multī, -ae, -a; **so many,** tot **15; very many,** plūrimī, -ae, -a

march, iter, itineris, *n.* 46, **8; line of march,** agmen, agminis, *n.* **57**

master, dominus, -ī, *m.* 18

matter, rēs, reī, *f.* 69; māteria, -ae, *f.* 11, **7**

mean, significō, (1) **21**

means, facultās, -tātis, *pl.* **63**

meanwhile, intereā **41;** *(adv.)* interim **57**

meet, occurrō, -ere, occurrī, occursus 33; **meet (in battle),** congredior, congredī, congressus **62; meet with (find),** nancīscor, nansīscī, nactus **42**

memory, memoria, -ae, *f.* 8

mention, commemorō, (1) **79**

merchant, mercātor, -ōris, *m.* **12**

mercy, clēmentia, -ae, *f.*

messenger, nūntius, -tī, *m.* 17

midday, merīdiēs, -ēī, *m.* **45**

middle (of), medius, -a, -um 25

migrate, migrō, (1) 15

mile, mīlle passūs; *pl.* mīlia passuum **17**

military, mīlitāris, -e **32**

mind, animus, -ī, *m.* 15; mēns, mentis, *f.* **33**

mine, *(poss.)* meus, -a, -um 9; mi *(voc.)*

misfortune, cāsus, -ūs, *m.* 68

moderate, mediocris, -e **97**

molest, noceō, -ēre, nocuī, nocitūrus *(w. dat.)* 69

money, pecūnia, -ae, *f.* 6; aes, aeris, *n.* **31**

month, mēnsis, -is *m.* 58, **7**

monument, monumentum, -ī, *n.*

more, *(adj. and adv.)* plūs; *(adv.)* magis **71;** amplius **37** *or use comparative*

most, plērīque, plēraeque, plēraque **64**

mother, māter, mātris, *f.* 50, **2**

motion, mōtus, -ūs, *m.* **81**

motto, sententia, -ae, *f.* 25, **6**

mountain, mōns, montis, montium, *m.* 46, **9**

mouth, ōs, ōris, *n.* **23**

move, moveō, -ēre, mōvī, mōtus 13; afficiō, -ere, affēcī, affectus 23; migrō, (1) 15; **move away from,** cēdō, -ere, cessī, cessūrus 19; **move back,** removeō 32; **move deeply,** permoveō 37

much, multus, -a, -um 3

must, necesse est (+ *infin.*) **18; dēbeō, -ēre, debuī, dēbitus 17, 6; oportet, -ēre, oportuit 31;** *or use fut. pass. part.*

my, meus, -a, -um 9; mi *(voc.)*

myself, *(intens.)* ipse, ipsa, 54, **8;** *(reflex.),* mei 65

N

name, *(noun)* nōmen, nōminis, *n.* 45, **2;** *(verb)* appellō, (1) 28

narrow, angustus, -a, -um, **12**

nation, gēns, gentis, gentium, *f.* 62, **9;** nātiō, -ōnis, *f.* **80**

native land, patria, -ae, *f.* 10

nature, nātūra, -ae, *f.* 36

near, ad *(w. acc.); (adj.),* propinquus, -a, -um **33; be near,** *(verb)* adsum, adesse, adfuī, adfutūrus 34, **6**

nearest, proximus, -a, -um 64

necessary (it is), oportet, -ēre, oportuit **31;** necesse **18;** *(adj.)* necessārius, -a, -um **70**

neglect, neglegō, -ere, -lēxī, -lectus**38**

neighbor, finitimus, -ī, *m.* **27**

neighboring, fīnitimus, -a, -um **27**

neither (of two) *(adj. or pron.)* neuter, -tra, -trum **56**

neither ... nor *(conj.)* neque... neque **28**

never, numquam **26**

nevertheless, tamen **34**

new, novus, -a, -um **3, 4**

next, proximus, -a, -um **64**

night, nox, noctis, *f.;* **by night,** noctū *(adv.)* **40**

ninth, nōnus, -a, -um **10**

no, *(interj.)* minimē **3;** *(adj.)* nūllus, -a, -um **56; no longer,** *(adv.)* nōn iam **43**

noble, nōbilis, -e **53, 2**

nobility, nōbilitās, *f.* **51**

noise, clāmor, -ōris, *m.* **45**

none, nūllus, -a, -um **56**

noon, merīdiēs, -ēī, *m.* **45**

no one, nēmō, nēminī *(dat.),* nēminem *(acc.) (no other forms)* **62, 7**

nor, *(conj.)* neque **28;** nēve, (neu) **70**

not, nōn **1;** nē *(w. negative volitive and purpose clauses)* **11; and not,** neque *(conj.)* neque nēve (neu) **70; not even,** nē... quidem **16; not yet,** nōndum **17; not only ... but also,** nōn sōlum... sed etiam **23**

not at all, minimē **3**

noted, īnsignis, -e **16;** nōtus, -a, -um

nothing, nihil **51**

notice, animadvertō, -ere, -vertī, -versus **57**

nourish, alō, -ere, aluī, alitus **31**

now, nunc **4;** iam **30**

number, numerus, -ī, *m.* **5, 7; the same number,** totidem, *(indeclinable adj.)* **64**

O

oath, iūs iūrandum, iūris iūrandī, *n.* **49**

oar, rēmus, -ī, *m.* **43**

obey, pāreō, -ēre, pāruī, pāritūrus *(w. dat.)* **89**

obstruct, impediō, -īre, -īvī, -ītus **44**

obtain, obtineō, -ēre, obiniuī, obtentus **37, 1; obtain one's request,** impetrō, (1)

occur, intercēdō, -ere, -cessī, -cessūrus; occurrō, -ere, occurrī, occursūrus **33**

offer, prōpōnō, -ere, -posuī, -positus **33;** offerō, offerre, obtulī, oblātus **79;** dēferō, dēferre. dētulī, dēlātus **28**

offering, mūnus, mūneris, *n.* **59, 7**

office, magistrātus, -ūs, *m.* **31**

often, saepe **14**

old, vetus, *(gen.)* veteris **88;** senex, *(gen.)* senis **27**

old man, senex, senis, *m.* **27**

omen, ōmen, ōminis, *n.* **19**

on, in, *(w. abl.)* **11; on account of,** ob **35;** *or* propter, *(w. acc.);* **on this account,** *(adv.)* proptereā **50**

once (upon a time), ōlim **31;** quondam **53**

one, ūnus, -a, -um **56**

one at a time, one by one, singulī, -ae, -a **13; one ... another,** alius... alius **56; one ... the other,** alter... alter **56**

onto, in *(w. acc.)* **15**

open, apertus, -a, -um **46;** aperiō, -īre, aperuī, apertus **30**

opinion, sententia, -ae, *f.* **25, 6;** opīniō, -ōnis, *f.* **47**

opportune, opportūnus, -a, -um **77**

opportunity, cōpia, -ae, *f.* **5;** occāsiō, -ōnis, *f.* **44**

oppose, obiciō, -ere, obiēcī, obiectus **58**

opposite, adversus, -a, -um **71**

oppress, opprimō, -ere, oppressī, oppressus

or, *(conj.)* vel **55;** aut **28; or if** sīve (seu) **55; an 25**

oracle, ōrāculum, -ī, *n.*

order *(noun)* imperium, -rī, *n.* **66;** *(verb)* iubeō, -ēre, iussī, iussus **32, 3;** imperō, (1), *(w. dat.)* **70; in order to** *or* **that,** ut **11; in order not to** *or* **that,** nē **11**

ornament, īnsigne, -is, *n.* **56**

other, alius, alia, aliud **56; the other of two,** alter, -a, -um **56; others** *(see some)* **all other** *(see all); the others,** cēterī, -ae, -a **16**

ought, dēbeō, -ēre, dēbuī, dēbitus **17, 6;** oportet, -ēre, oportuit **31;** *(use fut. pass. part.)*

our, noster, -tra, -trum **14**

ourselves, *(intens.)* ipsī, ipsae **54, 8;** *(reflex.)* —, nostrum **65**

out of, ē, ex *(w. abl.)* **13**

outcome, exitus, -ūs, *m.* **10**

outside of, extrā *(w. acc.)* **34**

over, super *(w. acc.)* **67**

overcome, superō, (1) **49;** vincō, -ere, vīcī, victus **61, 8;** opprimō, -ere, oppressī, oppressus **57**

owe, dēbeō, -ēre, dēbuī, dēbitus **17**

own (one's), proprius, -a, -um **63**

P

pace, passus, -ūs, *m.* **17**

pacify, pācō, (1) **63**

pain, dolor, -ōris, *m.* **40**

part, pars, partis, partium, *f.* **52, 4**

pass, trānseō, -īre, -iī, -itūrus **52**

pay, pendō, -ere, pependī, pēnsus **33;** stīpendium, -dī, *n.* **30; pay the penalty,** poenam dō

peace, pāx, pācis, *f.* **40, 3;** ōtium, ōtī, *n.* **22**

people, populus, -ī, *m.* 18, **1;** gēns, gentis, gentium, *f.* 62, **9**

penalty, poena, -ae, *f.* 8, **6**

perform, administrō, (1) **70**

perhaps, fortasse 41

perish, intereō, -īre, -iī, -itūrus **90;** pereō, -īre, -iī, -itūrus **21**

permit, licet, -ēre, licuit *or* licitum est **31;** permittō, -ere, -mīsī, -missus 34; patior, patī, passus **54**

person, homō, hominis, *m.* 40, **4**

persuade, persuādeō, -ēre, -suāsī, -suāsūrus *(w. dat.)* **26**

pilot, gubernātor, ōris, *m.* **12**

pitch camp, castra pōnō

place, *(noun)* locus, -ī, *m.; pl.* loca, -ōrum, *n.* 21; *(verb)* pōnō, -ere, posuī, positus 19; collocō (1) **57;** locō, (1) **39; place in charge,** praeficiō, -ere, -fēcī, -fectus 69

plain, plānitiēs, -ēī, *f.* **97;** campus, -ī, *m.* 22

plan, *(noun)* cōnsilium, -lī, *n.* 16, **6;** *(verb)* in animō habeō

play, lūdus, -ī, *m.* 35

plead, orō, (1) **24**

please, be pleasing to, placeō, -ēre, placuī, placitūrus *(w. dat.)* **26; pleasing,** *(adj.)* grātus, -a, -um 7, **4**

pledge, spondeō, -ēre, spopondī, spōnsus 19

plot, īnsidiae, -ārum, *f. pl.* 30

plunder, dīripiō, -ere, dīripuī, dīreptus **32**

poem, carmen, carminis, *n.* 45

poet, poēta, -ae, *m.* 26

point out, mōnstrō, (1) 7

Pompey, Pompeius, -peī, *m.*

poor, miser, -era, -erum 29

port, portus, -ūs 13

portray, exprimō, -ere, -pressī, expressus 26

pour, fundō, -ere, fūdī, fūsus 37

power, potestās, -tātis, *f.* 54, **2;** imperium, -rī, *n.* 66; **powerful,** potēns, *(gen.)* potentis **64**

praetor, praetor, -ōris, *m.*

praise, *(verb)* laudō, (1) 4; *(noun)* laus, laudis, *f.* **94**

prayer, prex, precis, *f.* **49**

prefer, mālō, mālle, māluī, — **28**

prepare, parō, (1) 3; **prepared,** parātus, -a, -um 42

present (be), adsum, esse, adfuī, adfutūrus 34, **6**

present, prōpōnō, -ere, -posuī, positus 33; **(as a gift),** dōnō, (1) 7

preserve, servō, (1) 8; cōnservō, (1) 37

press (hard), premō, -ere, pressī, pressus 40; **press out,** exprimō, -ere, -pressī, expressus 26

pretend, simulō, (1) **39**

prevent, prohibeō, -ēre, -hibuī, -hibitus 58

price, pretium, -tī, *n.* 21

pride, superbia, -ae, *f.* 34

priest, pontifex, pontificis, *m.* **19**

prisoner, captīvus, -ī, *m.* 13

private, prīvātus, -a, -um **52**

proceed, prōcēdō, -ere, -cessī, -cessūrus 30, **9**

procession, pompa, -ae, *f.*

produce, efficiō, -ere, effēcī, effectus 21

promise, polliceor, pollicērī, pollicitus **18;** spondeō, -ēre, spopondī, spōnsus **19**

protection, praesidium, -dī, *n.* 28; fidēs, -eī, *f.* **63**

proud, superbus, -a, -um 34

prove, probō, (1) 7, **6**

provide, īnstruō, -ere, īnstrūxī, īnstrūctus 62

province, prōvincia, -ae, *f.* 8

public, pūblicus, -a, -um, *m.* 18

publish, ēdō, -ere, ēdidī, ēditus **15**

punishment, poena, -ae, *f.* 8, **6;** supplicium, -cī, *n.* 53

pursue, īnsequor, īnsequī, īnsecūtus 47

put, pōnō, -ere, posuī, positus 19, **5; put forward,** prōpōnō, -ere, -posui, -positus 33; **put in charge of,** praeficiō, -ere, -fēcī, -fectus 69; **put in flight,** in fugam dō 43; **put out,** expōnō, -ere, exposuī, expositus 81; **put aside, put down,** dēpōnō, -ere, -posuī, -positus 17; **put away,** abdō, abdidī, abditus 30; **put around,** circumdō, -dare, -dedī, -datus 30

Q

quaestor, quaestor, -ōris, *m.* **26**

queen, rēgīna, -ae, *f.* 5

question, interrogō, (1) **23**

quick, celer, celeris, celere 47; matūrus, -a, -um **12**

quickly, celeriter

quiet, quiētus, -a, -um **18**

R

raise, sublevō, (1) **43;** tollō, -ere, sustulī, sublātus **43**

rampart, vāllum, -ī, *n.* **58**

rank, ōrdō, ōrdinis, *m.* 45

rashly, temere **80**

rather, *(expressed by comparative degree);* **rather than,** potius quam

reach, attingō, -ere, attigī, attāctus **23**

read, legō, -ere, lēgī, lēctus 26, **4**

ready, parātus, -a, -um 42; **get ready,** parō, (1) 3

real, vērus, -a, -um 18

realize, sentiō, -īre, sēnsī, sēnsus 60, **6**

reason, causa, -ae, *f.* 18; ratiō, -ōnis, *f.* 70; **without reason,** *(adv.)* temere **80**

recall, revocō, (1)

receive, accipiō, -ere, accēpī, acceptus 20; excipiō, -ere, excēpī, exceptus **13;** recipiō, -ere, recēpī, receptus **52**

recent, recēns, *(gen.)* recentis **60**

recite, recitō, (1); prōnūntiō, (1) **23**

reconnoiter, explōrō, (1) 70

recover, recipiō, -ere, recēpī, receptus 32; recuperō, (1) **97**

reduce, redigō, -ere, redēgī, redāctus 32

reinforcements, auxilia, -ōrum, *n.* 17, **6**

refrain, abstineō, -ēre, -tinuī, -tentus

region, regiō, -ōnis, *f.* 62

relate, nārrō, (1) 21

relax, remittō, -ere, remīsī, remissus 52

religion, religiō, -ōnis, *f.* **89**

remain, maneō, -ēre, mānsī, mānsūrus 11, **4**

remaining, reliquus, -a, -um 26

remark, vōx, vōcis, *f.* 57, **6**

remember, memoriā teneō

remind, moneō, -ēre, -uī, -itus 38, **8**

remove, removeō, -ēre, remōvī, remōtus 32

repair, reficiō, -ere, refēcī, refectus 15

reply, respondeō, -ēre, respondī, respōnsus 49, **2**

report *(noun)* nūntius, -tī, *m.* 17; fāma, -ae, *f.* 2; *(verb)* nūntiō, (1) 7, **6;** renūntiō, (1) **40**

repulse, repellō, -ere, reppulī, repulsus 62

reserve, reservō, (1)

resist, resistō, -ere, restitī, — *(w. dat.)*

resources, opēs, -um, *f. pl.*

rest, quiēs, -ētis, *f.* **15**

rest (of), reliquus, -a, -um 26; cēterī, -ae, -a **16**

restore, reddō, -ere, reddidī, redditus 68; restituō, -ere, restituī, restitūtus **34**

retire, mē recipiō 32

retreat, cēdō, -ere, cessī, cessūrus 19

return *(verb)* redeō, -īre, rediī, reditūrus **20;** *(noun)* reditus, -ūs, *m.;* revertō, -ere, revertī, reversus **26**

reveal, aperiō, -īre, aperuī, apertus **30**

revolution, novae rēs, novārum rērum, *f. pl.*

reward, praemium, -ī, *n.* 16

right, iūs, iūris, *n.* 47; dexter, -tra, -trum **72**

rightly, rēctē 13

ripe, matūrus, -a, -um 12

rise, sublevō, (1) *(w. reflex.)* **43;** orior, orīrī, ortus **19; rise up to,** adorior, adorīrī, adortus **67;** surgō, -ere, surrēxī, surrēctūrus **15**

river, flūmen, flūminis, *n.* 45, **8**

road, via, -ae, *f.* 1; iter, itineris, *n.* 46, **8**

rock, saxum, -ī, *n.* **22**

roll, volvō, -ere, volvī, volūtus 14

Roman, Rōmānus, -a, -um

row, ōrdō, ōrdinis, *m.* 45

rule, regō, -ere, rēxī, rēctus 20; imperō, (1) *(w. dat.)* 70

rumor, rumor, -ōris, *m.* **63**

run, currō, -ere, cucurrī, cursūrus 50; **run away,** fugiō, -ere, fūgī, fugitūrus 22

rush against, mē offerō **79**

S

sacred, sacer, -cra, -crum 14

sad, tristis, -e **34**

safe, tūtus, -a, -um **31**

safety, salūs, -ūtis, *f.* 40, **2**

sail, nāvigō, (1) 6, **1**

sailor, nauta, -ae, *m.* 6

sake of (for the), causā *or* grātiā *(w. gen. preceding)*

sally, ēruptiō, -ōnis, *f.* 74

same, īdem, eadem, idem 53, **8; at the same time,** simul *(adv.)* **43; to the same place,** eōdem *(adv.)* **52**

save, servō, (1) 8, **2**

say, dīcō, -ere, dīxī, dictus 22, **4;** inquit *(w. direct quotations)* **28; say . . . not,** negō, (1) **21**

scarcely, *(adv.)* vix 36

scare, terreō, -ēre, terruī, territus 10, **8; scare thoroughly,** perterreō, -ēre, -terruī, -territus **14**

school, lūdus, -ī, *m.* 35

scout, explōrātor, -ōris, *m.* 55

sea, mare, maris, *n.* 46; **of the sea,** maritimus, -a, -um **77; seacoast,** ōra maritima **77**

second, secundus, -a, -um 59

secret, occultus, -a, -um **60**

secretly, *(adv.)* clam **44**

see, videō, -ēre, vīdī, vīsus 11, **4;** cernō, -ere, crēvī, crētus 42; cōnspiciō, -ere, -spexī, -spectus 65; **see clearly,** perspiciō, -ere, -spexī, -spectus **67**

seek, petō, -ere, petīvī, petītus 36; **seek for,** conquīrō, -ere, -quīsīvī, -quīsitus **58; seek from,** quaerō, -ere, quaesīvī, quaesītus **22**

seem, videor, vidērī, vīsus 4

seize, capiō, -ere, cēpī, captus 20, **8;** occupō, (1) 8, **3;** prehendō, -ere, -hendī, -hēnsus **14**

select, legō, -ere, lēgī, lēctus 26, **4;** dēligō, (1) **24**

-self, *(intens.)* ipse, ipsa, ipsum 54, **8;** *(or use reflexives)* 65

senate, senātus, -ūs, *m.* 68

senator, senātor, -ōris, *m.*

send, mittō, -ere, mīsī, missus 19, **5; send ahead,** praemittō, -ere, -mīsī, missus 67; **send away,** dīmittō 31, **6; send back,** remittō 52; **send for,** arcesso, -ere, -īvī, -ītus; **send out,** dīmittō, -ere, dīmīsī, dīmissus 31, **6**

senior, senex, senis, *m.* **27**

sensible, prūdēns, *(gen.)* prūdentis **25**

service, mūnus, mūneris, *n.* 59, **7**

set out, proficīscor, proficīscī, profectus **18; set on fire,** incendō, -ere, incendī, incēnsus **15; set free,** expediō, -īre, -īvī, -ītus 44

settler, colōnus, -ī, *m.* 15

seventh, septimus, -a, -um **11**

several, complūrēs, -a, *or* -ia **35**

severe, gravis, -e 57, **5;** tristis, -e **34**

shape, fōrma, -ae, *f.* 5

share, commūnicō, (1) **89**

sharp, ācer, ācris, ācre 60, **2;** acūtus, -a, -um **16**

sharply, ācriter

she, ea 31; haec 50; illa 50; *(often not expressed)*

shed, fundō, -ere, fūdī, fūsus 37

shepherd, pāstor, -ōris, *m.* 46

shield, scūtum, -ī, *n.* 24

ship, nāvis, nāvis, *f.* 46

shore, lītus, lītoris, *n.* 23

short, brevis, -e **40**

shout, *(verb)* clāmō, (1) 40, **4; shouting,** *(noun)* clāmor, -ōris, *m.* 45

show *(noun)* mōnstrō, (1) 7; mūnus, -eris, *n.* 59, **7;** *(verb)* ostendō, -ere, ostendī, ostentus 58, **7;** dēmōnstrō, (1) 68

shy, timidus, -a, -um 43

sick, aeger, -ra, -rum 15

side, pars, partis, partium, *f.* 52, **4**

sign, signal, signum, -ī, *n.* 16, **8;** ōmen, ōminis, *n.* **19**

sight, cōnspectus, -ūs, *m.* **28**

silence, silentium, -ī, *n.* **10**

since, quod 4; cum; quoniam; *(use abl. abs.)* **34**

sing, cantō, (1); **sing (about),** canō, -ere, cecinī, cantus 10

single one (not a), neque quisquam

sit, sedeō, -ēre, sēdī, sessūrus 54; **sit down,** cōnsīdō, -ere, sēdī, -sessūrus **36**

'situation, rēs, reī, *f.* 69

sister, soror, -ōris, *f.* 54, **2**

six, sex; **sixty,** sexāgintā

sixth, sextus, -a, -um **11**

size, magnitūdō, -dinis, *f.* **34**

skilled, perītus, -a, -um 14

slave, servus, -ī, *m.* 4, **1**

slavery, servitūs, servitūtis, *f.* **61**

slaughter, caedēs, -is, *f.,* **32**

sleep, somnus, -ī 14

slow, tardus, -a, -um 24, **6; slow up,** tardō, (1) **72**

small, parvus, -a, -um 2; exiguus, -a, -um **80**

so, *(adv.)* ita 22; tam **14; so great** *or* **so large,** *(adj.)* tantus, -a, -um **14; so that,** *(conj.)* ut **11; so as not to, so that not,** nē **11; so** *or* **so much,** *(adv.)* adeō **39;** *(adv.)* sīc 3

soldier, mīles, mīlitis, *m.* 40, **8**

some, nōn nūllī, -ae, -a **58;** aliquī, aliqua, aliquod **20;** quīdam, quaedam, quoddam **20; some . . . others,** aliī... aliī 56; **someone, something,** aliquis, aliquid **20**

sometimes, *(adv.)* nōn numquam **53**

son, fīlius, -lī, *m.* 14, **1**

song, carmen, -minis, *n.* 45

soon, mox 37; **soon as possible (as),** quam prīmum **17; as soon as,** simul atque (ac) **43**

source, fōns, fontis, *m.* **20**

space, spatium, -tī, *n.* 43

spare, parcō, -ere, pepercī, parsūrus *(w. dat.)* **32**

speak, dīcō, -ere, dīxī, dictus 22, **4;** loquor, loquī, locūtus **18;** verba faciō

spear, pīlum, -ī, *n.* **57**

spectacle, spectāculum, -ī, *n.*

speech, ōrātiō, -ōnis, *f.* 62; **make a speech,** verba faciō

speed, celeritās, -tātis, *f.* 49

spend, cōnsūmō, -ere, -sūmpsī, -sūmptus **18; (of time),** agō, -ere, ēgī, āctus 19; **spend the winter,** hiemō, (1)

spirit, animus, -ī, *m.* 15

spot, cōnspiciō, -ere, -spexī, -spectus 65

spring, fōns, fontis, fontium, *m.* **20**

stand, stō, stāre, stetī, stātūrus 41, **5; stand still,** cōnsistō, -ere, cōnstitī, cōnstitūrus 58; **stand before,** praestō, -āre, -stitī, stitūrus **34; stand open,** pateō, -ēre, patuī, — **51**

standard, signum, -ī, *n.* 16, **8**

star, stella, -ae, *f.*

start, proficīscor, proficīscī, profectus **18;** suscipiō, -ēre, -cēpī, -ceptus 33

state *(noun)* cīvitās, -tātis, *f.* 48, **3;** *(verb)* dīcō, -ere, dīxī, dictus 22

station, collocō, (1)

stay behind, remaneō, -ēre, remānsī, remānsūrus 34

steal, rapiō, -ere, rapuī, raptus 61, **7**

steep, praeceps, *(gen.)* praecipitis 50

step, *(noun)* passus, -ūs, *m.* **17;** *(verb)* gradior, gradī, gressus **22; step into,** ingredior, ingredī, ingressus **19; step forward,** prōgredior, prōgredī, prōgressus **22**

stick, haereō, -ēre, haesī, haesus 60; **stick (to),** adhaereō, -ēre, -haesī, -haesus **12**

still, adhūc **28**

stir up, incitō, (1) **8;** sollicitō, (1) **63**

stop, cōnsistō, -ere, -stitī, -stitūrus 58; intermittō, -ere, -mīsī, -missus 37

storm, tempestās, -tātis, *f.* **12**

story, fābula, -ae, *f.*

straight, dērēctus **94; straight down,** praeceps, *(gen.)* praecipitis 50

strange, novus, -a, -um 3, **4**

street, via, -ae, *f.* **1**

strength, vīs, vīs, vīrium 58

stretch, tendō, -ere, tetendī, tentus 47; **stretch out,** ostendō, -ere, ostendī, ostentus 58, 7

strive, contendō, -ere, -tendī, -tentūrus

strong, firmus, -a, -um 23; fortis, -e 47

struggle, labōrō, (1); contendō, -ere, -tendī, -tentus 57

studies, studia, -ōrum, *n.* 22

study, studeō, -ēre, studuī,— 19

stupidity, stultitia, -ae, *f.* 29

succeed, succēdō, -ere, -cessī, -cessūrus 27

successful, fēlīx, *(gen.)* -īcis 18

successive, continuus, -a, -um 84

such, tam 14

sudden, repentīnus, -a, -um 55; **suddenly,** *(adv.)* repente 88; subitō 19

suitable, commodus, -a, -um, 22; aptus, -a, -um 62; idōneus, -a, -um 42

summer, aestās, -ātis, *f.* 51

summon, ēvocō, (1) 16; convocō, (1) 25; arcessō, -ere, -īvī, -ītus 60

sun, sōl, sōlis, *m.* 63

superstition, religiō, -ōnis, *f.* 89

supplies, commeātus, -ūs, *m.*

supply, cōpia, -ae, *f.* 5

suppose, putō, (1) 59, 6

sure, certus, -a, -um 42; **to be sure,** *(adv.)* quidem *(follows the word it emphasizes)* 16

surpass, superō, (1) 49

surprise, opprimō, -ere, oppressī, oppressus 57

surrender, *(verb)* dēdō, dēdere, dēdidī, dēditus 69; trādō, -ere, -didī, -ditus 66; *(noun)* dēditiō, -ōnis, *f.* 58

surround, circumsistō, -ere, -stetī, — 77; circumveniō, -īre, -vēnī, -ventus 26

survive, supersum, -esse, -fuī, -futūrus 67

suspect, suspicor, (1) 49

swamp, palūs, palūdis, *f.* 11

swear, iūrō, (1) 88

swift, celer, celeris, celere 47, 7; **swiftly,** celeriter; **swiftness,** celeritās, -tātis, *f.* 49

T

tablet, tabula, -ae, *f.*

take, capiō, -ere, cēpī, captus 20; sūmō, -ere, sūmpsī, sūmptus 65; emō, -ere, ēmī, ēmptus 66; **take back,** recipiō, -ere, recēpī, receptus 32; **take on,** incipiō 23; **take up,** suscipiō 33

talk, loquor, loquī, locūtus 18; **talk with,** colloquor, colloquī, collocūtus 83

tall, altus, -a, -um 12

teach, doceō, -ēre, docuī, doctus 10, 1

teacher, magister, -trī, *m.* 14; magistra, -ae, *f.*

tell, dīcō, -ere, dīxī, dictus 22; nārrō, (1) 21; canō, -ere, cecinī, cantus 10

temple, templum, -ī, *n.* 20

tempt, temptō, (1)

tenth, decimus, -a, -um 11

terms, condiciō, -ōnis, *f.* 61, 2

terrify, terreō, -ēre, terruī, territus 10, 8

territory, fīnēs, -ium, *m. pl.* 46

terror, terror, -ōris, *m.*

test, probō, (1) 7, 6; temptō, (1) 62

than, quam 61

thank, grātiās agō *(w. dat.)*

that *(dem. pron.)* ille, illa, illud 50; is, ea, id 52; iste, ista, istud 45

that, in order that, *(conj.)* so that ut(ī) 11; **that . . . not** (purpose), nē 11; *(result)* ut... nōn

their *(poss.)* eōrum, eārum, eōrum; *(reflex.)* suus, -a, -um 65

themselves *(reflex.)* suī; *(intens.)* ipsī, -ae, -a 65

then, tum 6; deinde 12

there, ibi 11; eō 24

thereafter, deinde 12

therefore, igitur 40

they, eī, eae, ea; illī, illae, illa; *(often not expressed)*

thing, rēs, reī, *f.; (often not expressed)* 69

think, putō, (1) 59; existimō, (1) 16; arbitror, (1) 18; cēnseō, -ēre, cēnsuī, cēnsus 44; cōgitō, (1) 61

third, tertius, -a, -um 42

this, hic, haec, hoc 50; is, ea, id 52

thousand, *(adj.)* mīlle; pl. mīlia; **thousands,** *(pl. noun)* mīlia, mīlium 66

threaten, īnstō, -āre, īnstitī, — 60

three, trēs, tria 66

through, per *(w. acc.)* 33

throw, iaciō, -ere, iēcī, iactus 45; coniciō, -ere, -iēcī, -iectus 48; **throw down,** dēiciō, -ere, dēiēcī, dēiectus 33; proiciō, -ere, -iēcī, -iectus 34; **throw against,** obiciō, -ere, obiēcī, obiectus 58; **throw (to),** adigō, -ere, adēgī, adāctus 70; **throw into confusion,** perturbō (1) 10; **throw out,** ēiciō, -ere, ēiēcī, ēiectus 12

thrust (forward), prōiciō, -ere, -iēcī, -iectus 34

thus, *(adv.)* sīc 69; ita 14

tide, aestus, -ūs, *m.* 81

tie, ligō, (1) 44

till, colō, -ere, coluī, cultus 54

timber, māteria, -ae, *f.* 11, 7

time, tempus, temporis, *n.* 45, 7; aetās, -ātis, *f.* 61; spatium, -tī, *n.* 43; **one at a time,** singulī, -ae, -a 13; **at the same time,** *(adv.)* simul 43

tired, dēfessus, -a, -um 17

to, *(prep.)* w. acc., ad 6; in 15; *(conj.)* ut 11

toga, -ae, *f.* toga

tomorrow, crās 6, **6**

tongue, lingua, -ae 10

too (also), quoque **21; too (much),** *(use comp. adj.)*

top (of), summus, -a, -um 64

touch, tangō, -ere, tetigī, tactus 53; attingō, -ere, attigī, attāctus **23;** contingō, -ere, tigī, tāctus 29

torture, cruciātus, -ūs, *m.* 49

toward, ad, *(w. acc.)*

tower, turris, -is, *f.* **74**

town, oppidum, -ī, *n.*

train, instituō, -ere, instituī, institūtus **21;** exerceō, -ēre, exercuī, exercitus 67

training, disciplīna, -ae, *f.* 10

transport, trānsportō, (1) 41

travel, iter faciō

traveler, viātor, -ōris, *m.*

treachery, perfidia, -ae, *f.* **25**

tree, arbor, -oris, *f.* **20**

trench, fossa, -ae, *f.* **28**

tribe, gēns, gentis, *f.* 62, **9;** nātiō, -ōnis, *f.* **80**

tribune, tribūnus, -ī, *m.* **24**

troops, cōpiae, -ārum, *f. pl.*

true, vērus, -a, -um 18, **7**

trumpet, tuba, -ae, *f.* **36**

trust, fidēs, -eī, *f.* 63

try, cōnor, (1) **43;** temptō, (1) **62;** experior, experīrī, expertus **66**

turn, vertō, -ere, vertī, versūrus 44; **turn away,** āverto 65; **turn over,** versō, (1) **63;** volvō, -ere, voluī, volūtus **14; turn back,** revertō, -ere, revertī, reversus **26**

twenty, vīgintī 18

twice, bis *(adv.)* **39**

two, duo, duae, duo 66; **two at a time,** bīnī, -ae, -a **77**

U

uncertain, incertus, -a, -um 52

under, sub *(w. abl. or acc.)* 33

understand, intellegō, -ere, -lēxī, -lēctus 67; **17**

undertake, suscipiō, -ere, -cēpī, -ceptus 33

unencumbered, expedītus, -a, -um **52**

uneven, inīquus, -a, -um **33**

unfavorable, aliēnus, -a, -um 57

unfold, explicō, (1) 63

unfriendly, inimīcus, -a, -um 30, **8**

unhappy, miser, -era, -erum 29

unharmed, incolumis, -e **35**

unjust, inīquus, -a, -um **33**

unknown, ignōtus, -a, -um **26**

unless, nisi **35**

unlike, dissimilis, -e 63

until, dum 52

untouched, integer, -gra, -grum 31

unwilling (be), nōlō, nōlle, nōluī, — **25;** invītus, -a, -um **54**

up (to), *(adv.)* usque (ad) **77**

upon, in *(w. abl. or acc.)*

uproar, tumultus, -ūs, *m.* **67**

upset, permoveō, -ēre, -mōvī, -mōtus 37

urge, hortor, (1) **21;** impellō, -ere, impulī, impulsus; **urge on,** incitō, (1) 8

us, see **we**

use, ūtor, ūtī, ūsus *(w. abl.)* **41; use up,** cōnsūmō, -ere, -sūmpsī, sūmptus **18**

useful, ūtilis, -e 61, **8**

usually, plērumque **74**

utter, ēdō, -ere, ēdidī, ēditus **15**

V

vain (in), frustrā **48**

various, varius, -a, -um 22

very, *(use superlative);* **very many,** plūrimī, -ae, -a; **very (much),** *(adv.)* admodum **97**

victor, *(noun)* victor, -ōris, *m.* **60; victorious,** *(adj.)* victor, -ōris **60**

victory, victōria, -ae, *f.* 8

vigorous, vehemēns, *(gen.)* vehementis **33**

villa, vīlla, -ae, *f.*

village, vīcus, -ī, *m.* **52**

violence, vīs, vīs, vīrium, *f.* 58

Virgil, Vergilius, -lī, *m.*

voice, vōx, vōcis, *f.* 57, **6**

voluntarily, *(adv.)* ultrō **82;** sponte *(with* **suā***)* 54

W

wage war, bellum gerō

wagon, carrus, -ī, *m.* 4

wait, exspectō, (1) 19, **6**

walk, gradior, gradī, gressus **22**

wall, vāllum, -ī, *n.* **58;** mūrus, -ī, *m.* **28**

wander, vagor, (1) **51**

want, cupiō, -ere, cupīvī, cupītus 31, **4;** volō, velle, voluī **25; not want,** nōlō, nōlle, nōluī, — **25**

war, bellum, -ī, *n.* 17

warn, moneō, -ēre, monuī, monitus 38, **8**

waste, cōnsūmō, -ere, -sūmpsī, -sūmptus **18**

watch, spectō, (1) 3, **7**

water, aqua, -ae, *f.* 1

wave, unda, -ae, *f.* 6

way, via, -ae, *f.* 1; modus, -ī, *m.* 38, **5**

we, nōs, nostrum; *(often not expressed)* 31

wealth, ops, opis, *f.* **20**

weapons, arma 17, **9;** tēlā, -ōrum, *n. pl.;* **weapon,** tēlum, -ī, *n.* **53**

wedding, nūptiae, -ārum, *f. pl.*

weep (for), fleō, flēre, flēvī, flētus **11**

weigh, pendō, -ere, pependī, pēnsus **33**

weight, onus, oneris, *n.* **74**

well, *(adv.)* bene **64;** **(be),** *(verb)* valeō, -ēre, valuī, valitūrus 22, **8**

what *(pron)* quis, quid 18; 38; *(adj.)* quī, quae, quod 36; 38

whatever, quīcumque, quaecumque, quodcumque **82**

when, ubi 18; cum; *(expressed by participle or abl. abs.)*

where, ubi 4; quā **52**

whether, num *(introduces questions expecting negative answer)* **25; whether . . . or,** sīve... sīve **55**

which *(rel. pron.)* quī, quae, quod 36; **which (of two),** uter, utra, utrum

while, *(conj.)* dum 52; **for a little while,** *(adv.)* paulisper **66**

who *(rel. pron.)* quī, quae, quod 36; *(interrog. pron.)* quis, quid 18; 38

whoever, quīcumque, quaecumque, quodcumque **82**

whole, tōtus, -a, -um 56; integer, -gra, -grum 31

wholesome, salūbris, -e

why, cūr 36

wide, lātus, -a, -um 18

width, lātitūdō, -dinis, *f.* **51**

wife, mulier, mulieris, *f.* **10**

wild, ferus, -a, -um **60**

willing (be), volō, velle, voluī, — **25; not be willing,** nōlō, nōlle, nōluī, — **25**

win, mereō, -ēre, meruī, meritus **12**

wind, ventus, -ī, *m.* 27

wing, āla, -ae, *f.* **17; wing (of an army),** cornū, -ūs, *n.* **72**

winter, hiems, hiemis, *f.* 51; **winter quarters,** hīberna, -ōrum, *n. pl* **54**

wise, sapiēns, *(gen.)* -ntis, *m.* **20**

wisely, sapienter

wish, cupiō, -ere, -īvī, -ītus 31, **4;** volō, velle, voluī, — **25; wish not,** nōlō, nōlle, nōluī, — **25;** *(noun)* voluntās, -tātis, *f.* **37**

with, cum, *(w. abl.); (sometimes abl. alone)*

withdraw, concēdō, -ere, -cessī, -cessūrus **21;** discēdō, -ere, -cessī, -cessūrus 32

within, intrā *(w. acc.)* **30**

without, sine, *(w. abl.)* 30

woman, mulier, -eris, *f.* **10;** fēmina, -ae, *f.* **35**

wonder, mīror, (1) **19**

wonderful, mīrus, -a, -um **16**

woods, silva, -ae, *f.* 1

word, verbum, -ī, *n.* 24

work, *(noun)* opus, operis, *n.* 63; opera, -ae, *f.* **15;** labor, -ōris, *m.* 59; *(verb)* labōrō, (1) 3

worse, peior, peius; **worst,** pessimus, -a, -um

worry, cūra, -ae, *f.* 5

worship, colō, -ere, coluī, cultus 54

worthy, dignus, -a, -um **10**

wound, *(noun)* vulnus, vulneris, *n.* 45; *(verb)* vulnerō, (1) 40

write, scrībō, -ere, scrīpsī, scrīptus 26, **4;** cōnscrībō, -ere, scrīpsī, -scrīptus **54**

wrong, iniūria, -ae, *f.* 8

Y

year, annus, -ī, *m.* 16, **5**

yes, sīc 3

yield, cēdō, -ere, cessī, cessūrus 19; concēdō, -ere, -cessī, -cessūrus **21**

yoke, iugum, -ī, *n.* 45

you, tū, tuī *(sing.)* 31; vōs, vestrum *(pl.); often not expressed* 31

young man, iuvenis, -is, *m.* **12**

your, tuus, -a, -um *(sing.)* 9; vester, -tra, -trum, *pl.* 18; **yourself** *(reflex.)* tuī 31; *(intens.)* ipse, ipsa 54, **8;** *(reflex)* —, tuī *(sing.)* 65; —, vestrum 65

youth, adulēscēns, -entis, *m.* **21**

SUBJECT INDEX

The page numbers in italics refer to the illustrations.

Cumae, 488
Cupid, *480*
Curia Julia, 36; *37, 257*
Curiatian brothers, 169, 172f ; *167*
cursus honorum, 154
Cynthia, 459
Cyprus, 484

D

Dacians, *340*
dagger, 197
daily life and routine, Units I, IX
Damma Imparicrus, 406
Damon and Pythias, 460
dance, 69, 120, 154; *461*
Danube River, 340
Darius, 138
dates and events in Roman history, 492
David, Jacques Louis, *168f.*
David, King, 471
De Consolatione, 472
De Officiis, 453f.; *453*
De Rerum Natura, 450
Deal, England, 365
debt, 186, 288
Decemviri, 27
Declaration of Independence, 189
Delia, 459
Delphi and Delphic oracle, 74, 119, 121, 139,
     234f.; *111, 109, 119, 121, 180*
democracy, 131, 160
Demosthenes, 139, *140*
Denmark, 468
Descartes, 466
Deucalion and Pyrrha, 478f.
dictator, 186, 260, 424–27
Did You Know, 74, 84, 120, 138
Dido, 486ff.; *486,*
Dies Irae, 471
Diespiter (Jupiter), *397*
Dijon, France, 336
dinner, 68ff., *80,* 438, 462; *68, 70, 80, 461*
Dionysius, King of Sicily, 460
Dionysus (Bacchus), 153, 162; *210*
Dis (Pluto), 38, 488
Discus Thrower (discobolus), *137*

Diviciacus (Haeduus), 270, 288, 299, 301, 318,
     323, 328, 393
Diviciacus (Suessio), 316
Domitian, 464
Domus Aurea, 220
Doric order, *107, 161, 207*
dowries, 149, 400
dragons, 242, 244, 246f., 482
drama, *see* Greek drama, Roman comedy
dreams, 490
Druids, 394, 396, 398; *394, 396*
Dumnorix, 270, 279, 288, 380f.

E

eagles, 369; *264, 299, 317, 368, 421*
Earth Goddess, 111
earthquake, 429
Eburones, 316, 384
Echo and Narcissus, 480, *480*
Eclogues, 23, 365, 485f., 490; *485*
Egypt, 74, 138, 213, 216; *225*
El Djem (Tunisia), *62*
Elaver (Allier) River, 411
Eleusis, 74, 119
education, *see* schools, students, teachers
Elysian Fields, 459
Enchorion, 99f., 109, 119
Ennius, 206, 448
Entremont, France, 291
ephebes, 131
Epicurus, 450; *450*
epigram, 463
Epirus, 216
Epistles of Horace, 457
epistulae, 387, 458, 472, *see also* letters
equites, *see* cavalry, social classes
Erechtheum, *93*
Ericsson, Leif, 468
Esquiline Hill, 176, 220
etchings, *191*
Ethiopians (Aithiopes), 57
Etruria, 196
Etruscans, 76, 138, 160f.,172, 176, 183; *76, 172,
     181, 183, 239*
Euclid, 161
Eutropius, 171

exploratores, *see* scouts

of Cicero, 472

of Pliny, Unit IX, *see also* **epistles**

libraries, 425; *284*

Libya, *95*

lictors, 417

light-armed troops, 263, 323, 334

lighthouse, *381*

Lingones, 294

Liutprand, 468

Livia Drusilla, 18; *18*

Livy, 170ff., 177, 183, 186, 191, 432, 456, 466f.; *170*

Loire (Liger) River, 411

Louvre, Paris, 106, 305, 467, 483

love letters, 441

love poetry, 452f., 457

Lucanians, 161

Lucretia, 18, 177; *176*

Lucretius, 139, 450

ludi circenses, 154

gladiatorii, 56, *220;*

Romani, 176

scaenici, 154, *see also* **games, schools**

Luna, 402

Lupercalia, 45

Lycurgus, 127

Lyon (France), 283

M

Maccari, Cesare, 447

Macedonia, 138, 212, 216, 449

Macedonian War, 207

magician, *449*

Maison Carrée, *267*

majuscule writing, *485*

Mandubii, 418

Manlius, Torquatus (father and son), 199

manuscripts, *318, 344, 439, 453, 469, 485*

maps of: Gaul, *254f.*

Roman Empire, *158*

Rome, *222*

voyage of the Argonauts, *233*

see also **battlefields of Caesar**

Marathon, Battle of 134, 138

Marcus Aurelius, *196,* **Column of,** *323, 326*

marines, *202, 318*

Marius, C. 139, 145, 306, 308, 339

Mark Antony 99, 145, 212, 216, 453; *260*

Marne River, 266

marriage, 113, 275, 297, 435; *113*

Mars, 44, 398

marshes, *see* **swamps**

Martial, 463

masks, 308; *153, 449*

Massilia (Marseilles, France), 297

materfamilias, 2

mathematics, 161

matron, *see* **women**

Maxentius, 258

meals 68ff., 238, 438; *68, 70, 80*

Medea, 232, 242, 244, 246, 248, 250-53; *242, 250*

medicine, 86, 88f.,242, 247, 250ff.; *86, 88*

medical instruments, *89*

Mediterranean Sea, *83, 158f., 233, 238*

Medusa, 481f.; *475*

Menapii, 316, 360, 362, 392

Menelaus, 487

Menenius Agrippa, 187

Menicia, Marcella, 435

merchants, 263, 329, 345, 366

Mercury, 398, 488

Merida, Spain, *308*

Messal(l)a Corvinus, 75

Messalla (cos. 61 B.C.), 269

Messalla (cos. 31 B.C.), 457

metals, *see* **minerals**

Metamorphoses, 23, 98, 476–84

Metlosedum (Melun, France), 412

Metropolitan Museum of Art, 246

Michelangelo, 196

Middle Ages, 468–71, 486

Middle East, 33, 138, 486

mile, Roman, 108

Miles Gloriosus, 449

Mill Race Gorge, 272, 283

Milton, 480

minerals, 382, *see also* **bronze, gold,**

Minerva, 21, 195, 398

temple of, 104

Misenum, 430

mistletoe, 394, 396

Mnemosyne, 120

models, Caesar's bridge over the Rhine, *363*

Paestum (Poseidonia), *161*
Paetus, 440
pagans, 286, 289
Painted Stoa, 90; *90*
paintings, *142, 168f.,, 176, 183, 186, 230f. 260,*
390f., 418, 472, 474f., 476
palace, 220, 468
Palatine Hill, 22, 37, 172, 220; *22, 37*
Palazzo Nuovo, 196
Pales, 45
Palladium, 21
Palmyra, Syria, *217*
Pannonians, *326*
panpipe, *397*
pantomimus, 154
pants, *306*
Parentalia, 45
Parilia (Palilia), 45
Paris (Lutecia), 392, 411f.; *410*
Paris (Trojan prince), 487
Parisii, 392, 410f.
Parthenon, 104, 127; *67*
Pas de l'Ecluse, 272
paterfamilias, *1, 2*
patria potestas, 2, 11, 400, 437
patrician, 138
patrons, 27
Pax Romana (Augusta), 2, 20, 216
pearls, 427
pedagogue, 69
Pedius, Q., 312, 324
Peleus, 234; *234*
Pelias, 232, 234ff., 236, 248-251; *248, 250*
Periander of Corinth, 126
Pericles, 127, 131f., 139, 260; *127*
peristyle, *1, 3*
Perseus, 475, 481f.
Persians, 104, 134, 138, 139
Petrarch, *472*
Petronius, 461f.
pets, 382, 437
Phaedrus, 459
Pharsalus, 213, 259
Phasis River (Colchis), 242
Pheidippides, 134
Philip of Macedon, 138, 140, 207, 451
Philippi, Battle of, 145, 216

Philippics, 140
philosophers, 68, 142, 436; *99*
see also Aristotle, Carneades, Cicero,
Epicurus, Plato, Seneca, Stoicism, Zeno
philosophy, 450, 453, 460, 462
Phineus, 238ff., 240
Phocion, 451
Phoenicians, 181, 202, 486
Phorcys, 475
Phrixus, 236
Piazza del Campidoglio, *196*
Picts, 365
Picturae Mobiles, 190
Pierpont Morgan Library, New York, *439*
Piloty, Karl Theodor von, 418
Pirustae, 381
Piso Aquitanus, 363
Piso, L. Calpurnius (cos. 112 B.C.), 284
Piso, L. Calpurnius (cos. 58 B.C.), 273
Piso, M., 269
Pittacus of Mytilene, 126
place names, ancient in U.S., 94, 198, 205, 207,
215
plans of battles, *see* battlefields of Caesar
Plato, 120, 146, 349; *142*
platters, *80*
Plautus, 154, 449
plebeians, 138, 186f., 190, 195, 258, 394
plebiscite, 190
Pliny the Elder, 225, 430-433
Pliny the Younger, 170, 430ff., 439f., 442f., 464
Pliny's *Letters,* 429-45; *439*
Plutarch, 258
Pluto, 398, 483
podium, *267*
Poeni *see* Carthaginians 203
poetry, 448–53, 457ff., 463f., 469ff., Unit XI
for metrics 477 *and* Grammar Index
Poggio, 473
political campaigns, 258f.,460
Pollux, 51
Pompeii, 139, 428-32, 449, 458, 462; *1, 3, 100,*
162, 358, 428f., 458f.
Pompey, Cn., 85f., 86, 95, 139, 145, 212f., 258f.,
273, 361, 392; *259, 273*
Pont du Gard, 311; *266, 310f.*
Pontifex Maximus 17

Valerius Maximus, 460
Varro, M. Terentius, 425, 466
vases, *234, 246, 250, 417*
Vatican Museum, 22, 142, 485
Vegetius, 287
Veii, 191, 195
Veliocasses, 316
Venetans, 354ff., 358f., 366, 378, 407
Venus and Rome, Temple of, *258*
Venus Genetrix, Temple of, 353
Venus, 258, 484, 486
Verbigenus, 295
Vercassivellaunus, 420
Vercingetorix, 336, 407-13, 419-23; *407, 421, 423*
Vergil, 23, 139, 153, 161f., 448, 457f., 472, 485-491, 486; *23, 485f., 490*
Verona, Italy, 280; *280*
Vertico, 385
Verulamium (St. Albans, England), 371
Vesontio (Besançon, France), 305, 307
Vespasian, 433, 462
Vesta, 196, 487
    atriun Vestae, *17*
Vesta, Temple of, *21*
Vestals, 18, 21, 44; *17*
    House of, *50*
veto, 186, 190
Veturia, 17
Via Appia, *see* Appian Way
Vichy, France, 411
victor's wreath, *see* wreaths
Victory (Nike), *106; 340*
vigiliae (watches), 217, 284
Villa of the Mysteries, *162*, 458
villas, 76, 373; *203, 452*
Viminal Hill, 176
Virgin Mary, 470, *471*
Viromandui, 316
Virtues, 469
vitis (centurion's staff), 385; *385*
Volscians, 17, 186, 196, 454
Volubilis, Morocco, *224*
Volusenus, C., 366, 368, 379
Vorenus, L., 385
voting, 186, 190, 465
Vulcan, 402
vulgar (spoken) Latin, 309

Vulgate, 466f.

W

wagons, see **carriages and carts**
wall paintings, *44, 100, 160, 162, 242, 248, 358, 432, 435, 452, 458, 471*
walls, *177, 312, 340, 415*
warfare, 216-65, 378ff.
    ancient vs. modern, 347–51
warships, *202, 344, 358, 368*
Washington, George, **171**, 217, 260
weapons, 196f., 347-51; *168, 197, 323, 326, 333, 344, 347f., 359, 361, 368, 385, 387, 421, 465*
    pungee-stakes (stimuli), 419
    spears, 197, 219, 323, 338, 387, 394; *387*
    swords, 197, 294, 336, 385; *168, 289, 294*
    wolf-pits (scrobes), 419
    Roman vs. modern weapons, 347
wells and fountains, *6*
Western civilization, 163
wills, 271, 444
wine, 438, *444*
woad, 382
Wolf and the Lamb, 459
women, 17f., 113, 149f., 202f., 266, 327, 435, 440, 450, 456; *1, 2, 6, 20, 100, 134, 149, 162, 176, 391, 457, 458*
World Wars I and II, 206, 208, 299, 303, 307, 318f., 326, 334, 347-51, 364, 378-80, 413
wreaths, 359; *33, 305, 472*
wrestling, 133
writing, writing implements, 439; *91, 485*

X

Xerxes, 138

Z

Zeno, 90
Zetes, 240
Zeus, 120, 398

GRAMMAR INDEX

A

ablative case, absolute, 33, 60, 212, 344, 499;
accompaniment, 14, 60, 499; accordance, 276,
500; agent, 33, 60, 498; attendant
circumstances, 312; cause, 499; comparison,
404, 452, 498; description, 216, 500; manner,
14, 60, 499; manner as adverb, 14; means
(instrument), 20, 60, 499; measure of
difference, 97, 216, 500; origin, 385, 498; place
from which, 498; place where, 7, 60, 178, 500;
respect (specification), 47, 60, 500; separation,
60, 214, 266, 276, 321, 498; time when or
within which, 7, 60, 500; with *dignus/indignus,*
410, 500; with prepositions, 2, 60, 214, 500;
with special verbs, 251, 294, 418, 421, 499;
summary of uses, 60f., 498

accent, 8, 477

accompaniment, ablative of, 14, 60f., 499

accordance, ablative of, 276, 500

accusative case, adverbial use of, 281; subject of
infinitive, 41, 188, 497; direct object, 7, 497;
extent, 97, 497; place to which, 204, 497; two
accusatives, 497; with prepositions, 497

ad, place to which, 497.3; with gerund or future
passive participle, 142, 507; with numerals,
272

adjectives, agreement of, 7, 494; as nouns, 494;
comparison of, 52f., 58f.,515; dative with, 53,
496; declension of comparatives, 52, 515;
demonstrative, 46, 51f., 517f.; first and
second declension, 5, 513; genitive with, 269,
495; indefinite, 121ff., 209, 518f.;
interrogative, 40, 151, 518; irregular, 58, 514;
numerals, 45,78, 514ff.; participles as, 30f.,
514; predicate, 147, 494f.; pronominal, 45;
relative, 518; third declension, 13, 52f., 514

adverbial clauses, 502

adverbs, formation and comparison of, 52f., 59,
515

adversative *cum* clauses, 193, 505

agent, ablative of, 33, 60, 498; dative of, 128f., 497

agreement, adjectives, 7, 494; appositives,
8, 494; relative pronouns, 39–40, 494; verbs,
187 (n. 9), 494

aliquī, 121, 510

aliquis, 121, 200, 518f.

ambō, declension of, 45, 515

antepenult, 8

antequam, 285, 505

anticipatory clauses, 285, 505

appositives, agreement of, 8, 494

assimilation, 63

attraction, subjunctive by, 338, 252, 505

auxiliary verbs, 72

B

bases, 5f., 9, 13, 118, *see also* **Word Study**

basic forms, 512–531

basic syntax, 494–511

C

cardinal numerals, 45, 57, 78, 193, 514, 516

causā, with genitive, 142, 507f.

causal clauses, relative descriptive clauses, 341;
with *cum,* 193, 504; with *quod* and *quoniam,*
292, 341, 505.16

cause, ablative of, 499

characteristic (descriptive) relative clauses, 504

clauses
  ablative absolute as, 33
  adjectival
    relative: 502.1; descriptive relative, 504.10
    expressing cause, 292, 341, 504.10, 505.16
    use of relative pronoun in, 39, 494

adverbial

  anticipatory, 285, 505.12

  causal: cum, 193, 504.11a; *quod* and
    quoniam, 292, 505.16

  concessive, 193, 505.llb

  conditional, 506

  purpose, 77, 503.2; relative purpose, 221,
    503.3; *quō* purpose, 503.4

  result, 504.8

  temporal, 101f., 502.2, 505.12

noun (substantive)

  indirect commands (volitive noun
    clauses), 503.5; (imperatives in
    ind. disc.), 506

  indirect questions, 505.13

  quod clauses of fact, 502.3

  result, 135, 504.9

  with verbs of fearing, 504.7

  with verbs of hindering, 503.6

participles as, 32, 507

subordinate clauses in indirect statement,
  277, 505.14

commands, indirect, 135, 506

comparison, ablative of, 404, 452, 498; of
  adjectives, 52f., 58f., 515; of adverbs, 52f.,
  59, 515

complementary infinitive, 20, 508

compound tenses, 32, 519–531

compound verbs, dative with, 173f., 496

concessive *cum* clauses, 193, 505

conditions, outline of, 506

conjugations, 5f., 19, 519–531

connecting relative, 204, 494

contracted forms of verbs, 238, 326, 531

correlatives, 49

cum (conj.), *cum prīmum* with indicative, 502;
  adversative (concessive) clauses, 193, 505;
  causal clauses, 193, 504; time clauses, 101f.,
  106, 165, 504f.

cum (prep.), as intensive prefix *com-, con-,* 509;
  joined to *mē, tē,* etc., 499

D

dactylic hexameter, 477

dates, counting, 212, 273

dative, of agent, 128f., 497; double dative, 156;
  indirect object, 14, 155, 496; possession, 252,
  279, 285, 303, 497; purpose, 155f., 165, 302,
  497; reference, 155f., 302, 496; separation,
  332, 336, 496; with adjectives, 53, 496; with
  compound verbs, 173f., 302, 324, 496; with
  future passive participle, 128f., 332, 507; with
  licet and *placet,* 188, 303, 496; with special
  verbs, 155, 270, 279, 303, 496; summary of
  uses, 128f.

declensions

  first, nouns and adjectives, 4, 512ff.

  second, nouns and adjectives, 4f., 512f.

  third, nouns, 12f., 512; adjectives, 13, 514;
    (comparatives), 515; (participles), 514

  fourth, 70, 157, 513

  fifth, 96, 513

  irregular adjectives, 514

  irregular nouns, 513

defective verbs, 531

degree, *see* **comparison**

demonstratives, 46, 51f., 517f.

deponent verbs, 110, 209, 525f.; perfect participle
  translated as present, 284

derivatives, *see* **Word Study**

description, ablative of, 500; genitive of, 495;
  descriptive relative clauses, 499

Developing "Word Sense," *see* **Word Study**

dignus/indignus, ablative with, 500

direct object, 497

diminutives, 452

doubting, verbs of, 240 (n. I)

dum, with indicative, 285, 502; with subjunctive,
  285, 505; with present tense, 235 (n. 7), 501

duo, declension of, 45, 515

E

ego, declension of, 517

eō, conjugation of, 123, 529

result clauses, subjunctive clauses of, 92f.,164, 504; used as nouns, 135, 504; with *ut* and *ut nōn,* 92f., 164

roots, *see* **Word Study**

S

scansion, 477f.

second conjugation, 5–6, 520–526

second declension, adjectives, 5, 513f.; nouns, 4f., 512

semideponent verbs, 293, 525f.

sentence structure, 184

separation, ablative of, 60, 214, 498; dative of, 332, 496

sequence of tenses, 82, 106, 117, 135, 165, 501f.; subjunctive, 82, 102, 106

simul ac, with indicative, 502

Spanish, *see* **Word Study**

special verbs, with ablative, 499; with dative, 155, 342, 496

specification (respect), ablative of, 47, 60, 500

spelling, *see* **Word Study**

statement, indirect, 41, 117; direct, 41

stem, present, 5, 19, 29, 38, 141, 128, 208; perfect, 38, 101; stem vowel, 147

subject, 7, 494; of infinitive, 41, 497

subjunctive mood, 70ff., 81f., 87, 502–506; formation of, 71, 81, 87, 97, 101, 105; anticipatory clauses, 285, 505; by attraction, 252, 297, 321, 505; in conditions, 505–506; *cum* adversative and causal clauses, 193, 504f.; *cum* clauses, 101, 165, 193, 504f.; descriptive relative clauses, 332, 336, 504; doubting, with verbs of, 240; fearing, with verbs of, 234, 314, 504; hindering, with verbs of, 300, 503; hortatory, 72; independent uses of, 72, 77; indirect questions, 116f., 504f.; jussive, 72; noun clauses, 135, 164f., 503f.; purpose clauses, 77, 93, 153, 221, 503; compared with result clauses, 93; tense sequence in, 82; with *quī,* 221, 503; with *quō,* 503; with *ut (uti)* and *nē,* 77, 503; *quod* causal

clauses, 292, 505; result with *ut* and *ut nōn,* 92f., 504.8; noun (substantive) clauses of result, 504.9; sequence of tenses in, 82, 102, 106; subordinate clauses in indirect statement, 82, 207, 236, 277, 398, 505; volitive noun (substantive) clauses, 135, 503f., volitive, 72, 502–503f.; summary of uses, 70ff., 164f., 502–506

subordinate clauses, in indirect statement, 82, 277, 398, 505

substantive, 31; clauses, 135, 164, 502f., 507

suffixes, 43, 48, 84, 108, 137, 157, 205, 219, 343, 397, 510f.; *see also* **Word Study**

suī, declension of, 517

sum, conjugation of, 6f., 24f., 81, 97, 105, 527f.; infinitives of, 39; omission of, 197, with future active participle, 128f.

superlative degree, 52f., 209

syllable quantity, 8, 477

syntax, basic, 494–509; review of, 164

T

tenses, 501; of infinitives, 41f., 508–509; of participles, 30, 507; progressive, 33; sequence of, 82, 102,106, 501f.; tense sign, 5, 19, 24, 29, 71

third conjugation, 19, 520–526

third declension, adjectives, 13, 52f., 514; nouns, 12ff., 512–512f.

time clauses, with *ubi, postquam, cum,* 101, 165

time when or within which, ablative of, 7, 60, 500

trādūcō, with two accusatives, 497

Translation Strategies, *see* **Reading Strategies**

trānsportō, with two accusatives, 497

trēs, declension of, 45, 514

tū, declension of, 517

two accusatives, with *trādūcō,* and *trānsportō,* 497; with verbs of calling, naming, etc., 495

U

ubi, 101, 502

ūnus, declension of, 41

ut(i), in purpose clauses, 77, 503; in result clauses, 92, 135, 504; with indicative, 502; with verbs of fearing, 314, 503

ūtor, with ablative, 499

V

verbs, agreement with subject, 494; conjugations, 5f., 19, 194, 223, 519–525; contracted forms, 238, 531; defective, 531; deponent, 110, 525f.; future perfect tense, 24f.; future tense, 5f.; imperfect tense, 5f.; impersonal, 188, 319, 344, 397; irregular, 527–530; past perfect (pluperfect) tense, 24f., 101, 105; perfect tense, 24f., 105; present tense, 5f.

vocative case, 4f., 104, 501

volitive subjunctive, 72, 77, 164, 502f.; noun clauses, 135, 164; 503

volō, 150f., 530

vowel changes, *see* **Word Study,** 74

vowel quantity, 70, 81 (n. 5), 477

W

whole, genitive of the, 25, 193, 495

word order, 9f., 16, 184, 244, 269, 477

Word Study

Aviation Terms from Latin, 201

Bases, 9

Derivatives, 9, 15,78, 175, 182, 235, 237,

239, 241, 243, 2445, 247, 249, 251, 253, 278, 282, 290, 293, 296, 298, 301, 304, 307, 315, 319, 322, 325, 327, 330, 333, 335, 337, 357, 360, 362, 364, 367, 370, 372, 375, 377, 383, 386, 389, 393, 395, 399, 401, 403, 405, 409, 415, 417, 420

Developing "Word Sense," 281, 422

Latin in Medicine, 89

Place Names, in Latin America, 296; in the United States, 94, 125, 137, 198, 205, 215

Latin Phrases, 152

Legal Phrases, 125, 275

Loan Words, 9, 89, 112, 125, 271, 346, 411

Musical Terms, 103

Portuguese, 315

Prefixes, 15, 21, 26, 35, 55, 98, 148, 179

Roots, 271, 286, 340

Science Derivatives, 112

Spanish, 78, 144, 221, 268, 296, 317

Spelling, 63, 94, 118, 185, 198, 215

Suffixes, 43, 48, 84, 108, 137, 157, 205, 219

Terms Used in Geometry, 189

Vowel Changes, 74